ARCHAEOLOGY 95/96

D1309027

Editor

Linda L. Hasten

Linda Hasten received both her B.A. and M.A. from UCLA. Her background is in archaeology, and she has done fieldwork in several areas including California, the Southwest United States, Peru, Europe, Mexico, and British Columbia. She taught anthropology and archaeology full time as a professor at Pasadena City College from 1971 to 1991. She has also taught experimental anthropology classes to children at UCLA. Currently, she is continuing her career as an author of fictional works, and she is a member of the Author's Guild of America.

Annual Editions

A Library of Information from the Public Press

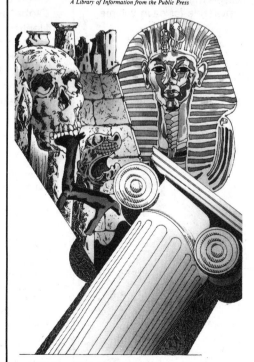

Cover illustration by Mike Eagle

The Dushkin Publishing Group, Inc.
Sluice Dock, Guilford, Connecticut 06437

The Annual Editions Series

Annual Editions is a series of over 60 volumes designed to provide the reader with convenient, low-cost access to a wide range of current, carefully selected articles from some of the most important magazines, newspapers, and journals published today. Annual Editions are updated on an annual basis through a continuous monitoring of over 300 periodical sources. All Annual Editions have a number of features designed to make them particularly useful, including topic guides, annotated tables of contents, unit overviews, and indexes. For the teacher using Annual Editions in the classroom, an Instructor's Resource Guide with test questions is available for each volume.

VOLUMES AVAILABLE

Africa
Aging
American Foreign Policy
American Government
American History, Pre-Civil War
American History, Post-Civil War
Anthropology
Archaeology
Biology
Biopsychology
Business Ethics
Canadian Politics
Child Growth and Development
China
Comparative Politics
Computers in Education
Computers in Business
Computers in Society
Criminal Justice
Drugs, Society, and Behavior
Dying, Death, and Bereavement
Early Childhood Education
Economics
Educating Exceptional Children
Education
Educational Psychology
Environment
Geography
Global Issues
Health
Human Development
Human Resources
Human Sexuality
India and South Asia
International Business

Japan and the Pacific Rim
Latin America
Life Management
Macroeconomics
Management
Marketing
Marriage and Family
Mass Media
Microeconomics
Middle East and the Islamic World
Money and Banking
Multicultural Education
Nutrition
Personal Growth and Behavior
Physical Anthropology
Psychology
Public Administration
Race and Ethnic Relations
Russia, the Eurasian Republics, and
    Central/Eastern Europe
Social Problems
Sociology
State and Local Government
Third World
Urban Society
Violence and Terrorism
Western Civilization,
    Pre-Reformation
Western Civilization,
    Post-Reformation
Western Europe
World History, Pre-Modern
World History, Modern
World Politics

Cataloging in Publication Data
Main entry under title: Annual Editions: Archaeology. 1995/96.
        1. Archaeology—Periodicals. I. Hasten, Linda L., comp. II. Title: Archaeology.
ISBN 1–56134–335–8   930.1′05

First Edition

Manufactured in the United States of America

Printed on Recycled Paper

Editors/ Advisory Board

EDITOR

Linda Hasten

ADVISORY BOARD

Elvio Angeloni
Pasadena City College

Cliff Boyd
Radford University

Christopher R. DeCorse
Syracuse University

Michael Finnegan
Kansas State University

Josef A. Gamper
Monterey Peninsula College

Nicholas Honerkamp
University of Tennessee

Melinda Leach
University of North Dakota

Michael G. Michlovic
Moorhead State University

Kevin Rafferty
Community College of
Southern Nevada

Thomas Rocek
University of Delaware

Members of the Advisory Board are instrumental in the final selection of articles for each edition of Annual Editions. Their review of articles for content, level, currentness, and appropriateness provides critical direction to the editor and staff. We think you'll find their careful consideration well reflected in this volume.

To the Reader

In publishing ANNUAL EDITIONS we recognize the enormous role played by the magazines, newspapers, and journals of the *public press* in providing current, first-rate educational information in a broad spectrum of interest areas. Within the articles, the best scientists, practitioners, researchers, and commentators draw issues into new perspective as accepted theories and viewpoints are called into account by new events, recent discoveries change old facts, and fresh debate breaks out over important controversies.

Many of the articles resulting from this enormous editorial effort are appropriate for students, researchers, and professionals seeking accurate, current material to help bridge the gap between principles and theories and the real world. These articles, however, become more useful for study when those of lasting value are carefully *collected, organized, indexed,* and *reproduced* in a *low-cost format,* which provides easy and permanent access when the material is needed. That is the role played by *Annual Editions.* Under the direction of each volume's *Editor,* who is an expert in the subject area, and with the guidance of an *Advisory Board,* we seek each year to provide in each *ANNUAL EDITION* a current, well-balanced, carefully selected collection of the best of the public press for your study and enjoyment. We think you'll find this volume useful, and we hope you'll take a moment to let us know what you think.

The first edition of *Annual Editions: Archaeology 95/96* consists of a number of articles specifically selected to present a lively, broad-based overview of the field of archaeology as it is practiced today. Each article was chosen to make the old bones, shards of pottery, and stone tools *pop* into the living cultural context in which they once existed.

The guiding concept behind this book is to present a *show me* approach in which archaeologists can speak for themselves of their own special experiences. Thus, the student will be exposed to a holistic perspective about archaeology as a living and applied science. In good writing, an author does not say "Darwin was a very tall man," but rather that "Darwin had to duck his head to pass through his seven-foot-tall front doorway." A *show me* literature can energize the necessary basics and enable the student to transform passive learning into active learning in a way in which information is both conceptualized and perceptualized. Simply said, the "light bulb" goes on.

This book is organized into eight general units, each of which contains several articles on various aspects of practicing archaeology. In the first part of the book, the *table of contents* provides a short synopsis of each article. This is followed by a *topic guide* that cross references general areas of interest as they appear in the various articles. At the end of the book there is a comprehensive *index.* Each unit is introduced by an *overview* that provides commentary on the unit topic, and *challenge questions* are offered to provoke thought and discussion of the articles.

The organization of this book is both suggestive and subjective. The articles may be assigned or read in any fashion that is deemed desirable. Each article stands on its own and may be assigned in conjunction to or contrast to any other article. The book may serve as a supplement to a standard textbook used in introductory archaeology classes. Or it might be used in conjunction with other books to replace the standard textbook altogether. Such an anthology might be useful in a general course in anthropology as well.

Annual Editions: Archaeology 95/96 is a premiere issue. Unlike most academic books, this book will be updated frequently to keep pace with its rapidly changing subject matter and to allow for greater exposure to the vast literature available in the field of archaeology. Those involved in the production of this volume wish to make each edition a valuable and provocative teaching tool. We welcome your criticisms, advice, and suggestions in order to carefully hone this book into a finer artifact of education. Please use the form at the end of the book for your comments.

Linda L. Hasten
Editor

Contents

Unit 1

About Archaeology

Six articles present overviews of the definition of archaeology and how archaeologists view themselves and each other. Emphasis is placed on the role of archaeologists as anthropologists.

The concepts in bold italics are developed in the article. For further expansion please refer to the Topic Guide and the Index.

Unit 2

Thinking Like an Archaeologist

Four selections illustrate a variety of approaches to viewing archaeological information. They range from the formality of the scientific method to more casual juxtapositions of fact and speculation.

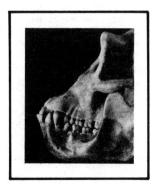

Unit 3

Problem-oriented Archaeology

The five unit articles deal with the contemporary goal of archaeology to solve problems rather than to make discoveries. Problems range from the larger issues of why do civilizations collapse to general issues of when did the earliest peoples first migrate to the New World.

The concepts in bold italics are developed in the article. For further expansion please refer to the Topic Guide and the Index.

Unit 5

History and Ethnoarchaeology

Four unit articles deal with the use of the studies of contemporary societies, including but not limited to primitive societies, to extrapolate back to the past in order to recreate a kind of living social archaeology.

Unit 6

Paleoanthropology: The Archaeology of Early Humans

Six selections in this section address the vast prehistory of our species. To gain a proper perspective of archaeology, it should be recognized that about 98 percent of human history is prehistory and is designated the Paleolithic or Stone Age.

The concepts in bold italics are developed in the article. For further expansion please refer to the Topic Guide and the Index.

35. When My Grandmother Is Your Database: Reactions to Repatriation, Nathalie F. S. Woodbury, *Anthropology Newsletter,* March 1992.   205

The *polarization* of the issue of *repatriation* is examined by Nathalie Woodbury. One opinion is expressed by a long-time field archaeologist, with another view by a major spokesperson for the *Native Americans,* a professor of political science. Woodbury contends that neither viewpoint is altogether accurate.

36. Tales from a Peruvian Crypt, Walter Alva and Christopher B. Donnan, *Natural History,* May 1994.   208

The *looting* of an *ancient pyramid* led to an operation in *salvage archaeology* during which one of greatest archaeological finds in the Western Hemisphere was recently made. The discovery of the fantastically preserved *burial chamber* of an ancient warrior priest revealed the art, rituals, and religion of the Mochica people of ancient Peru.

37. Indians, Archaeologists, and the Future, Vine Deloria Jr., *American Antiquity,* Volume 57, Number 4, 1992.   212

The conflict regarding *repatriation* of *American Indian skeletal remains* and *artifacts* is discussed in terms of materialism versus spiritualism. Vine Deloria addresses the needed reconciliation of Indian and archaeological goals from the *Native American viewpoint* in a manner filled with humorous barbs directed at archaeologists.

38. Damming the Past, Daniel J. Lenihan, *Natural History,* November 1993.   215

Dam building not only *buries archaeological sites,* but it *destroys* the *ecology* of the *sites.* The subtle clues contained in the soil, pollen, and plant life are lost forever. The *Native American* is another loser of this action. Their *ancestral lands* and people must now rest with the fish, well-preserved at times, but, for all its worth, unattainable.

Overview   218

39. The Beginning of a Partnership, Mary Leakey, from *Disclosing the Past: An Autobiography,* Doubleday & Company Publishers, 1984.   220

The great dame of archaeology, *Mary Nicol Leakey,* tells the story of meeting her future husband, *Louis S. B. Leakey,* when she was 20 years old. Their developing relationship is an intricate study of the manners and mores of the so-called lost generation. Their personal relationship grew while Mary Nicol's intense professionalism as an archaeologist equally grew.

40. Lucy: The Beginnings of Humankind, Donald Johanson and Maitland A. Edey, from *Lucy: The Beginnings of Humankind,* Simon & Schuster, 1981.   225

Donald Johanson got lucky as a young man and made one of the most spectacular finds in *paleoanthropology*—"Lucy in the sky with Diamonds," or just plain *Lucy,* as the famous female fossil hominid is known. In this essay, Johanson tells of the profound thrill of finding Lucy.

Unit 8

Archaeologists as People

Four selections take a look at the people behind the trowel; what they hold in common is the curiosity and respect for the history that lies just beneath our feet all over the world.

The concepts in bold italics are developed in the article. For further expansion please refer to the Topic Guide and the Index.

Topic Guide

This topic guide suggests how the selections in this book relate to topics of traditional concern to students and professionals involved with the study of archaeology. It is useful for locating articles that relate to each other for reading and research. The guide is arranged alphabetically according to topic. Articles may, of course, treat topics that do not appear in the topic guide. In turn, entries in the topic guide do not necessarily constitute a comprehensive listing of all the contents of each selection.

TOPIC AREA	TREATED IN:	TOPIC AREA	TREATED IN:
African American Archaeology	24. Bones and Bureaucrats	**Ethnographic Analogy and Ethnoarchaeology**	12. Who Were the Israelites?
Antiquities, Antiquarians, and Amateur Archaeologists	1. Quest for the Past 5. 'Reverse Archaeologists' 31. Antiquities Market	**Experimental Archaeology**	7. Epistemology 16. Yes, Wonderful Things 17. Paleolithic Paint Job 18. Bushmen 19. Ancient Indians 20. Arrow of Disease
Burials, Reburials, and Skeletal Remains	1. Quest for the Past 3. Enlightened Archaeologist 8. Death Cults of Prehistoric Malta 14. Mummies of Xinjiang 24. Bones and Bureaucrats 31. Antiquities Market 33. Anthropological Culture Shift 35. When My Grandmother Is Your Database 36. Tales from a Peruvian Crypt 37. Indians, Archaeologists, and the Future	**Forensic Archaeology**	22. Murders from the Past 23. Post-Mortem at the Little Bighorn
		Garbology	1. Quest for the Past 16. Yes, Wonderful Things
		Gender and Sex Roles	1. Quest for the Past 4. Indiana Joans 13. Ever Since Eve 28. Lithic Technology and the Hunter-Gatherer 30. Primitive Prescription for Equality 39. Beginnings of a Partnership 41. Novel Notion of Neanderthal
Cannibalism	5. 'Reverse Archaeologists' 26. Infants, Cannibals, and the Pit of Bones		
Contract Archaeology	5. 'Reverse Archaeologists' 33. Anthropological Culture Shift	**History and Historical Archaeology**	1. Quest for the Past 10. Living Through the Donner Party 16. Yes, Wonderful Things 18. Bushmen 23. Post-Mortem at the Little Bighorn 24. Bones and Bureaucrats
Cultural Resource Management (CRM) and Cultural Resources	6. Archaeology and Relief 24. Bones and Bureaucrats 31. Antiquities Market 34. Saving Our World's Heritage 38. Damming the Past		
		Hunter-Collectors	18. Bushmen 28. Lithic Technology and the Hunter-Gatherer 30. Primitive Prescription for Equality
Culture and Culture History	2. Golden Marshalltown 5. 'Reverse Archaeologists' 10. Living Through the Donner Party 28. Lithic Technology and the Hunter-Gatherer 29. Dating Game		
		Linguistics	3. Enlightened Archaeologist 14. Mummies of Xinjiang
Epistemology	7. Epistemology	**Living Informants**	18. Bushmen
Ethics and Laws	2. Golden Marshalltown 5. 'Reverse Archaeologists' 31. Antiquities Market 32. Project Sting 33. Anthropological Culture Shift 34. Saving Our World's Heritage 35. When My Grandmother Is Your Database 36. Tales from a Peruvian Crypt 37. Indians, Archaeologists, and the Future	**Looters, Grave Robbers, and Pot Hunters**	1. Quest for the Past 6. Archaeology and Relief 31. Antiquities Market 32. Project Sting 36. Tales from a Peruvian Crypt

About Archaeology

What is the difference between archaeology and anthropology? Would the archaeologist or anthropologist who has *not* been asked this question please stand up and be counted!

If human behavior were a baseball game, the anthropologist would be in the broadcaster's booth. But long before the game was over, in a seeming paradox, the anthropologist would run into the stands to be a spectator and chow down a good mustard-covered hot dog, then rush onto the field to be a player and catch a high fly to right field. This is the eccentric nature of anthropology. This is why anthropologists are so interesting. Often they succeed.

Comparing anthropology, psychology, sociology, and history as four disciplines that study humankind, anthropology is the study of humankind that takes the biggest step back and uses a panorama camera that gives a 360° view. The psychologist stands nose to nose with a person, the sociologist steps back for the group shot, and the historian steps back in time as well as space. However, the anthropologist does all these things standing well behind the others, watching and measuring, in a sense using the data of all of these disciplines but weaving them into the uniqueness of the anthropological perspective.

Anthropology is the science of human behavior that studies all humankind starting with our biological and evolutionary origins into cultural beings and the continuation and diversification of our cultural selves. Humankind is the single species that has evolved culture as a unique way of adapting to the world.

Academically, anthropology is divided into the two major fields of physical and cultural anthropology. Cultural anthropologists hold a generally shared concept of culture. The basic question that cultural anthropologists address is how to explain the differences and similarities between different cultures. In order to achieve this, cultural anthropologists view people with a cross-cultural perspective. This means comparing all cultures, present and past, with each other. A grand task, indeed.

What is culture? Culture is the unique way in which our species adapts to its total environment. Total environment includes everything that affects human beings—the physical environment, plants, animals, the weather, beliefs, values, a passing insult, or an opportunistic virus. Everything! Human beings are both created by culture and are the creators of culture.

Culture is the human adaptive system in which all people live in groups defined by time, space, and place, pass on shared values and beliefs through a common language(s), and manipulate things in the environment through tool use and tool making. Cultures change and evolve through time. And perhaps most important, cultures, all cultures, whether they be high civilizations or small tribes, eventually cease to exist.

And it is the field of cultural anthropology that studies these extant cultures. Archaeologists dig up the physical remains, the tools, the houses, and the rubbish of these once living cultures. And from this spare data base, anthropologists try to reconstruct these past cultures. Is this important to anthropology? Yes, because these once living cultures represent approximately 98 percent of all cultures that have ever existed. They tell us where we have been, when we are there again, and they tell us where we might go in the future. As this anthology continues, we will see how these archaeologists ply their magical trade.

Looking Ahead: Challenge Questions

What is the general relationship between anthropology and archaeology?

What does it mean to say that archaeology started as an "underground" science?

When was archaeology recognized as a science? Why?

Is an archaeologist's reputation based on the excellence of their fieldwork?

Describe how archaeology raises questions of ethics.

In what measurable ways have archaeological methods changed over time?

What is engendered archaeology? Give some examples.

How do we characterize the relationship between amateur and professional archaeologists?

The Quest for the Past

Brian M. Fagan

Archaeologists are commonly thought to be eccentric people who wear rumpled khaki shorts and sun helmets and spend their lives unearthing crumbling ruins in the shadow of mighty pyramids. They live in a world of lost civilizations and buried treasure, deep mysteries and unexplained phenomena. The archaeologist of novel and television seems to be continually off on a "dig," searching for missing links and unwrapping innumerable Ancient Egyptian mummies. Sometimes, too, the angry mummies chase the unfortunate archaeologists, intoning dreadful curses that lead to their premature deaths. Many of us, at one time or another, have dreamed of pursuing such a romantic—if, in fact, mythical—career.

This is . . . about actual archaeological discoveries, about remarkable archaeologists whose explorations have dramatically expanded our understanding of human history. It is . . . about the excitement of archaeological discovery, about a scientific world that many consider to be one of the most engrossing frontiers of science. Its heroes are archaeologists of extraordinary ability who have made fascinating discoveries, often after years of patient effort. Each was a pioneer who pursued a dream, a conviction that spectacular archaeological finds awaited his or her spade.

The face of archaeology has changed considerably in recent years. Archaeologists of the 1840s, and even as late as the 1930s, could hope to uncover hitherto unknown civilizations: the Assyrians and Sumerians of Mesopotamia surfaced in the mid-nineteenth century, the Maya of Mexico in the 1840s, the Mycenaeans of Greece in the 1870s, the Shang civilization of China in the late 1920s. All of these discoveries captured the public imagination, for they were made under conditions of great difficulty, conditions that often required near-heroic efforts. The early archaeologists had few resources and no advanced excavation techniques. By constant improvisation, by drawing on their own wealth, and by acute political maneuvering, they frequently achieved miracles. They learned digging the hard way, made brilliant finds, and, regrettably, sometimes irreparably damaged vital clues to the past.

Some of our archaeologists belong to this heroic era, others to our own generation, where there are simply no lost civilizations left to find. But today's archaeologists still make remarkable discoveries, often as a result of applying such advanced tools as the computer to archaeological data. Modern archaeology is big business; thousands of people all over the world are currently involved in digging up the past. Practically every nation now employs a few archaeologists—as museum curators, university professors, or conservators of national culture. All of these archaeologists use excavation techniques that have evolved over generations of archaeological discovery. The newer techniques enable them to tackle problems that would have boggled the mind even a few years ago.

One of Mexico's earliest cities, Teotihuacán, is a case in point. Early archaeologists could only gasp at the size of Teotihuacán, sample a portion of a pyramid or a few houses, then turn away in despair. They simply did not have the technology needed to carry their explorations further. It has taken a team of modern archaeologists over a decade to map the entire twelve-and-a-half square miles of Mexico's largest prehistoric city. Their task would have been impossible without a mosaic of air photographs and highly sophisticated computer programs that enabled them to store inventories of archaeological finds and millions of other items of information on computer tape. When the time came to put the data together, the archaeologists could recall and classify thousands of data items in a few seconds. The result: a whole new picture of Teotihuacán.

How do archaeologists dig up the past? What makes archaeological excavation different from ditch digging or the treasure-hunting activities of our mythical, sun-helmeted archaeologist? To get some idea of just how far the field of archaeology has progressed, let's look back over its colorful history.

Archaeology has a long and disreputable line of descent: its ancestors were, quite literally, grave robbers and adventurers. A century and a half ago, even serious archaeological excavation was little more than licensed treasure hunting. Everyone, whether archaeologist or treasure hunter, had the same objective—to recover as many valuable objects as possible in the shortest time. Serious archaeologists would not hesitate to use gunpowder to blast their way into a burial chamber or a pyramid. Everything was cast aside in a frantic search for the valuable and spectacular. As a result, most excavations resembled untidy vegetable gardens.

Mummy hunters in Egypt literally waded through piles of discarded coffins to reach their prey. The famous Italian collector Giovanni Belzoni, who worked in Egypt from 1817 to 1820, would crawl hundreds of yards into the rocky hillsides behind Thebes in search of mummies and papyri. Exhausted, he would perch in the darkness for a few minutes on a convenient mummy. Once his perch collapsed in a cloud of smelly dust. "I sank altogether among the broken mummies, with a crash of bones, rags, and wooden cases," he remembered. It was a good quarter of an hour before Belzoni could extricate himself.

Belzoni and his contemporaries were quite open about their efforts to "rob the Egyptians of their papyri." No one thought this either eccentric or wrong. Rather, Belzoni's audiences would be agog as he related his eerie experiences in the dark burial chambers, where, in the flickering lamplight, the mummies seemed almost to converse with one another and the naked Arab workmen, coated in layers of dust, resembled mummies themselves. The audiences would gasp as Belzoni produced pieces of desiccated ancient Egyptians, remarking casually that "mummies are rather unpleasant to swallow."

In general, the nineteenth century was a time of frantic search for ancient sculptures and fine artifacts, whether from Egypt, Greece, Mesopotamia, or the Americas. Everyone wanted items for their collections and no one had any scruples about the means used to dig up their pet acquisitions. All too often we read in their early reports that such and such a find "crumbled to dust" on discovery or that exposure to the open air caused the finds to "dissolve before our very eyes."

One cannot entirely blame Belzoni and his successors. Basically, they were ignorant. No one had ever tried to dig a large archaeological site at all systematically. Even today, the technology of conservation is in relative infancy and modern archaeologists are still at a loss as to how to preserve many delicate finds satisfactorily. Considering the state of the art, it's a miracle that so much is preserved from early excavations. But the archaeological price of filling the British Museum, the Louvre, and other great museums was simply enormous: witness Austen Henry Layard's excavations in Mesopotamia at ancient Nineveh and Nimrud from 1845 to 1851.

Layard started digging Nimrud with precious little money and absolutely no archaeological experience. He simply tunneled into the huge mounds reputed to be the remains of these ancient cities and went on digging until he hit a fine sculpture or a stone-walled palace room. At Nimrud he was lucky enough to find two palaces. But, as he dug through mud-brick walls and houses, he failed to recognize invaluable inscribed tablets of unbaked clay. To his unskilled eyes, the bricks and tablets were indistinguishable from the brown soil of the mound. Later excavators recovered thousands of these tablets from areas of Nimrud that Layard left untouched. They had developed the skills and techniques to find them.

The deep tunnels that Layard dug along walls or lines of sculptured slabs at least sheltered him from the merciless sun and sweeping winds of the open plains. He would shovel out the contents of each room with dispatch, then sit down to record the intricate details of prancing horsemen and fighting warriors that flickered in the somber shadows. When his trenches were open to the elements, clouds of blinding dust stirred by savage gale-force winds would bombard the workmen. Layard himself would take refuge behind a giant sculpture until the sandstorm subsided. Under the circumstances, it is remarkable that he succeeded in excavating at all.

Austen Henry Layard shifted thousands of tons of soil, discovered nearly two miles of bas-reliefs, and cleared seventy rooms in the Palace of Sennacherib at Kuyunjik alone. Although he did keep some records, he more or less shoveled his way into the past. He tore Nimrud and Nineveh apart and, in the process, wiped out priceless archaeological information—data on daily life and ancient diet, details of houses and storerooms, and, above all, the complex sequence of layers that made up the occupation mounds.

Every Mesopotamian city mound was formed over centuries of occupation through complex processes of rebuilding houses, dumping garbage, and the natural actions of rain and wind. Many years before Layard came to Nineveh, geologists studying railway cuttings and canal excavations in Europe and America had observed the layered strata of the earth and established the classic principle of superposition. Very simply stated, this means that the lower levels of a succession of geological horizons were laid down earlier than the higher levels. The law of superposition had obvious applications to great city mounds like Nimrud or Nineveh, for every site started as a small settlement on a low ridge. The first occupation levels were soon covered by later settlements built in the same place. A thousand years later, the same city could look down from the top of a high mound of age-old occupation debris. The archaeologist wishing to understand the history of the city would have to dissect this mound layer by layer.

Layard himself was well aware that his mounds had gone through many changes. He knew that many kings had ruled his cities. But his excavation methods were simply too crude to permit him to dig the mounds period by period. One cannot blame Layard. If anything, he was more conscientious than his contemporaries, for he at least wrote popular accounts of his findings.

Many excavations of Layard's time were little more than picnic parties. Wealthy country gentlemen would open Indian burial mounds or Bronze Age earthworks for the sheer fun of it. When the English antiquarian Thomas Wright attended the opening of an ancient burial mound in 1844, he found a large party of interested gentry assembled for the sport. While the workmen opened eight burial mounds, the ladies and gentlemen "continued to spend [their] time, at intervals between digging and picnicking, in games of various descriptions . . . and in other amusements. The weather was fortunately exquisitely fine." When a sudden shower threatened to drench the party, they took refuge in the trench under a shield of umbrellas. The burial mounds contained "skeletons, more or less entire, with the remains of weapons in iron, bosses of shields, urns, beads, armlets, and occasionally more vessels." All of these finds vanished into the landowner's private collection, which the party inspected after partaking of a "sumptuous repast." This burial-mound dig was in no way exceptional; rather, it was typical of thousands.

The techniques of excavation were still in their infancy when Heinrich Schliemann began work on the great Hissarlik mound, site of ancient Troy. Schliemann, a millionaire, attacked archaeological problems with the same single-minded intensity he applied to business ventures. His wealth gave him the means to work on a truly grand scale, with resident experts and hundreds of workmen. He arrived on the site in 1871 with the vague notion that the mound contained many different settlements. So he set out to dig to bedrock, on a scale that almost beggars description. In 1872, for example, he borrowed a railroad engineer and employed three overseers to direct over a hundred men. They sliced into Hissarlik with a cutting over 230 feet wide that eventually penetrated over 40 feet into the huge mound. The city walls found in the upper-most strata were ruthlessly cleared away as Schliemann dug his way down through the centuries, toward his Homeric city.

Eventually, Schliemann identified the remains of seven cities, one above the other. His excavations exhibited a notable lack of finesse. In his books, he refers to the clearance of entire ancient streets, to the removal of "older walls which I am also having broken through," and to thousands upon thousands of potsherds, ornaments, and other small finds that were shoveled out as thousands of tons of soil were dug out of Hissarlik. At one point, he boasted that he had removed 325,000 cubic yards of soil from ancient Troy.

Schliemann's motto was speed, more speed, and yet still more. When he dug, he cleared an entire landscape. Every day he described his findings in a comprehensive diary, which he eventually published. Unlike many of his contemporaries, Schliemann kept his finds and recorded all of them, not just the spectacular pieces. And, although he has been castigated as little more than a treasure hunter, he in fact undertook the first large-scale dissection of a city mound where, unlike the situation at Nineveh or Nimrud, there were no sculptures to guide the way to ancient structures. As his digging experience increased, Schliemann began to rely more heavily on expert diggers, who were able to refine his methods drastically.

While Schliemann was working at Troy, German archaeologists had begun a quiet revolution in excavation methods that was to affect both the Troy excavations and many other digs as well. The Austrian archaeologist Alexander Conze dug at the site of Samothrace in Greece between 1873 and 1875. He dug with the help of architects and a photographer, who recorded the progress of the excavations. The Samothrace report was a beautiful production, the first to be illustrated with photographs. Conze's example was not lost on the German Archaeological Institute, which started work at Olympia in 1875. For six winters, Ernst Curtius directed a brilliant campaign of excavations on the site of the original Olympic Games. The Kaiser himself paid for part of the dig. Every find was carefully preserved and housed in a special museum built at the site. No artifacts were exported. Curtius and Wilhelm Dörpfeld worked out every detail of the stratigraphy at Olympia with the aid of new and very precise record-keeping methods. The Olympia excavations set new standards that the ever-energetic Dörpfeld took with him to Troy. In his later years at Hissarlik, Schliemann became what one authority has called "a constitutional monarch among expert ministers." Dörpfeld refined Schliemann's seven cities into the complex history of a mound that, he said, flourished from

about 3000–700 B.C., the Homeric city dating from 1500–1000 B.C.

Curtius and Dörpfeld were concerned with the trivial as well as the spectacular. Their excavations were far more meticulous than those of their predecessors, although still crude by modern standards. A retired British general named Augustus Pitt-Rivers revolutionized the art of excavation even further. The general, a formidable personality, spent much of his military career working on the development of army rifles. His experimental research involved him in the history of firearms and the study of different types of primitive artifacts from all over the world. Pitt-Rivers was deeply interested in the evolution of human technology. He became an avid collector of artifacts of all types—masks, shields, weapons, even canoes. His collections became so large that he donated them to Oxford University, where they are to this day.

In 1880, Pitt-Rivers inherited an enormous estate in southern England, an estate littered with ancient burial sites and earthworks. The general decided to devote the rest of his life to investigation of the sites on his property. He did so with ruthless efficiency, diverting enormous sums from his fortune into leisured excavations that lasted twenty years, until his death in 1901. Pitt-Rivers had a mania for records and detail. "Every detail should be recorded in the manner most conducive to facility of reference," he wrote. "I have endeavored to record the results of these excavations in such a way that the whole of the evidence may be available for those who are concerned to go into it." He had realized a cardinal point: all archaeological excavation is permanent destruction and all objects found in a site have a vital context in time and space that is just as important a piece of information as the find itself.

The learned general was far ahead of his time. He trained archaeological assistants, had "before" and "after" models of his sites constructed, built a special museum to display his finds, and even marked his filled-in trenches with special medallions that said, in effect, "Pitt-Rivers was here." His ideas were revolutionary. Consider some of his basic principles of digging: "No excavation ought to ever be permitted except under the immediate eye of a responsible and trustworthy superintendent." "Superfluous precision may be regarded as a fault on the right side." "Tedious as it may appear to some to dwell on the discovery of odds and ends that have, no doubt, been thrown away by the owners as rubbish . . . yet it is by the study of such trivial details that archaeology is mainly dependent for determining the date of earthworks."

Hundreds of man-hours went into each of Pitt-Rivers's sumptuous reports. Each was published privately, complete with detailed plans, accurate measurements of every artifact, and precise information on every aspect of the site from pottery to hut foundations, stratigraphy to animal bones. It was to be years before anyone would equal or surpass Pitt-Rivers's painstaking work. He deplored the destruction of earthworks by plowing, laid out picnic grounds for people visiting his museum, and urged his fellow landowners to follow his example. The general was not a particularly endearing gentleman, but his legacy to archaeology is unquestioned. An interesting glimpse into the man comes from a photograph of the excavations which is tersely captioned: "The figure standing at attention in the foreground gives the scale." Evidently Pitt-Rivers was a military man, as well as an archaeologist, to the very end.

Few people followed Pitt-Rivers's example. One could still become an excavator without any training at all, although well-known archaeologists like Wilhelm Dörpfeld and the immortal Egyptologist Flinders Petrie were busy training students to follow in their footsteps. Petrie begged his colleagues to be quit of "the brandy-and-soda young man . . . of the adventurous speculator. Without the ideal of solid continuous work, certain, accurate, and permanent, archaeology is as futile as any other pursuit." He went on to urge informal attire: "To attempt serious work in pretty suits, shiny leg-

gings or starched collars, would be like mountaineering in evening dress." "It is sickening to see the rate at which everything is being destroyed," he once remarked, "and the little regard paid to preservation."

Some of the better digging that stemmed from Pitt-Rivers's work took place on Roman sites in Britain. Still, to modern eyes, the efforts appear to have been terribly amateurish and the excavators incredibly ill-equipped. Young Leonard Woolley, for example, later to become famous for his skilled excavations of royal graves at Ur-of-the-Chaldees in Mesopotamia, found himself in charge of a major Roman excavation without any experience at all or the least idea of how to survey a site or make plans.

The early part of this century also seems to have been a difficult period for female archaeologists. When a little-known archaeologist named J. P. Droop wrote a small manual on excavation in 1915, he spent a lot of time worrying about male/female roles. "I have never seen a trained lady excavator at work," he admitted. "Of a mixed dig, however, I have seen something, and it is an experiment that I would be reluctant to try again." His reasons were twofold. "In the first place, there are the proprieties." Excavators should respect the etiquette and mores of the countries they are working in. Droop's other reasons were more personal. It seems that, in his experience, the "charm" of ladies vanishes during an excavation, for the dig lays on its mixed participants "a bond of closer daily intercourse than is conceivable." Droop found this irritating. "The ordinary male at least cannot stand it," he added. He cited the strain of "self-restraint in moments of stress, moments that will occur on the best regulated dig, when you want to say just what you think without translation, which before ladies, whatever their feelings about it, cannot be done." Droop was never to know of the key roles played by twentieth-century women in major archaeological excavations the world over.

Nevertheless, there were a handful of women who carried out important

work in the field long before female excavators became commonplace. One pioneer was the English novelist Amelia Edwards, a Victorian lady in the classic sense of the word, who embarked on a two-month journey up the Nile in 1874. She traveled in genteel company aboard a sailing ship complete with upright piano and proper chaperones. Edwards was horrified by the looting and destruction of Ancient Egyptian sites on every side, at the blatant forgery of antiquities, and the "black-robed, grave men, who always lay in wait ready to sell you anything." Nevertheless, she was entranced by the Pyramids, the Temple of Karnak, and Abu Simbel, by the columns of ancient temples which she compared to groves of redwood trees. Her *Thousand Miles Up the Nile* (1877) is one of the classics of early archaeological travel and still bears reading today. Edwards devoted the rest of her life to lecturing and writing about the destruction in Egypt and was instrumental in the founding of the Egypt Exploration Society, which works in the Nile Valley to this day.

Harriet Boyd Hawes, a Smith graduate who met Amelia Edwards while in college, was even more remarkable. In 1897, she traveled to Athens to study archaeology, one of the first women to do so. Archaeology soon took a back seat to nursing when Turkey declared war on Greece. For months, Hawes cared for wounded Greek soldiers within sound of artillery barrages, developing a passion for humanitarian causes that guided much of her life. Much to her surprise, she won a fellowship at the American School in Athens from Yale University, but was not allowed to excavate, this being considered a male domain. The British were more encouraging and she went over to Crete, where she combed the countryside for archaeological sites on the back of a mule. Her persistence was rewarded and she became the first woman to excavate a Minoan town. Hawes's monograph on Gournia is one of the classics of early Mediterranean archaeology. Not that Harriet did much more fieldwork, for she threw herself into humanitarian work among Serb soldiers in Corfu and served as a ward aid in American hospitals in France during World War I. But she opened doors into the narrow archaeological world for many talented women that followed in her footsteps.

There were other talented women pioneers, too, among them the redoubtable Gertrude Bell, who became an expert desert traveler and founded the Iraq Museum; Gertrude Caton-Thompson, who discovered what were then the earliest farmers in the world in Egypt's Fayum in the 1920s; and Dorothy Garrod, the first woman Professor of Archaeology anywhere in Europe, who excavated the Stone Age caves on Mount Carmel in the Levant in the 1930s. For the most part, they worked on shoestring budgets and often with few companions. But the discoveries they made contributed to the revolution in archaeological methods that took hold after World War I, in the hands of several capable excavators. Indeed the lax standards of Pitt-Rivers's contemporaries and successors were assaulted by archaeologists of the 1920s and 1930s. "There is no right way of digging but there are many wrong ones," wrote one of Pitt-Rivers's most avid disciples—Mortimer Wheeler. Wheeler, who was ten years old when Pitt-Rivers died, came to archaeology through the good offices of Arthur Evans, discoverer of the ancient palace of King Minos on Crete. Wheeler spent his lifetime digging large sites with meticulous precision and training new generations of archaeologists in methods that owed their inspiration to the Victorian general.

Wheeler worked first on Roman forts, then on the famous Iron Age fortress at Maiden Castle in southern Britain. From archaeological evidence, he was able to reconstruct a blow-by-blow account of the Roman storming of that fort. After a distinguished military career in World War II, Wheeler was asked to head up the Archaeological Survey of India. With characteristic and flamboyant energy, he took up the task of organizing archaeology out of chaos. He found Roman imported pottery in southern India and dug deeply into the ancient city mounds of Harappa and Mohenjo-daro in the In-dus Valley. There he sketched a fascinating picture of a long-extinct Indian civilization that had traded with Mesopotamia and developed its own distinctive, and still undeciphered, script. Mortimer Wheeler's excavations were, quite simply, meticulous, and the results remarkable. Most modern excavations build on the basic principles that he and Pitt-Rivers, as well as a handful of other pioneers, set out.

"The archaeologist is not digging up things, he is digging up people," Wheeler would begin. Good excavation takes imagination, an ability to understand what one is digging up. According to Wheeler, people who do not have this kind of imagination should collect bus tickets instead of digging. He believed the key to excavation was accurate observation and recording of occupation levels and architectural features, of the layout of burials and minute artifacts. The relationship between different objects in the ground can tell one much about the behavior of their makers, he taught his students. Wheeler's excavations were models of tidiness, with straight walls and carefully swept trenches to make the tasks of observation and discovery more precise. The observation of superimposed layers and the features and artifacts in them would give one an accurate chronology to work with, an essential framework for studying the numerous pot fragments and other finds from the dig. He pointed out how buildings should be dissected with great care, so that the foundations could be related to the underlying, dated strata and the contents isolated from those in other parts of the site. The burials Wheeler found were exposed bone by bone and carefully photographed in position before removal.

All of Wheeler's excavations were carefully designed not only to find artifacts but to answer specific questions about chronology or other matters. These questions were formulated in advance or as the dig was in progress. The staff of the excavation was organized into a hierarchy of specialists, led by the director himself, whose task was to "cultivate a scrupulous accuracy and completeness in the observation and record of his factual evidence." Wheeler's ideal director had "the combined virtues of the scholar and the man of action," an ability to achieve accuracy "not for accuracy's sake, but as a basis for using his imagination to interpret his finds." "Archaeology," wrote Wheeler, "is primarily a fact-finding discipline." But, he would always add, we have to dig sites as a means to an end, the end being the understanding of humanity's complex and changing relationship with its environment.

Schliemann dug up the past of Troy. He and many other early archaeologists taught us that archaeological sites contain many treasures. Curtius, Dörpfeld, Pitt-Rivers, and Wheeler developed techniques for recording the contents of each site in meticulous detail. And Wheeler himself threw down the gauntlet to his successors—he challenged them to apply these recording methods to such complex problems as "estimating the density and social structure of populations." His words were prophetic, for that is what leading archaeologists are now trying to achieve.

Mortimer Wheeler died in 1976 after witnessing a revolution in digging methods all over the world, a revolution whose impact is still being felt. His students and their students, as well as those of other pioneering archaeologists, have refined his methods even further. Some idea of the complexity of a modern excavation can be gained by a brief look at the investigation of an ancient site at Olduvai Gorge in Tanzania. The site dates to about 1.75 million years ago.

"Archaeology," wrote British archaeologist Stuart Piggott some years ago, "is the science of rubbish." And rubbish is precisely what Louis and Mary Leakey had to dissect when they excavated the scatters of bones and stone artifacts in the lowest levels of Olduvai Gorge. All that remained were small scatters of discarded animal bones, stone tools, and waste chips, lying in irregular concentrations on the very land surfaces ancient people once trod. Often the scatter of artifacts and bones was only a few inches thick and was sealed under dozens of feet of sterile sand and lake clay. How old were these scatters? What activities took place there? Could any information on prehistoric diet and food-getting methods be obtained from the scatters? These and many other questions came to mind as the Leakeys began clearing these small but complicated sites. They had no doubt as to the importance of their excavations: these were probably among the earliest traces of human behavior in the world. To avoid damaging any human fossils and to prevent disturbance of the artifacts from their original positions, only the most delicate methods could be used.

Each scatter lay within a major geological horizon of Olduvai Gorge, one that the Leakeys knew dated to the earliest millennia of the human experience. But dating samples had to be obtained, that is, lumps of lava that could be dated by laboratory tests for their radioactive content. These samples had to come from the scatters themselves, from lava fragments that had actually been carried to the site by those who had lived there. The Leakeys had no choice: they knew they must excavate each entire site, plot all the objects on them, and obtain dating samples from among the finds in the scatter.

One site yielded the famous skull of *Zinjanthropus* in 1959. . . . Mary Leakey originally found a portion of the fossil outcropping from the lower lake beds of the Gorge. A small excavation was immediately undertaken at the site of this discovery to aid both in the removal of the precious skull and in establishing the exact level from which the fossil came. The immediate surroundings of the skull were sifted carefully in case additional fragments had already fallen down the slope on which it was found. The trial excavation yielded broken animal bones, some rodent fragments, and a few stone tools that lay in place near the skull. There seemed a strong possibility that the skull was directly associated with the tools—indeed, its owner might have made them.

It was seven months before Mary Leakey could return to the site, for the skull had been found at the very end of the 1959 season. When the time came for larger-scale excavations, she did not attack the site at once. Her task was to establish the precise position of the artifact scatter in the Olduvai geological strata. To determine this, she dug a six-foot trial trench in steps through the entire forty feet of the geological bed the skull had come from, right down to bedrock. She found that the scatter was halfway up the bed.

Once the stratigraphical position of the fossil skull was established, Mary Leakey set out to determine the extent of the scatter itself. The workmen removed the sterile over-burden of lake bed from the area around the trial trench. This unproductive soil was removed with picks and shovels in rough levels. When they reached a whitish-yellow volcanic-ash zone that Mary Leakey knew directly overlay the precious scatter, they stepped aside. The trench was now divided into four-foot-wide strips that were worked one by one with great care. Skilled workers carefully pared away the volcanic ash to within a few inches of the underlying artifacts and bones. Sometimes bones and other finds protruded through into the ash. So dry was the soil that the excavators had to dampen it before removal to guard against damaging valuable fossils underneath.

The scatter proved to be about a foot thick. With great care, Mary Leakey worked each strip of the trench from one side of the floor to the other. Whenever possible, every find was cleared from the surrounding soil with dental probes and small paintbrushes. Every find of any size, whether a stone tool or an animal bone, was marked with black or white ink and plotted on the floor plan before being lifted. A complete photographic record of the site was maintained as well. Once the larger finds had been removed, the soil was wet- or dry-sifted through one-sixteenth-inch screens so that even the tiniest stone chips and bone fragments were recovered for laboratory analysis. As a result of this painstaking excavation, the position of every significant find on the site was known to within an inch or less. What a contrast

to Belzoni's burial chambers or Layard's palaces!

The man-hours expended on the *Zinjanthropus* site were well worth the expense. The amount of detail about early human lifeways that came from the *Zinjanthropus* floor was truly astonishing, all of it the result of meticulous excavation. In addition to the dating samples gathered—which proved the site to be 1.75 million years old—the Leakeys obtained data on the dimensions and layout of one of the earliest archaeological sites in the world. Mary Leakey found and took apart a concentration of stone tools and flakes and over a thousand broken bone fragments covering an area twenty-one feet by fifteen feet near the spot where *Zinjanthropus* was found. This central zone was separated from another concentration of bones by a less densely covered area that she felt might have been the site of a crude shelter. We know that the inhabitants used crude stone choppers and many flakes in the preparation of food and the butchering of small animals. They smashed the limb bones of antelope and zebra and broke open the skulls to remove the brain. But large scavengers like hyenas visited the site as well and chewed up some of the freshly broken bones—presumably after the inhabitants left. None of this information could have been obtained without rigorous excavation techniques. The Leakeys literally drained the site of information. . . .

Archaeology has come a long way since Leonard Woolley performed miracles with plaster at Ur. Today, it is a sophisticated science that calls on experts from dozens of academic disciplines. It owes much to the natural and physical sciences, to revolutionary dating techniques . . . that enable us to date 2.5-million-year-old archaeological sites or tiny fragments of a wooden spear shaft extracted from the socket of a bronze spearhead used three thousand years ago. Computers enable archaeologists to manipulate vast data bases of artifacts and food remains, to plot intricate jigsaw puzzles of water-logged timbers that once formed a prehistoric house. We can trace the sources of volcanic rock used to make mirrors in three-thousand-year-old Mexican villages, establish whether stone workers making tools in a Belgian hunting camp ten thousand years ago were left- or right-handed. Using minute pollen grains, we can reconstruct the landscape around twenty-thousand-year-old Stone Age winter camps. Thousands of bison bones from an ancient mass kill on the American Plains can be reassembled so precisely that we know exactly how bison hunters of eight thousand years ago butchered their prey.

But the greatest advances of all have not been in the field or the laboratory, where all the hi-tech wizardry of archaeology comes into play. They have been in the ways in which we think of archaeology and plan our research. Much early archaeology was designed to recover as many spectacular objects as possible. This is what Layard strove for at Nimrud and Nineveh, and Schliemann at Hissarlik. Today's archaeology has three much more sophisticated goals: to construct the culture history of the past, to reconstruct ancient lifeways, the ways in which people made their living, and, most important of all, to explain how and why ancient human cultures changed through prehistoric times. This is where the most important advances in archaeology have been made—in seeking to explain why humans took up farming and aban-doned hunting and gathering, or what caused people to congregate in cities, develop writing, and establish a literate civilization. Studying such topics has involved the development of sophisticated theoretical models for explaining and interpreting the past, models that owe much to evolutionary and ecological theory. Science now realizes that archaeology is about the only discipline that enables us to study human biological and cultural evolution over long periods of time. The development of the tools to do so ranks among the greatest scientific triumphs of this century. Not that archaeology is confined to such topics, for in recent years there has been an explosion of interest in such issues as gender roles in ancient societies, and in such fascinating problems as social inequality in the past. One of the great fascinations of modern archaeology is its sheer range and diversity that accommodates archaeologists who study everything from foraging camps that are millions of years old to Mayan cities and abandoned railroad stations from the Industrial Revolution.

. . . there is a tremendous satisfaction and excitement in searching out the past. Even today, most talented archaeologists, at one time or another, feel they are in touch with the people they are studying. They seem to have an instinct for discovery, to know where to search and dig, and a sense of identity with their subjects. This sense seems to have been highly developed in Louis Leakey, Heinrich Schliemann, and Howard Carter. Carter experienced an almost eerie bond with Tutankhamun. He summed it up well when he wrote: "I stood in the presence of a king who reigned three thousand years ago." One suspects Carter was not speaking strictly figuratively: he felt he *really had*. Sometimes, as I have stood gazing over a long-deserted prehistoric settlement, silent on a cool evening as the sun casts long shadows over earthworks and eroding occupation deposits, I have experienced a sudden collapse of time. The site comes to life: thatched huts rise from the ground, scented wood smoke ascends in the evening still, dogs bark and children laugh in play. Outside their huts, old men sit and gossip quietly for a brief evening hour. Then, just as quickly, the image recedes and the village once again becomes a deserted archive of archaeological information, a silent complex of mud-hut foundations, dusty pot fragments, and broken food bones. For a moment, the ancient inhabitants of that village sprang to life, shedding their cloaks of anonymity to reach out across the millennia. Heady emotions, perhaps, but, for a moment, one understands why archaeology is so much more than just a set of techniques and tools for digging up the past.

The Golden Marshalltown:
A Parable for the Archeology
of the 1980s

Kent V. Flannery

Kent V. Flannery is Professor of Anthropology and Curator of Environmental Archeology, Museum of Anthropology, University of Michigan, Ann Arbor, MI 48109. He presented the Distinguished Lecture to the American Anthropological Association at the national meetings in Los Angeles on December 5, 1981.

I am happily too busy *doing* science to have time to worry about philosophizing about it. [Arno Penzias, Nobel Laureate, 1978]

This is a story about archeological goals and rewards, and no one should look for anything too profound in it. It's really just the story of a ride I took on an airplane from San Diego to Detroit. That may not sound very exciting to those of you who fly a lot, but this particular trip was memorable for me. For one thing, it was my first time on a 747. For another, I met someone on the plane who became one of the most unforgettable characters I've ever run across.

The flight was taking me home to Ann Arbor after the Society for American Archaeology meetings in May of 1981. I was leaving San Diego a day early because I had endured all the physical stress I could stand. I didn't particularly feel like watching the movie, so as soon as the plane was airborne and the seat belt sign had been turned off, I went forward to the lounge area of the plane. There were only two people there, both archeologists, and both recognized me from the meetings. So I had no choice but to sit down and have a beer with them.

I want to begin by telling you a little about my two companions, but you have to understand, I'm not going to give their actual names. Besides, their real identities aren't important, because each considers himself the spokesman for a large group of people.

The first guy, I suppose, came out of graduate school in the late 1960s, and he teaches now at a major department in the western United States. He began as a traditional archeologist, interested in Pueblo ruins and Southwestern prehistory, and he went on digs and surveys like the rest of us. Unlike the rest of us, he saw those digs and surveys not as an end in themselves, but as a means to an end, and a means that proved to be too slow. After a few years of dusty holes in hot, dreary valleys he was no closer to the top than when he had started, and in fact, he was showing signs of lamentable fallibility. In 50 tries at laying out a 5-ft square, he had never come closer than 4 ft 10 in by 5 ft 3 in, and he'd missed more floors than the elevator in the World Trade Center. And then, just when all seemed darkest, he discov-

ered Philosophy of Science, and was born again.

Suddenly he found the world would beat a path to his door if he criticized everyone else's epistemology. Suddenly he discovered that so long as his research design was superb, he never had to do the research; just publish the design, and it would be held up as a model, a brass ring hanging unattainable beyond the clumsy fingers of those who actually survey and dig. No more dust, no more heat, no more 5-ft squares. He worked in an office now, generating hypotheses and laws and models which an endless stream of graduate students was sent out to test; for he himself no longer did any fieldwork.

And it was just as well, for as one of his former professors had said, "That poor wimp couldn't dig his way out of a kitty litter box."

In all fairness to the Born-Again Philosopher, he was in large measure a product of the 1960s, and there are lots more like him where he came from. And let us not judge him too harshly until we have examined my other companion in the lounge, a young man whose degree came not from 1968, but from 1978. I will refer to him simply as the Child of the Seventies.

Like so many of his academic generation, the Child of the Seventies had but one outstanding characteristic: blind ambition. He had neither the commitment to culture history of my generation nor the devotion to theory of the generation of the 1960s. His goals were simple: to be famous, to be well paid, to be stroked, and to receive immediate gratification. How he got there did not matter. Who he stepped on along the way did not matter. Indeed, the data of prehistory did not matter. For him, archeology was only a vehicle—one carefully selected, because he had discovered early that people will put up with almost anything in the guise of archeology.

As a graduate student, the Child of the Seventies had taken a course in introductory archeology from a man I will simply refer to as Professor H. Professor H. worked very hard on the course, synthesizing the literature, adding original ideas and a lot of his own unpublished data. The Child of the Seventies took copious notes. Sometimes he asked questions to draw the instructor out, and sometimes he asked if he could copy Professor H.'s slides. When the professor used handouts, he bound them in his notebook.

At graduation, the Child of the Seventies went off to his first job at Springboard University. The day he arrived, he went directly to Springboard University Press and asked if they would like a textbook on introductory archeology. Of course they did. The Child polished his notes from Professor H.'s course and submitted them as a book. It was published to rave reviews. Today it is the only textbook on the subject that Professor H. really likes, and he requires it in his course. The faculty at Springboard U overwhelmingly voted the Child of the Seventies tenure. Professor H., on the other hand, has been held back because he hasn't published enough. "He's a great teacher," his colleagues say. "If only he could write more. Like that student of his at Springboard U."

To his credit as an anthropologist, the child had merely discerned that our subculture not only tolerates this sort of behavior, it *rewards* people for it. But the story doesn't end there.

The Child of the Seventies had written a six-chapter doctoral dissertation. Now he xeroxed each chapter and provided it with an introduction and con-

clusion, making it a separate article. Each was submitted to a different journal, and all were published within a year. He then persuaded Springboard University Press to publish a reader composed of his six reprinted works. In that reader, the chapters of his dissertation were at last reunited between hard covers. He added an overview, recounting the ways his perspective had changed as he looked back over the full sweep of his 18 months as a professional archeologist.

His publisher asked him to do another reader. This time, he invited six colleagues to write the various chapters. Some were flattered. Some were desperate. All accepted. He wrote a three-page introduction and put his name on the cover as editor. The book sold. And suddenly, his path to the top was clear; he could turn out a book a year, using the original ideas of others, without ever having an original idea himself. And in the long run, he would be better known and better paid than any of his contributors, even though they worked twice as hard.

I ordered a Michelob, and paid my buck-fifty a can, and sat wondering exactly what I could say to these two guys. It isn't easy when you know that one will criticize any idea you put forth, and the other will incorporate it into his next book. Fortunately I never had to say anything, for it was at exactly that moment that the third, and most important, character of this story entered the lounge.

He stood for a moment with his battered carryon bag in his hand, looking down at the three of us. He was an Old Timer—no question about that—but how old would have been anybody's guess. When you're that tanned and weather-beaten you could be 50, or 60, or even 70, and no one could really tell. His jeans had been through the mud and the barbed-wire fences of countless field seasons, his hat had faded in the prairie sun, and his eyes had the kind of crow's feet known locally as the High Plains squint. I could tell he was an archeologist by his boots, and I could tell he was still a good archeologist by the muscle tone in his legs.

(You see, I have a colleague at Michigan—an ethnologist—who claims that since archeologists have strong backs and weak minds, when an archeologist starts to fade, it's the legs that go first. On the other hand, his wife informs me that when an ethnologist starts to fade, the first thing to go is not his legs.)

The Old Timer settled into the seat next to me, stowed his carryon bag, and turned to introduce himself. I failed to catch his name because the stewardess, somewhat out of breath, caught up with him at that moment and pressed a bourbon and water into his hand. "Thank you, ma'am," he said, sipping it down; and he stared for a moment, and said, "I needed that. And that's the God's truth."

"I know what you mean," I said, "The meetings can do that to you. Six hundred people crammed into the lobby of a hotel. Two hundred are talking down to you as if you're an idiot. Two hundred are sucking up to you as if you're a movie star. Two hundred are telling you lies, and all the while they're looking over your shoulder, hoping they'll meet somebody more important."

"This year it was worse than that, son. Last night my department retired me. Turned me out to pasture."

"I wouldn't have guessed you were retirement age," I lied.

"I'm not. I had two years to go. But they retired me early. Mostly because of an article in the *New York Times Sunday Magazine* by an ethnologist, Eric Wold. You remember that one?"

"I read it," I said, "but I don't remember him calling for your retirement."

The Old Timer reached into his pocket, past a half-empty pouch of Bull Durham, and brought out a yellowed clipping from the Sunday *Times* of November 30, 1980. I caught a glimpse of Wolf's byline, and below it, several paragraphs outlined in red ink. "See what he says here," said the Old Timer.

An earlier anthropology had achieved unity under the aegis of the culture concept. It was culture, in the view of anthropologists, that distinguished humankind from all the rest of the universe, and it was the possession of varying cultures that differentiated one society from another. . . . The past quarter-century has undermined this intellectual sense of security. The relatively inchoate concept of "culture" was attacked from several theoretical directions. As the social sciences transformed themselves into "behavioral" sciences, explanations for behavior were no longer traced to culture; behavior was to be understood in terms of psychological encounters, strategies of economic choice, strivings for payoffs in games of power. Culture, once extended to all acts and ideas employed in social life, was now relegated to the margins as "world view" or "values." [Wolf 1980]

"Isn't that something?" said the Old Timer. "The day that came out my department called me in. The chairman says, 'It has come to our attention that you still believe in culture as the central paradigm in archeology.' I told him yes, I supposed I did. Then he says, 'We've talked about it, and we all think you ought to take early retirement.' "

"But that's terrible. You should have fought it."

"I *did* fight it," he said. "But they got my file together and sent it out for an outside review. Lord, they sent it to all these distinguished anthropologists. Marvin Harris. Clifford Geertz. And aren't there a couple of guys at Harvard with hyphenated names?"

"At least a couple." I assured him.

"Well, they sent my file to one of them. And to some Big Honcho social anthropologist at the University of Chicago. And the letters started coming back.

"Harris said he was shocked to see that in spite of the fact that I was an archeologist, I had paid so little attention to the techno-eco-demo-environmental variables. Geertz said as far as he could tell, all I was doing was Thick Description. The guy from Harvard said he wasn't sure he could evaluate me, because he'd never even heard of our department."

"And how about the guy from Chicago?"

"He said that he felt archeology could best be handled by one of the local trade schools."

There was a moment of silence while we all contemplated the heartbreak of an archeologist forced into early retirement by his belief in culture. In the background we could hear our pilot announcing that the Salton Sea was visible off to the right of the aircraft.

"They sure gave me a nice retirement party, though," said the Old Timer. "Rented a whole suite at the hotel. And I want to show you what they gave me as a going-away present."

His hand groped for a moment in the depths of his battle-scarred overnight bag, and suddenly he produced a trowel. A trowel such as no one had ever seen. A trowel that turned to yellow flame in the rays of the setting sun as he held it up to the window of the 747.

"This was my first Marshalltown trowel," he said. "You know what an archeologist's first Marshalltown is like? Like a major leaguer's first Wilson glove. I dug at Pecos with this trowel, under A. V. Kidder. And at Aztec Ruin with Earl Morris. And at Kincaid with Fay-Cooper Cole. And at Lindenmeier with Frank Roberts. Son, this trowel's been at Snaketown, and Angel Mound, and at the Dalles of the Columbia with Luther Cressman.

"And then one night, these guys from my department broke into my office and borrowed it, so to speak. And the next time I saw it, they'd had that sucker plated in 24-karat gold.

"It sure is pretty now. And that's the God's truth."

The trowel passed from hand to hand around our little group before returning to the depths of the Old Timer's bag. And for each of us, I suppose, it made that unimaginably far-off day of retirement just a little bit less remote.

"What do you think you'll do now?" asked the Child of the Seventies, for whom retirement would not come until the year 2018.

"Well," said the Old Timer, "so far the only thing that's opened up for me are some offers to do contract archeology."

The Born-Again Philosopher snickered condescendingly.

"I take it," said the Old Timer, "you have some reservations about contract archeology."

"Oh, it's all right, I suppose," said the Philosopher. "I just don't think it has much of a contribution to make to *my* field."

"And what would that field be?"

"Method and theory."

"No particular region or time period?"

"No. I wouldn't want to be tied down to a specific region. I work on a higher level of abstraction."

"I'll bet you do," said the Old Timer. "Well, son, there are some things about contract archeology I don't like either. Occasional compromises between scientific goals and industrial goals. Too many reports that get mimeographed for the president of some construction company, rather than being published where archeologists can read them. But in all fairness, most of the contract archeologists I know express just as strong an interest in method and theory as you do."

"But they're law *consumers*," said the Philosopher. "I'm committed to being a law *producer*."

The Old Timer took a thoughtful drag on his bourbon. "Son," he said, "I admire a man who dispenses with false modesty. But you've overlooked what I see as one of the strengths of contract archeologists: they still deal directly with what happened in prehistory. If I want to know what happened in Glen Canyon, or when agriculture reached the Missouri Basin, or how long the mammoth hunters lasted in Pennsylvania, often as not I need to talk to a contract archeologist. Because the answers to the cultural-historical questions don't always lie on a 'higher level of abstraction.' "

"No," said the Born-Again Philosopher. "Only the *important* questions lie on that level."

"There was an interruption as the stewardess reappeared before us, pushing an aluminum beverage cart. We ordered another round of beer, and she picked up our empty cans, depositing them in a plastic trash bag attached to the cart.

1. ABOUT ARCHAEOLOGY

"I'd like to ask a favor," said the Born-Again Philosopher. "Before our 10-minute stopover in Tucson, I'd like to examine the contents of that bag."

"Now I've heard everything," said the stewardess.

"No, it's not a come-on," said the Philosopher. "It's a favor for a friend. I have a colleague, Bill Rathje, who's doing a study of garbage disposal patterns in the city of Tucson [Rathje 1974]. He's got the internal system pretty well mapped out, but he realizes that Tucson is not a closed system: garbage enters and leaves via planes, cars, and backpacks. I promised him if I were ever on a plane landing or taking off from Tucson, I'd sample the refuse on board."

The stewardess struggled to remove all trace of emotion from her face. "Well," she said, "I suppose if you clean up everything when you're done—."

"I'll be checking the refuse in the tourist-class cabin," said the Philosopher, "while my friend here" (indicating the Child of the Seventies) "will be checking the first-class cabin, and coauthoring the paper with me."

"And what do you call your profession?" she asked.

"Archeology."

"You guys are weird," she called over her shoulder as she and the cart disappeared down the aisle.

The Born-Again Philosopher settled back in his seat with a pleased smile on his face. "Now there's a perfect example of why archeologists should not restrict themselves to the study of ancient objects lying on the surface or underneath the ground. If we're to develop a truly universal set of covering laws, we must be free to derive them from any source we can.

"In my opinion," he said, "the greatest legacy we can leave the next generation is a body of robust archeological theory."

"Well, son, I'll give you my opinion," said the Old Timer. "I don't believe there's any such thing as 'archeological theory.' For me there's only *anthropological* theory. Archeologists have their own methodology, and ethnologists have theirs; but when it comes to theory, we all ought to sound like anthropologists."

"My God, are you out of it!" said the Born-Again Philosopher. "For ten years we've been building up a body of purely archeological laws. I myself have contributed 10 or 20."

"I'd love to hear a few," I said. And I could see I was not the only one: the Child of the Seventies was getting ready to write them down unobtrusively on his cocktail napkin.

"Number One," said the Philosopher: "Prehistoric people did not leave behind in the site examples of everything they made. Number Two: Some of the things they did leave behind disintegrated, and cannot be found by archeologists."

"I don't want to sound unappreciative," I said, "but I believe Schliemann already knew that when he was digging at Troy."

"If he did," and the B.A.P. ," he never made it *explicit*. I have made it *explicit*."

"Son," said the Old Timer, "I guess we can all sleep easier tonight because of that."

"I also came up with the following," the Philosopher went on. "Number Three: Objects left on a sloping archeological site wash downhill. Number Four: Lighter objects wash downhill farther than heavy objects."

"Hold it right there, son," said the Old Timer, "because you've just illustrated a point I was hoping to make. So often these things you fellows call archeological laws turn out not to be laws of human behavior, but examples of the physical processes involved in the formation of sites. And son, those are no more than the products of *geological* laws."

The Born-Again Philosopher's face lit up in a triumphant smile. "That objection has been raised many times before," he said, "and it was disposed of definitively by Richard Watson, who is both a geologist and a philosopher. In his 1976 *American Antiquity* article, Watson (1976:65) makes it clear (and here I am paraphrasing) that even when hypotheses are directly dependent on laws of geology, they are specifically archeological *when they pertain to archeological materials.*"

Now it was the Old Timer's turn to smile "Oh. Well. That's different," he said. "In that case, I guess, archeology just barely missed out on a major law."

"How's that?" asked the Child of the Seventies earnestly, his pencil at the ready.

"Well, following your argument, the Law of Uniform Acceleration could have been an archeological law if only Galileo had dropped a metate and mano from the Leaning Tower of Pisa."

"I don't think you're taking this seriously," the Born-Again Philosopher complained.

"Son," said the Old Timer. "I'm taking it fully as seriously as it deserves to be taken. And as far as I'm concerned, so far the only legitimate archeological law I know of is the Moss-Bennett Bill."

The Born-Again Philosopher drew himself erect. "I think I'd better go back and start my inventory of the tourist-class trash," he said, and he began working his way down the aisle toward the galley.

"You're being awfully hard on him," said the Child of the Seventies. "You have to remember that he's the spokesman for a large number of theoretical archeologists who hope to increase archeology's contribution to science and philosophy."

The Old Timer took a long, slow pull on his bourbon. "Son, do you watch Monday Night Football?" he asked.

"Occasionally," said the Child. "When I'm not correcting page proofs."

"I have a reason for asking." said the Old Timer. "I just want to try out an analogy on you.

"During Monday Night Football there are 22 players on the field, 2 coaches on the sidelines, and 3 people in the broadcast booth. Two of the people in the booth are former players who can no longer play. One of the people in the booth never played a lick in his life. And who do you suppose talks the loudest and is the most critical of the players on the field?"

"The guy who never played a lick," I interrupted. "And the guys with him, the former players, are always saying things like, 'Well, it's easy to criticize from up here, but it's different when you're down on the field.'"

"Well said, son," the Old Timer chuckled. "And I want you to consider the symbolism for a moment. The field is lower than everything else; it's physical, it's sweaty, it's a place where people follow orders. The press box is high, detached, Olympian, cerebral. And it's verbal. Lord, is it verbal.

"Now football is a game of strategy, of game plans (or 'research designs,' if you will), and what are called differing philosophies. In our lifetime we've witnessed great innovations in strategy: the nickel defense, the flex, the shotgun, the wishbone—and the list goes on. How many of them were created in the press box?"

"None," I said. "They were created by coaches."

"By coaches, many of them former players, who are still personally involved in the game, and who diligently study their own mistakes, create new strategies, and return to the field to test them in combat," said the Old Timer.

"I think I see what you're driving at," said the Child of the Seventies, but we knew he was lying.

"There are estimated to be more than 4,000 practicing archeologists in the United States," said the Old Timer. "Most of them are players. Sure, many of us are second- or third-string, but when we're called upon to go in, we do the best we can. And we rely on the advice and strategy of a fair number of archeological 'coaches'—veterans, people we respect because they've paid their dues the same as we have.

"What's happening now is that we're getting a new breed of archeologist. A kind of archeological Howard Cosell. He sits in a booth high above the field, and cites Hempel and Kuhn and Karl Popper. He second-guesses our strategy, and tells us when we don't live up to his expectations. 'Lew Binford,' he says, 'once the fastest mind in the field, but frankly, this season he may have lost a step or two.' Or, 'It's shocking to see a veteran like Struever make a rookie mistake like that.'

"What I worry about, son, is that every year there'll be fewer people down on the field and more up in the booth. There's a great living to be made in the booth, but it's a place that breeds a great deal of arrogance. No one in the booth ever fumbles a punt or, for that matter, misclassifies a potsherd or screws up a profile drawing. They pass judgment on others, but never expose themselves to criticism. The guys in the booth get a lot of exposure, and some even achieve celebrity status. What rarely gets pointed out is that the guys in the booth have had little if any strategic and theoretical impact on the game, because they're far removed from the field of play.

"But the players know that. Especially the contract archeologists, and those of us who perennially work in the field. Because we have the feeling the guys in the booth look down on us as a bunch of dumb, sweaty jocks. And we're damn sick of it, son, and that's the God's truth."

"But you surely don't deny the importance of theory in archeology," said the Child of the Seventies. "I'm sure you've used what Binford [1977] calls middle-range theory in your own work."

"Of course," said the Old Timer. "I've used it to organize and make sense out of my data. Which is, when you stop to think about it, one of the main purposes for theory. The problem came when the guys in the booth began to think of 'archeological theory' as a subdiscipline in its own right—a higher and more prestigious calling than the pursuit of data on prehistory, which they see as a form of manual labor. As if that weren't bad enough, some of them are now beginning to think of themselves as philosophers of science."

"I find that exciting," said the Child of the Seventies.

"Son," said the Old Timer, "it would be exciting, if they were any good at it. Unfortunately, in most cases, it's the only thing they're worse at than field archeology."

"But some are establishing a dialogue with philosophers," said the Child.

"That's right," said the Old Timer. "Now we're going to have philosophers who don't know anything about archeology, advising archeologists who don't know anything about philosophy."

"They want archeology to make a contribution to philosophy," said the Child.

"I'll tell you what," said the Old Timer. "I'd settle for making a contribution to *archeology*. I guess I'd rather be a second-rate archeologist than a third-rate philosopher."

"But doesn't archeology have more to offer the world than that?"

The Old Timer leaned back in his seat and sipped at his bourbon. "That's a good question," he said. "We hear a lot about archeology's relevance to anthropology in general. To the social sciences. To the world. And of course, we're all waiting for our recently departed friend to come up with his first Great Law. But I'd like to turn the question around and ask What does the world really want from archeology?

"If I turn on television, or walk through a paperback bookstore, I'll tell you what I see. I see that what the world wants is for archeology to teach it something about humanity's past. The world doesn't want epistemology from us. They want to hear about Olduvai Gorge, and Stonehenge, and Macchu Picchu. People are gradually becoming aware that their first three million years took place before written history, and they look at archeology as the only science—the *only one*—with the power to uncover the past.

"I remember Bill Sanders telling me once that the only legitimate reason to do archeology was to satisfy your intellectual curiosity. And I suspect that if we just try to do a good job at that, the more general contributions will follow naturally. I don't think Isaac Newton or Gregor Mendel ran around saying 'I'm a law producer.' Their laws grew unself-consciously out of their efforts to satisfy their own curiosity.

"Son, if the world wants philosophy, it will surely turn to philosophers, not archeologists, to get it. I'd hate to see us get so confused about what the world wants from archeology that we turn our backs on what we do best. In my opinion, our major responsibility to the rest of the world is to do good, basic archeological research."

1. ABOUT ARCHAEOLOGY

"You know," said the Child of the Seventies, "as I listen to you talk, I'm thinking how nice it would be to have you write an overview for the book I'm editing right now. A book on future directions in archeology."

"I'm not sure how excited I am about some of the future directions," said the Old Timer.

That's why your overview would give us needed balance," said the Child. "Why, you're our link with the past. You've stepped right out of the pages of archeology's rich, much maligned empiricist tradition."

"You overestimate me, son."

"No. You're too modest," said the Child, who was not used to being turned down. "I feel that you may well be the most significant figure of your generation, and I'd consider myself deeply honored to have your overview in my book."

"Horsefeathers," said the Old Timer.

The Child of the Seventies stood up with a gesture of frustration. "I've got to inventory the trash in the first-class cabin, or I won't get to coauthor that article," he said. "But think over what I said. And don't say anything important until I get back."

We watched him disappear through the curtain into the first-class section.

"You must have been inoculated against soft soap," I told the Old Timer.

"Son," he said, "if that young fellow's nose were any browner, we'd need a Munsell Soil Color Chart to classify it."

"If you think he's at all atypical," I suggested, "take a good look around you at the next archeology meeting."

"And you know," said the Old Timer, "we're partly to blame for that. All of us in academic departments.

"We hire a young guy, right out of graduate school, and we give him all our introductory courses to teach. Then we tell him it's publish or perish. His only choices are to write something half-baked, or make an article out of an attack on some already established figure. You take those two kinds of papers out of *American Antiquity,* and you got nothing left but the book review."

"What we *ought* to do, if we really want these young people to grow, is give them their first year off, so they can go collect their own data and make their own positive contribution. How can we give them eight courses to teach and then put pressure on them to publish?"

"You're right," I said. "But our two friends here have discovered how to beat the system. One has created a specialty that never requires him to leave his office, and the other has figured out how to get other people to write his books for him. And we reward both of them for it."

"But not without some reservations," said the Old Timer. "You know, archeologists don't really like having a colleague who's so ambitious he'd kick his own grandmother's teeth in to get ahead. Businessmen, or perhaps showbusiness people, will tolerate it. They'll say, 'He's a real S.O.B., but he gets things done.' But archeologists don't want a colleague who's a real S.O.B. They're funny that way."

The stewardess with the beverage cart paused by our seats for a moment to see if we needed a refill. We did. And I took that opportunity to ask how our friends were coming with their inventory of her garbage.

"The one in the aft cabin seems to have hit a snag," she said thoughtfully. "I think he ran into a couple of airsickness bags."

"Well," said the Old Timer, "nobody said fieldwork was easy."

"What are those guys trying to find out, anyway?" she asked.

"As I understand it," I said, "they're trying to provide us with a better basis for archeological interpretation. Since archeologists study the garbage of ancient peoples, they hope to discover principles of garbage discard that will guide us in our work."

The Old Timer's eyes followed the stewardess as she passed through the curtain into the next cabin.

"Son," he said, "I want to hit you with a hypothetical question. Let's say you're working on a 16th-century Arikara site in South Dakota. There's lots of garbage—bison scapula hoes, Catlinite pipes, Bijou Hills quartzite, cord-marked pottery—you know the kind of stuff. You got to interpret it. You got an 18th-century French account of the Arikara, and you got a report on Tucson's garbage in 1981. Which would you use?"

"I think you already know the answer to that one," I smiled.

"Then why do I have the distinct impression that these two kids would use the report on Tucson's garbage?" he demanded.

"Because *you* still believe in *culture,*" I said, "and these kids are only concerned with *behavior.*"

"I guess that's right," he said thoughtfully. "I guess I believe in something called 'Arikara culture,' and I think you ought to know something about it if you work on Arikara sites."

"But suppose, as Eric Wolf suggests in that *Times* article, you're one of those people who no longer looks to culture as an explanation for behavior," I suggested. "Suppose you believe that behavior is explained by universal laws, or psychological encounters, or strategies of economic choice. Then it really doesn't matter whether your interpretive framework comes from tribal ethnohistory or 20th-century industrial America, does it?"

"Nope. And that's sure going to simplify archeology," said the Old Timer. "For one thing, we can forget about having to master the anthropological literature."

He fell silent as the Born-Again Philosopher and the Child of the Seventies returned to their seats, their notebooks filled with behavioral data and their faces flushed with success.

"Did we miss much?" asked the Child.

"Not much," said the Old Timer. "I was just fixing to ask my friend here where he thinks anthropology will go next, now that it no longer has culture as its central paradigm."

"I'm kind of worried about it," I admitted. "Right now I have the impression that anthropology is sort of drifting, like a rudderless ship. I have the feeling it could fragment into a dozen lesser disciplines, with everybody going his own way. Somehow it's not as exciting as it used to be. Enrollments are down all over the country. The job market sucks. I suspect one reason is that anthropology is so lacking in consensus as to what it has to offer, it just can't sell itself compared to more unified and aggressive fields."

"Doesn't Wolf tell you in his *Times* article what the next central paradigm will be?" asked the Child of the Seventies. He was hoping for a title for his next book.

"No," said the Old Timer. "He mentions other things people have tried, like cultural materialism, cultural ecology, French structuralism, cognitive and symbolic anthropology, and so on. But you know, none of those approaches involves more than a fraction of the people in the field."

"But it's useful to have all those approaches," I suggested.

"That's the God's truth," he agreed. "But what holds us all together? What keeps us all from pursuing those things until each becomes a separate field in its own right? What is it that makes a guy who works on Maori creation myths continue to talk to a guy who works mainly on Paleoindian stone tools?"

"In my department," I said, "they *don't* talk any more."

"Nor in mine," he said. "But they used to. And they *used* to talk because however obscure their specialties, they all believe in that 'integrated whole,' that 'body of shared customs, beliefs, and values' that we called culture."

"That's right," I said. "But now the Paleoindian archeologist would tell you his stone tools were best explained by Optimal Foraging Strategy. And the Maori ethnologist would tell you his creation myths are the expression of a universal logic inside his informants' heads."

"You know," said the Old Timer, "we've got an ethnologist like that on our faculty. He told me once, 'I'm not interested in anything you can feel, smell, taste, weigh, measure, or count. None of that is real. What's real is in my head.' Kept talking and talking about how what was in his head was what was important. For a long time, I couldn't figure it out.

"Then one day he published his ethnography, and I understood why

what was in his head was so important. He'd made up all his data."

The Born-Again Philosopher stirred restlessly in his seat. "It's incredible to me," he said, "that you people haven't realized that for more than a decade now the new paradigm has been Logical Positivism. It's hard to see how you can do problem-oriented archeology without it."

Slowly the Old Timer rolled himself a cigarette. The Child of the Seventies sat up momentarily, leaned forward to watch, then slumped back in his seat with disappointment when he realized it was only Bull Durham.

"Have you considered," said the Old Timer deliberately, "the implications of doing problem-oriented archeology without the concept of culture?"

"Now you're putting us on," said the Philosopher.

For just a moment, the Old Timer allowed himself a smile. "Consider this," he said. "An ethnologist can say, 'I'm only interested in myth and symbolism, and I'm not going to collect data on subsistence.' He can go to a village in the Philippines and ignore the terraced hillsides and the rice paddies and the tilapia ponds, and just ask people about their dreams and the spirits of their ancestors. Whatever he does, however selective he is in what he collects, when he leaves the village, it's still there. And next year, if a Hal Conklin or an Aram Yengoyan comes along, those terraces and paddies and fish ponds will still be there to study.

"But suppose an archeologist were to say, 'I'm only interested in Anasazi myth and symbolism, and I'm not going to collect data on subsistence.' Off he goes to a prehistoric cliff dwelling and begins to dig. He goes for the pictographs, and figurines, and ceremonial staffs, and wooden bird effigies. What, then, does he do with all the digging sticks, and tumplines, and deer bones that he finds while he's digging for all the other stuff? Does he ignore them because they don't relate to his 'research problem?' Does he shovel them onto the dump? Or does he pack them up and put them in dead storage, in the hope that he can farm them out to a student some day to ease

his conscience? Because, unlike the situation in ethnology, no archeologist will be able to come along later and find that stuff in its original context. It's *gone,* son."

"It's as if—well, as if your Philippine ethnologist were to interview an informant on religion, and then kill him so no one could ever interview him on agriculture," I ventured.

"Exactly, son," he said. "Archeology is the only branch of anthropology where we kill our informants in the process of studying them."

"Except for a few careless physical anthropologists," I said.

"Well, yes, except for that."

"But hasn't that always been the conflict between 'problem-oriented' archeology and traditional archeology?" asked the Born-Again Philosopher. "Surely you have to have a specific hypothesis to test, and stick pretty much to the data relevant to that hypothesis, rather than trying to record everything."

"And what about other archeologists with other hypotheses." I asked. "Don't you feel a little uncomfortable destroying data relevant to their problem while you're solving yours?"

"Well, *I* don't, because I really don't do any digging now," said the Philosopher. "I see my role as providing the hypotheses that will direct the research efforts of others. There are lots of archeologists around who can't do anything *but* dig. Let *them* do the digging.

"Look," he said, "I can't say it any better than Schiffer [1978:247] said it in Dick Gould's 1978 volume on ethnoarcheology. To paraphrase him: I feel free to pursue the study of laws wherever it leads. I do *not* feel the need to break the soil periodically in order to reaffirm my status as archeologist."

"Son," said the Old Timer, "I think I just heard 10,000 archeological sites breathe a sigh of relief."

There was a moment of air turbulence, and we all reached for our drinks. The sleek ribbon of the Colorado River shimmered below us, and over the audio system we could hear the captain advise us to keep our seat belts loosely fastened. Hunched in his seat, reflective, perhaps just a little sad, the Old Timer whispered in my ear: "That's what the ethnologists will never understand, son. There's a basic conflict between problem-oriented archeology and archeological ethics. Problem orientation tells you to pick a specific topic to investigate. Archeological ethics tell you you *must* record everything, because no one will ever see it in context again. The problem is that except for certain extraordinary sites, archeological data don't come packaged as 'cognitive' or 'religious' or 'environmental' or 'economic.' They're all together in the ground—integrated in complex ways, perhaps, but integrated. That's why the old concept of culture made sense as a paradigm for archeology. And it still does, son. That's the God's truth."

I wish I could tell you how the rest of the conversation went, but at this point I could no longer keep my eyes open. After all, you wear a guy out at the meetings, and then give him six beers and start talking archeological theory, and that guy's going to fall asleep. So I slept even through those bumpy landings in the desert where the Child of the Seventies and the Born-Again Philosopher retired to their respective universities, and then somewhere between St. Louis and Detroit, I started to dream.

Now, I don't know whether it was because of the beer or the heated discussion we'd had, but my dream was a nightmare. I don't really know what it means, but my friends who work with the Walbiri and the Pitjandjara tell me that Dream Time is when you get your most important messages. So let me talk about it for a minute.

In this dream, I'd been released by the University of Michigan—whether for moral turpitude or believing in culture is really not clear. No job had opened up anywhere, and the only work I could find was with Bill Rathje's Garbage Project in Tucson. And not as a supervisor, just as a debagger. Sorting through the refuse of a thousand nameless homes, Anglo and Chicano, Pima and Papago, hoping against hope for that discarded wallet or diamond ring that could underwrite my retirement program.

And then, one day, I'm standing on the loading dock with my gauze mask on, and my pink rubber gloves, and my white lab coat with "Le Projet du Garbage" embroidered on the pocket, and this *huge* garbage truck pulls up to the dock and unloads a 30-gallon Hefty Bag. The thing is heavy as the dickens, and I wrestle it onto a dolly, and wheel it inside the lab; and we dump it onto the lab table, where the thing splits under its own weight and its contents come out all over the place.

And you know what's in it?
Reprints.
Reprints of *my* articles. Every single reprint I ever mailed out. All of them. And I'm not just talking reprints; I'm talking *autographed* reprints. The kind where I'd written something in the upper right-hand corner like, "Dear Dr. Willey, I hope you find this of interest."

You know, you can mail 'em out, but you never know whether they *keep* 'em or not.

And I suddenly realize that my whole career—my entire professional output—is in that Hefty Bag. Along with a couple of disposable diapers, and a pair of pantyhose, and a copy of *Penthouse* with the Jerry Falwell interview torn out.

But that's not the worst part.
The worst part is that the form Rathje's people fill out doesn't have a space for "discarded reprints." So my whole career, my entire professional output, simply has to be recorded as "other."

And that's where the nightmare ended, and I woke up on the runway at Detroit. I was grabbing my carryon bag as I bumped into the stewardess on her way down the aisle. "The Old Timer who was sitting next to me," I said. "What stop did he get off at?"

"What Old Timer?" she asked.

"The old guy in the boots and the faded hat with the rattlesnake hatband."

"I didn't see anybody like that," she said. "The only 'old guy' in the lounge was you."

"Have a nice day," I said sweetly. And I caught the limousine to Ann Arbor, and all the way home to my front door I kept wondering whether I had dreamed the whole thing.

Now I'll bet some of you don't think this all really happened. And I was beginning to doubt it myself until I started to unpack my carryon bag, and I was almost blinded by a gleam. A 24-karat gleam.

And there, hastily stuffed into my bag with a note wrapped around the handle, was the golden Marshalltown.

And the note read: "Son, where I'm going, I won't be needing this. I know you and I see eye to eye on a lot of things, so I'm going to ask a favor. I want you to save it for—well, just the right person.

"First off, I don't see any paradigm out there right now that's going to replace culture as a unifying theme in archeology. If some ethnologists want to go their separate ways—into sociobiology, or applied semeiotics, or social psychology—well, fine, they can call themselves something else, and let *us* be the anthropologists. I sort of felt that the concept of culture was what distinguished us from those other fields and kept us all from drifting apart for good.

"Because of the way our data come packaged in the ground, we pretty much have to deal with all of them to deal with any of them. It's harder for us to abandon the traditional concerns of anthropology, and we can't afford sudden fads, or quixotic changes in what's 'in' this year. We need long-term stability. And because we kill our informants as we question them, we have to question them in ways that are less idiosyncratic and more universally interpretable. And we have to share data in ways they don't.

"Because of that, we have to have a kind of integrity most fields don't need. I need your data, and you need mine, and we have to be able to trust each other on some basic level. There can't be any backstabbing, or working in total isolation, or any of this sitting on a rock in the forest interpreting culture in ways no colleague can duplicate.

"That's why we can't afford too many S.O.B.s. We can't afford guys whose lives are spent sitting in a press box criticizing other people's contributions. Son, all of prehistory is hidden in a vast darkness, and my generation was taught that it was better to light one tiny candle than curse the darkness. Never did I dream we'd have people whose whole career was based on cursing our *candles.*

"In the old days we mainly had one kind of archeologist: a guy who scratched around for a grant, went to the field, surveyed or excavated to the best of his ability, and published the results. Some guys labored patiently, in obscurity, for years. And one day, their colleagues would look up and say, 'You know, old Harry's doing good, solid work. Nothing spectacular, mind you, but you know—I'd trust him to dig on my site.' I believe that's the highest compliment one archeologist can pay another. And that's the God's truth.

"Now that doesn't sound like much, son, but today we got archeologists that can't even do that. What's more, they're too damn ambitious to labor in obscurity. So they've decided to create a whole new set of specialties around the margins of the field. Each defines himself (or herself) as the founder of that specialty, and then sets out to con the rest of us into believing that's where all the action is.

"And because archeologists will believe *anything,* pretty soon you've got a mass migration to the margins of the field. And pretty soon that's where the greatest noise is coming from.

"Now, don't get me wrong. A lot of these kids are shrewd and savvy, and they'll make a contribution one way or another. But that's one out of ten. The other nine are at the margins because things weren't moving fast enough for them in the main stream. You know,

some of these kids think archeology is a 100-meter dash, and they're shocked and angry when no one pins a medal on them after the first 100 meters. But I'll tell you a secret: archeology is a marathon, and you don't win marathons with speed. You win them with character.

"Son, after our talk this afternoon, I got to wondering about what archeology needed the most.

"I decided there probably isn't an urgent need for one more young person who makes a living editing other people's original ideas. I decided there probably wasn't an urgent need for one more kid who criticizes everyone else's research design while he or she never goes to the field. And I decided we probably didn't need a lot more of our archeological flat tires recapped as philosophers. There seem to be enough around to handle the available work.

"What I don't see enough of son, is first-rate archeology.

"Now that's sad, because after all, archeology is fun. Hell, I don't break the soil periodically to 'reaffirm my status.' I do it because archeology is still the most fun you can have with your pants on.

"You know, there are a lot of awards in archeology. The Viking Fund Medal, the Kidder Medal, the Aztec Eagle, the Order of the Quetzal. But those awards are for intellectual contributions. I'd like to establish an award just for commitment to plain, old-fashioned basic research and professional ethics. And that's what this trowel is for.

"So, son, some day when you meet a kid who still believes in culture, and

in hard work, and in the history of humanity; a kid who's in the field because he or she loves it, and not because they want to be famous; a kid who'd never fatten up on somebody else's data, or cut down a colleague just to get ahead; a kid who knows the literature, and respects the generations who went before—you give the kid this golden Marshalltown."

And the note ended there, with no signature, no address, and no reply required.

So that, I guess, is what I'm really here for tonight: to announce an award for someone who may not exist. But if any of you out there know of such a kid coming along—a kid who still depends on his own guts and brains instead of everyone else's—a kid who can stand on the shoulders of giants, and not be tempted to relieve himself on their heads—have *I* got an award for *him.*

And that's the God's truth.

REFERENCES CITED

Binford, Lewis R., 1977. General Introduction. *In* For Theory Building in Archeology: Essays on Faunal Remains, Aquatic Resources, Spatial Analysis, and Systemic Modeling. Lewis R. Binford, ed. pp. 1–10. New York: Academic Press.

Rathje, William L., 1974. The Garbage Project: A New Way of Looking at the Problems of Archaeology. Archaeology 27:236–241.

Schiffer, Michael B., 1978. Methodological Issues in Ethnoarchaeology. *In* Explorations in Ethnoarchaeology. Richard A. Gould, ed. pp. 229–247. Albuquerque: University of New Mexico Press (for the School of American Research).

Watson, Richard A., 1976. Inference in Archaeology. American Antiquity 41(1):58–66.

Wolf, Eric, 1980. They Divide and Subdivide, and Call It Anthropology. The New York Times Sunday Magazine, Nov. 30, 1980.

The Enlightened Archaeologist

*Thomas Jefferson's exploration of an Indian burial mound was, for its time,
an extraordinary achievement. Recent excavations in Virginia offer
new insights into his goals and interpretations.*

Jeffrey L. Hantman and Gary Dunham

Jeffrey L. Hantman, an associate professor of anthropology at the University of Virginia, has conducted research on the prehistory of the Pueblo Southwest and the late prehistoric and contact periods in Virginia. He is currently writing a book on Monacan archaeology and ethnohistory.

Gary Dunham, a doctoral candidate in anthropology at the University of Virginia, directed the excavations at the Rapidan Mound.

Thomas Jefferson's excavation of an Indian burial mound near Charlottesville, Virginia, has earned him the title "Father of American Archaeology." Jefferson described his dig on the South Fork of the Rivanna River in his book, *Notes on the State of Virginia.* He also reported that "many [mounds] are to be found all over this country [though] cleared of their trees and put under cultivation [they] are much reduced in their height, and spread in width, by the plough, and will probably disappear in time." In fact, the mound excavated by Jefferson has disappeared from view, despite several attempts to locate it earlier in this century. Jefferson's description of it remains the sole documentation that it existed at all.

In 1988, an opportunity arose to study a burial mound quite similar to the one dug by Jefferson. Known as the Rapidan Mound, it is located just 14 miles from the one Jefferson excavated. It had been placed on the endangered sites list of the Virginia Department of Historic Resources, and money was available to help excavate and preserve the remaining portions of it. Once prominent in the middle of a floodplain, it had been steadily eroded by the shifting course and destructive flooding of the Rapidan River. Early nineteenth-century accounts of the Rapidan Mound suggest it was then a 12- to 15-foot-high conical mound with a diameter of some 50 feet. In 1892, the Smithsonian's Gerard Fowke, who had been an assistant to Cyrus Thomas on the great mound surveys of the late nineteenth century, recorded the mound as being reduced to six feet in height, though the width had remained stable. Fowke dug a large trench through the mound, even then severely eroded by the river and partially leveled by farmers. In 1979, Archaeological Society of Virginia members Charlton G. Holland, Sandra Spieden, and David van Roijen opened two small excavation units on the river's edge and described apparently random deposits of human bone and a submound pit. By 1988 those units had been washed away, and only a small fragment of the mound's south edge remained. The rate of destruction had quickened even in the past few years, and there was no way possible to secure the site without flooding farm fields downstream.

On a cold spring day, we met with archaeologists Keith Egloff, David Hazzard, Randy Turner, and Catherine Slusser from the Virginia Department of Historic Resources and discussed the possibility of salvaging the site. Because preservation was simply not possible, we decided to record what was left of the mound, in accordance with Virginia's new burial laws that include a commitment to rebury human remains.

Initially we were skeptical that there would be anything left within the mound to record. Although respectfully protected in recent years by the family that owned the land on which it was located, the mound's condition was rapidly deteriorating. Recent floods had eroded the north face exposed to the river; a few abandoned cars buried off the south edge of the mound acted as a makeshift flood wall. Despite the erosion, we felt a season of testing was worth the effort. Funds from the Virginia Department of Historic Resources provided for a professional staff to oversee the excavation; students from the University of Virginia's summer field school joined in the dig after receiving extensive training at nearby sites. It would be three years before we finished our work.

Most of our first season was spent clinging to the riverbank, our feet in small rests cut into the submound soils, cleaning off flood debris and roots to reveal the mound's inner levels. We could see the clear outline of the trench that Fowke had made. Having located the old trench, we could focus our attention on undisturbed areas. What we discovered was an astonishing similarity between the profiles of our mound and the one excavated by Jefferson—layers of dark stained soil with bone in it, interrupted by lighter colored soils brought to the site. Where Jefferson had seen seven such levels near the center of his mound, we could see three.

Jefferson had actually employed two excavation strategies. One was trenching, which allowed him to look at the internal structure of the mound and its stratigraphy. In this he was about 100 years ahead of his time. But he also wrote: "I first dug superficially in several parts of it, and came to collections of human bones, at different depths, from six inches to three feet below the surface. These were lying in the utmost confusion, some vertical, some oblique, some horizontal, and directed to every point of the compass, entangled, and held together in clusters by the earth. Bones of the most distant part were found together. . . ." What Jefferson could not see or fully appreciate with his narrow trenching and random digging was the internal structure of each of the separate burial features he had carefully identified.

In 1989 and 1990 we excavated the Rapidan River mound by exposing broad horizontal areas in an effort to study the spatial relationships among the mound's burial features, as well as the internal configuration of each burial. We were able to identify six burial features, three of which we excavated completely. We found that the bones were not "lying in utmost confusion," as Jefferson described them, nor were they random placements as posited by later excavators. Instead, the bones, after an initial burial or exposure of the body to remove the flesh, had been recovered and reburied as part of a mortuary ritual. The skulls had been placed in concentric circles with long bones distributed around them in linear arrangements. Our excavations also revealed a pattern of change in burial practice over time from earlier individual or small multiple burials in pits, to later secondary

burials containing up to 20 individuals. Jefferson did not record any submound pits, although they are common in most Virginia mounds, and we, as well as Fowke, found them at Rapidan Mound. Like the careful arrangement of bones, Jefferson probably missed them because he dug only narrow trenches and excavation pits.

We estimate that between 1,000 and 1,500 people were buried in the Rapidan Mound. Remarkably, with considerably less information in hand, Jefferson wrote of the Rivanna River mound, "I conjectured that in this barrow might have been a thousand skeletons." Based on our study of the Rapidan Mound, we now have good reason to believe his conjecture was accurate. The central Virginia mounds may not be extraordinary in terms of size, but the number of burials they contained and the generations it took for them to accumulate, is quite extraordinary.

A page from Jefferson's personal copy of the 1787 edition of Notes on the State of Virginia *includes comments in his own hand, mostly in Greek, which he hoped to include in a new edition to be published in his lifetime. They stress his interest in the similarities in Greek, Roman, and Native American burial practices.*

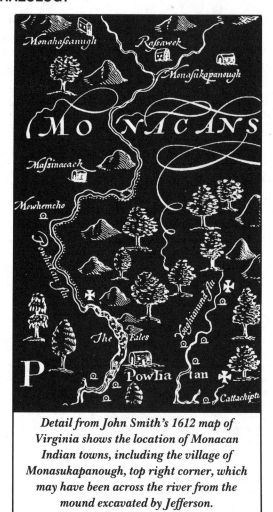

Detail from John Smith's 1612 map of Virginia shows the location of Monacan Indian towns, including the village of Monasukapanough, top right corner, which may have been across the river from the mound excavated by Jefferson.

Jefferson accurately described the variety of mounds in central Virginia, noting how they were of different sizes, some built of loose earth and others of stone. More than many twentieth-century archaeologists, he was aware of how the mound he was excavating fit into a regional archaeological perspective. He was also fairly accurate in describing the function of the mounds as community burial places, and the development of the mounds over an unstated period of time. He wrote: "Appearances certainly indicate that [the mound] has derived both origin and growth from the accustomary collection of bones, and deposition of them together; that the first collection had been deposited on the common surface of the earth, a few stones put over it, and then a covering of earth, that the second had been laid on this, had covered more or less of it in proportion to the numbers of bones, and was then also covered with earth, and so on."

To what extent did Jefferson's excavation contribute to an understanding of Native American history? The area in which his mound was located was the territory of the Monacan Indians. He noted that the mound was located across the river from an Indian town, most likely the Monacan town of Monasukapanough, or any one of a number of Late Woodland and possibly early contact period villages identified in archaeological surveys along the Rivanna. But of the Monacans, Jefferson only wrote that he thought they had merged with the Tuscarora and were now part of the Iroquois Confederacy to the north. He did not connect the mound to local Indian history. In fact, in his description of the excavation in *Notes,* Jefferson did not use archaeology to comment on Indian history at all. His focus was not on time, or cultural history, but on the inner construction of an odd feature on the landscape.

Why did he describe the mound at all? Because he was asked to do so. In 1780, a French diplomat in Philadelphia, François Marbois, circulated a letter to representatives of all the newly formed states requesting infor-

Analysis of bones from Rapidan Mound has provided interesting new insights. Sandra Olsen, an archaeologist at the Carnegie Museum of Natural History, who was then on the staff of the Virginia Museum of Natural History, performed a scanning electron microscope analysis of five detached skull caps and two skulls missing caps that were found in a single burial feature. Separating skulls from skull caps, presumably with a sharp instrument, was a practice described in local histories relating to the treatment of an enemy prisoner after death. Of further interest was an intact cranium that had an unusual depressed fracture and V-shaped linear groove indicating a blow to the head with a sharp weapon. We inferred from this that some of those buried in the mound may have been killed in warfare. Such evidence, though tentative, contrasts with Jefferson's finding that "no holes were discovered in any of them, as if made by

bullets, arrows or other weapons." In the absence of scanning electron microscopy, Jefferson may well have missed some tell-tale signs of violent death.

On so many other points, however, it is quite remarkable how well Jefferson's interpretations hold up in the late twentieth century. His reading of the stratigraphy of the mound has been well supported by excavations at other mounds in Virginia. Our own work also sheds light on the question of why Jefferson didn't mention any artifacts, and didn't appear to keep any from his excavation. At Rapidan Mound we found very little in the way of artifacts. Using screens and flotation, we did find small potsherds that appear to have been intentionally broken into small pieces as part of the burial ritual, and some stone tools including triangular projectile points. It is not likely that a trenching operation like Jefferson's, without screening, would have turned up such inconspicuous items.

mation on 22 separate topics such as their natural history, resources, population, climate, Indian population, etc. Jefferson was the Virginian who elected to answer this questionnaire, and his response became *Notes on the State of Virginia.* When Jefferson wrote *Notes,* he abbreviated the Indian question put to him by the Frenchman as: "A description of the Indians established in that state." In fact, Marbois' letter had requested: "A description of the Indians established in the state before the European settlements and of those who are still remaining. An indication of the Indian Monuments in that state."

Jefferson's chapter on Indians in *Notes,* titled "Aborigines," is in answer to these three questions posed by Marbois. First, he described the Indians established in the state before the Europeans, but he based this discussion entirely on his reading of colonist John Smith's account of Indians in the Jamestown area at the beginning of the seventeenth century—not on archaeological evidence. He then described the current distribution of the Indian tribes in Virginia, but argued that most had moved away, been greatly reduced in number or now "have more negro than Indian blood in them." Then he added, "I know of no such thing existing as an Indian monument for I would not honour with that name arrow points, stone hatchets, stone pipes, and halfshapen images." Jefferson then described his mound excavation. His archaeology was done in response to the request for information on Indian monuments, and was not undertaken as a matter of historical interest. In fact, in the section on Indian history in *Notes* he did not even mention the mounds. Jefferson concluded, however, with a moving personal memory that must have dated to his childhood: "But on whatever occasion they may have been

made, they are of considerable notoriety among the Indians: for a party passing, about thirty years ago, through the part of the country where this barrow is, went through the woods directly to it, without any instructions or inquiry, and having staid about it some time, with expressions of sorrow, they returned to the high road, which they had left about half a dozen miles to pay this visit, and pursued their journey."

There is little reason to doubt the veracity of this account. We know that Indians were still living in central Virginia into the eighteenth century, even if they had relocated away from the Charlottesville area. The moundbuilder myth that would soon sweep the country and which denied any tie between ancient mounds and contemporary Indians was apparently not a temptation to Jefferson. Such myths are often attributed to the period of American expansion and the pushing west of American Indians, and Jefferson was, as governor of Virginia and later president, a prominent agent in such forced relocation. In 1781, the very year he wrote *Notes,* he was also authorizing and closely monitoring the removal of the Cherokees from the western part of Virginia. Difficult as it is to comprehend such contradictory sides of Jefferson, we simply note here that he apparently did not rationalize his actions by manipulating his archaeological writing as some nineteenth-century scholars did.

At the time he wrote *Notes,* Jefferson did not see archaeological research as the key to understanding Native American origins. In *Notes* he followed the description of his archaeological excavation with a consideration of Indian origins based on linguistics, and suggested a close tie between Asians and Indians. However, seven years after publishing *Notes,* he wrote in a

letter to a colleague that he would be interested in hearing more of his colleague's linguistic theory of the descent of the Creek Indians from the Carthaginians, noting that he "saw nothing impossible in this conjecture." Clearly, his archaeological excavations had not dissuaded him from considering rather spectacular theories of Indian origins. But his opinions were subject to change. By 1813, in a lengthy letter to John Adams, he dismissed as "really amusing" notions of Indian origins in a distant Trojan or Hebrew past, concluding that "the question of origins was so unresolved that it could not be deciphered; Thus it was not a very practical question to ask."

Jefferson's excavation stands as one of many original scientific achievements in a lifetime of remarkable achievements. That it was intended to answer a particular question, not merely to collect relics, is notable, although Jefferson *was* a notable relic collector. And the publication of his excavation strategy, hypotheses, observations, and conclusions was extraordinary for his time. In moving from speculation to empirical observation, his concern was with the inner construction of a man-made phenomenon. In this regard, as in his interest in architecture, landscape, and so much else, Jefferson was particularly concerned with form and function rather than history. Yet, in his sympathetic depiction of the mound visit by Indians, he hinted at a continuity between present and past Indian cultures. And his description of the mound excavation preserved information that would otherwise have been lost, and provides a comparative base for our own excavations and interpretations of the prehistoric and early historic period in Virginia.

Indiana Joans

Lauren E. Talalay

Lauren E. Talalay is assistant to the director and curator of education at the Kelsey Museum of Archaeology, University of Michigan.

Although archaeology has spawned an impressive array of pioneering female scholars, it is only recently that the potential for a "feminist" or an "engendered" archaeology has received substantial play in the literature. Feminist scholarship is now enjoying explosive growth in the pages of archaeological journals and books. Since the initial call-to-arms in 1984 by Margaret Conkey and Janet Spector ("Archaeology and the Study of Gender"), several hundred articles have appeared on women and gender roles in antiquity.

Like many new marriages, the union of archaeology, feminism, and gender studies is marked by excitement, unexpected squabbling, and a healthy dose of self-reflection. The interested reader venturing into the literature might begin by perusing Elisabeth Bacus *et al.*, *A Gendered Past* (1993), an annotated bibliography of approximately 200 articles on the subject of gender and archaeology. Other widely cited books that are fast becoming classics include Joan Gero and Margaret Conkey, *Engendering Archaeology: Women and Prehistory* (1991); Dale Walde and Noreen Willows, *The Archaeology of Gender* (1991); and Cheryl Claassen, *Exploring Gender through Archaeology* (1992). Several journals have also devoted entire issues to the subject of women, gender, and the past, in particular. *Archaeological Review from Cambridge* 7 (1988), *Historical Archaeology* 25 (1991), and the *Norwegian Archaeological Review* 25 (1992). Finally, two recent articles are both instructive and eminently readable: Shelby Brown's "Feminist Research in Archaeology: What Does It Mean? Why Is It Taking So Long?" in *Feminist Theory and the Classics* (1993), and Lucia Nixon's "Gender Bias in Archaeology," in *Women in Ancient Societies: "An Illusion of the Night"* (1993).

Since this short overview can hardly do justice to the diversity of topics recently broached in the literature, the following introduction only touches upon the nature of feminist scholarship and several case studies on archaeology and gender.

Labels such as feminist theory and the feminist critique do not lend themselves to simple definitions. Feminism encompasses a range of issues, admitting into its ranks radical and measured, political and apolitical perspectives. In broad terms, feminist scholarship explores at least three explicit agendas: 1) the ways in which women are perceived, treated, and behave in various cultures; 2) the importance of gender as a fundamental organizing principle in all human societies; and 3) the practical and theoretical effects of androcentrism (reviewing the world from a male-defined perspective).

Many writers make distinctions between feminist research and gender studies. The former is usually considered to be more circumscribed, principally concerned with the role of women in society. Moreover, terms such as feminist and feminism are intended to be explicitly political and confrontational, connoting a challenge to the status quo. Gender studies, on the other hand, are more inclusive, exploring not only women's roles but relationships among and between all genders. The term is purposely depoliticized.

One of the significant contributions that feminist/gender-driven research has made to the social sciences is a reexamination and clarification of gender-related vocabularies. The labels sex and gender have come under particular scrutiny and discussions on the topic have special relevance for archaeology. As feminist scholars have correctly observed, the two, though clearly related, cannot be equated. Sex is biologically defined by certain physical attributes. Genders, though linked to sex, is culturally determined—there are certain expectations, norms, and behaviors that are linked to being a man or a woman in a given society. In the archaeological record, sex and gender have different degrees of visibility—sex can often be readily determined via skeletal remains, for example, while determining gender roles is an infinitely more complex enterprise.

Being culturally based, gender varies among societies, both past and present. We know from present anthropological research that, while Western cultures tend to recognize two clear-cut genders, other societies work with multiple gender categories and expectations for sexual behaviors that are not necessarily in keeping with traditional Western notions. The Etoro, a small group in the Trans-Fly region of Papua New Guinea, provide a striking, if somewhat extreme, example. For this group, heterosexual behavior is discouraged, while homosexual acts are not only encouraged, but also deemed essential for the maturation of men within the group as well as for the growth and vitality of society as a whole. The two gender/two sex paradigm is inadequate for understanding behaviors in cultures that include transvestites, eunuchs, castrati, and female impersonators—none of which is a modern phenomenon.

Ethnographic studies also indicate that in many societies mothering and child-care activities do not devolve exclusively on the biological mother but rather on siblings, grandparents, specialists, and fathers.

What is significant in all of these gender-conscious studies is that non-traditional behaviors (as measured by Western standards) are clearly evident in many parts of the world. These alternate configurations call into question whether current Western models should be those we use to interpret the past.

Feminist archaeologists, then, see gender constructs as central to the functioning of all societies, just as Marxist archaeologists would, for comparison, see class and economics as pivotal axes. Ultimately, the particular concepts that a society has about gender and sexual behavior dictate the social roles people play, the division of labor, and the allocation of authority and power. So defined, it would seem that feminist concerns should be at the very core of archaeological investigations. Ironically, archaeology resisted responding to feminist initiatives until the mid-1980s.

Recent attempts to engender the past range from the theoretical to the practical, and from well-conceived to slipshod studies. Some of the more indepth examples derive from an edited volume titled *Engendering Archaeology: Women and Prehistory.* Among the many provocative studies in the volume, those by Elizabeth Brumfiel, Christine Hastorf, and Joan Gero, are of particular note.

Brumfiel's article, "Weaving and Cooking: Women's Production In Aztec Mexico," examines the effects of these two household activities, which are known from ethnohistorical documents to be conducted by women. The author measures increases and decreases in the production of cloth (used as tribute, currency, and a mark of social status) and the ratio of pots to griddles (used for different types of cooking activities) before and after the Aztec conquest. Marked changes in these activities are found to be linked to demographic growth, agricultural intensification and, ultimately, the military success of the Aztec empire.

Hastorf's article, "Gender, Space, and Food in Prehistory," examines links between the distribution of food and the development of gender relationships in pre-Inka and Inka-dominated societies of the Andes. Hastorf employs various types of data, including archaeobotanical remains from residential and mortuary contexts and bone collagen samples from skeletons of known sex. The results suggest that over the course of approximately two centuries (ca. A.D. 1300–1530), women's roles became increasingly circumscribed and their contribution to the production—not the consumption—of corn beer increased. Since corn beer was laden with sociopolitical importance for the Inka, Hastorf suggests that women's status diminished from pre- to post-Inka times and that women's labor increasingly supported male-dominated activities.

Gero explores a very different kind of activity in a series of articles on stone tools. She argues that researchers have developed misconceptions about women's roles in prehistoric stone tool production. In one of her studies (published in *Engendering Archaeology*), Gero analyzes data from a ritual habitation center in highland Peru and demonstrates that women not only controlled access to local flint sources but were responsible for the production of tools used for domestic activities. Men, on the other hand, controlled non-local raw materials routinely employed for ritual activities.

Other studies in various books and journals have investigated class relations and gender inequalities in ancient Sumerian society, the rise of gender inequality in prehistoric Italy, adornment and gender identity in ancient Iran, gender bias in sixteenth- and seventeenth-century Spanish documents of the American Southwest, the effects that Western gender identities have on museum displays of the ancient world, and the possibilities of determining gender relationships on the basis of prehistoric figurines, to name only a few areas of research. A host of theoretical articles have also appeared that exhort archaeologists to unshackle themselves from a tradition bound by gender bias.

Exciting and controversial as this new thread of research is, it faces a knotty future. I attended a lecture some years ago at the University of Michigan by Margaret Conkey, an eminent archaeologist and one of the pioneers in the study of gender and archaeology, that boldly underscored some of the more obvious obstacles that a feminist-driven archaeology will have to scale. Two introductory slides at the lecture were especially instructive: one slide reproduced a page from a well-respected textbook on human evolution, the other displayed the front cover of a recent edition of *Newsweek.* The first image graphically illustrated human evolution from *Australopithecus* to *Homo sapiens.* Marching inevitably through time, small human figures became increasingly more erect, less hirsute, and whiter. The universal symbol was, however, recognizably male. The companion slide of *Newsweek* portrayed the head of a slightly unkempt Neanderthal, sporting a pelt. Above the head, bold letters announced the story within: THE WAY WE WERE. "WE," however, were decidedly white and male.

Admittedly these two slides were carefully chosen examples. Nonetheless, they effectively spotlighted the speaker's point: in this age of alleged enlightenment, alternate lifestyles, and heated feminist debate, androcentric perspectives of the past apparently still prevail.

To some extent, however, the problems that a feminist archaeology faces transcend the matter of androcentrism. Part of archaeology's initial reluctance to embrace feminist research stemmed from a belief that these fledgling endeavors were often subjective and politically driven. The need to prove a point appeared stronger than the drive to maintain rigor in analyzing data. These criticisms should not, however, be laid only at the feet of intransigent men. Archaeologists of both sexes found fault with some of the initial writings. Admittedly, extracting gender from the archaeological record is a complex endeavor; the data cannot always be measured and quantified. The question of what constitutes valid research, however, is not a sexist issue. It is critical to all disciplines and of particular concern today when the scientific method and scientific inquiry are being rejected in favor of interpretive narrative. Feminist scholars are acutely aware of these issues and continue to debate them vigorously.

Despite these problems, the future of archaeology, gender studies, and feminism is promising and exciting. Conferences, books, and papers continue to abound and theoretical discussions about gender are helping to "raise the consciousness" of all scholars who are, wittingly or unwittingly, guilty of gender bias. Some of the most promising work in this new field of inquiry may ultimately shed light on the universality of gender divisions of labor, how and why gender relations evolved, how gender roles and gender ideology varied in the past, and whether truly egalitarian societies ever existed—or can exist.

BIBLIOGRAPHY

Bacus, Elisabeth A., *et al.*, eds., *A Gendered Past.* Ann Arbor: University of Michigan Museum of Anthropology (*Technical Report 25*), 1993.

Brown, Shelby, "Feminist Research in Archaeology: What Does It Mean? Why Is It Taking So Long?" in Nancy Sorkin Rabinowitz and Amy Richlin, eds., *Feminist Theory and the Classics.* New York: Routledge 1993, pp. 238–71.

Claassen, Cheryl, ed., *Exploring Gender through Archaeology: Selected Papers from the 1991 Boone Conference.* Madison, WI: Prehistory Press, 1992.

Conkey, Margaret W., and Janet D. Spector, "Archaeology and the Study of Gender," in Michael B. Schiffer, ed., *Advances in Archaeological Method and Theory 7.* New York: Academic Press, 1984, pp. 1–38.

Gero, Joan M., and Margaret W. Conkey, eds., *Engendering Archaeology: Women and Prehistory.* Cambridge, MA: Basil Blackwell, 1991.

Nixon, Lucia, "Gender Bias in Archaeology," in Leonie J. Archer and Susan Fishler, eds. *Women in Ancient Societies: "An Illusion of the Night."* London: Macmillan, 1993, pp. 1–23.

Walde, Dale, and Noreen D. Willows, eds., *The Archaeology of Gender: Proceedings of the Twenty-Second Annual Conference of the Archaeological Association of the University of Calgary.* Calgary: Archaeological Association, The University of Calgary, 1991.

'Reverse Archaeologists' Are Tracing the Footsteps of a Cowboy-Explorer

A century ago rancher Richard Wetherill found the remnants of an ancient culture; finally his efforts are being recognized.

David Roberts

David Roberts is at work on his next book, a personal narrative of his travels throughout Anasazi country.

It was a bitter day in December 1888, with snow on the wind. Across the top of the remote Mesa Verde in southwestern Colorado, Richard Wetherill and his brother-in-law Charlie Mason rode horse-back, tracking cattle that had strayed from the family ranch in the Mancos Valley. Twenty-five miles from home, the ranchers faced a cold bivouac under the pines before they could bring the cattle in.

A looping track drew the two men near the mesa's edge, where the sandstone cliff dropped sheer to the talus below. They dismounted, walked to the rim and gazed east across a canyon they had never explored. Suddenly Wetherill blurted out a cry of astonishment.

Half a mile away, in the cliff forming the canyon's opposite wall, loomed an overhang that sheltered a natural cavern fully 400 feet long by 90 feet deep. Inside it stood the pristine ruins of an ancient city, more than 200 rooms built of stone and mud, dominated by a round three-story tower. "It looks just like a palace," murmured Mason.

Wetherill named the ruin Cliff Palace. The two men forgot about their cattle. Roping together dead trees with their lariats, they improvised a ladder to descend the cliff, then scrambled down to the canyon floor and up the opposite slope to enter the majestic ruin.

A PASSION FOR DISCOVERY YIELDS STILL MORE RUINS

It was as if the vanished inhabitants had walked off a few hours before, leaving everything in place. The rooms were strewn with intact ceramic pots sitting in the dust. On one floor the ranchers found a heavy stone ax, still hafted to its wooden handle. A perfunctory dig in the rubble uncovered three skeletons.

Wild with the passion of discovery, the men split up to search for other ruins in the few hours of daylight they had left. Wetherill headed north and west across the mesa top and stumbled upon another great ruin, which he named Spruce Tree House. He rejoined Mason at dusk; they built a fire and talked into the night.

In the morning, the pair found yet a third village, whose most startling feature was a soaring four-story tower. Square Tower House was the obvious name.

Today, more than 600,000 visitors come to Mesa Verde National Park every year. On the standard tour, they walk through the stabilized ruins of Cliff Palace and Spruce Tree House, and peer from a lookout point down on Square Tower House. The three villages are among the half-dozen cynosures of the park, with Cliff Palace—the best known of all Anasazi sites—one of the most famous ruins in the world.

The finding of Cliff Palace changed Wetherill's life utterly. The eldest of six siblings in a tight-knit Quaker clan from Pennsylvania, Richard struggled to keep the family's Alamo Ranch afloat through years of failed crops and dubious investments. Meanwhile he transformed himself into a self-taught archaeologist. During the next 14 years, with his four brothers, Charlie Mason and a handful of other partners, Wetherill discovered and excavated far more Anasazi sites than any researcher before or since. Their number includes 182 ruins on Mesa Verde alone, as well as dozens in the tortured canyon of Grand Gulch in Utah; the exquisite village of Keet Seel in Arizona; and Pueblo Bonito in New Mexico's Chaco Canyon, the hub of Anasazi civilization in its most complex phase.

One might expect that Wetherill's achievement, which rivals that of

Of Wetherill (center, with brothers, c. 1893) his wife remarked: "his eyes looked a hole right into you."

Heinrich Schliemann at Troy or of Hiram Bingham at Machu Picchu, should be hailed as a landmark in American archaeology. For nearly a century, however, the reputation of the rancher-turned-savant has lingered under a cloud of controversy. Schliemann and Bingham had their own critics, but the places of both men in the pantheon of prehistoric discovery are secure. Wetherill's is not.

An ambivalence toward the Mancos rancher remains particularly acute regarding his early work at Mesa Verde. By his own later admission, when he began digging in the ruins Wetherill was little more than a pothunter. For that matter, in 1888 true archaeology had scarcely been practiced in the United States, and many a professional in Wetherill's time excavated as crudely as he.

As a cowboy whose formal education ended in high school, Wetherill later earned the scorn of a number of university-trained academics. One of them was Jesse Nusbaum, himself a

pioneer in Anasazi archaeology as well as the superintendent of Mesa Verde National Park from 1921 through 1927. To the end of his life, Nusbaum dismissed Wetherill's work at Mesa Verde as "ravaging and looting" and as "commercial exploitation" of the ruins. He insisted that the Wetherills had used dynamite to open one ruin at Mesa Verde. No evidence of such a practice has ever been produced. Nusbaum even denied Wetherill credit for discovering Cliff Palace.

On a visit to Mesa Verde last June, I found that mixed feelings about Wetherill persist. As District Interpreter Linda Martin told me, "There's long been a controversy within our staff over Wetherill. I think what Wetherill did here a hundred years ago is what I would have done."

Research archaeologist Jack Smith was more critical. "I can't condemn the Wetherill brothers, but I can't praise them either," he said. "It's hard not to conclude that their excavating techniques were pretty brutal. I've seen

three backcountry sites where somebody has used [Anasazi] roof beams as levers to tear out the back walls of ruins. At these sites, you find Wetherill's signature scrawled on the cave walls. Yes, that's only circumstantial evidence, but I think it's convincing."

At first, as he hauled artifacts out of the Mesa Verde ruins, Wetherill hoped to display them in Durango and Denver and sell them to collectors. Gradually, however, he realized that science would be better served if the intact collections could find their way into museums. He began to search for altruistic patrons.

One of the first was a young Swedish baron, Gustaf Nordenskiold, who was traveling across the West. Trained in geology, Nordenskiold had visited digs in Italy and was aware of the best European techniques. Hiring Richard Wetherill to supervise ambitious excavations at Mesa Verde in 1891, he taught the rancher to use a trowel instead of a shovel and stressed the importance of written and photographic documentation.

Wetherill was an eager student. Soon he had devised his own field-note forms, and the records he kept grew more and more detailed and precise. As he wrote a later patron, "This whole subject . . . is in its infancy and the work we do must stand the most rigid inspection, and we do not want to do it in such a manner that anyone in the future can pick flaws in it."

Eventually, the vast collections of Anasazi artifacts assembled by Wetherill would anchor the Southwest holdings of half a dozen major institutions, including the Field Museum in Chicago, as well as the American Museum of Natural History and the National Museum of the American Indian, both in New York City. Nordenskiold's assemblage found its way to the National Museum of Finland in Helsinki.

In nearly every case, Wetherill's field notes were sent to the museums along with the relics. Over the years, however, these records were sometimes misinterpreted, ignored or even misplaced—contributing in a perverse twist to Wetherill's reputation as a mere pothunter.

Wetherill's passion for the Anasazi soon became an obsession. No longer content to work the ruins of Mesa Verde, he launched far-flung expeditions into the unmapped canyons of Utah, Arizona and New Mexico. These jaunts usually took place during the winter, the only season the brothers could spare from ranch work. The sheer logistics of Wetherill's archaeological toil—up before dawn, working long into the night, camping in snowstorms, digging in frozen ground, packing artifacts by horseback more than a hundred miles back to Mancos—testify to his diligence.

The Alamo Ranch, however, continued to fail. To supplement their income, the Wetherill brothers began guiding visitors through the ruins they had discovered. Among the Wetherill clients in 1895 were the Palmers, a family of traveling musicians from Kansas. Richard fell deeply in love with the 18-year-old harpist and soprano Marietta Palmer. With the family, Wetherill made his first trip to Chaco Canyon, then so remote as to be all but unknown to white explorers. On the way back from their two-month outing, Marietta was the only passenger who dared ride Wetherill's wagon as he forced it through a perilous ford of the swollen San Juan River. On the far bank, both drenched, Richard looked hard at Marietta: "Were you frightened?" "Why sure," she answered, "I was scared to death." "Will you marry me?" he asked.

Abandoning any hope of a "civilized" life back in Kansas, Marietta became Richard's wife, staying at his side through the last 14 eventful years of his life.

INSPIRING TRUST BY SPEAKING THEIR LANGUAGES

Wetherill was a parcel of contradictions. Though he had never gone to college, he read widely and ambitiously. He was miserably insecure about his shortcomings as a scholar, yet his letters reveal a frank, clear

Handsome masonry marks 600-plus rooms of Pueblo Bonito, which Wetherill began excavating in 1896.

prose that many an academic might emulate. A crack shot, he nonetheless, as a Quaker, often refused to carry a rifle even when he rode through hostile Indian country. He had the knack of inspiring trust among the Utes and Navajos, in part because he learned to speak well the languages of both tribes.

In 1902 the family bowed to the inevitable and sold Alamo Ranch. Meanwhile, Richard and Marietta and their infant son had moved to Chaco Canyon, where the rancher built a trading post next to Pueblo Bonito. Masoned with the finest Anasazi stonework ever seen, Pueblo Bonito incorporates astronomical alignments and stands at the center of a mysterious network of far-reaching Anasazi roads.

No archaeologist had ever touched this colossal ruin of some 600 rooms. Here, in 1896, Wetherill had gone to work with a will. He had won the steady patronage of Talbot and Frederick Hyde, millionaire brothers from New York. Incorporated as the Hyde Exploring Expedition, Wetherill dug

190 rooms at Pueblo Bonito over four years and shipped tens of thousands of artifacts to New York, which the Hydes donated to the American Museum of Natural History.

Inevitably, Wetherill's one-man monopoly of what was coming to be recognized as the most important Anasazi site in the Southwest aroused professional attention. A campaign to halt his unsupervised research was launched by Edgar L. Hewett, president of New Mexico Normal University and an archaeologist who had his own eye on Chaco. Decrying Wetherill's work as mere "vandalizing," Hewett persuaded the General Land Office to launch an investigation of the cowboy's doings. The upshot of the prolonged inquiry was dramatic: in 1902 Richard Wetherill was forbidden to dig at Chaco. For the last eight years of his life, the self-taught archaeologist turned not another shovelful of Anasazi soil.

Despite Hewett's antipathy, at Chaco Culture National Historical Park Wetherill's memory is now hon-

"Reverse archaeologist" Fred Blackburn, guide Tommy May, rest at Sandal House; "CW" was Clate Wetherill.

ored. Says Chief of Interpretation Kim McLean, "As far as archaeology is concerned, Wetherill's work was as good as or better than that of many professionals of his day."

Over the years, the criticisms of Nusbaum, Hewett and others have taken their toll on Richard Wetherill's reputation. Yet the strictures of his detractors are balanced by the praises of some of the Southwest's leading archaeologists. In 1946 John Otis Brew, of Harvard's Peabody Museum, hailed the sum of Wetherill's work as "the most far-reaching single event in Southwestern archaeology." Last spring Jeffrey Dean, of the University of Ari-

zona's Laboratory of Tree-Ring Research in Tucson, told me, "Wetherill was a far better archaeologist than"— Dean then named a well-regarded archaeologist whose career overlapped Wetherill's.

Much of the credit for the rehabilitating of Wetherill's name belongs to a loose band of Westerners—nearly all of them amateurs in archaeology, as Wetherill himself was—who call themselves the Wetherill-Grand Gulch Research Project. Their central figure is 43-year-old Fred Blackburn, a feisty wilderness guide and educator who lives in Cortez, Colorado. In the 1970s, as a Bureau of Land Manage-

ment ranger in Grand Gulch, Utah, Blackburn became preoccupied with retracing the rancher's footsteps across the Southwest.

The cloud over Wetherill's name had much to do with certain museums' negligence in handling his field notes and glass-plate photographs. Without good records of provenance—the stratigraphic context of each artifact in its original site—matchless collections like the ones Wetherill gathered reduce to little more than grab bags of pretty objects.

Blackburn and his colleagues learned, however, that in most cases the notes and photographs still existed. The team realized that it might be possible to relink the artifacts in the museums with their provenances. This sort of "reverse archaeology"—the term is Blackburn's coinage—could hold a vast potential for rejuvenating "dead" collections.

The effort depended crucially on Blackburn's deep knowledge of the obscure topography the cowboy had explored: he could peer at a photograph that Wetherill had made in 1893 and say, "Oh, that's Fishmouth Cave, back of Butler Wash." But the project had a hard time getting a foot in the door at Eastern museums. Curators used to dealing with doctoral candidates looked askance at the uncredentialed pleadings of a band of apparent dilettantes. And, as the team came to recognize, its own proposals were rife with naiveté and imprecision.

From 1986 on, the initially testy back-and-forth between the project and the museums gradually thawed into a good working arrangement. As Anibal Rodriguez, senior technician for anthropology at the American Museum of Natural History, recalls, "They were so ambitious, we finally realized the best thing for us to do was listen, to see what they had to offer."

Last June, Blackburn and another project member, archaeologist Winston Hurst, gave photographer Terrence Moore and me a vivid demonstration of the fruits of reverse archaeology as they guided us on a hike into Whiskers Draw, a minor tributary of Cottonwood Wash in southeastern Utah.

One hundred years ago this month, Wetherill made perhaps his greatest discovery. Working in an unprepossessing rock shelter he called Cave 7, he dug beneath a scattering of Anasazi relics, the likes of which he had found many a time. Finally, five feet down, he began to uncover something remarkable. The cave was riddled with bottle-shaped pits that had been used as burial cists. Eventually Wetherill unearthed more than 90 skeletons in Cave 7. Some four-fifths of them showed evidence of violent harm, and scattered among the bones were many deadly flint points, including one embedded in a backbone.

The importance of Wetherill's discovery lay not in the skeletons per se, but in the cowboy's acute recognition that these deep-buried remains belonged to a different people from those he had found at Cliff Palace and other sites. Almost at once he put his finger on the crucial distinguishing characteristics. The earlier humans had no pottery but made superb baskets of yucca and willow, some woven so tightly they could hold water; they used the atlatl, or spear-thrower, rather than the bow and arrow; and they had round skulls, rather than the artificially flattened craniums of the later cliff dwellers (now known to have been caused by the use of hard cradleboards in infancy).

Wetherill used the term "Basket People," and the Hyde brothers coined the name "Basketmaker." Today, the distinction between the Basketmaker and the Pueblo phases of Anasazi culture—with the transition taking place around A.D. 700—is one of the cornerstones of Southwest archaeology. By correlating depth with prehistoric age, moreover, Wetherill took another intellectual leap. Six decades later, the great archaeologist Alfred V. Kidder tipped his hat to the Mancos rancher: "[Nels] Nelson and I have often been credited with doing the first stratigraphic work in the Southwest, but Richard, in recognizing the greater antiquity of the Basketmakers than that of the Cliff Dwellers, used the method many years before anyone else in that field."

Archaeologist Winston Hurst makes notes in Cave 7, rediscovered by Wetherill-Grand Gulch Project in 1990.

After Wetherill's death, the location of Cave 7 was forgotten. In Frank McNitt's excellent biography *Richard Wetherill: Anasazi,* published in 1957, one of Wetherill's photographs of the site appeared, with a caption erroneously suggesting it was in Grand Gulch. Hurst, Blackburn and a few other members of the Wetherill Project became determined to find the cave again.

The search took two years. The sleuths had only a few tantalizing clues: a sketch map and description of the site among Wetherill's notes, a pair of photographs, and the heading of the letter in which the cowboy excitedly described his find to his patron back East: "First Valley Cottonwood Creek 30 Miles North Bluff City."

As Hurst and Blackburn took me into Whiskers Draw last June, I could appreciate what must have been the needle-in-a-haystack nature of the search for the ordinary-looking cave. It was a blazing day, with the temperature in the 90s; bullflies stung our arms, while tamarisk thickets lashed our faces as we bushwhacked up the draw. The surrounding country was crisscrossed for miles with mazes of virtually identical side canyons.

A crucial clue lay in the dated signatures Wetherill and his cohorts were wont to scrawl in charcoal or scratch with a bullet cartridge on the cave walls. To later generations, these inscriptions have often seemed offensive graffiti; at Mesa Verde, a number of Wetherill signatures were effaced in the 1950s or '60s. Yet in the 1890s, to leave one's name on an archaeological site was the normal practice, followed by professional excavators and government explorers alike. The deed amounted to no mere braggart "Kilroy was here"; it was an integral part of the documentation of the dig.

As Hurst's team searched the tributaries of Cottonwood Wash, the dates got "warm," clustering within days of December 17, 1893—the date on the letter to Wetherill's patron. But as it turned out, the real Cave 7 was the very last of all the possible rock shelters Hurst and his colleagues looked into. With the photograph from McNitt's book in hand, I stood on the exact spot where Wetherill had exposed the glass plate in 1893. The crumbling Pueblo wall on the left still stood, albeit more ravaged than a century before. In the old picture, Basketmaker skulls litter the floor of the cave. Now I could see the deep depressions in the dirt, a mute memorial to the 90 skeletons Wetherill had extracted.

Before the team relocated Cave 7, Christy Turner of Arizona State University, the leading expert on Anasazi cannibalism (a phenomenon revealed only within the past decade), traveled to the American Museum of Natural History where he examined the very bones and projectile points Wetherill had dug out of the cave nearly a century before. Reintegrating the site and the artifacts, Turner and Hurst demonstrated that Cave 7 had been the scene of a wholesale massacre some 1,500 years ago; the carnage involved stabbing by daggers, shooting with atlatl darts, bludgeoning, scalping, possibly even torture.

Hurst and Turner's work represents a major step in revealing what one might call the dark side of Anasazi culture—its occasional propensity to erupt into internecine violence. As the two archaeologists write in a forthcoming paper, the evidence from Cave 7 "document[s] yet another example of our species' strange capacity for both terrible destructiveness and the creation of beautiful works of art."

As the Wetherill Project's work gathered steam after 1986, some of the leading Anasazi archaeologists, such as Turner, Brigham Young University's

Joel Janetski and Washington State University's William Lipe, began to collaborate with these hardworking amateurs. The project's focus became the Basketmakers. Scholars had done less work on those early Anasazi than on the more accessible Pueblo people succeeding them. The culmination of this effort was a three-day scholarly symposium on the Basketmakers, held in Blanding, Utah, in 1990. With some 500 participants, it was arguably the best-attended Anasazi conference ever. The papers from the symposium have been published in book form by the BLM Utah Cultural Resource Series. In addition, Blackburn and archaeo-astronomer Ray Williamson have written *In Search of the Basketmaker,* a scholarly overview to be published next year by the School of American Research. And in 1995 the Utah Museum of Natural History will mount an exhibition on the Basketmakers featuring the project's work.

The rehabilitation of the Wetherill name has meant much to the brothers' descendants. Last June I met 63-year-old Tom Wetherill, the grandson of Richard's brother Al. A contractor living in Farmington, New Mexico, Tom has inherited the family records. Opening the yellowed pages of the Alamo Ranch guest register, he showed me Nordenskiold's signature from 1891.

A week later, photographer Moore and I were joined by Fred Blackburn and Marietta Davenport on a jaunt into Grand Gulch. Marietta, named for her

great-grandmother, is an archaeologist employed by the U.S. Forest Service. All through college and graduate school she heard her professors cast aspersions on Richard Wetherill. "I wouldn't say anything in class," Marietta recalled. "Afterwards I'd go up to the professor and say, 'Wait a minute, let's talk about this.' I wouldn't let on right away that Richard was my great-grandfather."

Winding our way into Bullet Canyon, a tributary of Grand Gulch, we retraced the stock trail, now faint, that Wetherill had built in 1893 and that Blackburn's team had rediscovered a few years ago. By midafternoon we had reached Jailhouse Ruin, one of the eeriest of all Anasazi sites in Grand Gulch, where huge, baleful "full-moon" pictographs dominate an airy, masoned ledge. It was a glorious, hot afternoon, with canyon wrens singing on the breeze. As we sat on the bedrock sandstone below the ruin, Marietta said quietly, "It's pretty exciting for me to visit a site he dug. It's very powerful."

We camped out, then spent the next day in Sheik's Canyon, another Grand Gulch tributary. By midday we reached Green Mask Spring, a Basketmaker site so profusely decorated with pictographs that in four hours of staring we only began to sort out the enigmatic paintings. Here Wetherill had camped in January 1897.

One evening as dusk approached, Wetherill had dug behind some rocks against the cliff. The burial he uncov-

Anthropomorphic figures painted onto cliff (left) stand guard near where "Princess" was found. Wetherill cut his signature (above), following a 19th-century practice.

ered, working into the night by lantern, would be the most striking find in all his years of Anasazi work. A 66 inch-wide basket covered another; under them lay a turkey-feather blanket decorated with bluebird feathers, and another blanket spangled with canary yellow spots. A final basket covered the perfectly mummified head of a woman. Her body was painted yellow, her face red.

The stunned archaeologist nicknamed his discovery "the Princess." Wetherill had found many a mummy, but never did he excavate one more carefully or pack one more delicately to be carried out of Grand Gulch and back to Durango and the railroad East.

Using Wetherill's field notes and photographs, Blackburn's team had been able to pinpoint the pit at Green Mask Spring from which the Princess had been removed. Now I stood on the spot and pondered a pair of haunting pictographs that had been painted directly above the grave. The androgynous human figures in white, each decorated with a red circle covering its chest, stood solemn and rigid, side by side, almost like some bridal couple. Here was another tantalizing promise spun out of reverse archaeology. Almost nowhere in the world has rock art been convincingly associated with burials. Yet if these pictographs commemorated the woman buried beneath them, then the paintings themselves might tell us more about the Princess— and vice versa.

Two weeks later, Terrence Moore and I went to New York City to view a pair of Wetherill collections. At the American Museum of Natural History, Anibal Rodriguez opened many drawers of Wetherill materials: splendid Chaco black-on-white pots, intricately woven baskets, atlatls, cradleboards and rabbit clubs.

The next day we visited the research branch of the National Museum of the American Indian in The Bronx. Assistant collections manager Mark Clark pulled out a dazzling variety of fine Anasazi artifacts: blankets made of rabbit fur, splendidly woven willow baskets with checkerboard red-and-

Misspelling of his name on tombstone was just the first of many indignities Wetherill's memory has suffered.

black designs, scrapers made from bighorn sheep horns, black lignite beads that had once been strung as a necklace, bowls shaped like pipes.

Barred from digging after 1902, Wetherill stayed on at his Chaco Canyon trading post. No white settlement in the United States lay farther from the beaten path. For Marietta, these were hard years, but Richard was in his element. As he traded regularly with the Chaco Navajos, he got to know these former nomads better than any white man ever had. Realizing the quality of the best Navajo rugs and blankets, Wetherill encouraged the weavers by crossbreeding sheep to produce an animal that bore a better wool.

Trouble struck one day in June 1910. A dispute between Wetherill and several Navajos flared out of control. At sunset, as Wetherill drove cows along the Chaco Canyon wash, a young Navajo man raised his rifle. The first bullet struck Wetherill in the chest; a second, from close range, blew half his face away.

Last June I hiked with Fred Blackburn to Sandal House. Here, a dozen miles down the Mancos River from Alamo Ranch, the Wetherills had dug in their first ruin a few years before the discovery of Cliff Palace. Naming the

site for the scores of yucca sandals they unearthed, they caught the bug of Anasazi exploration.

Sandal House lies only five miles east of thronged Cliff Palace, yet it is in Ute Mountain Ute Tribal Park, can be approached only with a Ute guide and is almost never visited. Blackburn himself had never been there.

Now, sketch pad in hand, he found on the cave's walls the signatures or initials of four of the five Wetherill brothers; no other site had yielded so many. And he discovered his first "Mamie Palmer," Marietta's maiden name, carved in neat capitals that summer when she first got to know the gruff cowboy.

After two hours of inching our way through the jumbled ruin our Ute guide, Tommy May, found a very faint inscription written in pencil on a stone in a kiva wall. Blackburn squatted in the rubble and flashed mirrored light across the evanescent message. After half an hour he had sketched out the memorandum: Wetherill had found a huge Anasazi pot, which he was caching in the ruin and would return to retrieve in four days. Blackburn paused, wiped his sweaty brow with a bandana and said to no one in particular, "This is as close as we're ever going to get to talking to him."

Archaeology and Relief

F. M. Setzler and W. D. Strong

F. M. Setzler, Acting Head Curator, Department of Anthropology, U.S. National Museum, Washington, D.C. and W. D. Strong, Anthropologist, Bureau of American Ethnology, Smithsonian Institution, Washington, D.C.

In December 1933, under the Civil Works Administration, a number of archaeological projects were organized with the primary purpose of reducing unemployment. The scientific direction of these particular emergency measures was given to the Smithsonian Institution which, since its founding in 1846, has carried on much important prehistoric research for the National Government. In the nature of the case it was the primary purpose of the C.W.A. to set a large number of unemployed persons to work with the least possible delay, while it was the duty and desire of the Smithsonian Institution to see that the scientific results attained might be as extensive and complete as the unusual opportunity warranted. The present article aims to sum up briefly the nature and results of these particular projects and their bearing on the wider problems of scientific archaeology as a channel for relief employment.

In this case the choice of archaeological sites was limited by climatic and economic factors. First, the work must be done in regions where winter conditions were mild, and second, it must be carried on at sites where unemployed labor was abundant and close at hand. In all, eleven C.W.A. archaeological projects, employing about 1,500 persons, were launched within a month. Seven of these were in Florida, and one each in Georgia, North Carolina, California, and Tennessee.

The seven sites excavated in Florida were selected with the above qualifications in view and also with a scientific aim: to secure a cross-section of the aboriginal cultures in the state. The northern half of the Florida peninsula was formerly occupied by tribes belonging to the Timucuan linguistic stock. In this region excavations were begun on the Canaveral peninsula, and a number of habitation and burial mounds that yielded many skeletons and a limited number of artifacts were opened. These structures apparently pertained to the Surruque Indians who occupied this part of Florida when it was discovered by the Spaniards. Hitherto Surruque history has consisted solely of a brief catalogue of repeated disasters ending with the extermination of this tribe slightly more than a century after its first contact with Europeans. At Ormond Beach, in what the Spanish called "the fresh-water provinces", another important excavation was made. A mound containing scattered burials was opened and below this were found two concentric circles of extended burials apparently contemporaneous with the village-site materials which also underlay the mound.

Pottery vessels, pipes, and carved shell and stone ornaments occurred in these levels, their specific styles throwing considerable light on the civilization and antecedents of the Mayaca Indians, also of Timucuan stock, who occupied the area at the time of discovery.

South of Lake Okeechobee in the central portion of Florida is a rather different archaeological area, once occupied by the Calusa Indians. Excavations in this region were made at Belle Glade, at sites on the Little Manatee River and near Englewood. The Belle Glade site was exceptionally significant since it consisted of a true refuse heap or midden, not a shell heap, above muck deposits. There was also a burial mound in association with it. Particularly striking were a number of elaborately carved wooden specimens that had been preserved in the muck. Many years ago Cushing found almost identical specimens at Key Marco on the west coast, but so rarely are perishable materials preserved in this general area and so unique were the finds that many questioned the authenticity of the first discovery. The Belle Glade specimens prove their authenticity and prehistoric age beyond any doubt. In addition the Belle Glade excavations yielded numerous skeletons, broken pottery, and bone, stone and shell artifacts, all of which throw much light on the nature and extent of the Calusa culture. Several mounds on the Little Manatee River, quite similar in external appearance, proved to contain quite different burial and ceramic types. In

From *American Antiquity*, Volume 4, 1936, pp. 301-309. Originally published in *The American Scholar*, Volume 5, Number 1, Winter 1936, pp. 109-117. © 1935 by the Phi Beta Kappa Society. Reprinted by permission.

one all burials were cremated, in another all were flexed, and in still another all were secondary—that is merely bundles of previously exposed bones. The mound containing the cremations also revealed the complete floor plan of a mortuary temple, the first yet reported from this area. Certain of these sites dated from early post-Spanish times whereas others were prehistoric, indicating a complex history which is being worked out as the data are studied. Near Englewood, under two superimposed mounds, was found a large pit containing more than 100 burials. These were covered by a sterile sand mound which in turn was covered by a layer of white sand on top of which was another mound containing numerous secondary burials. The pottery from this complex site is of the finest quality yet known in the Southeast and represents a southern thrust of a more northern ceramic type.

In Georgia a large group of mounds near Macon yielded especially valuable and picturesque results. One large mound in the Lamar Group was found to have a spiral causeway rising from base to summit. Another, on the Macon plateau, showed at least five successive levels of construction. The top of each level had been sealed with gray or else with vivid red clay, and the vertical profiles showing these successive colored layers are extremely striking. Beneath the base of this mound was a human skeleton covered with thousands of bone and shell beads. The manner in which these were placed indicated that they had formed necklaces, arm bands, and probably decorations on a woven mantle. Careful technique in opening this tomb revealed details of the timbered walls and log mould uprights, with crosspieces clearly indicated on the floor of the grave beneath the bundled bones. Under a small mound nearby was uncovered the entire floor of a still earlier ceremonial house or temple. The floor of this structure was of hard clay, polished by thousands of moccasined feet, and around the circular wall ran a bench on which fifty individual seats had been modelled from clay. Before each seat was a rectangular hollow

where the occupant probably placed his smoking and ceremonial apparatus. Opposite the entrance, which faced the southeast, was the modelled head and body of a great bird, probably an eagle, which was raised above the encircling seats. This was apparently the great altar. Details of construction, such as the conventionalized, decorative design around the eagle's eye suggest similar devices carved on pottery and shell from the great aboriginal mound site near Moundville, Alabama. The fact that the subterranean passageway of this structure is so placed that the rays of the early morning sun enter the building and fall directly upon the central fireplace and altar is further evidence of the complex ceremonialism once carried on in this early American temple. The Macon site has proved to be so important scientifically and so intrinsically interesting that the earlier work begun under the C.W.A., the Smithsonian Institution, and the Society for Georgia Archaeology was continued under the Georgia F.E.R.A., and then by the W.P.A. for twenty-eight months of continuous excavations. Plans to have this area constituted a National Monument have now been completed.

His chroniclers say that when, in 1540, Hernando De Soto passed through the western portion of what is now known as North Carolina he found an Indian town, called Guasili, of some 600 wooden houses. Although its size may have been exaggerated it was undoubtedly an important native metropolis. Garcilaso de la Vega records that "the lord who bore the name of the province left the capital half a league to meet the Spaniards, accompanied by 500 of the principal persons of the country, very gaily dressed after their fashion. His lodge was upon a mound with a terrace round it, where six men could promenade abreast". Here the hungry explorers were given a hearty welcome after their tedious journey through the Blue Ridge Mountains. To the amazement of the natives the "Spaniards caught and cooked some of the Indian dogs, whereupon their hosts immediately rounded up some 300 of the creatures and presented them.

Since the geographic location of this native capital seems to have been at the junction of Peachtree Creek and Hiwassee River, near Murphy, North Carolina, a large mound located at this place was chosen for excavation. As the work progressed three cultural levels were determined: the surface of the mound which yielded intrusive burials (possibly of Cherokee origin) with associated European objects; the mound horizon itself; and the village-site deposit beneath the mound. Burials in stone-lined cists occurred in the mound horizon. Study of the distribution of the stamped and incised pottery and the red and black painted ware from the different structures may indicate occupation by different ethnic groups at different times. Here, as at other sites chosen for such work, the occurrence of an historic dated period of occupation permits the archaeologist to proceed logically from the known to the unknown in reading the record.

The area now included in the Shiloh National Park, located on the Tennessee River near Pittsburg Landing, is famous as a major battlefield of the Civil War, but comparatively few people are aware that this action took place over and among the mounds of an important aboriginal site. Since no complete scientific excavations had ever been made at this place it was selected for the C.W.A.-Smithsonian project in Tennessee. Mapping and excavation, amidst the dense deciduous forest that covers the site, revealed seven large earth mounds, six of which had been used for dwellings and one for burial, as well as numerous low elevations marking the places where prehistoric Indian houses once stood. The natives recognized the strategic nature of the site as well as did the Union and Confederate generals for, flanked by two steep ravines, the bluff village was also protected by an embankment which formed the foundation for a stockade. Abundant broken pottery vessels, artifacts, and burials occurred in the village site. The excavations here yielded much evidence on the varied aspects of native life during the later prehistoric period. Since the general region is still very little known from the archaeological standpoint, the present work serves as a promising beginning toward a more complete understanding of an important culture area.

In California work was prosecuted in the southern tip of the great San Joaquin Valley, at present an important center for oil production. Two large refuse and shell heaps and several burial sites on Buena Vista Lake were excavated. The most recent of these large middens was the early historic village of Tulamniu where Father Zalvidea visited the Yokut Indians in 1772. Scientific investigation indicated that behind this early historic date stretched an occupation period of perhaps two millenia at this one site. By detailed stratigraphic work, house plans and burial methods during the different periods of occupation were revealed, and a considerable section of early California history reconstructed. On a hilltop behind the more recent of the two village sites 600 massed burials were uncovered. Near some of these were juniper posts, still preserved below the ground. It is hoped that when the study of annual tree-ring changes has been extended farther, these can be read to give the exact dates at which different burials occurred. California shell-heaps are noted for being very poor in artifacts but, thanks to the large-scale operations permitted by the abundant labor, as well as to the careful screening techniques employed, sufficient specimens were secured to permit full comparison with neighboring regions. These studies indicate that the ancient inhabitants of the Buena Vista middens were closely related to the occupants of the early shell mounds around San Francisco Bay, and that the remote ancestors of the modern Yokuts probably moved up the valley from that direction.

In passing, an important F.E.R.A. project near Marksville, Louisiana, directed by the Smithsonian Institution in 1933, should also be mentioned. A large archaeological site marked by mounds and earthworks was acquired by the city as a park, and the local officials invited the Smithsonian Institution to direct excavations there prior to reconstruction. These revealed a native civilization in the Southeast closely related to the most impressive mound-building culture of the Ohio region. The latter horizon, designated Hopewell after the site where it was first found, is entirely prehistoric yet advanced far beyond the status of the historic Indians of Ohio. At Marksville many of the distinctive northern objects, such as mica, obsidian, pearls, utensils and ornaments of copper, as well as modelled pipes and figurines are lacking, but the advanced pottery from the two regions is practically identical. Other features such as mounds, platform pipes, and surrounding earthworks are likewise very similar. Since the Marksville variant of the Hopewell culture appears to be very early in the South and lacks many of the fully developed traits of the northern Hopewell, it may prove to be the hitherto unknown basic complex from which the exotic northern civilization arose.

From the scientific standpoint these various projects have thrown much new light on the status and nature of the native civilizations which preceded that of the white man in the regions investigated. In Florida the excavations on the Canaveral Peninsula tended to disprove the theory that the mainland has been strongly influenced by the aboriginal cultures of the Greater Antilles. Practically nothing was found to strengthen this widely held belief, whereas the evidence was strong that the higher cultures of native Florida had been derived from centers farther west, toward the Mississippi River. In so far as the artifacts themselves were concerned the discoveries at Belle Glade verified the earlier work of Cushing but indicated, contrary to Cushing's belief, that they pertained to the Calusa Indians and not to any exotic culture. In Georgia the Macon site yielded a stratigraphic series of ceramic types which will go far toward elucidating the sequence of prehistoric cultures over a considerable part of the Southeast. The same is true of the discoveries at Marksville, Louisiana, where the important connections established extend still farther afield. In North Carolina and Tennessee new archaeological areas were opened, and in California more light was thrown on the long and amazingly conservative development of native culture which characterized that region from early prehistoric to historic times. Since laboratory study of the specimens and data secured is still in progress, further consideration of the scientific results would be premature. The above merely indicates their probable importance from the standpoint of New World prehistory.

Considering the speed with which they were put in motion, the above-mentioned archaeological projects under the C.W.A. were surprisingly successful. From the standpoint of relief they provided immediate work for numerous people. Over 90 per cent of the funds expended went for labor, since the tools for manual work, both skilled and unskilled, as well as the materials for the preservation of the archaeological remains, cost very little; and because the values produced were entirely scientific and educational, there was no resultant over-production. The main difficulties encountered were due to the failure of the original plans to provide for the supervision of the various aspects of each project by staffs adequately manned by technically-trained archaeological assistants, and to the fact that the exact amount of time and expenditure allotted to each project was constantly uncertain. This last factor prevented the accurate planning essential for the completion of a thoroughly productive piece of scientific excavation. So much for the immediate lessons acquired.

The actual application of large bodies of relief labor to scientific archaeological excavation must, however, be carefully considered in the light of broader scientific and educational principles. First, it must be remembered that the number of archaeological sites in the United States is strictly limited and that once a site has been carelessly excavated its value is totally destroyed. Such ancient ruins are really material documents that comprise the very stuff of American history. They are all that remain to enable future generations to trace out the story of the original settlement of the New World and the manner in which its strongly individualized and remarkable native civilizations came into being. No national monuments are more truly American than the great temple mounds of the Mississippi Valley, the cliff-dwellings and pueblos of the Southwest, and the great fortified villages of the Upper Missouri. These and all lesser sites contain valuable records which can only be read by those trained for such scientific work.

Recent years have opened new vistas in American prehistory and the work is still in its infancy. In New Mexico, Nevada, Colorado, Nebraska, and elsewhere, human artifacts have been found in association with fossil bison, the giant sloth, and the mammoth. Such finds indicate that the ancestors of the American Indian pushed into the North American continent at a very early period while the great Pleistocene ice sheet was still retreating to the north. Some competent students favor the theory that man arrived here even earlier, during certain inter-glacial periods. Certain stratified camp levels found in the Great Plains show the slow development of these early hunting cultures in their various stages. In the same area it has recently been demonstrated that the earliest hunting life was superseded by the advent of native farmers who grew corn and lived in permanent villages. These in turn were routed when the first white man brought in the horse, which was rapidly taken over by the Indians. Mounted, the hunting tribes swept over the Great Plains, setting up the nomadic, militaristic mode of life encountered by our first pioneers and later by our army. In the Southwest the long complex story of the rise of the Pueblo peoples is now

well known. Originally basket-making, seed-gathering, cave-dwelling, these people later moved into the open and built small adobe villages which in the course of time developed into the great communal apartment houses of the modern pueblo. Thanks to the newly discovered method of dating by tree rings, most of these larger ruins can now be assigned an actual date. Space forbids further details regarding the rise of the unique mound-building cultures of the Mississippi and Ohio River regions. Some of these may have been forced to migrate to other regions by the incoming Algonkians and the Iroquois, the latter a powerful people who pushed from the Southeast into the New York region; others were encountered by the first Spanish explorers in the South.

This is a mere suggestion of the long and important history patiently being pieced together by American archaeologists; no local problem but a vital and integral part of the larger picture of world prehistory that transcends all state or national boundaries. The earliest stages found in the prehistoric United States already suggest certain Paleolithic horizons in Europe and, when more work has been done here and in northern Asia, the human connections between the continents will become known facts instead of pure hypotheses.

The present actual status of archaeological conservation in the United States, however, is deplorable. Whereas the Scandinavian countries, France, Italy, Mexico, and many other nations, have nationalized their prehistoric remains in the belief that the objects themselves and the history they represent belong to the people as a whole and not to acquisitive individuals and curio dealers, no effort of this kind has

yet been made in the United States. From motives of mere curiosity or greed, dealers and relic hunters in practically every state are steadily destroying an irreplaceable heritage. The Antiquities Act of 1906 forbids unauthorized archaeological excavation on public lands, but the law is difficult to enforce and, so long as archaeological specimens can be sold on the open market, can have at best a very limited effect. This annihilation of our "readable past" which, due to the great popularity of "relic hunting", is steadily growing worse, indicates the need for a carefully planned archaeological program before it is too late. At present a race between the scientist and the curio seeker is on. Scientists are relatively few in number and must work slowly and carefully, whereas relic hunters are extremely numerous, and loot sites with great rapidity. The probable outcome, unless definite action is taken very soon, is only too obvious. Consequently, in mapping out any archaeological program, whether for emergency relief or for purely scientific purposes, the basic need for national conservation should be primary. Not only should each site opened be excavated with the greatest care, the material completely studied, and the results fully published, but certain sites in every area should be carefully preserved for research in the future, when new techniques have been developed. It is a sad paradox that at this time, when trained men are becoming available and new techniques for determining archaeological history are reaching a high pitch of development, the materials themselves should be vanishing like snow before the sun. It is even more tragic since an enlightened national policy in this regard could save them for all time.

Thinking Like an Archaeologist

Thinking like an archaeologist can make you a better consumer. It can help you in making decisions about your job choice, marriage partner, or where to take a vacation. It can help you get a job, get the best buy on cereal at the grocery store, and make life and death decisions. It can even cure ingrown toenails. So what is this magic archaeologists are hoarding and why don't they share it with everyone? Well, they try to but sometimes it seems to get lost somewhere between the pottery shards, the stone tools, and what is going on inside the pith helmet.

The greatest mystery of archaeology is the same thing that solves mysteries. It is called *thinking.* But not just any thinking. It is not thinking in the ordinary, everyday multimedia sense. The popular media gives us information but that information is usually constructed so that we do not have to think. We only think we are thinking because we are suddenly filled with novel information that we forget five minutes later. We do not have to think because the conclusions are inherent in the information. How is this done? Well, think. "Maniac murders chicken farmer and his wife and five children, sets chickens free! Film at eleven!" Hyperbole? It gets your attention. You are disgusted but you secretly want to know what is this person's thing about chickens. This is not a criticism of the media, just an observation. We are still talking about archaeology, but the media is a major source of the epistemology of the modern world and thus underscores cultural values as well as creating the necessary cultural myths by which all humans must live. The media is as much a response to our demands as we are to its manipulations. We are the media. Our conversations are the media. But in the same manner that modern cultures have moved away from labor-intensive production, we have moved away from communication-intensive language.

Most of our everyday conversations, if we should have any, are usually characterized by "fuzzy thinking." It is the state in which it seems brains are made of cotton balls and all our senses are hazy and dulled by the alpha waves of short-cut thinking. Brain drugged. Of course, the whole world cannot be populated by cantankerous scientists and academics challenging every syllable we speak, every action we take, every artifact we discard. But there is a very practical science of thinking, which may be learned and applied to defining, analyzing, and solving problems.

If our minds are trained to be articulate, our mouths and actions will follow suit. Scientific thinking is the real secret of archaeology. If the IRS is knocking on your door, you had better be able to think. Scientific thinking involves a very strict set of unchanging rules and regulations by which you test the veracity of your conclusions and decisions. Also it is best used before sending in your tax return.

But is scientific thinking really worth bothering with? Yes, it is. It may be called scientific thinking or using the scientific method, but it is also known as "being smart." Smart is more than the accumulation of trial and error learning, wherein you build up a repertoire of the do's and don'ts of life. And smart is not how many advanced degrees you have hanging on a wall. Smart is the systematic application of scientific thinking to this acquired body of information. And what do you get? You get good judgment and a predictably high number of desirable outcomes based on your decision-making processes. Call it game theory, call it science, but call it "smart"!

Looking Ahead: Challenge Questions

What is a hypothesis? How is it different from a theory? Give an example of general theory.

What is the relationship between thinking and communicating?

What are the four rules of science? Do they ever change?

Give short examples of inductive and deductive logic using the same information.

Do you believe an idea can bring about the end of a high civilization? Explain.

What is cultural historical reconstruction?

Epistemology: How You Know What You Know

Kenneth L. Feder

KNOWING THINGS

The word *epistemology* means the study of knowledge—how you know what you know. Think about it. How does anybody know anything to be actual, truthful, or real? How do we differentiate the reasonable from the unreasonable, the meaningful from the meaningless—in archaeology or in any other field of knowledge? Everybody knows things, but how do we really know these things?

I know that there is a mountain in a place called Tibet. I know that the mountain is called Everest, and I know that it is the tallest land mountain in the world (there are some a bit taller under the ocean). I even know that it is precisely 29,028 feet high. But I have never measured it; I've never even been to Tibet. Beyond this, I have not measured all of the other mountains in the world to compare them to Everest. Yet I am quite confident that Everest is the world's tallest peak. But how do I know that?

On the subject of mountains, there is a run-down stone monument on the top of Bear Mountain in the northwestern corner of Connecticut. The monument was built toward the end of the nineteenth century and marks the "highest ground" in Connecticut. When the monument was built to memorialize this most lofty and auspicious of peaks—the mountain is all of 2,316 feet high—people knew that it was the highest point in the state and wanted to recognize this fact with the monument.

There is only one problem. In recent times, with more accurate, sophisticated measuring equipment, it has been determined that Bear Mountain is not the highest point in Connecticut. The slope of Frissell Mountain, which actually peaks in Massachusetts, reaches a height of 2,380 feet on the Connecticut side of the border, eclipsing Bear Mountain by about 64 feet.

So, people in the late 1800s and early 1900s "knew" that Bear Mountain was the highest point in Connecticut. Today we *know* that they really did not "know" that, because it really was not true—even though they thought it was and built a monument saying so.

Now, suppose that I read in a newspaper, hear on the radio, or see on television a claim that another mountain has been found that is actually ten (or fifty, or ten thousand) feet higher than Mount Everest. Indeed, recently, new satellite data convinced a few, just for a while, that a peak neighboring Everest was, in actuality, slightly higher. You and I have never been to Tibet. How do we know if these reports are true? What criteria can we use to decide if the information is correct or not? It all comes back to epistemology. How indeed do we know what we think we "know"?

Collecting Information: Seeing Isn't Necessarily Believing
In general, people collect information in two ways;

1. Directly through their own experiences

2. Indirectly through specific information sources like friends, teachers, parents, books, TV, etc.

People tend to think that number 1—obtaining firsthand information, the stuff they see or experience themselves—is always the best way. This is unfortunately a false assumption because most people are poor observers.

For example, the list of animals alleged to have been observed by people that turn out to be figments of their imaginations is staggering. It is fascinating to read Pliny, a first-century thinker, or Topsell, who wrote in the seventeenth century, and see detailed accounts of the nature and habits of dragons, griffins, unicorns, mermaids, and so on (Byrne 1979). People claimed to have seen these animals, gave detailed descriptions, and even drew pictures of them. Many folks read their books and believed them.

Some of the first European explorers of Africa, Asia, and the New World could not decide if some of the native people they encountered were human beings or animals. They sometimes depicted them with hair all over their bodies and even as having tails.

Neither are untrained observers very good at identifying known, living animals. A red or "lesser" panda escaped from the zoo in Rotterdam, Holland, in December 1978. Red pandas are very rare animals and are indigenous to India, not Holland. They are distinctive in appearance and cannot be readily mistaken for any other sort of animal. The zoo informed the press that the panda was missing, hoping the publicity would alert people in the area of the zoo and aid in its return. Just when the newspapers came out with the panda story, it was found, quite dead, along some railroad tracks adjacent to the zoo. Nevertheless, over one hundred sightings of the panda *alive* were reported to the zoo from all over the Netherlands *after* the animal was obviously already dead. These reports did not stop until several days after the newspapers announced the discovery of the dead panda (van Kampen 1979). So much for the absolute reliability of firsthand observation.

Collecting Information: Relying on Others

When we explore the problems of secondhand information, we run into even more complications. Now we are not in place to observe something firsthand; we are forced to rely on the quality of someone else's observations, interpretations, and reports—as with the question of the height of Mount Everest. How do we know what to believe? This is a crucial question that all rational people must ask themselves, whether talking about medicine, religion, archaeology, or anything else. Again, it comes back around to epistemology; how do we know what we think we know, and how do we know what or whom to believe?

Science: Playing by the Rules

There are ways to knowledge that are both dependable and reliable. We might not be able to get to absolute truths about the meaning of existence, but we can figure out quite a bit about our world—about chemistry and biology, psychology and sociology, physics and history, and even prehistory. The techniques we are talking about to get at knowledge that we can feel confident in—knowledge that is reliable, truthful, and factual—are referred to as *science*.

In large part, science is a series of techniques used to maximize the probability that what we think we know really reflects the way things are, were, or will be. Science makes no claim to have all the answers or even to

be right all of the time. On the contrary, during the process of the growth of knowledge and understanding, science is often wrong. The only claim that we do make in science is that if we honestly, consistently, and vigorously pursue knowledge using some basic techniques and principles, the truth will eventually surface and we can truly know things about the nature of the world in which we find ourselves.

The question then is, What exactly is science? If you believe Hollywood, science is a mysterious enterprise wherein old, white-haired, rather eccentric bearded gentlemen labor feverishly in white lab coats, mix assorted chemicals, invent mysterious compounds, and attempt to reanimate dead tissue. So much for Hollywood. Scientists don't have to look like anything in particular. We are just people trying to arrive at some truths about how the world and universe work. While the application of science can be a slow, frustrating, all-consuming enterprise, the basic assumptions we scientists hold are really very simple. Whether we are physicists, biologists, or archaeologists, we all work under four underlying principles. These principles are quite straightforward, but equally quite crucial.

1. There is a real and knowable universe.
2. The universe (which includes stars, planets, animals, and rocks, as well as people, their cultures, and their histories) operates according to certain understandable rules or laws.
3. These laws are immutable—that means they do not, in general, change depending on where you are or "when" you are.
4. These laws can be discerned, studied, and understood by people through careful observation, experimentation, and research.

Let's look at these assumptions one at a time.

There Is a Real and Knowable Universe

In science we have to agree that there is a real universe out there for us to

study—a universe full of stars, animals, human history, and prehistory that exists whether we are happy with that reality or not.

The Universe Operates According to Understandable Laws

In essence, what this means is that there are rules by which the universe works: stars produce heat and light according to the laws of nuclear physics; nothing can go faster than the speed of light; all matter in the universe is attracted to all other matter (the law of gravity).

Even human history is not random but can be seen as following certain patterns of human cultural evolution. For example, the development of complex civilizations in Egypt, China, India/Pakistan, Mesopotamia, Mexico, and Peru was not based on random processes (Lamberg-Karlovsky and Sabloff 1979; Haas 1982). Their evolution seems to reflect similar general patterns. This is not to say that all of these civilizations were identical, any more than we would say that all stars are identical. On the contrary, they existed in different physical and cultural environments, and so we should expect that they be different. However, in each case the rise to civilization was preceded by the development of an agricultural economy. In each case, civilization was also preceded by some degree of overall population increase as well as increased population density in some areas (in other words, the development of cities). Again, in each case we find monumental works (pyramids, temples), evidence of long-distance trade, and the development of mathematics, astronomy, and methods of record keeping (usually, but not always, in the form of writing). The cultures in which civilization developed, though some were unrelated and independent, shared these factors because of the nonrandom patterns of cultural evolution.

The point is that everything operates according to rules. In science we believe that, by understanding these rules or laws, we can understand stars, organisms, and even ourselves.

2. THINKING LIKE AN ARCHAEOLOGIST

THE LAWS ARE IMMUTABLE

That the laws do not change under ordinary conditions is a crucial concept in science. A law that works here, works there. A law that worked in the past will work today and will work in the future.

For example, if I go to the top of the Leaning Tower of Pisa today and simultaneously drop two balls of unequal mass, they will fall at the same rate and reach the ground at the same time, just as they did when Galileo performed a similar experiment in the seventeenth century. If I do it today, they will. Tomorrow, the same. If I perform the same experiment countless times, the same thing will occur because the laws of the universe (in this case, the law of gravity) do not change through time. They also do not change depending on where you are. Go anywhere on the earth and perform the same experiment—you will get the same results (try not to hit any pedestrians or you will see some other "laws" in operation). This experiment was even performed by U.S. astronauts on the moon. A hammer and a feather were dropped from the same height, and they hit the surface at precisely the same instant (the only reason this will not work on earth is because the feather is caught by the air and the hammer, obviously, is not). We have no reason to believe that the results would be different anywhere, or "anywhen" else.

If this assumption of science, that the laws do not change through time, were false, many of the so-called historical sciences, including prehistoric archaeology, could not exist.

For example, a major principle in the field of historical geology is that of *uniformitarianism*. It can be summarized in the phrase, "the present is the key to the past." Historical geologists are interested in knowing how the various landforms we see today came into being. They recognize that they cannot go back in time to see how the Grand Canyon was formed. However, since the laws of geology that governed the development of the Grand Canyon have not changed through time, and since these laws are still in operation, they do not need to. Historical geologists can study the formation of geological features today and apply what they learn to the past. The same laws they can directly study operating in the present were operating in the past when geological features that interested them first formed.

The present that we can observe is indeed the "key" to the past that we cannot. This is true because the laws or rules that govern the universe are constant—those that operate today operated in the past. This is why science does not limit itself to the present, but makes inferences about the past and even predictions about the future (just listen to the weather report for an example of this). We can do so because we can study modern, ongoing phenomena that work under the same laws that existed in the past and will exist in the future.

This is where science and theology are often forced to part company and respectfully disagree. Remember, science depends on the constancy of the laws that we can discern. On the other hand, advocates of many religions, though they might believe that there are laws that govern things (and which, according to them, were established by a Creator), usually (but not always) believe that these laws can be changed at any time by their God. In other words, if God does not want the apple to fall to the ground, but instead, to hover, violating the law of gravity, that is precisely what will happen. As a more concrete example, scientists know that the heat and light given off by a fire results from the transformation of mass (of the wood) to energy. Physical laws control this process. A theologian, however, might agree with this ordinarily, but feel that if God wants to create a fire that does not consume any mass (like the "burning bush" of the Old Testament), then this is exactly what will occur. Most scientists simply do not accept this assertion. The rules are the rules. They do not change, even though we might sometimes wish that they would.

The Laws Can Be Understood

This may be the single most important principle in science. The universe is knowable. It may be complicated, and it may take years and years to understand even apparently simple phenomena. However, little by little, bit by bit, we expand our knowledge. Through careful observation and objective research and experimentation, we can indeed know things.

So, our assumptions are simple enough. We accept the existence of a reality independent of our own minds, and we accept that this reality works according to a series of unchanging laws or rules. We also claim that we can recognize and understand these laws or at least recognize the patterns that result from these universal rules. The question remains then: how do we do science—how do we explore the nature of the universe, whether our interest is planets, stars, atoms, or human prehistory?

THE WORKINGS OF SCIENCE

We can know things by employing the rules of logic and rational thought. Scientists—archaeologists or otherwise—usually work through a combination of the logical processes known as *induction* and *deduction*. The dictionary definition of induction is "arguing from specifics to generalities," while deduction is defined as the reverse, arguing from generalities to specifics.

What is essential to good science is objective, unbiased observations—of planets, molecules, rock formations, archaeological sites, and so on. Often, on the basis of these specific observations, we induce explanations called *hypotheses* for how these things work.

For example, we may study the planets Mercury, Venus, Earth, and Mars (each one presents specific bits of information). We then induce general rules about how we think these inner planets in our solar system were formed. Or, we might study a whole series of different kinds of molecules and then induce general rules about how all molecules interact chemically. We may study different rock formations and make general conclusions about their origin. We can study a number of specific prehistoric sites and make generalizations about how cultures evolved.

Notice that we cannot directly observe planets forming, the rules of molecular interaction, rocks being made, or prehistoric cultures evolving. Instead, we are inducing general conclusions and principles concerning our data that seem to follow logically from what we have been able to observe.

This process of induction, though crucial to science, is not enough. We need to go beyond our induced hypotheses by testing them. If our induced hypotheses are indeed valid—that is, if they really represent the actual rules according to which some aspect of the universe (planets, molecules, rocks, ancient societies) works—they should be able to hold up under the rigors of scientific hypothesis testing.

Observation and suggestion of hypotheses, therefore, are only the first steps in a scientific investigation. In science we always need to go beyond observation and hypothesizing. We need to set up a series of "if . . . then" statements; "if" our hypothesis is true "then" the following deduced "facts" will also be true. Our results are not always precise and clear-cut, especially in a science like archaeology, but this much should be clear—scientists are not just out there collecting a bunch of interesting facts. Facts are always collected within the context of trying to explain something or in trying to test a hypothesis.

As an example of this logical process, consider the health effects of smoking. How can scientists be sure that smoking is bad for you? After all, it's pretty rare that someone takes a puff on a cigarette and immediately drops dead. The certainty comes from a combination of induction and deduction. Observers have noticed for about three hundred years that people who smoked seemed to be more likely than people who did not to get certain diseases. As long ago as the seventeenth century, people noticed that habitual pipe smokers were subject to tumor growths on their lips and in their mouths. From such observations we can reasonably, though tentatively, induce a hypothesis of the unhealthfulness of smoking, but we still need to test such a hypothesis. We need to set up "if . . . then" statements. If, in fact, smoking is a hazard to your health (the hypothesis we have induced based on our observations), then we should be able to deduce some predictions that must also be true. Sure enough, when we test specific, deduced predictions like

1. Smokers will have a higher incidence than nonsmokers of lung cancer
2. Smokers will have a higher incidence of emphysema
3. Smokers will take more sick days from work
4. Smokers will get more upper respiratory infections
5. Smokers will have diminished lung capacity
6. Smokers will have a shorter life expectancy

we see that our original, induced hypothesis—cigarette smoking is hazardous to your health—is upheld.

That was easy, but also obvious. How about an example with more mystery to it, one in which scientists acting in the way of detectives had to solve a puzzle in order to save lives? Carl Hempel (1966), a philosopher of science, provided the following example in his book *The Philosophy of Natural Science.*

THE CASE OF CHILDBED FEVER

In the 1840s things were not going well at the Vienna General Hospital, particularly in Ward 1 of the Maternity Division. In War 1 more than one in ten of the women brought in to give birth died soon after of a terrible disease called "childbed fever." This was a high death rate even for the 1840s. In one year 11.4 percent of the women who gave birth in Ward 1 died of this disease. It was a horrible situation and truly mystifying when you consider the fact that in Ward 2, another maternity division in the *same* hospital at the *same* time, only about one in fifty of the women (2 percent) died from this disease.

Plenty of people had tried their hand at inducing some possible explanations or hypotheses to explain these facts. It was suggested that more women were dying in Ward 1 due to "atmospheric disturbances," or perhaps it was "cosmic forces." However, no one had really sat down and considered the deductive implications of the various hypotheses—those things that would necessarily have been true if the proposed, induced explanation were in fact true. No one, that is, until a Hungarian doctor, Ignaz Semmelweis, attacked the problem in 1848.

Semmelweis made some observations in the maternity wards at the hospital. He noted some differences between Wards 1 and 2 and induced a series of possible explanations for the drastic difference in the mortality rates. Semmelweis suggested:

1. Ward 1 tended to be more crowded than Ward 2. The overcrowding in Ward 1 was the cause of the higher mortality rate there.
2. Women in Ward 1 were from a lower socioeconomic class and tended to give birth lying on their backs, while in Ward 2 the predominate position was on the side. Birth position was the cause of the higher mortality rate.
3. There was a psychological factor involved; the hospital priest had to walk through Ward 1 to administer the last rites to dying patients in other wards. This sight so upset some women already weakened by the ordeal of childbirth that it contributed to their deaths.
4. There were more student doctors in Ward 1. Students were rougher than experienced physicians in their treatment of the women, unintentionally harming them and contributing to their deaths.

These induced hypotheses all sounded good. Each marked a genuine difference between Wards 1 and 2 that might have caused the difference in the death rate. Semmelweis was doing what most scientists do in such a situation; he was relaying on creativity and imagination in seeking out an explanation.

Creativity and imagination are just as important to science as good observation. But being creative and imaginative was not enough. It did not help the women who were still dying at an alarming rate. Semmelweis had to go beyond producing possible explanations; he had to test each one of them. So, he deduced the necessary implications of each:

1. If hypothesis 1 were correct, then cutting down the crowding in Ward 1 should cut down the mortality rate. Semmelweis tried precisely that. The result: no change. So the first hypothesis was rejected. It had failed the scientific test; it simply could not be correct.

2. Semmelweis went on to test hypothesis 2 by changing the birth positions of the women in Ward 1 to match those of the women in Ward 2. Again, there was no change, and another hypothesis was rejected.

3. Next, to test hypothesis 3, Semmelweis rerouted the priest. Again, women in Ward 1 continued to die of childbed fever at about five times the rate of those in Ward 2.

4. Finally, to test hypothesis 4 Semmelweis made a special effort to get the student doctors to be more gentle in their birth assistance to the women in Ward 1. The result was the same; 10 or 11 percent of the women in Ward 1 died compared to about 2 percent in Ward 2.

Then, as so often happens in science, Semmelweis had a stroke of luck. A doctor friend of his died, and the way he died provided Semmelweis with another possible explanation for the problem in Ward 1. Though Semmelweis's friend was not a woman who had recently given birth, he did have precisely the same symptoms as did the women who were dying of childbed fever. Most importantly, this doctor had died of a disease just like childbed

fever soon after accidentally cutting himself during an autopsy.

Viruses and bacteria were unknown in the 1840s. Surgical instruments were not sterilized, no special effort was made to clean the hands, and doctors did not wear gloves during operations and autopsies. Semmelweis had another hypothesis; perhaps the greater number of medical students in Ward 1 was at the root of the mystery, but not because of their inexperience. Instead, these students, as part of their training, were much more likely than experienced doctors to be performing autopsies. Supposing that there was something bad in dead bodies and this something had entered Semmelweis's friend's system through his wound—could the same bad "stuff" (Semmelweis called it "cadaveric material") get onto the hands of the student doctors, who then might, without washing, go on to help a woman give birth? Then, if this "cadaveric material" were transmitted into the woman's body during the birth of her baby, this material might lead to her death. It was a simple enough hypothesis to test. Semmelweis simply had the student doctors carefully wash their hands after performing autopsies. The women stopped dying in Ward 1. Semmelweis had solved the mystery.

SCIENCE AND NONSCIENCE: THE ESSENTIAL DIFFERENCES

Through objective observation and analysis, a scientist, whether a physicist, chemist, biologist, psychologist, or archaeologist, sees things that need explaining. Through creativity and imagination, the scientist suggests possible hypotheses to explain these "mysteries." The scientist then sets up a rigorous method through experimentation or subsequent research to deductively test the validity of a given hypothesis. If the implications of a hypothesis are shown not to be true, the hypothesis must be rejected and then it's back to the drawing board. If the implications are found to be true, we can uphold or support our hypothesis.

A number of other points should be made here. The first is that in order for a hypothesis, whether it turns out to be upheld or not, to be scientific in the first place, it must be testable. In other words, there must be clear, deduced implications that can be drawn from the hypothesis and then tested. Remember the hypotheses of "cosmic influences" and "atmospheric disturbances"? How can you test these? What are the necessary implications that can be deduced from the hypothesis, "More women died in Ward 1 due to atmospheric disturbances"? There really aren't any, and therefore such a hypothesis is not scientific—it cannot be tested. Remember, in the methodology of science, we ordinarily need to:

1. Observe
2. Induce general hypotheses or possible explanations for what we have observed.
3. Deduce specific things that must also be true if our hypothesis is true
4. Test the hypothesis by checking out the deduced implications

If there are no specific implications of a hypothesis that can then be analyzed as a test of the validity or usefulness of that hypothesis, then you simply are not doing and cannot do "science."

For example, suppose you observe a person who appears to be able to "guess" the value of a playing card picked from a deck. Next, assume that someone hypothesizes that "psychic" ability is involved. Finally, suppose the claim is made that the "psychic" ability goes away as soon as you try to test it (actually named the "shyness effect" by some researchers of the paranormal). Such a claim is not itself testable and therefore not scientific.

Beyond the issue of testability, another lesson is involved in determining whether an approach to a problem is scientific. Semmelweis induced four different hypotheses to explain the difference in mortality rates between Wards 1 and 2. These "competing" explanations are called *multiple working hypotheses*. Notice that Semmelweis did not simply proceed by a process of elimination. He did not, for example, test the first three hypotheses and—after finding them invalid—declare that the fourth was necessarily correct since it was the only one left that he had thought of.

Some people try to work that way. A light is seen in the sky. Someone hypothesizes it was a meteor. We find out that it was not. Someone else hypothesizes that it was a military rocket. Again this turns out to be incorrect. Someone else suggests that it was the Goodyear Blimp, but that turns out to have been somewhere else. Finally, someone suggests that it was the spacecraft of people from another planet. Some will say that this must be correct, since none of the other explanations panned out. This is nonsense. There are plenty of other possible explanations. Eliminating all of the explanations *we* have been able to think of except one (which, perhaps, has no testable implications) in no way allows us to uphold that final hypothesis. . . .

It's like seeing a card trick. You are mystified by it. You have a few possible explanations: the magician did it with mirrors, there was a helper in the audience, the cards were marked. But when you approach the magician and ask which it was, he assures you that none of your hypotheses is correct. Do you then decide that what you saw was an example of genuine, supernatural magic? Of course not! Simply because you or I cannot come up with the right explanation does not mean that the trick has a supernatural explanation. We simply admit that we do not have the expertise to suggest a more reasonable hypothesis.

Finally, there is another rule to hypothesis making and testing. It is called *Occam's Razor* or *Occam's Rule*. In essence it says that when a number of hypotheses are proposed through induction to explain a given set of observations, the simplest hypothesis is probably the best.

Take this actual example. During the eighteenth and nineteenth centuries, huge, buried, fossilized bones were found throughout North America and Europe. One hypothesis, the simplest,

was that the bones were the remains of animals that no longer existed. This hypothesis simply relied on the assumption that bones do not come into existence by themselves, but always serve as the skeletons of animals. Therefore, when you find bones, there must have been animals who used those bones. However, another hypothesis was suggested: the bones were deposited by the Devil to fool us into thinking that such animals existed (Howard 1975). This hypothesis demanded many more assumptions about the universe than did the first: there is a Devil, that Devil is interested in human affairs, he wants to fool us, he has the ability to make bones of animals that never existed, and he has the ability to hide them under the ground and inside solid rock. That is quite a number of unproven (and largely untestable) claims to swallow. Thus, Occam's Razor says the simpler hypothesis, that these great bones are evidence of the existence of animals that no longer exist—in other words, dinosaurs—is better. The other one simply raises more questions than it answers.

THE ART OF SCIENCE

Don't get the impression that science is a mechanical enterprise. Science is at least partially an art. It is much more than just observing the results of experiments.

It takes great creativity to recognize a "mystery" in the first place. In the apocryphal story, countless apples had fallen from countless trees and undoubtedly conked the noggins of multitudes of stunned individuals who never thought much about it. It took a fabulously creative individual, Isaac Newton, to even recognize that herein lay a mystery. Why did the apple fall? No one had ever articulated the possibility that the apple could have hovered in midair. It could have moved off in any of the cardinal directions. It could have gone straight up and out of sight. But it did not. It fell to the ground as it always had, in all places, and as it always would. It took great imagination to recognize that in this simple observation (and in a bump on the

head) rested the eloquence of a fundamental law of the universe.

Further, it takes great skill and imagination to invent a hypothesis in this attempt to understand why things seem to work the way they do. Remember, Ward 1 at the Vienna General Hospital did not have written over its doors, OVERCROWDED WARD or WARD WITH STUDENT DOCTORS WHO DON'T WASH THEIR HANDS AFTER AUTOPSIES. It took imagination first to recognize that there were differences between the wards and, quite importantly, that some of the differences might logically be at the root of the mystery. After all, there were in all likelihood many, many differences between the wards: their compass orientations, the names of the nurses, the precise alignment of the windows, the astrological signs of the doctors who worked in the wards, and so on. If a scientist were to attempt to test all of these differences as hypothetical causes of a mystery, nothing would ever be solved. Occam's Razor must be applied. We need to focus our intellectual energies on those possible explanations that require few other assumptions. Only after all of these have been eliminated, can we legitimately consider others. As summarized by that great fictional detective, Sherlock Holmes:

> It is of the highest importance in the art of detection to be able to recognize, out of a number of facts, which are incidental and which are vital. Otherwise, your energy and attention must be dissipated instead of being concentrated.

Semmelweis concentrated his attention on first four, then a fifth possible explanation. Like all good scientists he had to use some amount of what we can call "intuition" to sort out the potentially vital from the probably incidental. Even in the initial sorting we may be wrong. Overcrowding seemed a very plausible explanation to Semmelweis, but it was wrong nonetheless.

Finally, it takes skill and inventiveness to suggest ways for testing the hypothesis in question. We must, out of our own heads, be able to invent the "then" part of our "if . . . then" statements. We need to be able to suggest those things that must be true if our hypothesis is to be supported. There really is an art to that. Anyone can claim there was a Lost Continent of Atlantis, but often it takes a truly inventive mind to suggest precisely what archaeologists must find if the hypothesis of its existence were indeed to be valid.

Semmelweis tested his hypotheses and solved the mystery of childbed fever by changing conditions in Ward 1 to see if the death rate would change. In essence, the testing of each hypothesis was an experiment. In archaeology, the testing of hypotheses often must be done in a different manner. There is a branch of archaeology called, appropriately enough, "experimental archaeology" that involves the experimental replication and utilization of prehistoric artifacts in an attempt to figure out how they were made and used. In general, however, archaeology is largely not an experimental science. Archaeologists more often need to create "models" of some aspect of cultural adaptation and change. These models are simplified, manipulable versions of cultural phenomena.

For example, James Mosimann and Paul Martin (1975) created a computer program that simulated or modeled the first human migration into America some 12,000 years ago. By varying the size of the initial human population and their rate of growth and expansion, as well as the size of the big-game animal herds in the New World, Mosimann and Martin were able to test their hypothesis that these human settlers caused the extinction of many species of game animals. The implications of their mathematical modeling can be tested against actual archaeological and paleontological data.

Ultimately, whether a science is experimentally based or not makes little logical difference in the testing of hypotheses. Instead of predicting what the results of a given experiment must be if our induced hypothesis is useful or valid, we predict what new data we must be able to find if a given hypothesis is correct.

For instance, we may hypothesize that long-distance trade is a key ele-

ment in the development of civilization based upon our analysis of the ancient Maya. We deduce that if this is correct—if this is, in fact, a general rule of cultural evolution—we must find large quantities of trade items in other parts of the world where civilization also developed. We might further deduce that these items should be found in contexts that denote their value and importance to the society (for example, in the burials of leaders). We must then determine the validity of our predictions and, indirectly, our hypothesis by going out and conducting more research. We need to excavate sites belonging to other ancient civilizations and see if they followed the same pattern as seen for the Maya relative to the importance of trade.

Testing a hypothesis certainly is not easy. Sometimes errors in testing can lead to incorrectly validating or rejecting a hypothesis. Some of you may have already caught a potential problem in Semmelweis's application of the scientific method. Remember hypothesis 4? It was initially suggested that the student doctors were at the root of the higher death rate in Ward 1, because they were not as gentle in assisting in birthing as were the more experienced doctors. This hypothesis was not borne out by testing. Retraining the students had no effect on the mortality rate in Ward 1. But suppose that Semmelweis had tested this hypothesis instead by removing the students altogether prior to their retraining. From what we now know, the death rate would have indeed declined, and Semmelweis would have concluded incorrectly that the hypothesis was correct. We can assume that once the retrained students were returned to the ward (gentler, perhaps, but with their hands still dirty) the death rate would have jumped up again since the students were indeed at the heart of the matter, but not because of their presumed rough handling of the maternity patients.

This should point out that our testing of hypotheses takes a great deal of thought and that we can be wrong. We must remember: we have a hypothesis, we have the deduced implications, and

we have the test. We can make errors at any place within this process—the hypothesis may be incorrect, the implications may be wrong, or the way we test them may be incorrect. Certainty in science is a scarce commodity. There are always new hypotheses, alternative explanations, and more deductive implications to test. Nothing is ever finished, nothing is set in concrete, nothing is ever defined or raised to the level of religious truth.

Beyond this, it must be admitted that scientists are, after all, ordinary human beings. They are not isolated from the cultures and times in which they live. They share many of the same prejudices and biases of other members of their societies. Scientists learn from mentors at universities and often inherit their perspectives. It often is quite difficult to go against the scientific grain, to question accumulated wisdom, and to suggest a new approach or perspective.

For example, when German meteorologist Alfred Wegener hypothesized in 1912 that the present configuration of the continents resulted from the breakup of a single inclusive landmass and that the separate continents had "drifted" into their current positions (a process called *continental drift*), most rejected the suggestion outright. Yet today, Wegener's general perspective is accepted and incorporated into the general theory of *plate tectonics*.

Philosopher of science Thomas Kuhn (1970) has suggested that the growth of scientific knowledge is not neatly linear, with knowledge simply building on knowledge. He maintains that science remains relatively static for periods and that most thinkers work under the same set of assumptions—the same *paradigm*. New ideas or perspectives, like those of Wegener or Einstein, that challenge the existing orthodoxy, are usually initially rejected. Only once scientists get over the shock of the new ideas and start testing the new frameworks suggested by these new paradigms are great jumps in knowledge made.

That is why in science we propose, test, tentatively accept, but never prove a hypothesis. We keep only those hypotheses that cannot be disproved. As long as an hypothesis holds up under the scrutiny of additional testing through experiment and/or is not contradicted by new data, we accept it as the best explanation so far. Some hypotheses sound good, pass the rigors of initial testing, but are later shown to be inadequate or invalid. Others—for example, the hypothesis of biological evolution—have held up so well (all new data either were or could have been deduced from it) that they will probably always be upheld. We usually call these very well supported hypotheses *theories*. However, it is in the nature of science that no matter how well an explanation of some aspect of reality has held up, we must always be prepared to consider new tests and better explanations.

We are interested in knowledge and explanations of the universe that work. As long as these explanations work, we keep them. As soon as they cease being effective because new data and tests show them to be incomplete or misguided, we discard them and seek new ones. In one sense, Semmelweis was wrong after all, though his explanation worked at the time—he did save lives through its application. We now know that there is nothing inherently bad in "cadaveric material." Dead bodies are not the cause of childbed fever. Today we realize that it is a bacteria that can grow in the flesh of a dead body that can get on a doctor's hands, infect a pregnant woman, and cause her death. Semmelweis worked in a time before the existence of such things was known. Science in this way always grows, expands, and evolves.

SCIENCE AND ARCHAEOLOGY

The study of the human past is a science and relies on the same general logical processes that all sciences do. Unfortunately, perhaps as a result of its popularity, the data of archaeology have often been used by people to attempt to prove some idea or claim. Too often, these attempts have been bereft of science.

Archaeology has attracted frauds and fakes. Myths about the human past have been created and popularized. Misunderstandings of how archaeologists go about their tasks and what we have discovered about the human story have too often been promulgated. As I stated . . . my purpose is to describe the misuse of archaeology and the nonscientific application of the data from this field. . . .

The Death Cults of Prehistoric Malta

New archaeological excavations reveal that as the ancient island societies suffered from environmental decline, they developed an extreme religious preoccupation with life and death.

Caroline Malone, Anthony Bonanno, Tancred Gouder, Simon Stoddart and David Trump

Caroline Malone, Anthony Bonanno, Tancred Gouder, Simon Stoddart and David Trump have extensively explored the ruins of ancient Maltese culture and contributed to the modern understanding of it. Malone and Stoddart are both lecturers in archaeology at the University of Bristol in England. Bonanno is professor of archaeology at the University of Malta. Gouder is director of museums at the National Museum of Malta. Trump is a lecturer in extramural studies at the University of Cambridge. Between 1958 and 1963 he was also curator of archaeology at the University of Malta.

The Mediterranean region is a fine laboratory for the scientific study of early religions because so many emerged there. Everyone has heard of the mythology of Greece and the cults surrounding the Roman emperors. Yet those were the religions of city-states not far removed from our own modern societies. Far less well known are the religions of the agricultural communities that preceded the advance of Greco-Roman civilization.

In several of the latter, images of corpulent human figures played an important role. Because some of these figures are recognizably female in shape, archaeologists sometimes refer to them as "fat ladies" and associate them with the celebration of fertility, both human and agricultural. On one small group of islands, those of Malta, such figures became the object of an infatuation that was closely linked to the construction of the earliest free-standing public stone buildings in the world.

Those temples and the underground burial chambers related to them contained many images of obese humans—some no larger than a few centimeters, others the size of giants—as well as of animals and phallic symbols. A collaborative project between British and Maltese archaeologists, of which we are the directors, has recently made spectacular discoveries about the artistic representations of the so-called mother goddesses. These findings have cast new light on how certain religious practices evolved on Malta and perhaps on why they eventually disappeared. They suggest the religion itself encompassed much more than a worship of human fecundity. They also tell a cautionary tale about what happens when a people focus too much energy on worshiping life rather than sustaining it.

Traditionally, archaeological discoveries in Malta have been interpreted—or perhaps we should say misinterpreted—against a backdrop of broad conjecture about the significance of mother goddesses. Figurines fitting that general description date from the Upper Paleolithic era (about 25,000 years ago) to the dawn of metal-using societies in the Neolithic era. A few have been found in western Europe, but the yields have been much richer at sites in Egypt, the Levant, Turkey, Greece, Cyprus and the Balkans. The most elaborate figures come from the islands of Malta in the third millennium B.C.

Unfortunately, many of these figurines are far less informative than they might once have been because of the unscientific ways in which they were collected. The dating of the figures is often inaccurate. The records of where and how they were situated are often incomplete, so we cannot know whether the figures were peculiar to burial sites, shrines or houses. We do know that in the Balkans such figures were kept in houses inside specially constructed niches in the walls. In Turkey, at the site of the eighth millennium B.C. settlement Çatal Hüyük, the finest figurines of clay and stone were associated with the burials of high-status people in special shrines, whereas cruder figurines were found in houses. The discovery of similar figurines at far-flung sites and from disparate eras inspired a long tradition of scholarly speculation about a widespread prehis-

SEATED PAIR of human figures (*bottom of page*) is helping archaeologists revise their views of Maltese prehistory. The statue was unearthed (*below*) from a subterranean burial complex on the island of Gozo.

toric religion based on the worship of the mother goddess. In the middle decades of this century, for example, some archaeologists tried to show that a cult of the Eye Goddess (so called because of eye motifs on Mesopotamian idols) diffused throughout the entire Mediterranean. More recently, claims have been made that the Balkans were the center of an Old European religion.

Most modern scholars appreciate that the early cults were radically different in each prehistoric society and that the cults of domestic life were distinct from the cults of death and burial. The example of Malta demonstrates that variation most emphatically. Elsewhere in the Mediterranean, the cults generally involved simple domestic rituals; little effort was invested in religious art or architecture. In Malta, however, the worship of corpulent images gradually blossomed into a consuming passion. That fixation may have been able to take root because conditions there enabled a closed, isolated, introverted society to develop.

Today the dry, rocky, hilly islands of Malta seem inhospitable to farming communities. Little soil or vegetation is present, and obtaining fresh water is a problem. Yet the geologic evidence suggests that between 5,000 and 7,000 years ago, a far more inviting scene greeted the early inhabitants. Those people probably cleared the fragile landscape of its natural vegetation fairly rapidly. Thereafter, severe soil erosion gradually robbed the islands of their productivity. The resulting environmental fragility may have caused agricultural yields to be unpredictable. That stress may well have shaped the strange and often extreme society that one finds portrayed in the archaeological record of ancient Malta.

The prehistoric archaeology of the Maltese islands is famed for its many huge stone temples. The number of them is staggering: some 20 groups of temples dot the islands, most containing two or three individual massive structures. Radiocarbon dating has indicated that they developed over roughly a millennium, from approximately 3500 to 2500 B.C. Because of their prominence in the landscape of Malta and Gozo, the two largest and most populous of the islands, the temples were always obvious targets for enthusiastic archaeological investigations, particularly during the 19th century. Those early workers cleared the rubble and other deposits from the

temples long before scientific archaeology had developed. Little effort was made to specify the exact positions of the unearthed artifacts; in particular, the contexts of the cult idols were rarely recorded. Not much can be done now with that incomplete evidence, other than to appreciate the sculptors' high level of skill.

Although mostly stripped of its cult images and other decoration, the architecture of the Maltese temples still survives. The design of the temples is regular: each consists of a curved stone façade overlooking an open forecourt. The façade usually has a formal entrance, marked by enormous carved stones and a capstone, that leads to a central corridor. Lobe-shaped apses open onto this corridor at either side and ahead, as in a cloverleaf. The apses often had stone altars (which were frequently carved with spiral or animal designs), carefully plastered floors and walls and other decorations painted with red ocher, a pigment probably imported from Sicily. They also feature tie-holes, which in some cases were perhaps for fastening animals to the walls, and holes in the ground that were evidently for draining liquids. In many instances, substantial quantities of animal bones, particularly those of sheep and goats, were found together with drinking vessels and sharp flint knives. All these details suggest that sacrifices and feasting may

have played an important part in the rituals performed in the temples.

Some information about the layout of the furnishings survived in the temples of Tarxien, which were excavated between 1915 and 1919. The lower half of an enormous statue of a "fat lady" was found in the temple precinct. Next to it is an altar within which the remains of food were found. The altar faced the carved figures of animals that may have represented sacrifices. Deeper within the recesses of the temple, excavators found the images of people who may have been priests, caches of precious pendants and even architectural models of the temples themselves.

The discovery in 1902 of the hypogeum, or subterranean burial chamber, at Hal Saflieni added another dimension to the cults of early Malta. Construction workers stumbled across this remarkable site while excavating cellars and foundations for new buildings in the surrounding town of Pawla. Before any skilled archaeologist was called to the scene, most of the chambers were emptied without documenting their contents; the rich assemblage of human remains and grave goods they must have contained probably ended up as fertilizer in nearby fields. A proper study of the hypogeum was finally conducted a few years later by Themistocles Zammit, the curator of the National Museum of Malta and the father of Maltese prehistory. He attempted to salvage what information he could from the near-empty chambers cut in the rock.

Zammit estimated that a fantastic number of individuals—between 6,000 and 7,000—had been buried in the 32 chambers of the hypogeum complex. They had been interred along with grave gifts of pots, obsidian and flint tools, jewelry consisting of beads and stone pendants, and clay and stone figures of obese people and animals. One of the most striking figures is the Sleeping Lady of the Hypogeum. This statuette shows a rotund female lying on her side on an elaborate woven bed. She is clothed in gathered skirts, and her hair is dressed in a small neat bun.

The various passages and chambers of the site strongly resembled the temples aboveground, with upright stone blocks spanned by lintels, steps, hinge holes for barriers and perhaps painted decorations. Nevertheless, the primary function of the hypogeum was clearly for burial, as the thousands of bones attest. Yet it may have been more than

simply a huge tomb. Its elaborately carved form, so similar in design to the temples, hints that it was also a temple for the dead, central to the rituals of death, burial and the afterlife.

The great number of figurines from both the temples and the ornate burial hypogeum of Hal Saflieni have fueled ideas (some plausible, some fantastic)

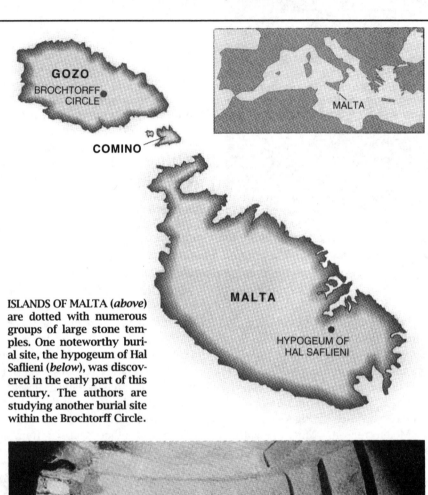

ISLANDS OF MALTA (*above*) are dotted with numerous groups of large stone temples. One noteworthy burial site, the hypogeum of Hal Saflieni (*below*), was discovered in the early part of this century. The authors are studying another burial site within the Brochtorff Circle.

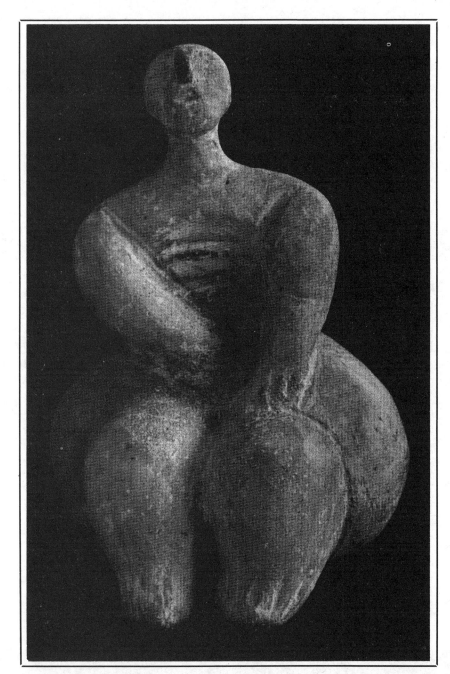

"FAT LADY" figurines representing mother goddesses were made by many early Mediterranean cultures, but those from Malta are the most elaborate. Not all the human figures from Malta are clearly female, however, which suggests that the ancient religion there involved much more than just the worship of human and agricultural fertility.

that consists of a stone wall and entrance that encircle a huge rough hole at the center; several megaliths also stand within the enclosure. In one drawing, a man is shown climbing from the hole, holding an object shaped like a human skull.

That series of pictures was the only clue left to suggest that an archaeological site was located on the plateau. It served as a starting point for our team, which set out to rediscover whatever remained underneath the flat field. Using the most up-to-date scientific techniques, such as ground-penetrating radar, we conducted topographic and geophysical surveys of the area to assess the nature of the buried rock. In 1987 we succeeded in once again locating the Bayer excavation within a circle that had been found 20 years earlier.

Since then, months of hard reexcavation have been spent at the site. Over an area of about a quarter acre, we needed to remove not only the 19th-century backfill but also the rubble from cave collapses that had filled several deep natural cavities to a depth of more than four meters. By the end of five work seasons, the true nature of the site was clear, and the rich array of recovered artifacts and human remains testified to its importance.

After the previous depredations at the site, we wanted to ensure that it was reexcavated with all the care and precision available to late 20th-century science. We therefore recorded and photographed every item at the base level of the caves in situ from several directions for a three-dimensional record of its position and appearance. Samples were taken for dating and also for studies of the local environment and subtle stratigraphy of the site. Paleoanthropological methods helped us to reconstruct a profile of the buried

about the supposed fertility cults and rituals of Malta. Some archaeologists have hypothesized that Maltese society may have been a powerful matriarchy dominated by priestesses, female leaders and mother goddesses. Those theories were always based on an implicit faith in the meaning of the artifacts—a faith as devout, in its way, as the prehistoric religion itself but lacking much scientific foundation.

During the past five years, a new excavation at the site of the Brochtorff Circle on Gozo has uncovered important evidence about the prehistoric rituals of death. The Brochtorff Circle, a megalithic enclosure on the summit of the Xaghra plateau, was first discovered in the 1820s by Otto Bayer, the lieutenant governor of Gozo. Vague historical records suggest that a typically haphazard treasure hunt at the site followed, from which no findings or documentation survived. Those efforts obliterated all surface traces of the structure. Fortunately, though, a roving Maltese artist, Charles Brochtorff, made several sketches of the work while it was in progress. His accurate, detailed watercolors and engravings show a site

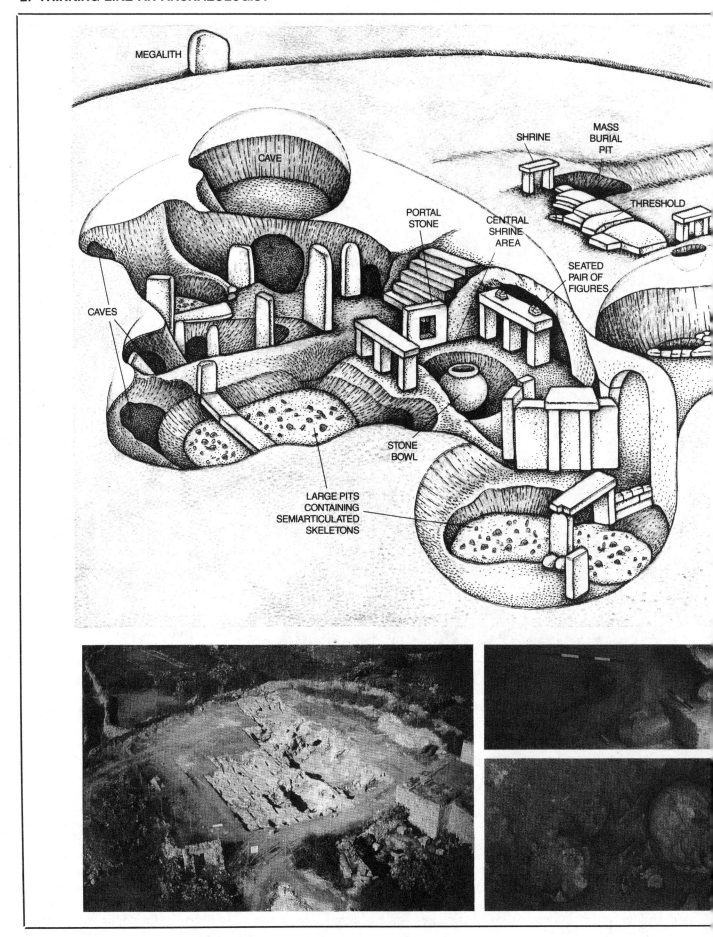

MEGALITH

CAVE

SHRINE

MASS
BURIAL
PIT

THRESHOLD

PORTAL
STONE

CENTRAL
SHRINE
AREA

SEATED
PAIR OF
FIGURES

CAVES

STONE
BOWL

LARGE PITS
CONTAINING
SEMIARTICULATED
SKELETONS

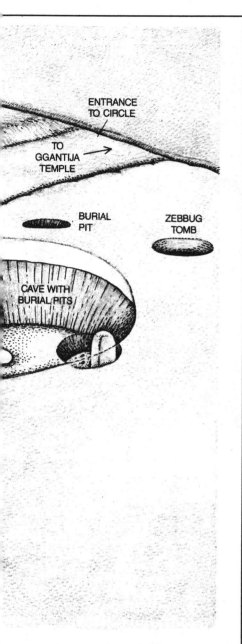

**Underground
Burial Chambers**

Brochtorff Circle marks a cave complex that the inhabitants of Gozo used for burials between 4000 and 2500 B.C. Treasure hunters found the site and then obliterated it in the 19th century, but in 1987 the authors and their colleagues found it again and re-excavated it. An aerial photograph (*far left*) shows the site as it appears today. The drawing (*above*) shows a partial reconstruction of the burial complex based on the most recent work. Thousands of human remains, many still adorned with ceremonial red ocher pigment, are clearly identifiable within certain pits in the cave floor (*near left*).

human population. We kept scrupulous computer records.

Unlike the great hypogeum of Hal Saflieni on Malta, which consists mainly of artificial carved chambers, the Brochtorff site on Gozo is fundamentally a series of natural caves with numerous interconnecting chambers. Erosion and perhaps earthquakes have cracked the thin rocky roof of the caves, resulting in several meters of rockfall and jumbled archaeological deposits. The caves were crumbling even 5,000 years ago. The prehistoric community, which by that time had already been using the caves for the burial of the dead for perhaps 1,000 years, began to insert carved stone supports under the cave roof in a vain attempt to control the collapse.

The burial complex at the Brochtorff site was in use for about 1,500 years, a period spanning several stages in the evolution of Maltese religion and society. In the early Zebbug period between 4000 and 3500 B.C., burial rituals were simple. The dead were placed in collective chambers that were either in caves or in tombs cut into the rock. Each chamber may have held the members from a single family or lineage group. One such tomb was found inside the circle in 1988. The burial rites evidently included the progressive removal of bones from earlier burials to allow space for later ones; the large removed bones may have been dumped in other parts of the caves.

A variety of gifts were interred with the dead: pottery, bone and stone beads and pendants, stone axes made of metamorphic rocks, flint and obsidian blades, shell pendants, and shell and bead necklaces. The bone pendants often have budlike appendages suggestive of arms and heads. Red ocher was spread lavishly over the grave goods and also over the dry white bones of the dead (perhaps in a symbolic attempt to restore them to life). At the entrance to one of the chambers stood a small upright monolith, a so-called menhir, bearing a crudely carved face that guarded the doorway.

The later burials, which were contemporary with the great Tarxien period of temple building, were different.

The emphasis on small family groups appears to have been supplanted by a more ritualized and elaborate cult of the dead. Part of the evidence for that conclusion comes from the megalithic construction of the Brochtorff Circle itself. The builders enclosed the opening to the cave with a wall and oriented its entrance eastward through the massive upright stones. In so doing, they integrated the entire site with the Ggantija temple, 300 meters away and on a lower terrace of the plateau.

Inside the caves the Tarxien builders leveled the earlier burials to provide a fresh (albeit bone-riddled) surface for the installation of stone monuments. The niches and smaller caverns were subdivided with pairs of upright stones and rough walls, which created additional, enclosed places for burials. At the center of the main cavern, the Maltese builders set up megalithic slabs in a semicircle, at the heart of which was a huge carved stone bowl. The stonework surrounding this bowl was elegant, and there is evidence that some of it included animal figures and pitted patterns. The builders did not apply red ocher as liberally as their predecessors did, and they painted only a few of the nearby slabs.

Bodies were buried in the compartments around this central shrine. One noteworthy burial site was a natural cavity in the cave floor where hundreds of bodies were laid to rest. At first sight, the remains seemed incomplete and in confusion. Our further work has shown, however, that the bones from many bodies had been carefully sorted and stacked by type: skulls in one place, femurs in another and so on. This pattern suggests that as part of the burial ritual, old bodies being removed from compartments were disarticulated.

The thousands of human bones, which probably represent hundreds if not thousands of individuals, are now being studied. The early results paint the ancient Maltese as a typically Mediterranean people—stockily built and of medium height. They show some distinctive characteristics, such as a digastric fossa, a well-formed groove on both sides of the skull that is found in some other populations. Their health was apparently very good, with few dental problems or other detectable illnesses. The same anthropological features are present from the earliest Zebbug people to the late Tarxien population, which evinces little or no change in the genetic makeup of the early Maltese community. The changes in their customs and cults were therefore probably not the result of foreign immigration. Scientific studies of the bones will continue for the next few years, providing one of the first and possibly the biggest samples of research on an early Mediterranean population ever undertaken.

The only grave goods with these Tarxien people (which have been dated by the radiocarbon method to around 2800 B.C.) were small, carefully modeled ceramic statuettes of obese human figures. These figurines are almost certainly female because of the distinctive accumulations of fat on the buttocks. Their discovery in that location was highly significant: it marked the first secure association of "fat ladies" with burial sites instead of shrines or temple altars.

On the ground surface, at the monumental entrance leading down into the caverns, another pit was also filled with human remains. Among them were many males whose body parts had been rearranged after being taken from some other burial place. Almost no grave gifts accompanied the bones. Small altars at either end of the megalithic pavement beside the burial pit may have been used for preliminary sacrifices and obeisances before the priest and the assembled mourning community ventured down into the foul, reeking caves of the dead.

The most exciting discoveries from the Brochtorff site, aside from the human remains themselves, are small stone sculptures that have changed our views about the role of art in the ancient local religion. The prehistoric Maltese of the Tarxien period seem to have invested most of their artisanship and craft into cult objects that were more than mere grave gifts. For example, a ceramic strainer and a unique stone sculpture

SMALL CERAMIC POT was used to hold red ocher, a pigment daubed on ritual figures and human bones during Maltese burial rites.

were unearthed from near the stone bowl in the megalithic shrine. The strainer was probably meant to be used with the bowl, perhaps for straining out unwanted objects or for sprinkling liquids onto bodies.

The sculpture shows a beautifully carved and painted pair of obese figures. They are seated on an intricately carved bed, daubed with red ocher, that shows woven struts on the underside and curvilinear designs on the upper. The fat figures are not explicitly male or female. They wear the familiar pleated skirts, painted black, of the finest Maltese cult figures. The head of one figure sports a haircut that includes a pigtail at the back. The other's head is missing, and we can only hope to find it in future seasons of excavation. Both figures hold objects on their laps: one a tiny dressed person (who may be a baby), the other a cup.

Aside from the sculpture's fine craftsmanship, it is astonishing because the portrayal of several humans together is almost unknown from that period in Europe: even individual figures, other than the "fat ladies," are uncommon. A few artifacts with features that are reminiscent of this sculpture have been found elsewhere in ancient Malta, such as the fragments of carved beds and the terra-cotta Sleeping Lady of the Hypogeum. Nevertheless, this discovery is one of the earliest and most thought-provoking groups of sculpture from European prehistory.

The other major find was a cache of nine carved stone idols, which were also closely associated with the stone bowl in the central shrine. The objects must originally have been wrapped tightly in a bag or box: when they were discovered in 1991, they were all lying one above the other, having fallen from the structures surrounding the bowl. Six of the objects represent human figures: flat, triangular shapes attached to carvings of human heads. The six range from poorly detailed rough-outs

SMALL STONE IDOLS were probably used by priests or other specialists in burial rituals at the Brochtorff Circle during the Tarxien period. The three on the left representing human figures show very different levels of detail and artistic execution. The other three, which invoke animal and phallic imagery, are more fanciful and individualized.

to skillfully executed cult idols. Two of the most detailed figures have pleated skirts and belts, and one wears an elaborate crested circlet, seemingly of metal, around its head. The faces of both these figures show eyes and lips and well-defined noses. A third figure is simpler and has no costume other than an exquisitely sculpted cowl headdress. Two more have plain bodies and bobbed hair. The last of the six is a crude rough-out that shows only the lines that the finished sculpture was to follow.

The three other idols of the nine are small and individual. One has a pig's head, the second a well-carved human head on a phallus-shaped pedestal and the third a head supported by two legs. Along with these extraordinary objects was a miniature Tarxien pot filled with ocher, perhaps for smearing on idols.

No parallels for any of these strange objects have ever been found elsewhere in Malta or the central Mediterranean. Even so, our knowledge of the context in which they appear is informative. Whereas the figures associated with the dead in their burial chambers are "fat ladies," those from the central shrine are much more complex. One cannot find an emphasis on images of female fertility in the shrine. Indeed, where the imagery is interpretable, it

seems to be male and animal. The context of their discovery suggests that the shrine objects were the paraphernalia employed by the ritual specialists or priests and that their symbolism was meant to evoke much more than just a mother goddess.

Unprecedented discoveries at the Brochtorff Circle have encouraged us to reconsider the whole basis of ancient cults and religions in prehistoric Malta and Gozo. As the old ideas had supposed, the worship of fertility may well have been a component of the prehistoric religion. But the recent findings argue that it would be a mistake to concentrate exclusively on any one facet or historical period: the prehistoric religion of Malta was not only an infatuation with fat females.

During the Zebbug period between 4000 and 3500 B.C., the cult focused on the provision of caves and underground tombs as burial places. Accurate depictions of people do not seem to have played a part in the local rituals: the closest representations of human forms in the tombs are the very crude faces on the menhirs and the curious bone pendants with budlike arms and heads. Red ocher was the predominant decoration. Exotic axes of green stones and

other objects made of flint and obsidian were also used as grave goods. In many ways, the early ritual developments appear to have paralleled similar trends in Sicily, where rock-cut tombs and simple collective burial rites were developing at the same time. The Maltese islands during this early period were still relatively fruitful and may not have been overpopulated.

But by half a millennium later Malta seems to have been shaken by major changes. The erosion of the soil and other signs of environmental degradation may have become apparent; in this environment, population levels almost certainly began to pose problems. Artifacts from that period—the obese human and animal figurines and the phallic symbols carved in stone or bone and modeled in clay—point to the idea that the people had an obsession with the living world and its successful propagation. Malta seems to have become an island world under powerful economic and environmental stress, where the communities were struggling to maintain their former standards of living and to feed the population. Yet fewer materials were imported into the islands during this time of crisis than in the more fruitful era. The prehistoric Maltese society seems to have let a fixation on sculpture and art replace contact with the world beyond the islands' rocky coasts.

That debilitating fixation may explain why the temples are so numerous on so small a group of islands. Some scholars have theorized that they were built by perhaps half a dozen rival clans or tribes, each competing for land and water. The colossal size of the temples, and the later architectural additions that made them even more prominent, could have been inspired by such a competitive spirit. Religious and cult influence and social control over the population may also have been influential.

Cult activities seem to have reached a feverish pitch in the final phases of the Tarxien period around 2500 B.C. The society was becoming increasingly dominated by a religious hierarchy in which cult specialists or priests controlled much of the industry of the people. Vast amounts of human time and energy were invested in temple building, artistic endeavors and ritual feasts. The dead were honored within cults and linked to animals and human obesity. The people seem to have expended relatively little effort on the building of villages or domestic structures, on terracing or on farming methods. The obsession with the cults of the temples seems to have been complete.

Such obsessions are dangerous, and so it proved to be on ancient Malta. By about 2500 B.C. the community of the temple builders had ceased to build and perhaps even to use the monumental burial sites prepared by earlier generations. By 2000 B.C. the entire culture had disappeared and been replaced by very different religious practices that favored cremation burials. The burial hypogea, the cult of the "fat ladies" and the other symbols of the living and the dead were completely abandoned.

The prehistoric religion of Malta might appear to be a failed experiment in the Mediterranean laboratory. Like many failures, however, it tells us more than a success might have. The extreme religious fervor of ancient Malta shows one of the possible results when societies are placed under severe pressures. Further careful excavations and reconstructions on Malta and at other Mediterranean sites should extend our understanding of the complexities and diversity of prehistoric society. To that end, the excavations at the Brochtorff Circle continue.

FURTHER READING

THE PREHISTORIC ANTIQUITIES OF THE MALTESE ISLANDS: A SURVEY. J. Evans. Athlone Press, London, 1971.

MALTA AND THE CALIBRATED RADIOCARBON CHRONOLOGY. Colin Renfrew in *Antiquity*, Vol. 46, No. 182, pages 141–144; June 1972.

THE COLLAPSE OF THE MALTESE TEMPLES. D. H. Trump in *Problems in Economic and Social Archaeology*. Edited by G. Sieveking, I. Longworth and K. E. Wilson. Duckworth, 1977.

MONUMENTS IN AN ISLAND SOCIETY: THE MALTESE CONTEXT. A. Bonanno, T. Gouder, C. Malone and S. Stoddart in *World Archaeology*, Vol. 22, No. 2, pages 190–205; October 1990.

CULT IN AN ISLAND SOCIETY: PREHISTORIC MALTA IN THE TARXIEN PERIOD. S. Stoddart, A. Bonanno, T. Gouder, C. Malone and D. Trump in *Cambridge Archaeological Journal*, Vol. 3, No. 1, pages 3–19; April 1993.

The Mysterious Fall of the Nacirema

Neil B. Thompson

Many archeologists consider themselves to be cultural anthropologists because their ultimate aim is to make interpretations about cultural systems. They use artifacts to infer the nature of both the social organization and cultural orientation of a people. The following article draws such inferences from the few artifacts left by the Nacirema. Neil Thompson attempts to explain why these people suddenly vanished from the face of the earth. His study suggests that a cultural drive to change the land, water, and air may have caused their demise.

The revival of concern in the recently extinct culture of the Nacirema is, to say the least, most interesting, and perhaps reflects an increasing state of concern for our own society. (Aspects of the Nacirema culture were first described by Horace Miner in "Body Ritual Among the Nacirema," American Anthropologist (1956) 58:503–507.) The use of a multidisciplined approach in deciphering this puzzling culture is gratifying, for it is only by bringing all our methodological techniques to bear on the fragments of evidence in our possession that we will be able to rationally study and understand the history of this apparently vigorous but short-lived culture.

Through exploratory digs by our archeological expeditions, we are able to say with some confidence that the Nacirema were the dominant group in the complex of North American cultures. Although the Nacirema left a large number of documents, our linguists have been unable to decipher any more than a few scattered fragments of the Nacirema language. Eventually, with the complete translation of these documents, we will undoubtedly learn a great deal about the reasons for the sudden disappearance of what, from the physical evidence, must have been an explosive and expansive culture. For the present however, we must rely upon the physical evidence we have uncovered and analyzed in order to draw any conclusions concerning its extinction.

When we examine the area occupied by these people in a single overview, it is immediately apparent that the Nacirema considered it of primary importance to completely remake the environment of the lands they occupied. On studying the fringes of their territory, particularly their penetration of the Cree cultural area to the north, one is struck by the energy that they expended on this task. Trees, if in large enough numbers and size to influence the appearance of the landscape, were removed. In treeless regions, hills were leveled and large holes were dug and partially filled with water. In a few areas the Nacirema imported structural steel with which they erected tall, sculpturesque towers. Some of these towers were arranged in series, making long lines that extended beyond the horizon, and were linked by several cables running through the air. Others, particularly in the northern fringe area, were erected in no discernible geometric pattern and were connected by hollow pipes laid on the surface of the earth.

When one views areas normally considered to be within their cultural suzerainty, one sees evidence of similar activity. Most trees were removed. In some areas, however, trees were replanted or areas were allowed to reforest themselves without assistance. Apparently, the fetish against trees went by fits and starts, for the Nacirema would sometimes move into a reforested area and again remove the trees.

Most of the land, however, was kept clear of trees and was sowed each year with a limited variety of plants. Esthetic considerations must have led to the cultivation of plants poisonous to human life because, while the products of the cropland were sometimes used as food, few were consumed without first being subjected to long periods of complicated processing. Purifying chemicals, which radically changed the appearance and the specific weights of the seeds or fibers, were added. These purification rituals were seldom performed in the living quarters, but rather in a series of large temple-like buildings devoted to this purpose. A vast hierarchy of priests dressed in white (a symbol of purity) devoted their lives to this liturgy. Members of another group, the powerful ssenisub community (whose position will be explained later), constantly examined the efforts of the first group and, if they approved, would affix to the finished product one of several stamps, such as "ADSU" or "Doog Gnipeekesouh." Still a third group, the repeekkoobs, accepted and recorded on permanent memorial rolls the gifts of the general population to their priestly order.

On a more limited territorial basis, the Nacirema spent great time and energy constructing narrow ribbons, called steers, across the landscape. Some steers were arranged and connected in patterns, and in regions with a great concentration of people, the patterns, when viewed from the air, increased in size and became more elaborate. Other ribbons did not follow any particular pattern but aimlessly pushed from one population center to another. In general, their primary function seems to have been to geometricize the landscape into units that could be manipulated by a few men. The steers also served as environmental dividers; persons of a lower caste lived within the boundaries of defined areas while those of the upper caste were free to live where they chose. Exploratory digs have shown that the quality of life in the different areas varied from very luxurious to poverty stricken. The various areas were generically referred to as ottehgs.

The task of completely altering the appearance of the environment to fit the Nacirema's ideology was given such high priority that the ssenisub community completely controlled the amassing of resources, manpower, and intelligence for this purpose. This group, whose rank bordered on that of a non-regimented priestly caste, lived in areas that were often guarded by electronic systems. There is no evidence to suggest that any restraints—moral, sociological, or engineering—were placed on their self-determined enterprises.

For a period of about 300 solar cycles (a determination made on the basis of carbon-dating studies), the Nacirema devoted a major part of their effort to the special environmental problem of changing the appearance of air and water. Until the last 50 solar cycles of the culture's existence, they seemed to have had only indifferent success. But during the short period

before the fall of the culture, they mastered their art magnificently. They changed the color of the waters from the cool end of the spectrum (blues and greens) toward the warm end (reds and browns).

The air was subjected to a similar alteration: it was changed from an azure shade to a uniform gray-yellow. This alteration of water and air was effected by building enormous plants in strategic locations. These are usually found by our archeologists in or near large population centers, although, as success rewarded the Nacirema's efforts, they seem to have built smaller plants in outlying areas where environmental changes had not yet been effected. These plants constantly produced a variety of reagents, each appropriate to its locale, which were then pumped into the rivers and lakes or released into the atmosphere in the form of hot gases. The problem of disposing of the many by-products of this process was solved by distributing them among the general population, which retained them as venerated or decorative objects in their living quarters for a short time, then discarded them in the huge middens that were established near every population center.

In regions where colder temperatures apparently prevented the reagents from changing the color of the water sufficiently, the Nacirema, near the end of their cultural explosion, built special plants that economically raised the water temperature to an acceptable level for the desired chemical reaction.

The idea of a man-made environment was so pervasive that in some areas, notably in the provinces called Ainrofilac and Anaisiuol, the Nacirema even tried to alter the appearance of the ocean currents. In these regions they erected steel sculptures in the sea itself and through them released a black and slick substance, which stained the waters and the beaches. This experiment, however, was relatively unsuccessful since the stains were not permanent and the Nacirema apparently never mastered a technique for constantly supplying the reagent.

Early research has disclosed the importance of ritualistic observance

among the Nacirema. In support of these observations, we should note the presence of the quasi-religious Elibomotua Cult, which sought to create an intense sense of individual involvement in the community effort to completely control the environment. This pervasive cult was devoted to the creation of an artistic symbol for a man-made environmental system.

The high esteem of the cult is demonstrated by the fact that near every population center, when not disturbed by the accumulation of debris, archeologists have found large and orderly collections of the Elibomotua Cult symbol. The vast number of these collections has given us the opportunity to reconstruct with considerable confidence the principal ideas of the cult. The newest symbols seem to have nearly approached the ultimate of the Nacirema's cultural ideal. Their colors, material, and size suggest an enclosed mobile device that corresponds to no color or shape found in nature, although some authorities suggest that, at some early time in the development, the egg may have been the model. The device was provided with its own climate control system as well as a system that screened out many of the shorter rays of the light spectrum.

The object was designed to eliminate most sounds from the outside and to fill the interior with a hypnotic humming sound when the machine was in operation. This noise could be altered in pitch and intensity by the manipulation, through simple mechanical controls, of an ingenious mechanism located outside the operator's compartment. This mechanism also produced a gaseous substance that, in a small area, could change the appearance of the air in a manner similar to the permanent plant installations.

In the early stages of the symbol's development, this was probably only a ritualistic performance since the production plant was small and was fueled by a small tank. This function, however, may have been the primary reason for the cult's symbol: to provide each family with its own device for altering the environment by giving it a private microuniverse with a system of producing the much desired air-changing reagent.

The complete machined piece was somewhat fragile. Our tests of the suspension system indicate that it was virtually immobile on unimproved terrain; by all of our physical evidence, its movement was restricted to the surfaced steerts that the Nacirema had built to geometricize the landscape.

We are relatively certain that a specially endowed and highly skilled group of educators was employed to keep the importance of these enclosed mobile devices constantly in the public eye. Working in an as yet unlocated area that they referred to as Euneva Nosidam, these specialists printed periodical matter and transmitted electronic-impulse images to boxlike apparatus in all homes.

While some of the information was aimed at describing the appearance and performance characteristics of the various kinds of machines, the greatest portion of the material was seemingly aimed at something other than these factors. A distinguished group of linguists, social psychologists, and theologians, who presented the principal symposium at our most recent anthropological conference, offered the hypothesis that the elibomotua symbols, also known as racs, replaced the processes of natural selection in the courtship and mating rituals of the Nacirema. Through unconscious suggestion, which derived from Euneva Nosidam's "mcnahulesque" materials, the female was uncontrollably driven to select her mate by the kind of elibomotua he occupied. The males of the culture were persuaded to believe that any handicap to masculine dominance could be overcome by selecting the proper cult symbol. In this way, the future of the race, as represented by Nacirema culture, was determined by unnatural man-made techniques.

The symposium was careful to point out that we have not yet uncovered any hard evidence to show whether or not this cultural trait actually had any effect on the race or its population growth. We have found, however, one strange sculpture from the Pop Loohcs depicting a male and female mating in an elibomotua's rear compartment, indicating a direct relationship. The hypothesis has the virtue of corresponding to the standard anthropological interpretations of the Nacirema culture—that it was ritual ridden and devoted to the goal of man's control of the environment.

Further evidence of the Nacirema's devotion to the Elibomotua Cult has been discovered in surviving scraps of gnivom serutcip. Some of these suggest that one of the most important quasi-religious ceremonies was performed by large groups who gathered at open-air shrines built in imitation of a planetary ellipse and called a keartecar. There, with intensely emotional reactions, these crowds watched a ritual in which powerful gnicar racs performed their idealized concept of the correct behavior of the planets in the universe. Apparently, their deep-seated need for a controlled environment was thus emotionally achieved.

The racs did not hold a steady position in the planetarium. but changed their relationship to the other racs rather frequently. Occasionally a special ritual, designed to emphasize man's power over his universe, was enacted. On these unannounced occasions one or more of the planet symbols was destroyed by crashing two of them together or by throwing one against a wall. The emotional pitch of the worshipers rose to its highest level at this moment. Then on command of the high priest of the ceremony, all the gnicar racs were slowed to a funereal speed and carefully held in their relative positions. After an appropriate memorial period honoring man's symbolic control of the universe, the machines were given the signal to resume their erratic speeds and permitted to make unnatural position changes.

We can only speculate on the significance of this ritual, but it seems reasonable to conclude that it served as an educational device, constantly imprinting in the individual the society's most important values.

Many of the findings of archeological explorations suggest that these symbols of universal power took up a large portion of the time and energy of the Nacirema society. Evidence indicates that a sizable portion of the work force and enormous amounts of space must have been devoted to the manufacture, distribution, and ceremonial care of the devices. Some of the biggest production units of the economy were assigned this function; extensive design laboratories were given over to the manipulation of styles and appearances, and assembly lines turned out the pieces in serial fashion. They were given a variety of names, although all of those made in the same time period looked remarkably alike.

Every family assumed the responsibility for one of the machined pieces and venerated it for a period of two to four solar cycles. Some families who lived in areas where a high quality of life was maintained took from two to four pieces into their care. During the time a family held a piece, they ritually cleansed it, housed it from the elements, and took it to special shrines where priests gave it a variety of injections.

The Nacirema spent much of their time inside their elibomotuas moving about on the steerts. Pictures show that almost everyone engaged, once in the morning and once in the evening, in what must have been an important mass ritual, which we have been unable to decipher with any surety. During these periods of the day, people of both sexes and all ages, except the very young and the very old, left their quarters to move about on the steerts in their racs. Films of these periods of the day show scenes analogous to the dance one can occasionally see in a swarm of honeybees. In large population centers this "dance of the racs" lasted for two or three hours. Some students have suggested that since the swarm dances took place at about the time the earth completed one-half an axial rotation, it may have been a liturgical denial of the natural processes of the universe.

Inasmuch as we are reasonably certain that after the rite most of the adults and all of the children left the racs and were confined inside man-made structures variously called loohcs, eciffos, tnalps, or emohs and, when released, went immediately to their racs and engaged in the next swarming, the suggestion may be apropos. The ardent involvement of the whole population from ages six through sixty five indicates that it was one of the strongest mores of the culture, perhaps approaching an instinctual behavior pattern.

It should also be mentioned that, when inside their racs, people were not restricted to their ottehgs, but were free to go anywhere they chose so long as they remained on the steerts. Apparently, when they were confined inside a rac, the Nacirema attained a state of equality, which eliminated the danger of any caste contamination.

These, then, to the best of our present state of knowledge, were the principal familial uses of the Elibomotua

Cult symbols. After a family had cared for a piece long enough to burnish it with a certain patina, it was routinely replaced by another, and the used rac was assigned to a gallery keeper, who placed it on permanent display in an outdoor gallery, sometimes surrounded by trees or a fence, but usually not concealed in any way. During their free time, many persons, especially those from the ottehgs of the lesser sorts, came to study the various symbols on display and sometimes carried away small parts to be used for an unknown purpose.

There seems to be little doubt that the Cult of the Elibomotua was so fervently embraced by the general population, and that the daily rituals of the rac's care and use were so faithfully

performed, that the minute quantities of reagent thus distributed may have had a decisive effect on the chemical characteristics of the air. The elibomotua, therefore, may have contributed in a major way toward the prized objective of a totally man-made environment.

In summary, our evaluation of both the Nacirema's man-made environmental alterations and the artifacts found in their territories lead us to advance the hypothesis that they may have been responsible for their own extinction. The Nacirema culture may have been so successful in achieving its objectives that the inherited physiological mechanisms of its people were unable to cope with its manufactured environment.

Living Through the Donner Party

The nineteenth-century survivors of the infamous Donner Party told cautionary tales of starvation and cannibalism, greed and self-sacrifice. But not until now are we learning why the survivors survived.

Jared Diamond

Jared Diamond is a contributing editor of DISCOVER, *a professor of physiology at* UCLA *School of Medicine, a recipient of a MacArthur genius award, and the author of* The Third Chimpanzee.

"Mrs. Fosdick and Mrs. Foster, after eating, returned to the body of [Mr.] Fosdick. There, in spite of the widow's entreaties, Mrs. Foster took out the liver and heart from the body and removed the arms and legs. . . . [Mrs. Fosdick] was forced to see her husband's heart broiled over the fire." "He eat her body and found her flesh the best he had ever tasted! He further stated that he obtained from her body at least four pounds of fat!" "Eat baby raw, stewed some of Jake and roasted his head, not good meat, taste like sheep with the rot."

—GEORGE STEWART,
*Ordeal by Hunger: The Story
of the Donner Party*

Nearly a century and a half after it happened, the story of the Donner Party remains one of the most riveting tragedies in U.S. history. Partly that's because of its lurid elements: almost half the party died, and many of their bodies were defiled in an orgy of cannibalism. Partly, too, it's because of the human drama of noble self-sacrifice and base murder juxtaposed. The

Donner Party began as just another nameless pioneer trek to California, but it came to symbolize the Great American Dream gone awry.

By now the tale of that disastrous journey has been told so often that seemingly nothing else remains to be said—or so I thought, until my friend Donald Grayson at the University of Washington sent me an analysis that he had published in the *Journal of Anthropological Research*. By comparing the fates of all Donner Party members, Grayson identified striking differences between those who came through the ordeal alive and those who were not so lucky. In doing so he has made the lessons of the Donner Party universal. Under more mundane life-threatening situations, who among us too will be "lucky"?

Grayson's insights did not depend on new discoveries about the ill-fated pioneers nor on new analytical techniques, but on that most elusive ingredient of great science: a new idea about an old problem. Given the same information, any of you could extract the same conclusions. In fact, on page 65 you'll find the roster of the Donner Party members along with a few personal details about each of them and their fate. If you like, you can try to figure out for yourself some general rules about who is most likely to die when the going gets tough.

The Lewis and Clark Expedition of 1804 to 1806 was the first to cross the continent, but they didn't take along ox-drawn wagons, which were a requirement for pioneer settlement. Clearing a wagon route through the West's unmapped deserts and mountains proved far more difficult than finding a footpath. Not until 1841 was the first attempt made to haul wagons and settlers overland to California, and only in 1844 did the effort succeed. Until the Gold Rush of 1848 unleashed a flood of emigrants, wagon traffic to California remained a trickle.

As of 1846, when the Donner Party set out, the usual wagon route headed west from St. Louis to Fort Bridger in Wyoming, then northwest into Idaho before turning southwest through Nevada and on to California. However, at that time a popular guidebook author named Lansford Hastings was touting a shortcut that purported to cut many miles from the long trek. Hastings's route continued west from Fort Bridger through the Wasatch mountain range, then south of Utah's Great Salt Lake across the Salt Lake Desert, and finally rejoined the usual California Trail in Nevada.

In the summer of 1846 a number of wagon parties set out for California from Fort Bridger. One, which left shortly before the Donner Party, was guided by Hastings himself. Using his shortcut, the party would eventually make it to California, albeit with great difficulty.

The pioneers who would become the members of the Donner Party were in fact all headed for Fort Bridger to join the Hastings expedition, but they arrived too late. With Hastings thus unavailable to serve as a guide, some of these California-bound emigrants opted for the usual route instead. Others, however, decided to try the Hastings Cutoff anyway. In all, 87 people in 23 wagons chose the cutoff. They consisted of 10 unrelated families and 16 lone individuals, most of them well-to-do midwestern farmers and townspeople who had met by chance and joined forces for protection. None had had any real experience of the western mountains or Indians. They became known as the Donner Party because they elected an elderly Illinois farmer named George Donner as their captain. They left Fort Bridger on July 31, one of the last parties of that summer to begin the long haul to California.

Within a fortnight the Donner Party suffered their first crushing setback, when they reached Utah's steep, brush-covered Wasatch Mountains. The terrain was so wild that, in order to cross, the men had first to build a wagon road. It took 16 backbreaking days to cover just 36 miles, and afterward the people and draft animals were worn out. A second blow followed almost immediately thereafter, west of the Great Salt Lake, when the party ran into an 80-mile stretch of desert. To save themselves from death by thirst, some of the pioneers were forced to unhitch their wagons, rush ahead with their precious animals to the next spring, and return to retrieve the wagons. The rush became a disorganized panic, and many of the animals died, wandered off, or were killed by Indians. Four wagons and large quantities of supplies had to be abandoned. Not until September 30—two full months after leaving Fort Bridger—did the Donner Party emerge from their fatal shortcut to rejoin the California Trail.

By November 1 they had struggled up to Truckee Lake—later renamed Donner Lake—at an elevation of 6,000 feet on the eastern flank of the Sierra Nevada, west of the present-day California-Nevada border. Snow had already begun to fall during the last days of October, and now a fierce snowstorm defeated the exhausted party as they attempted to cross a 7,200-foot pass just west of the lake. With that storm, a trap snapped shut around them: they had set out just a little too late and proceeded just a little too slowly. They now faced a long winter at the lake, with very little food.

Death had come to the Donner Party even before it reached the lake. There were five casualties: on August 29 Luke Halloran died of "consumption" (presumably tuberculosis); on October 5 James Reed knifed John Snyder in self-defense, during a fight that broke out when two teams of oxen became entangled; three days later Lewis Keseberg abandoned an old man named Hardkoop who had been riding in Keseberg's wagon, and most of the party refused to stop and search for

---

They cut off and roasted flesh from the corpses, restrained only by the rule that no one partook of his or her own relative's body.

---

him; sometime after October 13 two German emigrants, Joseph Reinhardt and Augustus Spitzer, murdered a rich German named Wolfinger while ostensibly helping him to cache his property; and on October 20 William Pike was shot as he and his brother-in-law were cleaning a pistol.

In addition, four party members had decided earlier to walk out ahead to Sutter's Fort (now Sacramento) to bring back supplies and help. One of those four, Charles Stanton, rejoined the party on October 19, bringing food and two Indians sent by Sutter. Thus, of the 87 original members of the Donner Party, 79—plus the two Indians—were pinned down in the winter camp at Donner Lake.

The trapped pioneers lay freezing inside crude tents and cabins. They quickly exhausted their little remaining food, then killed and ate their pack animals. Then they ate their dogs. Finally they boiled hides and blankets to make a gluelike soup. Gross selfishness became rampant, as families with food refused to share it with destitute families or demanded exorbitant payment. On December 16 the first death came to the winter camp when 24-year-old Baylis Williams succumbed to starvation. On that same day 15 of the strongest people—5 women and 10 men, including Charles Stanton and the two Indians—set out across the pass on homemade snowshoes, virtually without food and in appallingly cold and stormy weather, in the hope of reaching outside help. Four of the men left behind their families; three of the women left behind their children.

On the sixth morning an exhausted Stanton let the others go on ahead of him; he remained behind to die. On the ninth day the remaining 14 for the first time openly broached the subject of cannibalism which had already been on their minds. They debated drawing lots as to who should be eaten, or letting two people shoot it out until one was killed and could be eaten. Both proposals were rejected in favor of waiting for someone to die naturally.

Such opportunities soon arose. On Christmas Eve, as a 23-year-old man named Antoine, a bachelor, slept in a heavy stupor, he stretched out his arm such that his hand fell into the fire. A companion pulled it out at once. When it fell in a second time, however, no one intervened—they simply let it burn. Antoine died, then Franklin Graves, then Patrick Dolan, then Lemuel Murphy. The others cut off and roasted flesh from the corpses, restrained only by the rule that no one would partake of his or her own relative's body. When the corpses were consumed, the survivors began eating old shoes.

On January 5, 23-year-old Jay Fosdick died, only to be cut up and boiled by Mrs. Foster over the protests of Mrs. Fosdick. Soon after, the frenzied

Mr. Foster chased down, shot, and killed the two Indians to eat them. That left 7 of the original 15 snowshoers to stagger into the first white settlement in California, after a midwinter trek of 33 days through the snow.

On January 31 the first rescue team set out from the settlement for Donner Lake. It would take three more teams and two and a half months before the ordeal was all over. During that time many more people died, either in the winter camp or while fighting their way out with the rescue teams. There was never enough food, and by the end of February, cannibalism had established itself at the lake.

When William Eddy and William Foster, who had gotten out with the snowshoers, reached the lake with the third rescue team on March 13, they found that Keseberg had eaten their sons. The Foster child's grandmother accused the starving Keseberg of having taken the child to bed with him one night, strangling him, and hanging the corpse on the wall before eating it. Keseberg, in his defense, claimed the children had died naturally. When the rescuers left the lake the next day to return to California, they left Keseberg behind with just four others: the elderly Lavina Murphy, the badly in-

Manifest of a Tragic Journey

DONNER FAMILY

Name	Sex	Age	Notes
Jacob Donner	M	65	died in Nov. in winter camp
George Donner	M	62	died in Apr. in winter camp
Elizabeth Donner	F	45	died in Mar. in winter camp
Tamsen Donner	F	45	died in Apr. in winter camp
Elitha Donner	F	14	
Solomon Hook	M	14	
William Hook	M	12	died Feb. 28 with first rescue team
Leanna Donner	F	12	
George Donner	M	9	
Mary Donner	F	7	
Frances Donner	F	6	
Isaac Donner	M	5	died Mar. 7 with second rescue team
Georgia Donner	F	4	
Samuel Donner	M	4	died in Apr. in winter camp
Lewis Donner	M	3	died Mar. 7 or 8 in winter camp
Eliza Donner	F	3	

MURPHY-FOSTER-PIKE FAMILY

Name	Sex	Age	Notes
Lavina Murphy	F	50	died around Mar. 19 in winter camp
William Foster	M	28	
William Pike	M	25	died Oct. 20 by gunshot
Sara Foster	F	23	
Harriet Pike	F	21	
John Landrum Murphy	M	15	died Jan. 31 in winter camp
Mary Murphy	F	13	
Lemuel Murphy	M	12	died Dec. 27 with snowshoers
William Murphy	M	11	
Simon Murphy	M	10	
George Foster	M	4	died in early Mar. in winter camp
Naomi Pike	F	3	
Catherine Pike	F	1	died Feb. 20 in winter camp

GRAVES-FOSDICK FAMILY

Name	Sex	Age	Notes
Franklin Graves	M	57	died Dec. 24 with snowshoers
Elizabeth Graves	F	47	died Mar. 8 with second rescue team
Jay Fosdick	M	23	died Jan. 5 with snowshoers
Sarah Fosdick	F	22	
Mary Graves	F	20	
William Graves	M	18	
Eleanor Graves	F	15	
Lavina Graves	F	13	
Nancy Graves	F	9	
Jonathan Graves	M	7	
Franklin Graves Jr.	M	5	died Mar. 8 with second rescue team
Elizabeth Graves	F	1	died soon after rescue by second team

BREEN FAMILY

Name	Sex	Age	Notes
Patrick Breen	M	40	
Mary Breen	F	40	
John Breen	M	14	
Edward Breen	M	13	
Patrick Breen Jr.	M	11	
Simon Breen	M	9	
Peter Breen	M	7	
James Breen	M	4	
Isabella Breen	F	1	

REED FAMILY

Name	Sex	Age	Notes
James Reed	M	46	
Margaret Reed	F	32	
Virginia Reed	F	12	
Patty Reed	F	8	
James Reed Jr.	M	5	
Thomas Reed	M	3	

EDDY FAMILY

Name	Sex	Age	Notes
William Eddy	M	28	
Eleanor Eddy	F	25	died Feb. 7 in winter camp
James Eddy	M	3	died in early Mar. in winter camp
Margaret Eddy	F	1	died Feb. 4 in winter camp

KESEBERG FAMILY

Name	Sex	Age	Notes
Lewis Keseberg	M	32	
Phillipine Keseberg	F	32	
Ada Keseberg	F	3	died Feb. 24 with first rescue team
Lewis Keseberg Jr.	M	1	died Jan. 24 in winter camp

McCUTCHEN FAMILY

Name	Sex	Age	Notes
William McCutchen	M	30	
Amanda McCutchen	F	24	
Harriet McCutchen	F	1	died Feb. 2 in winter camp

WILLIAMS FAMILY

Name	Sex	Age	Notes
Eliza Williams	F	25	
Baylis Williams	M	24	died Dec. 16 in winter camp

WOLFINGER FAMILY

Name	Sex	Age	Notes
Mr. Wolfinger	M	?	killed around Oct. 13 by Reinhardt and Spitzer
Mrs. Wolfinger	F	?	

UNRELATED INDIVIDUALS

Name	Sex	Age	Notes
Mr. Hardkoop	M	60	died around Oct. 8, abandoned by Lewis Keseberg
Patrick Dolan	M	40	died Dec. 25 with snowshoers
Charles Stanton	M	35	died around Dec. 21 with snowshoers
Charles Burger	M	30	died Dec. 29 in winter camp
Joseph Reinhardt	M	30	died in Nov. or early Dec. in winter camp
Augustus Spitzer	M	30	died Feb. 7 in winter camp
John Denton	M	28	died Feb. 24 with first rescue team
Milton Elliot	M	28	died Feb. 9 in winter camp
Luke Halloran	M	25	died Aug. 29 of consumption
William Herron	M	25	
Samuel Shoemaker	M	25	died in Nov. or early Dec. in winter camp
James Smith	M	25	died in Nov. or early Dec. in winter camp
John Snyder	M	25	killed Oct. 5 by James Reed
Jean Baptiste Trubode	M	23	
Antoine	M	23	died Dec. 24 with snowshoers
Noah James	M	20	

jured George Donner, his 4-year-old nephew Samuel and his healthy wife Tamsen, who could have traveled but insisted on staying with her dying husband.

The fourth and last rescue team reached the lake on April 17 to find Keseberg alone, surrounded by indescribable filth and mutilated corpses. George Donner's body lay with his skull split open to permit the extraction of his brains. Three frozen ox legs lay in plain view almost uneaten beside a kettle of cut-up human flesh. Near Keseberg sat two kettles of blood and a large pan full of fresh human liver and lungs. He alleged that his four companions had died natural deaths, but he was frank about having eaten them. As to why he had not eaten ox leg instead, he explained that it was too dry: human liver and lungs tasted better, and human brains made a good soup. As for Tamsen Donner, Keseberg noted that she tasted the best, being well endowed with fat. In a bundle held by Keseberg the rescuers found silk, jewelry, pistols, and money that had belonged to George Donner.

After returning to Sutter's Fort, one of the rescuers accused Keseberg of having murdered his companions, prompting Keseberg to sue for defamation of character. In the absence of legal proof of murder the court verdict was equivocal, and the issue of Keseberg's guilt remains disputed to this day. However, Tamsen Donner's death is especially suspicious since she had been in strong physical condition when last seen by the third rescue team.

Thus, out of 87 Donner Party members, 40 died: 5 before reaching Donner Lake, 22 in their winter camp at the lake, and 13 (plus the two Indians) during or just after efforts to leave the lake. Why those particular 40? From the facts given in the roster, can you draw conclusions, as Grayson did, as to who was in fact the most likely to die?

As a simple first test, compare the fates of Donner Party males and females irrespective of age. Most of the males (30 out of 53) died; most of the females (24 out of 34) survived. The 57 percent death rate among males was nearly double the 29 percent death rate among females.

Next, consider the effect of age irrespective of sex. The worst toll was among the young and the old. Without exception, everyone over the age of 50 died, as did most of the children below the age of 5. Surprisingly, children and teenagers between the ages of 5 and 19 fared better than did adults in their prime (age 20 to 39): half the latter, but less than one-fifth of the former, died.

By looking at the effects of age and sex simultaneously, the advantage the women had over the men becomes even more striking. Most of the female deaths were among the youngest and oldest, who were already doomed by their age. Among those party members aged 5 to 39—the ones whose ages left them some reasonable chance of survival—half the men but only 5 percent of the women died.

The dates of death provide deeper insight. Of the 35 unfortunates who died after reaching the lake, 14 men but not a single woman had died by the end of January. Only in February did women begin to buckle under. From February onward the death toll was essentially equal by sex—11 men, 10 women. The differences in dates of death simply underscore the lesson of the death rates themselves: the Donner Party women were far hardier than the men.

Thus, sex and age considered together account for much of the luck of the survivors. Most of those who died (39 of the 40 victims) had the misfortune to be of the wrong sex, or the wrong age, or both.

Experience has taught us that the youngest and oldest people are the most vulnerable even under normal conditions, and their vulnerability increases under stress. In many natural disasters, those under 10 or over 50 suffered the highest mortality. For instance, children under 10 accounted for over half the 240,000 deaths in the 1970 Bangladesh cyclone, though they constituted only one-third of the exposed population.

Much of the vulnerability of the old and young under stress is simply a matter of insufficient physical strength: these people are less able to walk out through deep snow (in the case of the Donner Party) or to cling to trees above the height of flood waters (in the case of the Bangladesh cyclone). Babies have special problems. Per pound of body weight a baby has twice an adult's surface area, which means double the area across which body heat can escape. To maintain body temperature, babies have to increase their metabolic rate when air temperature drops only a few degrees below body temperature, whereas adults don't have to do so until a drop of 20 to 35 degrees. At cold temperatures the factor by which babies must increase their metabolism to stay warm is several times that for adults. These considerations place even well-fed babies at risk under cold conditions. And the Donner Party babies were at a crippling further disadvantage because they had so little food to fuel their metabolism. They literally froze to death.

But what gave the women such an edge over the men? Were the pioneers practicing the noble motto "women and children first" when it came to dividing food? Unfortunately, "women and children last" is a more accurate description of how most men behave under stress. As the *Titanic* sank, male crew members took many places in lifeboats while leaving women and children of steerage class below decks to drown. Much grosser male behavior emerged when the steamship *Atlantic* sank in 1879: the death toll included 294 of the 295 women and children on board, but only 187 of the 636 men. In the Biafran famine of the late 1960s, when relief agencies tried to distribute food to youngsters under 10 and to pregnant and nursing women, Biafran men gave a brutally frank response: "Stop all this rubbish, it is we men who shall have the food, let the children die, we will make new children after the war." Similarly, accounts by Donner Party members yield no evidence of hungry men deferring to women, and babies fared especially poorly.

Instead, we must seek some cause other than male self-sacrifice to account for the survival of Donner Party women. One contributing factor is that the men were busy killing each other. Four of the five deaths before the pioneers reached the lake, plus the deaths of the two Indians, involved male victims of male violence, a pattern that fits widespread human experience.

However, invoking male violence still leaves 26 of 30 Donner Party male deaths unexplained. It also fails to explain why men began starving and freezing to death nearly two months before women did. Evidently the women had a big physiological advantage. This could be an extreme expression of the fact that, at every age and for all leading causes of death—from cancer and car accidents to heart disease and suicide—the death rate is far higher for men than for women. While the reasons for this ubiquitous male vulnerability remain debated, there are several compelling reasons why men are more likely than women to die under the extreme conditions the Donner Party faced.

First, men are bigger than women. Typical body weights for the world as a whole are about 140 pounds for men and only 120 pounds for women. Hence, even while lying down and doing nothing, men need more food to support their basal metabolism. They also need more energy than women do for equivalent physical activity. Even for sedentary people, the typical metabolic rate for an average-size woman is 25 percent lower than an average-size man's. Under conditions of cold temperatures and heavy physical activity, such as were faced by the Donner Party men when doing the backbreaking work of cutting the wagon road or hunting for food, men's metabolic rates can be double those of women.

To top it all off, women have more fat reserves than men: fat makes up 22 percent of the body weight of an average nonobese, well-nourished woman, but only 16 percent of a similar man. More of the man's weight is instead made up of muscle, which gets burned up much more quickly than does fat. Thus, when there simply was no more food left, the Donner Party men burned up their body reserves much faster than did the women. Furthermore, much of women's fat is distributed under the skin and acts as heat insulation, so that they can withstand cold temperatures better than men can. Women don't have to raise their metabolic rate to stay warm as soon as men do.

These physiological factors easily surpass male murderousness in accounting for all those extra male deaths in the Donner Party. Indeed, a microcosm of the whole disaster was the escape attempt by 15 people on snowshoes, lasting 33 days in midwinter. Of the ten men who set out, two were murdered by another man, six starved or froze to death, and only two survived. Not a single one of the five women with them died.

Even with all these explanations, there is still one puzzling finding to consider: the unexpectedly high death toll of people in their prime, age 20 to 39. That toll proves to be almost entirely of the men: 67 percent of the men in that age range (14 out of 21) died, a much higher proportion than among the teenage boys (only 20 percent). Closer scrutiny shows why most of those men were so unlucky.

Most of the Donner Party consisted of large families, but there were also 16 individuals traveling without any relatives. All those 16 happened to be men, and all but two were between 20 and 39. Those 16 unfortunates bore the brunt of the prime-age mortality. Thirteen of them died, and most of them died long before any of the women. Of the survivors, one—William Herron—reached California in October, so in reality only 2 survived the winter at the lake.

Of the 7 men in their prime who survived, 4 were family men. Only 3 of the 14 dead were. The prime-age women fared similarly: the 8 survivors belonged to families with an average size of 12 people, while Eleanor Eddy, the only woman to die in this age group, had no adult support. Her husband had escaped with the snowshoers, leaving her alone with their two small children.

The Donner Party records make it vividly clear that family members stuck together and helped one another at the expense of the others. A notorious example was the Breen family of nine, every one of whom (even two small children) survived through the luck of retaining their wagons and some pack animals much longer than the others, and through their considerable selfishness toward others. Compare this with the old bachelor Hardkoop, who was ordered out of the Keseberg family wagon and abandoned to die, or the fate of the young bachelor Antoine, whom none of the hungry snowshoers bothered to awaken when his hand fell into the fire.

Family ties can be a matter of life and death even under normal conditions. Married people, it turns out, have lower death rates than single, widowed, or divorced people. And marriage's life-promoting benefits have been found to be shared by all sorts of social ties, such as friendships and membership in social groups. Regardless of age or sex or initial health status, socially isolated individuals have well over twice the death rate of socially connected people.

For reasons about which we can only speculate, the lethal effects of social isolation are more marked for men than for women. It's clear, though, why social contacts are important for both sexes. They provide concrete help in case of need. They're our source of advice and shared information. They provide a sense of belonging and self-worth, and the courage to face tomorrow. They make stress more bearable.

All those benefits of social contact applied as well to the Donner Party members, who differed only in that their risk of death was much greater and their likely circumstances of death more grotesque than yours and mine. In that sense too, the harrowing story of the Donner Party grips us because it was ordinary life writ large.

Problem-oriented Archaeology

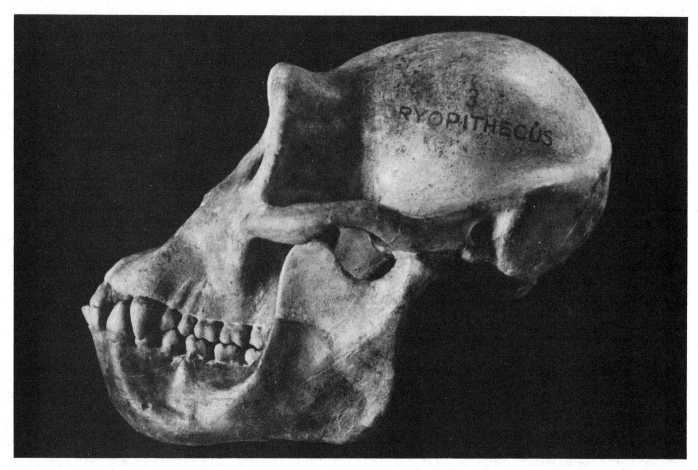

What are the goals of archaeology? What kinds of things motivate well-educated people to go out and dig square holes in the ground and sift through their diggings like it was flour for a cake? How do they know where to dig? What are they looking for? What do they do with the things they find? Let's drop in and eavesdrop on an archaeology class at Big City University.

"Good afternoon, class, I'm Dr. Penny Pittmeyer. Welcome to Introductory Archaeology. Excuse me, young man, uh, yes, you in the back with the pith helmet. I don't think you'll need to bring that shovel to class this semester. We aren't going to be doing any digging."

A noise like a bowling ball rolling down the alley calling "Whaaaat!" as it thudded into the gutter sounded as eyes bugged out, bodies contorted, foreheads receded, and mouths formed dark, damp caves at this pronouncement.

"That's right, no digging. You are here to learn about archaeology."

"But archaeology *is* digging. What are we going to do in the classroom all semester?" protested a blond girl wearing a safari suit with a trowel hooked firmly into her belt.

Dr. Pittmeyer calmly surveyed the class and quietly repeated, "You are here to learn about archaeology." In a husky but compelling voice, she went on. "Archaeology is not digging, nor is it about Egyptian pyramids, or lost civilizations, or ancient astronauts. It's a science. First you have to learn the basics of that science. Digging is just a technique. Digging comes later. Digging comes after you know *why* you are going to dig."

"No Egyptian pyramids," a hollow, sad whisper floated through the silent classroom.

"You can have your pyramids later. Take a class in Egyptian archaeology, fine. If you want ancient civilizations, take a course in world prehistory. This class is the prerequisite to all those other classes. I hate to be the one to tell you this, people, but there ain't no Indiana Jones!"

Dr. Pittmeyer said this with a slightly lopsided smile and a veiled look in her light eyes that sent an "uh-oh" to the brain stems of all of the students so that they uniformly felt that the lady had something to teach them.

Dr. Pittmeyer half sat on the old desk at the front of the classroom leaning one elbow onto the podium to her right and picked up a tall, red opaque glass, and took a long and greedy drink from it. Behind her large black eyeglasses her eyes watered noticeably. She wiped away an invisible mustache from her upper lip and settled onto the desk, holding the red glass in her left hand, letting it sway slightly as she unhurriedly looked over the students. Her right eyebrow raised unconsciously and made a few of the more imaginative students think she looked like Scarlet O'Hara in glasses. The quiet lengthened into a place where the students filling out the bright orange drop cards stopped writing, conscious of the now loud silence in the room.

"O.K! Let's go!" Dr. Pittmeyer said with a slap in her voice as if the class were going to run a relay. The startled students went straight-backed in unison.

"Archaeology is a science, ladies and gentlemen. It's part of the larger science of anthropology. The goals of both are to understand and predict human behavior. Let's look at an area or subfield of archaeology we may designate as 'problem-oriented archaeology.' Humans evolved in Africa, Asia, and Europe or what we refer to as the Old World."

Dr. Pittmeyer had clicked on an overhead projector and was writing rapidly with a harshly bright purple pen in a hieroglyphic scrawl that appeared suspended behind her and over her head on a large screen. She had a microphone dangling from her neck, which was plugged into a speaker, which was then plugged back into the cart where the overhead projector was, which was then plugged into an old cracked wall socket. The only one in the large, old, high ceilinged room whose floor tiles and ceiling tiles were packed with asbestos.

"In the New World, in the Americas, from Alaska down to the tip of Tierra del Fuego, people didn't live here until about 13,000 years ago. Whereas, in the Old World people have been living there for 100,000 years or more. People in the sense of *Homo sapiens.*"

"So what took them so long to get here?" a perplexed female voice asked.

"The continents weren't connected most of the time. But let's leave the geology until later. Let me point out that your question contains a very telling assumption. You said what took them so long to get *here.* The question is moot because they were not trying to get *here.* We're talking about the Paleolithic. People were migratory. They hunted and collected their food every day. Some of them followed the migrations of big game animals. So it is a nonquestion. Let me explain, please.

"In archaeology, you have to ask the right questions before you can get any useful answers. That's why archaeologists dig. Not to make discoveries. But to answer questions. Now here's what I want you to do. Go home and try to think yourself back into the Paleolithic Age. It's 100,000 years ago and mostly you hang out with your family and other close relatives. You get your food and shelter, and you have a lot of free time. Everybody cooperates. The point is that wherever you are, you are *there.* There is no place to try to get to. There's no notion of private property or ownership of land. Nobody needs to conquer anybody. There are no cities, no freeways, no clocks, no rush. Think about it. It's a concept of time without measurements or urgencies."

"But they must have been pretty stupid back that long ago!" the lady with the trowel protested.

"Please think about that assumption! No, these were people just like you and me. In fact, we're a little on the soft side. If they were here today, they probably could program their VCRs. Seriously, these were people with many skills and accomplishments, but they also had the wisdom to be *there.* That is, they lived every day in the present. There's a lot to be learned from our prehistoric ancestors. And tomorrow's another day."

Alone in the classroom, Dr. Penny Pittmeyer finished her cola and let her eyes glaze over as the bright orange drop cards fluttered to the floor.

Looking Ahead: Challenge Questions

How long ago did modern humans migrate to the New World? How do we know this?

What assumptions can we make about the subsistence patterns of these natives?

What is the importance of the Clovis-point as a time marker?

View the Bible as history. How does it compare to the archaeological record?

If two stories explain the same facts, how does scientific thinking apply?

What are some of the ways in which culture change comes about? Give examples.

Birth control through the ages? What can archaeology show us about this issue?

Coming to America

When did humans arrive here? Was it the long-accepted date of 11,200 years ago, or 10,000 years earlier? A remarkably detailed site in Chile may finally give us the answer.

David J. Meltzer

David J. Meltzer is an archeologist at Southern Methodist University in Dallas, a frequent contributor to New Scientist, *and the author of* Search for the First Americans.

The Southern High Plains were dusted with snow, and from 30,000 feet they appeared to be a vast marble slab. Since the flight from San Francisco to Dallas wasn't full, I slipped back and forth across the aisle, peering out the windows, hoping to spot a landmark. There aren't many on this flat, feature-less terrain. I was looking, in vain, for a sign that we were passing over Clovis, New Mexico, home of the ar-cheological site that's given its name to the people who first set foot in Amer-ica. That is supposed to have been about 11,200 years ago.

I'd been thinking about Clovis since we took off from San Francisco that morning last December, mostly be-cause I'd heard so much about it the day before, at the American Anthro-pological Association's annual meet-ing. There molecular biologists who use human DNA as a "clock" to date population migrations gave a message to us hands-in-the-dirt archeologists: the Clovis-based arrival date is wrong. Very wrong.

The messenger was molecular an-thropologist Tad Schurr, representing the Emory University laboratory of geneticist Douglas Wallace. Schurr and Wallace had examined the mitochondrial DNA of various Native American peo-ples. This DNA exists in little organ-elles—mitochondria—outside a cell's nucleus, and you inherit it solely from your mother. Because it doesn't get mixed up with DNA from your father, any changes in the molecule as it moves from generation to generation are a result only of random mutations. These, it turns out, happen at the con-veniently steady rate of 2 to 4 percent per million years. That makes mito-chondrial DNA a genetic clock.

Schurr and Wallace found that the Native Americans belong to four dis-tinct lineages. The Emory researchers then counted the mitochondrial DNA mutations in each lineage, figured out how much time was needed for them to occur, and deduced when these lin-eages were last together—that is, when they first diverged from a common maternal ancestor. That ancestor was someone who walked across the land bridge that once connected Siberia with Alaska, and the genetic clock started ticking when her descendants then spread across the New World. According to the biologists, that ances-tor took her stroll long before Clovis time. "Upwards of 21,000 to 42,000 years ago," Schurr told us, without batting an eye.

That's hearsay testimony, of course: genes cannot be directly dated. Still, the news caused something of a buzz, and not just because modern genetics was failing to uphold a cherished tenet of old-fashioned archeology. What got people talking was that Schurr's date provided support, from an unexpected quarter, for one of the most talked-about archeological finds of the last decade. From 1978 to 1985, researchers working in southern Chile excavated a site they claim was occupied earlier than Clovis times—some 2,000 years earlier, in fact. Ever since the news began spreading, that site, called Monte Verde, has received a lot of attention from archeologists seeking traces of a pre-Clovis human presence in the Americas. Schurr's date fits beautifully with the Monte Verde evi-dence, and together they may revolu-tionize our views on the peopling of the Americas.

That won't come as much of a sur-prise to those of us who were at an-other meeting, three years earlier, on the Orono campus of the University of Maine. A couple hundred archeolo-gists had assembled to wrangle over the origin and antiquity of the first Americans. We were there for three long days and three very long nights, and by the last afternoon session I was—all of us were, I suppose—tired, hungry for dinner, and ready to go home. The *New York Times* reporter had already left: no more news fit to print.

And then Tom Dillehay of the Uni-versity of Kentucky, the final speaker, began to tell us about Monte Verde.

Ten minutes into the talk, the fellow sitting next to me whistled softly in astonishment, then asked aloud of no one in particular, "What planet is this stuff from?" I was wondering that my-

Reed and Cane

A LOOP OF REED ONCE
BOUND TOGETHER
TIMBERS OF A HUT. THE
PIECE OF CANE WAS
PART OF A HANDLE ON
A TOOL OR WEAPON.

self. The evidence from Monte Verde was unlike anything most of us—who early in our careers learned to be thankful just for stone tools and scraps of bone—had ever encountered before in our archeological earth. When Dillehay finished 45 minutes later, the hall erupted in applause. I forgot about dinner.

That day in Maine many of us saw for the first time pictures of the extraordinary archeological treasures of Monte Verde: artifacts of stone and bone, of course, but also of wood and ivory; freshly preserved leftovers from meals of leaves, fruits, nuts, and seeds; the remains of crayfish and paleo-camel; the torn flesh of an extinct mastodon; even the footprint of a child.

Those are hardly the usual contents of an archeological site. They are un-heard of for one in the Americas dating to some 13,000 years before the present. The pros in the hall that afternoon

knew exactly what *that* meant: the Clovis-first barrier to the peopling of the Americas, standing strong at 11,200 years, was threatened.

Established in the 1930s with the discovery of the Clovis site, and buttressed with radiocarbon dating in the 1950s, the idea that Clovis people were the first Americans once made perfect sense. As envisioned, they came out of northeast Asia across the Bering land bridge (Beringia) to Alaska, then headed south. Their migration was thought to be timed to the rhythm of glaciers. By 25,000 years ago those vast ice sheets had frozen 5 percent of the oceans' water on land, plunging global sea levels and uncovering the land bridge. But 20,000 years ago the glaciers had grown so much that they blocked the routes south from Alaska. Only around 12,000 years ago, once the glaciers had melted back and the terrain dried and was reforested,

did a passable southern route reopen, roughly along the present border of Alberta and British Columbia.

The first Americans must have headed south soon thereafter, and fast, for by 11,200 years ago groups were camping at a freshwater pond at Clovis, and by 11,000 years ago they had reached Tierra del Fuego, at the southern tip of South America. One can recognize traces of the Clovis people in the fluted stone spear points they left behind—a design first noted at the New Mexico pond. The explosive move to the south corresponded neatly with the extinction of over 150 million mammoths, mastodons, ground sloths, and other giant Ice Age mammals. To some that was no coincidence: these rapacious hunters, encountering big game that had never before peered down the shaft of a spear, would have had easy pickings and been spurred onward by visions of still more prey.

Not a bad model, all things considered, and for six decades it held up well while pretenders came and went. But the Clovis-first model has problems, and one of them is enormous: How and why, did people race from Alaska—where archeologists have found Clovis-like traces in sites about 11,300 years old—down to Tierra del Fuego, *nearly 10,000 miles away,* in scarcely 300 years?

Granted, that's only 33 miles a year, unbearably slow by today's standards; many of us have longer daily commutes. Yet it's a breakneck pace for hunter-gatherers, easily four times faster than the current world record for prehistoric colonization of an empty area, set by ancestral Thule Eskimos. In just a couple of centuries around A.D. 1000, the Thule flashed from Alaska to Greenland. But they had it easy, following a familiar corridor of animals they had lived with for millennia. The corridor had just stretched thousands of miles eastward following a long period of warmer-than-average temperatures.

The first Americans had no such advantage. They were pioneering an infinitely trackless, ever changing, and (to former Siberians) ecologically exotic realm, from high mountains to high plains, and near-polar deserts to tropical forests. They were slowed each time they entered a new habitat and had to find plants, animals, water, stone, and other resources vital to their survival. Sadly, the romantic vision of fast-moving, mammoth-chasing hunters has no archeological reality. They were slowed by obstacles along the way, such as rivers swollen by glacial meltwater, mountains shrouded in ice, and freshly deglaciated barren landscapes. They were also slowed by the demands of keeping contact with kin, finding mates, and raising families. (Ever try to go *anywhere* fast with kids?)

But if the first Americans didn't race through the continent, why do Clovis sites suddenly spring like dragon's teeth from the ground in the centuries around 11,000 years ago? Maybe Schurr and his colleagues have the answer. Assume for the moment that the Americas were peopled 21,000 to 42,000 years ago, and then around 11,200 years ago someone invented the Clovis point—a handy, versatile tool useful in dozens of applications. How fast might such a good invention travel among groups?

Of course, if Schurr's group is right, then we ought to find lots of pre-Clovis archeological sites. Some pre-Clovis proponents say we already have, pointing to sites throughout the hemisphere that brandish dates of 13,000, 33,000, and even 200,000 years ago.

But these sites have few believers—and for good reason. Of the scores of pre-Clovis archeological finds made in the last 60 years, none so far has withstood the harsh glare of critical scrutiny. Either their ages were inflated, their artifacts proved of natural and not human origin, or they hid some other fatal flaw. Exposing these flaws usually takes less than a decade, and then the site is tossed on the archeological scrap heap. Archeologists have long memories—it's part of the job, after all—and in the face of many false alarms over the years, they have grown deeply skeptical of any and all pre-Clovis claims. The first site to topple the Clovis barrier will have to have undeniable artifacts in an undisturbed setting accompanied by unimpeachable dates, and it will have to win over the severest pre-Clovis critics: the Jackie Robinson rule, my colleague Mott Davis calls it.

That's why Monte Verde rivets our attention. It may well be archeology's Jackie Robinson.

Monte Verde sits along a small tributary creek of the Rio Maullín, some 30 miles inland from the Pacific Ocean. This is a region shrouded in mist and clouds and a thick, verdant cover of forest and marsh that softens and rounds the landscape. At the site itself the land opens into a grassy plain about the size of a football field, through which shallow Chinchihuapi Creek slowly meanders. The sharp, snow-capped spine of the

Stone-Age Missiles
HUNTING GEAR AT
MONTE VERDE
INCLUDED ROUNDED
STONES AS LARGE
AS SOFTBALLS (LEFT),
WHICH WERE THROWN
OR SLUNG, AND
SPEAR POINTS (RIGHT).

Andes looms to the east, but only on a clear summer's day can you see the steam and smoke rising from its active volcanoes. And those days are rare enough in this damp and chilly climate.

But it's the damp climate that makes the site special. The archeological debris that Dillehay told us about in Maine rests on a sandy bank, which, soon after the residents departed, was blanketed by water-saturated, grass-matted, oxygen-deprived peat. Beneath this anaerobic quilt the normal decay of organic materials was checked, preserving the site. Monte Verde came to light only in the mid-1970s, when local woodsmen, cutting back the banks of the creek to widen trails for their oxcarts, dislodged some buried wood and mastodon bones from their resting place.

Dillehay's subsequent excavation showed that the bank was littered with the roots, stems, fruits, and nuts of nearly 70 species of plants, and even 3 types of marine algae. That's many more plant species than might be expected in a comparable-size *natural* deposit. We know that because Dillehay's excavators hiked about a mile upstream from Monte Verde to dig where there was no hint of any human presence, just to see what was deposited naturally on surfaces of the same age. Such preemptive shoveling helps muffle critics who argue that the plants could as easily have been left at the site by flood-waters, for instance, as by people.

If nature was responsible for depositing the plants on the site, then nature is awfully hardworking—and more than a little bit devious. More than a third of the plants were imports, brought from their native habitats on the Pacific coast, high in the Andes, or from grasslands and other settings 30 to 250 miles distant. Coincidence or not, 42 of the species found on the sandy bank are still used by contemporary native Mapuche for food, drink, or medicine. Only the usable parts of many of those plants made it to Monte Verde and were found burned in some food pits, on the floors of what once were huts, and in shallow hearths. Even more unusual was the discovery of several plugs of chewed boldo leaves—prehistoric chaw, they'd call that here in Texas—mixed with what appears to be seaweed and a third, as yet unidentified, plant. Boldo leaves are still used today to cure stomach ills and relieve colds and congestion.

The chaw was lying on a wishbone-shaped foundation of sand and gravel, which appeared to be glued together by animal fat. Along the foundation's edges were vertical wood stubs and scraps of animal skin, the remnants of a hide-draped frame hut that once stood there. Fronting the structure was a small cache of salt crystals, plant remains, mastodon bones, a chunk of animal meat (which, based on preliminary DNA analysis, most likely belonged to a mastodon), hearths, and stone tools.

Tools of the Trade
FROM THESE STONE CORES (LEFT), MONTE VERDEANS STRUCK OFF SHARP FLAKES. THE MASTODON TUSKS (RIGHT) MAY HAVE BEEN USED AS GOUGES.

Monte Verde's stone artifact inventory, now 700 pieces strong, includes finely crafted spear points, a slender and polished basalt drill, and cores, choppers, and flakes, several dozen of which are made of rock quarried many miles from the site. One can imagine that with these tools the Monte Verdeans worked, ate, and took cures in the wishbone structure. Most of them, however, lived 40 yards away in a group of 12 rectangular huts, each some 45 feet square. Nine of these huts were arranged in two rows, like row houses, lined by log planks staked together, framed by poles, and draped with a common roof of mastodon hide. Their floors were of sediments high in nitrogen and phosphate—a sure chemical sign of human waste—and littered with ash and grit. The huts surrounded two large communal hearths, two dozen smaller hearths (the child's footprint alongside one of them), and more tools: digging sticks, mastodon-tusk gouges, grinding slabs, knives, spear points, and bola stones (rounded, grooved stones; when sinew is wrapped around the groove, the stone can be whirled and flung). Some of the artifacts were still speckled with the tar that bound them to their wooden or bone handles. In the huts were still more traces of the Monte Verdeans' meals: plant remains, animal remains large and small (mastodon and camel bones, as well as a bird's charred feathers, eggshells, and bone), and even a few human coprolites (the politely scientific word for fossilized excrement).

The age of Monte Verde is anchored by a chain of radiocarbon dates run on artifacts and samples of different materials, including charcoal, wood, bone, and ivory. The dates range in age from 11,790 to 13,565 years ago. Dillehay thinks the oldest one, from charcoal that was sealed and preserved in a clay-lined hole, best represents the age of the site, making it a good 2,000 years older than Clovis times.

But there the skeptics pounce. University of Massachusetts archeologist Dena Dincauze, for example, accuses Dillehay of "uncritical use" of the radiocarbon ages. A better approach, she argues, is to discard the oldest date, then look at the time ranges for each radiocarbon date and use their overlap as the best age for the site. In response, Dillehay suggests dropping the younger dates on bone and ivory (which are more susceptible to contamination) and averaging the dates run on charcoal and wood. Doing so, he says, puts the occupation at around 12,250 years ago, which, as retired archeologist Tom Lynch happily observes, lies "at the very margin of Paleo-Indian time."

Of course, the passage south from Alaska didn't open up for another 250 years, making the trip to Monte Verde an unlikely matter of time travel. But let's assume there's some slop in both dates, and that both the passage and the site appear a little before 12,000 years

If the first Americans left Siberia soon after 21,000 years ago, they could have moved south before ice became an obstacle and been at Monte Verde exactly on time.

ago, with the passage opening first. Monte Verde is still 6,000 miles farther south than Clovis. To reach the Chilean site on time, these first Americans had to have left Alaska immediately after the passage opened up—giving them maybe 200 or 300 years to make the trip (our record-setting Thule could never have kept up). Leaving Alaska before the glaciers advanced 20,000 years ago, or earlier, seems a little more plausible.

So is Monte Verde just another Paleo-Indian site, albeit slightly older than most? Lynch growls that we cannot be sure, since so few of the artifacts have been illustrated or described in print. Dillehay's first published volume on Monte Verde said next to nothing about the site's artifacts or architecture, saving them for the (yet unpublished) second volume. This was a novel gambit on Dillehay's part to convince his readers, solely on the testimony of the

nonarcheological remains, that Monte Verde was a genuine archeological site. It caused a fair amount of grumbling, but he nearly pulled it off. Lynch, for example, admits the plant remains didn't get to the site by chance—he's just not willing to have them be there as early as Dillehay is.

Ultimately, making the case for Monte Verde—as Dillehay knows—will require more detailed descriptions and photographs of the artifacts. It will require precise maps of the layout of the huts and hearths, showing why these features are demonstrably of human origin. And it will require showing the distribution of the artifacts, organic remains, and dated samples within these features. Jackie Robinson didn't have it easy his first few years in the majors, either.

But will the publication of Dillehay's second volume be all that's needed to reach consensus on this site, and perhaps break the Clovis barrier? I put the question to University of Arizona archeologist Vance Haynes, the dean of the skeptics:

"No."

"But why not?"

"Have you ever visited a site," Haynes asked me, "that looked just the way you thought it would, based on what you'd read of it beforehand?" I had to admit I hadn't (truth is, sometimes I have trouble recognizing sites I've dug from descriptions I've written of them). In archeology, what one reads and what one sees are often very different. Archeology is like that: unlike researchers in the experimental sciences, we cannot replicate a crucial study in our own labs nor fully recreate a site's evidence in words and pictures. Having Haynes visit Monte Verde for a guided tour of the site and an explanation of its history would be the best way for Dillehay to dispose of any lingering doubts the hard-boiled skeptics might have.

"The next book's important," Haynes said, "but one day on the site of Monte Verde would be worth all the words they could write."

Dillehay's response: "Fine. I've been inviting people since 1979 to come to the site. Let's go look at it."

So the wrangling over Monte Verde will last several more years, while we wait for Dillehay and his team of specialists to wrap up volume two, and for Haynes and the other skeptics to hustle funds for the plane tickets to Chile. In the meantime, though, Emory's molecule hunters are doing their part to hasten the end of the Clovis hegemony.

Wallace and his colleagues inaugurated their mitochondrial DNA studies among Native Americans in the mid-1980s, just about the time excavations at Monte Verde were winding down. Almost immediately their results were extraordinarily encouraging. In analyzing mitochondrial DNA from Arizona's native Pima, Wallace's group spotted a mutation that occurs in 1 to 2 percent of Asian people (*Hinc*II morph 6 at bp 13259, in the alphabet-soup idiom of genetics). Among the Pima, however, the mutation's incidence was 20 times higher. That telltale clue does more than affirm the Pima's shared ancestry with Asians. The mutation is so frequent among them that the Pima must have descended from a small number of Asian immigrants, nearly all of whom carried that mutation in their genetic baggage.

Half a dozen years and a couple of hundred more samples later (including mitochondrial DNA samples from Navajo and Apache in North America, Yucatán Maya in Central America and Ticuna in South America), Wallace's team was able to show that all native peoples throughout the Americas share four mitochondrial DNA founding lineages. That's powerful evidence that the very first Americans were few in number. Genetically speaking, they left their Siberian sisters carrying but a fraction of the mitochondrial DNA gene pool.

If Wallace's group is right, the genetic clock started ticking the moment those first Americans left Siberia, at least 21,000 years ago by mitochondrial DNA reckoning. As it happens, the first Siberians appear archeologically

Marching to the New World
MONTE VERDE LIES 30 MILES INLAND FROM THE PACIFIC—AND OVER 9,000 MILES FROM SIBERIA, WHERE ITS SETTLERS CAME FROM.

about then. If they left Siberia soon thereafter, they could have crossed Beringia, moved south before glacial ice became an obstacle, and been at Monte Verde exactly on time (and without having to break any hunter-gatherer speed records).

Of course, Wallace's group may not be right. There are biologists who think the genetic clock was already ticking back in Siberia—long before the future first Americans departed—and some of those naysayers were at the San Francisco meeting to say so. Ryk Ward, of the University of Utah, and Svante Pääbo, of the University of Munich, have also analyzed mitochondrial DNA variation among Native Americans—in their case, the Nuu-Chah-Nulth of Vancouver Island. Of the 63 individuals they studied, they found 28 separate molecular variants. That's an astonishingly high rate of molecular diversity in just one tribe. Measured by the mitochondrial DNA clock, the Nuu-Chah-Nulth's ancestors had to have left Siberia up to 78,000 years ago.

That startling number implies one of two things: either that Americans are

of an antiquity inconceivable to all but the most passionate pre-Clovis crusaders—a humbling prospect for archeologists, because it means people were here for tens of thousands of years before Clovis and we've utterly failed to detect them—or that the Emory group is dead wrong about how the Americas were colonized.

Ward thinks the latter. The genetic diversity evident in the Nuu-Chah-Nulth, he believes, cannot have evolved in America, at least not until archeologists find some evidence of a 70,000-year-old occupation. Therefore, it must have originated in Asia long before the first Americans left Siberia. In other words, the first emigrants were already genetically diverse at departure, and the mitochondrial DNA clock says nothing about when the populations departed for America. "Even if we are able to use molecular data to define the divergence times of a set of lineages," Ward told his Bay Area audience, "we cannot state at what time the representative populations themselves split."

But Wallace's group isn't giving an inch. "We're looking at the genetic tree very differently," Schurr says. For the Emory researchers, the separate branches on which Asians and Native Americans perch are so genetically distinct that there must have been a branching event somewhere near Siberia. But for Ward, the twigs on the American branch are too numerous for the branching to have happened only here.

Are we back where we started? Not entirely—the archeology is proceeding apace. Dillehay expects to complete the second volume on Monte Verde next year, and he, Haynes, and others are planning to visit the site together. If the skeptics leave converted, then the biologists will have a reason to pick one molecular-clock scenario over another. And the rest of us will have a much clearer picture of the hardy pioneers who long ago slipped across the unmarked border between Siberia and Alaska and found a truly new world.

Who Were the Israelites?

"Thus the Lord gave to Israel all the land which He swore to give to their fathers; and having taken possession of it, they settled there. And the Lord gave them rest on every side just as He had sworn to their fathers; not one of all their enemies had withstood them, for the Lord had given all their enemies into their hands. . . ."

Joshua 21: 43–44

Neil Asher Silberman

The story of the Israelites' conquest of the Promised Land has long been an article of faith wherever the Bible is widely read and respected. For centuries familiar scenes of the Israelite tribes crossing the Jordan River and encircling the walls of Jericho with their blasting trumpets have been vividly described in fire-and-brimstone sermons and solemn hymns, and depicted in heroic paintings and other works of art. Yet a new generation of archaeologists working in Israel has come to challenge the scriptural account in a manner that might seem heretical to some. Their survey, excavation, and analysis of finds from hundreds of Early Iron Age settlements in the rugged hill country of the West Bank and Galilee have led them to conclude that the ancient Israelite confederacy did not arise in a divinely directed military conquest from the desert but through a remarkable socioeconomic change in the lives of a few thousand herders, farmers, and villagers in Canaan itself.

Today's archaeologists are certainly not the first to challenge the Book of Joshua—its historical reliability has been a matter of dispute for more than two centuries. At issue are the Book's first 12 chapters, which describe how,

after the death of Moses in the wilderness, Joshua, his chosen successor, led the Tribes of Israel across the Jordan River to conquer the powerful Canaanite cities of Jericho, Ai, Gibeon, Makkedah, Libnah, Lachish, Eglon, Hebron, Debir, and Hazor in quick succession. By destroying these cities and exterminating or otherwise driving the pagan Canaanites from the land, the Israelite tribes fulfilled their God-given mission and each received a parcel of the conquered territory. These allotments became permanent territorial divisions in the later Israelite and Judean kingdoms, and the force of tradition is so strong that tribal names are still used for many administrative districts of modern Israel. Yet the precise identity of those conquering tribesmen—and the nature of their conquest—remains one of the most persistent riddles of biblical archaeology.

MIRACLES AND METAPHORS

As far back as the eighteenth century, many European scholars, relying more on reason than reverence, began to question many of the miraculous details in the Exodus and Conquest narratives. Noting the implausibility of the sudden parting of a body of water as large as the Red Sea, the survival of

two million wandering Israelites in a scorching desert for 40 years subsisting on *manna,* or the sudden stopping of the sun above the city of Gibeon so that the Israelites could complete their conquest in daylight, biblical scholars turned to naturalistic explanations. Unpredictable riptides, unusually nutritious tamarisk sap, and the gravitational effects of a passing comet were invoked to explain these biblical events. Even more important was the tendency to see the Israelite conquest as an instructive metaphor, phrased in the progressive vocabulary of the times. In 1829, the English historian H. H. Milman noted "the remarkable picture" that the story of the conquest of Canaan presented "of the gradual development of human society." With the arrival of the Israelites, Milman explained that "the Land of Milk and Honey began to yield its fruits to a simple, free, and pious race of husbandmen."

INVADERS FROM THE DESERT

The nineteenth-century archaeological exploration of Egypt, Sinai, and Palestine moved the Israelite conquest from the realm of social metaphor to that of vivid historical fact. The decipherment of Egyptian hieroglyphics provided substantiation for biblical ref-

Reprinted with permission from *Archaeology* magazine, Volume 45, Number 2, March/April 1992, pp. 22, 24-30. © 1992 by the Archaeological Institute of America.

erences to the "store cities" of Pithom and Ramesses, where the Israelites reportedly labored in captivity. Even more telling was the discovery of the name "Israel" on a commemorative stele of the late thirteenth century B.C. On this monument, Pharaoh Merneptah boasted of his triumph over this hostile group. Ironically, the tools of prehistoric archaeology, used in Europe in the nineteenth century to attack the credibility of the Book of Genesis, were put to use in Palestine in the twentieth century to defend the Book of Joshua. Though no indisputable physical proof was ever found of the Israelites' exodus and wandering in the desert, European, American, and Israeli archaeological teams interpreted the thick destruction levels of charred beams, collapsed walls, and smashed pottery blanketing the Late Bronze Age levels at ancient Canaanite cities as evidence of concerted military attacks by the advancing Israelites. The discovery of poor squatters' hovels and silos built in the ruins of the once mighty Canaanite cities seemed additional proof of the triumph of primitive semi-nomads over the city folk. Earlier doubts about the historical reliability of the biblical narrative were therefore confidently brushed aside by scholars like William F. Albright of The Johns Hopkins University and Yigael Yadin of Hebrew University in Jerusalem who ascribed the violent destruction and subsequent occupation of the conquered Canaanite cities in the late thirteenth century B.C. to arriving Israelite warriors, perhaps even led by an historical figure named Joshua—just as the Bible said.

There were, however, differences between the archaeological evidence and details of the biblical story. At Jericho, for instance, repeated, intensive excavations uncovered no trace of a city wall or destruction level at the supposed date of the arrival of the Israelites. At Yarmuth, Arad, and Ai (cities all specifically mentioned as being conquered), surveys and excavations found no trace of thirteenth-century B.C. occupation. While supporters of the biblical narrative initially suggested that these inconsistencies were

minor, the discrepancies grew wider as the years went on. With the increasing precision of pottery dating, it became clear that the destruction of individual Canaanite cities occurred at various times over more than a century—far longer than even the longest concerted military campaign. Even more damaging was the realization that in many cases the ruined Canaanite cities lay desolate and abandoned for many decades before their occupation by new settlers. And in recognizing the relative slowness of the transition, a new theory of Israelite origins was born.

PEACEFUL IMMIGRANTS

In the 1920s, two German scholars, Albrecht Alt and Martin Noth, suggested a radically different explanation for the Israelite "conquest." Relying on ancient Egyptian records rather than biblical tradition, they suggested that the Israelite settlement of Canaan was the result of gradual immigration, not a unified military campaign. In particular, they based their reconstruction on evidence from the fourteenth-century B.C. Tell el-Amarna Letters, a collection of diplomatic correspondence between an Egyptian pharaoh and various Canaanite princes. These cuneiform tablets, which were discovered by chance in Middle Egypt in 1887, were filled with vivid reports of the chaotic political situation in Late Bronze Age Canaan, and frequently mentioned the activities of a restive and rebellious group called 'apiru on the frontiers of the settled land.

While Alt and Noth followed earlier scholars with their equation of 'apiru with "Hebrews," they went much further in assessing the term's historical significance. On the evidence of the Amarna Letters, 'apiru/Hebrews were already present in Canaan and hostile to the Canaanite rulers more than a century before the estimated date of the Israelite conquest. Alt and Noth theorized that the ancient Israelites, like the modern Bedouin settling down on the desert fringes of Palestine in the early twentieth century, must have been pastoral nomads who slowly filtered into

the settled land from the desert and, after a long period of uneasy coexistence with the population of Canaan, overran and destroyed the Canaanite city-states.

This "peaceful immigration" theory gained influential supporters, and for many years seemed the best explanation for the growing body of archaeological evidence. In the early 1950s, Israeli archaeologist Yohanan Aharoni believed that he found conclusive proof for the Alt-Noth theory in the Upper Galilee. There, he discovered a group of small, unfortified settlements in the traditional territory of the tribe of Naphtali that, he suggested, represented the arrival of an early wave of 'apiru or "proto-Israelites." And after the 1967 war, throughout the West Bank—in the traditional tribal territories (and new Israeli administrative districts) of Manasseh, Ephraim, Benjamin, and Judah—the theory of peaceful immigration was seemingly bolstered as other archaeologists located the remains of approximately 250 more Early Iron Age herdsmen's enclosures, hilltop hamlets, and unfortified villages whose architecture and artifacts were much simpler than those found in the Canaanite cities of the preceding Late Bronze Age.

In 1978, Adam Zertal of the University of Haifa began the most painstaking survey of sites connected with the Israelite settlement of Canaan, in his exploration of the 800-square-mile territory of the tribe of Manasseh in the northern West Bank. Carefully recording the locations and relative dates of 136 Early Iron Age sites in the region, Zertal also collected information on each site's topography, geology, available water sources, and soil quality. Never before had so much environmental information been correlated with remains of Early Israelite sites. When he listed the scattered sites in chronological order, Zertal detected evidence of a gradual population movement from the eastern desert fringe into the interior valleys and finally to the hills *during* the Early Iron Age, suggesting progressive ecological adaptation from herding to grain-growing to intensive terrace agriculture. Through this process of economic intensification, he contended, the ancient Israelites came in from the desert and, abandoning their wanderings, inherited their Promised Land.

PASTORALISTS AND FARMERS

The ecologically based picture of "peaceful immigration" had its problems—some would say even a fatal flaw. Like the more militant "unified conquest" theory, it presumed that in the thirteenth century B.C. a discrete ethnic group of semi-nomads had entered Canaan. This theory further suggested that the material culture of this group was far more primitive than that of the native Canaanites. The Israelite conquest of Canaan, whether by sudden military campaign or gradual infiltration, was therefore placed in the timeless, often violent conflict between Middle Eastern farmers and nomads—between "the Desert and the Sown."

This neat historical reconstruction, however, was based on some outdated ideas about Middle Eastern pastoralism. The first and most important of these was the nineteenth-century belief that throughout antiquity the Syrian and Arabian deserts contained vast numbers of turbulent nomads who periodically invaded and ravaged the settled land, a theory apparently spawned by romantic images of the Muslim Conquest with flashing scimitars and thundering camels. By the 1960s, however, there was a growing consensus among anthropologists that the great deserts had been unable to support more than a handful of pure nomads before the widespread domestication of the camel around 1100 B.C. Since this development took place *after* the Israelites were already presumably in Canaan, a "bedouin invasion" seemed an unlikely explanation for their arrival. Far more probable was that the Israelites were not pure nomads but rather primarily sheep- and goat-herders, pastoralists who roamed with their flocks—not in the midst of the desert but on the fringes of the heavily populated, settled land.

So if the Israelites' lonely desert origins were only a mirage, what of

their hostility to the peoples of Canaan whom they had supposedly driven from the land? When anthropologists working in Central Asia, the Middle Euphrates Valley, and North Africa began to study the economic links between pastoralists and farmers, they discovered how closely the two groups are bound together. Since the summer grain harvest throughout much of the Middle East coincides with the drying up of grazing lands on the deserts' edges, the natural movement of pastoralists and their flocks toward the well-watered agricultural regions brings them into contact with the settled population. There, the pastoralists may be hired as seasonal agricultural workers and their flocks may be allowed to graze in and fertilize the stubble of the harvested fields. In some cases, as with the modern Agedat people in the Middle Euphrates Valley, pastoralists and farmers may be members of a single community whose nomadic members wander off to the desert steppe in the winter, while the more sedentary members stay behind to prepare and plant the community's fields.

This pastoral/agricultural society was apparently common in the ancient Near East. In a study of the cuneiform archives of the Middle Bronze Age city of Mari, also on the Euphrates, John Luke of the University of Michigan convincingly demonstrated that the ancient records did not differentiate between populations of settled farmers and wandering pastoralists; the distinction was, instead, between those peasants who tended animals and peasants who tended crops. The situation in ancient Canaan was probably not much different. "Israelite" pastoralists and "Canaanite" peasants would have been members of the same Canaanite society.

PEASANT REBELS

Israelites from Canaan? The thought clashes with everything we've been taught to believe. Yet in the 1960s, based on this understanding, a fascinating new theory of the Israelite "conquest" of Canaan arose. George Mendenhall, a feisty biblical scholar

and one of John Luke's teachers at Michigan, rejected both the "immigration" and "conquest" theories of Israelite settlement. For years he had claimed that the rise of the Israelite religion and tribal confederacy could be explained solely on the basis of internal social developments in Canaan. As early as 1947 he had reviewed the evidence of the Amarna Letters and insisted that the 'apiru, long identified as invading Hebrews, were not an ethnic group at all but a well-defined social class.

Mendenhall argued that the Late Bronze Age city-states of Canaan were organized as highly stratified societies, with the king or governor at the top of the pyramid, with princes, court officials, and chariot warriors right below him, and the rural peasants at the base. The 'apiru were apparently outside this scheme of organization, and they seem to have threatened the social order in a number of ways. Besides being pastoralists on the fringes of the settled land, they sometimes also served as mercenaries for the highest bidder and, when that work was not forthcoming, some 'apiru actively encouraged the peasants to rebel. This social unrest, Mendenhall asserted, was not a conflict between nomads and a settled population but between the rural population and the rulers of the city-states. The Amarna Letters are filled with reports of famine and hardship and the increasingly onerous exactions by the kings. It was no wonder, noted Mendenhall, that the 'apiru had great success in stirring up the peasants and that many Canaanite royal cities were destroyed at that time. "There was no real conquest of Palestine in the sense that has usually been understood," he wrote in 1970. "What happened instead may be termed, from the point of view of the secular historian interested only in socio-political processes, a peasants' revolt against the network of interlocking Canaanite city-states."

At the heart of Mendenhall's "peasant revolt" theory was a novel explanation of how the Israelite religion began. Mendenhall maintained that the 'apiru and their peasant supporters could never have united and overcome

Canaanite feudal domination without a compelling ideology to unify and inspire them. He believed that their worship of a single, transcendent god—Yahweh—was a brilliant response to the religion of the Canaanite kings. Instead of relying on a pantheon of divinities and elaborate fertility rituals that could be performed only by the king and his official priesthood, the new religious movement, Mendenhall believed, placed its faith in a single god who established egalitarian laws of social conduct and who communicated them *directly* to each member of the community. The hold of the kings over the people was therefore effectively broken by the spread of this new faith. And for Mendenhall the true Israelite conquest was accomplished—without invasion or immigration—when large numbers of Canaanite peasants overthrew their masters and became "Israelites."

Mendenhall did not deal with the archaeological evidence directly, but biblical scholar Norman K. Gottwald, who accepted and expanded Mendenhall's theories, confronted it. While Mendenhall had merely dismissed all talk of semi-nomads in the hill country, Gottwald believed that the Early Iron Age sites discovered there were, in fact, Israelite. He theorized that the remote frontier and forest regions were naturally attractive to the members of an independence movement who had fled from the more heavily populated, and more closely controlled, cities of the coastal plain to establish a new way of life. Adherents of the "peaceful immigration" theory had explained that the simplicity of the artifacts in the Early Iron Age villages was due to the Israelites' primitive, semi-nomadic origins. Gottwald, however, countered by suggesting that the absence of luxury goods was evidence of the breakdown in the high-status trade that had been carried on exclusively by the Canaanite nobility.

The "peasant revolt" theory of Israelite origins had obvious rhetorical power in the 1970s, a time of modern national liberation movements and Third World insurgency. Yet it, too, had its shortcomings—chief of which

was that it simply did not fit the accumulating archaeological evidence. Through the 1980s Adam Zertal's explorations in the territory of Manasseh were complemented by major new surveys in the Galilee and in the territories of the tribes of Ephraim and Judah farther south. Unfortunately for the supporters of the peasant revolt theory, no evidence could be discerned for a major demographic shift from the coastal cities toward the hill country. The area of unoccupied hills immediately to the east of the coastal plain apparently experienced no intense wave of settlement during the Early Iron Age. Even more important, the pattern Zertal discovered in Manasseh seemed to apply to other parts of the hill country as well. The earliest of the new settlements were clustered far to the east, in the grazing lands of the desert fringe. And their characteristic sprawling layout of rustic structures surrounding a communal animal pen was dramatically different from what might have been expected from city-bred Canaanite peasants who headed out to establish independent farmsteads on the frontier.

INVISIBLE ISRAELITES

Though rejecting the idea of a peasant revolt, the conquest story that has emerged in recent years may be the most revolutionary version of all. It is framed as an epic struggle—not between Israelites and Canaanites, pastoralists and settled populations, feudal lords and rebellious peasants, but between the human populations of Canaan and a changing economic environment. Israel Finkelstein of Tel Aviv University, who directed the survey of the territory of Ephraim, has gone far beyond the conventional chronological limits imposed by the biblical story in crafting a new reconstruction of events. Having traced settlement patterns and ecological adaptation in the hill country of Canaan over hundreds of years, Finkelstein is convinced that the demographic revolution of the Early Iron Age can no longer be seen in isolation. In fact, he believes that the

phenomenon of Israelite settlement is intimately connected to developments that began half a millennium before.

As recent archaeological surveys have indicated, the hill country of Canaan was thickly settled and dotted with fortified cities, towns, and hamlets in the period beginning around 1750 B.C. Yet the surveys also showed that around 1550 B.C., toward the end of what is called the Middle Bronze IIC period, the settled population in the hill country declined dramatically. During the succeeding Late Bronze Age (1550–1200 B.C.), while the large cities along the coast and in the major valleys continued to flourish, more than 90 percent of the permanent settlement sites in the hill country were abandoned and the few surviving sites became much smaller in size. But that is not to say that the hill country of Canaan was empty. Far from it. According to Finkelstein, the people who would later become Israelites were already there.

His basic argument, put simply, is that the model of pastoral nomads settling down and farming, long regarded as the main avenue of human progress, was always something of a two-way street. While Enlightenment thinkers and early-twentieth-century archaeologists pointed to the economic and social conditions that prompted pastoralists to become farmers, they neglected to think about the kinds of conditions that might encourage the reverse. Such was precisely what happened among the Canaanite population of the hill country, according to Finkelstein, at the end of the Middle Bronze Age. Population pressure, competition for scarce agricultural land in this rugged region, or perhaps even political change in the administration of the Canaanite city-states caused a shift in the balance between farmers and pastoralists. A large portion of the population of the hill country gradually abandoned their villages. While some may have gone to the coast to find work, toiling in the fields and orchards, others—perhaps the majority, according to Finkelstein—may have adopted a new, wandering way of life.

These hill-country farmers-turned-herdsmen (almost invisible to archaeologists when compared to populations that built permanent houses) were able to establish a stable, alternative way of life on the desert fringe. For two or three centuries they lived in symbiosis with the settled populations of the large cities along the coasts and in the major valleys—presumably to trade milk, meat, wool, and leather for agricultural produce. It was only when the Canaanite city-state system finally broke down completely and its agricultural surplus evaporated in the great upheavals of the thirteenth century B.C. that the lifestyle of the hill-country Canaanites shifted again.

Sometime shortly after 1250 B.C., far to the west in the Aegean, a combination of political, climatic, and economic factors brought an end to the power of the Mycenaean kingdoms—and this dramatic collapse disturbed the delicate balance of economic and political power in the entire eastern Mediterranean world. In an era of social, political, and economic disaster, the elaborate rituals of diplomacy and exchange of luxury goods that had legitimized the rule of hundreds of Bronze Age princes, kings, priests, and warlords throughout the region simply could not be maintained. The economic life of the cities was disrupted. The scattered pastoralists in the hill country of Canaan could no longer depend on the periodic markets in the coastal and valley cities—where they had grown accustomed to trading their sheep and goats for grain. Those cities could now hardly support their own inhabitants; the pastoralists were left on their own. When the first clans of wandering herders began to choose unoccupied hilltops for permanent settlements—and started to clear nearby fields in preparation for planting—they became what archaeologist might call Early Israelites.

The finds from the hundreds of Early Iron Age settlements in the hill country can be seen as evidence of this social process: architectural forms, pottery vessels, and even a few cult objects reflect the slow crystallization of a new, settled culture on the fringes of Canaanite society. No massive immigration from the outside is necessary to explain the sudden establishment of these Israelite settlements. New methods of estimating ancient population through studying site size and the economic carrying capacity of the land have also helped to place the Israelite settlement of Canaan in a more reasonable perspective. While the Book of Exodus relates that the Israelites fleeing Egypt numbered 600,000 warriors (bringing the incredible total to more than two million), recent archaeological assessments suggest that the Israelite population at the beginning of the Early Iron Age—which may indeed have included a small number of refugees from Egypt—probably did not exceed 20,000 souls.

Thus, the founding fathers of the Israelite nation can now be seen as scattered groups of pastoralists living in small family groups and grazing their flocks on hilltops and isolated valleys in the hill country of Canaan, reacting in their own way to the far-reaching social and economic changes that swept over the entire eastern Mediterranean world. Whether they possessed a unique, monotheistic religion—whether it was inspired and first articulated by refugees from Egypt—these are questions that are simply impossible to determine on the basis of current archaeological evidence. What seems almost certain, however, is that the story of the bloody conquest of the Land of Canaan as a unified military campaign led by a single, divinely directed leader was woven together centuries later—an anachronistic saga of triumph on the battlefield, crafted and compiled by loyal court poets anxious to flatter the later Israelite and Judean kings.

WHO WERE THE ISRAELITES?

This new understanding of Israelite origins as a socio-economic transformation is not really a religious challenge. It is a fulfillment of one of the most time-honored traditions of the West. For wherever the biblical faith has spread across the globe, the image of the Tribes of Israel conquering their Promised Land has been a medium of self-reflection as well as an episode of sacred history. For the seventeenth-century English Puritans, Canaan was the rolling hills and forests of New England. For the Boer settlers of South Africa, the Promised Land was the rich farmland of the Transvaal, with its own indigenous Canaanites. And the self-affirming visions continued throughout the nineteenth and twentieth centuries, as Western scholars formulated vivid images of manifest destiny, evolutionism, sociological analysis, and, now in the 1990s, hardheaded reflections on demographic pressure and economic change. Yet the historians of each age do not merely deceive themselves into believing that what is familiar is true. Generations of scholars are drawn to the problems of most immediate relevance to their society, viewing the ancient Israelites through an ever changing sequence of lenses. Each generation's reinterpretation of the biblical story has deepened historical understanding by addressing contemporary concerns.

"The crystallization of the People of Israel in their land," Finkelstein recently wrote, "was not a unique or miraculous event that occurred to a unique or peculiar people, but part of a wider, familiar phenomenon shared by many peoples appearing for the first time on the historical stage." In some earlier epochs, the suggestion that the Israelites, in their struggle to adapt and survive, were no different from hundreds of other groups throughout history would have earned its author a public stoning, or excommunication at the least. Yet one era's heresy is often another's article of faith. That's perhaps why in our own late-twentieth-century society—torn by economic stress, burdened with belated ecological awareness, and astounded by sweeping political changes—the new social explanation of Israelite origins can be seen as our generation's powerful and distinctive variation on a timeless biblical theme.

Ever Since Eve . . .
Birth Control in the Ancient World

John M. Riddle, J. Worth Estes, and Josiah C. Russell

John M. Riddle is professor of history at North Carolina State University and author of Contraception and Abortion from the Ancient World to the Renaissance.

J. Worth Estes is professor of pharmacology at the Boston University School of Medicine. His books include The Medical Skills of Ancient Egypt.

Josiah C. Russell is professor emeritus of medieval history at the University of New Mexico and the author of The Control of Late Ancient and Medieval Population.

Today, women's reproductive rights are a hotly debated issue. In ancient times, contrary to what historians have been telling us for the past several centuries, many women practiced birth-control with little interference from religious or political authorities. The knowledge of the plants that allowed them to do so and the loss of that knowledge by the time of the Renaissance is a story that is only now emerging with clarity.

In the seventh century B.C., Greek colonists from Thera founded the coastal city of Cyrene in what is now Libya. According to the Greek botanist Theophrastus (ca. 370–288 B.C.), they soon discovered a plant that made some of them wealthy and all of them famous. They called it *silphion;* its name was later latinized to *silphium.*

The pungent sap from its stems and roots was good in cough syrups and gave food a rich, distinctive taste. Of far greater significance, however, was its use as a contraceptive.

Silphium was a member of the genus *Ferula,* commonly known as giant fennel, a large group of plants with deeply divided leaves and yellow flowers. These plants were known in antiquity to have contraceptive and abortifacient properties. Anecdotal testimony about silphium's reputation as a birth-control agent is found in nonmedical classical literature. The first-century B.C. Roman poet Catullus wondered how many kisses he and his Lesbia might partake. Why "as many grains of sand as there are on Cyrene's silphium shores." Demand for the plant drove prices so high in fifth-century Athens that Aristophanes would write in his play *The Knights,* "Don't you remember when a stalk of silphium sold so cheap?" Fortunately for the Cyrenians, attempts to cultivate it in Syria and Greece failed, leaving them the sole exporters of the plant, which soon became the city's distinctive symbol. One of a series of Cyrenian four-drachma coins shows a seated woman touching the plant with one hand while the other points to her genitals.

Within a few centuries, the supply of silphium could not keep up with demand. The plant grew only in a band about 125 miles long and 35 miles wide on the dry mountainsides facing the Mediterranean Sea. By the first century A.D., it was scarce from overharvesting. Pliny the Elder reported in his *Natural History* that silphium had become worth more than its weight in silver and that in Emperor Nero's time, "only a single stalk had been found there [in Cyrene] within our memory." By the third or fourth century A.D. silphium was extinct. Related plants survived, including asafoetida, also of the genus *Ferula,* which gives Worcestershire Sauce its aroma. Though less effective than silphium, asafoetida was widely used as a contraceptive in antiquity because it was more abundant and less expensive.

For centuries, historians paid no attention to ancient accounts that claimed certain plants provided an effective means of birth control. Keith Hopkins, an English scholar who studied ancient contraception in the mid-1960s, for example, described ancient oral contraceptives as "ineffectual potions." The French historian Philippe Ariès has suggested that when people in ancient and medieval times wanted a small family, they simply engaged in sexual practices that did not result in pregnancy. Modern laboratory analysis of various plants, however, gives us reason to believe that the classical potions *were* effective, and that women in antiquity had more control over their reproductive lives than previously thought.

Besides silphium and asafoetida, the seeds of Queen Anne's Lace, or wild carrot, may also have been effective. Hippocrates, among others, declared that such seeds, when taken orally, both prevent and terminate pregnancy. In a test conducted in 1976, doses of 80 to 120 milligrams of seeds from Queen Anne's Lace given to mice on the fourth to the sixth day of pregnancy prevented fetal growth. Other experiments on rodents reported in 1984 and 1987 suggest that the seeds inhibit both fetal and ovarian growth and disrupt the reproductive cycle. In 1986, chemical compounds in Queen Anne's Lace were reported to block the production of progesterone, the hormone that prepares the uterus for the development of the fertilized ovum. The evidence suggests that these seeds are effective as a postcoital antifertility agent. Indeed, a small number of women in Watauga County, North Carolina, in the Appalachian Mountains, drink a glass of water containing a teaspoonful of Queen Anne's Lace seeds immediately after intercourse to prevent pregnancy. And women living in rural areas of Rajasthan, India, chew dry seeds of Queen Anne's Lace to reduce fertility. Both practices were known to women 2,000 years ago.

Other plants used in classical times as contraceptives or abortifacients included pennyroyal, artemisia, myrrh, and rue. In Aristophanes' comedy *Peace*, first performed in Athens in 421 B.C., Hermes provides Trigaius with a female companion. Trigaius wonders if the woman might become pregnant. "Not if you add a dose of pennyroyal," advises Hermes. Nearly contemporary Hippocratic works on gynecology also mention pennyroyal as a birth-control agent.

Pennyroyal grows wild and would have been generally available to ancient women. It is toxic, however, and had to be taken in precise amounts in a tea. Recent American studies show that pennyroyal contains a substance called pulegone that terminates pregnancies in humans and animals. Galen (A.D. 129–199), the foremost physician in classical antiquity, and Dioscorides, a first-century A.D. herbalist and writer on pharmacology, also reported that willow, date palm, and pomegranate were used for birth control. The best known literary reference to the pomegranate's contraceptive power is in the Greek myth of Persephone and Hades; for every pomegranate kernel that Persephone ate, that many months were

alloted to the infertile fall and winter. Studies in the 1930s showed that all three of these plants stimulated the production of female sex hormones and reduced fertility in laboratory animals, much as modern contraceptive pills do.

Long before the Greeks and Romans, the ancient Egyptians were practicing birth control. The Ebers Papyrus, a medical document of 1550–1500 B.C. (but containing ideas that date much earlier), lists substances that it claims "stop pregnancy in the first, second, or third period [trimester]." According to the papyrus, unspecified amounts of acacia gum, dates, and an unidentified plant are mixed with plant fiber and honey and formed into a pessary (vaginal suppository). The Kahun gynecological papyrus, compiled around 1900 B.C., lists three similar contraceptive pessaries. Several of them also include acacia gum. Modern researchers have found acacia to be spermatocidal. When compounded, it produces the lactic acid anhydride, which is used in modern contraceptive jellies and is

Queen Anne's Lace, or wild carrot, is common to North America, where it has been used in rural communities to prevent pregnancy.

An ancient abortifacient, pennyroyal contains pulegone, a chemical compound that ends pregnancies in humans and animals.

Named after Artemis, the goddess of women and protector of childbirth, artemisia was believed in antiquity to induce abortion.

THE ROYAL HORTICULTURAL SOCIETY

bonded to vaginal diaphragms to prevent sperm from passing around the edges of the device. When, in one study, an acacia leaf was fed to rats twice a day for five days, litters were reduced by 88 to 100 percent, while acacia seed reduced pregnancy by 100 percent.

How many ancient people actually practiced birth control? Historical demographic studies suggest that premodern peoples of Europe regulated family size. Between A.D. 1 and 500, the population within the bounds of the Roman Empire declined. Overall, the population of Europe is estimated to have declined from 32.8 million to 27.5 million. By the year 1000 the

---

Ancient Recipes to Avoid Conception

Early in the second century A.D., Soranus, antiquity's foremost writer on gynecology, clearly distinguished between contraceptives and abortifacients. Writing in his treatise *Gynaecology*, he described procedures he thought would inhibit conception. First, a woman should avoid intercourse during her most fertile period—thought to be the time when menstruation was "ending and abating." During intercourse the woman could avoid deep penetration; afterward she was to squat down, induce sneezing, wipe the vagina, and, possibly, drink something cold. Finally, he gave a series of "aids," with the prefatory phrase "They assist the inconception."

The aids, all ointments to smear on the cervix, were: old olive oil; honey; cedar resin, or juice of the balsam tree, alone or together with white lead; a salve with myrtle oil and white lead; moist alum (a crystalline substance with astringent properties); galbanum (a gum resin from the genus *Ferula,* or giant fennel); a lock of fine wool; or, before intercourse vaginal suppositories that have the power to contract and condense the entry into the uterus.

According to Soranus, "Such of these things are as styptic [astringent], clogging, and cooling cause the orifice of the uterus to shut before the time of coitus and do not let the seed pass beyond its opening." The gums and resins may have had a mild antiseptic effect and, as such, acted as spermicides. In antiquity, cedar oil came mostly from the juniper tree. White lead has been employed in modern medicine in dermatological salves, for poison ivy as an example. Because of its toxicity, it has been dropped for the most part from our pharmacy. Both myrtle oil and galbanum have an anti-fertility effect. The wool pad and old olive oil were seen as lubricants and devices to block the cervix mechanically.

Soranus recommended four oral contraceptives, but warned, "These things not only prevent conception but also destroy any already existing. In our opinion, moreover, the evil from these things is too great, since they damage and upset the stomach, and besides cause congestion of the head and induce sympathetic [distress the nervous system] reactions." Soranus's prescriptions follow:

"To some people it seems advisable once a month to drink Cyrenaic juice (or sap) in the amount of the size of a chick-pea in two cups of water so as to induce menstruation. Or, of opopanax, Cyrenaic juice, and seeds of rue, up to two obols [1 obol = ca. $\frac{1}{3}$ ounce, 6 obols = 1 drachma = 2 ounces], mold round with wax and give to swallow; then follow with a drink of weak [or diluted] wine or let it be drunk in weak wine. [Or] the seeds of *leukoion* [a plant of the mustard family] and myrtle, three obols each; of myrrh, a drachma; of white pepper, two seed-pods; give to drink with wine for three days. [Or] of rocket seed, one obol; of cow parsnip, one-half obol; drink with oxymel [a vinegar-honey mixture]."

In evaluating Soranus's four recipes, the first obstacle is determining the meaning of "Cyrenaic juice" in the first two prescriptions. References from classical writers, especially Pliny the Elder and Isidore, Bishop of Seville (A.D. 602–636), show that Cyrenaic juice was derived from the now extinct silphium. Low doses of ferujol, a substance that occurs in the genus *Ferula,* to which silphium belonged, has been nearly 100 percent successful in preventing pregnancy in female rats up to three days after coitus. One species, *Ferula moschata* (Reinsch), is employed in folk medicine in Central Asia to abort. Because plants of the same family, especially closely related species, tend to have similar chemistries, we can be reasonably sure that Cyrenaic juice was a contraceptive and an abortifacient.

Besides Cyrenaic juice, the second prescription mentions opopanax, an odorous gum resin that is closely related to *Ferula.* Like other giant fennels, opopanax was regarded as a contraceptive, but one inferior to silphium. The third plant in this prescription, rue, contains a compound similar to pilocarpine, which has induced abortions in horses. Rue is a traditional abortifacient among the Hispanic people in New Mexico and has been used as a tea for abortion purposes throughout Latin America.

There is some evidence that the contents of the third prescription might have been effective, but confirmatory evidence is lacking. It contains leukoinos, either of two plants belonging to the mustard family. Both plants are known in modern Indian medicine as abortifacients and emmenagogues, which provoke menstruation regardless of whether a fertilized egg is present and implantation has occurred. The effectiveness of the fourth recipe is equally uncertain. Neither rocket nor cow parsnip has been evaluated as a contraceptive.

—J.M.R.

population was 38.5 million, a net increase of less than six million in a millennium. Many scholars have hypothesized that infanticide explains low population and family size in both ancient and medieval times. They argue that infanticide, because it was not illegal, was widely practiced.

The late J. Lawrence Angel, a Smithsonian anthropologist, studied skeletons in ancient cemeteries of Athens, Corinth, and the Roman Empire. While the number of skeletons in his samples varied and the remains of very young children were not included, his data indicate that people were living longer during the pre-

---

From Plato to Pius: The Ethics of Birth Control

In 1869 Pope Pius IX outlawed abortion among Catholics, declaring that the human soul was born at conception. The decree reflected a very old debate. Greco-Roman, Hebrew, and early medieval sources all contain sophisticated discussions of the issues surrounding contraception and abortion. While there was never uniform opinion among them as to the ethics and medical advisability of birth control practices, Hebrew, Greek, and Roman law generally did not protect the fetus; but there was a religious distinction made once the fetus had formed recognizable features. Before that point women could abort without fear of religious or legal reprisal.

The most famous medical statement from classical antiquity, the Hippocratic oath, was misinterpreted early on as forbidding physicians to perform abortions. In reading the oath, formulated in the fifth century B.C., initiates swore not to administer an abortive suppository. Scribonious Largus, a Roman physician writing in the first century A.D., was among the first to interpret Hippocrates' injunction against abortive suppositories as a blanket condemnation of abortion. In his book *Compositiones,* Scribonius wrote: "Hippocrates, who founded our profession, laid the foundation for our discipline by an oath in which it was proscribed to give a pregnant woman a kind of medicine that expels the embryo or fetus." Scribonius's misreading survived into modern times. The error became particularly important in the nineteenth century, when so many American states passed anti-abortion laws based in part on this misreading

of a doctor's sacred obligations. Despite its fame, the Hippocratic oath regarding abortion was not generally followed by ancient physicians. While the oath outlawed abortive suppositories and pessaries, its implicit meaning was that a physician was left free to employ contraceptives, oral abortifacients, and the various surgical and manipulative procedures available.

Both Plato and Aristotle advocated population control to ensure population stability in the ideal city-state. Plato wrote: "There are many devices available: if too many children are being born, there are measures to check propagation." Aristotle also considered population control desirable, writing, "If conception occurs in excess of the limit so fixed . . . have abortion induced before sense and life have begun in the embryo." Roman stoic philosophers, on the other hand, were more hesitant. They believed that the human soul appeared when the baby was first exposed to cool air, but that the potential for a soul existed at conception.

Hebrew sources give idiosyncratic interpretations of the Biblical directive to "Be fruitful and multiply." The Babylonian Talmud, *Yebamoth,* records: "A man is commanded concerning the duty of propagation, but not a woman." In other words, men were encouraged to spread their seed, but women, who had to suffer pregnancy, childbirth, and child rearing, were excused by God from the command to be fruitful. Hebrew religious law did not regard a woman as pregnant until 40 days after conception.

Early church fathers were divided about the ethics of abortion. In a sermon around 390, John Chrysostom, the bishop of Constantinople, decried those who used contraceptives, likening the practice to sowing a field in order to destroy fruit, and raising the question whether it was not the same as murder. Jerome (348–420), who revised and translated the Bible into Latin, condemned those who drank potions causing "sterility and murder[ing] those not yet conceived." Augustine of Hippo (354–430), on the other hand, appears to have been influenced on this subject by pagan authors, principally Aristotle. "If what is brought forth is unformed," he wrote, "but at this stage some sort of living, shapeless thing, then the law of homicide would not apply, for it could not be said that there was a living soul in that body, for it lacks all sense, if it be such as is not yet formed and therefore not endowed with its senses." Gregory, Bishop of Nyssa (330–395), expressed the same sentiments when he wrote that the unformed embryo could not be considered a human being.

We tend to believe that quandaries over birth control are recent, brought on by the presence of effective contraceptives and safe abortion procedures. In fact, the ethical dilemmas are much the same as they were when Juvenal wrote, almost 2,000 years ago, "we have sure-fire contraceptives." Hundreds of generations—saints and sinners, people in distress, kings, queens, merchants, and peasants—have faced many of the same problems we do. At the very least, let us be consoled by the thought that our times are not as unique as we think they are.

—J.M.R.

Dioscorides, Galen, and other ancient medical writers believed that the pomegranate possessed antifertility properties.

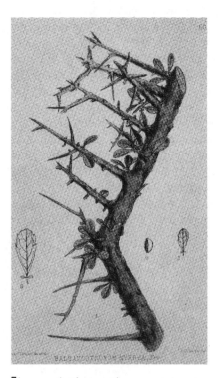

The aromatic plant myrrh was a component of many antifertility potions in ancient and medieval Western medicine.

Known to the Greeks and Romans as a contraceptive and abortifacient, rue is still used throughout Latin America.

Christian centuries from the second millennium until about the first century A.D. Other data suggest that the population of pharaonic Egypt underwent a parallel increase in life-span. Life expectancy then declined in both Egypt and the European Roman Empire into the Middle Ages.

Scarring and pitting of bones in the pelvic region provide clues to the number of full-term pregnancies in these cemeteries. Each time childbirth occurs, one or more of these features is produced. Data compiled from Mediterranean cemeteries by Angel and the late Sarah Bisel, also with the Smithsonian, imply that birthrates in Roman times had fallen below what was necessary to maintain the population. The life-span of adults was increasing as the number of pregnancies or, more accurately, births was declining. This conclusion is also inferred from the archaeological evidence of the size of cities, as well as contemporary literary evidence. The Greek historian Polybius (ca. 200–118 B.C.), speaking of what was happening in cities during his lifetime, said that families were limiting their size to one or two children.

Similarly, demographic profiles of the Middle Ages provide persuasive evidence that women used oral contraceptives and early term abortifacients. Such demographic research, laboratory studies, and scrutiny of ancient texts have given us new hints concerning the efficacy of ancient "family planning."

We can now understand why the ancient Greeks and Romans valued silphium, and why they tried to develop substitutes when it disappeared from the marketplace. It is more difficult to discover why such herbal birth-control agents faded from common usage. Although they are described in medical texts of the early and late Middle Ages, by the onset of the Renaissance physicians were no longer writing about them. Did doctors no longer know what plants to use, when to use them, or what doses would prevent conception or end pregnancy? Why was that knowledge passed down through generations of women but not physicians? The research question now becomes not what the ancients knew about birth control, but why we lost what was once so well known.

We do know that by the twelfth century, medical training had moved from apprenticeships to the universities. By the fourteenth century in most of the towns and cities of Europe, guilds required that one be a university graduate in order to practice medicine. The university curriculum was geared more toward medical theory and less toward clinical practice. Increasingly, the compounding and dispensing of drugs fell out of the realm of the physicians' offices and into the domain of the pharmacists' guilds.

Although women had studied medicine at some universities in the early Middle Ages, men gradually came to dominate the profession. At the same time, gynecology became more and more the province of midwives who had learned the uses of herbs in the fields. They knew, for instance, how to identify the necessary plants, how and when to harvest their appropriate parts, how to make extracts and administer them, in what dose, and, perhaps most important, when to administer them in relation to the last coitus or missed menstruation. However, such complex knowledge may have slowly faded from common usage simply because, perhaps, it became increasingly difficult to transmit this information orally.

Indeed, by the fifteenth and sixteenth centuries, physicians were being summoned to women's bedsides only when their medical problems called for drastic or nonroutine action. Few physicians knew about birth-control agents since they were not part of their training, nor was there an easy way to learn about them. The learning chain broke, and the folk knowledge chain nearly broke. Dioscorides and Galen had learned about herbal agents from people who knew what and how much to take. Physicians of the Renaissance, however, distrusted folk medicine and had no occupational or professional means to acquire this knowledge. In time, Christian church doctrine, canon law, and eventually the laws of states came to restrict women's claims that they should regulate their own reproduction.

In any case, we can now be reasonably certain that many women in antiquity knew what only a few women know today. Many twentieth-century historians still assume that these women relied solely on magic, superstition, and ineffectual folklore to limit their reproductive capacities. They are wrong. Women in antiquity had significant control over their reproductive lives. The evidence is there in the documents, where it has been all along.

The Mummies of Xinjiang

Evan Hadingham

Evan Hadingham is the science editor of the PBS series Nova, *now in its twentieth season. Author of many books and articles on prehistoric art and archeology, Hadingham's most recent volumes are* Early Man and the Cosmos *and* Lines to the Mountain Gods: Nazca and the Mysteries of Peru. *He is currently helping to develop a series on ancient technology for* Nova.

In the dry hills of this central Asian province, archeologists have unearthed more than 100 corpses that are as much as 4,000 years old. Astonishingly well preserved—and Caucasian. One glimpse of the corpses was enough to shock Victor Mair profoundly. In 1987, Mair, a professor of Chinese at the University of Pennsylvania, was leading a tour group through a museum in the Chinese city of Ürümqi, in the central Asian province of Xinjiang, when he accidentally strayed into a gloomy, newly opened room. There, under glass, lay the recently discovered corpses of a family—a man, a woman, and a child of two or three—each clad in long, dark purple woolen garments and felt boots. "Even today I get chills thinking about that first encounter," says Mair. "The Chinese said they were 3,000 years old, yet the bodies looked as if they were buried yesterday."

But the real shock came when Mair looked closely at their faces. In contrast to most central Asian peoples, these corpses had obvious Caucasian, or European, features—blond hair, long noses, deep-set eyes, and long skulls. "I was thunderstruck," Mair recalls. "Even though I was supposed to be leading a tour group, I just couldn't leave that room. The questions kept nagging at me: Who were these people? How did they get out here at such an early date?"

The corpses Mair saw that day were just a few of more than 100 dug up by Chinese archeologists over the past 16 years. All of them are astonishingly well preserved. They come from four major burial sites scattered between the arid foothills of the Tian Shan ("Celestial Mountains") in northwest China and the fringes of the Taklimakan Desert, some 150 miles due south. All together, these bodies, dating from about 2000 B.C. to 300 B.C., constitute a significant addition to the world's catalog of prehistoric mummies. Unlike the roughly contemporaneous mummies of ancient Egypt, the Xinjiang mummies were not rulers or nobles; they were not interred in pyramids or other such monuments, nor were they subjected to deliberate mummification procedures. They were preserved merely by being buried in the parched, stony desert, where daytime temperatures often soar over 100 degrees. In the heat the bodies were quickly dried, with facial hair, skin and other tissues remaining largely intact.

Where exactly did these apparent Caucasians come from? And what were they doing at remote desert oases in central Asia?

Any answers to these questions will most likely fuel a wide-ranging debate about the role outsiders played in the rise of Chinese civilization. As far back as the second century B.C., Chinese texts refer to alien peoples called the Yuezhi and the Wusun, who lived on China's far western borders; the texts make it clear that these people were regarded as troublesome "barbarians." Until recently, scholars have tended to downplay evidence of any early trade or contact between China and the West, regarding the development of Chinese civilization as an essentially homegrown affair sealed off from outside influences; indeed, this view is still extremely congenial to the present Chinese regime. Yet some archeologists have begun to argue that these supposed barbarians might have been responsible for introducing into China such basic items as the wheel and the first metal objects. Exactly who these central Asian outsiders might have been, however—what language they spoke and where they came form—is a puzzle. No wonder, then, that scholars see the discovery of the blond mummies as a sensational new clue.

Although Mair was intrigued by the mummies, the political climate of the late 1980s (the Tiananmen Square massacre occurred in 1989) guaranteed that any approach to Chinese archeological authorities would be fraught with difficulties. So he laid the riddle to one side as he returned to his main area of study, the translation and analysis of ancient Chinese texts. Then, in September 1991, the discovery of the 5,000-year-old "Ice Man" in the Alps electrified the world press. The frozen body is thought to be that of a late Neolithic trader, apparently caught by a storm while hiking at an altitude of 10,500 feet. Photos of the Ice Man's corpse, dried by the wind and then buried by a glacier, reminded Mair of the desiccated mummies in the Ürümqi museum. And he couldn't help wondering whether some of the scientific detective methods now being applied to the Ice Man, including DNA analysis of the preserved tissue, could help solve the riddle of Xinjiang.

With China having become more receptive to outside scholars, Mair decided to launch a collaborative investigation with Chinese scientists. He contacted Ninjiang's leading archeologist, Wang Binghua, who had found the first of the mummies in 1978. Before Wang's work in the region, evidence of early settlements was virtually unknown. In the late 1970s, though, Wang had begun a systematic search for ancient sites in the northeast corner of Xinjiang Province. "He knew that ancient peoples would have located their settlements along a stream to have a reliable source of water," says Mair. As he followed one such stream from its source in the Tian Shan, says Mair, "Wang would ask the local inhabitants whether they had ever found any broken bowls, wooden artifacts, or the like. Finally one older man told him of a place locals called Qizilchoqa, or 'Red Hillock.' "

It was here that the first mummies were unearthed. This was also the first site visited last summer by Mair and his collaborator, Paolo Francalacci, an anthropological geneticist at the University of Sassari in Italy. Reaching Qizilchoqa involved a long, arduous drive east from Ürümqi. For a day and a half Mair, Wang, and their colleagues bounced inside four-wheel-drive Land Cruisers across rock-strewn dirt roads

from one oasis to the next. Part of their journey eastward followed China's Silk Road, the ancient trade route that evolved in the second century B.C. and connected China to the West. Finally they reached the village of Wupu; goats scattered as the vehicles edged their way through the back streets. Next to the village was a broad green ravine, and after the researchers had maneuvered their way into it, the sandy slope of the Red Hillock suddenly became visible.

"It wasn't much to look at," Mair recalls, "about 20 acres on a gentle hill ringed by barbed wire. There's a brick work shed where tools are stored and the visiting archeologists sleep. But you could spot the shallow depressions in the sand where the graves were." As Mair watched, Wang's team began digging up several previously excavated corpses that had been reburied for lack of adequate storage facilities at the Ürümqi museum. Mair didn't have to wait long; just a couple of feet below the sand, the archeologists came across rush matting and wooden logs covering a burial chamber lined with mud bricks. Mair was surprised by the appearance of the logs; they looked as if they had just been chopped down. Then the first mummy emerged from the roughly six-foot-deep pit. For Mair the moment was nearly as charged with emotion as that first encounter in the museum. "When you're standing right next to these bodies, as well preserved as they are, you feel a sense of personal closeness to them," he says. "It's almost supernatural—you feel that somehow life persists even though you're looking at a dried-out corpse."

Mair and Francalacci spent the day examining the corpses, with Francalacci taking tissue samples to identify the genetic origins of the corpses. "He took small samples from unexposed areas of the bodies," says Mair, "usually from the inner thighs or underarms. We also took a few bones, usually pieces of rib that were easy to break off, since bone tends to preserve the DNA better than muscle tissue or skin." Francalacci wore a face mask and rubber gloves to avoid contaminating the samples with any skin flakes

that would contain his own DNA. The samples were placed in collection jars, sealed, and labeled; Mair made a photographic and written record of the collection.

So far 113 graves have been excavated at Qizilchoqa; probably an equal number remain to be explored. Based on carbon-14 dating by the Chinese and on the style of painted pots found with the corpses, all the mummies here appear to date to around 1200 B.C. Most were found on their backs with their knees drawn up—a position that allowed the bodies to fit into the small burial chambers. They are fully clothed in brightly colored woolen fabrics, felt and leather boots, and sometimes leather coats. The men generally have light brown or blond hair, while the women have long braids; one girl has blue tattoo marks on her wrist. Besides pottery, resting alongside them are simple items from everyday life: combs made of wood, needles of bone, spindle whorls for spinning thread, hooks, bells, loaves of bread, and other food offerings. The artifacts provide further proof that these were not the burial sites of the wealthy: had the graves been those of aristocrats, laden with precious bronzes, they probably would have been robbed long ago.

However, Wang and his colleagues have found some strange, if not aristocratic, objects in the course of their investigations in Xinjiang. At a site near the town of Subashi, 310 miles west of Qizilchoqa, that dates to about the fifth century B.C., they unearthed a woman wearing a two-foot-long black felt peaked hat with a flat brim. Though modern Westerners may find it tempting to identify the hat as the headgear of a witch, there is evidence that pointed hats were widely worn by both women and men in some central Asian tribes. For instance, around 520 B.C., the Persian king Darius recorded a victory over the "Sakas of the pointed hats"; also, in 1970 in Kazakhstan, just over China's western border, the grave of a man from around the same period yielded a two-foot-tall conical hat studded with magnificent gold-leaf decorations. The Subashi woman's formidable headgear, then, might be an ethnic badge or a symbol of prestige and influence.

Subashi lies a good distance from Qizilchoqa, and its site is at least seven centuries younger, yet the bodies and their clothing are strikingly similar. In addition to the "witch's hat," clothing found there included fur coats and leather mittens; the Subashi women also held bags containing small knives and herbs, probably for use as medicines. A typical Subashi man, said by the Chinese team to be at least 55 years old, was found lying next to the corpse of a woman in a shallow burial chamber. He wore a sheepskin coat, felt hat, and long sheepskin boots fastened at the crotch with a belt.

Another Subashi man has traces of a surgical operation on his neck; the incision is sewn up with sutures made of horsehair. Mair was particularly struck by this discovery because he knew of a Chinese text from the third century A.D. describing the life of Huatuo, a doctor whose exceptional skills were said to have included the extraction and repair of diseased organs. The text also claims that before surgery, patients drank a mixture of wine and an anesthetizing powder that was possibly derived from opium. Huatuo's story is all the more remarkable in that the notion of surgery was heretical to ancient Chinese medical tradition, which taught that good health depended on the balance and flow of natural forces throughout the body. Mair wonders if the Huatuo legend might relate to some lost Asian medical tradition practiced by the Xinjiang people. One clue is that the name Huatuo is uncommon in China and seems close to the Sanskrit word for medicine.

The woolen garments worn by the mummies may provide some clue to where exactly the Xinjiang people came from. A sample of cloth brought back by Mair was examined by University of Pennsylvania anthropologist Irene Good, a specialist in early Eurasian textiles. Examining the cloth under a low-power microscope, she saw that the material was not, strictly speaking, wool at all. Wool comes from the undercoat of a sheep; this material appeared to have been spun from the coarse outer hair (called kemp) of a sheep or goat. Despite the crudeness of the fibers, they were carefully dyed green, blue, and brown to make a plaid design. They were also woven in a diagonal twill pattern that indicated the use of a rather sophisticated loom. The overall technique, Good believes, is "characteristically European" and, she says, the textile is "the easternmost known example of this kind of weaving technique." Similar textile fragments, she notes, have been recovered from roughly the same time period at sites in Germany, Austria, and Scandinavia.

Another hint of outside connections struck Mair as he roamed across Qizilchoqa. Crossing an unexcavated grave, he stumbled upon an exposed piece of wood, which he quickly realized had once belonged to a wagon wheel. The wheel was made in a simple but distinctive way, by doweling together three carved, parallel wooden planks. This style of wheel is significant: wagons with nearly identical wheels are known from the grassy plains of the Ukraine from as far back as 3000 B.C.

Most researchers now think the birthplace of horse-drawn vehicles and horse riding was in the steppes east and west of the Urals rather than in China or the Near East. As archeologist David Anthony and his colleagues have shown through microscopic study of ancient horse teeth, horses were already being harnessed in the Ukraine 6,000 years ago. The Ukraine horses, Anthony found, show a particular kind of tooth wear identical to that of modern horses that "fight the bit." The world's earliest high-status vehicles also seem to have originated in the steppes; recent discoveries of wooden chariots with elaborate spoked wheels were reported by Anthony to date to around 2000 B.C. Chariots do not seem to have appeared in China until some 800 years later.

A number of artifacts recovered from the Xinjiang burials provide important evidence for early horse riding. Qizil-choqa yielded a wooden bit and leather reins, a horse whip consisting of a single strip of leather attached to a wooden handle, and a wooden cheekpiece with leather straps. This last object was decorated with an image of the sun that was probably religious in nature and that was also found tattooed on some of the mummies. And at Subashi, archeologists discovered a padded leather saddle of exquisite workmanship.

Could the Xinjiang people have belonged to a mobile, horse-riding culture that spread from the plains of eastern Europe? Does this explain their European appearance? If so, could they have been speaking an ancient forerunner of modern European, Indian, and Iranian languages? Though the idea is highly speculative, a number of archeologists and linguists think the spread of Indo-European languages may be linked to the gradual spread of horse-riding and horse-drawn-vehicle technology from its origins in Europe 6,000 years ago. The Xinjiang mummies may help confirm these speculations.

Intriguingly, evidence of a long-extinct language belonging to the Indo-European family does exist in central Asia. This language, known as Tocharian, is recorded in manuscripts from the eighth century A.D., and solid evidence for its existence can be found as far back as the third century. Tocharian inscriptions from this period are also found painted in caves in the foothills of the mountains west of Ürümqi, along with paintings of swashbuckling knights wielding long swords. The knights are depicted with full red beards and European faces. Could the Xinjiang people have been their ancestors, speaking an early version of Tocharian? "My guess is that they would have been speaking *some* form of Indo-European," comments Don Ringe, a historical linguist at the University of Pennsylvania, "but whether it was an early form of Tocharian or some other branch of the family, such as Indo-Iranian, we may never know for sure."

Perhaps a highly distinctive language would help explain why the Xinjiang people's distinctive appearance and culture persisted over so many centuries. Eventually they might well have assimilated with the local population—the major ethnic group in the area today, the Uygur, includes people with unusually fair hair and complexions. That possibility will soon be investigated when Mair, Francalacci, and their Chinese colleagues compare DNA from ancient mummy tissue with blood and hair samples from local people.

Besides the riddle of their identity, there is also the question of what these fair-haired people were doing in a remote desert oasis. Probably never wealthy enough to own chariots, they nevertheless had wagons and well-tailored clothes. Were they mere goat and sheep farmers? Or did they profit from or even control prehistoric trade along the route that later became the Silk Road? If so, they probably helped spread the first wheels and certain metalworking skills into China.

"Ultimately I think our project may end up having tremendous implications for the origins of Chinese civilization," Mair reflects. "For all their incredible inventiveness, the ancient Chinese weren't cut off from the rest of the world, and influences didn't just flow one way, from China westward."

Unfortunately, economics dictates that answers will be slow in coming. The Chinese have little money to spare for this work, and Wang and his team continue to operate on a shoestring. Currently most of the corpses and artifacts are stored in a damp, crowded basement room at the Institute of Archeology in Ürümqi, in conditions that threaten their continued preservation. If Mair's plan for a museum can be financed with Western help, perhaps the mummies can be moved. Then, finally, they'll receive the study and attention that will ultimately unlock their secrets.

The Search for a Bronze Age Shipwreck

**Cemal Pulak
and Donald A. Frey**

The Late Bronze Age shipwreck discovered by Peter Throckmorton in 1959 at Cape Gelidonya, Turkey, is a milestone in the history of underwater archaeology. Excavated by George Bass and Throckmorton, it was the first ancient wreck studied in its entirety on the floor of the Mediterranean (ARCHAEOLOGY 14 [1961]: 78–87). No less important has been the scholarly controversy stirred by the publication of the excavation.

Based on artifacts from the site, Bass—today the Archaeological Director of the Institute of Nautical Archaeology—concluded that the wreck at Cape Gelidonya was all that remained of a Canaanite (Bronze Age Phoenician) or Cypriote vessel that sank in the thirteenth or very early twelfth century B.C. This agreed with the fact that its cargo of four-handled copper ingots, superficially shaped like dried ox-hides, represented the distinct type usually associated with Syrian traders on fourteenth and thirteenth-century Egyptian tomb paintings. Restudy of earlier finds in Greece, Cyprus and the Levant, combined with the evidence from Cape Gelidonya, now suggested that a greater role should be attributed to Semitic seafarers in those centuries than was generally accepted.

These conclusions were subsequently questioned by some scholars. Could the ship not have been Mycenaean

Greek, its Syro-Palestinian seal, lamp, weights, scarabs, pottery, and stone mortars simply bric-a-brac taken on board by Mycenaean sailors? Was its cargo not the product of twelfth-century Mycenaean colonists on Cyprus? Was there not, in fact, a Mycenaean monopoly on maritime trade in the eastern Mediterranean?

In an attempt to answer these questions, a number of efforts were made to relocate the other Late Bronze Age wrecks, almost certainly earlier, which yielded "ox-hide" ingots in the opening decades of this century. Peter Throckmorton looked in vain for the wreck off Euboea; he fears it might now be covered by modern harborworks. Donald Frey, using directions given to Throckmorton by an elderly Greek sponger who knew the site, searched unsuccessfully for a wreck not far from Cape Gelidonya, in the Bay of Antalya.

Although scattered copper and tin ingots later were found off the coast of Israel, and although the first mold for casting the same type of "ox-hide" ingot was found in a thirteenth-century Ugaritic palace in Syria, decades passed without the discovery of another ingot-carrying Late Bronze Age shipwreck. If one were to be found at all, it seemed, it would be only by chance. But archaeologists must strive to improve their chances!

First, a method of locating wrecks is needed. We cannot, as do archaeologists seeking wrecks of much later periods, depend on archival work for clues to the whereabouts of specific disasters. Nor are magnetometers, so useful in sensing the iron remains from later ships, helpful in locating such early vessels. Metal detectors are of limited range. Random search by sonar has proven to be possible but extremely inefficient. Visual search, then, re-

Underwater archaeologists in the Mediterranean rely heavily on sightings of ancient underwater remains by sponge divers. A typical sponge boat has four divers, a captain who may also be a diver, and the captain's son who helps out with daily chores. This boat is appropriately named "May You Succeed."

mains the best means of spotting exposed cargoes of ancient shipwrecks.

For visual search, a diver is sometimes towed on a wing-like diving plane, but this method is limited by the length of time a diver can stay at depth without risking decompression sickness. To overcome this limitation, we have used a device called a Towvane, a sealed capsule which is towed with a pilot controlling his depth from inside; because the pressure in the capsule remains the same as that at the surface, the pilot may stay down indefinitely. Although the Towvane can be maneuvered up and down by its occupant, it is difficult to steer to the left or right for close inspection of sighted objects. Yet another technique is to tow a television camera instead of a person, but the scope of view is limited, and it is difficult to return exactly to objects that have passed briefly by on the screen.

At present our best "remote-sensing device" remains that used by Peter Throckmorton—the Turkish sponge diver. Every year about 50 of the 150 to 200 registered sponge boats in southern Turkey sail out for sponges. Sponges have been so depleted, and their prices have dipped so low, that about half of these boats supplement or even earn the major part of their income by illegal spear fishing. In spite of the small number of boats that deal only with sponges, the total amount of time their divers spend exploring the seabed is considerable.

Each sponge boat has a minimum crew of about five divers, and usually the captain's son to help out with the daily chores of shipboard life. The captain himself may or may not be a diver. The boats usually set out to sea sometime in late May or early June and do not return until the end of September or early October. The so-called "romantic" and "adventurous" lives of these men are, in reality, unfortunate dramas. They dive at least twice and often three times a day to depths that are not even registered on air-diving tables. Their equipment consists of a shared, well-patched rubber suit (one size for all!), a face mask, fins, and diving weights probably cast from an-

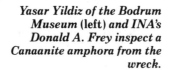

Yasar Yildiz of the Bodrum Museum (left) *and INA's Donald A. Frey inspect a Canaanite amphora from the wreck.*

cient lead anchor stocks recovered from the sea. Their breathing system, known as *narghile,* or *hookah,* utilizes an industrial air compressor "souped up" to deliver greater pressure for the deeper dives through a hose connected to a vintage regulator. Most of the spongers are ignorant of diving facts, and those who seem to understand the mechanism involved in decompression rely on undigested information mingled with old wives' tales. Time seems to have stood still in the sponge industry.

Four months are usually spent at sea in a small, overcrowded and miserable boat. Port calls are made only if the divers are short of victuals or diesel fuel to run their engines and diving compressors. Occasionally the sponges

have to be unloaded to make room on the already cramped boats. They are spread out on a pier and allowed to dry under the sun. The inferior pieces are culled and the remaining collection is sorted according to size, shape, quality, and species. Throughout the procedure, great care is taken not to mix the individual batches of sponges belonging to specific divers—and the inexperienced divers stand out with their modest collections. Once dried, the sponges are stuffed into large sacks to be shipped home for storage until the market season in the fall.

Usually each sponge diver gives half of his share to the captain and owner of the boat in return for his food and the use of the vessel. A seasoned diver on a very lucky day can collect nearly a kilo of sponges, but the average usually does not exceed half a kilo per day. At best, a kilo of sponges sold for about 8,000 T.L. ($27) in 1983. A hardworking diver, then, could expect to earn about $1,500 to $2,500 for the whole season, half of which would be given to the captain—hardly worth the risk of losing the use of an arm, leg or entire body, or, for some, even their lives.

Five spongers diving three times a day for half an hour on the seabed totals an incredible seven-and-a-half hours of bottom time per boat per day (not including decompression time). For the full season of four months, or 100 working days, divers on 25 boats would spend 18,750 hours scanning the seabed along the Mediterranean coast. This amounts to over two years spent under water! This lifestyle is an invaluable resource for archaeologists to tap; no amount of remote sensing or any other means could accomplish so much for so little. The only input required by archaeologists is advising the divers as to what to look for under water. Most of the sponge divers do not know what ancient wrecks are, and instead look for modern steel hulls with high scrap values. Therefore, continued marginal efforts on our part—giving slide shows and talks during the dormant winter months, and contacting the sponge boats during summers while all information is still fresh—are well worthwhile. The rewards are certainly high.

During the past 13 years, the Institute of Nautical Archaeology (INA) has located 73 wrecks along the coast of Turkey. Only two were discovered by remote sensing equipment, while the remainder were either shown to us by sponge divers or relocated following their leads. In recent years, a few wrecks have been discovered purely by the efforts of our staff through surveying areas that were dangerous to sailing vessels of antiquity. Even then, we found sponge divers who remembered the same wrecks after we described them. Many other sites, with their exact locations clouded over the years,

"Ox-hide" ingots from the Cape Gelidonya wreck are displayed in the Bodrum Museum of Underwater Archaeology. On the wall is a replica of the painting from the Tomb of Huy at Thebes, Egypt, depicting the Syrian chieftains of Retnu bringing tribute to the pharaoh. (Below) This sketch plan of the site made in 1983 gives some indication of the wealth of finds.

are imprinted on the minds of this dying breed of weathered old men.

Early INA surveys were somewhat haphazard affairs. If we learned of a wreck from a sponge diver, it was necessary to wait for a full-scale survey project, requiring weeks of outfitting a local trawler as a mobile diving platform, and gathering an adequate team. By that time, it often was impossible to find the sponge diver, who might be at sea.

The purchase of the *Virazon* by the Institute of Nautical Archaeology in 1978 changed the picture radically. Now INA has a 65-foot, steel-hulled vessel, fully outfitted with a double-lock recompression chamber, high and low pressure compressors, radar, sonar, a photographic darkroom, living quarters for a dozen diving archaeologists, and an eight-foot drafting table. For the first time we have at our disposal the means to practically, economically and safely search for ship-wrecks along the coast of Turkey. Now we can visit a site within a few days of learning of it, accompanied by the diver who reported it, even during the course of an excavation campaign.

With the acquisition of the *Virazon*, INA President Donald A. Frey insti-tuted a long-range survey program in cooperation with the Bodrum Museum of Underwater Archaeology. Frey travels the coast, meeting dozens of sponge divers. During the off-season he and other Turkish-speaking mem-bers of the survey team visit the vil-lages where spongers winter, and every autumn he directs a one to two-month survey from the *Virazon*.

During the fall of 1982 a diver named Mehmet Çakir told another sponge diver that he had seen "metal biscuits with ears" on the seabed at Ulu Burun near Kaş, at a depth exceed-ing 40 meters. Çakir's friend already knew the INA survey team, and asked him to draw one of the "biscuits." He immediately recognized the familiar "ox-hide" ingot shape and advised Çakir to report his discovery to the Bodrum Museum, where, he was told, a group of underwater archaeologists were looking for wrecks with ingots of similar shape. A team from INA and the Bodrum Museum soon dived on the site and raised an ingot for identi-fication. So began the excitement of a landmark discovery.

In 1983 Pulak received permission from the Turkish Ministry of Culture and Tourism to direct another INA survey. As part of the survey, we ar-rived in the town of Kaş on August 18 to investigate the Bronze Age wreck in preparation for its full-scale excavation starting in 1984.

We located the wreck area imme-diately and moored the *Virazon* di-rectly above it. At the end of a week INA director Jack W. Kelley, a driving force behind our search for a Bronze Age ship, had made a plan of the site based on photomosaics and direct mea-surements. We established that the wreck lay between 43 and 51 meters deep, spread over an area 10 by 18 meters. Gigantic limestone blocks which had toppled from the cliffs

Archaeologists survey the wreck site. The large, boulder-like outcrop to the left and the large storage jar covered with sea-growth are directly beneath the diver on the right.

In this common scene dur-ing the sponge season, sponges are spread out to dry on the pier at Kaş before being shipped home.

above the wreck dominated the up-slope portion of the site. A large, boul-der-like outcrop marked the center of the visible wreckage. Some artifacts lay scattered on the inclined rocky bottom surrounding the boulder, while others were caught in the abounding sand pockets.

The wreck appeared to be far larger than that at Cape Gelidonya. Visible cargo included 84 full and half-size "ox-hide" ingots, some still stacked as they once had been stowed on the ship. Surveying with a metal detector revealed additional ingots buried in the sand pockets. Small plano-convex "bun" ingots lay among the "ox-hide" ingots.

Six large storage jars (*pithoi*) in three sizes were completely covered with sea-growth and originally were mistaken for boulders. The largest, along with two medium-sized pithoi, occupied the central part of the visible wreckage, directly above the boulder, while the others had rolled down the terraced seabed. The sixth and smallest jar still remained upslope where it probably came to rest with the ship. Eight Canaanite amphoras also were seen upslope of the outcrop. The intact pithoi and amphoras contained sediments that can be collected and analyzed, as is now routine on our excavations, providing new knowledge of the perishable export goods of the East.

Two large stone anchors of the type built into temple walls at Byblos and Ugarit on the Syrian coast, and Kition on Cyprus, lay close to the amphoras. The larger, rectangular stone had slid into the base of one of the medium-sized pithoi and caused it to fracture, while the second slab, with a square hole for a hawser, was partially hidden under "ox-hide" ingots. Lying on the latter slab, miraculously intact, was a ladle-shaped, terracotta wall bracket of a type found on Cyprus and at Ugarit in Syria. Similar objects found on land bear smoke-blackened stains suggesting their use as lamps, torch holders or, most likely, incense burners. Three pilgrim flasks of Canaanite type were also visible, one on the outer edge of the site, while the others were half buried, mouth down, between the two prominent rows of stacked ingots.

Another fully exposed stone anchor estimated at weighing about 200 kilograms could be observed on the deeper end of the wreck. It is pierced at the narrower end of its slightly tapered body for the securement of a hawser. Bronze Age stone anchors have been recovered in some numbers from the sea in the past, but never before from a datable ship.

The discovery of even the slightest hull remnants, we knew, would immensely increase our almost non-existent knowledge of Bronze Age ship construction in the Mediterranean. Sand from the area thought most likely to yield hull remains was brushed gently away. After a few hand strokes, a well-preserved piece of wood, perhaps an element of the ship's hull, emerged from beneath its protective blanket of sand. A smaller, contorted fragment, most probably part of the ship's dunnage, was recovered for analysis and later identified as pistachio.

A small sample removed from larger lumps of grayish-white, brittle material found in the vicinity of the wood was later shown in a laboratory to be 99.5 percent pure tin. To establish a tentative date for the wreck we also raised one bun ingot, one pilgrim flask, the hanging wall lamp, and one amphora, all of which were transported to the Bodrum Museum of Underwater Archaeology. Preliminary studies showed these to fit most comfortably in the fourteenth century B.C., with the first half of that century providing the closest parallel for the pilgrim flask.

Information gained during the survey was sufficient to plan a full-scale excavation of the shipwreck at Ulu Burun. INA's first summer campaign, in 1984, was directed by George F. Bass, with Pulak serving as assistant director. The excavation was financed by the Institute, Texas A&M University and the National Geographic Society.

Finds in 1984 were extraordinary. No other single site—on land or under water—will have provided so much primary evidence for the movement of raw materials in the Late Bronze Age.

Both copper and tin ingots of ox-hide shape were in abundance. The first evidence for shipments of raw glass appeared in the form of nearly 20 blue, discoid ingots. About seven inches in diameter, and two inches thick, the ingots were probably used to fashion jewelry and perhaps even drinking vessels. Both elephant and hippopotamus ivory appeared. One Canaanite amphora was filled with glass beads, and others among the three dozen raised contained resin, yellow arsenic, grape seeds, olive pits, and materials still being analyzed. A gold pectoral in the form of a hawk, probably of Canaanite origin, was found near a Mycenaean (probably IIIA:2) *kylix;* nearby were a gold chalice, faience and amber beads, a Syrian pilgrim flask, and a Cypriote White-Slip "milk bowl." Not far distant were other Mycenaean wares and a seemingly Syrian gold medallion. Bronze weapons, at least some Canaanite, abound.

One of the pithoi contained stacks of Cypriote pottery—Bucchero, Base-Ring II, White-Slip II, and White-Shaved wares—along with terracotta lamps of apparent Syro-Palestinian origin. Other finds included weights, silver bracelets, bronze tools, a stone macehead, a stone tray, astragals, and, perhaps most important, a Mycenaean seal. Beneath a row of six anchors running across the ship was found a section of the ship's hull, its fir keel and planks secured with pegged mortise-and-tenon joints similar to those used in the construction of the Kyrenia ship of a millennium later.

Such exciting finds will surely continue as future seasons progress. We estimate it will take four or five summers to complete the job. Although its excavation may not resolve the controversy over early metallurgy and trade in the eastern Mediterranean, the Ulu Burun shipwreck will certainly provide exciting new data for a better understanding of the Late Bronze Age.

Experimental Archaeology

Some archaeologists would like to see experimental archaeology become a major subfield of the science of archaeology. Until recently, most archaeologists have viewed this approach as a supplementary technique to enhance archaeological data.

The criteria of experimental archaeology in the strictest sense is that an experiment must be set up in the present that will in some way reenact or recreate a past archaeological process. The idea underlying experimental archaeology is similar to the principle of *uniformitarianism* that Charles Lyell presented in the nineteenth century in order to interpret geological phenomena.

This principle is based on two ideas. One is that geological processes that occur in the present also occurred in the past. This would include such things as earthquakes, water erosion, mountain building, continental drift, volcanic activity, and so forth. The second idea is that the rate at which geological processes modified the crust of Earth is uniform (the same) in the present as it was in the past. For example, consider the Grand Canyon in the United States. This great wonder of geology was formed by water erosion. The canyon's depth consists of about one mile of sedimentary rock layers leveled down by the tremendous pressure of ages of water literally cutting into the rock. It is this same process that continues to erode rock at Niagara Falls. The processes that modify Earth's crust are universal.

In the case of Niagara Falls, for many years observers have been monitoring the rate at which the rock recedes each year due to water erosion. In this manner they have been able to establish a *uniform* rate of erosion. This does not mean that the rate of erosion at Niagara Falls is necessarily exactly the same every year. It means that given X amount of water pressure, a rock density of Y will erode at the rate of Z inches per year. Usually the sum total of the different rates of erosion over a period of years will be averaged, which may lead to a statement such as "the average rate of erosion per year at Niagara Falls is four and one half inches of rock."

Experimental archaeology is based on the same general principles. Usually archaeologically derived processes involved shorter time spans and can be stated with greater accuracy. However, archaeological processes also involve the eccentricities of human behavior and must be treated with considerable caution.

One variable in archaeology in which experimental archaeology may be used is with respect to questions about the state of preservation of archaeological materials. In archaeology there are many absolute dating methods that give good approximations of how old a thing is. One of the most frequently used is the radiocarbon dating method. However, people have a tendency to unconsciously assume that the more recent an artifact is, the better its state of preservation will be. And likewise, that the older an artifact is, the more deteriorated it will be.

The state of preservation of archaeological materials is dependent upon many variables, most particularly the original material of the artifact and the conditions of the medium (site) in which it is preserved. A nineteenth-century adobe mission in the Mojave desert in California may be so weathered as to be unrecognizable. This is because the extreme temperatures from very hot to very cold, which are typical of a low desert climate, tend to rapidly destroy any kind of matter. On the other hand, consistently wet or consistently dry conditions will tend to preserve organic matter in a relatively pristine state for long periods of time. The preservation of human remains is therefore very good in bogs (such as in Denmark) that are consistently damp, or in the coastal deserts of Peru, where the conditions are consistently dry over the millennia.

But archaeologists need not wait for such discoveries to be made. They may set up their own experiments in terms of preservation. Both material (artifacts) and medium (soil) may be infinitely varied and repeatedly tested and fine-tuned under laboratory conditions. Not only does this generate a set of relationships that may be used as a basis in any archaeological situation, it also acts as a cross check on other dating methods. For example, radiocarbon dates can be seriously skewed by unusual chemical conditions in the artifact, the soil, or by inadvertent contamination in the process of excavation or laboratory analysis. These dates may be salvaged by using experimentally generated data to correct for such contamination, or it may be shown that the samples are not correctable.

Keep in mind that preservation is only one of many archaeological concerns that may be enhanced through experimental archaeology. Experimental archaeology may also elucidate cultural historical reconstruction and questions of human behavior. In this unit, the University of Arizona's famous "Garbage Project" is examined. Modern garbology presents archaeologists with an opportunity to practice a kind of "sociology of garbage." What people say they do, eat, or practice is often quite different from what their garbage tells of their actual behavior. And furthermore, these deviations seem to vary in predictable patterns based on chosen variables such as income level, occupation, family unit, and so forth.

This study of modern garbology has also reinforced what archaeologists already know. That is, the recognition that written history or the information received from living informants is sometimes heavily biased in certain directions. These biases may be discerned through archaeological excavation. In fact, all anthropologists have to be somewhat wary of both the written and spoken word. Often the fish was not as long as the tale. A healthy dose of skepticism is always part of the recipe for scientific thinking.

Looking Ahead: Challenge Questions

Why do archaeologists study modern garbage? Does any other discipline do this?

Have you ever looked at your own garbage after a week? What might it tell you?

How much misinformation given to archaeologists is purposeful? Accidental?

Cultural anthropologists use "participant observation." Would an archaeologist do this?

If you want to know how something was done, what is the best way to find out?

Why do people give lip service to values they no longer practice?

What kinds of practical things can modern peoples learn from ancient peoples?

Diseases will spread differently among peoples due to what kinds of variables?

Yes, Wonderful Things

William Rathje and Cullen Murphy

On a crisp October morning not long ago the sun ascended above the Atlantic Ocean and turned its gaze on a team of young researchers as they swarmed over what may be the largest archaeological site in the world. The mound they occupied covers three thousand acres and in places rises more than 155 feet above a low-lying island. Its mass, estimated at 100 million tons, and its volume, estimated at 2.9 billion cubic feet, make it one of the largest manmade structures in North America. And it is known to be a treasure trove—a Pompeii, a Tikal, a Valley of the Kings—of artifacts from the most advanced civilization the planet has ever seen. Overhead sea gulls cackled and cawed, alighting now and then to peck at an artifact or skeptically observe an archaeologist at work. The surrounding landscape still supported quail and duck, but far more noticeable were the dusty, rumbling wagons and tractors of the New York City Department of Sanitation.

The site was the Fresh Kills landfill, on Staten Island, in New York City, a repository of garbage that, when shut down, in the year 2005, will have reached a height of 505 feet above sea level, making it the highest geographic feature along a fifteen-hundred-mile stretch of the Atlantic seaboard running north from Florida all the way to Maine. One sometimes hears that Fresh Kills will have to be closed when it reaches 505 feet so as not to interfere with the approach of aircraft to Newark Airport, in New Jersey, which lies just across the waterway called Arthur Kill. In reality, though, the 505-foot elevation is the result of a series of calculations designed to maximize the landfill's size while avoiding the creation of grades so steep that roads built upon the landfill can't safely be used.

Fresh Kills was originally a vast marshland, a tidal swamp. Robert Moses's plan for the area, in 1948, was to dump enough garbage there to fill the marshland up—a process that would take, according to one estimate, until 1968—and then to develop the site, building houses, attracting light industry, and setting aside open space for recreational use. ("The Fresh Kills landfill project," a 1951 report to Mayor Vincent R. Impelliteri observed, "cannot fail to affect constructively a wide area around it. It is at once practical and idealistic.") Something along these lines may yet happen when Fresh Kills is closed. Until then, however, it is the largest active landfill in the world. It is twenty-five times the size of the Great Pyramid of Khufu at Giza, forty times the size of the Temple of the Sun at Teotihuacan. The volume of Fresh Kills is approaching that of the Great Wall of China, and by one estimate will surpass it at some point in the next few years. It is the sheer physical stature of Fresh Kills in the hulking world of landfills that explains why archaeologists were drawn to the place.

To the archaeologists of the University of Arizona's Garbage Project, which is now entering its twentieth year, landfills represent valuable lodes of information that may, when mined and interpreted, produce valuable insights—insights not into the nature of some past society, of course, but into the nature of our own. Garbage is among humanity's most prodigious physical legacies to those who have yet to be born; if we can come to understand our discards, Garbage Project archaeologists argue, then we will better understand the world in which we live. It is this conviction that prompts Garbage Project researchers to look upon the steaming detritus of daily existence with the same quiet excitement displayed by Howard Carter and Lord George Edward Carnarvon at the unpillaged, unopened tomb of Tutankhamun.

"Can you see anything?" Carnarvon asked as Carter thrust a lighted candle through a hole into the gloom of the first antechamber. "Yes," Carter replied. "Wonderful things."

Garbage archaeology can be conducted in several ways. At Fresh Kills the method of excavation involved a mobile derrick and a thirteen-hundred-pound bucket auger, the latter of which would be sunk into various parts of the landfill to retrieve samples of garbage from selected strata. At 6:15 a.m. Buddy Kellett of the company Kellett's Well Boring, Inc., which had assisted with several previous Garbage Project landfill digs, drove one of the company's trucks, with derrick and auger collapsed for travel, straight up the steep slope of one of the landfill mounds. Two-thirds of the way up, the Garbage Project crew directed Kellett to a small patch of level ground. Four hydraulic posts were deployed from the stationary vehicle, extending outward to keep it safely moored. Now the derrick was raised. It supported a long metal rod that in turn housed two other metal rods; the apparatus, when pulled to its full length, like a telescope, was capable of penetrating the landfill to a depth of ninety-seven feet—enough at this particular spot to go clear through its bottom and into the original marsh that Fresh Kills had been (or into what was left of it). At the end of the rods was the auger, a large bucket made of high-tension steel: four feet high, three feet in diameter, and open at the bottom like a cookie cutter, with six graphite-and-steel teeth around the bottom's circumference. The bucket would spin at about thirty revolutions per minute and with such force that virtually nothing could impede its descent. At a Garbage Project excavation in Sunnyvale, California, in 1988, one of the first things the bucket hit in the cover dirt a few feet below the surface of the Sunnyvale Landfill was the skeleton of a car. The bucket's teeth snapped the axle, and drilled on.

The digging at Fresh Kills began. Down the whirring bucket plunged. Moments later it returned with a gasp, laden with garbage that, when released, spewed a thin vapor into the chill autumnal air. The smell was pungent, somewhere between sweet and disagreeable. Kellett's rig operator, David Spillers, did his job with the relaxation that comes of familiarity, seemingly oblivious to the harsh grindings and sharp clanks. The rest of the archaeological crew, wearing cloth aprons and heavy rubber gloves, went about their duties with practiced efficiency and considerable speed. They were veteran members of the Garbage Project's A-Team—its landfill-excavating arm—and had been through it all before.

Again a bucketful of garbage rose out of the ground. As soon as it was dumped Masakazu Tani, at the time a Japanese graduate student in anthropology at the University of Arizona (his Ph.D. thesis, recently completed, involves identifying activity areas in ancient sites on the basis of distributions of litter), plunged a thermometer into the warm mass. "Forty-three degrees centigrade," Tani called out. The temperature (equivalent to 109.4 degrees Fahrenheit) was duly logged. The garbage was then given a brusque preliminary examination to determine its generic source and, if possible, its date of origin. In this case the presence of telltale domestic items, and of legible newspapers, made both tasks easy. Gavin Archer, another anthropologist and a research associate of the Garbage Project, made a notation in the running log that he would keep all day long: "Household, circa 1977." Before the next sample was pulled up Douglas

Wilson, an anthropologist who specializes in household hazardous waste, stepped up to the auger hole and played out a weighted tape measure, eventually calling out, "Thirty-five feet." As a safety precaution, Wilson, like any other crew member working close to the sunken shaft on depth-measure duty, wore a leather harness tethered to a nearby vehicle. The esophagus created by the bucket auger was just large enough to accept a human being, and anyone slipping untethered a story or two into this narrow, oxygen-starved cavity would die of asphyxiation before any rescue could be attempted.

Most of the bucketfuls of garbage received no more attention than did the load labeled "Household, circa 1977." Some basic data were recorded for tracking purposes, and the garbage was left on a quickly accumulating backdirt pile. But as each of what would finally be fourteen wells grew deeper and deeper, at regular intervals (either every five or every ten feet) samples were taken and preserved for full-dress analysis. On those occasions Wilson Hughes, the methodical and serenely ursine co-director and field supervisor of the Garbage Project, and the man responsible for day-to-day logistics at the Fresh Kills dig, would call out to the bucket operator over the noise of the engine: "We'll take the next bucket." Then Hughes and Wilson would race toward the rig in a running crouch, like medics toward a helicopter, a plywood sampling board between them. Running in behind came a team of microbiologists and civil engineers assembled from the University of Oklahoma, the University of Wisconsin, and Procter & Gamble's environmental laboratory. They brought with them a variety of containers and sealing devices to preserve samples in an oxygen-free environment—an environment that would allow colonies of the anaerobic bacteria that cause most of the biodegradation in landfills (to the extent that biodegradation occurs) to survive for later analysis. Behind the biologists and engineers came other Garbage Project personnel with an assortment of wire mesh screens and saw horses.

Within seconds of the bucket's removal from the ground, the operator maneuvered it directly over the sampling board, and released the contents. The pile was attacked first by Phillip Zack, a civil engineering student from the University of Wisconsin, who, as the temperature was being recorded, directed portions of the material into a variety of airtight conveyances. Then other members of the team moved in—the people who would shovel the steaming refuse atop the wire mesh; the people who would sort and bag whatever didn't go through the mesh; the people who would pour into bags or cannisters or jars whatever did go through the mesh; the people who would label everything for the trip either back to Tucson and the Garbage Project's holding bins or to the laboratories of the various microbiologists. (The shortest trip was to the trailer-laboratory that Procter & Gamble scientists had driven from Cincinnati and parked at the edge of the landfill.) The whole sample-collection process, from dumping to sorting to storing, took no more than twelve minutes. During the Fresh Kills dig it was repeated forty-four times at various places and various depths.

As morning edged toward afternoon the bucket auger began to near the limits of its reach in one of the wells. Down through the first thirty-five feet, a depth that in this well would date back to around 1984, the landfill had been relatively dry. Food waste and yard waste—hot dogs, bread, and grass clippings, for, example—were fairly well preserved. Newspapers remained intact and easy to read, their lurid headlines ("Woman Butchered-Ex-Hubby Held") calling to mind a handful of yesterday's tragedies. Beyond thirty-five feet, however, the landfill became increasingly wet, the garbage increasingly unidentifiable. At sixty feet, a stratum in this well containing garbage from the 1940s and 1950s, the bucket grabbed a sample and pulled it toward the surface. The Garbage Project team ran forward with their equipment, positioning themselves underneath. The bucket rose majestically as the operator sat at the controls, shouting something over the noise. As near as anyone can reconstruct it now, he was saying, "You boys might want to back off some, 'cause if this wind hits that bucket. . . ." The operator broke off because the wind did hit that bucket, and the material inside—a gray slime, redolent of putrefaction—thoroughly showered the crew. It would be an exaggeration to suggest that the victims were elated by this development, but their curiosity was certainly piqued, because on only one previous excavation had slime like this turned up in a landfill. What was the stuff made of? How had it come to be? What did its existence mean? The crew members doggedly collected all the usual samples, plus a few extra bottles of slime for special study. Then they cleaned themselves off.

It would be a blessing if it were possible to study garbage in the abstract, to study garbage without having to handle it physically.* But that is not possible. Garbage is not mathematics. To understand garbage you have to touch it, to feel it, to sort it, to smell it. You have to pick through hundreds of tons of it, counting and weighing all the daily newspapers, the telephone books; the soiled diapers, the foam clamshells that once briefly held hamburgers, the lipstick cylinders

*A note on terminology. Several words for the things we throw away—"garbage," "trash," "refuse," "rubbish"—are used synonymously in casual speech but in fact have different meanings. *Trash* refers specifically to discards that are at least theoretically "dry"—newspapers, boxes, cans, and so on. *Garbage* refers technically to "wet" discards—food remains, yard waste, and offal. *Refuse* is an inclusive term for both the wet discards and the dry. *Rubbish* is even more inclusive: It refers to all refuse plus construction and demolition debris. The distinction between wet and dry garbage was important in the days when cities slopped garbage to pigs, and needed to have the wet material separated from the dry; it eventually became irrevelant, but may see a revival if the idea of composting food and yard waste catches on. We will frequently use "garbage" in this book to refer to the totality of human discards because it is the word used most naturally in ordinary speech. The word is etymologically obscure, though it probably derives from Anglo-French, and its earliest associations have to do with working in the kitchen.

coated with grease, the medicine vials still encasing brightly colored pills, the empty bottles of scotch, the half-full cans of paint and muddy turpentine, the forsaken toys, the cigarette butts. You have to sort and weigh and measure the volume of all the organic matter, the discards from thousands of plates: the noodles and the Cheerios and the tortillas; the pieces of pet food that have made their own gravy; the hardened jelly doughnuts, bleeding from their side wounds; the half-eaten bananas, mostly still within their peels, black and incomparably sweet in the embrace of final decay. You have to confront sticky green mountains of yard waste, and slippery brown hills of potato peels, and brittle ossuaries of chicken bones and T-bones. And then, finally, there are the "fines," the vast connecting mixture of tiny bits of paper, metal, glass, plastic, dirt, grit, and former nutrients that suffuses every landfill like a kind of grainy lymph. To understand garbage you need thick gloves and a mask and some booster shots. But the yield in knowledge—about people and their behavior as well as about garbage itself—offsets the grim working conditions.

To an archaeologist, ancient garbage pits or garbage mounds, which can usually be located within a short distance from any ruin, are always among the happiest of finds, for they contain in concentrated form the artifacts and comestibles and remnants of behavior of the people who used them. While every archaeologist dreams of discovering spectacular objects, the bread-and-butter work of archaeology involves the most common and routine kinds of discards. It is not entirely fanciful to define archaeology as the discipline that tries to understand old garbage, and to learn from that garbage something about ancient societies and ancient behaviors. The eminent archaeologist Emil Haury once wrote of the aboriginal garbage heaps of the American Southwest: "Whichever way one views the mounds—as garbage piles to avoid, or as symbols of a way of life—they nevertheless are features more productive of information than any others." When the British archae-

ologist Sir Leonard Woolley, in 1916, first climbed to the top of the ancient city of Carchemish, on the Euphrates River near the modern-day Turkish-Syrian border, he moistened his index finger and held it in the air. Satisfied, he scanned the region due south of the city—that is, downwind—pausing to draw on his map the location of any mounds he saw. A trench dug through the largest of these mounds revealed it to be the garbage dump Woolley was certain it was, and the exposed strata helped establish the chronological sequence for the Carchemish site as a whole. Archaeologists have been picking through ancient garbage ever since archaeology became a profession, more than a century ago, and they will no doubt go on doing so as long as garbage is produced.

Several basic points about garbage need to be emphasized at the outset. First, the creation of garbage is an unequivocal sign of a human presence. From Styrofoam cups along a roadway and urine bags on the moon there is an uninterrupted chain of garbage that reaches back more than two million years to the first "waste flake" knocked off in the knapping of the first stone tool. That the distant past often seems misty and dim is precisely because our earliest ancestors left so little garbage behind. An appreciation of the accomplishments of the first hominids became possible only after they began making stone tools, the debris from the production of which, along with the discarded tools themselves, are now probed for their secrets with electron microscopes and displayed in museums not as garbage but as "artifacts." These artifacts serve as markers—increasingly frequent and informative markers—of how our forebears coped with the evolving physical and social world. Human beings are mere placeholders in time, like zeros in a long number; their garbage seems to have more staying power, and a power to inform across the millennia that complements (and often substitutes for) that of the written word. The profligate habits of our own country and our own time—the sheer volume of the garbage that we create and must dispose of—

will make our society an open book. The question is: Would we ourselves recognize our story when it is told, or will our garbage tell tales about us that we as yet do not suspect?

That brings up a second matter: If our garbage, in the eyes of the future, is destined to hold a key to the past, then surely it already holds a key to the present. This may be an obvious point, but it is one whose implications were not pursued by scholars until relatively recently. Each of us throws away dozens of items every day. All of these items are relics of specific human activities—relics no different in their inherent nature from many of those that traditional archaeologists work with (though they are, to be sure, a bit fresher). Taken as a whole the garbage of the United States, from its 93 million households and 1.5 million retail outlets and from all of its schools, hospitals, government offices, and other public facilities, is a mirror of American society. Of course, the problem with the mirror garbage offers is that, when encountered in a garbage can, dump, or landfill, it is a broken one: our civilization is reflected in billions of fragments that may reveal little in and of themselves. Fitting some of the pieces back together requires painstaking effort—effort that a small number of archaeologists and natural scientists have only just begun to apply.

A third point about garbage is that it is not an assertion but a physical fact—and thus may sometimes serve as a useful corrective. Human beings have over the centuries left many accounts describing their lives and civilizations. Many of these are little more than self-aggrandizing advertisements. The remains of the tombs, temples, and palaces of the elite are filled with personal histories as recorded by admiring relatives and fawning retainers. More such information is carved into obelisks and stelae, gouged into clay tablets, painted or printed on papyrus and paper. Historians are understandably drawn to written evidence of this kind, but garbage has often served as a kind of tattle-tale, setting the record straight.

It had long been known, for example, that French as well as Spanish forts had been erected along the coast of South Carolina during the sixteenth century, and various mounds and depressions have survived into our own time to testify to their whereabouts. Ever since the mid-nineteenth century a site on the tip of Parris Island, South Carolina, has been familiarly known as the site of a French outpost, built in 1562, that is spelled variously in old documents as Charlesfort, Charlesforte, and Charles Forte. In 1925, the Huguenot Society of South Carolina successfully lobbied Congress to erect a monument commemorating the building of Charlesfort. Subsequently, people in nearby Beaufort took up the Charlesfort theme, giving French names to streets, restaurants, and housing developments. Gift shops sold kitschy touristiana with a distinctly Gallic flavor. Those restaurants and gift shops found themselves in an awkward position when, in 1957, as a result of an analysis of discarded matter discovered at Charlesfort, a National Park Service historian, Albert Manucy, suggested that the site was of Spanish origin. Excavations begun in 1979 by the archaeologist Stanley South, which turned up such items as discarded Spanish olive jars and broken majolica pottery from Seville, confirmed Manucy's view: "Charlesfort," South established, was actually Fort San Marcos, a Spanish installation built in 1577 to protect a Spanish town named Santa Elena. (Both the fort and the town had been abandoned after only a few years.)

Garbage, then, represents physical fact, not mythology. It underscores a point that can not be too greatly emphasized: Our private worlds consist essentially of two realities—mental reality, which encompasses beliefs, attitudes, and ideas, and material reality, which is the picture embodied in the physical record. The study of garbage reminds us that it is a rare person in whom mental and material realities completely coincide. Indeed, for the most part, the pair exist in a state of tension, if not open conflict.

Americans have always wondered, sometimes with buoyant playfulness, what their countrymen in the far future will make of Americans "now." In 1952, in a monograph he first circulated privately among colleagues and eventually published in *The Journal of Irreproducible Results,* the eminent anthropologist and linguist Joseph H. Greenberg—the man who would one day sort the roughly one thousand known Native American languages into three broad language families—imagined the unearthing of the so-called "violence texts" during an excavation of the Brooklyn Dodgers' Ebbets Field in the year A.D. 2026; what interpretation, he wondered, would be given to such newspaper reports as Yanks Slaughter Indians" and "Reese made a sacrifice in the infield"? In 1979 the artist and writer David Macaulay published *Motel of the Mysteries,* an archaeological site-report setting forth the conclusions reached by a team of excavators in the year A.D. 4022 who have unearthed a motel dating back to 1985 (the year, Macaulay wrote, in which "an accidental reduction in postal rates on a substance called third- and fourth-class mail literally buried the North Americans under tons of brochures, fliers, and small containers called FREE"). Included in the report are illustrations of an archaeologist modeling a toilet seat, toothbrushes, and a drain stopper (or, as Macaulay describes them, "the Sacred Collar . . . the magnificent 'plasticus' ear ornaments, and the exquisite silver chain and pendant"), all assumed to be items of ritual or personal regalia. In 1982 an exhibit was mounted in New York City called "Splendors of the Sohites"—a vast display of artifacts, including "funerary vessels" (faded, dusky soda bottles) and "hermaphrodite amulets" (discarded pop-top rings), found in the SoHo section of Manhattan and dating from the Archaic Period (A.D. 1950–1961), the Classical Period (1962–1975), and the Decadent Period (1976– c.1980).

Greenberg, Macaulay, and the organizers of the Sohites exhibition all meant to have some fun, but there is an uneasy undercurrent to their work, and it is embodied in the question: What are we to make of ourselves? The Garbage Project, conceived in 1971, and officially established at the University of Arizona in 1973, was an attempt to come up with a new way of providing serious answers. It aimed to apply *real* archaeology to this very question; to see if it would be possible to investigate human behavior "from the back end," as it were. This scholarly endeavor has come to be known as garbology, and practitioners of garbology are known as garbologists. The printed citation (dated 1975) in the *Oxford English Dictionary* for the meaning of "garbology" as used here associates the term with the Garbage Project.

In the years since its founding the Garbage Project's staff members have processed more than 250,000 pounds of garbage, some of it from landfills but most of it fresh out of garbage cans in selected neighborhoods. All of this garbage has been sorted, coded, and catalogued—every piece, from bottles of furniture polish and egg-shaped pantyhose packaging to worn and shredded clothing, crumpled bubble-gum wrappers, and the full range of kitchen waste. A unique database has been built up from these cast-offs, covering virtually every aspect of American life: drinking habits, attitudes toward red meat, trends in the use of convenience foods, the strange ways in which consumers respond to shortages, the use of contraceptives, and hundreds of other matters.*

*A question that always comes up is: What about garbage disposers? Garbage disposers are obviously capable of skewing the data in certain garbage categories, and Garbage Project researchers can employ a variety of techniques to compensate for the bias that garbage disposers introduce. Studies were conducted at the very outset of the Garbage Project to determine the discard differential between households with and without disposers, and one eventual result was a set of correction factors for various kinds of garbage (primarily food), broken down by subtype. As a general rule of thumb, households with disposers end up discarding in their trash about half the amount of food waste and food debris as households without disposers. It should be noted, however, that the fact that disposers have ground up some portion of a household's garbage often has little relevance to the larger issues the Garbage Project is trying to address. It means, for example, not that the Garbage Project's findings about the extent of food waste are invalid, but merely that its estimates are conservative.

The antecedents of the Garbage Project in the world of scholarship and elsewhere are few but various. Some are undeniably dubious. The examination of fresh refuse is, of course, as old as the human species—just watch anyone who happens upon an old campsite, or a neighbor scavenging at a dump for spare parts or furniture. The first systematic study of the components of America's garbage dates to the early 1900s and the work of the civil engineers Rudolph Hering (in New York) and Samuel A. Greeley (in Chicago), who by 1921 had gathered enough information from enough cities to compile *Collection and Disposal of Municipal Refuse,* the first textbook on urban trash management. In academe, not much happened after that for quite some time. Out in the field, however, civil engineers and solid-waste managers did now and again sort and weigh fresh garbage as it stood in transit between its source and destination, but their categories were usually simple: paper, glass, metal. No one sorted garbage into detailed categories relating to particular consumer discard patterns. No one, for example, kept track of phenomena as specific as the number of beer cans thrown away versus the number of beer bottles, or the number of orange-juice cans thrown away versus the number of pounds of freshly squeezed oranges, or the amount of candy thrown away in the week after Halloween versus the amount thrown away in the week after Valentine's Day. And no one ever dug into the final resting places of most of America's garbage: dumps (where garbage is left in the open) and sanitary landfills (where fresh garbage is covered every night with six to eight inches of soil).

Even as America's city managers over the years oversaw—and sometimes desperately attempted to cope with—the disposal of ever-increasing amounts of garbage, the study of garbage itself took several odd detours—one into the world of the military, another into the world of celebrity-watching, and a third into the world of law enforcement.

The military's foray into garbology occurred in 1941, when two enlisted men, Horace Schwerin and Phalen Golden, were forced to discontinue a survey they were conducting among new recruits about which aspects of Army life the recruits most disliked. (Conducting polls of military personnel was, they had learned, against regulations.) Schwerin and Golden had already discovered, however, that the low quality of the food was the most frequently heard complaint, and they resolved to look into this one matter with an investigation that could not be considered a poll. What Schwerin and Golden did was to station observers in mess halls to record the types of food that were most commonly wasted and the volume of waste by type of food. The result, after 2.4 million man-meals had been observed, was a textbook example of how garbage studies can produce not only behavioral insights but also practical benefits. Schwerin and Golden discovered that 20 percent of the food prepared for Army mess halls was eventually thrown away, and that one reason for this was simply excess preparation. Here are some more of their findings, as summarized in a wartime article that appeared in the *The Saturday Evening Post:*

Soldiers ate more if they were allowed to smoke in the mess hall. They ate more if they went promptly to table instead of waiting on line outside—perhaps because the food became cold. They ate more if they fell to on their own initiative instead of by command. They cared little for soups, and 65 percent of the kale and nearly as much of the spinach went into the garbage can. Favorite desserts were cakes and cookies, canned fruit, fruit salad, and gelatin. They ate ice cream in almost any amount that was served to them.

"That, sergeant, is an excellent piece of work," General George C. Marshall, the Army chief of staff, told Horace Schwerin after hearing a report by Schwerin on the research findings. The Army adopted many of Schwerin and Golden's recommendations, and began saving some 2.5 million pounds of food a day. It is perhaps not surprising to learn that until joining the Army Horace Schwerin had been in market research, and, among other things, had helped CBS to perfect a device for measuring audience reaction to radio shows.

The origins of an ephemeral branch of garbage studies focused on celebrities—"peeping-Tom" garbology, one might call it—seem to lie in the work of A. J. Weberman. Weberman was a gonzo journalist and yippie whose interest in the songs of Bob Dylan, and obsession with their interpretation, in 1970 prompted him to begin stealing the garbage from the cans left out in front of Dylan's Greenwich Village brownstone on MacDougal Street. Weberman didn't find much—some soiled Pampers, some old newspapers, some fast-food packaging from a nearby Blimpie Base, a shopping list with the word vanilla spelled "vannilla." He did, however, stumble into a brief but highly publicized career. This self-proclaimed "garbage guerrilla" quickly moved on to Neil Simon's garbage (it included a half-eaten bagel, scraps of lox, the Sunday *Times*), Muhammad Ali's (an empty can of Luck's collard greens, an empty roach bomb), and Abbie Hoffman's (a summons for hitchhiking, an unused can of deodorant, an estimate of the cost for the printing of *Steal This Book,* and the telephone numbers of Jack Anderson and Kate Millet). Weberman revealed many of his findings in an article in *Esquire* in 1971. It was antics such as his that inspired a prior meaning of the term "garbology," one very different from the definition established today.

Weberman's work inspired other garbage guerrillas. In January of 1975, the *Detroit Free Press* Sunday magazine reported on the findings from its raids on the garbage of several city notables, including the mayor, the head of the city council, the leader of a right-wing group, a food columnist, a disk jockey, and a prominent psychiatrist. Nothing much was discovered that might be deemed out of the ordinary, save for some of the contents of the garbage taken from a local Hare Krishna temple: a price tag from an Oleg Cassini garment, for example, and four ticket stubs from the Bel-Aire Drive-In Theater, which at the time was showing *Horrible House on the*

Hill and *The Night God Screamed.* Six months after the *Free Press* exposé, a reporter for the *National Enquirer,* Jay Gourley, drove up to 3018 Dumbarton Avenue, N.W., in Washington, D.C., and threw the five garbage bags in front of Secretary of State Henry A. Kissinger's house into the trunk of his car. Secret Service agents swiftly blocked Gourley's departure, but after a day of questioning allowed him to proceed, the garbage still in the trunk. Among Gourley's finds: a crumpled piece of paper with a dog's teeth marks on it, upon which was written the work schedules of the Secret Service agents assigned to guard the Secretary; empty bottles of Seconal and Maalox; and a shopping list, calling for a case of Jack Daniel's, a case of Ezra Brooks bourbon, and a case of Cabin Still bourbon. Gourley later returned most of the garbage to the Kissingers—minus, he told reporters, "several dozen interesting things."

After the Kissinger episode curiosity about the garbage of celebrities seems to have abated. In 1977 the *National Enquirer* sent a reporter to poke through the garbage of President Jimmy Carter's press secretary, Jody Powell. The reporter found so little of interest that the tabloid decided not to publish a story. In 1980 Secret Service agents apprehended A. J. Weberman as he attempted to abduct former President Richard Nixon's garbage from behind an apartment building in Manhattan. Weberman was released, without the garbage.

The third detour taken by garbage studies involves police work. Over the years, law enforcement agents looking for evidence in criminal cases have also been more-than-occasional students of garbage; the Federal Bureau of Investigation in particular has spent considerable time poring over the household trash of people in whom it maintains a professional interest. ("We take it on a case-by-case basis," an FBI spokesman says.) One of the biggest criminal cases involving garbage began in 1975 and involved Joseph "Joe Bananas" Bonanno, Sr., a resident of Tucson at the time and a man with alleged ties to organized crime that

were believed to date back to the days of Al Capone. For a period of three years officers of the Arizona Drug Control District collected Bonanno's trash just before the regular pickup, replacing it with "fake" Bonanno garbage. (Local garbagemen were not employed in the operation because some of them had received anonymous threats after assisting law enforcement agencies in an earlier venture.) The haul in evidence was beyond anyone's expectations: Bonanno had apparently kept detailed records of his various transactions, mostly in Sicilian. Although Bonanno had torn up each sheet of paper into tiny pieces, forensic specialists with the Drug Control District, like archaeologists reconstructing ceramic bowls from potsherds, managed to reassemble many of the documents and with the help of the FBI got them translated. In 1980 Bonanno was found guilty of having interfered with a federal grand jury investigation into the business operations of his two sons and a nephew. He was eventually sent to jail.

Unlike law-enforcement officers or garbage guerrillas, the archaeologists of the Garbage Project are not interested in the contents of any particular individual's garbage can. Indeed, it is almost always the case that a given person's garbage is at once largely anonymous and unimaginably humdrum. Garbage most usefully comes alive when it can be viewed in the context of broad patterns, for it is mainly in patterns that the links between artifacts and behaviors can be discerned.

The seed from which the Garbage Project grew was an anthropology class conducted at the University of Arizona in 1971 that was designed to teach principles of archaeological methodology. The University of Arizona has long occupied a venerable place in the annals of American archaeology and, not surprisingly, the pursuit of archaeology there to this day is carried on in serious and innovative ways. The class in question was one in which students undertook independent projects aimed precisely at showing links between various kinds of artifacts and various kinds of behavior. For example, one student, Sharon Thomas, decided to look into the relationship between a familiar motor function ("the diffusion pattern of ketchup over hamburgers") and a person's appearance, as manifested in clothing. Thomas took up a position at "seven different hamburger dispensaries" and, as people came in to eat, labeled them "neat" or "sloppy" according to a set of criteria relating to the way they dressed. Then she recorded how each of the fifty-seven patrons she studied—the ones who ordered hamburgers—poured ketchup over their food. She discovered that sloppy people were far more likely than neat people to put ketchup on in blobs, sometimes even stirring it with their fingers. Neat people, in contrast, tended to apply the ketchup in patterns: circles, spirals, and crisscrosses. One person (a young male neatly dressed in a body shirt, flared pants, and patent-leather Oxfords) wrote with ketchup what appeared to be initials.

Two of the student investigations, conducted independently by Frank Ariza and Kelly Allen, led directly to the Garbage Project. Ariza and Allen, wanting to explore the divergence between (or correlation of) mental stereotypes and physical realities, collected garbage from two households in an affluent part of Tucson and compared it to garbage from two households in a poor and, as it happens, Mexican-American part of town. The rich and poor families, each student found, ate about the same amount of steak and hamburger, and drank about the same amount of milk. But the poor families, they learned, bought more expensive child-education items. They also bought more household cleansers. What did such findings mean? Obviously the sample—involving only four households in all—was too small for the results even to be acknowledged as representative, let alone to provide hints as to what lay behind them. However, the general nature of the research effort itself—comparing garbage samples in order to gauge behavior (and, what is more, gauging behavior unobtrusively, thereby avoiding one of the great biases inher-

ent in much social science)—seemed to hold great promise.

A year later, in 1972, university students, under professorial direction, began borrowing samples of household garbage from different areas of Tucson, and sorting it in a lot behind a dormitory. The Garbage Project was under way. In 1973, the Garbage Project entered into an arrangement with the City of Tucson, whereby the Sanitation Division, four days a week, delivered five to eight randomly selected household pickups from designated census tracts to an analysis site that the Division set aside for the Project's sorters at a maintenance yard. (Wilson Hughes, who as mentioned earlier is the Garbage Project's co-director, was one of the first undergraduate garbage sorters.) In 1984 operations were moved to an enclosure where many of the university's dumpsters are parked, across the street from Arizona Stadium.

The excavation of landfills would come much later in the Garbage Project's history, when to its focus on issues of garbage and human behavior it added a focus on issues of garbage management. The advantage in the initial years of sorting fresh garbage over excavating landfills was a basic but important one: In landfills it is often quite difficult and in many cases impossible to get some idea, demographically speaking, of the kind of neighborhood from which any particular piece of garbage has come. The value of landfill studies is therefore limited to advancing our understanding of garbage in the aggregate. With fresh garbage, on the other hand, one can have demographic precision down to the level of a few city blocks, by directing pickups to specific census districts and cross-tabulating the findings with census data.

Needless to say, deciding just which characteristics of the collected garbage to pay attention to posed a conceptual challenge, one that was met by Wilson Hughes, who devised the "protocol" that is used by the Garbage Project to this day. Items found in garbage are sorted into one of 150 specific coded categories that can in turn be clustered into larger categories representing food

(fresh food versus prepared, health food versus junk food), drugs, personal and household sanitation products, amusement-related or educational materials, communications-related materials, pet-related materials, yard-related materials, and hazardous materials. For each item the following information is recorded on a standardized form: the date on which it was collected; the census tract from which it came; the item code (for example, 001, which would be the code for "Beef"); the item's type (for example, "chuck"); its original weight or volume (in this case, derived from the packaging); its cost (also from the packaging); material composition of container; brand (if applicable); and the weight of any discarded food (if applicable). The information garnered over the years from many thousands of such forms, filled out in pursuit of a wide variety of research objectives, constitutes the Garbage Project's database. It has all been computerized and amounts to some two million lines of data drawn from some fifteen thousand household-refuse samples. The aim here has been not only to approach garbage with specific questions to answer or hypotheses to prove but also to amass sufficient quantities of information, in a systematic and open-minded way, so that with the data on hand Garbage Project researchers would be able to answer any future questions or evaluate any future hypotheses that might arise. In 1972 garbage was, after all, still terra incognita, and the first job to be done was akin to that undertaken by the explorers Lewis and Clark.

From the outset the Garbage Project has had to confront the legal and ethical issues its research involves: Was collecting and sorting someone's household garbage an unjustifiable invasion of privacy? This very question has over the years been argued repeatedly in the courts. The Fourth Amendment unequivocally guarantees Americans protection from unreasonable search and seizure. Joseph Bonanno, Sr., tried to invoke the Fourth Amendment to prevent his garbage from being used as evidence. But garbage placed in a garbage can in a public thoroughfare, where it awaits removal by impersonal refuse collectors, and where it may be picked over by scavengers looking for aluminum cans, by curious children or neighbors, and by the refuse collectors themselves (some of whom do a thriving trade in old appliances, large and small), is usually considered by the courts to have been abandoned. Therefore, the examination of the garbage by outside parties cannot be a violation of a constitutional right. In the Bonanno case, U.S. District Court Judge William Ingram ruled that investigating garbage for evidence of a crime may carry a "stench," but was not illegal. In 1988, in *California v. Greenwood*, the U.S. Supreme Court ruled by a margin of six to two that the police were entitled to conduct a warrantless search of a suspected drug dealer's garbage—a search that led to drug paraphenalia, which led in turn to warrants, arrests, and convictions. As Justice Byron White has written, "The police cannot reasonably be expected to avert their eyes from evidence of criminal activity that could have been observed by any member of the public."

Legal issues aside, the Garbage Project has taken pains to ensure that those whose garbage comes under scrutiny remain anonymous. Before obtaining garbage for study, the Project provides guarantees to communities and their garbage collectors that nothing of a personal nature will be examined and that no names or addresses or other personal information will be recorded. The Project also stipulates that all of the garbage collected (except aluminum cans, which are recycled) will be returned to the community for normal disposal.

As noted, the Garbage Project has now been sorting and evaluating garbage, with scientific rigor, for two decades. The Project has proved durable because its findings have supplied a fresh perspective on what we know—and what we think we know—about certain aspects of our lives. Medical researchers, for example, have long made it their business to question people about their eating habits in order to uncover relationships between patterns of diet and patterns of disease. These researchers have also long suspected that people—honest, well-meaning people—may often be providing information about quantities and types and even brands of food and drink consumed that is not entirely accurate. People can't readily say whether they trimmed 3.3 ounces or 5.4 ounces of fat off the last steak they ate, and they probably don't remember whether they had four, five, or seven beers in the previous week, or two eggs or three. The average person just isn't paying attention. Are there certain patterns in the way in which people wrongly "self-report" their dietary habits? Yes, there are, and Garbage Project studies have identified many of them.

Garbage archaeologists also know how much edible food is thrown away; what percentage of newspapers, cans, bottles, and other items aren't recycled; how loyal we are to brand-name products and which have earned the greatest loyalty; and how much household hazardous waste is carted off to landfills and incinerators. From several truckloads of garbage and a few pieces of ancillary data—most importantly, the length of time over which the garbage was collected—the Garbage Project staff can reconstruct the community from which it came with a degree of accuracy that the Census Bureau might in some neighborhoods be unable to match.

Garbage also exposes the routine perversity of human ways. Garbage archaeologists have learned, for example, that the volume of garbage that Americans produce expands to fill the number of receptacles that are available to put it in. They have learned that we waste more of what is in short supply than of what is plentiful; that attempts by individuals to restrict consumption of certain foodstuffs are often counterbalanced by extra and inadvertent consumption of those same foodstuffs in hidden form; and that while a person's memory of what he has eaten and drunk in a given week is inevitably wide of the mark, his guess as to what a family member or even neighbor has eaten and drunk usually turns out to be more perceptive.

Some of the Garbage Project's research has prompted unusual forays into arcane aspects of popular culture. Consider the matter of those "amulets" worn by the Sohites—that is, the once-familiar detachable pop-top pull tab. Pull tabs first became important to the Garbage Project during a study of household recycling practices, conducted on behalf of the federal Environmental Protection Agency during the mid-1970s. The question arose: If a bag of household garbage contained no aluminum cans, did that mean that the household didn't dispose of any cans or that it had recycled its cans? Finding a way to answer that question was essential if a neighborhood's recycling rate was to be accurately determined. Pull tabs turned out to hold the key. A quick study revealed that most people did not drop pull tabs into the cans from which they had been wrenched; rather, the vast majority of people threw the tabs into the trash. If empty cans were stored separately for recycling, the pull tabs still went out to the curb with the rest of the garbage. A garbage sample that contained several pull tabs but no aluminum cans was a good bet to have come from a household that recycled.

All this counting of pull tabs prompted a surprising discovery one day by a student: Pull tabs were not all alike. Their configuration and even color depended on what kind of beverage they were associated with and where the beverage had been canned. Armed with this knowledge, Garbage Project researchers constructed an elaborate typology of pull tabs, enabling investigators to tease out data about beverage consumption—say, beer versus soda, Michelob versus Schlitz—even from samples of garbage that contained not a single can. Detachable pull tabs are no longer widely used in beverage cans, but the pull-tab typology remains useful even now. Among other things, in the absence of such evidence of chronology as a newspaper's dateline, pull tabs can reliably help to fix the dates of strata in a landfill. In archaeological parlance objects like these that have been widely diffused over a short period of time, and then abruptly disappear, are known as horizon markers.

The unique "punch-top" on Coors beer cans, for example, was used only between March of 1974 and June of 1977. (It was abandoned because some customers complained that they cut their thumbs pushing the holes open.) In landfills around the country, wherever Coors beer cans were discarded, punch-top cans not only identify strata associated with a narrow band of dates but also separate two epochs one from another. One might think of punch-tops playfully as the garbage equivalent of the famous iridium layer found in sediment toward the end of the Cretaceous Era, marking the moment (proponents of the theory believe) when a giant meteor crashed into the planet Earth, exterminating the dinosaurs.

All told, the Garbage Project has conducted nine full-scale excavations of municipal landfills in the United States and two smaller excavations associated with special projects. In the fall of 1991 it also excavated four sites in Canada, the data from which remains largely unanalyzed (and is not reflected in this book). The logistics of the landfill excavations are complex, and they have been overseen in all cases by Wilson Hughes. What is involved? Permission must be obtained from a raft of local officials and union leaders; indemnification notices must be provided to assure local authorities that the Garbage Project carries suffi-

cient insurance against injury; local universities must be scoured for a supply of students to supplement the Garbage Project team; in many cases construction permits, of all things, must be obtained in advance of digging. There is also the whole matter of transportation, not only of personnel but also of large amounts of equipment. And there is the matter of personal accommodation and equipment storage. The time available for excavation is always limited, sometimes extremely so; the research program must be compressed to fit it, and the staff must be "tasked" accordingly. When the excavation has been completed the samples need to be packed and shipped—frequently on ice—back to headquarters or to specialized laboratories. All archaeologists will tell you that field work is mostly laborious, not glamorous; a landfill excavation is archaeology of the laborious kind.

For all the difficulties they present, the Garbage Project's landfill digs have acquired an increasing timeliness and relevance as concerns about solid-waste disposal have grown. Even as the Garbage Project has trained considerable attention on garbage as an analytical tool it has also taken up the problem of garbage itself—garbage as a problem, garbage as symbolized by *Mobro 4000,* the so-called "garbage barge," which sailed from Islip, Long Island, on March 22, 1987, and spent the next fifty-five days plying the seas in search of a place to deposit its 3,168

tons of cargo. Strange though it may seem, although more than 70 percent of America's household and commercial garbage ends up in landfills, very little reliable data existed until recently as to a landfill's contents and biological dynamics. Much of the conventional wisdom about garbage disposal consists of assertions that turn out, upon investigation, to be simplistic or misleading: among them, the assertion that, as trash, plastic, foam, and fast-food packaging are causes for great concern, that biodegradable items are always more desirable than nonbiodegradable ones, that on a per capita basis the nation's households are generating a lot more garbage than they used to, and that we're physically running out of places to put landfills.

This is not to say that garbage isn't a problem in need of serious attention. It is. But if they are to succeed, plans of action must be based on garbage realities. The most critical part of the garbage problem in America is that our notions about the creation and disposal of garbage are often riddled with myth. There are few other subjects of public significance on which popular and official opinion is so consistently misinformed. . . .

Gaps—large gaps—remain in our knowledge of garbage, and of how human behavior relates to it, and of how best to deal with it. But a lighted candle has at least been seized and thrust inside the antechamber.

Paleolithic Paint Job

Two French archeologists are trying to get closer—much closer—to an ancient act of creation.

Roger Lewin

Roger Lewin is a writer in Washington, D.C., who specializes in human prehistory. His most recent book on the subject, Origins Reconsidered, *written with anthropologist Richard Leakey, was published last November. In 1989 Lewin was the recipient of the inaugural Lewis Thomas Award for Excellence in the Communication of Life Sciences. "Ancient human fossils stir the imagination," Lewin says, "but nothing matches the immediacy of prehistoric cave paintings in their ability to connect us with our past."*

"You have to be dressed right for this job," says Michel Lorblanchet, whose beret-capped head and white goatee make him a virtual caricature of a Frenchman. Lorblanchet, an archeologist with France's National Center for Scientific Research, slips out of mud-caked overalls and, with a colleague's help, struggles free of a pair of snug rubber boots. "It's pretty tight in there," he says, referring to a cave he has been working in, not to his boots. "You have to crawl a long way," he adds. "That's how we get so filthy." Lorblanchet is describing his efforts to study the ancient paintings deep inside the caves of the Lot Valley in southwest France. These depictions of a lost world—of Ice Age bison, horses, mammoths, and deer—were painted between 30,000 and 10,000 years ago.

They remain among the most haunting of all archeological finds.

The region here, known as Quercy, is dominated by rugged gray limestone plateaus intermittently sliced by fertile valleys and farmland. The cuisine of the area—a matter of constant and weighty discussion among the locals—is rich and robust: truffles, foie gras, duck confit, deeply flavorful lamb, and strong, dark wines. There is an earthy sensuosity about the place. When Lorblanchet, a native son of the area, describes it simply as "my country," you know he is speaking not only for himself but for generations of people whose roots are planted in this land. The Quercy sensuosity also apparently imbues Lorblanchet's unorthodox approach to studying cave art.

Traditionally cave art archeologists, perhaps to beef up their scientific credentials, have striven to understand the meaning of these paintings through objective inquiry. They have relied heavily on statistical analysis (which animals were represented where in the caves, for example) to test their hypotheses about the art. Lorblanchet's approach, by contrast, is freewheeling, subjective, experimental. He wants to get inside the minds of the early artists by reproducing some of their most famous works—not merely by tracing their outlines onto paper, as others have done in the past, but by replicating whole paintings on rock. Although he hopes to gain new insights, he has

no theory to prove or disprove. "Some of my colleagues think that experimentation without a preliminary theory is a waste of time," says Lorblanchet, the usual soft timbre of his voice gaining a slight edge of defiance. "But I totally disagree with them. I don't know what I will learn by temporarily becoming a Paleolithic painter, but I know I'll learn something."

Actually, for all its apparent unorthodoxy, Lorblanchet's work fits right into a new trend in cave art archeology. The Quercy archeologist is interested in how the early artists went about painting. Jean Clottes, another French archeologist, working in the Pyrenees, studies what their pigments were composed of. Although the two men's styles could hardly be more dissimilar—one personal and intuitive, the other extremely high-tech—they converge on the same novel question: What can we learn from the *paint* in these paintings? This investigative avenue doesn't ignore all that has gone before, of course, but builds on it.

The scholarly study of Ice Age art began in the 1920s with the great French prehistorian Abbé Henri Breuil, who saw it as an expression of hunting magic. Breuil based his conclusions on contemporary anthropological observations of the Arunta aborigines in central Australia. To ensure a plentiful supply of prey, the Arunta performed rituals during which they painted images of the prey—principally kangaroos—on rock faces. (Rituals of this kind are now well known among many of the world's remaining foraging peoples.)

Gradually though, archeologists began to doubt that hunting magic alone could explain all prehistoric cave art. The overthrow of this hypothesis in the 1960s was led by another French prehistorian, André Leroi-Gourhan. After surveying more than 60 painted caves, Leroi-Gourhan came to see order in the images' distribution. Stags often appeared in entrance-ways, ibex at the caves' peripheries, and horses, bison, oxen, and mammoths in the main chambers. As Leroi-Gourhan saw it, this structure represented the division of the world into males and females—or, more mystically, maleness and femaleness. The horse, the stag, and the ibex embodied maleness; the bison, the mammoth, and the ox embodied femaleness. According to this "structuralist" interpretation, all caves were decorated systematically to reflect this male-female duality, which suffused the mythology of Upper Paleolithic people.

This mode of structuralism was eventually done in by its all-embracing scope. It could be true, but there was no way of knowing: How could you test a rule with no exceptions? These days archeologists are taking more diverse approaches. Structure could still play a role, for example, but a more limited one—individual caves may well have been decorated with an overall pattern in mind. More attention is now being paid to the art's context. For example, Margaret Conkey, an archeologist at the University of California at Berkeley, argues that to understand what made the art meaningful you have to understand its social context. Which members of society produced the images? Was it the sacred right of a few important males? Were females involved, or even responsible for the art?

Still, even with a diversity of approaches, you can only hope for shadowy glimpses of Paleolithic life. "You know we should admit that it may never be possible to bridge the gap between the Paleolithic mind and the modern mind," cautions Lorblanchet. "There are many barriers that stop us." The most immediate barrier, he says, is that our perspective on the world is so utterly different from that of the Ice Age artists. The country here was once a frigid steppe, roamed by herds of exotic species that have long since gone extinct; and the lives of the hunters, so intimately attuned to the rhythms of nature, were vastly different from our own. "We are city dwellers, surrounded by angular build-ings, following artificial rhythms of life," says Lorblanchet. "How can we expect to be able to view the art as Upper Paleolithic people did?" Lorblanchet hopes his new approach will help answer that.

Lorblanchet's recent bid to re-create one of the most important Ice Age images in Europe was an affair of the heart as much as the head. "I tried to abandon my skin of a modern citizen, tried to experience the feeling of the artist, to enter the dialogue between the rock and the man," he explains. Every day for a week in the fall of 1990 he drove the 20 miles from his home in the medieval village of Cajarc into the hills above the river Lot. There, in a small, practically inaccessible cave, he transformed himself into an Upper Paleolithic painter. And not just any Upper Paleolithic painter, but the one who 18,400 years ago crafted the dotted horses inside the famous cave of Pech Merle.

You can still see the original horses in Pech Merle's vast underground geo-

Spit-painting in action: Michel Lorblanchet blows paint under his left hand to achieve an outline with a soft lower edge for the horse's back; spits pigment between parallel hands to paint the legs; makes a handprint; and spits dots through a hole in an animal skin.

logic splendor. You enter through a narrow passageway and soon find yourself gazing across a grand cavern to where the painting seems to hang in the gloom. "Outside, the landscape is very different from the one the Upper Paleolithic people saw," says Lorblanchet. "But in here, the landscape is the same as it was more than 18,000 years ago. You see what the Upper Paleolithic people experienced." No matter where you look in this cavern, the eye is drawn back to the panel of horses.

The two horses face away from each other, rumps slightly overlapping, their outlines sketched in black. The animal on the right seems to come alive as it merges with a crook in the edge of the panel, the perfect natural shape for a horse's head. But the impression of naturalism quickly fades as the eye falls on the painting's dark dots. There are more than 200 of them, deliberately distributed within and below the bodies and arcing around the right-hand horse's head and mane. More cryptic still are a smattering of red dots and half-circles and the floating outline of a fish. The surrealism is completed by six disembodied human hands stenciled above and below the animals.

Lorblanchet began thinking about re-creating the horses after a research trip to Australia over a decade ago. Not only is Australia a treasure trove of rock art, but its aboriginal people are still creating it. "In Queensland I learned how people painted by spitting pigment onto the rock," he recalls. "They spat paint and used their hand, a piece of cloth, or a feather as a screen to create different lines and other effects. Elsewhere in Australia people used chewed twigs as paintbrushes, but in Queensland the spitting technique worked best." The rock surfaces there were too uneven for extensive brushwork, he adds—just as they are in Quercy.

When Lorblanchet returned home he looked at the Quercy paintings with a new eye. Sure enough, he began seeing the telltale signs of spit-painting—lines with edges that were sharply demarcated on one side and fuzzy on the other, as if they had been airbrushed—instead of the brushstrokes he and others had assumed were there. Could you produce lines that were crisp on both edges with the same technique, he wondered, and perhaps dots too? Archeologists had long recognized that hand stencils, which are common in prehistoric art, were produced by spitting paint around a hand held to the wall. But no one had thought that entire animal images could be created this way. Before he could test his ideas, however, Lorblanchet had to find a suitable rock face—the original horses were painted on a roughly vertical panel 13 feet across and 6 feet high. With the help of a speleologist, he eventually found a rock face in a remote cave high in the hills and set to work.

Following the aboriginal practices he had witnessed, Lorblanchet first made a light outline sketch of the horses with a charred stick. Then he prepared black pigment for the painting. "My intention had been to use manganese dioxide, as the Pech Merle painter did," says Lorblanchet, referring to one of the minerals ground up for paint by the early artists. "But I was advised that manganese is somewhat toxic, so I used wood charcoal instead." (Charcoal was used as pigment by Paleolithic painters in other caves, so Lorblanchet felt he could justify his concession to safety.) To turn the charcoal into paint, Lorblanchet ground it with a limestone block, put the powder in his mouth, and diluted it to the right consistency with saliva and water. For red pigment he used ocher from the local iron-rich clay.

He started with the dark mane of the right-hand horse. "I spat a series of dots and fused them together to represent tufts of hair," he says, unself-consciously reproducing the spitting action as he talks. "Then I painted the horse's back by blowing the pigment

below my hand held so"—he holds his hand flat against the rock with his thumb tucked in to form a straight line—"and used it like a stencil to produce a sharp upper edge and a diffused lower edge. You get an illusion of the animal's rounded flank this way."

He experimented as he went. "You see the angular rump?" he says, pointing to the original painting. "I reproduced that by holding my hand perpendicular to the rock, with my palm slightly bent, and I spat along the edge formed by my hand and the rock." He found he could produce sharp lines, such as those in the tail and in the upper hind leg, by spitting into the gap between parallel hands. The belly demanded more ingenuity; he spat paint into a V-shape formed by his two splayed hands, rubbed it into a curved swath to shape the belly's outline, then finger-painted short protruding lines to suggest the animals' shaggy hair. Neatly outlined dots, he found, could not be made by blowing a thin jet of charcoal onto the wall. He had to spit pigment through a hole made in an animal skin.

"I spent seven hours a day for a week," he says. "Puff . . . puff . . . puff. . . . It was exhausting, particularly because there was carbon monoxide in the cave. But you experience something special, painting like that.

> *"You experience something special, painting like that. You are breathing the image onto the rock."*

You feel you are breathing the image onto the rock—projecting your spirit from the deepest part of your body onto the rock surface."

Was that what the Paleolithic painter felt when creating this image? "Yes, I know it doesn't sound very scientific," Lorblanchet says of his highly personal style of investigation, "but the intellectual games of the structuralists haven't got us very far, have they? Studying rock art shouldn't be an intellectual game. It is about understanding humanity. That's why I believe the experimental approach is valid in this case."

In contrast to Lorblanchet's free-wheeling style, Jean Clottes's research looks much more like science as usual—technical and analytical. Clottes, a scientific adviser on rock art to the French Ministry of Culture, works in the Midi-Pyrénées, a wild and mountainous region that abuts France's border with Spain. Many of

the caves in these mountains contain fine examples of Ice Age art. The most celebrated of the decorated caves is Niaux, which is approached by a gaping entrance on the steep northern slope of the Vicdessos Valley. About half a mile into this long, meandering cave is the Salon Noir, a towering cavern containing black images of horses, bison, ibex, and deer. Among the questions that preoccupied Clottes during his many visits to the Salon Noir was the age of these images. Were they all created at about the same time? And who created them?

One of the toughest problems in the study of rock art is accurately dating it. Radiocarbon dating, the surest method can be done only if charcoal is present in the paint. (The first such dates were obtained in 1989, when a technological advance—carbon dating by accelerator mass spectrometry—made it possible to use much smaller paint samples.) For the most part, however, archeologists have had to rely on what they term stylistic chronology. This basically depends on a subjective assessment of painting styles and on the assumption that particular conventions—such as the use of perspective—belong to particular periods. According to Leroi-Gourhan's chronology, nearly universally accepted, the paintings in the Salon Noir were painted in a uniform style typical of the period known as the Middle Magdalenian, which occurred some 13,000 to 14,000 years ago. But the pigment analysis that Clottes undertook with physicists Michel Menu and Philippe Walter revealed a different story.

Clottes's study was inspired by some work that Menu and Walter had done previously at the cave of La Vache, some 450 feet from Niaux, as the crow flies, on the southern side of the Vicdessos Valley. Although La Vache had no paintings, it did contain engraved bone objects, along with charcoal remains, that carbon dating established as being between 12,000 and 13,000 years old, an age corre-

Lorblanchet's re-creation of the ancient dotted horses; it took him a week to complete his Paleolithic masterpiece.

sponding to the period known as the Late Magdalenian. Trapped within the grooves of the engraved artifacts were residues of red and black paint Menu and Walter decided to find out what these paints were made from.

Back in Paris, at the Research Laboratory of the Museums of France, the two physicists used scanning electron microscopy, X-ray diffraction, and proton-induced X-ray emission to examine the physical and chemical properties of these paints. The pigment minerals held no surprises: the red was hematite and the black was basically manganese dioxide. The interest lay in the extender, a general term for materials that artists use to stretch pigment and, along with water, enhance its ease of application. Menu and Walter's analysis revealed that the extender in the La Vache paint was a mixture of biotite and feldspar, minerals easily obtained in the valley. But what intrigued the researchers was that biotite and feldspar don't occur together. "The Paleolithic painters had to mix them together, then grind them with the pigment to form paint," says Clottes. Quartz grinding stones bearing traces of paint production were discovered in the caves. "This tells us that the Paleolithic painters didn't just use whatever was available," Clottes points out "They had a specific recipe."

Was the La Vache recipe—call it recipe B, for biotite and feldspar—also used at Niaux? "Because of their proximity, there seemed a good chance that the hunters of La Vache belonged to the same social group that frequented Niaux," explains Clottes. "If so, they probably used the same pigments." Traditionally archeologists would have hesitated to take paint from prehistoric

Flightless Bird in Waterlogged Cave

The cave has been hailed as a sort of underwater Lascaux, the most exciting find since Lascaux's painted galleries were discovered five decades ago in southwest France. The hyperbole is understandable. The Cosquer cave, whose discovery was formally documented last year, can't really match Lascaux for artistry, but its images are unique and its place in prehistory is pivotal. The cave was found in 1991 by Henri Cosquer, a professional diver, while he was exploring the underwater grottoes at Cap Morgiu, near Marseilles. Its narrow entrance lies 121 feet below the surface of the Mediterranean, making it inaccessible to all but the most expert scuba divers—and enormously frustrating for landlubbing archeologists like Jean Clottes.

"I'd love to visit the Cosquer cave," says Clottes, who heads the committee formed by the French Ministry of Culture to plan future work at the promising site. "But I'm no diver, and the passage to it is very dangerous." Already the cave has claimed three lives. Shortly after its discovery, three diving enthusiasts died in the water darkness while worming their way along the 500-foot-long tunnel that leads from the entrance to the partially flooded inner caverns. The French government has since blocked the entrance to prevent further tragedy. Clottes himself has seen only video images of the paintings, transmitted by the cameras of the diving research team to a TV monitor on dry land.

The cave is important for several reasons, explains Clottes. While painted caves are common in southwest France and in the Pyrenees, nothing like Cosquer had ever been found in the country's southeast. Although Cosquer is half underwater, the walls above sea level are covered in decorations. There are hand stencils, finger tracings, cryptic symbols, and cross-hatchings and more than 100 engraved and painted animal images. Many of these show horses, bison, and ibex, which are typical of Ice Age art from Europe. But the images of marine animals—what look like jellyfish, and a kind of seabird—are unlike anything seen before. Early English-language reports referred to the large, portly birds with stunted wings as penguins. In fact, says Clottes, they are auks, flightless seabirds that became extinct in the Mediterranean about a century and a half ago.

The cave is all the more important because it is possible to carbon-date some of the images from charcoal flakes in the paint and from charcoal in hearths found on the cave floor. Carbon dating has shown that the hand stencils were done between 27,800 and 26,500 years ago, which makes them contenders for the oldest known paintings in the world. The animal images, some of which appear on top of the negative handprints, were crafted more than 8,000 years later. "In the short time since its discovery, Cosquer has become the most thoroughly dated painted cave known," observes Clottes.

Although getting to the cave is hard nowadays—a sort of athletic event in itself, as Clottes puts it—the prehistoric people who used the cave for their ancient rituals would have had no trouble reaching it. Sea levels at the time were at least 300 feet lower than they are today, so the cave was dry. Archeologists hope to make access easier by sinking a shaft through the limestone to a passage near the caverns. But first they will have to determine what effect such an opening would have on very fragile paintings that have been sealed in an air pocket for thousands of years. "Our first priority," says Clottes, "is the preservation of the paintings."

—Roger Lewin

images to test the idea, but Menu and Walter's methods required only a tiny quantity—less than half a milligram. In 1989 they received permission to lift 59 pinhead-size pieces of pigment from images in the Salon Noir and other locations in the cave. When these paint samples were analyzed, Clottes's intuition was proved correct: most were indeed recipe B, suggesting that they, too, might be 12,000 to 13,000 years old, just like those in the cave across the valley. His deductions were recently confirmed in a follow-up study capitalizing on one of the surprises of the Niaux pigment analysis. Tests revealed that the recipe B paint was layered: there were traces of charcoal under the black manganese pigment. Carbon dating on the charcoal flakes under one of the images corroborated that the paint was 12,800 years old, consistent with the paint at La Vache.

T he confirmation of Clottes's hunch, however, opened a can of worms. Based on Leroi-Gourhan's stylistic chronology, the Niaux paintings were up to 14,000 years old. Yet at least some of the Niaux paintings employed a paint recipe—recipe B—that carbon dating established as 12,000 to 13,000 years old. Did this mean that the recipe had been in use for at least 1,000 years? Or could there be something wrong with the chronology based on stylistic similarity?

"We didn't know what to make of it," says Clottes. "And the situation became more complicated, because in *some* paint samples from Niaux, we found a different recipe." In this paint mixture, call it recipe F the extender was only feldspar. It contained no biotite, and there was no charcoal beneath it. "We toyed with the idea of different paint recipes being used by groups of different social status, or even one recipe for men, the other for women. But it seemed just as likely that the different recipes were used during different periods."

To settle this puzzle, Clottes, Menu, and Walter analyzed the paint recipes

from a wide range of decorated caves in the region that have been firmly carbon-dated. Would the two recipes at Niaux turn out to correspond to two different prehistoric periods? So far—and Clottes points out that the sample is small, about ten sites—recipe B has been found consistently with Late Magdalenian work (about 12,000 to 13,000 years old), while recipe F is exclusively Middle Magdalenian (about 13,000 to 14,000 years old). "We don't know why Paleolithic painters changed the recipe for the extender around 13,000 years ago," asserts Clottes. Perhaps, he speculates, it made the paint easier to apply or gave it a slightly different color. "But whatever the reason, it gives us a way of attaching a date to paintings when radiocarbon methods are not possible."

Thus the Niaux paint studies answered Clottes's question in a completely unexpected way: despite their similarity, the paintings in the cave were not all created within a short period of time. Many generations could have separated recipe B and recipe F paintings. The more general implication—one that archeologists will have to struggle with in the years to come—is that style is no certain guide to chronology. The methodology that supported years of archeological work has suddenly crumbled. But that isn't the only ripple the studies have left in their wake.

Archeologists have long believed that the Salon Noir at Niaux was a sanctuary—a sort of Ice Age cathedral where important ceremonies were held. Clottes himself subscribes to this gut feeling. "There is something special about the Salon Noir," he says, as he leads the way along the uneven corridor that takes you to the cave's inner chamber. "When you enter with a small lamp, you naturally follow the right-hand wall, retreating from that great black void to the left. Eventually, inevitably, you reach the Salon Noir, with its soaring ceiling beyond the reach of torchlight. It's as if the place draws you here." Clottes shifts the beam of light to the walls, dramatically revealing the panels of black bison, horses, ibex, and deer. He swings the

beam from panel to panel, creating an eerie sense of movement in the ancient images as he points out how stylistically homogeneous they are. "This homogeneity," he explains, "has been very important to our perception of the cave as a sanctuary."

When archeologists speak of a sanctuary, they typically imagine a richly decorated cave in which the paintings seem to form a planned, cohesive body of work. The two most famous examples are Altamira in Spain, with its huge polychrome extravaganzas, and Lascaux in France, with its fabulous friezes. But by that logic, wouldn't the discovery of different paint recipes in the Salon Noir, spanning as much as two millennia, cast doubt on Niaux's status as a sanctuary? "That *seems* logical, but it turns out to be wrong," asserts Clottes. For evidence, he returns to the pigment studies that uncovered charcoal fragments under the most commonly used paint in the Salon Noir. "That indicated to us that the

"There it was, my hand, very definitely me, a more powerful signature than any writing."

Upper Paleolithic artists first made a sketch using a charcoal stick, then painted over the outline," says Clottes.

This technique—a preliminary sketch followed by careful painting—is not common in Paleolithic art. The combination of sketch and painting not only takes more time, says Clottes, but also implies premeditation. It suggests that the artist had some sort of composition in mind, sketching first and only filling in the outlines with paint after he or she was satisfied with the overall effect. That kind of care, argues Clottes, is much more consistent with paintings found in heavily decorated sanctuaries than in the more run-of-the-mill caves with their scattered images that look as if they've been hastily dashed off on brief visits.

"I believe people repeatedly came to the spot we're standing on now," says Clottes. It was, he is sure, a gathering place of lasting social and mythological significance. "You know," he finally confides, "I've been in this cave many times. I've stood in the place where the Upper Paleolithic painter stood. I've traced the images. You put your hand where his or her hand once was; you move it, producing the same lines. Sometimes it feels uncanny. It brings you closer to them. Closer, but still frustratingly distant."

At moments like this the differences in style between Clottes and Lorblanchet seem to evaporate. "The first time I did my own hand stencil, I was shocked," recalls Lorblanchet. "There it was, my hand, separate and distant from me, but very definitely me, a more powerful signature than any writing. I had put myself into the rock, become part of another world." For Paleolithic people, that "other world," a potent mythological world mediated by simple images, was probably as real as life on the frigid steppe. Today we see only images on the rock.

BUSHMEN

John Yellen

John Yellen, director of the anthropology program at the National Science Foundation, has returned to the Kalahari four times since 1968.

I followed Dau, kept his slim brown back directly in front of me, as we broke suddenly free from the dense Kalahari bush and crossed through the low wire fence that separated Botswana from Namibia to the West. For that moment while Dau held the smooth wires apart for me, we were out in the open, in the full hot light of the sun and then we entered the shadows, the tangled thickets of arrow grass and thorn bush and mongongo trees once again. As soon as the bush began to close in around us again, I quickly became disoriented, Dau's back my only reference point.

Even then, in that first month of 1968, while my desert boots retained their luster, I knew enough to walk behind, not next to Dau. I had expected the Kalahari Desert to be bare open sand. I had imagined myself looking out over vast stretches that swept across to the horizon. But to my surprise, I found that the dunes were covered with trees and that during the rains the grasses grew high over my head. The bare sand, where I could see it, was littered with leaves, and over these the

living trees and brush threw a dappled pattern of sunlight and shade. To look in the far distance and maintain a sense of direction, to narrow my focus and pick a way between the acacia bushes and their thorns, and then to look down, just in front of my feet to search out menacing shapes, was too much for me. Already, in that first month, the Bushmen had shown me a puff adder coiled motionless by the base of an acacia tree, but not until Cumsa the Hunter came up close to it, ready to strike it with his spear, could I finally see what all those hands were pointing at.

As Dau walked, I tried to follow his lead. To my discomfort I knew that many of these bushes had thorns—the Kalahari cloaks itself in thorns—some hidden close to the ground just high enough to rake across my ankles and draw blood when I pushed through, others long and straight and white so they reflected the sun. That morning, just before the border fence, my concentration had lagged and I found myself entangled in wait-a-bit thorns that

curved backwards up the branch. So I stopped and this short, brown-skinned Bushman pushed me gently backwards to release the tension, then worked the branch, thorn by thorn from my shirt and my skin.

In the mid-1960s, the South African government had decided to accurately survey the Botswana border, mark it with five-strand fence, and cut a thin firebreak on either side. At intervals they constructed survey towers, strange skeletal affairs, like oil drilling rigs, their tops poking well above the highest mongongo trees. It was to one of these that Dau led me across the border, through the midday sun. Although he would not climb it himself, since it was a white man's tower, he assumed I would. I followed his finger, his chain of logic as I started rather hesitantly up the rusted rungs. I cleared the arrow grass, the acacia bushes, finally the broad leafy crowns of the mongongo nut trees. Just short of the top I stopped and sat, hooked my feet beneath the rung below, and wrapped my arms around the metal edges of the sides.

For a month now I had copied the maps—the lines and the circles the !Kung tribesmen had drawn with their fingers in the sand. I had listened and tried to transcribe names of those places, so unintelligible with their clicks, their rising and falling tones. I had walked with Dau and the others to some of those places, to small camps near ephemeral water holes, but on the ground it was too confusing, the changes in altitude and vegetation too subtle, the sun too nearly overhead to provide any sense of where I was or from where I had come.

For the first time from the tower, I could see an order to the landscape. From up there on the tower, I could see that long thin border scar, could trace it off to the horizon to both the north and south. But beyond that, no evidence, not the slightest sign of a human hand. The Bushmen camps were too few in number, too small and well-hidden in the grass and bush to be visible from here. Likewise, the camp where we anthropologists lived, off to the east at the Dobe waterhole, that also was too small to see.

As Dau had intended, from my perch on that tower I learned a lot. At least now I could use the dunes, the shallow valleys, to know whether I was walking east and west or north and south.

In those first years with the Dobe Bushmen, I did gain at least a partial understanding of that land. And I learned to recognize many of those places, the ones that rate no name at all but are marked only by events—brief, ephemeral happenings that leave no mark on the land. I learned to walk with the Bushmen back from a hunt or a trip for honey or spear-shaft wood and listen. They talked, chattered almost constantly, decorating the bus, these no-name places as they went, putting ornaments of experience on them: "See that tree there, John? That's where we stopped, my brother and I, long before he was married, when he killed a kudu, a big female. We stopped under that tree, hung the meat up there and rested in the shade. But the flies were so bad, the biting flies, that we couldn't stay for long."

It took me a long time to realize that this chatter was not chatter at all, to

understand that those remarks were gifts, a private map shared only among a few, an overlay crammed with fine, spidery writing on top of the base map with its named waterholes and large valleys, a map for friends to read. Dau would see a porcupine burrow, tiny, hidden in the vastness of the bush. And at night he could sit by the fire and move the others from point to point across the landscape to that small opening in the ground.

But as an archeologist, I had a task to do—to name those places and to discover what life had been like there in the past. "This place has a name now," I told Dau when I went back in 1976. Not the chicken camp, because when I was there I kept 15 chickens, or the cobra camp, for the cobra we killed one morning among the nesting hens, but Dobe Base Camp 18. Eighteen because it's the eighteenth of these old abandoned camps I've followed you to in the last three days. See? That's what goes into this ledger, this fat bound book in waterproof ballpoint ink. We could get a reflector in here—a big piece of tin like some metal off a roof and get some satellite or a plane to photograph it. We could tell just where it is then, could mark it on one of those large aerial maps down to the nearest meter if we wanted.

We came back to these camps, these abandoned places on the ground, not once but month after month for the better part of a year. Not just Dau and myself but a whole crew of us, eight Bushmen and I, to dig, to look down into the ground. We started before the sun was too high up in the sky, and later Dau and I sat in the shade sipping thick, rich tea. I asked questions and he talked.

"One day when I was living here, I shot a kudu: an adult female. Hit it with one arrow in the flank. But it went too far and we never found it. Then another day my brother hit a wildebeest, another adult female and that one we got. We carried it back to camp here and ate it."

"What other meat did you eat here, Dau?"

"One, no two, steenbok, it was."

1948: 28 years ago by my counting was when Dau, his brothers, his family were here. How could he remember the

detail? This man sat in the shade and recalled trivial events that have repeated themselves in more or less the same way at so many places over the last three decades.

We dug day after day in the old camps—and found what Dau said we should. Bones, decomposing, but still identifiable: bones of wildebeest and steenbok among the charcoal and mongongo nut shells.

We dug our squares, sifting through the sand for bones. And when I dumped the bones, the odd ostrich eggshell bead, the other bits and pieces out onto the bridge table to sort, so much of what my eyes and ears told me was confirmed in this most tangible form. If excavation in one square revealed the bones of a wildebeest or kudi or other large antelope, then the others would contain them as well. In an environment as unpredictable as the Kalahari, where the game was hard to find and the probability of failure high, survival depended on sharing, on spreading the risk. And the bones, distributed almost evenly around the individual family hearths confirmed that. What also impressed me was how little else other than the bones there was. Most archeological sites contain a broad range of debris. But in those years the Bushmen owned so little. Two spears or wooden digging sticks or strings of ostrich eggshell beads were of no more use than one. Better to share, to give away meat or extra belongings and through such gifts create a web of debts, of obligations that some day would be repaid. In 1948, even in 1965, to accumulate material goods made no sense.

When it was hot, which was most of the year, I arranged the bridge table and two chairs in a patch of nearby shade. We sat there with the bound black and red ledger and dumped the bones in a heap in the center of the table, then sorted them out. I did the easy stuff, separated out the turtle shells, the bird bones, set each in a small pile around the table's edge. Dau did the harder part, separated the steenbok from the duiker, the wildebeest from kudu, held small splintered bone fragments and turned them over and over in his hands. We went through the

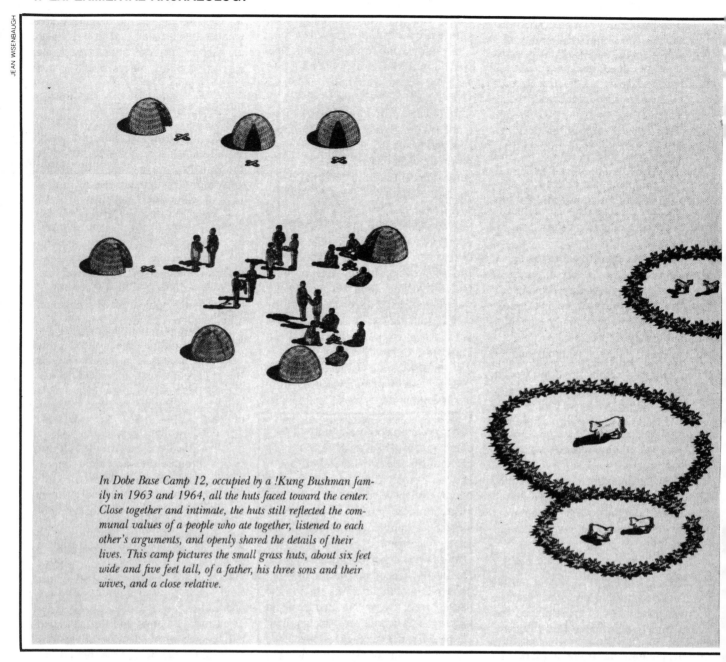

In Dobe Base Camp 12, occupied by a !Kung Bushman family in 1963 and 1964, all the huts faced toward the center. Close together and intimate, the huts still reflected the communal values of a people who ate together, listened to each other's arguments, and openly shared the details of their lives. This camp pictures the small grass huts, about six feet wide and five feet tall, of a father, his three sons and their wives, and a close relative.

piles then, one by one, moved each in its turn to the center of the table, sorted them into finer categories, body part by body part, bone by bone. Cryptic notes, bits of data that accumulated page by page. The bones with their sand and grit were transformed into numbers in rows and columns, classes and subclasses which would, I hoped, emerge from some computer to reveal a grander order, a design, an underlying truth.

Taphonomy: That's the proper term for it. The study of burial and preservation. Archeologists dig lots of bones out of the ground, not just from recent places such as these but from sites that span the millions of years of mankind's existence. On the basis of the bones, we try to learn about those ancient people. We try to reconstruct their diet, figure out how the animals were hunted, how they were killed, butchered, and shared.

What appealed to me about the Dobe situation, why I followed Dau, walked out his youth and his early manhood back and forth around the waterhole was the neat, almost laboratory situation Dobe offered. A natural experiment. I could go to a modern camp, collect those discarded food bones even before the jackals and hyenas had gotten to them, examine and count them, watch the pattern emerge. What happened then to the bones after they'd been trampled, picked over, rained on, lain in the ground for five years? Five years ago? Dobe Base Camp 21, 1971. I could go there, dig up a sample and find out.

What went on farther and farther back in time? Is there a pattern? Try eight years ago. 1968, DBC 18. We could go there to the cobra camp and see. Thirty-four years ago? The camp where Tsaa with the beautiful wife was

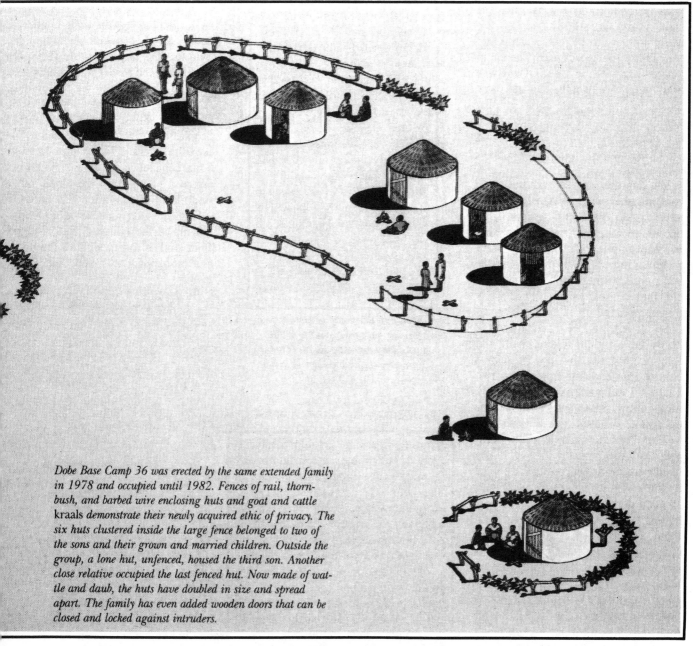

Dobe Base Camp 36 was erected by the same extended family in 1978 and occupied until 1982. Fences of rail, thornbush, and barbed wire enclosing huts and goat and cattle kraals demonstrate their newly acquired ethic of privacy. The six huts clustered inside the large fence belonged to two of the sons and their grown and married children. Outside the group, a lone hut, unfenced, housed the third son. Another close relative occupied the last fenced hut. Now made of wattle and daub, the huts have doubled in size and spread apart. The family has even added wooden doors that can be closed and locked against intruders.

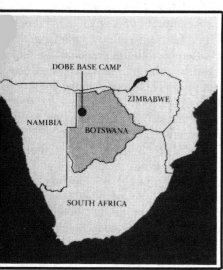

born. One can watch, can see how things fall apart, can make graphs, curves, shoot them back, watch them arc backwards beyond Dau, beyond Dau's father, back into the true archeological past.

We dug our way through the DBCs, back into the early 1940s, listening day after day to the South African soap operas on the short-wave radio, and our consumption of plastic bags went down and down. Slim pickings in the bone department. And the bones we did find tended to be rotten: They fragmented, fell apart in the sieve.

So we left the 1940s, collapsed the bridge table and the folding chairs and went to that site that played such a crucial role for anthropologists: DBC 12, the 1963 camp where those old myths about hunters and gatherers came up against the hard rock of truth.

They built this camp just after Richard Lee, the pioneer, arrived. They lived there through the winter and hunted warthog with spears and a pack of dogs so good they remember each by name to this day. Richard lived there with them. He watched them—what they did, what they ate, weighed food on his small scale slung with a rope from an acacia tree. He weighed people, sat in camp day after day with his notebook and his wristwatch and scale. He recorded times: when each person left camp in the morning, when each returned for the day.

In this small remnant group, one of the last in the world still living by hunting and gathering, it should be possible, he believed, to see a reflection, a faint glimmer of the distant universal past of all humanity, a common condition that had continued for millions and millions of years. He went there because of that and for that reason, later on, the rest of us followed him.

What he found in that desert camp, that dry, hard land, set the anthropological world back on its collective ear. What his scale and his wristwatch and his systematic scribbles showed was that we were fooled, that we had it all wrong. To be a hunter and gatherer wasn't that bad after all. They didn't work that hard, even in this land of thorns: For an adult, it came to less time than a nine-to-five office worker puts in on the job. They lived a long time, too, didn't wear out and die young but old-looking, as we had always thought. Even in this camp, the camp with the good hunting dogs, it was plants, not meat, which provided the staff of life. Women walked through the nut groves and collected nuts with their toes, dug in the molapos and sang to each other through the bush. Unlike the game, which spooked so easily and followed the unpredictable rains, the nuts, roots, and berries were dependable, there in plenty, there for the picking. Another distinguished anthropologist, Marshall Sahlins, termed those DBC 12 people "the original affluent society"— something quite different from the traditional conception of hunting and gathering as a mean, hard existence half a step ahead of starvation and doom.

Over the years that name has held— but life in the Kalahari has changed. That kind of camp, with all the bones and mongongo nuts and dogs, is no more.

By the mid-1970s, things were different at Dobe. Diane Gelburd, another of the anthropologists out there then, only needed to look around her to see how the Bushman lifestyle had changed from the way Richard recorded it, from how Sahlins described it. But what had changed the people at DBC 12 who

believed that property should be commonly held and shared? What had altered their system of values? That same winter Diane decided to find out.

She devised a simple measure of acculturation that used pictures cut from magazines: an airplane, a sewing machine, a gold mine in South Africa. (Almost no one got the gold mine right.) That was the most enjoyable part of the study. They all liked to look at pictures, to guess.

Then she turned from what people knew to what they believed. She wanted to rank them along a scale, from traditional to acculturated. So again she asked questions:

"Will your children be tattooed?"

To women: "If you were having a difficult childbirth and a white doctor were there, would you ask for assistance?"

To men: "If someone asked you for permission to marry your daughter would you demand (the traditional) bride service?"

Another question so stereotyped that in our own society one would be too embarassed to ask it: "Would you let your child marry someone from another tribe—a Tswana or a Herero—a white person?"

First knowledge, then belief, and finally material culture. She did the less sensitive questions first. "Do you have a field? What do you grow? What kind of animals do you have? How many of what?" Then came the hard part: She needed to see what people actually owned. I tagged along with her one day and remember the whispers inside one dark mud hut. Trunks were unlocked and hurriedly unpacked away from the entrance to shield them from sight. A blanket spread out on a trunk revealed the secret wealth that belied their statements: "Me? I have nothing." In the semidarkness she made her inventory. Then the trunks were hastily repacked and relocked with relief.

She went through the data, looked at those lists of belongings, itemized them in computer printouts. Here's a man who still hunts. The printout shows it. He has a bow and quiver and arrows on which the poison is kept fresh. He has a spear and snares for birds. He has a small steenbok skin bag, a traditional

carryall that rests neatly under his arm.

He also has 19 goats and two donkeys, bought from the Herero or Tswana, who now get Dobe Bushmen to help plant their fields and herd their cows. They pay in livestock, hand-me-down clothing, blankets, and sometimes cash. He has three large metal trunks crammed full: One is packed to the top with shoes, shirts, and pants, most well-worn. He has two large linen mosquito nets, 10 tin cups, and a metal file. He has ropes of beads: strand upon strand—over 200 in all, pounds of small colored glass beads made in Czechoslovakia that I had bought in Johannesburg years earlier. He has four large iron pots and a five-gallon plastic jerry can. He has a plow, a gift from the anthropologists. He has a bridle and bit, light blankets, a large tin basin. He has six pieces of silverware, a mirror and hairbrush, two billycans. His wife and his children together couldn't carry all that. The trunks are too heavy and too large for one person to carry so you would have to have two people for each. What about the plow, those heavy iron pots? Quite a job to carry those through bush, through the thick thorns.

But here is the surprising part. Talk to that man. Read the printout. See what he knows, what he believes. It isn't surprising that he speaks the Herero language and Setswana fluently or that he has worked for the Herero, the anthropologists. Nothing startling there. A budding Dobe capitalist. But then comes the shock: He espouses the traditional values.

"Bushmen share things, John. We share things and depend on each other, help each other out. That's what makes us different from the black people."

But the same person, his back to the door, opens his trunks, unlocks them one by one, lays out the blankets, the beads, then quickly closes each before he opens the next.

Multiply that. Make a whole village of people like that, and you can see the cumulative effect: You can actually measure it. As time goes on, as people come to own more possessions; the huts move farther and farther apart.

In the old days a camp was cosy, initimate and close. You could sit there by one fire and look into the other grass huts, see what the other people were doing, what they were making or eating. You heard the conversations, the arguments and banter.

We ask them why the new pattern?

Says Dau: "It's because of the livestock that we put our huts this way. They can eat the grass from the roofs and the sides of our houses. So we have to build fences to keep them away and to do that, you must have room between the huts."

I look up from the fire, glance around the camp, say nothing. No fences there. Not a single one around any of the huts, although I concede that one day they probably will build them. But why construct a lot of separate small fences, one around each hut? Why not clump the huts together the way they did in the old days and make a single large fence around the lot? Certainly a more efficient approach. Why worry about fences now in any case? The only exposed grass is on the roofs, protected by straight mud walls and nothing short of an elephant or giraffe could eat it.

Xashe's answer is different. Another brief reply. An attempt to dispose of the subject politely but quickly. "It's fire, John. That's what we're worried about. If we put our houses too close together, if one catches fire, the others will burn as well. We don't want one fire to burn all our houses down. That's why we build them so far apart."

But why worry about fire now? What about in the old days when the huts were so close, cheek by jowl? Why is it that when the huts were really vulnerable, when they were built entirely of dried grass, you didn't worry about fires then?

You read Diane's interviews and look at those lists of how much people own. You see those shielded mud huts with doors spaced, so far apart. You also listen to the people you like and trust. People who always have been honest with you. You hear their explanations and realize the evasions are not for you but for themselves. You see things they can't. But nothing can be done. It would be ludicrous to tell these brothers: "Don't you see, my friends, the lack of concordance between your values and the changing reality of your world?"

Now, years after the DBC study, I sit with data spread out before me and it is so clear. Richard's camp in 1963: just grass huts, a hearth in front of each. Huts and hearths in a circle, nothing more. 1968: more of the same. The following year though the first *kraal* appears, just a small thorn enclosure, some acacia bushes cut and dragged haphazardly together for their first few goats. It's set apart way out behind the circle of huts. On one goes, from plot to plot, following the pattern from year to year. The huts change from grass to mud. They become larger, more solidly built. Goats, a few at first, then more of them. So you build a fence around your house to keep them away from the grass roofs. The *kraals* grow larger, move in closer to be incorporated finally into the circle of huts itself. The huts become spaced farther and farther apart, seemingly repelled over time, one from the next. People, families move farther apart.

The bones tell the same story. 1947: All the bones from wild animals, game caught in snares or shot with poisoned arrows—game taken from the bush. By 1964 a few goat bones, a cow bone or two, but not many. Less than 20 percent of the total. Look then at the early 1970s and watch the line on the graph climb slowly upwards—by 1976 over 80 percent from domesticated stock.

But what explains the shattering of this society? Why is this hunting and gathering way of life, so resilient in the face of uncertainty, falling apart? It hasn't been a direct force—a war, the ravages of disease. It is the internal conflicts, the tensions, the inconsistencies, the impossibility of reconciling such different views of the world.

At Dobe it is happening to them all together. All of the huts have moved farther apart in lockstep, which makes it harder for them to see how incompatible the old system is with the new. But Rakudu, a Bushman who lived at the Mahopa waterhole eight miles down the valley from Dobe, was a step ahead of the rest. He experienced, before the rest of them, their collective fate.

When I was at the Cobra Camp in 1969, Rakudu lived down near Mahopa, off on his own, a mile or so away from the pastoral Herero villages. He had two hats and a very deep bass voice, both so strange, so out of place in a Bushman. He was a comical sort of man with the hats and that voice and a large Adam's apple that bobbed up and down.

The one hat must have been a leftover from the German-Herero wars because no one in Botswana wore a hat like that—a real pith helmet with a solid top and a rounded brim. It had been cared for over the years because, although soiled and faded, it still retained the original strap that tucks beneath the chin. The second hat was also unique— a World War I aviator's hat, one of those leather sacks that fits tightly over the head and buckles under the chin. Only the goggles were missing.

I should have seen then how out of place the ownership of two hats was in that hunter-gatherer world. Give two hats like that to any of the others and one would have been given away on the spot. A month or two later, the other would become a gift as well. Moving goods as gifts and favors along that chain of human ties. That was the way to maintain those links, to keep them strong.

When I went to Rakudu's village and realized what he was up to, I could see that he was one of a kind. The mudwalled huts in his village made it look like a Herero village—not a grass hut in sight. And when I came, Rakudu pulled out a hand-carved wood and leather chair and set it in the shade. This village was different from any of the Bushman camps I had seen. Mud huts set out in a circle, real clay storage bins to hold the corn—not platforms in a tree—and *kraals* for lots of goats and donkeys. He had a large field, too, several years before the first one appeared at Dobe.

Why shouldn't Bushmen do it—build their own villages, model their subsistence after the Herero? To plant a field, to tend goats, to build mud-walled houses like that was not hard to do. Work for the Herero a while and get an axe, accumulate the nucleus of a herd, buy or borrow the seeds. That year the rains were long and heavy. The sand held the water and the crickets and the birds didn't come. So the harvest was good, and I could sit there in the carved chair and look at Rakudu's herd of goats and their young ones and admire him for his industry, for what he had done.

Only a year later I saw him and his eldest son just outside the Cobra Camp. I went over and sat in the sand and listened to the negotiations for the marriage Rakudu was trying to arrange. His son's most recent wife had run away, and Rakudu was discussing a union between his son and Dau the Elder's oldest daughter who was just approaching marriageable age. They talked about names and Dau the Elder explained why the marriage couldn't take place. It was clear that the objection was trivial, that he was making an excuse. Even I could see that his explanation was a face-saving gesture to make the refusal easier for all of them.

Later I asked Dau the Elder why he did it. It seemed like a good deal to me. "Rakudu has all that wealth, those goats and field. I'd think that you would be anxious to be linked with a family like that. Look at all you have to gain. Is the son difficult? Did he beat his last wife?"

"She left because she was embarrassed. The wife before her ran away for the same reason and so did the younger brother's wife," he said. "Both brothers treated their wives well. The problem wasn't that. It was when the wives' relatives came. That's when it became so hard for the women because

Rakudu and his sons are such stingy men. They wouldn't give anything away, wouldn't share anything with them. Rakudu has a big herd just like the Herero, and he wouldn't kill goats for them to eat."

Not the way Bushmen should act toward relatives, not by the traditional value system at least. Sharing, the most deeply held Bushman belief, and that man with the two hats wouldn't go along. Herero are different. You can't expect them to act properly, to show what is only common decency; you must take them as they are. But someone like Rakudu, a Bushman, should know better than that. So the wives walked out and left for good.

But Rakudu understood what was happening, how he was trapped—and he tried to respond. If you can't kill too many goats from the herd that has become essential to you, perhaps you can find something else of value to give away. Rakudu thought he had an answer.

He raised tobacco in one section of his field. Tobacco, a plant not really adapted to a place like the northern Kalahari, has to be weeded, watered by hand, and paid special care. Rakudu did that and for one year at least harvested a tobacco crop.

Bushmen crave tobacco and Rakudu hoped he had found a solution—that they would accept tobacco in place of goats, in place of mealie meal. A good try. Perhaps the only one open to him. But, as it turned out, not good enough. Rakudu's son could not find a wife.

Ironic that a culture can die yet not a

single person perish. A sense of identity, of a shared set of rules, of participation in a single destiny binds individuals together into a tribe or cultural group. Let that survive long enough, let the participants pass this sense through enough generations, one to the next, create enough debris, and they will find their way into the archeological record, into the study of cultures remembered only by their traces left on the land.

Rakudu bought out. He, his wife, and his two sons sold their goats for cash, took the money and walked west, across the border scar that the South Africans had cut, through the smooth fence wire and down the hard calcrete road beyond. They became wards of the Afrikaaners, were lost to their own culture, let their fate pass into hands other than their own. At Chum kwe, the mission station across the border 34 miles to the west, they were given numbers and the right to stand in line with the others and have mealie meal and other of life's physical essentials handed out to them. As wards of the state, that became their right. When the problems, the contradictions of your life are insoluble, a paternalistic hand provides one easy out.

Dau stayed at Dobe. Drive there today and you can find his mud-walled hut just by the waterhole. But he understands: He has married off his daughter, his first-born girl to a wealthy Chum kwe man who drives a tractor—an old man, more than twice her age, and by traditional Bushmen standards not an appropriate match. Given the chance, one by one, the others will do the same.

Ancient Indians Sought Shadows and Ice Caves

Daniel J. Lenihan and James E. Bradford

Shoveling dirt on a bright summer day in Canyon de Chelly, a deep ravine carved into the western slope of the Chuska Mountains of northern Arizona, archeological field crews cast longing glances at the approaching shadows. The prehistoric inhabitants who lived here also paid attention to solar orientation. On the arid Colorado Plateau, despite an average elevation of 5,000 feet, temperatures often exceed 100° F during the summer. In lower, moister locales, a thicker atmosphere tends to steam-cook a person more evenly, but in the Southwest the sun really counts.

The Anasazi ("ancient ones," in the Navajo language), first occupied Canyon de Chelly more than 2,000 years ago. The earliest Anasazi, known to archeologists as the Basket Makers, took advantage of subtle alignments of the landscape for protection from the sun at critical times of the year. Realizing that a narrow ledge in the canyon wall faced north, they would dedicate the entire site to the construction of storage units, digging small pits in the dirt and debris fallen from the overhanging roof of the rock-shelter. They lined the pits with sandstone slabs bonded by mud mortar and roofed them with beehive constructions of

sticks and mud. This enabled the Basket Makers to store food (corn, beans, pine nuts, squash) for a long time in a cool, dry environment in the middle of a sandstone hotbox.

In the winter months, the canyon rims and flat country outside the canyon entrance provided prehistoric inhabitants with easy exposure to the sun's warming rays, while the cooling shade of the canyon bottoms afforded refuge in the heat of summer. The later Anasazi, or Puebloans, constructed elaborate buildings of stone and mud mortar, which they nestled in shady canyon alcoves. To this day, the resident Navajo live on the canyon bottom in the summer and the rim in the winter.

Another basic strategy of Native Americans in the Southwest was to burrow into the earth, roofing semisubterranean homes with earth-covered wooden frameworks or digging underground dwellings. In the earliest recorded description of a Navajo dwelling, dating to 1630, Fray Alonso de Benavides mentions a *vivienda debaxo de tierra*, "a dwelling under the ground" or "dwelling under earth." He probably was referring to an ancestral version of the hogan, perhaps a hole with hide stretched over the top. The typical hogan of today is constructed from logs, bark, earth, and stone and possesses a sunken floor that provides a cooler environment. Some hogans

have root cellars, rooms with still deeper floors insulated with additional dirt and logs. Their inside temperatures are significantly cooler for storage of perishable foods.

Caves, a source of protection from many types of meteorological mayhem, are also excellent insulators against heat. Limestone caves provide natural air conditioning, maintaining a nearly constant temperature year-round. The contrast is even more dramatic when the cave lies in dark rock, such as basalt, or hardened lava, whose surface absorbs much radiant heat.

Near Acoma, a still-occupied pueblo in western New Mexico, lies El Malpais—the badlands. The meager tree cover to be found, consisting of low-lying junipers, piñon pines, and ponderosas, affords little refuge from the black, jagged basaltic blanket. Not far below ground, however, are natural cavities that are oases of coolness. Lava tubes that hardened around molten rivers of rock provide makeshift thoroughfares to these sanctums, into which the dense, cold air of winter settles and remains. Ice forms in them as well, and depending on a cave's size and shape and the location of its entrance hole, it may be preserved throughout the year. Ice cave temperatures hover around freezing throughout the summer, in some cases maintaining ice that is 2,000 years old. A prehistoric woven mat, probably used to cushion and insulate the knees of an ancient ice gatherer, is still captured in the frozen interior of one such cave.

Through the centuries, the hundred-mile-long trail connecting the pueblos of Acoma and Zuni traversed El Malpais, presenting a formidable passage. With their ice, the caves provided not only respite from the heat but also a source of water. When the ancient icemen came, they chipped off a supply and apparently used fire to melt the precious resource. Nearly every ice-yielding cave contains charcoal from their fires. The drinking water thus obtained was consumed during the trip or sealed in pottery jars and cached for later use. Today, the Acoma, Zuni, and Navajo who hunt in El Malpais still use the caves to store their butchered meat until they are ready to return home.

The miracle of ice in an oven made of molten rock has engendered a sense of reverence in those who benefit from its presence. The Acoma, for instance, do not approach the caves without performing the requisite rites, including prayers and small offerings—gestures that acknowledge unique gifts, to be used within limits and with proper respect.

The now-dominant Anglo and Hispanic cultures in the Southwest have rediscovered some of the basic principles of the ancients. The homes of these newcomers (who will probably be known to future archeologists as the Plastic Makers) incorporate solar-design features. Although these are primarily aimed at keeping warm in the winter, rather than cool in the summer, most are fairly obvious extensions of Native American strategies.

But the newcomers have been slow to pick up on the ancient life style. One important key to keeping cool is choosing when to raise your metabolic rate. Just as the Arabs marveled at the propensity of English overlords to keep mad dogs company in the midday sun, many a Navajo has marveled at the antics of tourists—even some archeologists—who follow an activity schedule developed for use in Northern Europe.

The Arrow of Disease

When Columbus and his successors invaded the Americas, the most potent weapon they carried was their germs. But why didn't deadly disease flow in the other direction, from the New World to the Old?

Jared Diamond

Jared Diamond is a contributing editor of Discover, *a professor of physiology at the UCLA School of Medicine, a recipient of a MacArthur genius award, and a research associate in ornithology at the American Museum of Natural History. Expanded versions of many of his* Discover *articles appear in his book* The Third Chimpanzee: The Evolution and Future of the Human Animal, *which won Britain's 1992* copus *prize for best science book. Not least among his many accomplishments was his rediscovery in 1981 of the long-lost bowerbird of New Guinea. Diamond wrote about pseudohermaphrodites for* Discover*'s special June issue on the science of sex.*

The three people talking in the hospital room were already stressed out from having to cope with a mysterious illness, and it didn't help at all that they were having trouble communicating. One of them was the patient, a small, timid man, sick with pneumonia caused by an unidentified microbe and with only a limited command of the English language. The second, acting as translator, was his wife, worried about her husband's condition and frightened by the hospital environment. The third person in the trio was an inexperienced young doctor, trying to figure out what might have brought on the strange illness. Under the stress, the doctor was forgetting everything he had been taught about patient confidentiality. He committed the awful blunder of requesting the woman to ask her husband whether he'd had any sexual experiences that might have caused the infection.

As the young doctor watched, the husband turned red, pulled himself together so that he seemed even smaller, tried to disappear under his bed sheets, and stammered in a barely audible voice. His wife suddenly screamed in rage and drew herself up to tower over him. Before the doctor could stop her, she grabbed a heavy metal bottle, slammed it onto her husband's head, and stormed out of the room. It took a while for the doctor to elicit, through the man's broken English, what he had said to so enrage his wife. The answer slowly emerged: he had admitted to repeated intercourse with sheep on a recent visit to the family farm; perhaps that was how he had contracted the mysterious microbe.

This episode, related to me by a physician friend involved in the case, sounds so bizarrely one of a kind as to be of no possible broader significance. But in fact it illustrates a subject of great importance: human diseases of animal origins. Very few of us may love sheep in the carnal sense. But most of us platonically love our pet animals, like our dogs and cats; and as a society; we certainly appear to have an inordinate fondness for sheep and other livestock, to judge from the vast numbers of them that we keep.

Some of us—most often our children—pick up infectious diseases from our pets. Usually these illnesses remain no more than a nuisance, but a few have evolved into far more. The major killers of humanity throughout our recent history—smallpox, flu, tuberculosis, malaria, plague, measles, and cholera—are all infectious diseases that arose from diseases of animals. Until World War II more victims of war died of microbes than of gunshot or sword wounds. All those military histories glorifying Alexander the Great and Napoleon ignore the ego-deflating truth: the winners of past wars were not necessarily those armies with the best generals and weapons, but those bearing the worst germs with which to smite their enemies.

The grimmest example of the role of germs in history is much on our minds this month, as we recall the European conquest of the Americas that began with Columbus's voyage of 1492. Numerous as the Indian victims of the murderous Spanish conquistadores were, they were dwarfed in number by the victims of murderous Spanish microbes. These formidable conquerors killed an estimated 95 percent of the New World's pre-Columbian Indian population.

Why was the exchange of nasty germs between the Americas and Europe so unequal? why didn't the reverse happen instead, with Indian diseases decimating the Spanish invaders, spreading back across the Atlantic, and causing a 95 percent decline in *Europe's* human population?

Similar questions arise regarding the decimation of many other native peoples by European germs, and regarding the decimation of would-be European conquistadores in the tropics of Africa and Asia.

Naturally, we're disposed to think about diseases from our own point of view: What can we do to save ourselves and to kill the microbes? Let's stamp out the scoundrels, and never mind what *their* motives are!

In life, though, one has to understand the enemy to beat him. So for a moment, let's consider disease from the microbes' point of view. Let's look beyond our anger at their making us sick in bizarre ways, like giving us genital sores or diarrhea, and ask why it is that they do such things. After all, microbes are as much a product of natural selection as we are, and so their actions must have come about because they confer some evolutionary benefit.

Basically, of course, evolution selects those individuals that are most effective at producing babies and at helping those babies find suitable places to live. Microbes are marvels at this latter requirement. They have evolved diverse ways of spreading from one person to another, and from animals to people. Many of our symptoms of disease actually represent ways in which some clever bug modifies our bodies or our behavior such that we become enlisted to spread bugs.

The most effortless way a bug can spread is by just waiting to be transmitted passively to the next victim. That's the strategy practiced by microbes that wait for one host to be eaten by the next—salmonella bacteria, for example, which we contract by eating already-infected eggs or meat; or the worm responsible for trichinosis, which waits for us to kill a pig and eat it without properly cooking it.

As a slight modification of this strategy; some microbes don't wait for the old host to die but instead hitchhike in the saliva of an insect that bites the old host and then flies to a new one. The free ride may be provided by mosquitoes, fleas, lice, or tsetse flies, which spread malaria, plague, typhus, and sleeping sickness, respectively. The

dirtiest of all passive-carriage tricks is perpetrated by microbes that pass from a woman to her fetus—microbes such as the ones responsible for syphilis, rubella (German measles), and AIDS. By their cunning these microbes can already be infecting an infant before the moment of its birth.

Other bugs take matters into their own hands, figuratively speaking. They actively modify the anatomy or habits of their host to accelerate their transmission. From our perspective, the open genital sores caused by venereal diseases such as syphilis are a vile indignity. From the microbes' point of view, however, they're just a useful device to enlist a host's help in inoculating the body cavity of another host with microbes. The skin lesions caused by smallpox similarly spread microbes by direct or indirect body contact (occasionally very indirect, as when U.S. and Australian whites bent on wiping out "belligerent" native peoples sent them gifts of blankets previously used by smallpox patients).

From our viewpoint, diarrhea and coughing are "symptoms" of disease. From a bug's viewpoint, they're clever evolutionary strategies to broadcast the bug. That's why it's in the bug's interests to make us "sick."

More vigorous yet is the strategy practiced by the influenza, common cold, and pertussis (whooping cough) microbes, which induce the victim to cough or sneeze, thereby broadcasting the bugs toward prospective new hosts. Similarly the cholera bacterium induces a massive diarrhea that spreads bacteria into the water supplies of potential new victims. For modification of a host's behavior, though, nothing matches the rabies virus, which not only gets into the saliva of an infected dog but drives the dog into a frenzy of

biting and thereby infects many new victims.

Thus, from our viewpoint, genital sores, diarrhea, and coughing are "symptoms" of disease. From a bug's viewpoint, they're clever evolutionary strategies to broadcast the bug. That's why it's in the bug's interests to make us "sick." But what does it gain by killing us? That seems self-defeating, since a microbe that kills its host kills itself.

Though you may well think it's of little consolation, our death is really just an unintended by-product of host symptoms that promote the efficient transmission of microbes. Yes, an untreated cholera patient may eventually die from producing diarrheal fluid at a rate of several gallons a day. While the patient lasts, though, the cholera bacterium profits from being massively disseminated into the water supplies of its next victims. As long as each victim thereby infects, on average, more than one new victim, the bacteria will spread, even though the first host happens to die.

So much for the dispassionate examination of the bug's interests. Now let's get back to considering our own selfish interests: to stay alive and healthy, best done by killing the damned bugs. One common response to infection is to develop a fever. Again, we consider fever a "symptom" of disease, as if it developed inevitably without serving any function. But regulation of body temperature is under our genetic control, and a fever doesn't just happen by accident. Because some microbes are more sensitive to heat than our own bodies are, by raising our body temperature we in effect try to bake the bugs to death before we get baked ourselves.

Another common response is to mobilize our immune system. White blood cells and other cells actively seek out and kill foreign microbes. The specific antibodies we gradually build up against a particular microbe make us less likely to get reinfected once we are cured. As we all know there are some illnesses, such as flu and the common cold, to which our resistance is only temporary; we can eventually contract the illness again. Against other illnesses, though—including measles, mumps, rubella, pertussis, and the now-defeated menace of smallpox—antibodies stimulated by one infection confer lifelong immunity. That's the principle behind vaccination—to stimulate our antibody production without our having to go through the actual experience of the disease.

Alas, some clever bugs don't just cave in to our immune defenses. Some have learned to trick us by changing their antigens, those molecular pieces of the microbe that our antibodies recognize. The constant evolution or recycling of new strains of flu, with differing antigens, explains why the flu you got two years ago didn't protect you against the different strain that arrived this year. Sleeping sickness is an even more slippery customer in its ability to change its antigens rapidly.

We and our pathogens are now locked in an escalating evolutionary contest, with the death of one contestant the price of defeat, and with natural selection playing the role of umpire.

Among the slipperiest of all is the virus that causes AIDS, which evolves new antigens even as it sits within an individual patient, until it eventually overwhelms the immune system.

Our slowest defensive response is through natural selection, which changes the relative frequency with which a gene appears from generation to generation. For almost any disease some people prove to be genetically more resistant than others. In an epidemic, those people with genes for resistance to that particular microbe are more likely to survive than are people lacking such genes. As a result, over the course of history human populations repeatedly exposed to a particular pathogen tend to be made up of individuals with genes that resist the

appropriate microbe just because unfortunate individuals without those genes were less likely to survive to pass their genes on to their children.

Fat consolation, you may be thinking. This evolutionary response is not one that does the genetically susceptible dying individual any good. It does mean, though, that a human population as a whole becomes better protected.

In short, many bugs have had to evolve tricks to let them spread among potential victims. We've evolved countertricks, to which the bugs have responded by evolving counter-counter-tricks. We and our pathogens are now locked in an escalating evolutionary contest, with the death of one contestant the price of defeat, and with natural selection playing the role of umpire.

The form that this deadly contest takes varies with the pathogens: for some it is like a guerrilla war, while for others it is a blitzkrieg. With certain diseases, like malaria or hook-worm, there's a more or less steady trickle of new cases in an affected area, and they will appear in any month of any year. Epidemic diseases, though, are different: they produce no cases for a long time, then a whole wave of cases, then no more cases again for a while.

Among such epidemic diseases, influenza is the most familiar to Americans, this year having been a particularly bad one for us (but a great year for the influenza virus). Cholera epidemics come at longer intervals, the 1991 Peruvian epidemic being the first one to reach the New World during the twentieth century. Frightening as today's influenza and cholera epidemics are, though, they pale beside the far more terrifying epidemics of the past, before the rise of modern medicine. The greatest single epidemic in human history was the influenza wave that killed 21 million people at the end of the First World War. The black death, or bubonic plague, killed one-quarter of Europe's population between 1346 and 1352, with death tolls up to 70 percent in some cities.

The infectious diseases that visit us as epidemics share several characteris-

tics. First, they spread quickly and efficiently from an infected person to nearby healthy people, with the result that the whole population gets exposed within a short time. Second, they're "acute" illnesses: within a short time, you either die or recover completely. Third, the fortunate ones of us who do recover develop antibodies that leave us immune against a recurrence of the disease for a long time, possibly our entire lives. Finally, these diseases tend to be restricted to humans; the bugs causing them tend not to live in the soil or in other animals. All four of these characteristics apply to what Americans think of as the once more-familiar acute epidemic diseases of childhood, including measles, rubella, mumps, pertussis, and smallpox.

It is easy to understand why the combination of those four characteristics tends to make a disease run in epidemics. The rapid spread of microbes and the rapid course of symptoms mean that everybody in a local human population is soon infected, and thereafter either dead or else recovered and immune. No one is left alive who could still be infected. But since the microbe can't survive except in the bodies of living people, the disease dies out until a new crop of babies reaches the susceptible age—and until an infectious person arrives from the outside to start a new epidemic.

A classic illustration of the process is given by the history of measles on the isolated Faeroe Islands in the North Atlantic. A severe epidemic of the disease reached the Faeroes in 1781, then died out, leaving the islands measles-free until an infected carpenter arrived on a ship from Denmark in 1846. Within three months almost the whole Faeroes population—7,782 people—had gotten measles and then either died or recovered, leaving the measles virus to disappear once again until the next epidemic. Studies show that measles is likely to die out in any human population numbering less than half a million people. Only in larger populations can measles shift from one local area to another, thereby persisting until enough babies have been born in the originally infected area to permit the disease's return.

Rubella in Australia provides a similar example, on a much larger scale. As of 1917 Australia's population was still only 5 million, with most people living in scattered rural areas. The sea voyage to Britain took two months, and land transport within Australia itself was slow. In effect, Australia didn't even consist of a population of 5 million, but of hundreds of much smaller populations. As a result, rubella hit Australia only as occasional epidemics, when an infected person happened to arrive from overseas and stayed in a densely populated area. By 1938, though, the city of Sydney alone had a population of over one million, and people moved frequently and quickly by air between London, Sydney, and other Australian cities. Around then, rubella for the first time was able to establish itself permanently in Australia.

What's true for rubella in Australia is true for most familiar acute infectious diseases throughout the world. To sustain themselves, they need a human population that is sufficiently numerous and densely packed that a new crop of susceptible children is available for infection by the time the disease would otherwise be waning. Hence measles and other such diseases are also known as "crowd diseases."

Crowd diseases could not sustain themselves in small bands of hunter-gatherers and slash-and-burn farmers. As tragic recent experience with Amazonian Indians and Pacific Islanders confirms, almost an entire tribelet may be wiped out by an epidemic brought by an outside visitor, because no one in the tribelet has any antibodies against the microbe. In addition, measles and some other "childhood" diseases are more likely to kill infected adults than children, and all adults in the tribelet are susceptible. Having killed most of the tribelet, the epidemic then disappears. The small population size explains why tribelets can't sustain epidemics introduced from the outside; at the same time it explains why they could never evolve epidemic diseases of their own to give back to the visitors.

That's not to say that small human populations are free from all infectious diseases. Some of their infections are caused by microbes capable of maintaining themselves in animals or in soil, so the disease remains constantly available to infect people. For example, the yellow fever virus is carried by African wild monkeys and is constantly available to infect rural human populations of Africa. It was also available to be carried to New World monkeys and people by the transatlantic slave trade.

Other infections of small human populations are chronic diseases, such as leprosy and yaws, that may take a very long time to kill a victim. The victim thus remains alive as a reservoir of microbes to infect other members of the tribelet. Finally, small human populations are susceptible to nonfatal infections against which we don't develop immunity, with the result that the same person can become reinfected after recovering. That's the case with hookworm and many other parasites.

All these types of diseases, characteristic of small, isolated populations, must be the oldest diseases of humanity. They were the ones that we could evolve and sustain through the early millions of years of our evolutionary history, when the total human population was tiny and fragmented. They are also shared with, or are similar to the diseases of, our closest wild relatives, the African great apes. In contrast, the evolution of our crowd diseases could only have occurred with the buildup of large, dense human populations, first made possible by the rise of agriculture about 10,000 years ago, then by the rise of cities several thousand years ago. Indeed, the first attested dates for many familiar infectious diseases are surprisingly recent: around 1600 B.C. for smallpox (as deduced from pockmarks on an Egyptian mummy), 400 B.C. for mumps, 1840 for polio, and 1959 for AIDS.

Agriculture sustains much higher human population densities than does hunting and gathering—on average, 10 to 100 times higher. In addition, hunter-gatherers frequently shift camp, leaving behind their piles of feces with their accumulated microbes and worm larvae. But farmers are sedentary and live amid their own sewage, providing microbes with a quick path from one person's body into another person's drinking water. Farmers also become surrounded by disease-transmitting rodents attracted by stored food.

Some human populations make it even easier for their own bacteria and worms to infect new victims, by intentionally gathering their feces and urine and spreading it as fertilizer on the fields where people work. Irrigation agriculture and fish farming provide ideal living conditions for the snails carrying schistosomes, and for other flukes that burrow through our skin as we wade through the feces-laden water.

If the rise of farming was a boon for our microbes, the rise of cities was a veritable bonanza, as still more densely packed human populations festered under even worse sanitation conditions. (Not until the beginning of the twentieth century did urban populations finally become self-sustaining; until then, constant immigration of healthy peasants from the countryside was necessary to make good the constant deaths of city dwellers from crowd diseases.) Another bonanza was the development of world trade routes, which by late Roman times effectively joined the populations of Europe, Asia, and North Africa into one giant breeding ground for microbes. That's when smallpox finally reached Rome as the "plague of Antonius," which killed millions of Roman citizens between A.D. 165 and 180.

Similarly, bubonic plague first appeared in Europe as the plague of Justinian (A.D. 542–543). But plague didn't begin to hit Europe with full force, as the black death epidemics, until 1346, when new overland trading with China provided rapid transit for flea-infested furs from plague-ridden areas of Central Asia. Today our jet planes have made even the longest intercontinental flights briefer than the duration of any human infectious disease. That's how an Aerolíneas Argentinas airplane, stopping in Lima, Peru, earlier this year, managed to deliver dozens of cholera-infected people the same day to my city of Los Angeles, over 3,000 miles away. The explosive increase in world travel by Americans, and in immigration to the United States, is turning us into another melting pot—this time of microbes that we previously dismissed as just causing exotic diseases in far-off countries.

The explosive increase in world travel by Americans, and in immigration to the United States, is turning us into another melting pot— this time of microbes that we'd dismissed as causing disease in far-off countries.

When the human population became sufficiently large and concentrated, we reached the stage in our history when we could at last sustain crowd diseases confined to our species. But that presents a paradox: such diseases could never have existed before. Instead they had to evolve as new diseases. Where did those new diseases come from?

Evidence emerges from studies of the disease-causing microbes themselves. In many cases molecular biologists have identified the microbe's closest relative. Those relatives also prove to be agents of infectious crowd diseases—but ones confined to various species of domestic animals and pets! Among animals too, epidemic diseases require dense populations, and they're mainly confined to social animals that provide the necessary large populations. Hence when we domesticated social animals such as cows and pigs, they were already afflicted by epidemic diseases just waiting to be transferred to us.

For example, the measles virus is most closely related to the virus causing rinderpest, a nasty epidemic disease of cattle and many wild cud-chewing mammals. Rinderpest doesn't affect humans. Measles, in turn, doesn't affect cattle. The close similarity of the measles and rinderpest viruses suggests that the rinderpest virus transferred from cattle to humans, then became the measles virus by changing its properties to adapt to us. That transfer isn't surprising, considering how closely many peasant farmers live and sleep next to cows and their accompanying feces, urine, breath, sores, and blood. Our intimacy with cattle has been going on for the 8,000 years since we domesticated them—ample time for the rinderpest virus to discover us nearby. Other familiar infectious diseases can similarly be traced back to diseases of our animal friends.

Given our proximity to the animals we love, we must constantly be getting bombarded by animal microbes. Those invaders get winnowed by natural selection, and only a few succeed in establishing themselves as human diseases. A quick survey of current diseases lets us trace four stages in the evolution of a specialized human disease from an animal precursor.

In the first stage, we pick up animal-borne microbes that are still at an early stage in their evolution into specialized human pathogens. They don't get transmitted directly from one person to another, and even their transfer from animals to us remains uncommon. There are dozens of diseases like this that we get directly from pets and domestic animals. They include cat scratch fever from cats, leptospirosis from dogs, psittacosis from chickens and parrots, and brucellosis from cattle. We're similarly susceptible to picking up diseases from wild animals, such as the tularemia that hunters occasionally get from skinning wild rabbits.

In the second stage, a former animal pathogen evolves to the point where it does get transmitted directly between people and causes epidemics. However, the epidemic dies out for several reasons—being cured by modern medicine, stopping when everybody has been infected and died, or stopping when everybody has been infected and become immune. For example, a previously unknown disease termed *o'nyong-nyong* fever appeared in East Africa in 1959 and infected several million Africans. It probably arose from a virus of monkeys and was transmitted to humans by mosquitoes. The fact that patients recovered quickly and became immune to further attack helped cause the new disease to die out quickly.

The annals of medicine are full of diseases that sound like no known disease today but that once caused terrifying epidemics before disappearing as mysteriously as they had come. Who alive today remembers the "English sweating sickness" that swept and terrified Europe between 1485 and 1578, or the "Picardy sweats" of eighteenth- and nineteenth-century France?

A third stage in the evolution of our major diseases is represented by former animal pathogens that establish themselves in humans and that do not die out; until they do, the question of whether they will become major killers of humanity remains up for grabs. The future is still very uncertain for Lassa fever, first observed in 1969 in Nigeria and caused by a virus probably derived from rodents. Better established is Lyme disease, caused by a spirochete that we get from the bite of a tick. Although the first known human cases in the United States appeared only as recently as 1962, Lyme disease is already reaching epidemic proportions in the Northeast, on the West Coast, and in the upper Midwest. The future of AIDS, derived from monkey viruses, is even more secure, from the virus's perspective.

The final stage of this evolution is represented by the major, long-established epidemic diseases confined to humans. These diseases must have been the evolutionary survivors of far more pathogens that tried to make the jump to us from animals—and mostly failed.

Diseases represent evolution in progress, as microbes adapt by natural selection to new hosts. Compared with cows' bodies, though, our bodies offer different immune defenses and different chemistry. In that new environment, a microbe must evolve new ways to live and propagate itself.

The best-studied example of microbes evolving these new ways involves myxomatosis, which hit Australian rabbits in 1950. The myxoma virus, native to a wild species of Brazilian rabbit, was known to cause a lethal epidemic in European domestic rabbits, which are a different species. The virus was intentionally introduced to Australia in the hopes of ridding the continent of its plague of European rabbits, foolishly introduced in the nineteenth century. In the first year, myxoma produced a gratifying (to Australian farmers) 99.8 percent mortality in infected rabbits. Fortunately for the rabbits and unfortunately for the farmers, the death rate then dropped in the second year to 90 percent and eventually to 25 percent, frustrating hopes of eradicating rabbits completely from Australia. The problem was that the myxoma virus evolved to serve its own interests, which differed from the farmers' interests and those of the rabbits. The virus changed to kill fewer rabbits and to permit lethally infected ones to live longer before dying. The result was bad for Australian farmers but good for the virus: a less lethal myxoma virus spreads baby viruses to more rabbits than did the original, highly virulent myxoma.

For a similar example in humans, consider the surprising evolution of syphilis. Today we associate syphilis with genital sores and a very slowly developing disease, leading to the death of untreated victims only after many years. However, when syphilis was first definitely recorded in Europe in 1495, its pustules often covered the body from the head to the knees, caused flesh to fall off people's faces, and led to death within a few months. By 1546 syphilis had evolved into the disease with the symptoms known to us today. Apparently, just as with myxomatosis, those syphilis spirochetes evolved to keep their victims alive longer in order to transmit their spirochete offspring into more victims.

How, then, does all this explain the outcome of 1492—that Europeans conquered and depopulated the New World, instead of Native Americans conquering and depopulating Europe?

Part of the answer, of course, goes back to the invaders' technological advantages. European guns and steel swords were more effective weapons than Native American stone axes and wooden clubs. Only Europeans had ships capable of crossing the ocean and horses that could provide a decisive advantage in battle. But that's not the whole answer. Far more Native Americans died in bed than on the battlefield—the victims of germs, not of guns and swords. Those germs undermined Indian resistance by killing most Indians and their leaders and by demoralizing the survivors.

The role of disease in the Spanish conquests of the Aztec and Inca empires is especially well documented. In 1519 Cortés landed on the coast of Mexico with 600 Spaniards to conquer the fiercely militaristic Aztec Empire, which at the time had a population of many millions. That Cortés reached the Aztec capital of Tenochtitlán, escaped with the loss of "only" two-thirds of his force, and managed to fight his way back to the coast demonstrates both Spanish military advantages and the initial naïveté of the Aztecs. But when Cortés's next onslaught came, in 1521, the Aztecs were no longer naive; they fought street by street with the utmost tenacity.

What gave the Spaniards a decisive advantage this time was smallpox, which reached Mexico in 1520 with the arrival of one infected slave from Spanish Cuba. The resulting epidemic proceeded to kill nearly half the Aztecs. The survivors were demoralized by the mysterious illness that killed Indians and spared Spaniards, as if advertising the Spaniards' invincibility. By 1618 Mexico's initial population of 20 million had plummeted to about 1.6 million.

Pizarro had similarly grim luck when he landed on the coast of Peru in 1531 with about 200 men to conquer the Inca Empire. Fortunately for Pizarro, and unfortunately for the Incas, smallpox had arrived overland around 1524, killing much of the Inca population, including both Emperor Huayna Capac and his son and designated successor, Ninan Cuyoche. Because of the vacant throne, two other sons of Huayna Capac, Atahuallpa and Huáscar, became embroiled in a civil war that Pizarro exploited to conquer the divided Incas.

In the century or two following Columbus's arrival in the New World, the Indian population declined by about 95 percent. The main killers were European germs, to which the Indians had never been exposed.

When we in the United States think of the most populous New World societies existing in 1492, only the Aztecs and Incas come to mind. We forget that North America also supported populous Indian societies in the Mississippi Valley. Sadly, these societies too would disappear. But in this case conquistadores contributed nothing directly to the societies' destruction; the conquistadores' germs, spreading in advance, did everything. When De Soto marched through the Southeast in 1540, he came across Indian towns abandoned two years previously because nearly all the inhabitants had died in epidemics. However, he was still able to see some of the densely populated towns lining the lower Mississippi. By a century and a half later, though, when French settlers returned to the lower Mississippi, almost all those towns had vanished. Their relics are the great mound sites of the Mississippi Valley. Only recently have we come to realize that the mound-building societies were still largely intact when Columbus arrived, and that they collapsed between 1492 and the systematic European exploration of the Mississippi.

When I was a child in school, we were taught that North America had originally been occupied by about one million Indians. That low number helped justify the white conquest of what could then be viewed as an almost empty continent.

However, archeological excavations and descriptions left by the first European explorers on our coasts now suggest an initial number of around 20 million. In the century or two following Columbus's arrival in the New World, the Indian population is estimated to have declined by about 95 percent.

The main killers were European germs, to which the Indians had never been exposed and against which they therefore had neither immunologic nor genetic resistance. Smallpox, measles, influenza, and typhus competed for top rank among the killers. As if those were not enough, pertussis, plague, tuberculosis, diphtheria, mumps, malaria, and yellow fever came close behind. In countless cases Europeans were actually there to witness the decimation that occurred when the germs arrived. For example, in 1837 the Mandan Indian tribe, with one of the most elaborate cultures in the Great Plains, contracted smallpox thanks to a steamboat traveling up the Missouri River from St. Louis. The population of one Mandan village crashed from 2,000 to less than 40 within a few weeks.

The one-sided exchange of lethal germs between the Old and New worlds is among the most striking and consequence-laden facts of recent history. Whereas over a dozen major infectious diseases of Old World origins became established in the New World, not a single major killer reached Europe from the Americas. The sole possible exception is syphilis, whose area of origin still remains controversial.

That one-sidedness is more striking with the knowledge that large, dense human populations are a prerequisite for the evolution of crowd diseases. If recent reappraisals of the pre-Columbian New World population are correct, that population was not far below the contemporaneous population of Eurasia. Some New World cities, like Tenochtitlán, were among the world's most populous cities at the time. Yet Tenochtitlán didn't have awful germs waiting in store for the Spaniards. Why not?

One possible factor is that the rise of dense human populations began somewhat later in the New World than in the Old. Another is that the three most populous American centers—the Andes, Mexico, and the Mississippi Valley—were never connected by regular fast trade into one gigantic breeding ground for microbes, in the way that Europe, North Africa, India, and China became connected in late Roman times.

The main reason becomes clear, however, if we ask a simple question: From what microbes could any crowd diseases of the Americas have evolved? We've seen that Eurasian crowd diseases evolved from diseases of domesticated herd animals. Significantly, there were many such animals in Eurasia. But there were only five animals that became domesticated in the Americas: the turkey in Mexico and parts of North America, the guinea pig and llama/alpaca (probably derived from the same original wild species) in the Andes, the Muscovy duck in tropical South America, and the dog throughout the Americas.

That extreme paucity of New World domestic animals reflects the paucity of wild starting material. About 80 percent of the big wild mammals of the Americas became extinct at the end of the last ice age, around 11,000 years ago, at approximately the same time that the first well-attested wave of Indian hunters spread over the Americas. Among the species that disappeared were ones that would have yielded useful domesticates, such as American horses and camels. Debate still rages as to whether those extinctions were due to climate changes or to the impact of Indian hunters on prey that had never seen humans. Whatever the reason, the extinctions removed most of the basis for Native American animal domestication—and for crowd diseases.

The few domesticates that remained were not likely sources of such diseases. Muscovy ducks and turkeys don't live in enormous flocks, and they're not naturally endearing species (like young lambs) with which we have much physical contact. Guinea pigs may have contributed a trypanosome infection like Chagas' disease or leishmaniasis to our catalog of woes, but

that's uncertain. Initially the most surprising absence is of any human disease derived from llamas (or alpacas), which are tempting to consider as the Andean equivalent of Eurasian livestock. However, llamas had three strikes against them as a source of human pathogens: their wild relatives don't occur in big herds as do wild sheep, goats, and pigs; their total numbers were never remotely as large as the Eurasian populations of domestic livestock, since llamas never spread beyond the Andes; and llamas aren't as cuddly as piglets and lambs and aren't kept in such close association with people. (You may not think of piglets as cuddly, but human mothers in the New Guinea highlands often nurse them, and they frequently live right in the huts of peasant farmers.)

The importance of animal-derived diseases for human history extends far beyond the Americas. Eurasian germs played a key role in decimating native peoples in many other parts of the world as well, including the Pacific islands, Australia, and southern Africa. Racist Europeans used to attribute those conquests to their supposedly better brains. But no evidence for such better brains has been forthcoming. Instead, the conquests were made possible by Europeans nastier germs, and by the technological advances and denser populations that Europeans ultimately acquired by means of their domesticated plants and animals.

So on this 500th anniversary of Columbus's discovery, let's try to regain our sense of perspective about his hotly debated achievements. There's no doubt that Columbus was a great visionary, seaman, and leader. There's also no doubt that he and his successors often behaved as bestial murderers. But those facts alone don't fully explain why it took so few European immigrants to initially conquer and ultimately supplant so much of the native population of the Americas. Without the germs Europeans brought with them—germs that were derived from their animals—such conquests might have been impossible.

History and Ethnoarchaeology

How many times have you misplaced your car keys? Locked yourself out of the house? Lost your wallet? Your address book? Sometimes these artifacts are recovered and brought back into the historical present. Sometimes they are lost forever, becoming part of the rubbish of a extant culture. Have you ever noticed that lost things, when found, are always in the *last* place you thought to look? Is this a law of science?

Here is an opportunity to practice historical archaeology. You may wish to try this puzzler in order to practice thinking like an archaeologist. (Do not forget to apply the basics discussed in unit 1.) The incident recounted here is true, only the names and places were changed to protect the privacy of the famous personages involved in this highly charged mystery.

Problem: Dr. Wheeler, an archaeologist at a large university, left his office on the evening of December 20, 1989, around 9 p.m. on a cold Wednesday evening, preceding the long holiday. Immediately before he left his office, he states that he placed a thin, reddish, three-ring notebook in an unlocked cupboard in his office.

Dr. Wheeler states he went directly to his designated campus parking lot, got into his motorcar, and drove directly home to Marshalltown Goldens. When he arrived at home, he went straight to his study.

Dr. Wheeler had a great holiday with his family and thought nothing more of his notebook until the university resumed its session on Wednesday, January 3, 1990. Upon returning to his office, Dr. Wheeler could not find his notebook in the cupboard, and he became very agitated.

He chased his assistant Mortimer around the office wielding a wicked-looking Acheulean hand ax. Poor Mortimer claimed he had no knowledge of the whereabouts of the notebook. But Dr. Wheeler had always suspected that Mortimer pinched pens and pencils from his desk, so, naturally. . . . But Mortimer protested so earnestly that Dr. Wheeler eventually calmed down, had a cup of tea, and decided that perhaps he had absent mindedly taken the notebook home after all.

However, a thorough search of his home indicated that the notebook was clearly not there. It was lost! Dr. Wheeler was almost jolly well lost himself when his wife, Leonora, caught him excavating her rose garden in the vain hope that the family dog had buried the lost article there. It was a professor's nightmare, since the notebook contained the only copy of all his class records for the entire term. What could he do? He knew he was in danger of being fired from his chair for moral ineptitude.

So, of course, Dr. Wheeler approached the problem in the manner of a proper, eccentric archaeologist. He had another cup of tea and generated several hypotheses about where his notebook might be. He tested these hypotheses, but none of them yielded his notebook. Considered a good archaeologist, he kept on generating hypotheses.

Now, as is sometimes the case, Lady Luck intervened when his faithful assistant Mortimer received a phone call on January 9 from a woman who had found the missing notebook on the evening of December 31 in a gutter! To be precise, she found it in a family neighborhood on the corner of Olduvai Drive and East Turkana Avenue in Hadar Heights, about one mile from the university. Please note that this area is in the opposite direction of Dr. Wheeler's home in Marshalltown Goldens. The notebook was wet and muddy, and it was wedged down on a gutter grill. The woman, a grammar school teacher, had been trying to call the university during the holiday without success.

Greatly relieved, Dr. Wheeler the next day sent Mortimer over to the kind lady's home, and thus he received his class records. Dr. Wheeler was so relieved when Mortimer returned with the notebook that he invited him to sit down and join him for a cup of tea. But Dr. Wheeler was not satisfied with merely recovering his notebook. He was curious to know what had happened to it and why. He continued to generate more sophisticated hypotheses until . . . ?

The Challenge: Now, it is your turn to be Dr. Wheeler. Trace the whereabouts of the lost three-ring notebook from the night of Wednesday, December 20, 1989, to the time of its return to Dr. Wheeler on January 10, 1990.

How do you do this? Review everything you know to be true, carefully. Using this as your initial data base, set up a hypothesis to account for the lost notebook. This means a plausible series of events to account for the mysterious traveling notebook. Continue to refine your hypothesis and/or make alternative hypotheses until you arrive at the simplest possible explanation that is largely supported by direct or deduced data.

Consider that you are doing historical archaeology. Ask your living informant(s) for information first. What could you ask Dr. Wheeler? You could ask, Did you go to the restroom before you left the building on December 20? Where was your motorcar parked? Was it raining? Did you stop and talk to anybody on your way to the car? Where were you on December 31? And don't forget Mortimer. And the lady who found the notebook. Let your imagination fly free. Creativity is the core of all science.

Hints: Dr. Wheeler's university office was never broken into. Poor Mortimer and the kind lady who found the notebook had nothing to do with the whereabouts of the notebook. Dr. Wheeler's family and his dog were not involved with the missing notebook. Do not look now, but you are thinking like an archaeologist. It is a lot of fun and it will reward you well.

Looking Ahead: Challenge Questions

How was archaeology used as propaganda to fuel the Nazi movement in World War II? In your judgment, did the Nazi archaeologists really believe their own lies? Can you think of other instances where archaeology has been used as propaganda?

What kinds of evidence do forensic archaeologists use to solve past murders?

Do you think the evidence is conclusive that the daughter of Russian czar Nicholas, Anastasia, was killed with the rest of her family during the Bolshevik Revolution? Defend your answer.

What is historical archaeology? How does it differ from other kinds of archaeology? What is the relationship between history and historical archaeology?

What do you think happens when the archaeological record rewrites history?

Germany's Nazi Past
The Past as Propaganda

*How Hitler's archaeologists distorted European prehistory to
justify racist and territorial goals.*

Bettina Arnold

The manipulation of the past for political purposes has been a common theme in history. Consider Darius I (521–486 B.C.), one of the most powerful rulers of the Achaemenid, or Persian, empire. The details of his accession to power, which resulted in the elimination of the senior branch of his family, are obscured by the fact that we have only his side of the story, carved on the cliff face of Behistun in Iran. The list of his victories, and by association his right to rule, are the only remaining version of the truth. Lesson number one: If you are going to twist the past for political ends, eliminate rival interpretations.

The use of the past for propaganda is also well documented in more recent contexts. The first-century Roman historian Tacitus produced an essay titled "On the Origin and Geography of Germany." It is less a history or ethnography of the German tribes than a moral tract or political treatise. The essay was intended to contrast the debauched and degenerate Roman Empire with the virtuous German people, who embodied the uncorrupted morals of old Rome. Objective reporting was not the goal of Tacitus's *Germania;* the manipulation of the facts was considered justified if it had the desired effect of contrasting past Roman glory with present Roman decline. Ironically, this particular piece of historical propaganda was eventually appropriated by a regime notorious for its use and abuse of the past for political, imperialist, and racist purposes: the Third Reich.

The National Socialist regime in Germany fully appreciated the propaganda value of the past, particularly of prehistoric archaeology, and exploited it with characteristic efficiency. The fact that German prehistoric archaeology had been largely ignored before Hitler's rise to power in 1933 made the appropriation of the past for propaganda that much easier. The concept of the *Kulturkreis,* pioneered by the linguist-turned-prehistorian Gustav Kossinna in the 1920s and defined as the identification of ethnic regions on the basis of excavated material culture, lent theoretical support to Nazi expansionist aims in central and eastern Europe. Wherever an artifact of a type designated as "Germanic" was found, the land was declared to be ancient Germanic territory. Applied to prehistoric archaeology, this perspective resulted in the neglect or distortion of data that did not directly apply to Germanic peoples. During the 1930s scholars whose specialty was provincial Roman archaeology were labeled *Römlinge* by the extremists and considered anti-German. The Römisch Germanische Kommission in Mainz, founded in 1907, was the object of numerous defamatory attacks, first by Kossinna and later by Alfred Rosenberg and his organization. Rosenberg, a Nazi ideologue, directed the Amt Rosenberg, which conducted ethnic, cultural, and racial research.

Altered prehistory also played an important role in rehabilitating German self-respect after the humiliating defeat of 1918. The dedication of the 1921 edition of Kossinna's seminal work *German Prehistory: A Preeminently National Discipline* reads: "To the German people, as a building block in the reconstruction of the externally as well as internally disintegrated fatherland."

According to Nazi doctrine, the Germanic culture of northern Europe was responsible for virtually all major intellectual and technological achievements of Western civilization. Maps that appeared in archaeological publications between 1933 and 1945 invariably showed the Germanic homeland as the center of diffusionary waves, bringing civilization to less developed cultures to the south, west, and east. Hitler presented his own views on this subject in a dinner-table monologue in which he referred to the Greeks as Germans who had survived a northern natural catastrophe and evolved a highly developed culture in southern contexts. Such wishful thinking was supported by otherwise reputable archaeologists. The *Research Report of the Reichsbund for German Prehistory,*

July to December 1941, for example, reported the nine-week expedition of the archaeologist Hans Reinerth and a few colleagues to Greece, where they claimed to have discovered major new evidence of Indogermanic migration to Greece during Neolithic times.

This perspective was ethnocentric, racist, and genocidal. Slavic peoples occupying what had once been, on the basis of the distribution of archaeological remains, Germanic territory, were to be relocated or exterminated to supply true Germans with *Lebensraum* (living space). When the new Polish state was created in 1919, Kossinna published an article, "The German Ostmark, Home Territory of the Germans," which used archaeological evidence to support Germany's claim to the area. Viewed as only temporarily occupied by racially inferior "squatters," Poland and Czechoslovakia could be reclaimed for "racially pure" Germans.

Prehistoric archaeologists in Germany, who felt they had been ignored, poorly funded, and treated as second-class citizens by colleagues specializing in the more honored disciplines of classical and Near Eastern archaeology, now seemed to have everything to gain by an association with the rising Nazi party. Between 1933, the year of Hitler's accession to power, and 1935, eight new chairs were created in German prehistory, and funding became available for prehistoric excavations across Germany and eastern Europe on an unprecedented scale. Numerous institutes came into being during this time, such as the Institute for Prehistory in Bonn in 1938. Museums for protohistory were established, and prehistoric collections were brought out of storage and exhibited, in many cases for the first time. Institutes for rune research were created to study the *futhark,* or runic alphabet in use in northern Europe from about the third to the thirteenth centuries A.D. Meanwhile, the Römisch Germanisches Zentral Museum in Mainz became the Zentral Museum für Deutsche Vor- und Frühgeschichte in 1939. (Today it has its pre-war title once again.)

Open-air museums like the reconstructed Neolithic and Bronze Age lake settlements at Unteruhldingen on Lake Constanz were intended to popularize prehistory. An archaeological film series, produced and directed by the prehistorian Lothar Zotz, included titles like *Threatened by the Steam Plow, Germany's Bronze Age, The Flames of Prehistory,* and *On the Trail of the Eastern Germans.* The popular journals such as *Die Kunde (The Message),* and *Germanen-Erbe (Germanic Heritage)* proliferated. The latter publication was produced by the Ahnenerbe ("Ancestor History") organization, run as a personal project of Reichs-führer-SS and chief of police Heinrich Himmler and funded by interested Germans to research, excavate, and restore real and imagined Germanic cultural relics. Himmler's interests in mysticism and the occult extended to archaeology; SS archaeologists were sent out in the wake of invading German forces to track down important archaeological finds and antiquities to be transported back to the Reich. It was this activity that inspired Steven Spielberg's *Raiders of the Lost Ark.*

The popular journals contained abundant visual material. One advertisement shows the reconstruction of a Neolithic drum from a pile of meaningless sherds. The text exhorts readers to "keep your eyes open, for every *Volksgenosse* [fellow German] can contribute to this important national project! Do not assume that a ceramic vessel is useless because it falls apart during excavation. Carefully preserve even the smallest fragment!" An underlined sentence emphasizes the principal message: "Every single find is important because it represents a document of our ancestors!"

Amateur organizations were actively recruited by appeals to patriotism. The membership flyer for the official National Confederation for German Prehistory (*Reichsbund für Deutsche Vorgeschichte*), under the direction of Hans Reinerth of the Amt Rosenberg, proclaimed: "Responsibility with respect to our indigenous prehistory must again fill every German with pride!" The organization stated its goals as "the interpretation and dissemination of unfalsified knowledge regarding the history and cultural achievements of our northern Germanic ancestors on German and foreign soil."

For Himmler objective science was not the aim of German prehistoric archaeology. Hermann Rauschning, an early party member who became disillusioned with the Nazis and left Germany before the war, quotes Himmler as saying: "The one and only thing that matters to us, and the thing these people are paid for by the State, is to have ideas of history that strengthen our people in their necessary national pride. In all this troublesome business we are only interested in one thing—to project into the dim and distant past the picture of our nation as we envisage it for the future. Every bit of Tacitus in his *Germania* is tendentious stuff. Our teaching of German origins has depended for centuries on a falsification. We are entitled to impose one of our own at any time."

Meanwhile archaeological evidence that did not conform to Nazi dogma was ignored or suppressed. A good example is the controversy surrounding the Externsteine, a natural sandstone formation near Horn in northern Germany. In the twelfth century Benedictine monks from the monastery in nearby Paderborn carved a system of chambers into the rock faces of the Externsteine. In the mid-1930s a contingent of SS Ahnenerbe researchers excavated at the site in an attempt to prove its significance as the center of the Germanic universe, a kind of Teutonic mecca. The excavators, led by Julius Andree, an archaeologist with questionable credentials and supported by Hermann Wirth, one of the founders of the SS Ahnenerbe, were looking for the remains of an early Germanic temple at the Externsteine, where they claimed a cult of solar worshipers had once flourished. The site was described in numerous publications as a monument to German unity and the glorious Germanic past, despite the fact that no convincing evidence of a temple or Germanic occupation of the site was ever found.

So preposterous were the claims made by Andree, Wirth, and their associates that numerous mainstream archaeologists openly questioned the findings of the investigators who became popularly known as *German omanen* or "Germanomaniacs." Eventually Himmler and the Ahnenerbe organization disowned the project, but not before several hundred books and pamphlets on the alleged cult site had been published.

By 1933 the Nazis had gone a step further, initiating a movement whose goal was to replace all existing religious denominations with a new pseudo-pagan state religion based loosely on Germanic mythology, solar worship, nature cults, and a Scandinavian people's assembly or *thing,* from which the new movement derived its name. Central to the movement were open-air theaters or *Thingstätten,* where festivals, military ceremonies, and morality plays, known as *Thingspiele,* were to be staged. To qualify as a Thingstätte, evidence of significant Germanic occupation of the site had to be documented. There was considerable competition among municipalities throughout Germany for this honor. Twelve Thingstätten had been dedicated by September 1935, including one on the summit of the Heiligenberg in Heidelberg.

The Heiligenberg was visited sporadically during the Neolithic, possibly for ritual purposes; there is no evidence of permanent occupation. It was densely settled during the Late Bronze Age (1200–750 B.C.), and a double wall-and-ditch system was built there in the Late Iron Age (200 B.C. to the Roman occupation), when it was a hillfort settlement. Two provincial Roman watchtowers, as well as several Roman dedicatory inscriptions, statue bases, and votive stones, have been found at the site.

When excavations in the 1930s failed to produce evidence of Germanic occupation the Heiligenberg was granted Thingstätte status on the basis of fabricated evidence in the published excavation reports. Ironically, most of the summit's prehistoric deposits were destroyed in the course of building the open-air arena. The Heiligenberg Thingstätte actually held only one Thingspiel before the Thing movement was terminated. Sensing the potential for resistance from German Christians, the Ministry of Propaganda abandoned the whole concept in 1935. Today the amphitheater is used for rock concerts.

Beyond its convenience for propaganda and as justification for expansion into countries like Czechoslovakia and Poland, the archaeological activities of the Amt Rosenberg and Himmler's Ahnenerbe were just so much window dressing for the upper echelons of the party. There was no real respect for the past or its remains. While party prehistorians like Reinerth and Andree distorted the facts, the SS destroyed archaeological sites like Biskupin in Poland. Until Germany's fortunes on the eastern front suffered a reversal in 1944, the SS Ahnenerbe conducted excavations at Biskupin, one of the best-preserved Early Iron Age (600–400 B.C.) sites in all of central Europe. As the troops retreated, they were ordered to demolish as much of the site's preserved wooden fortifications and structures as possible.

Not even Hitler was totally enthusiastic about Himmler's activities. He is quoted by Albert Speer, his chief architect, as complaining: "Why do we call the whole world's attention to the fact that we have no past? It's bad enough that the Romans were erecting great buildings when our forefathers were still living in mud huts; now Himmler is starting to dig up these villages of mud huts and enthusing over every potsherd and stone axe he finds. All we prove by that is that we were still throwing stone hatchets and crouching around open fires when Greece and Rome had already reached the highest stage of culture. We should really do our best to keep quiet about this past. Instead Himmler makes a great fuss about it all. The present-day Romans must be having a laugh at these revelations."

"Official" involvement in archaeology consisted of visits by Himmler and various SS officers to SS-funded and staffed excavations, like the one on the Erdenburg in the Rhineland, or press shots of Hitler and Goebbels viewing a reconstructed "Germanic" Late Bronze Age burial in its tree-trunk coffin, part of the 1934 "Deutsches Volk—Deutsche Arbeit" exhibition in Berlin. Party appropriation of prehistoric data was evident in the use of Indo-European and Germanic design symbols in Nazi uniforms and regalia. The double lightning bolt, symbol of Himmler's SS organization, was adapted from a Germanic rune. The swastika is an Indo-European sun symbol which appears in ceramic designs as early as the Neolithic in western Europe and continues well into early medieval times.

German archaeologists during this period fall into three general categories: those who were either true believers or self-serving opportunists; those (the vast majority) who accepted without criticism the appropriation and distortion of prehistoric archaeology; and those who openly opposed these practices.

Victims of the regime were persecuted on the basis of race or political views, and occasionally both. Gerhard Bersu, who had trained a generation of post–World War I archaeologists in the field techniques of settlement archaeology, was prematurely retired from the directorship of the Römisch Germanische Kommission in 1935. His refusal to condone or conduct research tailored to Nazi ideological requirements, in addition to his rejection of the racist Kossinna school, ended his career as a prehistorian until after World War II. The official reason given for the witch-hunt, led by Hans Reinerth under the auspices of the Amt Rosenberg, was Bersu's Jewish heritage. By 1950 Bersu was back in Germany, again directing the Römisch Germanische Kommission.

It should be noted that some sound work was accomplished during this period despite political interference. The vocabulary of field reports carefully conformed to the dictates of funding sources, but the methodology was usually unaffected. Given time this would have changed as politically motivated terms and concepts altered the intellectual vocabulary of the discipline. In 1935, for example, the entire prehistoric and early historic chronologies were officially renamed: the Bronze and pre-Roman Iron Ages became the "Early Germanic period," the Roman Iron Age the "Climax Germanic period," the Migration period the "Late Germanic period," and everything from the Carolingians to the thirteenth century the "German Middle Ages."

It is easy to condemn the men and women who were part of the events that transformed the German archaeological community between 1933 and 1945. It is much more difficult to understand the choices they made or avoided in the social and political contexts of the time. Many researchers who began as advocates of Reinerth's policies in the Amt Rosenberg and Himmler's Ahnenerbe organization later became disenchanted. Others, who saw the system as a way to develop and support prehistory as a discipline, were willing to accept the costs of the Faustian bargain it offered. The benefits were real, and continue to be felt to this day in the institutions and programs founded between 1933 and 1945.

The paralysis felt by many scholars from 1933 to 1945 continued to affect research in the decades after the war. Most scholars who were graduate students during the 12-year period had to grapple with a double burden: a humiliating defeat and the disorienting experience of being methodologically "deprogrammed." Initially there was neither time nor desire to examine the reasons for the Nazi prostitution of archaeology. Unfortunately prehistoric archaeology is the only German social-science discipline that has still to publish a self-critical study of its role in the events of the 1930s and 1940s.

The reluctance of German archaeologists to come to terms with the past is a complex issue. German prehistoric archaeology is still a young discipline, and first came into its own as a result of Nazi patronage. There is therefore a certain feeling that any critical analysis of the motives and actions of the generation and the regime that engendered the discipline would be ungrateful at

The reluctance of German archaeologists to come to terms with the past is a complex issue.

best and at worst a betrayal of trust. The vast majority of senior German archaeologists, graduate students immediately after the war, went straight from the front lines to the universities, and their dissertation advisers were men whose careers had been determined by their connections within the Nazi party.

The German system of higher education is built upon close bonds of dependence and an almost medieval fealty between a graduate student and his or her dissertation advisor. These bonds are maintained even after the graduate student has embarked on an academic career. Whistle-blowers are rare, since such action would amount to professional suicide. But in the past decade or so, most of the generation actively involved in archaeological research and teaching between 1933 and 1945 have died. Their knowledge of the personal intrigues and alliances that allowed the Nazi party machine to function has died with them. Nonetheless, there are indications that the current generation of graduate students is beginning to penetrate the wall of silence that has surrounded this subject since 1945. The remaining official documents and publications may allow at least a partial reconstruction of the role of archaeology in the rise and fall of the Nazi regime.

The future of prehistoric archaeology in the recently unified Germany will depend on an open confrontation with the past. Archaeologists in the former East Germany must struggle with the legacy of both Nazi and Communist manipulation of their discipline. Meanwhile, the legacy of the Faustian bargain struck by German archaeologists with the Nazi regime should serve as a cautionary tale beyond the borders of a unified Germany: Archaeological research funded wholly or in part by the state is vulnerable to state manipulation. The potential for political exploitation of the past seems to be greatest in countries experiencing internal instability. Germany in the years following World War I was a country searching for its own twentieth-century identity. Prehistoric archaeology was one means to that end.

Murders From the Past

*Sleuthing crimes of the past, forensic anthropologists open up files
on Lizzie Borden, the Colorado Cannibal, Zachary Taylor, and
Huey "Kingfish" Long, among others.*

James Dickerson

An electric saw buzzed through a lead container that had been sealed for 150 years. Slowly, the liner lid was removed, exposing the remains of Zachary Taylor, the twelfth president of the United States. Face to face with the former president, a blue-ribbon panel of investigators was surprised to see a thick mass of dark hair and a large cloth bow under the chin. Since the president's visit was meant to be brief, his hosts went to work immediately. University of Florida forensic anthropologist Bill Maples methodically cut away the president's clothing, finding abundant body hair beneath the one-piece, pleated shroud. Then he took hair, nail, and tissue samples, hoping they would prove whether the president had succumbed to arsenic poisoning or died of natural causes.

Ghoulish? Perhaps to most. But to forensic sleuths like Maples, who focus on murders and other mysteries a century or more old, exhuming and examining the remains of celebrities from presidents to political assassins is business as usual.

In another case, for instance, Maples seeks to identify the remains of Francisco Pizarro, the Spanish conqueror of Peru. And his colleague James Starrs, a lawyer and forensic scientist at George Washington University in Washington, DC, has exhumed the remains of Dr. Carl Austin Weiss, the alleged assassin of the controversial U.S. senator from Louisiana, Huey Long. When held up to the scrutiny of modern science, Weiss's remains and other buried evidence may show whether the doctor was truly Long's assassin or was innocent, as his descendants have claimed.

It's possible to resolve such issues today, thanks to the extraordinary range and power of modern forensic techniques. Today's high-resolution microscopes, for instance, can analyze knife marks on bone, distinguishing between different knives or the marks left by animals. X-rays can probe beneath the surface of grave sites. Sophisticated chemical and nuclear technologies can detect trace amounts of incriminating poisons. And using computers, experts can superimpose old photos of a victim or suspect on top of x-ray images of facial bones, determining whether or not the identities are a match.

In fact, whether it's determining the identity of an eighteenth-century cannibal or investigating the fate of the princess Anastasia Romanov, forensic anthropologists have begun to rewrite the history of murder, mayhem, and sensational crime. For a look at some of the most fascinating investigations to date, open *Omni*'s murder dossier, and read on.

WHO KILLED THE KINGFISH?

VICTIM: Huey Long, U.S. senator and former governor from Louisiana.
DEATH NOTES: The politically powerful Long was shot and killed while visiting the Louisiana State Capitol on September 8, 1935. The presumed assassin, a 29-year-old physician named Carl Weiss, was killed by Long's bodyguards in a hail of gunfire at the scene.
MURDER MYSTERY: Although the case against Weiss was considered open and shut at the time, questions began to emerge. First of all, officials were never able to establish a genuine motive. In addition, though police said Weiss's gun was found at the scene, no one could prove he had carried the gun into the Capitol. Did Carl Weiss really kill Huey Long, or was he just a patsy, a fall guy set up by one of the many bitter political enemies Long had cultivated over the years?
FORENSIC SLEUTHS: James Starrs, forensic scientist, George Washington University, Washington, DC; Douglas Ubelaker, curator of anthropology, National Museum of Natural History, Smithsonian Institution, Washington, DC; Lucien Haag, freelance "criminalist" and weapons expert, Phoenix; Irvin Sother, state medical examiner, West Virginia; and Alphonse Poklis, toxicologist, Medical College of Virginia at Richmond.
CLUES UNEARTHED: Weiss's remains were exhumed on October 20, 1991, at the Roselawn Cemetery in Baton Rouge and transported first to the Lafayette, Louisiana, pathology lab for cleaning, then to Ubelaker's lab at the National Museum of Natural History. To identify the remains as those of Weiss, Ubelaker used the technique of photographic imposition to

match the skull with old photos of the suspect. To rule out the likelihood that Weiss committed the act as a result of a brain tumor or while under the influence of drugs, toxicologist Poklis examined the anatomy of the skull and analyzed the chemical content of tissue and bones. Examining the remains, he also discovered that Weiss had been shot a minimum of 23 times, with half the wounds inflicted on his back. Several bullet wounds were found in his arms, suggesting a defensive posture. Ubelaker also found that Weiss had been shot from a "variety of angles, implying that his assailants came from many directions."

Then Haag, an expert in firearms and tool marks, stepped in to examine the contents of files squirreled away by the police superintendent. Perhaps most telling was a .32-caliber bullet thought to have come from the scene of the crime. After testing the bullet at the laboratory in Phoenix, Haag concluded it did not come from Weiss's gun. Since Long's bodyguards carried only larger .38- and .45-caliber pistols, Haag notes, the mysterious bullet raises the question of a second, never-reported .32-caliber pistol somewhere on the scene. It's possible, he proposes, that Weiss's gun was simply a plant to protect the identity of the true killer, the one that got away. Anyone who knew that Weiss carried a piece could have found one like it and committed the crime themselves, setting Weiss up for the fall, Haag says.

CONCLUSION: As a result of all the new evidence, the seemingly solid case against Weiss has been riddled with doubt.

WILL THE REAL PIZARRO PLEASE STAND?

VICTIM: Francisco Pizarro, Spanish conqueror of Peru.

DEATH NOTES: Francisco Pizarro, despised by native Peruvians because of his brutal reign, was stabbed to death by a crowd of angry subjects in 1541 at the age of 71 in full view of numerous witnesses. Pizarro subsequently faded into history where he remained a topic for academicians and scholars for more than 350 years.

QUESTION OF IDENTITY: The cir-

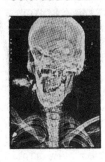

Back in time: To resolve some of the most gruesome and enigmatic murder mysteries of the past, physical anthropolo-gists like Bill Maples, top center, are digging up remains of both killers and victims as well as old murder weapons and more. Maples' colleagues, for instance, have exhumed the body of Dr. Carl Austin Weiss, top left, convicted, perhaps wrongfully, of assassinating the controversial U.S. senator Huey Long. Weiss's x-rayed skull is depicted, bottom right. Experts also want to study the hatchet supposedly used by Lizzie Borden, next page, top right, to kill her father, whose skull is shown, top right, and her stepmother, whose skull is depicted on the next page, bottom left. Bottom center on this page is another focus for forensic sleuthing: One Alferd Packer, convicted of the gruesome, cannibalistic murder of five prospectors seeking gold and silver in Colorado's San Juan Mountains. Though Packer was convicted by a jury of his peers, he always maintained his innocence and was eventually paroled. Packer died in 1907, leaving unanswered the question of whether he truly was the

vicious killer who ate his unwitting victims' remains. Shown above is a photo of the remains of the five victims shortly after exhumation in 1989. Another historical figure currently the subject of investigation is Meriwether Lewis, of Lewis and Clark fame, at right, who died of two gunshot wounds. The death was declared a suicide at the time but is now considered a murder. Also the topic of study was former U.S president Zachary Taylor, bottom right, who died suddenly, allegedly of gastroenteritis; despite this official cause of death, some experts have suggested arsenic poisoning instead. To unearth the truth, a team of forensic sleuths exhumed Taylor's remains in 1991, almost a century and a half after his untimely death. It's interesting to note that detailed chemical and nuclear tests at the Louisville medical examiner's office and at the Oak Ridge National Laboratory in Tennessee yielded no evidence of arsenic poisoning. But despite these results, say some experts, it's remotely possible that Taylor was poisoned with arsenic after all and that the evidence has simply leached from his body over the years.

cumstances of Pizarro's death are not in question, having been well documented at the time by the Spanish, who tortured witnesses to elicit the details. However, in the 1890s, Peruvian officials decided to put Pizarro's remains on exhibit as part of an upcoming celebration of Columbus's voyage. They asked officials at the Cathedral of the Plaza de Aramis in Lima for Pizarro's body and were directed to a mummy, which they put on view. Then, in 1978, workers in the cathedral uncovered a secret niche that had been walled over. On a shelf inside the niche was a lead box with a skull and an inscription identifying the contents as the head of Pizarro. Alongside this first box was another, this one containing the bones of several unidentified individuals. Who was the real Pizarro? The mummy that had been on display

for nearly a century or the skull and bones found in the cathedral crypt?

FORENSIC SLEUTHS: Bill Maples, anthropologist, University of Florida, Gainesville, and Bob Benfer, anthropologist, University of Missouri, Columbia.

CLUES UNEARTHED: A preliminary investigation by one of Benfer's students showed that postcranial bones in the second box matched the skull in the first. The matching bones were then assembled with the skull. The challenge for Maples and Benfer: determining whether the newly discovered bones contained marks consistent with knife or sword wounds and then determining whether similar wounds appeared on the mummy. Using straightforward visual observation, the researchers determined that the skeleton had been stabbed multiple times, consistent with

the reported demise of Pizarro. From the location of the wounds, Maples and Benfer concluded that Pizarro had been stabbed about the head and body and apparently had tried to shield himself with his arm, a reaction that is common in stabbing deaths. The mummy, on the other hand, exhibited no injuries whatsoever and could not have been Pizarro at all.

CONCLUSION: The remains of Pizarro had been hidden in the Cathedral crypt all along. The mystery solved, Peruvian officials exchanged the mummy with the bones, which are now on display instead. As for the mummy, it's on a piece of plywood down in the crypt. "Fame is fleeting," Maples observes, "even after death."

SEARCH FOR ANASTASIA

VICTIMS: Czar of Russia, Nicholas II; his wife, Alexandra; their five children, Olga, Tatlana, Marie, Anastasia, and Alexis; the royal physician; and several royal servants.

DEATH NOTES: On July 17, 1918, during the Bolshevik Revolution, the Russian czar and his family along with the royal physician and some servants were awakened and taken to the basement of the house in which they stayed. There, they were greeted by a hail of bullets and then stabbed with bayonets. According to one account, their bodies were hacked to pieces and soaked in acid. Two were burned.

MURDER MYSTERY: In what may

have been the ultimate game of Russian roulette, the assassins assigned to wipe out the royal family may have let two members slip through the cracks. According to rumors that have persisted ever since the fateful day, the princess Anastasia Romanov and her brother Alexis may have survived their grievous injuries and lived to tell the tale. One observer, for instance, recalled the czar's youngest daughter sitting up and screaming after the initial volley of bullets. And in the years that followed, a number of people have claimed to be Anastasia herself. Anna Anderson Manahan, who died in Charlottesville, Virginia, in 1984 at the age of 82, was probably the most publicized claimant. For 60 years she tried

to convince people she was Princess Anastasia and even filed a lawsuit in Germany for an $85 million dowry supposedly held in trust. German bankers were vague about the existence of a trust fund, however, and she lost the case. Although a movie was made of her struggle, her claims were discounted, primarily because she could not speak Russian. Was Manahan or another claimant the true Anastasia Romanov? Did the youngest czarist princess survive?

FORENSIC SLEUTHS: Bill Maples; Lowell Levine, codirector of the New York State Police Forensic Sciences Unit in Albany; Michael Baden, New York City pathologist; and Catherine

One of the biggest mysteries of the past involved the lost remains of

Francisco Pizarro, top left, Spanish conqueror of Peru, stabbed to death by native Peruvians who despised his brutal reign. While the circumstances of Pizarro's death are not in question, experts have debated the legitimacy of the explorer's mummified remains, put on exhibit at the Cathedral of the Plaza de

Aramis in Lima. The mummy in question showed no evidence of a brutal attack, and when workers found

another batch of remains hidden behind a secret cathedral wall,

the identity of the true Pizarro was up for grabs. A bit of forensic sleuthing proved the mummy an imposter and the bones behind the hidden wall real.

Maples, "even after death." This page, center, is George Washington University lawyer and forensic scientist James Starrs, who investigated the

The mystery solved, Peruvian officials put the true remains on display. "Fame is fleeting," observed investigator Bill

murder of Huey Long, bottom left, and the true guilt of his

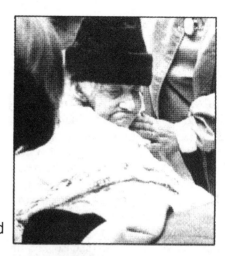

murderer, Carl Weiss, whose dead body is shown on the previous page on a Baton Rouge Capitol corridor floor. Forensic slueths investigating the Colorado Canni-bal have studied this sketch, above, created by artist John Randolph, the man said to have discovered the remains of the five unlucky victims brutally killed and then apparently filleted and eaten by Packer.

Photograph of the skull of victim George Noon, below, shows numerous hatchet marks. Finally,

experts trying to solve a royal murder mystery have compared photos of Anna Anderson Mana-han, right, with depictions of her royal high-ness Anastasia Romanov, bottom right, said to have been killed with the rest of the Russian royal family during the Bolshevik revolution. To her dying day, Manahan claimed she was the real Anastasia, whose remains have never been identified.

Did Anastasia survive? To get to the truth, scientists are hoping to find and study more royal bones at the bottom of a firepit.

Oakes, microtomist, New York State police.

CLUES UNEARTHED: In 1991, Russian authorities exhumed the remains of nine bodies thought to be the czar and those who perished with him. Also retrieved from the grave site were bullets and a broken acid jar. Soon after exhumation, American experts, including Maples and Levine, arrived at a lab in Yekaterinburg, a city some 800 miles east of Moscow. Their goal: to identify the bodies and determine the cause of death. The Americans quickly declared that historical accounts of the assassination were born out by the condition of the remains. "Three of the skulls showed clear evidence of gunshot wounds," Maples says, "and teeth and skulls showed evidence of etching and erosion by acid." There was even enough tissue on the remains of what was certainly the royal physician to hold the lower torso together. In fact, there was only one part of the story that could not be verified: the death of Anastasia. The skeleton of a 17-year-old female could not be found. Maples sees one last way to prove that Anastasia died: Locate a firepit containing the two bodies that were supposedly burned. According to historical accounts, the burned bodies belonged to Alexis, the czar's son, and a maid. But Maples says one of the burned bodies could turn out to be Anastasia. "If we found the bodies of two teenagers in a fire pit," he says, "I would feel confident that Anastasia did not survive."

CONCLUSION: DNA analysis conducted by British scientists confirmed the findings of forensic sleuths who went to Russia. After comparing blood samples taken from Prince Philip, a blood relative of the czar's wife, with tissue samples taken from the remains at Yekaterinburg, scientists were able to get a match. At the moment, the fate of Anastasia has been thrown into question. Russian investigators say Anastasia's remains were among those found. American experts are unsure. Recently, a lock of hair said to belong to Anna Anderson Manahan has been produced and will soon be subjected to DNA analysis. Hopefully, say the experts, they will be able to tell whether her genes and those of Prince Philip match.

PRESIDENTIAL POISON

VICTIM: Zachary Taylor, twelfth president of the United States.

DEATH NOTES: On July 4, 1850, President Taylor dedicated the cornerstone for the Washington Monument. After walking home from the ceremony, he ate a bowl of cherries and drank a glass of cold milk. A short while later, he became violently ill with diarrhea, severe vomiting, and dehydration. Five days later he died.

MURDER MYSTERY: At the time, Taylor's death was attributed to deadly gastroenteritis. But according to pundits, the same symptoms are characteristic of arsenic poisoning, and, they say, Taylor may have been murdered by enemies wishing to do him in. Historical novelist Clara Rising even has two prime suspects: then–Vice President Millard Fillmore and Kentucky senator Henry Clay. Taylor was opposed to the extension of slavery, Rising explains, and supported the admission of California as a free state, something that would have made free states more numerous than slave ones. After Taylor's death, however, Fillmore supported a compromise proposal by Clay in which California, a free state, was paired with New Mexico, a slave state; the balance of power was kept intact. Motive enough to assassinate a president? Rising and others say maybe so.

FORENSIC SLEUTHS: Clara Rising, Louisville; Bill Maples; Dr. Richard Greathouse, Jefferson County coroner, Louisville; Dr. George Nichols, medical examiner, Commonwealth of Kentucky, Louisville; and Dr. William Hamilton, medical examiner, Gainesville, Florida.

CLUES UNEARTHED: Before exhuming Taylor on June 17, 1991, researchers checked with White House historical records to determine if the president had been embalmed. In the 1800s, embalming almost always involved the use of arsenic, and if he had been embalmed, it would have been impossible to tell whether Taylor had in fact been poisoned. According to Rising, records show that Taylor's wife would not allow him to be embalmed.

Oxidation of the coffin's lead liner caused by large quantities of seeping body fluids offers additional evidence that embalming did not occur. The researchers also sent tissue samples to the Louisville medical examiner's toxicology lab and to the Oak Ridge National Laboratory in Tennessee, where it was placed in a powerful research reactor and bombarded with neutrons. When bombarded with neutrons, different metals give off different levels of radiation; arsenic, of course, has its own telltale signature. When the results were in, both the chemical and nuclear tests revealed only "normal levels of arsenic" consistent with neither embalming nor poisoning. The labs also checked for the presence of other heavy metals, including mercury and antimony, and found none.

CONCLUSION: The detailed tests found no evidence of arsenic poisoning. But despite the results, says Maples, it's remotely possible that Taylor was poisoned with arsenic after all and that the evidence has simply leached from his body over the years.

COLORADO CANNIBAL

VICTIMS: Shannon Bell, Israel Swan, James Humphrey, George Noon, and Frank Miller, five prospectors seeking gold and silver in Colorado's San Juan Mountains.

DEATH NOTES: In the winter of 1874, the five victims hired one Alferd Packer to guide them through the mountains. But when Packer returned to town after six weeks, he said he had lost the others in a snow storm. There had, indeed, been a raging storm, but authorities were suspicious because of Packer's appearance: Despite his claims of hardship and a shortage of food, he was noticeably fat and more interested in drinking than eating. In addition, he seemed to have far more money than he'd had *before* the trip. When a traveling artist located the remains of the missing men, he discovered evidence of foul play and even sketched the scene for *Harper's Weekly*. Finally authorities reported "marks of extreme violence" on the bodies of the victims and concluded that they had been murdered by ax or hatchet.

FORENSIC SLEUTHS: James Starrs; Douglas Ubelyker; Walter Birkby, forensic anthropologist, University of Arizona, Tucson; tool-mark expert Lucien Haag; and archeologist James Ayres, Tucson, Arizona.

MURDER MYSTERY: Before he could be charged with the murders, Packer escaped from authorities and remained at large for nine years. He was finally captured in 1883 and at his trial declared that four of the men had been murdered by Shannon Bell. He himself shot and then hacked Bell to death in self-defense, he claimed, after Bell attacked him. Packer was convicted and sentenced to death but won a new trial on a technicality. He was convicted a second time and sentenced to 40 years hard labor. At the turn of the century, however, a Denver newspaper columnist raised doubts about his guilt and succeeded in getting him paroled in 1901. He died in 1907. Was Packer innocent, or was he a vicious killer who ate the remains of his victims?

CLUES UNEARTHED: After the remains of the five prospectors were exhumed in July 1989, they were taken to the University of Arizona, where Walter Birkby is curator of physical anthropology. According to Birkby, the remains were in good condition, the result of soil with especially low levels of acid at the grave site. None of the bodies had been dismembered, he noted, but all had hatchet-like marks on the skull and had been defleshed. After the skeletons were assembled, Lucien Haag was called in to identify the marks found on the bones. Haag used a microscope to study the tool patterns and then made silicone rubber casts to preserve the marks for additional study.

According to investigators, the number, type, and location of implement marks leave no mystery as to how the prospectors died and what happened to them after death. "These individuals were all murdered," said Birkby. "All of them exhibited evidence of sharp implement marks on their bones, which is consistent with defleshing.

One individual had 14 hatchet marks on his skull." Some of the marks are clearly defensive, indicating some of the victims had held up their arms to ward off the blows of an ax or hatchet. Others received blows on the head, indicating they may have been sleeping when attacked. Many of the bones also showed very fine knife marks, Haag adds, an indication that these victims had, like steak, been filleted.

What about Packer's claim that Bell shot the others, causing him to shoot Bell in self-defense? Not likely, say the investigators. One individual probably committed all the murders, they explained, because the injuries were consistent from one cranium to the next. What's more, the researchers found only one bullet wound amongst all the victims—and that individual had been shot years before his death.
CONCLUSION: Packer's story did not hold up to scientific scrutiny. The jury that convicted him was right and his defenders were wrong. Alferd Packer was, indeed, "the Colorado Cannibal."

ON THE DOCKET:

Thanks to modern technology, the skeletal remains of historical figures have the potential to rewrite history by answering questions unanswerable at the time of death. Several cases still under study could rattle the cages of historians and law-enforcement officials:

Lizzie Borden. After an inept police investigation and a sensational murder trial in 1893, Lizzie Borden was found not guilty of hacking her father and 200-pound stepmother to death with an ax at their home in Fall River, Massachusetts. Despite her acquittal, Lizzie remained guilty in the eyes of the popular press and some historians. Enter forensic investigator James Starrs, who is convinced Lizzie Borden may have been innocent. Starrs wants permission from Borden family members to exhume the skulls of Lizzie's parents. If Lizzie is innocent, it can be proven scientifically, he says, "by comparing available physical evidence, such as the famous 'hoodoo hatchet,' with scientific analysis of the remains."

Meriwether Lewis. Also on Starrs' list of unsolved mysteries is the death of Meriwether Lewis (of Lewis and Clark fame). Lewis died in 1809 at an inn on the Natchez Trace southwest of Nashville, Tennessee. Governor of the Louisiana Territory at the time, he was on his way to Washington, DC, to meet with officials when he died of two gunshot wounds, one to the side and the other to the head. The death has long been labeled a suicide, but Starrs states that "the scientific evidence that he committed suicide is entirely deficient." Lewis may have been murdered,

---

'James Starrs hopes to exhume the skulls of Lizzie Borden's parents to compare with physical evidence such as the famous hoodoo hatchet.'

---

says Starrs. With the permission of Lewis's descendants, he hopes to exhume the remains and find out.

John Wilkes Booth. Abraham Lincoln was assassinated in April 1865 by John Wilkes Booth, who 12 days later was gunned down by soldiers in a barn—right? Wrong, according to Hugh Berryman, director of the Regional Forensic Center in Memphis; Nathaniel Orlowek, a religious educator at Beth Shalom Congregation in Potomac, Maryland; and Arthur Chitty, historian at the University of the South. They believe Booth may have escaped capture and lived another 38 years using the name John St. Helen before confessing his identity and committing suicide in Enid, Oklahoma. After his death, St. Helen's body was embalmed. But when the government showed no interest in investigating the claims, the lawyer to whom St. Helen confessed stored the mummy in his basement for 29 years. Eventually, the mummified body was sold to a carnival and then slipped out of sight. If the mummy can be recovered, says Berryman, it would be possible, using mod-

ern forensic technology, to make comparisons with known photographs of Booth. Meanwhile, Orlowek is attempting to exhume the body thought to belong to Booth and determine whether it is truly his.

Wild Bill Longley. On October 11, 1878, a notorious Texas outlaw named Wild Bill Longley was convicted of murder and hanged under the watchful eye of the local sheriff. His body was then buried in a cemetery near Giddings. Or was it? Family legend has it that he escaped the hangman's noose and relocated in Iberville Parish, Louisiana, where he adopted the sheriff's last name of Brown and lived a long life as a respected member of the community. According to family legend, in fact, Longley made a deal with the sheriff to fake the hanging using a harness to break his fall. Before burial, he escaped while the coffin was weighted with stones. The sheriff was subsequently killed in a gunfight with police in Chicago, and a man calling himself John Calhoun Brown began a new life in Louisiana. He fathered ten children, ran a successful timber business, and died around 1923.

These claims by the families of both the "original" Longley and the Brown descendants in Louisiana prompted Dr. Douglas Owsley, a forensic anthropologist at the Smithsonian Institution, to organize an investigative team. The first step was using a computer to compare photographs of the two men. "I was taken aback by the correspondence of the fit," he says. "They were very, very similar. "Betting on the "probability" that Longley and Brown were one and the same, Owsley worked with geologist Brooks Elwood at the University of Texas and Pat Mercado-Allinger of the Texas Historical Commission to excavate 25 graves at the cemetery where the outlaw's coffin, filled with stones, was said to lie. The outlaw's marker had been moved at least twice in more than a century, so it's no surprise that none of the 25 coffins turned out to be his. But the team will do some more historical research and then return to the cemetery, hoping to find a coffin full of stones.

Post-mortem at the Little Bighorn

Archeologists sift for clues at Custer's fatal battleground.

**Douglas D. Scott and
Melissa A. Connor**

The anniversary of the Battle of the Little Bighorn falls on June 26, the day 110 years ago when George Armstrong Custer led some 210 men to their death in the Montana Territory. In the years that followed, the story of Custer's Last Stand assumed legendary proportions, while much of the hard evidence of the battle remained unexamined. Then in August 1983, a wildfire scorched four-fifths of the 760 acres of Custer Battlefield National Monument (a cigarette tossed from a car on nearby State Route 212 may have ignited the drought-stricken vegetation), and the National Park Service, which administers the Monument, enlisted local archeologist Richard Fox to see whether artifacts might be recovered from the denuded landscape. The result has been a full-fledged study by the Midwest Archeological Center of the National Park Service and the University of Nebraska.

Along with Dick Harmon, of the U.S. Geological Survey, and Richard Fox, and aided by many volunteers, we have spent two field seasons encouraging the earth to yield its secrets about this historic battle. We chose to view the battleground as a crime scene, and by using forensic techniques, such as microscopic examination of firing-pin marks on cartridge cases and rifling marks on bullets, we have been able to

determine the weapons used by the various participants. These techniques, combined with the standard archeological practice of recording where artifacts are found, have enabled us to deduce the movement of individual firearms over the field of battle, verify cavalry positions, and pinpoint the previously unknown placement of the Indian warriors. Many human skeletal remains were also found, and these tell us of the wounds the men received, as well as the soldiers' general health and condition at the time of death.

The story of the battle begins in 1868, when the Treaty of Fort Laramie was signed with the Sioux and Cheyenne. Among other things, the treaty granted the Black Hills area to the Sioux for "as long as the grass was green and the sky was blue." In the early 1870s, however, rumors spread of gold in the Black Hills, and white miners began slipping into the reservation. In 1874, the U.S. government sent a geological team under Custer to check out these rumors. Gold was among the minerals found, and thereafter there was no stopping the hordes of miners who flowed onto the Indians' land.

The Sioux were disgusted with the government's inability to keep white people from trespassing, especially in the Black Hills, which they considered sacred. As the whites did not seem to be respecting the treaty, many of the Indians saw no reason to abide by its terms and stay on the reservation. Along with Cheyenne from other In-

dian agencies, thousands of Sioux spent the winter of 1875–76 on their traditional hunting grounds in Montana and the Dakotas, despite a government warning that unless they returned immediately, they would be considered hostile and subject to military action.

In May of 1876, a three-sided campaign was launched to shepherd the Sioux and Cheyenne back to their assigned lands. One column, under Gen. John Gibbon, marched east from Fort Ellis (near present-day Bozeman, Montana). A second column, led by Gen. Alfred Terry and including Custer, headed west from Fort Abraham Lincoln (near present-day Bismarck, North Dakota). The third column departed from Fort Fetterman (near present-day Sheridan, Wyoming) under the command of Gen. George Crook and moved north into Montana. These three units, totaling about 3,000 men, were to meet near the end of June in the vicinity of the Little Bighorn River.

Unknown to Terry and Gibbon, Crook encountered Indians near Rosebud Creek in southern Montana, was defeated by them on June 17, and withdrew his men to Wyoming. Meanwhile, Terry, with some 921 men, mostly cavalry, was moving west up the Yellowstone River to the Little Bighorn. On June 22, the cavalry, led by Custer, left Terry's command to scout ahead.

The 7th Cavalry consisted of twelve companies, each authorized to contain fifty to sixty-four men. In reality, most field units never operated at authorized strength, owing to low budget allotments from Congress, high desertion rates, and men on detached duty. Custer commanded about 715 men, about 160 men under authorized strength. Custer's rank was lieutenant colonel (brevet major general). A brevet rank was an honorific and temporary grade given for special service and as an award for gallantry in action. Custer's second-in-command was Maj. Marcus Reno. Next in line was Frederick Benteen, the regiment's senior captain.

Early on the morning of the 25th, the 7th Cavalry was on high ground, with Rosebud Creek behind them to the east and the Little Bighorn about sixteen and a half miles to the west. From a spot subsequently dubbed the Crow's Nest, Custer observed a large Indian camp on the far side of the Little Bighorn. Worried that the Indians might escape, Custer decided to attack and descended westward into the valley. Near the Crow's Nest, Captain Benteen was ordered to take three companies and keep to the south, to block a possible escape route. The pack train, carrying ammunition and guarded by one company, followed Benteen, while the other companies went ahead. At midday, a few miles from the Little Bighorn, Custer again divided his command, ordering Major Reno to take three companies along the river bottom and attack the Indian camp on its southern end. The remaining five companies followed Custer westward along the ridge to the north, preparing to support Reno.

About 3:00 P.M., Indian warriors engaged Reno and his men, forcing them to retreat back across the river and up the bluffs to a defensible position. Meanwhile, Custer must have realized the gravity of the situation as the north end of the Indian camp came into view. About 3:30, Custer's adjutant sent a message to Benteen: "Benteen, Come on. Big village, be quick, bring packs. P.S. Bring pacs [sic]. W. W. Cooke." The messenger, bugler John Martin, was the last to see Custer and the men in his five companies alive.

Summoned by the message, Benteen's forces and the pack train arrived some forty-five minutes later, joining Reno and his men on the hilltop. All were pinned down for two days, fighting to keep their defensive position and wondering when Custer would relieve them. The Indians finally retreated on June 27, when General Terry arrived, joined by General Gibbon's column. Reno sent two men to meet the advancing column, and they found Terry and Gibbon near the abandoned Indian camp. Here, a scout brought the news: Custer and his men lay dead on a ridge above the Little Bighorn.

From that moment until the present, Custer's movements after the messenger left him have been the subject of hot debate. Soon after the battle ended, however, eyewitness accounts began to appear in newspapers across the country. The witnesses were the survivors—the Indians. Weary of army pursuit, the warriors had returned to their reservations, where Indian agents interviewed them. Only then did the warriors learn for certain the identity of the commander they had defeated.

Different versions of Indian accounts of the battle appeared in different papers and journals, and many began to question their accuracy. People suspected distorted reporting by glory-seeking correspondents or faulty translations of Indian words or signs. The Indians, fearing retribution from the army, may also not have told the whole truth. As a result, the Indian accounts were long scorned, although in the past fifteen years, historians who have reviewed them have concluded that the gist of the reports rings true.

The Indians' accounts, collected from survivors up until the middle of this century, state that the camp on the Little Bighorn was established shortly after Crook's defeat at Rosebud Creek, and included the Sioux who had fought in that confrontation. Nevertheless, Custer's arrival apparently took the camp by surprise. As Custer and his men moved north along the ridge, a large contingent of Sioux pressed the attack from the south. A group of Cheyenne and some Sioux also attacked the soldiers from the north and northwest.

At first the shooting was from a distance, but as the soldiers stood their ground, apparently in a V-shaped formation, the intense fire thinned their ranks. It was then that the warriors were able to move in and essentially surround the cavalry. Once many of the

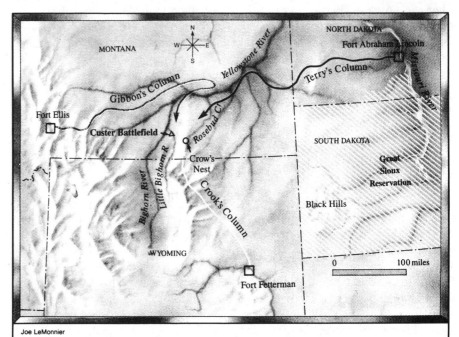

Joe LeMonnier

In May of 1876, approximately 3,000 soldiers, commanded by Generals Gibbon, Terry, and Crook, set out to round up Plains Indians who had left their reservations. The three columns were to meet near the Little Bighorn River in late June. The ill-fated 7th Cavalry, under Custer, made up the majority of Terry's command.

soldiers were dead or wounded, the Indians swooped in on those that remained, finishing them off in hand-to-hand combat. Accounts tell of killing wounded soldiers and of stripping the dead of their guns, ammunition, clothing, and other useful items. Some warriors scalped the dead or mutilated their remains, as was their custom in warfare.

In an attempt to make the battleground speak for itself, during the summers of 1984 and 1985 we used the techniques of archeology to unearth thousands of artifacts, despite events that had disturbed the area over the intervening years. After the battle, the Indians removed their dead and wounded, but the dead soldiers lay in the hot Montana sun for nearly three days. When the surviving members of the 7th Cavalry began the onerous task of burying the dead, the bodies were bloated, blackened, and almost unrecognizable. Because there were few shovels or other tools with which to do a proper job, cups, plates, and other available implements were used to mound dirt over the bodies. Afraid that the Indians would return and attack again, the soldiers covered most of the dead with just a little soil and sagebrush.

The powdery soil was not enough to keep coyotes and other scavengers from the graves, and the action of wind, rain, and snow compounded the problem of keeping the men buried. In 1877, the army reburied the exposed bones. All the officers' remains, however, were exhumed and shipped home, except those of Lt. John Crittenden, whose father asked that he be left where he fell. Persistent reports of exposed remains brought the army back in 1879 for another reburial. Finally, in 1881, the army exhumed all the remains from the battlefield and reburied them in a mass grave on Last Stand Hill, near where Custer's body had been found. A large granite marker was placed over the grave that same year.

While the reburial teams stripped the battlefield of its most conspicuous bones and artifacts, many important clues were left to await archeological exploration. We divided our work into

As he approached the Little Bighorn, Custer divided up the twelve companies under his command. While Captain Benteen trailed behind with four companies and a pack train, Custer ordered Major Reno to take three companies and attack the Indian camp from the south. Custer himself led the remaining five companies farther north. Reno and his men were driven back to a defensive position, where they were eventually joined by Benteen's forces. The detail map shows the battlefield where Custer deployed his men. One company, under Lieutenant Calhoun, was arranged in an arc, facing south. Another company, under Captain Keogh, was positioned farther north. Custer's other three companies stretched in a line from Deep Ravine to Last Stand Hill, confronting Indians attacking from the north and west.

Joe LeMonnier; Detail Map after Midwest Archeological Center, National Park Service

Archeological Finds at Custer Battlefield National Monument

Concentration of Cavalry Materials

Concentration of Indian Materials

three parts. The first was a metal detector survey of the battlefield. Volunteers, often experts in the use of detectors, walked about five yards apart, covering the field. Where their detectors beeped, they flagged the spot. Behind them came a recovery crew that excavated cautiously, searching for the object that had caused the detector to signal, but not moving it out of place. Finally, the survey crews came along to plot each artifact's position on a grid system. This crew also

recorded the depth at which the artifact lay and, in the case of bullets and cartridges, noted the orientation and the declination of the piece. Only then was the artifact collected.

The second part of the project was a search in a gully known as Deep Ravine, where twenty-eight men were said to have been buried in place and never subsequently exhumed. At first, we thought that the metal detectors would locate these men, but even after several close examinations, only a handful of scattered artifacts came to light. In 1985, C. Vance Haynes, a geomorphologist from the University of Arizona, volunteered to examine the ravine. Haynes found a deeply buried area that conforms to the historic descriptions of the burial locale; we hope to excavate it in a future field season.

In the third part of our work, we excavated the immediate areas around marble markers that had been placed to commemorate the locations where Custer's men fell. Set in place fourteen years after the battle and more than nine years after the bodies were disinterred and placed in a mass grave, these marble markers replaced wooden ones, many of which had fallen down or been burned by wildfire. Two hundred fifty-one markers dot the main battlefield, yet only about 210 men fell with Custer. One reason to excavate around the markers was to test the appropriateness of their locations.

These three activities—the metal detector survey, the search in Deep Ravine, and the excavations near the markers—uncovered about 2,200 artifacts, 300 human bones, and 200 bones of horses and other animals. Additional materials (still being analyzed) were collected in 1985 at the Reno-Benteen defense site.

The metal detector survey located hundreds of bullets and cartridge casings. In most cases we could assume that spent cartridges from Springfield carbines and Colt revolvers—the regulation cavalry weapons—had fallen in cavalry positions, and that bullets from these guns had been fired toward the Indians. Conversely, we assumed that bullets found in association with cavalry remains and artifacts came from Indian fire, and that cartridges of the corresponding calibers indicated the Indian positions.

Even before the analyses were complete, we knew that the Indians were much better armed than had been previously documented. The subsequent firearms analyses have identified twenty-five different types of guns used by the warriors. Metal arrowheads were also found, showing that the stereotypical bow and arrow was also used.

Indian arms included army issue Springfield carbines and Colt revolvers. These could have been captured either in the Rosebud skirmish with General Crook's forces or in the valley fight against Reno; some were no doubt taken from Custer's men. Antiquated muzzle-loading firearms were also well represented. Other Indian arms included the .44-caliber Henry, the .44-caliber Model 1866 Winchester, and the .44-caliber Model 1873 Winchester, all repeating rifles. The army did not issue repeating rifles in 1876. The army's single-shot Springfield was not as fast as the repeating rifles, although it was more powerful and more accurate than the majority of the Indian arms.

By using crime laboratory firearms-identification techniques, we could determine how many individual weapons were represented by the archeological artifacts. We estimate that if 1,500 Indian warriors took part in the battle (a conservative number by historical accounts), then about 375 would have been armed with muzzle-loaders and single-shot rifles such as Sharps and Ballards, and about 192 would have been armed with repeating weapons. The rest may have used bows and arrows and a few old pistols and revolvers. Based on these minimal figures, we can conclude that in terms of carbines, Custer's men were outgunned two to one.

There is historical information on the battle that derives from the examination of the battleground at the time of its discovery (including where the bodies of the officers and men were found) and from Indian accounts. Combining this information with the distribution of the recently uncovered buttons, spurs, bullets, and cartridge cases, we are able to make a detailed reconstruction of the battle.

The Indian camp that Custer sought to attack contained perhaps 3,000 to 4,000 people, including some 1,500 warriors. The Indians belonged to a number of different bands whose members were affiliated by common language and family ties. The majority were Sioux (Lakota, Teton, Brulé, and Blackfoot), a lesser number of Chey-

enne occupied the northern end of the camp, and there were also a few Arapahos. Although camped together for protection, the various bands lacked an overall organization. There were a number of important leaders—Sitting Bull, Crazy Horse, and Gall for the Sioux; Lame White Man and Two Moon for the Cheyenne—but in battle, strategy was determined by individual initiative and charisma, not by a chain of command. According to Indian accounts, Sitting Bull, sometimes thought of as Custer's adversary in battle, did not participate in the fighting but occupied himself with making medicine to strengthen the Indian warriors.

Our reconstruction begins after the messenger left Custer, with the command apparently moving aggressively toward the Indian camp. Encountering Sioux and Cheyenne warriors directed by Gall at about 4:00 P.M., Custer moved north and gained high ground at areas now known as Greasy Grass Ridge and Custer Ridge. Here he deployed one company, led by Lt. James Calhoun, in a broad, south-facing arc some 400 yards long. Then, probably to confront a group of Indians attacking from the north and west, Custer took the rest of his men and wheeled north. Leaving Capt. Myles Keogh in charge of a company between himself and Calhoun, Custer deployed his remaining three companies between a high point and a ravine, now called Last Stand Hill and Deep Ravine, respectively.

These deployments formed a broad V-shaped pattern—a classic offensive formation—with the angle to the north, at Last Stand Hill. The cartridge cases attributed to the soldiers are generally in the area of this V. There is very little archeological evidence to document any further troop movement. Although the fight may have been a running one until this final deployment, after this, the units apparently stood their ground.

We determined the soldiers' positions from the presence of spent cartridges from government-issue guns. Bullets fired from the soldiers' guns were found embedded in the ground, often within, or in front of, the areas in which quantities of Indian cartridge cases were found. Bullets corresponding to the calibers of cartridge cases at Indian positions were found embedded in army positions. A few were associated with human remains.

The most intense Indian fire came from a position about 300 feet southeast of Calhoun's position, where perhaps as many as sixty .44-caliber Henry and Winchester rifles were being fired. A second Indian position, on Greasy Grass Ridge, was southwest of Calhoun's men. A minimum of forty-five guns using .44-caliber rimfire ammunition were fired here, as well as at least seven other types of weapons. Calhoun's men probably were overrun by Indians firing from these two positions.

The only physical evidence we found for any movement among the soldiers' positions consists of some .45-caliber cartridge cases (U.S. Army issue for the Springfield carbine), fired from the same weapons. These were found, first, in the Calhoun position, then scattered along a line toward the Keogh position, and finally, intermixed with cartridges belonging to the Keogh group. Several of Calhoun's men, watching their comrades and then their position fall, must have finally retreated under fire to Keogh's position.

Some Indian weapons fired toward Calhoun's men were also fired toward the cavalry line that stretched from Deep Ravine to Last Stand Hill. This cavalry line was also under attack from the north and west by Crazy Horse, Two Moon, Lame White Man, and other Sioux and Cheyenne warriors. Judging by the numbers of cartridges that we found, these warriors were not as well armed as those fighting Calhoun's men. Indians joining the attack from the south, after Calhoun's position collapsed, may have added the firepower and numbers needed to overwhelm the cavalry.

The documented movement of a number of Indian weapons indicates that as the battle progressed, the Indians moved upslope toward Custer's final position on Last Stand Hill. Some of the Indians converged at a knoll north and east of the hill to shoot down into the knot of remaining men. We found little evidence that the soldiers fired their handguns. Indian accounts of the battle, gathered many years afterward, state that the soldiers only used their Colts near the end of the battle, when hand-to-hand fighting began, and that after emptying their Colts, the soldiers did not have time to reload before the Indians were upon them. The paucity of Colt bullets and casings among the archeological finds confirms these accounts. The battle was all over sometime between 5:00 and 6:00 in the afternoon.

Our excavations around the markers confirm that most were placed where a soldier fell, as shown by pieces of uniforms, weapons, and human bone found nearby. About thirty-eight pairs of markers (markers placed by twos around the battlefield) usually indicated a single soldier, thus accounting for many of the excess markers.

Although Custer's men were reburied in a mass grave in 1881, we found human remains belonging to at least thirty-two individuals. Dr. Clyde Snow, a forensics expert who is interpreting the remains, says this is not unusual. Whenever untrained people gather up bones, they may overlook small ones, such as hand and foot bones, or not recognize them as human. These were most of the bones we found.

The skull fragments we uncovered showed that the bone had been broken while still green, indicating what Dr. Snow calls "perimortem blunt instrument trauma." An Indian warrior, Black Elk, recounting the final moments of the battle, described how the Indians used hatchets and clubs to finish off the surviving soldiers. While some of the evidence of trauma we found was undoubtedly induced at the time of death, many of the cut marks and crushed skulls may have resulted from mutilation of the dead, a normal cultural expression of victory for Sioux and Cheyenne warriors. This battle was not exceptional in this regard, but to the soldiers who buried Custer's dead on June 28, 1876, the field was a scene of ghastly and sickening horror.

The excavations around one pair of markers near the Deep Ravine yielded many bones from one individual, some uniform buttons, bullets, and a metal arrowhead. Taking this data, the relative placement of the artifacts, and a little imagination, we could put together the following scenario. The soldier was about twenty-five years old and robust—probably strong for his 5' 8" stature. He wore regulation coat and pants and was hit by a bullet from a .44-caliber repeating rifle. The bullet was associated with a few rib bones, suggesting the shot was to the chest and may have been the mortal wound. Whether the man was dead or dying, someone also shot him in the head with a Colt revolver. When the Indians overran his position, they crushed his skull with a war club and hacked at his front and back with knives. The Indians did not remove his uniform for cloth; perhaps it was too bloody to be worthwhile.

So far the archeological data support much in the Indian accounts of the battle and contradict none of them. As the analysis of the material collected in 1985 progresses, we will learn more details of Custer's fight, as well as what happened to Reno and Benteen. The archeological finds provide historians with a new resource in the study of the battle. By itself, each button, bullet, or cartridge may seem unimportant, but both the Indians and the cavalry left behind arrangements of artifacts that reflected their fighting styles, their ideas of leadership, and their concepts of battle.

The Battle of the Little Bighorn epitomized the clash of cultures—the Native American versus the Euro-American—that differed in hundreds of ways, including perceptions of land ownership, treaties, and boundaries. It may not have been of strategic importance in military history, but it did affect the course of this struggle. In the years preceding the battle, individuals sympathetic to the Indians' plight had determined government dealings with them. If the debacle at the Little Bighorn did nothing else, it galvanized the anti-Indian forces in the U.S. government, influencing official policy toward the Plains Indians until nearly the close of the nineteenth century.

Bones and Bureaucrats

New York's Great Cemetery Imbroglio

Spencer P. M. Harrington

The bones of 420 enslaved Africans found last year under a parking lot two blocks north of New York's City Hall comprise the largest and earliest collection of African-American remains, and possibly the largest and earliest collection of American colonial remains of any ethnic group. The excavation of the old Negros Burial Ground has challenged the popular belief that there was no slavery in colonial New York, and has provided unparalleled data for the Howard University scholars who will study the remains of New York's first African Americans. But as archaeologists removed the remains one by one, they dug up age-old resentment and suspicion with every trowel-full of earth. Scholarly excitement was tempered by the protest of the city's black community, which felt its concerns were not being addressed in decisions about the excavation and disposition of the remains. In the flurry of protests, negotiations, and political maneuverings, the controversy took on an undeniably racial cast. The African Burial Ground, as it is known today, became a "microcosm of the issues of racism and economic exploitation confronting New York City," says Michael L. Blakey, a Howard University anthropologist and the burial ground's scientific director.

In a national context, the controversy over the burial ground excavation became an important episode in a larger struggle of descendant communities to reclaim their heritage. But more specifically, the story was about African-American empowerment: about how a black congressman, acting on the advice of New York City's first black mayor, stopped the excavation of the burial ground; about how the African-American community chose Washington D.C.'s Howard University, the country's most prestigious black research university, as a venue for the study of the remains, thereby ensuring that black researchers and students would study and interpret the remains of their ancestors; and about how the city's black community lobbied for and received a $3 million appropriation from Congress for a memorial and commemorative museum. Equally important were the hard lessons learned by the General Services Administration, the federal agency that supervised the excavation—lessons about the importance of descendant-community involvement in salvage archaeology.

The story of the African Burial Ground begins in 1626, when the Dutch West Indies Company imported its first shipment of slaves, 11 young men from today's Congo-Angola region of Africa. Two years later, the company brought over three African women "for the comfort of the company's Negro men," according to Dutch West Indies records. Like the British who governed Manhattan after them, the Dutch encountered difficulties attracting European settlers to the new colony. Grave manpower shortages threatened the profitability of the Dutch West Indies trading enterprise, and the company was quick to import slave labor to farm its fields. In 1664, just before the Dutch ceded Manhattan to the British, enslaved Africans made up about 40 percent of the colony's total population. The British continued the slave trade, importing as many as 6,800 Africans between 1700 and 1774, many of whom had worked previously on Caribbean plantations. By the mid-eighteenth century, New York had become a thriving port town, and enslaved Africans loaded and unloaded cargo at the docks, wharves, slips, and warehouses along the East River. They also piloted boats ferrying produce from the farming villages of Long Island, repaired and expanded city streets, and worked in shipbuilding and construction. On the eve of the American Revolution, New York City had the largest number of enslaved Africans of any English colonial settlement except Charleston, South Carolina, and it had the highest proportion of slaves to Europeans of any northern settlement. Though seldom acknowledged, Africans were essential to the functioning, as well as the building of colonial New York.

In November 1697, New York City adopted a policy of mortuary apartheid, declaring lower Manhattan churchyards off-limits to blacks. Forced to look for a place to bury its dead, New York's African population, which then numbered about 700, chose unappropriated property outside city limits two blocks north of today's City Hall. There, from 1712 until 1790, in an area characterized by David Valentine, an early city historian, as "unattractive and desolate," Africans conducted last rites for their people. "So little seems to have been thought of the race that not even a dedication of their burial place was made by church authorities," wrote Valentine of what was known then as the Negros Burial Ground. Under the British, Africans were subject to a sunset curfew and city ordinances that prohibited unsupervised gatherings of more than three slaves. They were, however, allowed to gather in large numbers and with regularity at the burial ground. Some 10,000 to 20,000 people, both black and lower-class white, are believed to have been buried in the five-to-six-acre plot of land.

The growth of the city's population in the late eighteenth and early nineteenth centuries led to a northward expansion along main thoroughfares such as Broadway. Street plans were drafted, and blocks over the burial ground were divided into lots for residential and commercial development. By the end of the century, ten- and 15-story buildings with deep foundations and with vaults that were used for storage and coal delivery were going up. The Negros Burial Ground, now paved or built over, was all but forgotten, noted only in a few historical maps and documents. Meanwhile, African Americans were now burying their dead on the Lower East Side, near what are now Chrystie and Delancey streets.

Nearly 200 years later a section of the burial ground lay beneath a parking lot between Duane and Reade streets. In December 1990, New York sold this property and another plot on nearby Foley Square to the General Services Administration (GSA), the federal agency charged with constructing and managing government buildings. The GSA paid $104 million for both properties, which it hoped to develop simultaneously. It planned to build a $276 million, 34-story office tower

and adjoining four-story pavilion on the parking lot area. A federal courthouse was envisioned for the Foley Square property. The tower, designated 290 Broadway, would contain the offices of the United States Attorney, a regional office of the Environmental Protection Agency, and the downtown district office of the Internal Revenue Service. The pavilion would house a day-care center, an auditorium, and a pedestrian galleria.

Five months before the GSA bought the sites from the city, the agency hired Historic Conservation and Interpretation (HCI), an archaeological salvage and consulting firm, to write the archaeological portion of an environmental impact statement for the 290 Broadway site. Such statements are a legal requirement before any new construction using federal funds can begin. HCI's report identified the area as a section of the old Negros Burial Ground and included historical maps indicating its approximate location. But the impact statement predicted that nineteenth- and twentieth-century construction at the site would have destroyed any significant archaeological deposits. It read in part: "The construction of deep sub-basements would have obliterated any remains within the lots that fall within the historic bounds of the cemetery."

Still, the statement left open the possibility of some human remains being preserved under an old alley that once bisected Duane and Reade streets. That the GSA purchased the land despite this possibility suggests that the agency was betting on HCI's overall assessment that few, if any, human remains would be found there. In retrospect, GSA regional director William Diamond admits that the agency would never have bought the land if it had known it would have to remove hundreds of skeletons before sinking the office tower foundation.

In May 1991, six months after purchasing the land, the GSA hired HCI to investigate the possibility that there were undisturbed burials in the alley area. By the end of the summer the firm started to find human bones. In September a full-scale excavation was

underway, and on October 8 Diamond held a press conference to announce the discovery of the remains. One year later, the last of some 420 skeletons had been removed from the site to Lehman College in the Bronx, where they were undergoing conservation before being transferred to Howard University for more detailed study.

African-American outrage over the handling of the excavation stemmed from a perception that the black community had no control over the fate of its heritage—that decisions about the burial ground were being made by white bureaucrats with little insight into African-American history and spiritual sensitivities. "Religious, Afrocentric people believe that to disturb burials in any way is the highest form of disrespect," says Gina Stahlnecker, an aide to State Senator David Patterson, who represents Harlem and the Upper West Side. "There were some people who believed the archaeologists were releasing evil." According to Peggy King Jorde, of the Mayor's Office of Construction, an early monitor of the project, the GSA initially was calling the site a "potters' field," which she felt divorced it from its African origin and diminished its importance. There were even rumors, she says, that the bones were to be removed without any archaeological study. Jorde says that the GSA had only vague ideas about what to do with the remains that were coming to light.

The black community was also upset because it was not alerted at the outset to what might lie beneath the parking lot between Duane and Reade streets. While the GSA did distribute both draft and final environmental impact statements to more than 200 federal, state, and city agencies and local community groups, the agency did not alert civic groups in predominantly black neighborhoods that the buildings would be constructed on top of the old burial ground. "I spoke to hundreds and hundreds of people in the black community, and no one had ever heard about it," says Stahlnecker. While distributing environmental impact statements to descendant communities may seem like a good idea, it is not customary for private or government developers to do so. Peter Sneed, the GSA's planning staff director, argues that the distribution list was formulated in accordance with federal regulations. "We didn't include the Harlem community board because the project isn't in Harlem, it's in lower Manhattan," he says. "We felt it was incumbent upon the Mayor's office to spread the word. It's unreasonable to expect a federal agency to know every interest group in the community."

African-American fury over the excavation increased dramatically after a backhoe operator digging the tower's foundation accidentally destroyed several of the burials. The incident was reported by Dan Pagano, an archaeologist for the city's Landmarks Preservation Commission, who was photographing the site through a telephoto lens when he spotted HCI archaeologists sifting through human remains outside the excavation area, where the backhoe had scooped up earth so that a concrete footing could be poured for the tower. Pagano says jawbones and leg and arm bones were among the remains scooped up by the backhoe. The GSA blamed the accident on an out-of-date drawing that the construction crews were using to determine which part of the site was "culturally sterile." Diamond halted tower construction pending further investigation by archaeologists. The incident led State Senator David Patterson to form an oversight committee to monitor the burial ground excavation.

Miriam Francis, a member of Patterson's committee, says that the involvement of African-American anthropologists in the excavation was among the group's most pressing concerns. "If it was an African find, we wanted to make sure that it was interpreted from an African point of view," she says. But the committee soon learned that the GSA had picked physical anthropologists from the city's Metropolitan Forensic Anthropology Team (MFAT) to conduct field analyses of the remains and that the bones would be stored at the group's Lehman College facility. "We didn't know anything about MFAT whether they were

butchers, bakers, or candlestick makers," says Francis. She notes that when the committee introduced the GSA to African-American specialists like Howard University's Michael Blakey, it was either stonewalled or ignored.

Meanwhile, the GSA was having difficulty getting HCI, its archaeological salvage contractor, to produce a research design stating conservation measures and scientific study goals for the burial project. The GSA had managed to obtain extensions on the report's due date from the Advisory Council on Historic Preservation, the government agency that reviews all federal projects that might have an impact on historic sites. Still, the missing research plan sent further signals to the black community that something was wrong with the way work was progressing. "Any archaeological excavation is useless without a research design," noted Landmarks Preservation Commission Chair Laurie Beckelman at a congressional hearing on the burial ground. "It's like driving a car in a foreign country without a road map or destination."

HCI's Edward Rutsch, the project's archaeologist, says that although he was responsible for the research design, he felt too overworked to get it done properly. "They [GSA] had us working seven days a week and overtime every day," says Rutsch. "Many times it was expressed to me that millions of dollars of public money were being lost. There was terrific pressure to get the excavation done—to finish it."

Last April, black activists staged a one-day blockade of the site in an effort to prevent the GSA from pouring concrete for the tower's foundation. Among other things, they were concerned that there was little African-American involvement in the scientific aspects of the excavation; they were visibly unhappy at the choice of Lehman College as the site for the conservation of the remains. Bones from the site had been wrapped in newspaper and placed in cardboard boxes before being shipped to Lehman. One problem, according to Dan Baer of Ed-

wards and Kelcey, an engineering firm hired to manage the site, was that "We were digging them out faster than [storage] cases could be made." But in the African-American community there was concern that the bones were being damaged at Lehman. "They had some remains up there in boxes ten or 11 months," says Abd-Allah Adesanya, director of the Mayor's Office of African American and Caribbean Affairs. "They were wrapped in newspaper longer than they should have been. They had to be rewrapped in acid-free paper." Baer says, "The bones were stored in newspaper, which may be scientific protocol, but it didn't appear respectful to those who visited the site. It was a mistake that was made. But the bones were in good shape and Dr. Blakey said so after touring the facility."

Blakey's tour of Lehman resulted from pressure by Senator Patterson's committee. "We kept asking them [MFAT], 'Can we go up there?' And that involved more waiting, more delays," says Miriam Francis. "It wasn't that we were against Lehman, we just wanted to see how our ancestors were being stored." Blakey's visit to the facility confirmed the community's suspicion of inadequate conservation. In a letter to ARCHAEOLOGY, Blakey wrote "We intervened in time to prevent the potential for further deterioration, such as the spread of mold in the skeletal remains due to inadequate environmental controls, and improper storage of skeletal materials on top of fragile bone."

As the excavation progressed, the GSA began briefing the public on the burial project's progress. But there was a widespread perception among African Americans that the GSA was merely paying lip-service to the public, that they were digging the bones as fast as they could so the tower foundation could be poured. "People would tell them [the GSA] their gripes, then they went off and did what they wanted," says Adesanya. "The community wanted to be let in on the decision-making process, to influence the direction of the project." While descendant-community input into decisions about

STORIES THE BONES WILL TELL

The skeletal remains and associated artifacts from the African Burial Ground are the only concrete evidence recovered to date of the life of Africans who lived in colonial New York City. The burials were found 16 to 28 feet below street level, many coffins stacked one on top of another—an urban mortuary practice of the period. Although the majority of burials are people of African descent, about seven percent appear to be Europeans. Physical anthropologists determine racial differences by studying characteristic features of the skull, pelvis, and limb bones. The 420 skeletons found at the New York City site represent a fraction of the entire graveyard population. The condition of the remains varies considerably, from good to extremely poor. There were no grave markers or burial maps, and other than wood, coffin nails, and shroud pins, few artifacts associated with the burials were found. "These were not wealthy graves," says Howard University's Michael L. Blakey, the African Burial Ground's scientific director. "The most striking artifacts were the glass beadwork on one woman, and cowrie shells," he says. "Cowrie shells had a symbolic function in West African funeral practice. They were symbols of the passage in death across the sea and have been variously interpreted as a return to Africa or the afterlife."

In the vast majority of the burials the deceased's head faces west, which prompted journalists to report that the bodies were arranged according to Christian burial practice so that they could sit up and see the rising sun on Judgment Day. But Blakey warns that there was considerable overlap between African and Western burial practices during this period, and it is unclear just how Christianized the Africans were. Blakey points out that a few graves facing east may indicate Moslem burials.

Spencer Turkel, an anthropologist with the Metropolitan Forensic Anthropology Team, estimates two-thirds of the remains found at the site were male, and that 40 percent of the sample were children. He says that sex ratios may change after lab study because the hard physical labor demanded by slavery affected the musculoskeletal structure in such a way that some female skeletons look male. The soil in which the bodies were buried was highly acidic and corrosive to human bone, causing further complications for researchers. "One problem we've been having is trying to determine the difference between damage to the bone caused by life experience and that caused by post-mortem soil exposure," says Turkel.

He notes that field examination revealed some obvious causes of death—a musket ball lodged in a rib cage, and a case of rickets, a nutritional deficiency. Diagnosis of other causes of death will have to await further study. "The major epidemics of that period were cholera and yellow fever, but here we're dealing with vague written descriptions," he says. "Many of the children would have died from diarrhea, which is a form of malnutrition. Poorly nourished children would also have been susceptible to pneumonia."

Meanwhile, Howard University scientists are contemplating the skeletal sample's research potential. Because seventeenth- and eighteenth-century historical sources tend to dismiss or ignore New York's enslaved Africans, anthropological research becomes all the more important for scholars interpreting what their life was like. "This is a unique opportunity to gain a better understanding of the biology, health, and culture of the first generation of people who would become the African-American people," says Blakey.

The primary focus of the research conducted at Howard, will be the social and economic conditions affecting the health of the enslaved Africans. The interdisciplinary team studying the skeletal population will consider questions dealing with demography, epidemiology, nutrition, social history, and cultural transformation. Demographic research will attempt to provide information on the African ethnicity of the sample. "We hope to bring attention to the great variety of cultural groups that were brought over from Africa," says Blakey. "Some of these individuals may have spent time in the West Indies or South America, and we may be able to pick that up," he says. Meanwhile, epidemiologists will study the Africans' adjustment to New York's disease environment. Turkel notes that such bone-scarring diseases as tuberculosis and syphilis were relatively rare in Africa, and finding them in this population would yield interesting data on the community's acculturation to Western diseases. Research on the skeletons may also reveal information about nutrition in the colonial period, while study of mortuary practices at the site will show the extent to which African burial traditions were retained or modified.

Because the sample is large enough to account for human variation, accurate statistical analysis will be possible. And because of the age of the burial population, the sample provides baseline data against which hypotheses about the development of specific pathologies in the African-American population can be tested, such as the relatively high incidence of hypertension in today's black community. The data will also yield information on toxic-element levels in preindustrial America.

The draft research design submitted by Blakey this past fall notes that earlier studies of African-American skeletal populations tended to be descriptive of physical characteristics such as sex, age, and height rather than focused on biohistorical information such as diet, African nationality, and adaptation to disease. According to Blakey, carefully conceived, large-scale academic research plans for African-American archaeological sites are rare. "The growth of African-American archaeology reflects the randomness of the discoveries resulting from development projects," he says, adding that specialists in African-American archaeology often find themselves responding to "emergency situations," in which burial grounds or other sites are threatened by development projects. Theresa Singleton, an archaeologist at the Smithsonian Institution, says that "quick and dirty" salvage archaeology has compromised historical sites in general, and African-American sites in particular, because "you need time to study sites thoroughly, and most contractors don't have time." She adds that "many contract archaeologists don't know much about African-American archaeology." Blakey notes that contract archaeologists "have not often taken advantage of the rich literature and perspectives of Afro-American scholarship on Afro-Americans. That needs to change. And that's one of the things all the protest in New York brought about."

—S.P.M.H.

the course of contract excavations seems desirable when human remains are involved, consultation is not part of standard archaeological practice. Nonetheless "the [African-American] community was very unhappy," says Diamond, "and I understood that and kept saying to them, 'I wish I could help you with this but my obligations by law are contrary to your wishes, and the only way we can get this changed is by an act of Congress or an agreement from the administrator of the GSA.' And I was in consultation with them [GSA administrator Richard G. Austin and members of Congress] and they were telling me to continue the construction."

At the GSA's public meetings, African Americans also questioned the propriety of continuing with the removal of remains from the area where the pavilion would be built. They also hoped that the GSA would consider not building the pavilion, or at least modify the plans so there would be no further removals. "There were several conflicting demands," recalls Diamond. "Some wanted the exhumation to stop, others wanted nothing built on the site, and still others wanted a museum built on the site. . . . But I had no authority but to continue under the law with the construction."

The GSA eventually replaced Historic Conservation and Interpretation with John Milner Associates (JMA), a West Chester, Pennsylvania, archaeological contractor. JMA had recently completed a successful excavation of an early nineteenth-century cemetery associated with the First African Baptist Church in Philadelphia that brought to light information on that city's early black history. "JMA had done this sort of job before," says Baer. "We didn't feel we had involved the community enough and we thought that JMA would improve that situation."

But reports by agencies monitoring the excavation were becoming increasingly critical. One report filed by the Advisory Council on Historic Preservation stated, in part, that: " . . . the GSA was proceeding without any clear focus on why the remains were being removed; how they were to be an-

alyzed; how many more bodies were involved; or, what the African-American community's desire was for the treatment of the burials." Mayor David Dinkins sent a letter to Diamond complaining about the lack of a research design and requesting "that the GSA suspend all excavation and construction activities in the pavilion area and bring the project into compliance with the terms outlined in the Memorandum of Agreement [a document specifying the terms of archaeological work to be undertaken in advance of construction]. . . ." There is "no basis for discontinuance of ongoing excavations" was Diamond's response a week later. "I would not be put in a position of abrogating important government contracts because of political pressure," he later recalled.

The final act in the drama was played out before the congressional committee that appropriates funds for the GSA, the House Subcommittee on Public Buildings and Grounds. Meeting in New York, the subcommittee was chaired by former Representative Gus Savage, an Illinois Democrat, who heard testimony from the GSA, the Advisory Council, the city's Landmarks Preservation Commission, and concerned citizens. At the meeting, the GSA argued that stopping the excavation would jeopardize the exposed human remains, and it estimated that relinquishing the pavilion site would cost taxpayers as much as $40 million: $5 million in interest payments, $10 million in land acquisition costs, and $25 million in initial construction costs.

Savage then subjected GSA representatives to intense questioning, during which it became apparent that at the outset the GSA was aware that a historic burial ground had once occupied the land it intended to purchase and develop, and that the agency had made no contingency plans for construction in the event that human remains were found. The meeting also revealed that the building prospectus for 290 Broadway the GSA had submitted for Congressional approval did not mention the burial ground, nor was Savage's subcommittee alerted by the

agency when HCI's impact statement mentioned the possibility of intact graves. Savage ended the hearing early, noting that he would not approve any further GSA projects until he received "a more honest and respectful response" from the agency regarding its excavation of the burial ground. "And don't waste your time asking this subcommittee for anything else as long as I'm chairman, unless you can figure out a way to go around me! I am not going to be part of your disrespect," Savage said.

Three days later, Savage halted excavation on the pavilion site, and last October former President Bush signed Public Law 102-393, ordering the GSA to cease construction of the pavilion portion of the project and approving $3 million for the construction of a museum honoring the contribution of African Americans to colonial New York City. Meanwhile, JMA removed the last of the exposed burials.

In a statement to the House Subcommittee on Public Buildings and Grounds, GSA head Richard G. Austin acknowledged that "in hindsight we could have handled some things better." Austin's statement made it clear to all parties that the GSA recognized the need for descendant-community cooperation in salvage excavations. Its office tower would be built, but African Americans would determine the course of research on the remains. The agency hired Blakey to develop a research design, which he produced in consultation with JMA and numerous black scholars. Blakey was also appointed scientific director of a five-year research program on the remains that will take place at Howard University. Sherill D. Wilson, an urban anthropologist and ethnohistorian, calls the sudden involvement of black scholars "very revolutionary." Such scholarship, she says, "is going to set a precedent for what happens to African burial grounds in the future, and how African heritage will be viewed by the public."

Meanwhile, a chastened GSA has also set up a federal advisory committee chaired by Howard Dodson of New York's Schomburg Center for Research in Black Culture that will address plans for reburial of the remains, an African Burial Ground memorial, a burial ground exhibition in the office tower, and a museum of African and African-American History in New York City. State Senator David Patterson's burial ground oversight committee seeks to create a museum that will honor African-American heritage, "a place similar to Ellis Island, something that can attest to Afro-American history." The city Landmarks Preservation Commission has also proposed that the burial ground be designated a city landmark and has requested that it be considered for National Historic Landmark status. These efforts stemmed in part from a massive petition drive spearheaded by Senator Patterson's oversight committee and jazz musician Noel Pointer that yielded more than 100,000 signatures.

Among other things, the petition called for the creation of a museum and landmark status for the burial ground.

The burial ground controversy and its attendant publicity have had important repercussions nationwide. "The media exposure has created a larger, national audience for this type of research," says Theresa Singleton, an archaeologist at the Smithsonian Institution who has done pioneering research on African-American sites. "I've been called by dozens of scholars and laypeople, all of them interested in African-American archaeology, all of them curious about why they don't know more about the field. Until recently, even some black scholars considered African-American archaeology a waste of time. That's changed now."

Things have indeed changed. Public curiosity about this country's African-American past has been aroused by the New York experience. And it is probably safe to assume that in the future government and private developers will take a hard look at how to include descendant communities in their salvage excavations, especially when human remains are concerned. "Everyone could have talked more to everyone else," concludes the GSA's planning staff director Peter Sneed. "There would have been a lot less heartache . . . the GSA has certainly been sensitized to archaeology."

DOMINIC G. DIONGSON *helped in the reporting of this article. Research assistance was provided by* ANDREW D. REINHARD.

Paleoanthropology: The Archaeology of Early Humans

Paleoanthropology is the study of the biological and cultural evolution of humankind. It is a discipline that juxtaposes the study of physical anthropology, cultural anthropology, and archaeology. It also incorporates many other disciplines such as biology, geology, paleontology, statistics, and taphonomy.

Fossilized bones represent the physical remains of early humans and their ancestors. Under the best of conditions human bones in their original organic state survive less than 10,000 years. It is the fossilized human bones that tell of the millions of years of human evolution.

Archaeologists designate these events by the term *Paleolithic.* They focus on the study of stone or "lithic" tools. The word *Paleolithic* literally means "old-stones." We can deduce, and we also have some direct evidence, that our prehistoric forebears used and made tools from other kinds of materials as well. However, as the name *Stone Age* indicates, it is mainly from the stone tools that the cultural evolution of our earliest ancestors is reconstructed. While other materials, such as bone, wood, shells, vegetation, and so forth, undoubtedly were utilized by early humans, only the stone tools have survived intact through the vast stretch of prehistory.

In the nineteenth century a Frenchman named Boucher de Perthes found odd-shaped stones on his property—stones that could comfortably be held by a human hand. So, undoubtedly, had thousands of other people throughout history. To de Perthes they suggested a novel meaning. He wondered if these odd rocks might not have been made by long-ago humans lost in the mists before history.

Other exciting changes were occurring in the epistemology of the nineteenth century that soon lent credibility to this hypothesis. Not the least of which was the publication of *On the Origin of Species* by Charles Darwin in 1859. In this book, which by the way never mentioned humans or any implied relationship they might have to contemporary apes, Darwin suggested a general process that became known as *natural selection* wherein species could change through time. This was a revolutionary idea because at the time even biologists believed that species were immutable. Now if species could change, the implication was that maybe even human beings (who were considered above nature) could change.

In addition, there was the concurrent emergence of the idea of *uniformitarianism,* which indicated that Earth was old, very old, perhaps hundreds of thousands of years old. (It is in fact about five billion years old.) But the revolutionary possibility that human beings could have existed before history became more plausible. Such a serious challenge to the established wisdom that Earth was about 6,000 years old gave rise to a new age of speculation on the very nature of human beings. Thus, when de Perthes published his hypothesis on the antiquity of humankind throughout the world, others answered that they too had found these same odd-shaped stones and had thought similar thoughts. The study of prehistory began.

Stop for a moment and think about this. Consider that all the bones and stones of prehistory had been sitting around for all of history waiting to be discovered, so to speak. However, they were never perceived in such a way because the idea of a human prehistoric past, while it had occurred many times to individuals throughout the ages, was never conceived in a cultural frame of knowledge that would make it a plausible or testable hypothesis. Simply stated, it was an idea whose time had come.

It is humbling to realize that today is tomorrow's past and that evidence abounds of truths whose questions we have not yet asked.

Looking Ahead: Challenge Questions

What kind of tool is an Acheulean hand ax? What kind of people used them? How might an Acheulean hand ax have been used? Criticize this hypothesis. What are the possible relationships between Neanderthals and modern humans? What is the currently favored theory or theories? What are the arguments?

In what ways could human cultures change when stone lamps were invented?

Explore the psychological changes in human cultures made possible by mobile lighting.

What are some of the absolute dating methods used in archaeology? Discuss thermoluminescence (TL).

What are the underlying similarities between Paleolithic people and modern urbanites. How is this particularly expressed in gender roles and why?

What Was the Acheulean Hand Ax?

Contrary to its name, this prehistoric stone tool may have been a projectile weapon

Eileen M. O'Brien

Eileen M. O'Brien is a research associate in the Department of Anthropology at Georgia State University.

About one and one-half million years ago, a new type of large, symmetrically shaped stone implement entered the prehistoric tool kit, signaling both an advance in early craftsmanship and the advent of *Homo erectus,* a small-brained but otherwise fairly recognizable form of human being. The tool was the hand ax, which these ancestral humans faithfully made for well over one million years. Named for archeological finds at Saint Acheul, France, examples of the Acheulean hand ax are found from the Vaal River of South Africa to the lakes, bogs, and rivers of Europe, from the shores of the Mediterranean to India and Indonesia. Such continuity over time and space speaks to us of use, success, and reuse—a design integral to some task, a task appropriate or essential to diverse environments. *Homo erectus* needed tools: tools to cut, slice, and chop; to dig, pound, and grind; tools to defend against predators and competitors, to procure and process food or other materials, even tools to make tools. But which task (or tasks) the hand ax performed is still being debated.

The average hand ax looks like a giant stone almond, although some are more ovate and others are triangular. Crafted from a stone core or flake, it can range in size from only a few inches to a foot or more, but most are six or seven inches long. Whether roughly finished or as refined as a work of art, the hand ax always has an eccentric center of gravity and a sharp edge around all or most of its perimeter. Thus in cross section lengthwise, it resembles a stretched-out teardrop.

Some have speculated that the hand ax's design was not functional but purely aesthetic or that it was a byproduct of the manufacture of the sharp flakes used in butchering. Most anthropologists, however, assume it was a practical implement. Initially, prehistorians thought it was a hafted, multipurpose tool and weapon like the stone hatchet, or ax, of the aboriginal Americans and Australians. But there is no evidence that it was hafted until much later in time, not until after the evolution of *Homo sapiens.* Another proposal, advanced to explain why excavators find some hand axes standing on edge, *in situ,* is that the hand ax acted as a stationary tool, one edge embedded in the earth while the exposed edge cut or scraped an object passed over it. But the common and traditional interpretation is that it was a hand-held tool for butchering, cutting, scraping, digging, or as its name implies, chopping.

Reprinted with permission from *Natural History,* July 1984, pp. 20, 22-23. © 1984 by the American Museum of Natural History.

Experiments show that these important tasks can be accomplished with a hand ax. But *Homo erectus* possessed other tools suitable for these purposes—tools that precede and continue alongside the hand ax in the archeological record. Compared with these, the hand ax was costly to produce in terms of time, labor, and skill, and required larger blocks of fine-grained, faultless stone such as flint or basalt. The hand ax also presented a hazard. Since a heavy object requires effort to wield and carry, we may assume the mass of the hand ax was important to its function. Force in the form of increased momentum would be useful for chopping, for example, as compared with a task like scraping, where the user exerts all the energy in the form of pressure. But without a safe handhold, the sharp edge of the hand ax, when used with force, was (and is) capable of inflicting as much damage on the user as on the material being worked.

Whatever its function, the hand ax represented to its users not only an investment of energy but also a source of raw material. They would have saved and reused a hand ax for as long as possible and retouched it when necessary. With time and repeated repair, it would have become smaller; once irreparably damaged, what remained could then have served as a core in the production of still smaller stone tools. Accordingly, except for those hand axes that were misplaced or lost, the hand ax should not be in the archeological record. Excavators, however, recover hand axes in abundance, mostly at sites that are within or alongside what were once (and may still be) watercourses or wetland environments. For example, at the Acheulean site of Olorgesailie (one of the East African sites southwest of Nairobi, Kenya, in the Eastern Rift Valley), hundreds of large hand axes were deposited about four hundred thousand years ago in what appears to have been a shallow stream bed. Elsewhere across the landscape, hand axes are rare, although they are occasionally found in some numbers in prehistoric cave sites. This suggests that during some activity that took place near water, hand axes were used and lost with astonishing frequency.

If we let the evidence speak for itself, the appropriate question is: What task would require force, call for a tool with a sharp edge around all (or most) of its perimeter but without a safe handhold, occur in or near water, and often result in the loss of a potentially reusable and valuable artifact? The possibility that occurred to me is that the hand ax was a projectile weapon. The idea, I have since discovered, has been thought of before, but not pursued. Use of the hand ax as a weapon has been suggested since at least the sixteenth century, and small hand axes have been proposed as projectiles since the nineteenth century, most enjoyably by H.G. Wells in his *Tales of Time and Space* (1899). More recently, M.D.W. Jeffreys, a South African anthropologist, wrote that the small- to medium-sized Vaal River hand axes would make good bird-hunting weapons if thrown overhand, like a knife ("The Handbolt." *Man,* 1965). But the idea that hand axes were in general used as projectiles has not taken hold, probably because it is not obvious how the larger hand axes could have been thrown.

By analogy with modern forms, we understand how prehistoric stone arrowheads and spearpoints were propelled and used as weapons or how a stone ball ("spheroid," to archeologists) could be thrown or used in a bola (a weighted thong or cord thrown to entangle prey). But what about the hand ax? One way might be overhand, as Jeffreys suggested. Other methods of throwing a small- to medium-sized hand ax might be the side/overhand throw used in baseball and perhaps the backhand throw used in both knife and frisbee throwing. To throw a large, heavy hand ax, however, a sidearm or underhand throw might be preferable. A few years ago, I decided that a practical experiment was what was needed. From my limited knowledge of track and field, I thought that for sidearm throwing, an analogy might be made between a hand ax and the Olympic discus.

Like a hand ax, the early discus of the ancient Greeks was unhafted, edged all around, and made of stone. It also varied in size from about half a foot to more than one foot in diameter, and in weight from about two and one-quarter pounds to more than fourteen and one-half pounds. (Actually, the word *discus* means "a thing for throwing" or "a thing thrown"; the discus thrown by Odysseus in Homer's *Odyssey,* for example, is thought by some scholars to refer to a beach cobble.) Unlike a hand ax, the classic Greek discus was perfectly round. (The modern regulation discus, which weighs 2 kilograms, or 4.4 pounds, is made of wood and weighted with metal around the edge to accelerate its spinning motion. The longer and faster it spins, the more stable the flight pattern and the longer the flight, all else being equal.)

The hand ax I chose for the throwing experiment was the largest I could find in the Olorgesailie collection at the National Museums of Kenya, Nairobi (I was in Africa at the time doing fieldwork unrelated to this topic). Because the original could not be used—and raw material for making a "real" hand ax of such size was difficult to obtain—a fiberglass replica was made. The original hand ax is a little more than a foot long, ovate shaped, and edged all around. It is made of basalt and weighs about four pounds, three ounces. J.D. Ambrosse Esa (then head of the museum's casting department) supervised the casting and the accurate weighting of the facsimile to within one and one-half ounces of the original.

The experiment took place in 1978, in the discus practice area at the University of Massachusetts, where I was then a student. Two student athletes participated: Karl Nyholm, a discus thrower, and George Peredy, a javelin thrower. One day in late April, and again two weeks later, both threw the hand ax discus-style. Peredy also threw it overhand. To maximize potential accuracy in the discus throw, the thrower did not whirl.

The first to throw the hand ax discus-style was Karl Nyholm. He took the unfamiliar object in his right hand, grasping it every which way before settling on the butt. He tossed it up and down for balance and "feel," then crouched and practiced his swing. Ready, he paced off from the release line. With his back to the field, he spread his legs apart, bent at the knees, and twisted his right arm far behind him. Then he began the throw: his outstretched left hand grasping at air, weight shifting from right foot to left, he rotated to face the field. The burdened right hand swung wide and low and then raced upward. With a great exhalation of breath, he hurled himself out straight and let go. Silently, gracefully spinning, the hand ax soared.

Like a discus, the hand ax spun horizontally as it rose, but changed its orientation in midair. On reaching its maximum altitude, it rolled onto its edge and descended in a perpendicular position, its spinning motion appearing to decline. Then, with a thud, it landed point first, slicing deeply into the thawing earth. In both throwing bouts, regardless of thrower, the hand ax repeated this flight pattern when thrown discus-style. It landed on edge forty-two out of forty-five throws, thirty-one of which were point first. The average throw was about one-third the length of a football field (almost 102 feet), and usually accurate to within two yards right or left of the line of trajectory.

The propensity of the hand ax to pivot onto its edge in mid-flight was unexpected and curious. But, as suggested to me by several track coaches, it may be related to the same factors that can produce the "peel-off" pattern in a thrown discus, some function of the manner of release and the thrower's expertise. A full explanation of the physical principles involved must await an interpretation by someone with the relevant expertise. What is important is that it does happen. By so doing, it makes on-edge impact of a thrown hand ax predictable. The further tendency of the hand ax to land point first does not appear accidental and adds to the implement's potential to inflict damage. If the hand ax can also be thrown so that it behaves exactly like the discus in both ascent and descent (more recent demonstrations support this possibility), then by simply changing the angle and manner of release it

should be possible to strike a target with either a horizontally or vertically directed edge.

Modern discus throwing is not known for its accuracy. But in terms of how far a hand ax might ideally be thrown, it is worth noting that the 1980 Olympic record in discus was 218.8 feet. Since the experimental hand ax weighs only two and a half ounces less than the modern Olympic discus, this suggests that as the thrower's skill and/or strength increase, the potential flight distance of the hand ax increases.

When grasped and thrown overhand, like a knife, the experimental hand ax performed like one, rotating symmetrically on edge in both ascent and descent. The average throw was just short of discus-style, but more accurate, about half a yard right or left of the line of trajectory. It always landed on edge, but less often point first. Unfortunately, these results are the product of only six throws; owing to its weight and the ovate, broad point, the experimental hand ax was difficult to grasp and throw overhand. George Peredy, who was the thrower, also appeared to tire more quickly using this method and probably could not have used it at all if he had not had large hands, in proportion to his six-foot six-inch frame. This overhand style would probably be more suitable for lighter, more triangular hand axes. In contrast, weight and shape were of no real concern when throwing the hand ax discus-style. Even a significant increase in weight might not have impeded the throwing motion, although it would have affected the distance of the throw.

Further testing is needed (and is currently under way), but these first trials showed that a hand ax could perform appropriately as a projectile. The hand ax demonstrated a propensity to land on edge when thrown overhand or discus-style, a tendency to land point first, and a potential for distant and accurate impact. Its overall shape minimizes the effects of resistance while in flight, as well as at impact. This is not true of an unshaped stone or a spheroid, for example. And despite its sharp edge, the hand ax could be launched without a safe handhold. The

only apparent limitations to the hand ax's use as a projectile weapon are the strength, coordination, and skill of the thrower.

Homo erectus was bipedal, probably dexterous enough to manipulate a hand ax in either of the tested throwing styles, and very much stronger than most modern humans. With their technique perfected over years of practice and use, our ancestors probably surpassed the accuracy shown in the experimental throws. I suspect the hand ax simply reflects a refinement in missile design, one that allowed for successful long-distance offense and defense against larger animals. This is consistent with evidence that big-game hunting appears for the first time in the archeological record along with *Homo erectus*.

Perfected through trial and error, the hand ax would not necessarily have replaced preexisting projectile or hand-held weapons, because weapons and strategies probably varied with the predator being deterred or the game being hunted. Hand axes would have been especially effective in a collective strategy, such as a group of hunters bombarding a herd. To overcome any difficulty in transporting hand axes, *Homo erectus* could have used carrying slings made from hide, stockpiled hand axes near hunting areas, or cached them (in caves, for example) prior to seasonal migrations.

Hunting near water, where game is relatively predictable and often concentrated, offers a simple explanation of why hand axes are recovered there in abundance—as well as the phenomenon of hand axes embedded on edge *in situ*. Hand axes that missed their mark, landing in water or dense vegetation on the banks of a river, might have been difficult or impossible to retrieve. Over time, with continued exploitation of an area, projectiles would accumulate like golf balls in a water trap. Elsewhere across the landscape, retrieval is more likely and the hand ax should be rare. This distribution pattern, as noted by English archeologist L.H. Keeley, resembles that of the Indian projectile points across the American Southwest. (Keeley, however, does not believe that the hand ax was a projectile.)

Homo erectus, like later *Homo sapiens,* was physically defenseless compared with the rest of the animal kingdom. Relatively slow, without canines, claws, tusks, or other natural means of defense, these early humans were easy prey when out of a tree. With handheld weapons they could defend themselves, once attacked. With projectile weapons they could wound, maim, or kill without making physical contact, avoiding assault or retaliation. Modern humans are notoriously expert at killing from a distance. The hand ax may be proof that this behavioral strategy was refined long ago, at a time when truly "giants strode the earth"— when by dint of size the megamammals of the Pleistocene asserted their dominance, when migrating game might pass in a continuous parade for days without a break in their ranks, and humankind struggled to survive, both consumer and consumed. At the other end of time, at the dawn of history, is it possible that the ancient Greeks preserved as a sport a tradition handed down from that distant yesterday?

Infants, Cannibals, and the Pit of Bones

James Shreeve

James Shreeve is the coauthor, with anthropologist Donald Johanson, of Lucy's Child: The Discovery of a Human Ancestor *and the author of a forthcoming book on the origins of modern humans.*

Pity the poor Neanderthals. Though the brainiest of all ancient hominids, they were destined to play the role of evolution's fool, a future race's synonym for idiocy. Their big mistake was to be almost human. After occupying Europe for hundreds of millennia, the Neanderthals disappeared just as human culture was taking off in an explosion of art, symbol, new social complexities, and technical innovations—most of which activity has been attributed to the Cro-Magnons, who lived after the Neanderthals. In the rearview mirror of that cultural juggernaut, any earlier version of humanity is bound to look diminished. As the exhaust clears, you can see Neanderthal standing by the wayside, blackened, blinking, and bewildered: the classic cartoon loser.

Yet in that image, too, may lie the attraction Neanderthals exert on us: we feel an uneasy sense of recognition, and we wonder to what extent they really are us. Who were the Neanderthals, how did they live, and what happened to them? Last year brought news of several exciting fossil finds that shed light on these questions—or at least fueled the contentious debate that surrounds them.

By far the most important news came from Spain. In the summer of 1992 a team led by Juan-Luis Arsuaga of the Complutense University in Madrid reached undisturbed fossil deposits in

the "pit of bones," a narrow recess in a complex of caves in the Sierra de Atapuerca of northern Spain. Hundreds of human fossil fragments have been dug up at the site since the mid-1970s, but because the deposits had been churned up earlier by amateur cavers, they've been difficult to date and interpret. Arsuaga and his team were forced by the deep, narrow passage to excavate while lying on planks and with dangerously limited oxygen. But finally they hit pay dirt: a trio of beautifully preserved fossil skulls located just below a layer of limestone that has been dated to around 300,000 years ago. Last spring the researchers published a paper describing their find.

The skulls have helped clarify the confusing muddle of Neanderthal origins. The record of human evolution in Europe begins with some early scraps traditionally assigned to the species *Homo erectus,* such as the famous 500,000-year-old Mauer jaw from Heidelberg, Germany. Fossils bearing the classic, indisputably Neanderthal stamp—the middle of the face thrust forward and amplified by the great projecting nose, the puffed-up cheekbones, the long jaw with its chinless finish, and the extrathick brow ridges shading it all like twin awnings—don't begin to turn up until around 130,000 years ago. (Not long after that, "modern humans"—people who look anatomically like humans today—began to appear in Africa.) Between these two points in time lies a teasing trail of skulls from Greece, France, England, and Germany whose origins are in doubt. These early archaic *sapiens,* as they're called, were found decades ago, when dating and excavation methods were imprecise. Some have large faces

but small braincases. Others have big brains but small faces. Some are more *erectus*-like, while others have an incipient Neanderthal tinge. Sometimes it seems to depend on whether you look at the specimen from the front or the back.

Sorting out the relationships among these poorly dated fossils has been a taxonomic nightmare. Some investigators thought these early European archaics were so varied that they should be split into two separate groups: one—often given the species name *Homo heidelbergensis*—the common ancestor of Neanderthals and modern humans; the other a younger bunch, firmly set on the path leading to classic Neanderthals. Other scientists have argued that the whole motley crew should be lumped into a single lineage of "pre-Neanderthals," reflecting the gradual emergence of Neanderthals from *Homo erectus.* Such disputes between "splitters" and "lumpers" have been cropping up for decades, and the scant fossil record rarely speaks clearly enough to say which side is right.

The new skulls from Atapuerca, however, do not mince their words. Though they preserve a few *erectus* characteristics, the three fossils collectively boast a bevy of traits that securely link them with the Neanderthals to come. But what really decides the issue is how different the Atapuercan pre-Neanderthals are one from another, in spite of being contemporaneous. The cranial capacity of one of the adult skulls, for instance, is among the largest ever found in its time period, while the other adult cranium is close to the smallest. (The third skull is a juvenile.) In this and other features, in fact, the variation among the individuals of this single population—which may even represent the remains of a single social group, killed by some catastrophe—equals that found among all the other known early archaics scattered across Europe. Indeed, the mix of traits revealed at this one spot sets limits for an anatomical range for pre-Neanderthals that can easily encompass all the other bones from the time period as well. In other words, all the skulls of unknown origin are pre-Neanderthal, and they should all be lumped into one lineage.

"Atapuerca shows that all that variation in Europe is normal for the population," says Milford Wolpoff of the University of Michigan, long a leader of the lumpers. "It anchors the Neanderthals as a lineage. They were not a static group but an evolving race. At Atapuerca you can see where that race comes from."

"There is no question that the new Atapuerca skulls show Neanderthal affinities," says Chris Stringer of the Natural History Museum in London. Stringer and Wolpoff have had some well-publicized disagreements, but in this case Stringer can't ignore the evidence. "In spite of all the variation they display, they get sucked in with the Neanderthals. Once that happens, it becomes very difficult to prevent the rest of the European material from getting sucked in as well."

Meanwhile, the question of what became of the Neanderthals is just as disputed as ever. Again it's a debate between taxonomic splitters and lumpers: between those who say Neanderthals belonged to a different species of human that long ago slid into the oblivion of extinction, and those who, like Wolpoff, view the Neanderthals not as a distinct species but merely as a distinct race that interbred with other races, contributed genes to the Cro-Magnons, and thus never truly went extinct. All Caucasians, says Wolpoff, are carrying around quite a bit of the Neanderthal genetic legacy.

The latest newcomer to this crusty debate is a baby: the skeleton of a ten-month-old hominid that, according to Yoel Rak of Tel Aviv University and his colleagues, appears to have been

purposely buried in a niche of a cave called Amud, near the Sea of Galilee, 50,000 to 60,000 years ago. Whose baby was it? Figuring out which taxonomic group an infant belongs to is notoriously hard because most of the characteristics that distinguish one ancient hominid from another only emerge later in life. But this case may be different. According to Rak, the baby bears three traits—the absence of a chin, an elongated shape to the hole where the spinal cord enters the skull, and some peculiarly overstated muscle-attachment markings on the inside of the jaw—that loudly, insistently wail "Neanderthal."

Whose baby was it? The skeleton bears several traits—including the absence of a chin—that insistently wail "Neanderthal."

Since the baby is far too young for such features to have been shaped by use, the traits must have been programmed in its genes. This bolsters Rak's belief that the Neanderthals were a separate species and were genetically distinct from the true ancestors of modern human beings. "The Amud baby tells us how profoundly different these traits are," says Rak. "They reach even into childhood."

Wolpoff, however, isn't ready to separate the Neanderthals from the rest of modern humans on account of one odd baby. "It's not that easy to tell Neanderthals from anybody else at that age," he says. "I'm surprised to find Yoel so certain about something so young."

Whether the Neanderthals died out or live on in our genes, the texture of their existence remains a separate mystery. They appear to have engaged in some disturbing practices. In March, Alban Defleur and Olivier Dutour, of the University of Provence, and their colleagues announced the discovery of some scattered Neanderthal limb and skull fragments from the Abri Moula rock shelter, near Valence in south-

eastern France. Four of the fragments bore "clear cut marks, undoubtedly resulting from a flint tool," as well as a distinctive breakage pattern. To put it delicately, they had been gastronomically exploited. Tim White of the University of California at Berkeley, an expert on discerning traces of cannibalism on ancient bones, is not surprised. "A lot of people have made claims about Neanderthals being cannibalized," he says. "Some of those claims have been discredited, but others have stood up."

The Abri Moula find is further evidence that Neanderthals ate one another, but sadly it sheds little light on why. People eat other people because they are starving, but they may also do it as a ritual act. In the prehistoric context, ritualistic cannibalism—like intentional burial—would be evidence of a more sophisticated mentality: it would suggest that the lives of Neanderthals included a symbolic, even religious aspect. Unfortunately the Neanderthals' motives cannot easily be read from the cut marks and breakage patterns in the bones of Abri Moula and other sites. As white points out, the motive is not always clear even in modern examples of man-eating.

"If you are starving to death and you eat Uncle Harry, there is probably going to be some ritual involved," he says. "Even so, your motive in eating him was still starvation. On the other hand, there are societies where they eat Uncle Harry purely because they thought he was a neat guy and want to be more like him."

However titillating the tales of cannibalism, the biggest news of 1993 by far remains the delicious promise of Atapuerca. Since the report of the three skulls, the dig has already yielded four additional human jawbones and enough cranial fragments to reconstruct another skull. And this is just one small site in a hill pockmarked with caves and fissures virtually spilling out ancient bones and artifacts. The Spanish excavators are slowly and carefully working a paleo-gold mine. "They've literally just scratched the surface," says Wolpoff "Atapuerca shows the promise of almost limitless science."

Ice Age Lamps

The invention of fat-burning lamps toward the end of the Ice Age helped to transform European culture. It coincided with several other major technological advances.

Sophie A. de Beaune and Randall White

Sophie A. de Beaune and Randall White share a fascination with the culture and technology of Ice Age humans. De Beaune is a member of the Laboratory of Prehistoric Ethnology at the National Center for Scientific Research (CNRS) in Paris. She also teaches biological and cultural anthropology to high school students in France. Her current research focuses on nonflint artifacts from the Paleolithic era; she has participated in and directed several excavations in southwest France. White is an associate professor of anthropology at New York University. He specializes in Upper Paleolithic art and technology and is currently preparing a monograph on the earliest forms of personal adornment among European cultures. White co-edited French Upper Paleolithic Collections in the Logan Museum of Anthropology, *which brought to light important late Ice Age art and artifacts in an important U.S. repository. De Beaune contributed most of the new research for this article, which White has helped place in a broader scientific context.*

The controlled use of fire, first achieved at least half a million years ago, is one of the great innovations in human culture. Although archaeologists and anthropologists generally emphasize the importance of fire for cooking, warmth and protection from predators, the light accompanying fire was also a precious resource, one that made it possible to extend human activity to times and places that are naturally dark. The invention of stone, fat-burning lamps, which happened in Ice Age Europe nearly 40,000 years ago, offered the first effective, portable means of exploiting this aspect of fire. The appearance of lamps broadly coincides with a number of other extraordinary cultural changes, including the emergence of art, personal adornment and complex weapons systems.

Many scholars have hypothesized about how Ice Age lamps functioned and were used, but nobody had ever undertaken a systematic study of them. One of us (de Beaune) therefore set out to examine these lamps in detail and to classify them by type. In conjunction with that project, we built working replicas of stone lamps in order to analyze their effectiveness as light sources and to learn about their design, fabrication and use. The results of this investigation provide a provocative insight into the technology and behavior of some of the earliest modern humans in Europe.

The first object explicitly identified as an Ice Age lamp was discovered in 1902, the year researchers authenticated the wall art in the cave at La Mouthe, France. Archaeologists had presumed that the creation of paintings and engravings hundreds of meters underground must have required an artificial light source. In the course of exploring La Mouthe, they uncovered compelling support of that notion: a carefully fabricated and heavily burned sandstone lamp bearing the engraved image of an ibex on its underside.

Since then, hundreds of more or less hollowed-out objects have been excavated and rather indiscriminately lumped into the category of lamps. The initial research goals were to sift through the potpourri, establish criteria for identifying lamps and examine variation within this category of objects. A search of the literature and of museum collections turned up 547 artifacts that had been listed as possible lamps. The first hurdle was to distinguish lamps from other similarly shaped implements, such as grinding stones. It quickly became obvious that the size and shape of an object are insufficient as defining criteria. For example, lamps need not have a bowl-shaped depression; many perfectly flat slabs show clear traces of localized burning, which in these and other instances provide only incontrovertible evidence that an object served as a lamp.

We judged that 245 of the 547 putative lamps clearly served other purposes (mortars, ocher receptacles and so on). The remaining 302 objects were of uncertain status as lamps. We then divided that sample (285 of which have a well-known site of origin) into two categories. We considered 169 of the items to be certain, probable or

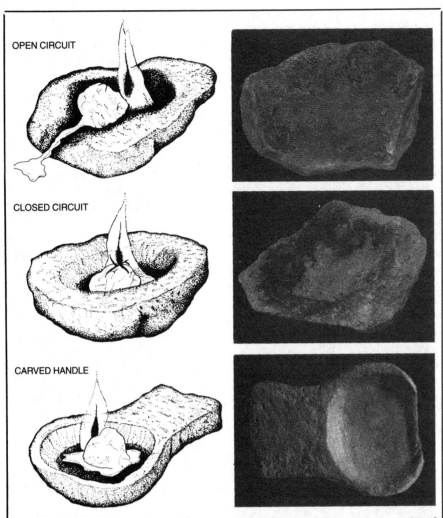

OPEN CIRCUIT

CLOSED CIRCUIT

CARVED HANDLE

LAMP DESIGNS fall into three main categories. Open-circuit lamps (*top*) consist of largely unaltered slabs of rock. When the lamp is lit, melted fat runs off through natural crevices in the rock. Closed-circuit lamps (*middle*) have carved depressions to contain the runoff. Carved-handle, closed-circuit lamps (*bottom*) also have bowl-shaped fuel chambers but are more finely finished and have formed extensions for easier handling. Burn marks indicate that the wick was placed away from the handle.

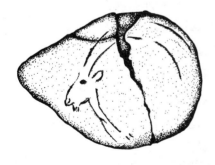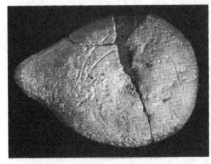

ENGRAVED DECORATIONS often appear on the sides or bottoms of closed-circuit lamps. This carved-handle lamp, which features the incised image of an ibex, was found at La Mouthe in 1902. It was the first object explicitly identified as a lamp.

possible lamps. The other 133 we classified as doubtful or unavailable for study. Markings left by the burning of fuel and wick tend to disappear over time, so the oldest lamps were the most likely to fall into the dubious category.

The lamps that we consider here all date from the Upper Paleolithic era, between 40,000 and 11,000 years ago.

The 285 lamps of known origin come from 105 different archaeological sites, mainly in southwest France. The

Aquitaine basin has yielded 60 percent of the lamps, the Pyrenean region 15 percent. Considerably fewer lamps have been recovered from other parts of France, and lamps found outside France—in Spain, Germany and Czechoslovakia—are exceedingly rare. Although this pattern may be explained in part by the historically greater intensity of research and the greater number of sites in southwest France, it seems that lamp-producing cultures were in fact restricted to a particular European region.

The vast majority of the known stone lamps consist of limestone or sandstone, both of which are fairly abundant. Limestone has the advantage of often occurring naturally in slab-like shapes that require little alteration. Moreover, limestone conducts heat poorly, so lamps of this material do not get hot enough to burn the user's fingers. Sandstone is a much better heat conductor, so simple sandstone lamps quickly become too hot to hold after they are lit. Paleolithic people solved this problem by carving handles into most sandstone lamps. Perhaps part of the appeal of sandstone lay in its attractive red color and smooth texture.

Our experiments suggest that the size and shape of the bowl are the primary factors that control how well a stone lamp functions. Setting bowl shape as our primary criterion, we divided the 302 Upper Paleolithic lamps into three main types: open-circuit lamps, closed-circuit bowl lamps and closed-circuit lamps with carved handles.

Open-circuit lamps are the simplest kind. They consist of either small, flat or slightly concave slabs or of larger slabs having natural cavities open to one side to allow excess fuel to drain away as the fat melts; the largest ones are roughly 20 centimeters across. Because open-circuit lamps show no noticeable signs of carving or shaping, large numbers of them may have gone unrecognized in premodern excavations. As a result, open-circuit lamps probably are underrepresented in the current sample.

Any slab of rock will work as an open-circuit lamp, so fashioning one requires extremely little effort. The trade-off is that these kinds of lamps inevitably waste a lot of fuel. Open-circuit lamps may be best interpreted as makeshift or expedient devices, easily made and freely discarded. Studies of the modern Inuit show that human groups, even those capable of building large, elaborate lamps, occasionally burn a piece of fat on a stone slab when no alternative lies readily at hand.

Closed-circuit bowl lamps are the most common variety. They are in all regions, in all periods and in all types of sites where lamps have been recovered. Closed-circuit bowl lamps have shallow, circular or oval depressions designed to retain the melted fuel. The recovered lamps of this kind range from crude to elaborate. Some bowl lamps are entirely natural, some have a slightly retouched bowl and others are completely fabricated. The exterior part of the lamp also may be natural, partly retouched or entirely sculpted. These lamps consist of oval or circular pieces of limestone that are usually the size of a fist or slightly larger. The bowl has sloping sides capable of retaining liquid when the lamp is placed on a horizontal surface. A typical bowl measures a few centimeters across but only 15 to 20 millimeters deep. The largest bowls can hold about 10 cubic centimeters of liquid.

Ice Age closed-circuit lamps resemble those employed by certain Inuit peoples—such as the Caribou, Netsilik and Aleut—who had access to wood for fuel and were therefore not dependent on lamps for heat. Inuit living north of the treeline, where wood was scarce, designed large lamps from slabs of soapstone that were up to a meter across. Those giant lamps (perhaps more correctly thought of as stoves) served many of the same functions as hearths elsewhere, including drying clothes, cooking and heating. There may be direct relations between the quality and abundance of locally available wood for fuel, the presence of fireplaces and the form of lamps at a site.

The most intricate lamps are those we classified as closed-circuit lamps with carved handles. The 30 such lamps in our sample are shaped, smoothed and finely finished entirely by abrasion. Each has a carved handle; 11 of them are decorated with engravings. These lamps appear in the archaeological record somewhat later than the others. The first carved-handle lamps show up in either the Solutrean (22,000 to 18,000 years ago) or Lower Magdalenian (18,000 to 15,000 years ago) cultures. They are particularly abundant in the Middle and Upper Magdalenian (15,000 to 11,000 years ago). Most carved-handle lamps are found in the Dordogne region of France. They are most abundant in rock-shelter sites but are also found in caves and open-air camps.

The elegant design, rarity and limited distribution in time and space of carved-handle lamps may imply that they served primarily ceremonial purposes. A well-known example from Lascaux, which has been dated to 17,500 years ago, was found on the cave floor at the bottom of a vertical shaft, below a drawing of a hunter confronting a wounded bison. This

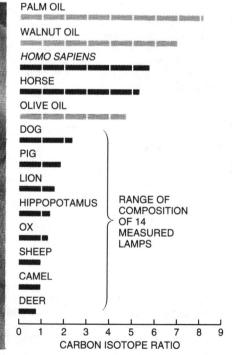

EXPERIMENTAL CLOSED-CIRCUIT LAMP (*left*) clarifies how these objects were used in Paleolithic times. A lump of fat serves as the fuel; the wick consists of bits of bark, lichen or moss. Melted fat collects in a depression in the rock and must occasionally be poured off. Chemical analysis of Ice Age lamps reveals the presence of residues whose composition resembles that of fat from animals that were common in Paleolithic France (*right*); vegetable fats clearly were not used.

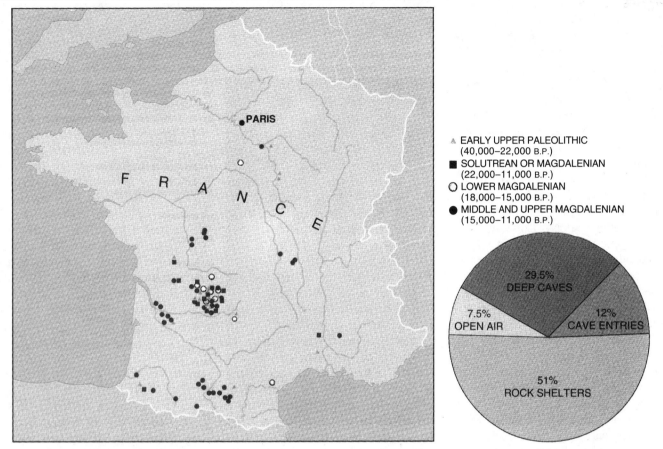

ICE AGE LAMPS have been found primarily in southwest France (*left*). Lamps appear in all eras of the Upper Paleolithic (40,000 to 11,000 years ago); more of them have been recovered from the later periods. Surprisingly, most lamps have been retrieved not from deep caves but from open-air sites and from under rock shelters (*right*).

lamp was discovered by the Abbé Glory, a Catholic lay priest who suggested that such lamps were used to burn aromatic twigs and hence were analogous to incense burners. Too few chemical analyses have been performed, however, to test this hypothesis adequately. The other kinds of stone lamps probably served exclusively as sources of light.

To be effective, a fat-burning lamp must be reliable, easy to handle and bright enough to throw usable light a distance of a few meters in, for example, a darkened cave. The form of lamp that predominates in our sample of Paleolithic lamps is precisely that which our experiments revealed to be optimally efficient. It is a closed-circuit lamp having an oval or circular depression and gently sloping rather than vertical sides. Sloping the side of the bowl facilitates emptying the lamp (so that the wick does not become swamped

in melted fat) without dislodging the wick. Carving a gap or notch in the rim of the lamp offers an alternative way to empty the bowl while keeping the wick in place. Eighty percent of the Paleolithic lamps we studied use the sloped-side approach.

Anthropologists have long assumed that animal fat was the fuel burned in Ice Age lamps. From our experiments, we learned that the best fats are those that melt quickly and at a low temperature. Also, they must not contain too much adipose tissue, the connective tissue in fat. Fat from seals, horses and bovids proved most effective in experimental lamps. But were these in fact the fuels favored by Paleolithic humans?

Guy L. Bourgeois of the University of Bordeaux and de Beaune analyzed residues from several Paleolithic lamps to identify the substances they con-

tained. Using two sensitive chemical analysis techniques (vapor-phase chromatography and mass spectrometry), they measured the carbon isotope ratios in fatty acids in the residues. The abundance ratios resemble those in animal fats from modern herbivores, such as cattle, pigs and horses. Unfortunately, scientists have no samples of fat from the actual animals that lived during the late Pleistocene. Nevertheless, the observed ratios of carbon isotopes are quite unlike those in vegetable fats, proving that animals were indeed the source of fuel for Ice Age lamps.

Our investigations also provided new information about the materials from which wicks were made. A good wick must be able to attract melted fat by capillary action and convey it to the free, burning end without being too quickly consumed. Of the wicks we tested, lichen (known to be used by modern Inuit), moss and then juniper worked best. Fritz H. Schweingrüber of the Swiss Federal Research Institute for Forest, Snow and Landscape analyzed several lamp residues. He detected remnants of conifers, juniper and grass, as well as nonwoody residues, possibly lichen or moss. In our experience, juniper wicks are never completely consumed by the flame and so may be better preserved than wicks composed of other plants.

The traces of use on our experimental lamps make it possible to interpret with confidence the markings observed on Paleolithic lamps. Those signs of usage come in three broad forms: light accumulations of soot, deposits of charcoal and reddening of the rock itself, a process known as rubefaction. In 80 percent of all the lamps observed, soot and charcoal deposits are situated within or on the rim of the fuel chamber, where one would expect the wick to lie. Occasional blackening of the side or underside of the lamp can be produced by trickles of melted fat that carried with them small particles of soot. Charcoal deposits result from carbonization of the wick or from the heat alteration, or calcination, of adipose tissue in the burning fat.

Thermal reddening often appears on the sides and undersides of lamps, but it, too, most frequently appears in or on the rim of the fuel chamber (in 67.5 percent of the cases). Experience with modern replicas indicates that such reddening took place when hot, melted fat ran onto the side or bottom of the lamp, either as the lamp was being emptied or when it overflowed on its own. Thermal reddening evidently can occur after only a few uses and so provides a helpful indicator of which artifacts served as lamps.

Repeated reuse of a lamp leaves distinct patterns. If a standard open- or closed-circuit lamp is lit on several occasions, the placement of the fat and wick tends to change from one time to the next. Because there is no preferred orientation for those simple lamps, they eventually become blackened and reddened over the entire bowl or surface. The carefully worked closed-circuit lamps that have handles display strikingly different signs of usage.

They are oriented the same way each time they are lit, so soot deposits build up on one part of the bowl only, generally the area opposite the handle.

Open-circuit and simple closed-circuit lamps probably were lit only a few times before being discarded. They are so easy to manufacture that there would have existed little incentive to carry them from site to site; we found that we could make a decent lamp in about half an hour. Decorated, carved-handle lamps, which represent a greater investment of labor, were more likely to have been used repeatedly.

To evaluate the effectiveness of Paleolithic fat-burning lamps, one needs to know how much light those lamps could provide. De Beaune investigated this matter by measuring the light output of modern replicas in the metrology laboratories of Kodak-Pathé, France. In quantity, intensity and luminescence, the experimental lamps provided distinctly less light than a standard candle but nonetheless would have been sufficient to guide a person through a cave or to illuminate fine work when placed nearby—assuming, of course, that the visual acuity of Paleolithic people was the same as ours.

The limitations of Ice Age lamps suggest that the creators of cave drawings never saw them as they appear in modern photographs. Human color perception is constrained and distorted at levels less than 150 lux (for comparison, 1,000 lux is typical in a well-lit office). It seems doubtful that the creators of the cave art worked under such bright conditions. Achieving full and accurate color perception of the cave images along a five-meter-long panel would require 150 lamps, each of them placed 50 centimeters from the cave wall. Torches could have provided supplementary light, but few traces of torches have been found in deep caves. On the other hand, the absence or scarcity of lamps in vast cave galleries such as those at Rouffignac, Niaux and Les Trois Frères implies that the creator of the paintings had access to some alternative light sources.

Today when one views the famous cave art in France and Spain, the artificial illumination creates an effect fundamentally unlike that experienced by Paleolithic visitors. Electric lights in the cave of Font de Gaume yield a steady light level of about 20 to 40 lux across a full panel of drawings. Ten to 15 thoughtfully placed stone lamps would be needed to attain 20 lux. A person carrying a single lamp would get a very different impression of the cave art and could view only small portions of the wall at a time. The dim illumination produced by flickering lamps may well have been part of the desired effect of viewing art deep within a cave. The illusion of animals suddenly materializing out of the darkness is a powerful one, and some cave images are all the more convincing if one cannot see them too well.

Of course, fat-burning lamps were employed for many tasks other than creating and viewing cave art. Lamps are found in such abundance at sites throughout southwest France that they must have been a fairly ordinary item of day-to-day existence. Only about 30 percent of the known lamps were recovered in deep caves. Open-air sites, rock shelters exposed to plentiful daylight and cave entries have provided the rest. The number of lamps at each site (two to three, on average) does not differ significantly from caves to rock shelters to open-air sites.

The location of lamps within sites provides clues to how people exploited them. In deep caves, lamps are often recovered from places where people had to pass, such as cave entrances, the intersections of different galleries and along walls. It would seem that lamps were placed at strategic or predictable points where they could easily be found and reused. The discovery of many lamps lying together—most notably at Lascaux, where 70 lamps have been recovered—implies that lamps were stored in particular locations between uses. Unfortunately, one cannot deduce how many of the lamps were lit at any one time.

Lamps are frequently discovered near fireplaces. Perhaps they were preheated in the fire in order to warm the fat and make it easier to ignite or were abandoned and reused as hearthstones. More likely, fireplaces served as central points of heat and light from which people departed into and returned from the darkness. Many lamps are found inverted in the soil, implying that on returning, people extinguished them simply by turning them over.

In at least one location, a lamp seems to have provided a permanent, fixed source of light within a campsite. Archaeologists found two lamps in a small, natural cavity in the wall of the rock shelter of La Garenne. One lamp had been turned over as if to extinguish the flame. The other was placed upright in a natural hollow in the rock that held it level. The cavity itself would have served as a natural reflector that maximized the lamp's light output.

Sorting through the sample of fat-burning lamps, we sought to learn how their abundance and design changed over time. That analysis is somewhat restricted by the paucity of data. Accurate radioactive dates are available for only the most recently discovered lamps. In most cases, ages are inferred from the archaeological levels in which the lamps were found, and in many early excavations even that information was not recorded. Nevertheless, enough information exists for us to make some general observations.

Many more lamps appear in the last cultural period of the Upper Paleolithic, the Magdalenian, than in preceding periods. This may reflect the fact that there are simply more Magdalenian sites known than is the case for earlier periods, as well as the fact that most deep-cave painting took place in the Magdalenian. Older lamps are also harder to identify with certainty.

The form of lamps seems to have evolved surprisingly little through the ages. Some variation in form, material and design occurred, but there is no clear progression from crude to elaborate. Although carved-handle lamps are more common in the later eras, all three primary types of lamp are found throughout the Magdalenian, and even the most elaborate lamp designs date back to the earliest Upper Paleolithic periods, which roughly corresponds to the time when Cro-Magnon, anatomically modern humans, appeared in Europe. The various forms of lamp most likely represent functional responses to particular contexts of use; the need for both simple, easy-to-make lamps and carved, aesthetically pleasing ones apparently was common to all Paleolithic cultures in France.

It is difficult to overstate the importance of artificial light in freeing humans from their evolutionary adaptation to the daylight world. Cave art specialist Denis Vialou of the Museum of Natural History in Paris lauds the Magdalenian cave artists as the people who conquered the world of the underground. But perhaps it is more accurate to see them as the most daring of a long line of our Cro-Magnon ancestors, who, through intelligence and technological innovation, changed the human experience forever by domesticating the realm of darkness.

FURTHER READING

DARK CAVES, BRIGHT VISIONS: LIFE IN ICE AGE EUROPE. Randall White. American Museum of Natural History and W. W. Norton & Company, 1986.

PALEOLITHIC LAMPS AND THEIR SPECIALIZATION: A HYPOTHESIS. S. de Beaune in Current Anthropology, Vol. 28, No. 4, pages 569–577; August/October 1987.

TECHNOLOGICAL CHANGES ACROSS THE MIDDLE-UPPER PALEOLITHIC TRANSITION: ECONOMIC, SOCIAL AND COGNITIVE PERSPECTIVES. P. Mellars in The Human Revolution: Behavioural and Biological Perspectives on the Origins of Modern Humans. Edited by P. Mellars and C. Stringer. Princeton University Press, 1989.

NONFLINT STONE TOOLS OF THE EARLY UPPER PALEOLITHIC. Sophie de Beaune in Before Lascaux: The Complex Record of the Early Upper Paleolithic. Edited by H. Knecht, A. Pike-Tay and R. White. CRC Press, 1993.

Lithic Technology and the Hunter-Gatherer Sexual Division of Labor

Kenneth E. Sassaman

South Carolina Institute of Archaeology and Anthropology, University of South Carolina

ABSTRACT

A technological change from formal to expedient core reduction marks the "transition" from mobile to sedentary prehistoric societies in many parts of the world. The phenomenon has often been attributed to changes in the organization of men's activities, particularly hunting. Considering, however, that the change coincides with the adoption of pottery, technology usually attributed to women, an alternative explanation must be considered. From the standpoint of archaeological systematics, the addition of pottery turns our focus away from places where hafted bifaces were discarded toward places where pottery was discarded. The latter are largely domestic contexts: locations at which women, as well as men, employed expedient core technology for a variety of tasks. Thus, the perceived change in core technology reflects the increased visibility of women's activities in the archaeological record. This recognition provides a basis for incorporating gender variables into our interpretations of prehistoric technology and labor organization.

Within American archaeology, studies of lithic technology are burgeoning in new and productive directions. Moving away from the traditional pursuits of chronology and function, lithic analysts are developing method and theory for relating stone tool technology to issues of broad anthropological relevance. These efforts have been particularly important in the study of hunter-gatherers, societies whose traces are often limited to stone tools and the by-products of their manufacture and use. Interpretations of hunter-gatherer settlement-subsistence organization (Amick, 1987; Jeffries, 1982; Raab et al., 1979), mobility (Kelly, 1988; Lurie, 1989; Parry and Kelly, 1987; Shott, 1986), time management (Torrence, 1983), and risk avoidance (Bleed, 1986; Myers, 1989; Torrence, 1989) have all been derived from studies of lithic technology (see Nelson, 1991 for recent review).

A common denominator in this work is that technology variation is referable to environmental variation—the geological occurrence of rock, the seasonality and spatial distribution of food resources, and so forth. Lithic studies that focus on social dimensions of technology are lagging behind the ecological or techno-environmental efforts. With few exceptions (e.g., Cross, 1990), studies addressing social issues—the organization of labor, inequality, control, and the like—concern relatively complex societies (e.g., Clark, 1987; Gero, 1989). The lack of similar approaches to hunter-gatherer technology might be traced to stereotypes about simple societies—that by being egalitarian, all members of the group have access to technology, including the materials and information needed to make and use tools, as well as the products of labor. We simply do not expect much social differentiation in the manufacture, distribution, and consumption of hunter-gatherer stone tools.

While this assumption is itself a subject of debate, there is one dimension of social variation that we accept in hunter-gatherers ethnographically, but do not explicitly incorporate into our models of hunter-gatherers archaeologically. That dimension is the division of labor by sex.

Nearly all recent attempts at modeling hunter-gatherer lithic technology have treated groups as if they were composed of undifferentiated members. The issue I want to address in this article is simply whether or not we can continue to develop models of lithic technology while ignoring the sexual division of labor. It seems apparent that most lithic analysts have implicitly assumed that only men made and used flaked stone tools. However, recent reviews of ethnographic literature render this position untenable (Bird, 1988; Gero, 1991). Moreover, even if women did not make and use stone tools in some prehistoric societies, it is unrealistic to assume that the economic activities of women were not factored into decisions about the production, use, and discard of men's technology.

I want to add to the growing recognition of women's roles in stone tool

From *North American Archaeologist*, Volume 13, Number 3, 1992, pp. 249-262. © 1992 by Baywood Publishing Company, Inc. Reprinted by permission.

production and use by pointing out how attention to gender variables can enhance extant interpretations of technological variation and change. My basic argument is quite simple: if we allow that women and men alike used stone tools, we should anticipate that any differences in the productive activities of men and women involving stone tools would contribute to technological variation in the material records of those activities. Such differences might include spatial patterns of work, work schedules, scale of production, access to raw materials, and discard behavior, to name but a few potential axes of variation. Needless to say, these sorts of variables are central to our perceptions and interpretations of prehistoric society.

I employ as a case study the purported change from formal to expedient core technology that is thought to mark the transition from mobile to sedentary prehistoric societies in many parts of the world. This shift has been recently attributed to changes in the organization of male hunting activities (Torrence, 1989) and to changes in patterns of residential mobility (Parry and Kelly, 1987). I will show how a consideration of gender provides alternative readings of the data.

ARCHAEOLOGICAL TIME-SPACE SYSTEMATICS

To begin, I propose that the perceived transition from formal to expedient core technology is in part shaped by the categories used to order archaeological time. As a foundation for this proposition, let us assume that there was a basic division of labor whereby men hunted game, and women collected plants and small animal resources. Let us also assume that hunting technology was distinct from other lithic technology, and that the technological requirements of hunting game contributed to regularities in tool design that are now useful in dividing archaeological time into meaningful phases or periods. It follows that time-space systematics in archaeology are largely based on continuity and change

in the design of tools used by men; in North America these consist largely of hafted bifaces, both projectiles and other bifacial tools associated with hunting activity.

While hafted bifaces comprise the primary diagnostic artifacts for early North American prehistory, pottery types replace bifaces as the chief time markers during late prehistory. Cross-cultural evidence allows us to safely assume that women made and used most of the pottery in these prehistoric societies (Arnold, 1985:108). It follows, then, that late prehistory is subdivided temporally by variation in technology usually attributed to women.

The significance of this observation becomes apparent when we consider the distinct disposal patterns of hafted bifaces versus pottery, and how these differences predetermine the distribution of associated archaeological remains (Figure 1). Specifically, hafted bifaces used in hunting are discarded at some domestic sites (where tools are replaced; represented in Figure 1 by the intersection of male and female activity loci), and at hunting-related and quarry-related locations used exclusively by men. In contrast, pottery is discarded at most, if not all domestic sites, and perhaps also at some locations where women conducted specialized activities. In short, the archaeological record of the preceramic period consists almost exclusively of locations at which hafted bifaces were discarded, while the ceramic period record consists largely of locations at which pottery was discarded. Inasmuch as the sexual division of labor ensures that these locations are not completely isomorphic, the preceramic and ceramic period archaeological records represent distinct samples of settlement variation. Our disregard for gender roles in this respect renders comparisons of the preceramic and ceramic periods untenable. As a result, observed differences in the records of these periods are interpreted as the result of anything other than gender.

I must interject at this point that the model I propose applies to the hunting of solitary game such as white-tailed deer, but not herd or migratory species

such as bison, reindeer, and caribou. In hunting the latter, entire co-resident groups relocate to kill sites after a successful hunt. Under these circumstances, we should not anticipate spatial separation of men's and women's activities at the intersite level of analysis. Unfortunately, equivalent analogs for the organization of white-tailed deer hunting are not available. I can only assume that some of the intersite assemblage variability observed in the archaeological record of temperate forest hunter-gatherers reflects a spatial (and sexual) dichotomy in the logistical organization of deer hunting. Even if this dichotomy is exaggerated, the addition of pottery to the archaeological record of temperate forest hunter-gatherers assures that we are focused on locations at which women worked. This alone creates a potential bias in the way we perceive functional differences between preceramic and ceramic period sites.

Such gender bias is illustrated in recent models for the apparent shift from formal to expedient core reduction in flaked stone industries. Because it seemingly reflects a degeneration of the art of flintknapping, the change is sometimes referred to as "devolutionary" (Torrence, 1989:58). What is interesting about the change is that it occurs in so many different places across the globe, and at similar junctures in the histories of local prehistoric populations. Two models have been developed to account for these broad patterns. One developed by Torrence (1989) points to changes in the risk avoidance strategies of hunters as societies become increasingly dependent on agricultural production. An alternative articulated by Parry and Kelly (1987) focuses on the diminishing need for portable bifacial cores as the residential mobility of hunter-gatherers decreased through time. Both arguments are logically sound and supported by evidence. However, because the technological change coincides with the adoption of pottery in many parts of the globe, our perceptions of it are partly shaped by a shift in focus from men's roles to women's roles in stone tool production and use. If we include

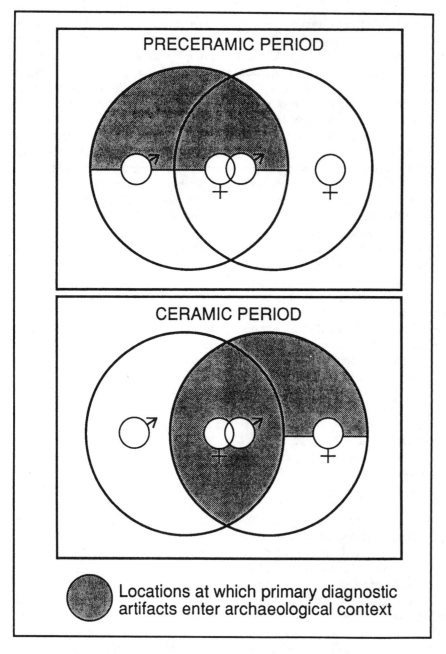

Figure 1. Model of the spatial relationships between the sexual division of labor and distributions of diagnostic artifacts in preceramic and ceramic period contexts.

gender in the extant models of this technological change, we not only eliminate this bias, but also introduce a variable that accounts for more of the variation in the design, use, and discard of lithic stone tools cross-culturally.

STONE TOOLS AND RISK AVOIDANCE

Robin Torrence (1989) proposes that cross-cultural variation in design and use of stone tools can be understood as a function of the risk avoidance strate-gies of hunter-gatherers. Of particular relevance is the short-term risk involved in capturing food. The abundance of a food resource at a particular point in space and time is an essential component of such risk, but the greatest risk arises when there is a dependence on mobile prey for food (Torrence, 1989:59). Conversely, relatively little short-term risk is expected when there is dependence on foods that are stationary, particularly plant foods. Torrence concludes that "the percentage of plant versus animal resources in the diet can be taken as a very rough indication of the strength of a potential risk faced by a hunter-gatherer group" (Torrence, 1989:60).

To illustrate the role of risk avoidance in tool design, Torrence draws a contrast between *instruments* on the one hand, and *weapons* and *facilities* on the other. She shows that instruments dominate the tool assemblages of hunter-gatherers whose diets consisted mainly of plant foods, while weapons and facilities characterized the technologies of groups dependent on mobile games (see Torrence, 1983). She further describes how hunting technology consists of complex, formalized tools designed for long-lasting, reliable service (see Bleed, 1986). That is, hunting tools are ready when needed, unlikely to fail, and easy to repair. These properties, Torrence argues, avert much of the uncertainty of hunting by minimizing the chance of technological failure.

In contrast, the instruments of the more vegetarian hunter-gatherers need not be maintainable or reliable because the timing and severity of risk are insignificant. Instruments are thus simple in design and rarely maintained for continuous or long-term use. In this regard, instruments are equivalent to the *expedient* technology described by Lewis Binford (1979).

Torrence (1989) employs this model to explain the shift from complex to simple lithic technology that characterizes archaeological sequences throughout the world. In eastern North America, the change is characterized as a decrease in the use of formal bifaces (weapons), and an increase in the use of informal, expedient tools (instruments). Torrence claims that the technological change coincides with the shift in subsistence from hunting and gathering to food production. As a consequence of this fundamental subsistence change, she argues, the nature of short-term risk changed. Hunting no longer occupied a risk-prone position in the economy, and thus did not require the application of elaborate and costly technology to avert failure.

My criticism of Torrence's model is that it downplays the importance of plant foods in nonagricultural economies, and thus portrays the technological change from formal to expedient core technology as abrupt. To be fair, Torrence confesses to the oversimplification of her model and points out that most assemblages will reflect a mix of technological responses to risk avoidance. The challenge, she suggests, is to determine how particular tool forms, not entire technologies, are subject to different levels and types of risk.

Her challenge offers a point of departure for addressing gender roles. If we can develop predictions about the types of subsistence activities men and women respectively perform and relate these to the timing and severity of risk, we can begin to refer the bridging arguments Torrence makes between risk and tool design to gender-specific technology. We can expect, as Torrence notes, that the risks of hunting mobile game are different than the risks of collecting plant foods, and that tools will be designed and used accordingly. That hunting and gathering were conducted simultaneously through a sexual division of labor suggests that technologies will indeed contain a mix of formal and expedient core technology. The co-occurrence of these distinct core types will depend on local factors such as the organization of land-use, duration of occupation, and site reoccupation, as well as the availability of raw materials. In more general terms, however, the relative contributions that formal and amorphous core technology make to hunter-gatherer technology can be a gauge to the relative contribution of women to subsistence production.

In eastern North America, bifaces and other formalized core tool forms dominate assemblages dating to the late Pleistocene and early Holocene. Many of these assemblages also contain expedient cores that were used for on-site flake production, and these lend indirect support to the increasing awareness that plant foods comprised a significant portion of Paleoindian and Early Archaic diet (Meltzer and Smith, 1986). Expedient tool technology becomes increasingly important over subsequent millennia, at times eclipsing biface technology. The manufacture of formal unifacial tools likewise abates. Following Torrence, these changes probably reflect the waning need for risk-averting technology, presumable due to the increasing importance of plant foods and, presumably, women's contribution to production. However, hunting did not cease, and, indeed, it probably intensified in areas of high population density. Nor did biface technology disappear altogether. Changes are evident in the design and production of bifaces and, at certain times and places, the production of bifaces and expedient cores converged. It is important to keep in mind that these trends are nonlinear. Because they appear to fluctuate from region to region, and at different rates, we should be able to track changes in the relative contributions of men and women through changes in flaked stone technology. Importantly, the model that Torrence provides, with its emphasis on hunting technology, permits us to view changes in men's technology as a response to changes in the subsistence activities of women, and this indeed is a promising avenue for future research.

STONE TOOLS AND MOBILITY

An alternative to Torrence's model is an argument posed by William Parry and Robert Kelly (1987) on the relationship between flaked stone technology and hunter-gatherer mobility. Building upon the work of several authors (Binford, 1977, 1979; Goodyear, 1979; Kelly, 1988; Nelson 1987), they look at biface technology as an adaptive solution to the spatial and temporal incongruity between tool production and tool use. This relates not only to the constraints of tool function and tool design, but also to "behavioral variables which mediate the spatial and temporal relations among activity, manufacturing, and raw material loci" (Kelly, 1988: 717). They consider mobility to be the key behavioral factor that mediates these relations. Because there is no necessary relationship between geologic sources of rock and the locations of other resources people require, particularly food and water, stone tools have to be transported (see also Shott, 1986). And, because the functional requirements for stone tools cannot always be predicted, stone tool technology must also be flexible (see also Goodyear, 1979). Thus, mobility simultaneously dictates access to raw material, tool needs, and portability. Throughout prehistoric North America, bifacial core technology was used to meet the organizational contingencies of mobility.

Several authors have commented on the advantages of bifacial core technology to mobile hunter-gatherers (Goodyear, 1979; Kelly, 1988; Nelson, 1987; Parry and Kelly, 1987). For instance, Kelly (1988) suggests that formalized bifacial technology was selected whenever mobile settlement systems included occupations in areas lacking lithic raw material. Under these conditions, bifaces served as portable cores that could be reduced for usable flakes and shaped into formal tools that were flexible, maintainable, and recyclable. As this was a long-term, planned reduction strategy that hinged on one's ability to predictably flake stone, good-quality raw material was obviously a must (Goodyear, 1979). Parenthetically, the need to utilize good quality rock perpetuated the need for biface technology. That is, because sources of good material generally have spotty distributions, a reliance on these sources by mobile peoples created spatial incongruity between locations of procurement and locations of tools use.

Like the dichotomy set up by Torrence, Parry and Kelly (1987) juxtapose bifacial core technology with expedient core technology. They argue that the transition from bifacial to expedient core technology in several parts of North America coincided with the rise of sedentism. Residential stability, they argue, allowed tool makers to stockpile rock for immediate use. They further suggest that the tool-using activities of sedentary people were largely restricted to residential bases, so there was little spatial incongruity between raw material and tool use. It follows that there was little need to make formal bifaces for the anticipated needs of a lithic-poor environment.

In contradiction to the argument posed by Parry and Kelly are numerous examples of expedient core technology throughout eastern North America by mobile hunter-gatherers who also employed formal biface technology. These cases have been attributed by a number of authors to the luxury of local raw material abundance (Bamforth, 1986; Custer, 1987; Johnson, 1986). Here a mixed strategy of biface technology for anticipated needs and expedient technology for immediate needs seems to be the case.

The other problem with Parry and Kelly's argument is that groups that spent long periods of time at bases, and/or reoccupied bases on a seasonal basis continued to practice logistical mobility, ostensibly for hunting game. Thus, the need for bifacial core technology, both as weapons and as cores, continued.

How do the shortcomings of Parry and Kelly's thesis play themselves out in the sexual division of labor? To begin, we need to disentangle the different types of mobility embedded in the seasonal rounds of hunter-gatherers. Parry and Kelly (1987) consider residential mobility—the mobility of entire coresident groups—to be the critical consideration in technological design. Alternatively, I agree with Torrence (1989:62) that the relevant amount of mobility for the transport of tools is the distance travelled by the tool-user.

In this sense, the distances and patterns of mobility of men and women differ. Thus, the sexual division of labor is a variable that potentially accounts for combinations of formal and expedient core technology in terms of the mobility parameters spelled out by Parry and Kelly. Rather than seeing the two technologies as being mutually exclusive, we should expect the use of these to be complementary and interdependent.

In terms of production, for example, bifacial and expedient core technologies varied from being independent to being interdependent. When occupying nonsource areas, portable tools provided all of the raw material needs of stone tool-uses. Insofar as men were responsible for producing bifacial cores, women may have had little direct access to usable flakes, and instead depended on the by-products of men's work. In contrast, at residential bases near source areas, both men and women could have procured, manufactured, and used tools. Bifacial cores still comprised an important male technology for hunting forays into areas with either uncertain or unreliable raw material sources. Under these conditions, the production of bifaces remained distinct from the production of flakes from expedient cores irrespective of the availability of raw material at domestic sites.

The two strategies of tool production converged when bifaces were made from flakes removed from expedient cores at residential sites. This occurred in parts of the Southeast during the Early Woodland, and continued into late prehistory. The strategy can be partly explained by changes in biface technology itself, not the least of which was the adoption of bow and arrow technology in the Late Woodland period. In addition, though, we need to consider how women's uses of flaked stone helped to support the shift from bifacial to expedient core technology within men's technology. In this respect, the celebrated trends toward increased residential stability that mark the Woodland period had immediate and significant ramifications for women's work. As residential mobility became more difficult to maintain, a

variety of other strategies was engaged to cope with the economic stresses that constraints on fissioning imposed. Many, if not most, of the economic changes associated with this trend are implicitly attributed to women: the adoption of pottery and the expansion of the food base to include starchy seeds, shellfishing, and incipient horticulture. As Cheryl Claassen (1991) observes, if we consider all the innovations and changes that we implicitly attribute to women, we have written into prehistory a time and energy crisis for women.

If this depiction of women's labor is correct, and I believe it may be, it goes without saying that women experienced a greater need for technology, including flaked stone technology. I think it is reasonable to propose that women sought raw materials and reduced rock for their own purposes. It is unrealistic to think that women depended solely on the by-products of men's flintknapping. Instead, women had intimate knowledge of the local landscape and were able to locate and exploit sources of rock that otherwise may have been ill-suited for biface manufacture. Women also had ample opportunity and motive for scavenging the lithic refuse of abandoned sites (Sassaman and Brooks, 1990). Both sources of raw material would have been well-suited to the needs of food processing and maintenance activities at residential bases.

Eventually, the roles that formal bifaces played in men's hunting activities were filled by more expedient forms made from flakes, and finally by bow and arrow technology that required only small modified flakes for tipping arrows. This change from long-lived, curated bifaces to short-lived, throwaway bifaces marks a significant change in the technology of men's hunting weapons, but it does not necessarily reflect a major organizational change in the men's activities *per se*. Rather, the change in men's technology may in part reflect the increased contribution of women to raw material procurement and core reduction at domestic sites. The removal of flakes for immediate on-site use and for the manufacture of projectiles for hunting now fell under a single production trajectory. It is likely that women, as well as men, participated in expedient core reduction. In any event, the process was simplified so that the steps of production no longer required spatial, temporal, technological or sexual differentiation.

Whatever became of the ill-fated formal biface? Across Eastern North America well-made formal bifaces do not disappear altogether, but they do seem to be relegated to special functions within society. Ceremonial uses of bifaces, including mortuary offerings, persisted well into late prehistory. It is tempting to suggest that formal bifacial technology remained under the domain of males and became relegated to ceremonial functions as an expression of male control over certain resources and productive processes. This idea might be further substantiated if we allow that within the secular world, flaked stone had developed into an androgynous technology, bearing little to no differentiation along lines of gender. Male rituals involving formal biface technology might therefore embody a form of male resistance to the changing conditions of technology.

SUMMARY AND CONCLUSION

The sexual division of labor that we accept as a basic feature of hunter-gatherer organization obviously contributed to the patterns of technological variation we read in the archaeological record. The extant models for explaining the shift from formal biface to expedient core technology stand to gain from a consideration of gender. The changes in risk avoidance strategies that Torrence identifies, and the effects of sedentism on tool design that Parry and Kelly identify, can be recast to include the sexual division of labor. If we deny women a role in stone tool production and use, a stance that now seems wholly unfounded, then the attention on division of labor may seem extraneous. However, the decisions men make about the design, production, and use of flaked stone tools obviously have some bearing on the

overall opportunities and constraints of the entire economy; so we should expect that changes in men's technology will reflect changes in the organization and success of women's activities.

Thus, models of the organization of hunter-gatherer technology need to be expanded to account for the social units that comprise divisions of labor involving stone tools. Perhaps separate models need to be developed for men and women (cf. Jochim, 1988). But we should also focus attention on variation in the integration or interdependence of male-female tool-using activities. Given the basic dichotomy we have between hunting and gathering, many of the well-developed bridging arguments of technological organization lend themselves to this problem. If we include gender in the models, we may begin to account for variation that cannot be fully explained by tool function, raw material constraints, or group mobility.

The goal, of course, is not to define particular men and women in the record, but to look for variation in gender relations and roles that can help us to model processes of culture changes and continuity. I have no doubt that stone tools hold answers to these issues, and, the lack of ethnographic analogs notwithstanding, significant gains in these areas can be made if serious attention is brought to the subject. This is not an issue of politics; rather it is simply a natural part of the ongoing process of improving our ability to describe and explain human variation. It is unfortunate, though explicable (Wylie, 1989), that the question of gender has taken so long to enter archaeological analysis (especially lithic studies), but it is fundamental to human organization and requires our further consideration.

ACKNOWLEDGMENTS

A shorter version of this article was presented in a plenary session on the Archaeology of Gender at the 1991 Middle Archaeological Conference. My thanks to Joe Dent and Christine Jirikowic for inviting me to participate in the session. Support for this re-search was provided by the United States Department of Energy-Savannah River Operations Office. Revisions of an earlier draft of this article benefitted from the comments of Mark Brooks, Joan Gero, Bill Green, Alice Kehoe and Keith Stephenson. These colleagues did not agree with all of my claims, so only I, not they, can be held responsible for the final version.

REFERENCES CITED

AMICK, D. S., 1987. *Lithic Raw Material Variability in the Central Duck River Basin: Reflections of Middle and Late Archaic Organizational Strategies,* Report of Investigation 46, Department of Anthropology, University of Tennessee, Knoxville.

ARNOLD, D. E., 1985. *Ceramic Theory and Cultural Process,* Cambridge University Press, Cambridge.

BAMFORTH, DOUGLAS B., 1986. Technological Efficiency and Tool Curation, *American Antiquity, 51,* pp. 38–50.

BINFORD, LEWIS R., 1977. Forty-seven Trips: A Case Study in the Character of Archaeological Formation Processes, in *Stone Tools as Cultural Markers: Change, Evolution and Complexity,* R. V. Wright (ed.), pp. 24–36, Australian Institute of Aboriginal Studies, Canberra.

————, 1979. Organization and Formation Processes: Looking at Curated Technologies, *Journal of Anthropological Research, 35,* pp. 255–273.

BIRD, C. F. M., 1988. Women and the Toolmaker: Evidence of Women's Use and Manufacture of Flaked Stone Tools in Australia and New Guinea, paper presented at the Second New England Conference on Technological Analysis in Australian Archaeology.

BLEED, P., 1986. The Optimal Design of Hunting Weapons: Maintainability or Reliability, *American Antiquity, 51,* pp. 737–747.

CLAASSEN, CHERYL, 1991. Shellfishing and the Shellmound Archaic, in *Engendering Archaeology: Women in Prehistory,* J. M. Gero and M. W. Conkey (eds.) pp. 276–300, Blackwell, Cambridge.

CLARK, J. E., 1987. Politics, Prismatic Blades, and Mesoamerican Civilization, in *The Organization of Core Technology,* J. K. Johnson and C. A. Morrow (eds.), pp. 259–284, Westview Press, Boulder, Colorado.

CROSS, J. R., 1990. *Craft Specialization in Nonstratified Society: An Example from the Late Archaic in the Northeast,* Ph. D. dissertation, Department of Anthropology, University of Massachusetts, Amherst.

CUSTER, JAY F., 1987. Core Technology at the Hawthorne Site, New Castle County, Delaware: A Late Archaic Hunting Camp, in *The Organization of Core Technology,* J. K. Johnson and C. A. Morrow (eds.), pp. 45–62, Westview Press, Boulder, Colorado.

GERO, J. M., 1989. Assessing Social Information in Material Objects: How Well Do Lithics Measure Up?, in *Time, Energy and Stone Tools,* R. Torrence (ed.), pp. 92–105, Cambridge University Press, Cambridge.

_____, 1991. Genderlithics: Women in Stone Tool Production, in *Engendering Archaeology: Women in Prehistory,* J. M. Gero and M. W. Conkey (eds.), pp. 163–193, Blackwell, Cambridge.

GOODYEAR, ALBERT C., 1979. *A Hypothesis for the Use of Cryptocrystalline Raw Materials Among Paleo-Indian Groups in North America,* Research Manuscript Series 165, South Carolina Institute of Archaeology and Anthropology, University of South Carolina, Columbia.

JEFFRIES, R. W., 1982. Debitage as an Indicator of Intraregional Activity Diversity in Northwest Georgia, *Midcontinental Journal of Archaeology, 7,* pp. 94–132.

JOCHIM, M. A., 1988. Optimal Foraging and the Division of Labor, *American Anthropologist, 90,* pp. 130–136.

JOHNSON, JAY K., 1986. Amorphous Core Technologies in the Midsouth, *Midcontinental Journal of Archaeology, 11,* pp. 135–151.

KELLY, ROBERT L., 1988. The Three Sides of a Biface, *American Antiquity, 53,* pp. 717–731.

LURIE, R., 1989. Lithic Technology and Mobility Strategies: The Koster Site Middle Archaic, in *Time, Energy and Stone Tools,* R. Torrence (ed.), pp. 46–56, Cambridge University Press, Cambridge.

MELTZER, DAVID J. and B. D. SMITH, 1986. Paleoindian and Early Archaic Subsistence Strategies in Eastern North America, in *Foraging, Collecting and Harvesting: Archaic Period Subsistence and Settlement in the Eastern Woodlands,* S. W. Neusius (ed.), pp. 3–31, Occasional Papers 6, Center for Archaeological Investigations, Southern Illinois University, Carbondale.

MYERS, A., 1989. Reliable and Maintainable Technological Strategies in the Mesolithic of Mainland Britain, in *Time, Energy and Stone Tools,* R. Torrence (ed.), pp. 78–91, Cambridge University Press, Cambridge.

NELSON, M. C., 1987. The Role of Biface Technology in Adaptive Planning, paper presented at the 27th Annual Meeting of the Northeastern Anthropological Association, Amherst, Massachusetts.

_____, 1991. The Study of Technological Organization, in *Archaeological Method and Theory,* Vol. 3, M. B. Schiffer (ed.), pp. 57–100, University of Arizona Press, Tucson.

PARRY, WILLIAM J. and ROBERT L. KELLY, 1987. Expedient Core Technology and Sedentism, in *The Organization of Core Technology,* J. K. Johnson and C. A. Morrow (eds.), pp. 285–304, Westview Press, Boulder, Colorado.

RABB, L. MARK, R. F. CANDE and D. W. STAHLE, 1979. Debitage Graphs and Archaic Settlement Patterns, *Midcontinental Journal of Archaeology, 4,* pp. 167–182.

SASSAMAN, KENNETH E. and MARK J. BROOKS, 1990. Cultural Quarries: Scavenging and Recycling Lithic Refuse in the Southeast, paper presented at the Southeastern Archaeological Conference, Mobile, Alabama.

SHOTT, M. J., 1986. Technological Organization and Settlement Mobility: An Ethnographic Examination, *Journal of Anthropological Research, 42,* pp. 15–52.

TORRENCE, ROBIN, 1983. Time-Budgeting and Hunter-Gatherer Technology, in *Hunter-Gatherer Economy in Prehistory: A European Perspective,* G. Bailey (ed.), pp. 11–22, Cambridge University Press, Cambridge.

_____, 1989. Re-tooling: Towards a Behavioral Theory of Stone Tools, in *Time, Energy and Stone Tools,* R. Torrence (ed.), pp. 57–66, Cambridge University Press, Cambridge.

WYLIE, A., 1989. Feminist Critiques and Archaeological Challenges, paper presented at the CHACMOOL Conference, Calgary.

The Dating Game

*By tracking changes in ancient atoms, archeologists are establishing
the astonishing antiquity of modern humanity.*

James Shreeve

*James Shreeve wrote fiction before
turning to science writing. He is the
coauthor (with anthropologist Donald
Johanson) of* Lucy's Child: The Discovery of a Human Ancestor *and the
author of* Nature: The Other Earthlings.

Four years ago archeologists Alison
Brooks and John Yellen discovered
what might be the earliest traces of
modern human culture in the world.
The only trouble is, nobody believes
them. Sometimes they can't quite believe it themselves.

Their discovery came on a sun-
soaked hillside called Katanda, in a
remote corner of Zaire near the Ugan-
dan border. Thirty yards below, the
Semliki River runs so clear and cool
the submerged hippos look like giant
lumps of jade. But in the excavation
itself, the heat is enough to make anyone doubt his eyes.

Katanda is a long way from the
plains of Ice Age Europe, which archeologists have long believed to be the
setting for the first appearance of truly
modern culture: the flourish of new
tool technologies, art, and body orna-
mentation known as the Upper Paleolithic, which began about 40,000 years
ago. For several years Brooks, an archeologist at George Washington University, had been pursuing the heretical
hypothesis that humans in Africa had
invented sophisticated technologies
even earlier, while their European
counterparts were still getting by with

the same sorts of tools they'd been
using for hundreds of thousands of
years. If conclusive evidence hadn't
turned up, it was only because nobody
had really bothered to look for it.

"In France alone there must be three
hundred well-excavated sites dating
from the period we call the Middle
Paleolithic," Brooks says. "In Africa
there are barely two dozen on the
whole continent."

One of those two dozen is Katanda. On an afternoon in 1988
John Yellen—archeology program director at the National Science
Foundation and Brooks's husband—
was digging in a densely packed litter
of giant catfish bones, river stones, and
Middle Paleolithic stone tools. From
the rubble he extricated a beautifully
crafted, fossilized bone harpoon point.
Eventually two more whole points and
fragments of five others turned up, all
of them elaborately barbed and polished. A few feet away, the scientists
uncovered pieces of an equally well
crafted daggerlike tool. In design and
workmanship the harpoons were not
unlike those at the very end of the
Upper Paleolithic, some 14,000 years
ago. But there was one important difference. Brooks and Yellen believe the
deposits John was standing in were at
least five times that old. To put this in
perspective, imagine discovering a
prototypical Pontiac in Leonardo da
Vinci's attic.

"If the site is as old as we think it
is," says Brooks, "it could clinch the

argument that modern humans evolved
in Africa."

Ever since the discovery the couple
have devoted themselves to chopping
away at that stubborn little word *if.* In
the face of the entrenched skepticism
of their colleagues, it is an uphill task.
But they do have some leverage. In
those same four years since the first
harpoon was found at Katanda, a
breakthrough has revived the question
of modern human origins. The breakthrough is not some new skeleton pulled out of the ground. Nor is it the
highly publicized Eve hypothesis, put
forth by geneticists, suggesting that all
humans on Earth today share a common female ancestor who lived in
Africa 200,000 years ago. The real
advance, abiding quietly in the shadows
while Eve draws the limelight, is simply a new way of telling time.

To be precise, it is a whole smorgas-
bord of new ways of telling time. Lately
they have all converged on the same
exhilarating, mortifying revelation: what
little we thought we knew about the
origins of our own species was hopelessly wrong. From Africa to the Middle East to Australia, the new dating
methods are overturning conventional
wisdom with insolent abandon, leaving
the anthropological community dazed
amid a rubble of collapsed certitudes.
It is in this shell-shocked climate that
Alison Brooks's Pontiac in Leonardo's
attic might actually find a hearing.

"Ten years ago I would have said it
was impossible for harpoons like these
to be so old," says archeologist Mi-

chael Mehlman of the Smithsonian's National Museum of Natural History. "Now I'm reserving judgment. Anything can happen."

An archeologist with a freshly uncovered skull, stone tool, or bone Pontiac in hand can take two general approaches to determine its age. The first is called relative dating. Essentially the archeologist places the find in the context of the surrounding geological deposits. If the new discovery is found in a brown sediment lying beneath a yellowish layer of sand, then, all things being equal, it is older than the yellow sand layer or any other deposit higher up. The fossilized remains of extinct animals found near the object also provide a "biostratigraphic" record that can offer clues to a new find's relative age. (If a stone tool is found alongside an extinct species of horse, then it's a fair bet the tool was made while that kind of horse was still running around.) Sometimes the tools themselves can be used as a guide, if they match up in character and style with tools from other, better-known sites. Relative dating methods like these can tell you whether a find is older or younger than something else, but they cannot pin an age on the object in calendar years.

The most celebrated *absolute* method of telling archeological time, radiocarbon dating, came along in the 1940s. Plants take in carbon from the atmosphere to build tissues, and other organisms take in plants, so carbon ends up in everything from wood to woodchucks. Most carbon exists in the stable form of carbon 12. But some is made up of the unstable, radioactive form carbon 14. When an organism dies, it contains about the same ratio of carbon 12 to carbon 14 that exists in the atmosphere. After death the radioactive carbon 14 atoms begin to decay, changing into stable atoms of nitrogen. The amount of carbon 12, however, stays the same. Scientists can look at the amount of carbon 12 and—based on the ratio—deduce how much carbon 14 was originally present. Since the decay rate of carbon 14 is constant and steady (half of it disappears every 5,730 years), the difference between the

amount of carbon 14 originally in a charred bit of wood or bone and the amount present now can be used as a clock to determine the age of the object.

Conventional radiocarbon dates are extremely accurate up to about 40,000 years. This is far and away the best method to date a find—as long as it is younger than this cutoff point. (In older materials, the amount of carbon 14 still left undecayed is so small that even the slightest amount of contamination in the experimental process leads to highly inaccurate results.) Another dating technique, relying on the decay of radioactive potassium rather than carbon, is available to date volcanic deposits *older* than half a million years. When it was discovered in the late 1950s, radiopotassium dating threw open a window on the emergence of the first members of the human family—the australopithecines, like the famous Lucy, and her more advanced descendants, *Homo habilis* and *Homo erectus*. Until now, however, the period between half a million and 40,000 years—a stretch of time that just happens to embrace the origin of *Homo sapiens*—was practically unknowable by absolute dating techniques. It was as if a geochronological curtain were drawn across the mystery of our species' birth. Behind that curtain the hominid lineage underwent an astonishing metamorphosis, entering the dateless, dark centuries a somewhat precocious bipedal ape and emerging into the range of radiocarbon dating as the culturally resplendent, silver-tongued piece of work we call a modern human being.

F ifteen years ago there was some general agreement about how this change took place. First, what is thought of as an *anatomically* modern human being—with the rounded cranium, vertical forehead, and lightly built skeleton of people today—made its presence known in Europe about 35,000 years ago. Second, along with those first modern-looking people, popularly known as the Cro-Magnons, came the first signs of complex human

behavior, including tools made of bone and antler as well as of stone, and art, symbolism, social status, ethnic identity, and probably true human language too. Finally, in any one region there was no overlap in time between the appearance of modern humans and the disappearance of "archaic" humans such as the classic Neanderthals, supporting the idea that one group had evolved from the other.

"Thanks to the efforts of the new dating methods," says Fred Smith, an anthropologist at Northern Illinois University, "we now know that each of these ideas was wrong."

The technique doing the most damage to conventional wisdom is called thermoluminescence, TL for short. (Reader take heed: the terrain of geochronology is full of terms long enough to tie between two trees and trip over, so acronyms are a must.) Unlike radiocarbon dating, which works on organic matter, TL pulls time out of stone.

If you were to pick an ordinary rock up off the ground and try to describe its essential rockness, phrases like "frenetically animated" would probably not leap to mind. But in fact minerals are in a state of constant inner turmoil. Minute amounts of radioactive elements, both within the rock itself and in the surrounding soil and atmosphere, are constantly bombarding its atoms, knocking electrons out of their normal orbits. All this is perfectly normal rock behavior, and after gallivanting around for a hundredth of a second or two, most electrons dutifully return to their normal positions. A few, however, become trapped en route—physically captured within crystal impurities or electronic aberrations in the mineral structure itself. These tiny prisons hold on to their electrons until the mineral is heated, whereupon the traps spring open and the electrons return to their more stable position. As they escape, they release energy in the form of light—a photon for every homeward-bound electron.

Thermoluminescence was observed way back in 1663 by the great English physicist Robert Boyle. One night Boyle took a borrowed diamond to bed with him, for reasons that remain obscure. Resting the diamond "upon a warm part of my Naked Body," Boyle noticed that it soon emitted a warm glow. So taken was he with the responsive gem that the next day he delivered a paper on the subject at the Royal Society, noting his surprise at the glow since his "constitution," he felt, was "not of the hottest."

Three hundred years later another Englishman, Martin Aitken of Oxford University, developed the methods to turn thermoluminescence into a geophysical timepiece. The clock works because the radioactivity bombarding a mineral is fairly constant, so electrons become trapped in those crystalline prisons at a steady rate through time. If you crush the mineral you want to date and heat a few grains to a high enough temperature—about 900 degrees, which is more body heat than Robert Boyle's constitution could ever have produced—all the electron traps will release their captive electrons at once, creating a brilliant puff of light. In a laboratory the intensity of that burst of luminescence can easily be measured with a device called a photomultiplier. The higher the spike of light, the more trapped electrons have accumulated in the sample, and thus the more time has elapsed since it was last exposed to heat. Once a mineral is heated and all the electrons have returned "home," the clock is set back to zero.

Now, our lineage has been making flint tools for hundreds of thousands of years, and somewhere in that long stretch of prehistory we began to use fire as well. Inevitably, some of our less careful ancestors kicked discarded tools into burning hearths, setting their electron clocks back to zero and opening up a ripe opportunity for TL timekeepers in the present. After the fire went out, those flints lay in the ground, pummeled by radioactivity, and each trapped electron was another tick of the clock. Released by laboratory heat, the electrons flash out photons that reveal time gone by.

In the late 1980s Hélène Valladas, an archeologist at the Center for Low-Level Radioactivity of the French Atomic Energy Commission near Paris, along with her father, physicist Georges Valladas, stunned the anthropological community with some TL dates on burned flints taken from two archeological sites in Israel. The first was a cave called Kebara, which had already yielded an astonishingly complete Neanderthal skeleton. Valladas dated flints from the Neanderthal's level at 60,000 years before the present.

In itself this was no surprise, since the date falls well within the known range of the Neanderthals' time on Earth. The shock came a year later, when she used the same technique to pin a date on flints from a nearby cave called Qafzeh, which contained the buried remains of early modern human beings. This time, the spikes of luminescence translated into an age of around 92,000 years. In other words, the more "advanced" human types were a full 30,000 years *older* than the Neanderthals they were supposed to have descended from.

If Valladas's TL dates are accurate, they completely confound the notion that modern humans evolved from Neanderthals in any neat and tidy way. Instead, these two kinds of human, equally endowed culturally but distinctly different in appearance, might have shared the same little nook of the Middle East for tens of thousands of years. To some, this simply does not make sense.

"If these dates are correct, what does this do to what else we know, to the stratigraphy, to fossil man, to the archeology?" worries Anthony Marks, an archeologist at Southern Methodist University. "It's all a mess. Not that the dates are necessarily wrong. But you want to know more about them."

Marks's skepticism is not entirely unfounded. While simple in theory, in practice TL has to overcome some devilish complications. ("If these new techniques were easy, we would have thought of them a long time ago," says geochronologist Gifford Miller of the University of Colorado.) To convert into calendar years the burst of luminescence when a flint is heated, one has to know both the sensitivity of that particular flint to radiation and the dose of radioactive rays it has received each year since it was "zeroed" by fire. The sensitivity of the sample can be determined by assaulting it with artificial radiation in the lab. And the annual dose of radiation received from *within* the sample itself can be calculated fairly easily by measuring how much uranium or other radioactive elements the sample contains. But determining the annual dose from the environment *around* the sample—the radioactivity in the surrounding soil, and cosmic rays from the atmosphere itself—is an iffier proposition. At some sites fluctuations in this environmental dose through the millennia can turn the "absolute" date derived from TL into an absolute nightmare.

Fortunately for Valladas and her colleagues, most of the radiation dose for the Qafzeh flints came from within the flints themselves. The date there of 92,000 years for the modern human skeletons is thus not only the most sensational number so far produced by TL, it is also one of the surest.

"The strong date at Qafzeh was just good luck," says Valladas. "It was just by chance that the internal dose was high and the environmental dose was low."

More recently Valladas and her colleague Norbert Mercier turned their TL techniques to the French site of Saint-Césaire. Last summer they confirmed that a Neanderthal found at Saint-Césaire was only 36,000 years old. This new date, combined with a fresh radiocarbon date of about 40,000 years tagged on some Cro-Magnon sites in northern Spain, strongly suggests that the two types of humans shared the same corner of Europe for several thousand years as the glaciers advanced from the north.

While Valladas has been busy in Europe and the Middle East, other TL timekeepers have produced some astonishing new dates for the first human occupation of Australia. As recently as the 1950s, it was widely believed that Australia had been colonized only some five thousand years ago. The reasoning was typically Eurocentric:

since the Australian aborigines were still using stone tools when the first white settlers arrived, they must have just recently developed the capacity to make the difficult sea crossing from Indonesia in the first place. A decade later archeologists grudgingly conceded that the date of first entry might have been closer to the beginning of the Holocene period, 10,000 years ago. In the 1970s radiocarbon dates on human occupation sites pushed the date back again, as far as 32,000 years ago. And now TL studies at two sites in northern Australia drop that first human footstep on the continent—and the sea voyage that preceded it—all the way back to 60,000 years before the present. If these dates stand up, then the once-maligned ancestors of modern aborigines were building ocean-worthy craft some 20,000 years *before* the first signs of sophisticated culture appeared in Europe.

"Luminescence has revolutionized the whole period I work in," says Australian National University archeologist Rhys Jones, a member of the team responsible for the new TL dates. "In effect, we have at our disposal a new machine—a new time machine."

With so much at stake, however, nobody looks to TL—or to any of the other new "time machines"—as a geochronological panacea. Reputations have been too badly singed in the past by dating methods that claimed more than they could deliver. In the 1970s a flush of excitement over a technique called amino acid racemization led many workers to believe that another continent—North America—had been occupied by humans fully 70,000 years ago. Further testing at the same American sites proved that the magical new method was off by one complete goose egg. The real age of the sites was closer to 7,000 years.

"To work with wrong dates is a luxury we cannot afford," British archeologist Paul Mellars intoned ominously earlier this year, at the beginning of a London meeting of the Royal Society to showcase the new dating technologies. "A wrong date does not simply inhibit research. It could conceivably throw it into reverse."

Fear of just such a catastrophe—not to mention the risk that her own reputation could go up in a puff of light—is what keeps Alison Brooks from declaring outright that she has found exquisitely crafted bone harpoons in Zaire that are more than 40,000 years older than such creations are supposed to be. So far the main support for her argument has been her redating of another site, called Ishango, four miles down the Semliki River from the Katanda site. In the 1950s the Belgian geologist Jean de Heinzelin excavated a harpoon-rich "aquatic civilization" at Ishango that he thought was 8,000 years old. Brooks's radiocarbon dating of the site in the mid-1980s pushed the age back to 25,000. By tracing the layers of sediment shared between Ishango and Katanda, Brooks and her colleagues are convinced that Katanda is much farther down in the stratigraphy—twice as old as Ishango, or perhaps even more. But even though Brooks and Yellen talk freely about their harpoons at meetings, they have yet to utter such unbelievable numbers in the unforgiving forum of an academic journal.

"It is precisely because no one believes us that we want to make our case airtight before we publish," says Brooks. "We want dates confirming dates confirming dates."

Soon after the harpoons were discovered, the team went to work with thermoluminescence. Unfortunately, no burned flints have been found at the site. Nevertheless, while TL works best on materials that have been completely zeroed by such extreme heat as a campfire, even a strong dose of sunlight can spring some of the electron traps. Thus even ordinary sediments surrounding an archeological find might harbor a readable clock: bleached out by sunlight when they were on the surface, their TL timers started ticking as soon as they were buried by natural processes. Brooks and Yellen have taken soil samples from Katanda for TL, and so far the results are tantalizing—but that's all.

"At this point we think the site is quite old," says geophysicist Allen Franklin of the University of Mary-

land, who with his Maryland colleague Bill Hornyak is conducting the work. "But we don't want to put a number on it."

As Franklin explains, the problem with dating sediments with TL is that while some of the electron traps might be quickly bleached out by sunlight, others hold on to their electrons more stubbornly. When the sample is then heated in a conventional TL apparatus, these stubborn traps release electrons that were captured perhaps millions of years before the sediments were last exposed to sunlight-teasing date-hungry archeologists with a deceptively old age for the sample.

Brooks does have other irons in the dating fire. The most promising is called electron spin resonance—or ESR, among friends. Like TL, electron spin resonance fashions a clock out of the steadily accumulating electrons caught in traps. But whereas TL measures that accumulation by the strength of the light given off when the traps open, ESR literally counts the captive electrons themselves while they still rest undisturbed in their prisons.

All electrons "spin" in one of two opposite directions—physicists call them up and down. (Metaphors are a must here because the nature of this "spinning" is quantum mechanical and can be accurately described only in huge mathematical equations.) The spin of each electron creates a tiny magnetic force pointing in one direction, something like a compass needle. Under normal circumstances, the electrons are paired so that their opposing spins and magnetic forces cancel each other out. But trapped electrons are unpaired. By manipulating an external magnetic field placed around the sample to be dated, the captive electrons can be induced to "resonate"—that is, to flip around and spin the other way. When they flip, each electron absorbs a finite amount of energy from a microwave field that is also applied to the sample. This loss of microwave energy can be measured with a detector, and it is a direct count of the number of electrons caught in the traps.

ESR works particularly well on tooth

enamel, with an effective range from a thousand to 2 million years. Luckily for Brooks and Yellen, some nice fat hippo teeth have been recovered from Katanda in the layer that also held the harpoons. To date the teeth, they have called in Henry Schwarcz of McMaster University in Ontario, a ubiquitous, veteran geochronologist. In the last ten years Schwarcz has journeyed to some 50 sites throughout Europe, Africa, and western Asia, wherever his precious and arcane services are demanded.

Schwarcz also turned up at the Royal Society meeting, where he explained both the power and the problems of the ESR method. On the plus side is that teeth are hardy remains, found at nearly every archeological site in the world, and that ESR can test a tiny sample again and again—with the luminescence techniques, it's a one-shot deal. ESR can also home in on certain kinds of electron traps, offering some refinement over TL, which lumps them all together.

On the minus side, ESR is subject to the same uncertainties as TL concerning the annual soaking of radiation a sample has received from the environment. What's more, even the radiation from *within* a tooth cannot be relied on to be constant through time. Tooth enamel has the annoying habit of sucking up uranium from its surroundings while it sits in the ground. The more uranium the tooth contains, the more electrons are being bombarded out of their normal positions, and the faster the electron traps will fill up. Remember: you cannot know how old something is by counting filled traps unless you know the rate at which the traps were filled, year by year. If the tooth had a small amount of internal uranium for 50,000 years but took in a big gulp of the hot stuff 10,000 years ago, calculations based on the tooth's current high uranium level would indicate the electron traps were filled at a much faster rate than they really were. "The big question is, When did the uranium get there?" Schwarcz says. "Did the tooth slurp it all up in three days, or did the uranium accumulate gradually through time?"

One factor muddying the "big ques-tion" is the amount of moisture present around the sample during its centuries of burial: a wetter tooth will absorb uranium faster. For this reason, the best ESR sites are those where conditions are driest. Middle Eastern and African deserts are good bets. As far as modern human origins go, the technique has already tagged a date of about 100,000 years on some human fossils from an Israeli cave called Skhul, neatly supporting the TL date of 92,000 from Qafzeh, a few miles away. If a new ESR date from a Neanderthal cave just around the corner from Skhul is right, then Neanderthals were also in the Middle East at about the same time. Meanwhile, in South Africa, a human jawbone from the site of Border Cave— "so modern it boggles the mind," as one researcher puts it—has now been dated with ESR at 60,000 years, nearly twice as old as any fossil like it in Europe.

But what of the cultural change to modern human behavior—such as the sophisticated technological development expressed by the Katanda harpoons? Schwarcz's dating job at Katanda is not yet finished, and given how much is at stake, he too is understandably reluctant to discuss it. "The site has good potential for ESR," he says guardedly. "Let's put it this way: if the initial results had indicated that the harpoons were not very old after all, we would have said 'So what?' to them and backed off. Well, we haven't backed off."

There are other dating techniques being developed that may, in the future, add more certainty to claims of African modernity. One of them, called ura-nium-series dating, measures the steady decay of uranium into various daughter elements inside anything formed from carbonates (limestone and cave stalactites, for instance). The principle is very similar to radiocarbon dating—the amount of daughter ele-ments in a stalactite, for example, indi-cates how long that stalactite has been around—with the advantage that ura-nium-series dates can stretch back half a million years. Even amino acid race-mization, scorned for the last 15 years, is making a comeback, thanks to the discovery that the technique, unreli-able when applied to porous bone, is quite accurate when used on hard os-trich eggshells.

In the best of all possible worlds, an archeological site will offer an oppor-tunity for two or more of these dating techniques to be called in so they can be tested against each other. When asked to describe the ideal site, Schwarcz gets a dreamy look on his face. "I see a beautiful human skull sandwiched be-tween two layers of very pure flow-stone," he says, imagining uranium-series dating turning those cave lime-stones into time brackets. "A couple of big, chunky hippo teeth are lying next to it, and a little ways off, a bunch of burned flints."

Even without Schwarcz's dream site, the dating methods used separately are pointing to a common theme: the alarming antiquity of modern human events where they are not supposed to be happening in the first place. Brooks sees suggestive traces of complexity not just at Katanda but scattered all over the African continent, as early as 100,000 years before the present. A classic stone tool type called the blade, long considered a trademark of the European Upper Paleolithic, appears in abundance in some South African sites 40,000 to 50,000 years before the Upper Paleolithic begins. The conti-nent may even harbor the earliest hints of art and a symbolic side to human society: tools designed with stylistic meaning; colorful, incandescent min-erals, valueless but for their beauty, found hundreds of miles away from their source. More and more, the Cro-Magnons of Europe are beginning to look like the last modern humans to show themselves and start acting "hu-man" rather than the first.

That's not an easy notion for anthro-pologists and archeologists to swallow. "It just doesn't fit the pattern that those harpoons of Alison's should be so old," says Richard Klein, a paleo-anthropologist at the University of Chi-cago. Then he shrugs. "Of course, if she's right, she has made a remarkable discovery indeed."

Only time will tell.

A Primitive Prescription for Equality

Helen Fisher, an anthropologist at the American Museum of Natural History, argues that the "traditional" role of women is a recent invention—and that human society is now rediscovering its ancient roots

Conversation with Kathleen McAuliffe

Men and women are moving toward the kind of roles they had on the grasslands of Africa millions of years ago. But this "backward" trend is a step forward, toward equality between the sexes.

The rise of economically autonomous women is a new phenomenon that is in reality very old. For more than 99 percent of human evolution, we existed as hunters and gatherers, and women in those cultures enjoyed enormous clout because they probably brought back 60 to 80 percent of the food. At least that's the case in most contemporary hunting-gathering communities, such as the Kung bushmen of Africa, whose lifestyle is thought to mirror that of earliest Homo sapiens.

The recent trend toward divorce and remarriage is another example of a throwback to earlier times. The constant making and breaking of marital ties is a hallmark of hunting-gathering societies. The trend only seems novel to us because we are just now emerging from an agricultural tradition—a male-dominated culture that, while recent, lasted for a flash in the night on the time scale of human evolution. A peculiarity of the farming lifestyle is that men and women functioned as an isolated, economically dependent unit. Marriage was "till death do us part" for the simple reason that neither part-

ner could pick up half the property and march off to town.

But when men and women left farms for jobs and came back with money—movable, divisible property—we slipped right back into deeply ingrained behavior patterns that evolved long ago. Money makes it easy to walk out on a bad relationship. A man is going to think a lot harder about leaving a woman who picks his vegetables than leaving a woman who is the vice president of Citibank, because she can fend for herself and vice versa. Indeed, around the globe, wherever women are economically powerful, divorce rates are high. You see it in the Kung, and you see it in the United States: Between 1960 and 1980, when the number of women in the work force doubled, the divorce rate doubled, too.

THE "NEW" EXTENDED FAMILY

That figure seems bleak until we recall that the vast majority of couples who split up remarry—and that's as true in hunting-gathering communities as in postindustrial America. This suggests that the so-called new extended family may actually have evolved millennia ago. If so, perhaps our tendency to equate divorce with failure has made us blind to the advantages of the extended family: Children grow up with more adult role models and a larger network of relatives, increasing their

range of power and influence within society.

The trend toward smaller families may not be as modern as we think, either. Although women gatherers had four or five children, only two typically survived childhood—the number found in the average American family today. Even our style of rearing children is starting to parallel hunting-gathering communities, in which girls and boys are permitted to play together from a young age, and consequently experiment at sex earlier and engage in trial marriages. Clearly we've moved away from the agricultural custom of arranged marriages and cloistering girls to preserve their virginity.

Moreover, the home is no longer the "place of production," as it was in farm days. We don't make our soap, grow our vegetables and slaughter our chicken for the dinner table. Instead, we hunt and gather in the grocery store and return to our "home base" to consume the food we have collected. No wonder we are so in love with fast foods. It probably harks back to an eating strategy our primate relatives adopted over 50 million years ago.

PUTTING OUR HEADS TOGETHER

There's no mistaking the trend: Humans are once again on the move. Husband and wife are no longer bound to a single plot of land for their livelihood. Women are back in production as well as reproduction. As we head back to the future, there's every reason to believe the sexes will enjoy the kind of equality that is a function of our birthright. By equality, I mean a more equitable division of power—not that our roles will converge. Alike men and women have never been and never will be. Very simply, we *think* differently, which is again tied to our long hunting-gathering heritage.

For 2 million years, women carried around children and have been the nurturers. That's probably why tests show they are both more verbal and more attuned to nonverbal cues. Men, on the other hand, tend to have superior mathematical and visual-spatial skills because they roamed long distances from the campsite, had to scheme ways to trap prey and then had to find their way back.

The specialization is reflected in genuine gender differences in the brain today. Nature not only intended men and women to put their bodies together; we're meant to put our heads together as well.

That's what is so thrilling about what's happening now. All those male and female skills are beginning to work together again. At long last, society is moving in a direction that should be highly compatible with our ancient human spirit.

Archaeologists Today

A trowel for your thoughts . . .

*"Good morning, ladies and gentlemen. Welcome to the first annual convention of WARP, the World Archaeological Research Project. I am Dr. Derk Digger. As we all know, from the very beginning archaeology was an underground science fraught with a lot of just plain dirt flying around. By the end of the nineteenth century, disagreement within the rank and file had elevated to mud slinging.

"During the 1960s, in the historical period known as the 'New Archaeology,' infighting among archaeologists reached new intellectual lows. A whole decade was spent arguing about the true meaning of Mousterian points. Heavies like 'Louie the Blade' and 'François the Flake' perpetuated pointed discussions ignoring core materials.

"When push came to shove in the 1970s, some archaeologists viciously attacked vending machines at professional meetings. Whole dynasties of stellar archaeological families fought others for sites and National Geographic funding, sometimes misplacing whole sites or taking over small nations. Rulers of sites rose and fell as espionage and counterespionage tossed reputations around like falling back dirt.

"There was much splitting and lumping of heads during these fluctuating dates and not much was salvaged. This pugnacious pattern of archaeological antics continued to worsen during the decades of the 1980s and 1990s until archaeology was in ruins. The garbage finally hit the pits, and archaeologists surrendered on July 4, 1999, at Point Clovis in New Mexico. The Marshalltowns hitting the ground made a sound the likes of which had not been heard since Howard Carter opened King Tut's tomb.

"Ah, but this is all history, or sort of like protohistory. In a way it could even be viewed as prehistory, but that might be stretching the point. At any rate, calibrated, of course, we remaining archaeologists hope to form a hypothetical agreement on the issues that concern all of us here today. That is, of course, the future of archaeological sites. Remember, as you sit here today, we are about to create TRASH (The Ruling Archaeological Sites Hierarchy). During this morning's session, we can consider about six demands from our various special interest groups. Please put your shards on the table before you speak.

*Any resemblance to real persons or events in this fictional story are purely coincidental with the exception of Howard Carter and King Tut's tomb.

"I would like to introduce our first speaker, Mr. Peter Potlooter of TPL, Inc. You all know of the importance to archaeology of this worldwide organization representing thieves, pothunters, and looters. We welcome our fellow enthusiasts and hope to incorporate a great deal of their views into TRASH. As archaeologists we are eager to make up for the past 200 years of tyranny when we tried to keep archaeological sites for ourselves.

"What was that? I cannot hear you! Oh yes, certainly, Mr. Sharp Arrow, this afternoon we will get to your proposal to bury the Smithsonian artifacts and all!"

And the tale above goes on, somewhere in someone's dust-clogged brain. In this unit the real state of the health of the science of archaeology is examined.

In any science, there is a good deal of infighting that goes on. It seems like there is something about archaeologists, most particularly paleoanthropologists, that makes for an emotional carriage that impresses even the most hardened veterans of other disciplines. A great deal of speculation has been spent on the eccentric stereotype of archaeologists. If there is an answer, it probably is to be found in the nature of the subject matter and its closeness to ultimate concerns such as the nature of human beings and their very origins. So far geneticists have not come up with a defective gene that causes people to become archaeologists.

However, there are other kinds of disagreements that may be truly harmful to a science. As a science evolves, it naturally diversifies. In the case of archaeology today, there is some concern that as archaeologists continue toward greater specialization, they will specialize themselves right out of mainstream archaeology. It is the practice of archaeology as cultural anthropology that unites the field. Mainstream archaeology at this time is definitely being pulled in different directions.

In this unit articles are addressed concerning the serious problems archaeology faces (as depicted in the beginning essay). There are other contenders for the rights to archaeological sites.

As long as there has been property, there have been thieves. As long as there have been archaeological sites, there have been looters. Wherein do we make the moral judgments? What about the interests of developers, dam

builders, or road builders? It is their livelihood to do these things even if it means destroying archaeological sites. What about the native or descendant generations who feel a continuity with their past either in a specific area or in a generalized sense? North American archaeology has been revolutionized by recent laws designating ownership of all archaeological sites to those who claim to be of the native descendant generation.

Archaeologists must walk an ethical tightrope on all of these issues. It is a very hard thing to do when our shared human past, and all the wisdom it can offer us, is at stake. Our species has always had an insatiable need to know. This is what we are.

Looking Ahead: Challenge Questions

There are many antiquity laws in the United States. Are they ever enforced?

What is meant by the term *native descendant generation* as used in archaeology? What arguments would an archaeologist use who feels natives have no claim to sites? What arguments would a native use? What compromise might the archaeologist and the native reach?

What is meant by repatriation of archaeological finds?

In some cases, salvage archaeology can lead to new discoveries. Give an example.

Give several examples of human activities that destroy archaeological sites.

The Antiquities Market

DAVID P. STALEY

David P. Staley (M.A. 1990, Washington State University) is a research associate at the University of Alaska Anchorage's Environment and Natural Resources Institute. He has 10 years' cultural-resource management experience in Alaska. Mailing address: University of Alaska Anchorage, Environment and Natural Resources Institute, 707A Street, Anchorage, Alaska 99501.

INTRODUCTION

The market in ancient human artifacts has always had a supply problem. Apart from the resale of objects in the possession of collectors—objects, that is, already in slow circulation—maintaining a profitable market tempo has left dealers with two major options. One possibility is to attempt to create new categories of objects deemed worthy of sale, purchase, and collection; this obviously involves the manipulation of tastes and perceptions so as to imbue previously disdained or ignored objects with new value. The other possibility is far more notorious: the encouragement of continued mining of known sources for objects of established saleability. The connection, overt or covert, between dealers and those non-archaeologists who dig for artifacts is well known.

Far less understood are the diggers themselves. These people, usually called looters, are strangely anonymous in the literature on the illicit market in antiquities. Their names are not known,

or, if known, not published. Usually only the empty trenches and gaping holes they leave behind are all that is left to mark their progress. For the most part, discussions of why the past is put up for sale conclude (without more than cursory investigation) that the economic straits in which these suppliers find themselves are so dire that looting is an attractive solution.

The following article by David P. Staley seeks to develop a better understanding of the market's supply side through a look at the lives of a group of Bering Sea natives who engage in what Staley calls "subsistence digging." Certain inhabitants of St. Lawrence Island spend some time every year excavating and selling ancient ivory and other artifacts, an activity which brings them some profit. These objects command high prices when they reach the centers of the art market. Recently, a New York dealer was asking $17,500 for an ivory anthropomorphic drum handle, with inlaid metal eyes, said to date to A.C. 600 and to have been excavated on St. Lawrence Island. The dealer, Jeffrey R. Myers, apparently makes a point of spending a part of his summers on St. Lawrence, which is when subsistence digging is done.

Staley's article will also be of interest to those who enjoy the ethical dilemma of who owns the past. Since St. Lawrence is owned by its natives, their excavations are not illegal. Since they are unearthing the possessions of their own ancestors, can any outsider object?

Timothy Kaiser
Editor

ST. LAWRENCE ISLAND'S SUBSISTENCE DIGGERS: A NEW PERSPECTIVE ON HUMAN EFFECTS ON ARCHAEOLOGICAL SITES

The problem of archaeological site destruction is receiving much deserved attention from the archaeological profession and from the public. Native subsistence diggers are significant agents of destruction in Alaska and their situation is representative of third world conditions. A case study, featuring the St. Lawrence Island community of Gambell, Alaska, describes the subsistence diggers' attitudes and motivations. This study provides insight into behavioral aspects of archaeological looting, causal factors underlying site destruction, and the internal workings of the artifact market. The Gambell case illustrates an ethical dilemma that needs to be addressed, since newly adopted policies to curtail site destruction may cause significant harm to a Native population that is compelled by economic forces to cannibalize its own heritage. The introduction of alternate sources of cash income through sensible economic development offers a possible solution.

Introduction
Archaeologists are shaping public policy through lobbying efforts in the area of cultural resource legislation and through their involvement in the U.S. public education campaign. The international archaeological community has been very much concerned with site looting, artifact trafficking, and the ethics of collecting (Messenger 1989; Neumann 1989; Smith and Ehrenhard

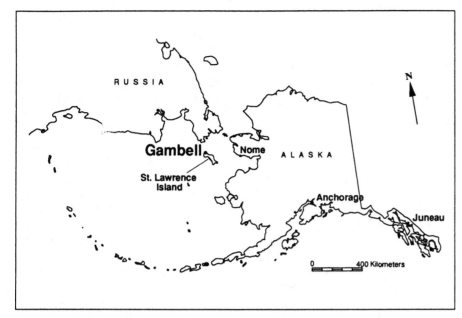

Figure 1. Map showing the location of the study ares. (By Ray Norman)

1991; Vitelli 1984). Major educational campaigns, supported by government agencies and professional organizations, have been launched to enlighten the public regarding the importance of heritage preservation (Hoffman and Lerner 1988; McManamon 1990; Rogge 1988). This is now the archaeologist's primary weapon against the destruction and degradation of historical and archaeological sites. While archaeologists are actively attempting to influence public attitudes and policies, we know very little about the people involved in site destruction. With few exceptions (Gramann and Vander Stoep 1986; Nickens, Larralde, and Tucker 1981; McAllister 1991), the behavioral aspects of looting and trafficking and the factors underlying the destruction of sites have not been evaluated.

Native subsistence diggers are significant agents in site looting in Alaska (Crowell 1985; King 1991; Morton 1989: 2; Staley 1990: 22–23). I opt for the term "digger" since both "looter" and "pothunter" have negative connotations and do not apply well in this situation. In this article, the subsistence digger is defined as a person who uses the proceeds from artifact sales to support his or her traditional subsistence lifestyle. My usage of "traditional subsistence" follows that of

Wenzel, who described the notion as having " . . . little to do with the technology used but much to do with internal relations . . ." of a culture (1991: 180). The term subsistence includes "cultural values that socially integrate the economic relations of a hunting peoples into their daily lives" (Wenzel 1991: 57). For the most part, subsistence diggers have been either overlooked by investigators of the problem or considered a limited regional phenomenon (Christensen et al. 1988; Nickens 1991; McAllister 1991). In contrast with other destructive agents, very little is known of the subsistence digger's situation, attitudes, or motivations.

On St. Lawrence Island, Eskimos are mining their ancestral archaeological sites (Scott 1984; Wardell 1986). The case study presented here, focusing on the community of Gambell, Alaska, contributes to an understanding of human impact on archaeological sites and highlights the Native subsistence digger. A brief summary of conditions and factors illustrates the extreme nature of the situation in Gambell. Economic conditions in the community are bleak (Little and Robbins 1984), yet St. Lawrence Island ivory artifacts are world renowned, and delicately carved pieces command high prices (Wardell 1986). Unlike raw or

fresh ivory, trade in old or fossil ivory is not restricted by the Marine Mammal Protection Act. St. Lawrence is one of the few sources for bulk ancient or fossil ivory sold to artisans and manufacturers. Unrestricted, fee simple title to the island is held by the Gambell and Savoonga village corporations established under the Alaska Native Claims Settlement Act (ANCSA) of 1971. Thus, since the entire island is privately owned, its lands are not covered under existing laws such as the Archaeological Resources Protection Act. Site access is relatively easy, as three sites are located in Gambell or within a short walking distance. Destruction of sites around Gambell has been so severe that the sites have lost their National Historic Landmark status (Morton 1989: 2).

During July and August of 1991, I monitored a municipal construction project in Gambell. In my "off" hours, I wandered about the sites, observed work in progress, and visited with local diggers and traders. Much of the information presented in this case study was personally observed or learned through these conversations.

The Setting

Gambell is a Yupik community located at the NW end of St. Lawrence Island (FIG. 1). Only one other community, Savoonga, is located on the 160 km-long island, which is situated less than 65 km from Siberia and 200 km from the Alaskan mainland. In 1990, Gambell had a total population of 525 people. At that time, 317 adults lived in the community and the median age was 24.2 years. There were 120 houses in Gambell with 4.38 persons per household (U.S. Department of Commerce, Bureau of the Census 1991: 33).

The people of Gambell are engaged in a mixed cash and subsistence economy, with the latter being more important (Little and Robbins 1984: 64; John Muir Institute, Inc. 1984: 112). A considerable amount of cash income is required for subsistence pursuits (Nowak 1977; VanStone 1960; Wenzel 1991: 106–133). A decade ago, a family would spend an average of $6700 each year on transportation, weapons, ammunition, and fishing equipment used in subsistence pursuits and an additional $1700 per year on gasoline. In 1984, the average family paid out $3800 for goods and food. This included primarily cereals, tea, coffee, sugar, pilot bread, soda, and cigarettes (John Muir Institute, Inc. 1984: 121). Of course, prices have increased over the last decade. For example, in 1991, a household of seven persons spent between $200 and $300 a month on food alone. A delayed barge delivery during the summer temporarily drove gasoline prices to $5.00 per gallon, although eventually prices returned to $2.50. Other monthly expenses included $74 for water and sewer services, $72 for cable television, $70 for electric service, and a heating fuel bill around $345 a month during winter.

Jobs are relatively scarce and extremely dependent upon State and Federal appropriations. Based on a community survey of Gambell conducted by the Norton Sound Health Corporation during 1990, 51% of 95 household respondents were unemployed. Only 22% of these households included a member with full time employment (Don Smith, Bering Strait Economic Development Corporation, personal communication, 1991). Monthly wage income in Gambell averaged $85 per person (Alaska Department of Labor, personal communication, 1991). This income was supplemented by food stamps, Aid to Families with Dependent Children, Energy Assistance, Longevity Bonus, and Permanent Fund Dividend programs. The production and sale of crafts, particularly ivory carvings, is a large source of locally generated income on the island. During the 1980s, ivory-carving sales volumes were estimated at approximately $100,000 per year (Little and Robbins 1984: 68). Between September, 1983, and October, 1984, sales of bulk ivory mined from sites netted more than $100,000. Sales of artifacts totalled around $40,000 in 1983 (Crowell 1985: 20). An analysis of average household income and expenses during 1991 demonstrated the critical importance of both the subsistence oriented economy,

48% of the expenses, and cash influx from ivory and artifacts, 13% of the income. Sales of ivory and artifacts are especially important because household budgets appear to be operating in a break-even or deficit mode.

Since 1983, Sivuqaq, Inc., Gambell's village corporation established under ANCSA, has been actively involved in the sale of bulk ivory (Crowell 1985: 21–22). The corporation acts as a middleman in the trade, providing a consistent, accessible market for the ivory diggers and attempting to maximize economic returns to the resident shareholders. The village corporation's perception of archaeological sites as economic resources is contrary to the perspective of most Native groups in the United States. Native groups generally advocate protection and conservation of historical and prehistoric sites (Nichols, Klesert, and Anyon 1989; Anyon 1991). Sivuqaq, Inc. sees archaeological sites as the source of extractable commodities, whereas other Native groups perceive cultural resources as a means to economic development but through a combined strategy of preservation and tourism (Parker 1990: 67).

Gambell's Subsistence Diggers
The entire demographic spectrum of the community participates in the excavation of Gambell's archaeological sites. Young and old, male and female, single individuals and entire families mine sites for old ivory and artifacts. Children brought to the site may help, but often bring toys to entertain themselves while the adults work. Both employed and unemployed residents work at the sites, although the latter have more time to devote to this activity.

Digging is limited to the summer season while permafrost sediments are thawing. Ardent diggers tend to work between four and 10 hours a day, while casual diggers are more likely to spend a few hours at a site one evening a week. Although digging may take place at any time, it seems to be predominantly an evening affair. The work is typically cold, wet, and arduous.

A variety of tools and apparatus is used at the sites including simple hand tools such as shovels, mattocks, picks, and buckets. Ice axes, manufactured for mountaineers, are preferred by both serious and casual diggers. This may be related to their easy access through mail-order catalogs. Wheelbarrows are in short supply; a village entrepreneur was recently renting one for $20 per day. At times, gasoline-powered portable pumps are used to drain pooled water from excavations. Hydraulic excavation occurs at some sites but not at those adjacent to Gambell. Many people leave their tools and equipment at the site between digging sessions.

The focus of excavation shifts around on the sites based on other diggers' findings or rumored findings. Rumored success of diggers under one of the few road beds in town caused substantial sections of the road to be torn up in a matter of days. Word of the recovery of potentially valuable pieces travels fast through the community and often stimulates others to get out and dig.

Excavation intensity and technique vary considerably. Men tend to excavate larger and deeper holes. When working by themselves, women and children dig numerous small shallow holes and never invest much time in any one location; but they tend to do more prospecting than the men, who concentrate on mining. Patterns of permafrost thawing also tend to influence excavation strategies and techniques. At present, diggers go to great lengths to find rare, undisturbed sections of the sites. The digging undercuts paths and roads and exposes various pipes, and phone and power lines. At times, diggers are forced to move tremendous piles of backdirt and disturbed sediments extending to depths of 4 m. Plastic covers surprisingly deep limits of previous mining efforts. Once undisturbed deposits are located, excavations proceed horizontally into the face, sometimes undercutting large blocks of sediments. These blocks frequently give way and negate the time and effort used to clear the area as well as burying equipment and diggers alike. Curious passersby are sharply warned not to walk above these excavations. Diggers often follow house wall logs, as whole walrus tusks are known to have been used to support vertical posts. Other structural elements are often chopped out of the way before they are completely exposed, and rock slab flooring is often torn up as the excavation proceeds.

Some of the techniques used by diggers in Gambell were learned directly from archaeologists who have worked in the area. In the late 1920s, Otto Geist experimented with boilers and steam thawing as well as using pumps, hoses, pressure nozzles, and screens to hydraulically excavate sites and water screen artifacts (Geist and Rainey 1976: 35, 42). The use of steel rod probes to differentiate subsurface bone and ivory was adopted from Hans-Georg Bandi, who used the technique to locate human burials. One digger stated she had been shown by archaeologists how small artifacts on the surface are more easily observed after a rain storm. Gambell diggers often toss faunal remains into a separate pile as they dig. This behavior may have been adopted from Otto Geist, who also segregated bone into large piles (Geist and Raney 1976: 246).

Artifacts

The relative importance of various artifact classes to the people of Gambell is expressed in the way they sort, accumulate, and conserve artifacts. Artifacts with certain monetary values are piled separately while digging and bagged at the end of the session. These include complete or fragmentary ivory artifacts with or without incised decoration, ivory scrap, walrus tusk and teeth, large sea mammal teeth, and walrus penis bones. Artifacts of marginal value or interest, such as seal teeth, groundstone ulus and endblades, palettes, chipped stone scrapers, points or blades, baleen bucket parts, scapula shovel blades, and various whole or broken wood and bone tools, are consistently sorted from the dirt and piled near the pit. Some of these artifacts are composite tool parts that are kept sep-

arately until the digger is certain that other components are lost. Artifacts are often shown to children, visitors, and other diggers and are the main topic of discussion. Artifacts of marginal value are often displayed on a whale or walrus scapula in or on the margins of the pit. Structural elements, faunal remains, flaking debitage, and small fragments of stone artifacts are either tossed into the backdirt or segregated into piles.

Valuable artifacts are typically amassed until sold to village visitors, professional artifact dealers or, if unmarketable as art or curio, eventually sold as scrap ivory. Diggers are anxious to show their artifacts even without any potential for sale. People will invite you into their houses to see their collections. In one home, I saw composite fish hooks, harpoon heads, buttons, and a wrist-guard fragment made of ivory and decorated with Punuk design elements. Most collections, however, included large varieties of mundane, undecorated artifacts. Although most household collections are awaiting sale, there are several families that keep groups of interesting artifacts in their homes with no intention of selling them.

Old ivory begins to crack, split, and peel after it is removed from the ground. Diggers attempt to conserve ivory artifacts using a variety of techniques and substances. Most understand that the problems are caused by too-rapid drying. Therefore, many try to control temperatures and humidity by drying specimens in a cool place inside sealed plastic bags. Others attempt to replace the water in the artifacts by soaking them in baby or gun oils.

Staking Claims and Territoriality

The passage of ANCSA legally made the natural resources on St. Lawrence Island common property and essentially gave all residents access to these resources. Control over the island's natural resources is shared by the village corporations of Gambell and Savoonga. This is the latest step in the liberalization of natural-resource use

rights. Prior to ANCSA, each community claimed control over a portion of the island's resources (Burgess 1974: 78). Preceding the consolidation of the population into these communities, territories were controlled by clans (Little and Robbins 1984: 82–83). Even at present, however, clans do maintain use rights over specific camping, hunting, and fishing locations.

The archaeological sites on St. Lawrence Island are also considered a common natural resource. There appear to be some differences in use rights, however, depending on the distance between the site and the main village. At sites close to Gambell, diggers who begin an excavation or adopt an abandoned, existing pit have use rights contingent on their consistent and continuous work in the location. Claimed areas are often shared between brothers who may work together or in staggered shifts. These rights may be traded or passed to other individuals, and permission is requested to dig in areas that are not clearly abandoned.

During the summer, many families leave Gambell to stay at subsistence camps, which are positioned within larger clan territories at prime subsistence-resource locations (Little and Robbins 1984: 184–205; Crowell 1985: 18). These same resources have drawn people to these locations for millennia. As clan members have use rights for the location, they also have exclusive control over any nearby archaeological resources. Unlike the Gambell sites, there is no requirement for consistent and continuous digging at these sites to maintain use rights.

Claims on digging areas at subsistence camps follow the historical, kinship-based pattern of use rights. Closer to Gambell, no clan can claim exclusive rights to an area, therefore, a different system has developed to define digging territories within sites. This system is a reflection of the liberalization of natural-resource use rights but only at the community scale. Future research on this subject may find even further communal ownership, with Savoonga residents freely digging at Gambell and vice versa.

Use rights to digging territories are generally respected although there are interlopers. It seems likely that incidents of encroachment are more common near Gambell than at subsistence camps. Diggers complain about trespassers more for their sloppy technique than for the potential loss of ivory and artifacts. Some diggers have threatened to place booby traps in their pits to discourage poaching by their fellow villagers.

Attitudes

The people of Gambell are very friendly, generous, and kind. Their attitudes toward the profession of archaeology are generally negative, however. Early archaeological investigations on the island were sophisticated for their time, although by today's standards the methods were coarse, and the large scale trenches through mounds would appear to the uninitiated as uncontrolled massive disturbances. Other than the excavation techniques described above, one can safely assume that little effort was expended toward explaining archaeological method and theory to the residents of Gambell.

Before the early archaeological investigations on the island by Otto Geist and Henry Collins, various superstitions and fears of the dead made most residents very reluctant to dig at the sites (Keim 1969: 114, 218). Archaeologists had a hand in changing this attitude by purchasing artifacts and hiring local assistants (Collins 1975: 25, 31, 35; Geist and Rainey 1976: 25, 31–32; Keim 1969: 150; Scott 1984: 48). Due to a lack of funds, Geist could not pay his assistants an hourly or daily wage. He paid the "volunteers" according to the amount of ivory they uncovered (Geist and Rainey 1976: 32). Geist soon realized the mistake of paying for unprovenienced artifacts, as residents became uncontrollable diggers. In his biography of Geist, Keim (1969: 115) describes the result: "The car Otto had oiled, greased, and carefully cranked was running away with him and there was not much he could do until it ran out of gas."

People frequently complain about archaeologists digging up their sites and, justifiably, about the removal of the artifacts from the island. Historically, collecting artifacts for museums was a primary reason for doing archaeology. At present, the lack of an appropriate facility prevents curation on the island. The excavation of artifacts by archaeologists is variously presented as a cultural or a financial loss. Crowell (1985: 26–27) has found that buyers and collectors tend to support or encourage the notion of the archaeologist as resource competitor. Portions of the population wish the artifacts returned, and some would like to profit from the sale of these returned items. Others have proposed placing the artifacts in a local museum to be used for educational purposes and also for generating tourist revenues.

Many Gambell residents disagree with the position that only archaeologists can extract worthwhile information through controlled excavation of the sites. Local diggers contend that they have learned much about their heritage through their excavations. Traditional craftsmanship, innovations, architecture, and natural history are all learned from digging. Although not written in reports, heritage learned from digging at the site has been expressed orally to other villagers. In contrast, few, if any, archaeologists have presented their findings to the people of Gambell.

Some diggers see their work at archaeological sites as a form of recycling, realizing that previous residents gleaned materials from the sites to be reused or remade into needed tools. Similar attitudes have been expressed to other researchers (Little and Robbins 1984: 194; Crowell 1985: 25).

The Gambell diggers do not want to intensify their extraction of artifacts. Intensification would merely cause the resource to be consumed too quickly and, thus, a slower pace is preferred. A slow pace maintains prices at current levels and also extends the financial gain into the future. The diggers fear that a sudden, large influx of money would be squandered. In this instance, people do not favor strict conservation

to preserve their heritage for posterity, but rather a conservative management style to provide a steady source of cash.

Motivations

Digging on St. Lawrence Island is fueled by a combination of motives including economic requirements, education, tradition, and recreation. Economic conditions provide the primary motive for digging at the sites, and the earlier overview of the Gambell economy and the cash requirements of modern subsistence practices provides a partial context for this discussion. A description of the Gambell ivory market, including rates, prices, and structure is critical for understanding residents' motivations.

The return for scrap ivory and artifacts is an important source of the community's cash income. Most of the return comes from the slow, steady recovery and sale of scrap ivory. The purchase price for this commodity varies depending upon the size and condition of the pieces, as well as seasonal supply and demand factors. During August, 1991, the prevailing rate for small ivory scrap was $20 per pound.

Prices for artifacts destined for the curio or native art markets vary considerably. Mundane utilitarian objects are sometimes sold for a few dollars to a tourist or visitor. More often, these same items are of more value if sold as scrap ivory. Those bound for the art market bring the greatest prices. These pieces include decorated ivory figurines, winged objects, tridents, and utilitarian objects of the Old Bering Sea and Punuk periods (Wardwell 1986). It is difficult to get an accurate estimate of sale prices in Gambell as these have become clouded by myth and legend. Gambell residents spoke of an ivory ulu handle in the form of a polar bear that was recently sold by a digger for $10,000. Other legendary prices paid to finders range from $45,000 up to as high as $60,000. These prices are most often mentioned in relation to the winged objects or "butterflies." Such large monetary returns, whether real and rare or purely imaginary, are a major driving force in the system.

Diggers have several avenues for converting scrap ivory and artifacts into cash. Scrap ivory is purchased by the Native store, the Native corporation, and various visiting private buyers. Visiting buyers may also buy ivory carvings and artifacts. These individuals advertise their upcoming visits through posters and flyers. It was said that in 1991 there was only one buyer, down from the annual average of three buyers, who tended to bid against each other.

Several recent developments may now be acting to preclude the necessity of actual buying trips on the part of brokers and/or collectors. A Gambell entrepreneur, particularly adept at negotiating and facilitating business deals, has established himself as a middleman between diggers and a New York City buyer. The middleman describes the find to his contact by telephone. If the buyer is interested in a piece, he asks for it to be sent along for viewing. A price is agreed upon and the middleman gets 10% of the sale price. This same middleman has sold a number of pieces for a group of diggers directly through Sotheby's auction house in New York City. He said Sotheby's gets a 5% commission on any of these sales. Many other diggers have the capability to sell directly to auction houses, brokers, and collectors. The names and telephone numbers of New York collectors are casually traded among allied diggers. Many have arrangements to call dealers collect or via toll-free numbers.

The participants in digging activities are not exclusively those in need of cash. Successful individuals and families, with economic, social, and political power, also dig at the sites. These people often have steady, full-time employment, are whaling captains and boat owners, and may hold or have held political office. Factors other than economic necessity, such as recreation, education, and tradition, apparently prompt these people. Excavation at the sites is often seen as family recreation that provides educational opportunities. Artifacts are shown to children and are placed in a context of modern and traditional lifeways. They are also used to substantiate legends and local oral history. Tradition is also cited as a factor, since people have now been digging in these sites for over 50 years; it has been a socially acceptable activity for several generations.

The casual nature of some digging at least partially reflects recreational motivations. The activity provides opportunities to leave the household, enjoy the outdoors, socialize or find solitude, and get exercise. Digging, as a form of gambling or treasure hunting, provides a recreational thrill. The popularity of this type of recreation is manifested by frequent participation in sweepstakes, lotteries, bingo, and card playing. In Gambell, many games of chance are well established; community bingo and pull-tabs are especially popular. Expended pull-tabs, also known as "rippies" or "ripoffs," are often found in backdirt piles at the sites. Extremely worn, small bills commonly observed in circulation are attributed by locals to heavy use during card games. The largest potential payoffs, however, are found in another popular game of chance: digging.

Finally, the sites are common property, and all people in Gambell have the right to dig. Perhaps families with no economic pressures are motivated to dig in order to maintain their rights to this resource or to guarantee a share of the resource before it is gone. Whatever the non-economic motives, the economic gains from digging are an added bonus.

The Ethical Dilemma

Current strategies for curtailing the looting problem in the United States include legislation, law enforcement, education, and public involvement. Legislation and law enforcement alone have not been effective. Education and public involvement are the newest approaches to the problem and may eventually have a significant effect, although doubts remain (King 1991). All of these strategies or policies have been advocated by individual archae-ologists and archaeological organizations. If these policies succeed in shutting down the demand for artifacts, quenching or deflecting collectors' desires to possess Native American artifacts, and protecting archaeological sites from looting, what will be the effect on the Native subsistence digger? Should archaeologists, as anthropologists, ignore the potentially substantial effects of archaeologist-influenced public policies regarding site looting on a group of Native Americans? How will they continue their "traditional" lifestyles which now include technology purchased and maintained by cash? Parallel dilemmas exist in Canada where policies have been generated by animal rights activists (Wenzel 1991: 175); native communities that once had their economic basis in seal hunting have been significantly disrupted by the seal fur ban. At present, there are no clear and easy solutions to the subsistence digger dilemma.

The introduction of alternate sources of cash income combined with present anti-looting strategies could stop site destruction and ameliorate any economic effects on Native groups. The Eskimos of St. Lawrence are extremely wary of large-scale natural resource development. They fear the land will be lost through sales to corporations or individuals who will become majority shareholders in the corporations (John Muir Institute, Inc. 1984: 125; Crowell 1985: 23). Elsewhere in the Arctic, non-indigenous development plans have not meshed with traditional subsistence pursuits and have not been productive (Wenzel 1991: 183). The people of St. Lawrence must have input into any development schemes if they are to be successful.

The two villages on St. Lawrence have joined together in a non-profit venture named St. Lawrence Economic Development Corporation (SLEDCO). Appointments to the 12 member board are evenly divided between the villages and represent Indian Reorganization Act (IRA) councils, City governments, and at-large members from both Gambell and Savoonga. The organization is intended to address all development issues (Don Smith, personal communication, 1991).

Several economic development plans currently are being considered for St. Lawrence Island, and short-term projects should continue to provide money to the local economy. The clean-up of World War II debris, airport runway expansions, and other government-sponsored public works projects will provide some employment, but not permanent, full-time jobs. Exploitation of other island-based resources might have more long-term effects. The feasibility of harvesting various seaweeds for sale to the health food and medical industries is actively being researched. The reindeer industry is being revived through herd expansions that may increase sales of meat and antler products to Asian markets. The expansion of eco-tourism, particularly bird-watching, is another possible development for the future (Don Smith, personal communication, 1991).

Alternatives must be found that will contribute cash to the local economy, decrease demands for ancient artworks and curios, promote conservation, and increase reverence for the island's antiquities. Hopi and Zuni artisans of the American Southwest use designs from ancient potsherds for inspiration (Stanislawski 1969: 13, 1978: 221–222), and St. Lawrence Island craftspeople could incorporate some of the aesthetic features of earlier works and use their own cultural heritage in a similar fashion. In this way, their traditional art and heritage would be continually revived and reinforced as something important and meaningful.

Summary
This case study reveals some of the behavioral aspects of looting, examines causal factors underlying site destruction, and illuminates the shadowy world of artifact trafficking. Mainly, however, this study has focused on Native subsistence diggers: their situation, attitudes, and motivations. As a group, subsistence diggers add a unique level of complexity to the site looting problem in Alaska and elsewhere in the world. The information

presented here contributes to a better understanding of the looting-trafficking/local economy dichotomy and may ultimately lead to appropriate solutions to the problem. As pointed out by Cheek (1991), what is lacking are Native perspectives on the subject. Further investigations in Gambell would doubtless identify a greater range of concerns and attitudes than those presented here and would more accurately represent the Native perspective. This study presents a complicated problem but does not provide solutions. Perhaps, however, it will stimulate professionals to apply some thought to this dilemma.

Acknowledgments
The anonymous Gambell diggers must be thanked for their candor in discussing this emotionally-charged issue. A number of scholars contributed useful comments, ideas, and information. In particular, I would like to thank Robert Ackerman, Stephen Braund, Aron Crowell, Steven Loring, Ken Pratt, and George Wenzel. Figure 1 is by Ray Norman.

REFERENCES

Anyon, Roger, 1991. "Protecting the Past, Protecting the Present: Cultural Resources and American Indians," in George Smith and John Ehrenhard, eds., *Protecting the Past*. Boca Raton: CRC Press, 215–222.

Burgess, Stephan, 1974. *The St. Lawrence Islanders of Northwest Cape: Patterns of Resource Utilization*. Ph.D. dissertation, University of Alaska Fairbanks. Ann Arbor: University Microfilms.

Cheek, Annetta, 1991. Review of Phyllis Messenger, ed., *The Ethics of Collecting Cultural Property: Whose Culture? Whose Property? American Antiquity* 56: 557–558.

Christensen, H., K. Maberry, M. McAllister, and D. McCormick, 1988. "Cultural Resource Protection: A Predictive Framework for Identifying Site Vulnerability, Protection Priorities, and Effective Protection Strategies," in J. Tainter and R. Hamre, eds., *Tools to Manage the Past: Research Priorities for Cultural Resource Management in the Southwest*. U.S. Forest Service, Southwestern Region and Rocky Mountain Forest and Range Experimentation Station, 62–67.

Collins, Henry, 1975. *Archaeology of St. Lawrence Island, Alaska*. (Originally published in 1937 as *Smithsonian Miscellaneous Collections* Vol. 96, No. 1.) Ann Arbor: University Microfilms.

Crowell, Aron, 1985. *Archeological Survey and Site Condition Assessment of Saint Lawrence Island, Alaska, 1984*. Report submitted to Department of Anthropology, Smithsonian Institution, Washington, D.C., and Sivuqaq, Incorporated, Gambell, Alaska.

Geist, Otto, and Froelich Rainey, 1976. *Archaeological Investigations at Kukulik, St. Lawrence Island, Alaska*. (Originally published in 1936 as Vol. 2 of *Miscellaneous Publications of the University of Alaska* by the U.S. Government Printing Office, Washington, D.C.). New York: AMS Press.

Gramann, J., and G. Vander Stoep, 1986. "Reducing Depreciative Behavior at Shiloh National Military Park," *Technical Report* No. 2. College Station: National Park Service Cooperative Park Studies Unit, Texas A&M University.

Hoffman, Teresa, and Shereen Lerner, 1988. "Arizona Archaeology Week: Promoting the Past to the Public," *Archaeological Assistance Program Technical Brief* No. 2. Washington, D.C.: U.S. Department of the Interior, National Park Service, Archaeological Assistance Division.

John Muir Institute, Inc., 1984. "A Description of the Socioeconomics of Norton Sound," *Technical Report* No. 99, *Contract No. AA851-CT2-38*. Prepared for the Minerals Management Service, Alaska Outer Continental Shelf Region, Leasing and Environmental Office, Social and Economic Studies Unit.

Keim, Charles, 1969. *Ahgvook, White Eskimo: Otto Geist and Alaskan Archaeology*. College: University of Alaska Press.

King, Thomas, 1991. "Some Dimensions of the Pothunting Problem," in George Smith and John Ehrenhard, eds., *Protecting the Past*. Boca Raton: CRC Press, 83–92.

Little, Ronald, and Lynn Robbins, 1984. "Effects of Renewable Resource Harvest Disruptions on Socioeconomic and Sociocultural Systems: St. Lawrence Island," *Contract No. AA851-CT1-59*. Prepared for The John Muir Institute, Napa, California, and Alaska Outer Continental Shelf Office, Socioeconomic Studies Program, Minerals Management Service, Anchorage, Alaska.

McAllister, Martin, 1991. "Looting and Vandalism of Archaeological Resources on Federal and Indian Lands in the United States," in George Smith and John Ehrenhard, eds., *Protecting the Past*. Boca Raton: CRC Press, 93–99.

McManamon, Francis, 1990. "A National Strategy for Federal Archaeology," *Federal Archeology Report* 3(1): 1, 13, 23. Washington, D.C.: U.S. Department of the Interior, National Park Service, Archaeological Assistance Division.

Messenger, Phyllis, ed., 1989. *The Ethics of Collecting Cultural Property? Whose Culture? Whose Property?* Albuquerque: University of New Mexico Press.

Morton, Susan, 1989. "The Archaeological Resources Protection Act and Alaska," *Federal Archeology Report* 2(3): 1–2. Washington, D.C.: U.S. Department of the Interior, National Park Service, Archaeological Assistance Division.

Neumann, Loretta, 1989. "Saving the Past for the Future: SAA Embarks on a Project to Prevent Looting," *Bulletin of the Society for American Archaeology* 6(1).

Nickens, Paul, 1991. "The Destruction of Archaeological Sites and Data," in George

Smith and John Ehrenhard, eds., *Protecting the Past.* Boca Raton: CRC Press, 73–81.

Nickens, Paul, S. Larralde, and G. Tucker, Jr., 1981. *A Survey of Vandalism to Archaeological Resources in Southwestern Colorado. Cultural Resources Series* No. 11. Denver: Bureau of Land Management, Colorado State Office.

Nichols, Deborah, Anthony Klesert, and Roger Anyon, 1989. "Ancestral Sites, Shrines, and Graves: Native American Perspectives on the Ethics of Collecting Cultural Properties," in Phyllis Messenger, ed., *The Ethics of Collecting Cultural Property: Whose Culture? Whose Property?* Albuquerque: University of New Mexico Press, 27–38.

Nowak, Michael, 1977. "The Economies of Native Subsistence Activities in a Village of Southwestern Alaska," *Arctic* 30: 225–233.

Parker, Patricia, 1990. *Keepers of the Treasures: Protecting Historic Properties and Cultural Traditions on Indian Lands.* A Report on Tribal Preservation Funding Needs Submitted to Congress by the United States Department of the Interior, National Park Service, Interagency Resources Division, Branch of Preservation Planning, Washington, D.C.

Rogge, A. E., ed., 1988. "Fighting Indiana Jones in Arizona," *American Society for Conservation Archaeology Proceedings 1988.*

Scott, Stuart, 1984. "St. Lawrence: Archaeology of a Bering Sea Island," *Archaeology* 37(1): 46–52.

Smith, George, and John Ehrenhard, eds., 1991. *Protecting the Past.* Boca Raton: CRC Press.

Staley, David, 1990. "Wait's Modest Proposal and Cultural Resource Reality in Alaska," *American Society for Conservation Archaeology Report* 17(1): 19–24.

Stanislawski, Michael, 1969. "What Good is a Broken Pot?" *Southwestern Lore* 35: 11–18.

———, 1978. "If Pots Were Mortal," in Richard Gould, ed., *Explorations in Ethnoarchaeology.* Albuquerque: University of New Mexico Press, 201–227.

U.S. Department of Commerce, Bureau of the Census, 1991. *1990 Census of Population and Housing. Summary: Population and Housing Characteristics, Alaska.* Washington, D.C.: Economics and Statistics Administration.

VanStone, James, 1960. "A Successful Combination of Subsistence and Wage Economies on the Village Level," *Economic Development and Cultural Change* 8: 174–191.

Vitelli, K., 1984. "The International Traffic in Antiquities: Archaeological Ethics and the Archaeologist's Responsibility," in E. L. Green, ed., *Ethics and Values in Archaeology.* New York: The Free Press, 143–155.

Wardwell, A., 1986. *Ancient Eskimo Ivories of the Bering Strait.* New York: Hudson Hills Press.

Wenzel, G., 1991. *Animal Rights, Human Rights: Ecology, Economy, and Ideology in the Canadian Arctic.* Toronto: University of Toronto Press.

Project Sting

The latest tactic in the war on illegal artifact trading is paying off in federal convictions and a flood of information about dealers and their clients.

John Neary

John Neary is a writer living in New Mexico.

It's Wednesday morning, and Judy Reed looks ahead to a busy few days of oddly melodramatic work for an archaeologist. A National Park Service undercover agent and the 41-year-old mother of two daughters, she frequently goes into the field with other agents to set up and execute sting operations intended to catch traffickers in stolen artifacts. On this day, with Park Service undercover specialist Phil Young, Reed flies from her home base in Santa Fe, New Mexico, to Austin, Texas, where she picks up from a federal museum a small satchel containing artifacts from Mexico and the southwestern United States, bait for a sting planned for that evening.

She and Young then drive to a motel in northern San Antonio, where they rendezvous with Park Service agent Al DeLaCruz and their boss Bill Tanner. Young, Tanner, and DeLaCruz next drive to a motel on San Antonio's south side, leaving Reed to put identifying code numbers on the artifacts. De-LaCruz checks in, taking two rooms, one for the sting, the other for surveillance. They quickly set up a radio receiver and tape recorder and begin testing them to make sure they pick up conversations through the microphone that Young has planted—along with his .357 magnum pistol—under the bed pillows in the room two doors away. Meanwhile, because Young is not sure whether their target might bring some friends, if he shows up at all, two more Park Service agents, Don Philpot and Dan Steed, arrive to provide backup. Reeds, en route with the artifacts, calls over her car phone to request help finding the motel.

The powerfully built DeLaCruz, his face scarred from years in the ring as an amateur prize-fighter, will lead the questioning of their target if the sting works. He straps on a shoulder holster, then changes from jeans into a business suit, the better to intimidate his quarry. Philpot hitches up his gun belt below his bulletproof vest and checks his handcuffs as Tanner readjusts the recorder. Young—slim, disarmingly youthful, and easy-going—slips into the room to give a last-minute briefing,

explaining that the target is a "dealer in prehistoric antiquities," a middle-aged real estate entrepreneur who augments his income from negotiating oil leases by trading in artifacts. It was Tanner who had first spotted their target at an antiquities show in Kentucky. "I go to all these shows," he says, "and look for people who buy and sell artifacts. If a person indicates any sort of willingness to do business illegally, we pursue it. Right now we probably have a hundred such cases we could pursue."

Young has no fixed appointment with the dealer, but had arranged days before to call him when he was in town. He had told the dealer he was selling artifacts, items taken from somewhere in the huge Amistad National Recreation Area, a vast reservoir and forest on the Mexican border near Del Rio, Texas. The dealer had expressed an interest in seeing them.

Reed arrives with the artifacts, takes them to Young's room, and spreads them out on the bed. They include three clay figurines from Jalisco, Mexico, and seven painted pebbles, three sandals made of woven yucca fiber, a piece of mat, a bit of wooden flute, a stone bead, a painted deer scapula, and

Outnumbered by pot hunters, federal undercover agents seek to curb a frenzy of looting before relics of the Native American past vanish forever.

A Legacy of WANTON THIEVERY

The challenge Judy Reed and fellow undercover agents face every day is overwhelming. The territory they are charged with protecting is vast, making it all but impossible to catch looters in the act. And the laws protecting archaeological sites and their artifacts are written so that if looters are not caught in the act, the only routes to a conviction lie through a confession, an inadvertent admission, or proof that an artifact came from a particular site—something that is hard to determine. By working undercover, agents like Reed gain access to the closed world of antiquities traffickers and to evidence otherwise unobtainable.

Undercover agents must painstakingly work their way through a bureaucratic labyrinth in which the Bureau of Land Management (BLM), the National Park Service (NPS), the U.S. Department of Agriculture Forest Service (FS), and other agencies vie for the spotlight. An interagency undercover team was abandoned last year when the BLM abruptly withdrew its support and reassigned its agent in charge, Gary Olson, after friction developed between some team members and their BLM boss. The team had also blown its cover over the course of two dozen criminal investigations. Each agency now pursues antiquities thieves independently.

The problem of illegal artifact trading almost defies comprehension. When Congress asked the General Accounting Office (GAO) in 1985 to survey the problem, the GAO turned in a nightmarish report. The three principal land management agencies—BLM, NPS, and FS—are responsible for safeguarding some two million archaeological sites presumed to exist on their 104.4 million acres of public land. Only about seven percent of those sites (136,000) had actually been surveyed, and there was a grand total of three staff members assigned to protect them. The GAO reported that federal records were not adequate to provide an accurate picture of the extent of looting and that "Because of the vast land areas the local agency offices are responsible for covering and the remote locations of many of the archaeological sites, agency staff rarely revisit most archaeological sites after they are initially recorded. Therefore the extent to which recorded sites have been recently looted is unknown. In addition, the numbers do not reflect the looting that is likely to have occurred on the estimated 1.8 million sites that have not been recorded."

The GAO hinted at the size of the looting problem, however, by saying that from Oc-

tober 1980 through March 1986 alone the three agencies had reported more than 1,200 looting incidents. "Commercial looting," the report concluded, "may be a relatively low-risk activity with a high-profit potential." Among the GAO's recommendations: employ undercover agents in the fight against looters.

Meeting outside Taos, New Mexico, in 1989, a group of BLM, NPS, and FS archaeologists and other experts held a conference on the looting crisis. Conclusions: vandals and thieves had attacked at least 90 percent on the known sites in the Southwest, including almost all of the classic Mimbres sites, and that between 1980 and 1987 looting on private and Indian land has skyrocketed (1,000 percent on Indian land alone). "Of course," observed Maryland archaeologist Thomas King in the Taos conference's formal statement, "reported incidents are only the tip of the iceberg. The National Park Service has estimated that reported cases represent only about a quarter of the actual ones in any given year. What is most clear is that the vast majority of pot hunters on public lands are getting away with it."

It is important to note that government statistics are based largely on the known incidents of looting on public lands. There is virtually no legal protection for sites on private land, other than burials in some states. The Archaeological Conservancy, a national nonprofit group committed to preserving sites, does attempt to *purchase* private land with sites that appear to be threatened, providing for their subsequent protection or turning the land over to federal or state agencies for monitoring.

Like the GAO investigators, the Taos conferees called for undercover retaliation and proposed mounting sting operations. Meanwhile, pressure had been growing within the agencies for the formation of a unit to carry out such aggressive investigations. When, in November 1990, federal investigators in New Mexico found a cache of stolen antiquities along with journals and maps pinpointing where the artifacts had come from and where some had gone, complete with the names of collectors and dealers, suddenly it appeared that the moment had come to launch just such an operation.

The laws Reed and her undercover teammates work under include the Antiquities Act of 1906, the Archaeological Resources Protection Act of 1979 (ARPA), and the Native American Grave Protection and Repatriation Act of 1990 (NAGPRA); these

and other statutes comprise an oddly feeble and for the agents a baroque and unwieldy set of ground rules that makes the game almost unwinnable. The 1906 law originally carried a fine of only $500, since boosted to $5,000 for individuals, $10,000 for organizations, and up to six months in jail. From 1906 to 1979 the Antiquities Act netted a grand total of 18 convictions, a paltry $4,000 in fines, and just two jail sentences of 90 days each. The 1979 law is more stringent: it allows the seizure of vehicles and tools used in looting, provides for rewards to informants, and requires that the locations of endangered archaeological sites be kept secret. It can also impose much tougher sanctions: up to a year in jail and fines up to $100,000 for a misdemeanor (when total damage to a site is $500 or less), up to two years in jail and fines up to $250,000 for a first felony conviction, and five years in jail and up to $250,000 for a second felony conviction. ARPA, however, requires Reed and her teammates to prove to a jury that an artifact is more than 100 years old and was taken from federal land or from private land without the owner's permission, and that archaeological damage to a site amounts to the total she claims. NAGPRA does much to close one loophole, forbidding the sale of artifacts looted from burials on public or private land.

Reed learned her way through the thicket of laws protecting American Indian artifacts and defining prosecutorial procedures by attending a week-long course at the government's ARPA training academy at Tallahassee, Florida. Martin E. McAllister, one of the teachers there, is a Minnesota archaeologist who (with coauthors Sherry Hutt, an Arizona judge, and Elwood Jones, another ARPA instructor) has written *Archaeological Resource Protection,* a book detailing the history of ARPA and how to go about investigating and prosecuting cases under it.

McAllister's course at Tallahassee introduces students to the network of artifact thieves, fences, and dealers. "Go to the Yellow Pages in any major city—Santa Fe, Palm Springs, Aspen," McAllister says, "and look up 'antiques,' or 'art consultants,' or 'Indian goods,' and you'll find dealers. Some of these people, in places like New York, Chicago, Los Angeles, make hundreds of thousands of dollars a year, if not millions, some not only domestically but internationally. In any major city there will be 20 to 25 dealers trading in prehistoric artifacts,

(Box continued)

so if there are 50 major cities in the U.S., maybe there are about 1,000 dealers."

Supplying these dealers are the looters, the pick-and-shovel lackeys who sneak into the ruins, often outfitted with metal detectors and fake government uniforms—and two-way radios to keep track of the whereabouts of the real government uniforms. Commercial full-time looters, McAllister estimates, number from 200 to 500, 50 to 100 of them in the Southwest. He thinks there may be as many as 1,000 part-time looters, 200 of whom work in the Southwest. "There is," he adds, "another vast group out there, people who collect, hundreds of thousands of them." How active are all these people? "I would say there are at least 10,000 violations every year," McAllister estimates. "For every violation that is detected, maybe there are 100 that go undetected."

As artifacts move from pot hunters, to regional centers, to major cities, the price rises with every change of hands. Somebody digging up a Mimbres pot in southern New Mexico might get as little as $200, or as much as $1,000 for it—but when it is sold in Albuquerque, the pot can fetch as much as $45,000. When it is auctioned in New York, it will bring $95,000—and in Europe, he says, prices as high as $400,000 have been reported. Most of the stolen artifacts that wind up overseas go to European and Japanese buyers, according to McAllister; the remainder end up in Korea, Taiwan, and Saudi Arabia.

McAllister doesn't know the total dollar volume of the trade, but he estimates the traffic must be in the multimillion dollar range. "One of the agencies not involved to date is U.S. Customs," he notes. "We need tougher laws regarding the export of artifacts. There is a very, very strong market for prehistoric and for historic artifacts. That market never abates. There aren't any prehistoric people out there making new sites, new artifacts. So their dollar value increases as they become more rare."

Experts like McAllister are virtually unanimous on two points that Judy Reed and her cohorts struggle with daily: the problem is vast and the costs to all of us are stagger-ing. Says Albuquerque BLM archaeologist Tony Lutonsky, "Congress said in 1974 that all federal agencies must inventory their lands. We estimate it would take over 100 years for us to do that, if that were all we did eight hours a day, 40 hours a week. As is, we've inventoried five percent. We have about 8,000 sites in my resource area, the Rio Puerco, which consists of some one million acres in six counties—and another 3,500 sites in those counties but not on BLM land. Most people don't realize the magnitude of the problem. The area is vast, the bulk of it is unrecorded. Within an hour and a half of Albuquerque there are ruins that a white person has probably never seen." Pondering the evidence contained in those ancient ruins, relics of the Anasazi culture that flourished and then vanished, Lutonsky adds, "I just fear that they will disappear so fast that we'll never understand how the prehistoric system worked—we won't know how it functioned and why it broke."

—John Neary.

a tiny snare net, all from the Amistad. Reed leaves, and Young, now in his undercover role as convicted felon and trader "Shawn O'Hara," telephones the target and invites him to come over. At 8:02, hunched over their tape monitor, the agents hear a faint knocking. Shawn O'Hara's visitor has arrived. Showtime.

"Looks like a little net used to catch a mouse when it comes out of a hole," a strange voice drawls as Young's guest admires the artifacts on the bed. "Little bamboo flute. You got any papers on this?"

"No, but I can get 'em," Young replies, and the agents two doors away listen intently as the bargaining begins, O'Hara asking $1,500 for the whole batch, the trader laconically countering, "I don't think everything here is worth $250." The agents are waiting for the trader to make his buy and for Young to say, "Hope we can do business again," the code words that will signal the agents to rush down the hall and handcuff the trader—and cuff Shawn O'Hara too, to protect Young's undercover identity.

The bargaining goes on for more than an hour, interspersed with good ol' boy banter about bass fishing and the hard, long highway miles it takes to be a trader. At last a deal is struck. At 9:22, Young accepts $100 in cash and an I.O.U. for $300. He says he hopes they can do business again. DeLaCruz, Steed, and Philpot speed down the corridor and grab the dealer as he is about to leave Young's room. "Federal officers!" DeLaCruz barks, "Back inside!"

But the evening is far from over. Questioning of the dealer goes on for about two hours. He is released, pending further interrogation, and warned that he faces a possible federal indictment. The agents hope he will choose to cooperate with the government and name others involved in the artifacts trade. Around midnight the agents return to their motel to review the day's work. "Good job," Young tells them. "I'm really pleased, because the ultimate goal is to get this guy to lead us to other people—and it looks like he will. Texas has a lot of collectors. He's been a collector and a minor dealer for a number of years. We want him to identify his business friends." Tanner tells the agents the next morning at breakfast, "When we get back to Santa Fe, we'll sit down and figure out how to milk this guy."

But before that happens, Judy Reed has another job back in Santa Fe preparing diagrams that will enable a federal court jury in Albuquerque to understand that damage another trafficker in artifacts has done by looting a rock-shelter in the Gila National Forest. She will explain to the jury how digging inside the shelter has diminished its archaeological integrity and the value to scholars of the artifacts taken from it. Confronted by her testimony and the rest of the evidence against him, the accused, a building supplies dealer from Milan, New Mexico, will abandon his efforts at a defense and plead guilty. He will be fined $5,000, given three years' probation, and ordered to perform 300 hours of community service. Reed's role in this case began more than a year before when she posed as the mistress of a wealthy collector, a ruse invented to explain where the money was coming from to buy the stolen artifacts—more than $10,000 worth before the sting was over—and to pay for a helicopter to take the agents to the rock-shelter in question.

Reed began working on such cases two years ago, after the body of a 35-year-old Santa Fe artifacts trader was found on secluded land near the village of Tesuque outside Santa Fe. The trader had shot himself in the chest with a .22 caliber rifle. Hearing that the dead man kept a stash of antiquities in a rented storage unit, Park Service agents checked out the lead and discovered a bonanza of looted artifacts along with journals and maps indicating where they had come from and to whom some had gone. It was a virtual client list of collectors and dealers.

A Park Service field director busy at the time with an exhaustive survey of the Native American ruins that dot Bandelier National Monument, Reed was asked to drop that assignment and undertake an inventory of the dead trader's collection. It was a tough job, made even more difficult by the fact that she had known the trader and his family for years. In time, she catalogued 2,952 artifacts worth $178,550, and traced each one to the site from which it had been taken. From the trader's files and journals, she and her fellow agents, working as a Park Service/Bureau of Land Management task force, created a wall map showing the whereabouts of more than 200 of the trader's clients throughout the country—and began investigating them.

Only once did Reed feel herself to be in danger in the field. A team member working undercover on a tip from an informant had visited a remote ruin southwest of Socorro, New Mexico. He had watched looters dig, but an assessment of the damage by an expert was needed to buttress the case. On a trip to the site, Reed was naturally apprehensive that the culprits might turn up at any moment, spoiling for a fight. "We drove from Santa Fe," she recalls, "taking the back roads, avoiding the small towns. These Broncos we use have antennas all over them, blacked-out windows, you can spot 'em a mile away. We parked at the drop-off the looters used, in the open. The five of us walked up through the trees to the ruin, up on a ridge 20 to 40 feet above the surrounding flatlands. Everybody else had a bulletproof vest. I didn't! I was thinking, if there's trouble, where should I be—under a tree? I'd never been in a position where my life might

be in danger." The assignment required two visits and eight hours of study, and helped obtain the convictions of a rural store owner and his son who pleaded guilty to federal charges of artifact theft. They were sentenced to probation of two years and one year, respectively.

In the rock-shelter case, Reed had to gain the confidence of the looter so she could go along on the helicopter ride. She felt the risk was worth it to get to the remote site and assess the damage. "I was supposed to be the spoiled mistress of a collector," she recalls. Her undercover teammate, BLM agent Mike Moomey posing as a scout for a wealthy export company owner, told the target, "Don't talk to her. She's a real bitch!" To live up to her advance billing, the slender five-foot six-inch Reed dolled herself up in hiking boots, a tank top, and Lycra tights under a long sweater that concealed a wire—"I wore a harness with two mikes and a recorder in back, so he wouldn't detect it if he touched me on the shoulders. I frowned a lot."

Reed recalls with undiminished astonishment the time she drove to the home of a California looter who told her and another undercover agent, "I've got skeletons in my closet." She laughs. "He really did!" The man had been excavating Chumash burials around Santa Barbara, and there in his utility room were two human skulls. The skeletons were in the basement. "I just can't believe that people can live with skeletons in their house!" she marvels. The looter was fined $2,500, given a five-year suspended jail term and 18 months of probation and ordered to perform 300 hours of community service with the Santa Barbara Trust for Historic Preservation. The skeletons were sent to the anthropology department of the University of California at Santa Barbara, pending their return to the Chumash.

A specialist in Pueblo ceramics, Reed signs a log every time she opens and closes the locked room that serves as the evidence vault in the suite of Santa Fe offices her team occupies but will soon vacate. The task force, having blown its cover over the course of

two dozen criminal investigations, is being disbanded. Park Service and BLM agents, between whom there had been considerable friction, will pursue their undercover work separately. Inside the vault, carefully swathed in blisterpak and plastic zip-loc bags, nestled in acid-free paper and cardboard boxes, are more than 4,000 artifacts, a miniature museum of the cultures of North, Central, and South America. Some of them get the special treatment that their status as cultural totems requires. Reed once invited a Navajo medicine man to inspect a ceremonial mask and to advise her on proper storage procedures. He told her the mask should be stored alone in a box, not rolled in paper, and kept face up—and that nothing should obstruct its vision. Mylar was okay. A plastic lid was eventually chosen.

Reed wears white cotton gloves so the oil of her skin won't contaminate these relics, which include a prehistoric ivory hair pin from Alaska; textiles, a comb still bearing the reddish hairs of its long-dead owner, copper money, a ceramic whistle in the shape of a bird effigy, a duck-shaped pot, a tripod-shaped stone metate and an intricate stirrup-shaped mano, and spindles from Peru; charred tubes of wood once packed with tobacco smoked as cigarettes by the Hohokam; tiny purses made from the bodies of rodents; a magnificent 2,000-year-old turkey feather robe from a cave in Utah; a hunter-warrior's oak bow; and a delicate wooden circlet enclosing a web of yucca fibers used by its Apache owner to snare bad dreams.

"I've seen more beautiful things than I probably ever would have otherwise," says Reed, "even in a museum." Her work imposes an emotional toll, the price she pays in the anger she feels. "Some people wouldn't want to do this at all, it irritates them so much, seeing all this contraband. They can't hold their temper." Packing a tiny woven cotton sandal from southeastern Utah, she murmurs, "Archaeologists *never* find these. *We* find little bits of cloth. Now I know why. Somebody's already been there!" She resents the targets she and her teammates pursue, especially the dealers. "They view these things as art rather than as things that lose their value when they lose their provenance."

Reed's boss, Phil Young, says stings like the San Antonio operation, in which artifacts Reed has authenticated as stolen are presented for sale—and identified as hot—are having a chilling effect on the trade. Says Young, "We don't want 'em even to trust the people they went to high school with!" But what is really needed, he adds, is a new law prohibiting the possession of stolen artifacts, period. "Until then," says Reed, as she prepares for her next court case, "We've got to concentrate on education, teaching people to respect things. It will take a long time. You won't see a return on it right away. It's like committing to research. There are all sorts of things people could do. But it means changing people's values."

Carefully, Reed packs up her cache of artifacts, some to be repatriated to their countries of origin, the rest destined for federal and tribal museums and storehouses. Meanwhile, Phil Young waits for a fresh supply for use in a new round of stings.

An Anthropological Culture Shift

A federal law that puts Native American rights and religion ahead of scientific curiosity is reshaping North American anthropology and archeology.

Museums, universities, and federal agencies are beginning to clean skeletons out of their closets all across the United States. They're clearing out other objects important to Native Americans as well, such as sacred shields and medicine bundles. This flurry of housecleaning is prompted not by a shortage of storage space, but by a law that recognizes Native Americans' claims to their past.

The Native American Graves Protection and Repatriation Act (NAGPRA) requires some 5000 federally funded institutions and government agencies to return Native American skeletons, funerary and sacred objects, and items of profound cultural importance to American Indian tribes and Native Hawaiians. Although NAGPRA was passed 4 years ago, it didn't really start to bite until last November, when facilities had to notify the tribes about the sacred and cultural items in their collections. That was just the first step in a process that will see tens of thousands of scientifically valuable items handed over, many of them for reburial, over the next few years. Hundreds of scientists who depend upon this material will be cut off from their research data, and North American anthropology and archeology will be changed forever.

"The reality is there's been a shift in the equation," says Dan Monroe, executive director of the Peabody Essex Museum in Salem, Massachusetts. "It's a matter of basic human rights versus scientific rights, and in this new equation in many instances those scientific rights have been constrained, no doubt about it." But NAGPRA isn't just placing skeletons and artifacts out of reach of scientific study. It's also giving Native Americans influence over what research is conducted and published. Scientists who were once accustomed to "doing as they damned well-pleased," as one anthropologist put it, must now involve Native Americans in almost every phase of their research—from requesting research permits to study collections to, in some cases, passing completed studies to tribal councils for prepublication review. "The shocking thing is that we really haven't spent time talking to the Indians," admits Thomas J. Green, director of the Arkansas Archeological Survey. "NAGPRA is forcing us to do that, and maybe once we get through these issues, we'll see that there's actually a natural alliance between the archeological and Indian communities."

But this bridge-building doesn't mean that the bitter debate that preceded passage of NAGPRA 4 years ago has died down. Many scientists still decry the repatriation as an improper melding of church and state, and they are particularly upset that the law provides Native Americans very broad ancestral claims—even on items that scientists say predate the origins of the tribes themselves.

From the Indians' perspective, however, the return of sacred items is long overdue. "The reality is, it's our stuff," says John Pretty On Top, cultural director for the Crow. "We made it and we know best how to use it and care for it. . . . And now because of the law, we're going to get it back." Leigh Jenkins, the director of the Hopi Cultural Preservation Office, notes that graves and religious icons of all other peoples in America were never treated the way Indian material was treated. "Every tribe has sad stories about graves being pillaged, the offerings and skeletons taken, and ritual objects removed," he says. "Scientists always had one standard for themselves and another for Indians."

A shift of power

Now that museums have notified tribes that they possess sacred and culturally important Indian material, the next step will be to determine exactly what will be returned. By 1995, the museums must provide detailed inventories of all skeletal remains and funerary goods, and the tribes can then request that the material be shipped back to them. NAGPRA provides a set of guidelines to help Native Americans and museums sort out what can and cannot be returned, but both sides anticipate disagreements—particularly over prehistoric remains and burial goods. "Those are emerging as the flash point," says Jonathan Haas, McArthur Curator of North American anthropology and archeology at Chicago's Field Museum of Natural History.

No anthropologist interviewed by Science objected to reburial when the

State Laws Provide a Glimpse of the Future

As researchers and museum officials begin to implement a new law requiring repatriation of Native American skeletons and artifacts, some clues to what lies ahead may be found in the operation of similar state laws already on the books. One of those laws in Idaho sent "Buhla," a 10,675-year-old female skeleton, back into the ground in 1992. Idaho state archeologists had recovered the bones from a gravel pit operation near the town of Buhl just 3 years earlier. During this time the remains had only been studied for 3 days, by a single physical anthropologist—research that was delayed because of technical problems in obtaining a radiocarbon date.

The remains and the artifacts found with the skeleton were reburied on the Shoshone-Bannock reservation, 100 miles from where it was found—although archeologists doubt any Shoshone-Bannock inhabited the region 10,000 years ago. In the tradition of the Shoshone-Bannock, the woman is perceived as "our Mother; the Mother of us all," explains Diana K. Yupe, a Shoshone-Bannock anthropologist. "To us, she is our ancestor, and hers is not just a decomposed body; she is alive."

"There are about 25 skeletons in North America older than 8500 [before present]," says Thomas J. Green, the former Idaho state archeologist and now director of the Arkansas Archeological Survey. "And of these, she was one of the oldest and certainly one of the best preserved. Now, probably the most signifi-

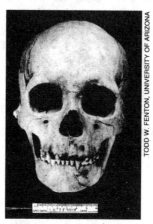

Reinterred. Skull of 10,675-year-old skeleton reburied under Idaho state law.

cant thing about Buhla is that she's reburied."

Archeologists expect to see a similar fate befall many of the funerary goods now stored in museums. A 1991 Arizona case, in which archeologists were complying with state law, suggests what might be in store on a broad scale. When a new highway in Phoenix was going to destroy a portion of a known, large Hohokam settlement called Pueblo Grande that dated from 900 to 1450 years ago, the state called in an archeological consulting firm to salvage and record what was found. Eventually, 2000 funerary vessels and 800 skeletons were recovered—the largest such collection of Hohokam pottery and individuals ever found. "It was the best collection of its kind," says Cory Breternitz, president of Soil Systems

Inc., the archeological firm that handled the dig. "And we'd worked out an agreement about the study of this material with the tribes ahead of time." But in the spring of 1991, the tribal council objected to the study of the human remains, and a few months later every item was reburied on the Ak-Chin Reservation.

Also destined for reburial is the Grasshopper Collection, skeletal and funerary material dating from 1300 to 1400 years ago that was recovered from a large Mogollan complex on the White Mountain Apache Reservation over the past 30 years. Consisting of more than 700 skeletons and thousands of artifacts, including arrow points, stone and bone tools, beads, shells, pottery, and hair ornaments, it is now housed in the Arizona State Museum. According to University of Arizona archeologist William A. Longacre, who oversaw much of the excavation, it is "the best documented and largest collection from a single Native American community that's been occupied consistently for 100 years.

But the collection is going back into the ground. Although the excavations took place on White Mountain Apache land, the material is culturally linked to the Zuni and Hopi—and the three tribes have decided they want all the skeletons and grave goods repatriated and reburied. "It's an incredible resource that we are going to lose," Longacre says. "From our perspective, it is a terrible loss. But from theirs [the Indians], it's a terrible thing that we've done." —V.M.

remains were those of a known individual—in fact, scientists expressed dismay that such items should have found their way to a museum in the first place. But the return and reburial of skeletal material several hundreds or thousands of years old, where ancestral relationships are not always clear, has researchers groaning—especially since these materials are often scientifically the most interesting. To American Indians, however, a skeleton's age

is immaterial. "We don't accept any artificial cutoff date set by scientists to separate us from our ancestors," says Walter R. Echo-Hawk, the attorney for the Native American Rights Fund, one of the groups that fought for NAGPRA. "What Europeans want do with their dead is their business," he says. "We have different values."

NAGPRA, in fact, places those values on an equal footing with scientific evidence. "The law explicitly says

that their oral traditions have standing in this process," explains C. Timothy McKeown, an ethnographer and program leader for the implementation of NAGPRA at the National Park Service, the federal agency charged with overseeing the law. Thus, a tribe can claim prehistoric remains if tribal tradition says that its people were created in the same region where the remains were found—a claim that has already led to reburial of some collections under existing state laws (see box). (If a museum objects to these claims, then a special NAGPRA review committee will make the final determination, weighing both the scientific and tribal evidence.)

Many museums, in order to maintain good relations with the tribes and salvage some material for study, have already handed over, or are in the process of doing so, large collections of skeletons. The Field Museum, where more than 300 scholars a year come to use the extensive Native American materials, has given back 62 of its 2000 remains, and expects to return the rest. At the Smithsonian Institution's physical anthropological collections, 2000 skeletons have been returned for reburial, with the remaining 14,000 skeletons set to follow.

Many scientists are troubled by the prospect of massive reburials of prehistoric materials because they shut the door on studies using new techniques. "Once the material is gone, it is no longer available for restudy or for future studies using new techniques, nor can anyone check the original data for observer error—something that is fundamental to science," says Jane Buikstra, a physical anthropologist at the University of Chicago. Douglas Owsley, a physical and forensic anthropologist at the Smithsonian, points out that "we can do studies now—on health and disease, demographic rates, settlement patterns—that we simply had no inkling of when I was in graduate school [in the 1970s]. To say that we have learned all we can from these skeletons is a serious mistake."

Take the case of Ethne Barnes, a physical anthropologist at Witchita State University, who recently developed a new method for identifying developmental defects in adult skeletons. "The data collected in the past on these skeletons has very little value to my work," says Barnes, "because I'm looking at them from a completely new perspective and scaling the growth patterns differently than others have done." Barnes began her study shortly before NAGPRA, using skeletal material housed in the Smithsonian and other museums. Initially, she needed

only the museums' permission to study the collections, but now she must also seek each tribe's permission, which is not always forthcoming. "The Cochiti Pueblo flat-out said no, while the Hopi were very interested," she says. However, the Hopi want to see her research results before she publishes. "It is a kind of censorship," she agrees, "but I also think we should be collaborating with the Indians."

So far, most of the attention has been focused on NAGPRA's impact on archeology and physical anthropology, but some scientists think it will eventually have a major effect on cultural anthropology as well. Lynne Goldstein, a mortuary archeologist at the University of Wisconsin, Milwaukee, says Native Americans aren't going to be satisfied with the return of bones and artifacts: "They'll ask next for field notes, tapes, photographs; and they'll insist that you have their permission before you publish." Goldstein's concern is more than hypothetical: The Hopi Tribe, in its response to the museums' inventory letters, asked museums to declare a moratorium on the study of any archival material pertaining to the Hopi people—a request that has stunned the museum community, although to the Hopi it seems a logical extension of NAGPRA. "We feel very strongly that there is a connection between the intellectual knowledge and the sacred objects that were collected from our religious altars: The knowledge and the object are one," says Leigh Jenkins. "The Hopi people want that esoteric knowledge protected right now."

An alliance out of adversity?
Despite all the turmoil NAGPRA has caused, scientists and Indians alike agree that the law has started to bring them together. Scientists, says Goldstein, "have to look at this situation pragmatically because the reality is, we lost. . . . [F]or those of us doing excavations, we're going to have to be a lot more responsible collecting information and sharing it with the people we're studying."

Not sharing information appears to be at the root of much of the distrust

now afflicting academic researchers. Archeologists, for example, excavated homes and burials of the Pawnee people for more than a half-century before they ever contacted the tribe, says Roger Echo-Hawk, a Pawnee graduate student studying the relationship between oral history and archeology at the University of Colorado, Boulder. Indeed, scientists admit they made little effort in the past to involve Native Americans. "We've had to move from the ethics of conquest to the ethics of collaboration," says Martin Sullivan, director of Phoenix, Arizona's Heard Museum.

Still, scientists should "not look at collaboration through rose-colored glasses," says Goldstein, who points to her excavation last summer of a cemetery in California's Fort Ross State Park as an example. It took her 18 months to acquire all the necessary permissions—from state agencies, California and Alaskan tribes, the Russian Orthodox Church, and the local coroner's office—and then she went out of her way to keep all parties informed as the dig progressed. "Was it the easiest way to do archeology?" she asks. "Hell, no. But it was effective. Everybody felt they were a part of it."

Similar alliances, if they take shape, will probably coalesce around a new series of tribal museums. Not every tribe is planning to rebury all returned material; many have opened or are planning to open museums of their own, as the Confederated Tribes of the Warm Springs Reservation did last summer in Oregon. Some 120 such institutions now exist, and although some are little more than cultural centers, others maintain small research centers, which are staffed with Indian scientists.

The museums will have the material, and much of it (aside from sacred objects) will be made available to academic researchers, who are willing to work with tribal councils. "We do have common ground," says Roger Echo-Hawk. "If we build on that, we may create a new science of North American archeology."

-Virginia Morell

199

Saving Our World's Heritage

Ellen Hoffman

On a potholed, dusty road a few miles south of the Mayan ruins of Tulum on Mexico's Caribbean coast, a crudely executed wall painting of a turtle advertises a primitive seaside bungalow camp. *PESCA, BUCEO, PATRIMONIO UNIVERSAL,* it says in Spanish. In English, its "FISHING, SKIN DIVING, WORLD HERITAGE." The causal tourist might never focus on or question the meaning of "WORLD HERITAGE." But to the diligent travel researcher or member of the eco-cognoscenti, that phrase signals a specific message: You are in or near a natural or cultural site "of outstanding universal value to mankind." In this case, the site a few miles down the road is the Sian Ka'an Biosphere Reserve, a 1.3-million-acre landscape of tropical forest, savannas and mangrove, and coastal and marine habitats that abound with white ibis and roseate spoonbills, manatees and monkeys, sea turtles, and the living corals of the world's second largest reef system.

Several hundred miles away, in the dense, vine-clogged jungle of Mexico's Chiapas state, the imposing stone temples of the Mayan city of Palenque attract thousands of visitors every year. But unless they search out the now-closed museum on the fringe of the site and read the plaque attached to the facade, they might never know that here—as in Sian Ka'an—they are in the presence of a monument that belongs to an elite club whose other "members" include the Great Wall of China, the Tower of London, Africa's Victoria Falls, and our Statue of Liberty.

The "club" is the World Heritage List, created by the World Heritage Convention, an international treaty approved in 1972 and since then signed by 134 of the world's 188 nations. The List consists of natural and cultural sites and monuments that meet specific criteria designed to verify their "outstanding universal value."

To get on the List, a site or monument must meet at least one of several criteria that emphasize both uniqueness and superlative qualities. A natural site, for example, might qualify because it is an "outstanding example" of a stage of the earth's evolutionary history or the habitat for an important threatened animal or plant species. A man-made site or monument, such as a building or a group of buildings, might make the List because it is a "unique artistic achievement" or because it represents a civilization that has disappeared.

"If we want to protect the world for future generations so they can enjoy the benefits of the work of nature, of millennia, the diversity of plants and species, the World Heritage List can help us do that," says Bernd von Droste, a German ecologist who directs the program from the World Heritage Centre at UNESCO headquarters in Paris.

A sedate, systematic bureaucrat on the podium when he was conducting business at the World Heritage Committee's annual meeting in Santa Fe, New Mexico, last December, in an interview von Droste revealed himself as a passionate advocate for the World Heritage Convention as a tool for nothing less than saving the world.

"Why do we need diversity of species? Of culture?" He answered his own question. "We need them for human survival. Since we don't know about the future, it's better to keep all the knowledge we have about how to adapt."

One purpose of the Santa Fe meeting was to celebrate 20 years of the World Heritage Convention—which the delegates did at a series of festive receptions and dinners sponsored by local officials and cultural institutions. But they also heard a clarion call from von Droste, who reported, "This year many more World Heritage sites are severely damaged or under threat than ever before in the history of the Convention," and cited examples including earthquake damage to the pyramids and other Egyptian monuments and war damage to the medieval city of Dubrovnik.

Population growth, widespread poverty and lack of education, global warming and acid rain ("It creates stone degradation that affects monuments"), climate change, the rising of the sea level—von Droste ticked off a series of physical threats to sites on the List. "If we believe what most scientists are saying," he said, "conservation will be in for a hard time."

To understand not just the physical but also the thorny political and finan-

LIST OF ENDANGERED PLACES

The following World Heritage sites have been inscribed on the Danger List because of threats to or deterioration of the characteristics for which they were placed on the List. The date signifies the year the site was placed on the List.

Benin: Royal Palaces of Abomey; damaged caused by tornado (1985).

Bulgaria: Srebarna Biosphere Reserve; drainage of wetlands has damaged the ecosystem and threatened bird habitats (1992).

Cambodia: Angkor; the former Khmer capital has suffered severe war damage and lacks a comprehensive plan for rehabilitation (1992).

Croatia: Plitvice Lakes National Park; near the border with Serbia, left without a comprehensive management structure and, due to the war, a total loss of tourism income (1992).

Ecuador: Sangay National Park; heavy poaching of wildlife, illegal livestock grazing, and a proposed road-construction project (1992).

Guinea and Cote d'Ivoire: Mount Nimba; lack of effective management, possible uncontrolled mining, and an influx of refugees from Liberia (1992).

Hashemite Kingdom of Jordan: Old City of Jerusalem; concern over the archaeological methods used to document the Old City and its walls (1982).

India: Manas Wildlife Sanctuary; damage to park infrastructure from invasion of Bodo tribespeople, including "illegal cultivation" (1992).

Mali: Timbuktu; enroachment of desert sand (1990).

Niger: Aïr-Ténéré National Nature Reserve; fighting between government forces of Niger and the Tuareg rebels. Six members of the park staff were held hostage for more than a year and a half. Four were released; two were killed (1992).

Oman: Bahia Fort; general deteriorating conditions and poor restoration practices (1988).

Peru: Chan Chan Archaeological Zone; damage from excavation work and plundering (1986).

Poland: Wieliczka Salt Mine; deterioration of salt carvings (1989).

Yugoslavia: Kotor and its Gulf; earthquake damage (1979). Old City of Dubrovnik; war damage to city walls and old buildings, especially their roofs (1991).

Zaire: Garamba National Park; alarming reduction in population of northern white rhinoceros (1984).

---

cial threats the sites on the List face, it's necessary to understand how the World Heritage Convention works. Individual governments nominate sites within their borders. They must convince the 21-member international World Heritage Committee (the group that met in Santa Fe) that each proposed site meets the criteria of "universal value to mankind," and pledge to conserve it.

'There is no way to ensure that sites are protected from environmental degradation, war, neglect, tourism, urbanization, and development.'

The Committee accepts or rejects nominations to the List on the basis of information supplied by two nonprofit organizations: the International Council on Monuments and Sites (ICOMOS) in the case of cultural or manmade sites, and the World Conservation Union

(IUCN) in the case of natural sites. Although neither of these groups is an official organ of UNESCO, their role is written into the Convention's guidelines.

Twenty years after its creation, the still-growing List consists of 378 sites. With an annual budget of around $2 million to implement the Convention, some sites have been named to the List without even being visited by impartial evaluators. And, although it's being discussed, there is no routine program of monitoring to ensure that all sites are protected from threats of environmental degradation, war, urbanization, tourism, and "development."

Once on the List, a site or monument the Committee believes faces "serious and specific dangers"—such as war damage, as in Dubrovnik, or in the case of Sangay National Park in Ecuador, "suffering from heavy poaching of wildlife, illegal livestock grazing, and encroachment"—may be placed on the World Heritage In Danger List, signifying the need for dramatic intervention or major financial or technical assistance. As of press time, the Danger List consisted of 15 sites, including six added at the December meeting.

The United States has 18 World Heritage sites, including Grand Canyon and Yellowstone national parks, Independence Hall in Philadelphia, and the Everglades. They are managed by the National Park Service and supported by tax dollars as well as admission fees. But many sites are in the developing world, where there is less tourism and a commitment to conservation poses wrenching decisions. "When people are living hand to mouth" as they do in some African game-reserve areas, for example, "you can't expect them not to poach," says Jim Thorsell, who evaluates natural sites for IUCN.

The Committee spends some of its funds on technical cooperation and training—restoring earthquake-damaged sites in Egypt or training natural-park managers, for example—but lacks the resources to support large-scale conservation projects.

During the week-long Santa Fe meeting, the delegates—some clad in colorful African robes or gauzy saris, others in the more severe attire of international diplomacy—attended marathon sessions in a hotel ballroom. UNESCO staff hurried up and down the aisles, distributing a blizzard of French- and English-language documents while the Committee discussed reports, guidelines, and budgets and made decisions via simultaneous translation, which were offered in French and English.

In addition to expanding the Danger List, the Committee added 21 new sites to the World Heritage List, including the Kasbah of Algiers and Angkor, the ancient Khmer capital of Cambodia. The tone of these sessions was primarily bureaucratic and politely diplomatic. Yet throughout this twentieth-anniversary meeting, there was a persistent undercurrent of urgency—of concern about the future of the World Heritage List. "The Convention is at a crossroads," said Andy Turner, who is involved with the World Heritage program in Australia. "It has got to deal with the difficult issues."

By the end of the week, the Committee's discussions had illuminated not only the physical threats facing the monuments, but also some of the thorny philosophical, political, and financial issues clamoring to be resolved. For example:

• How can the List be more "balanced"? Only 88 of the 378 sites are natural; 291 are cultural. Europe has a heavy concentration of sites, while other continents have only a few. The Committee has begun to address this by encouraging all countries that have signed the treaty to inventory sites they believe are eligible and want to nominate and by offering some funding to help prepare the nominations.

• Should the List even distinguish between natural and cultural sites? Too often, von Droste says, "culture and nature are artificially separated. They belong together. If you destroy the tropical forest, you also destroy the culture of the people who live there." To address this issue, the Committee has been trying to define a new category of sites called "cultural landscapes," which would recognize "combined works of nature and man."

• How can the World Heritage Centre find the resources to offer protection to so many sites? Publications sales and voluntary contributions by countries or individuals add to the budget, but von

Droste reported that as needs for both emergency funds and regular monitoring and technical assistance grow, the "overall budget at the disposal of the Committee is stagnating or even decreasing in real terms." A key reason for the decrease is that many countries lag far behind in their mandatory contributions. Argentina, for example, owed more than $65,000 for the years 1986 through 1993 as of last December.

Given these limitations, does the World Heritage Convention really have an impact on the future of the earth's most important, often threatened, monuments, natural habitats, and cultural sites? What has it accomplished? What challenges does it face, and what are its prospects for the future?

IUCN's Thorsell has compiled a list of 22 cases in which World Heritage Committee intervention, he says—through political pressure, funding, technical assistance, and the like—has helped protect or improve threatened sites. The success stories include Ecuador's Galápagos islands, where "tourism-control policies were introduced," and Tanzania's Ngorongoro conservation area, which received equipment needed for park management and was removed from the Danger List.

But these accomplishments seem like a drop in the bucket when compared with the size and needs of the entire List and von Droste's gloomy appraisal of the current state of World Heritage efforts.

One case in point—discussed at length in Santa Fe because of the difficulty of agreeing on what to do about it—is that of Mount Nimba, a natural reserve that straddles the borders of Guinea and Ivory Coast in West Africa. In 1980, Mount Nimba—which is described in a book about World Heritage as a "beautiful and isolated environment," the habitat of "rare species of bats, lichens, and other plants and animals"—was put on the List.

Twelve years later, at the Santa Fe meeting, the Committee placed Mount Nimba on the World Heritage In Danger List, citing two major threats to its integrity: a proposal by the Guinea government to open an iron mine adjacent to the site, and the presence of as

many as 60,000 "extremely poor Liberian refugees" in the region, who, von Droste told the Committee, "if not helped, will destroy the whole area."

Despite diplomatic conversations and meetings, technical missions to the reserve, and extensive debate at Santa Fe and previous meetings, the Committee can't even agree on the boundaries of the World Heritage site—and whether the proposed mine really is inside them. The Guinea government's delegate told the Committee in Santa Fe that the proposed mine—which the government has been developing for more than 20 years—"was never protected under World Heritage" because, he said, it was outside the site.

At the same time it put Mount Nimba on the Danger List, the Committee decided to send another mission to study the boundaries, determine the impact of the threats to its "universal values," and work toward development of a management plan to protect the reserve. The mission was successful. Participants generally agreed on new boundaries for the site. The Mount Nimba example illuminates several dilemmas that the World Heritage Convention confronts in its role as protector of our collective future:

• The Convention has lofty principles, but the Committee has limited ability to enforce them. Sites are put on the list because they're considered to be of great value and because individual governments agree to protect them. But, other than mobilizing world opinion, the Committee can do little to protect a site that's threatened by a government policy, such as the proposed iron-mine development, or by unforeseen events, such as the turmoil that led so many Liberians to seek refuge in another country. The case of Mount Nimba illustrates the difficult political and financial issues the Convention faces. The potential value of the iron mine to the country of Guinea is approximately $8 billion—money that could be spent to build an infrastructure and resolve pressing social problems.

• The Convention has lofty operational goals but few resources for implementing them. Even if contributions were paid up, the budget cannot support thorough investigation of proposed nominations or regular monitoring of 378 sites, let alone keep pace with demands generated by adding to the List. This dilemma also emerged in debates on whether to add sites to the Danger List. As long as the Committee cannot provide funds for conservation programs or compensate governments for what they see as an economic loss—not mining in the Mount Nimba reserve—placement on the Danger List appears more like a reprimand than a positive call for protection.

•The structure for implementing the Convention is sensitive to political pressures. The World Heritage Centre is physically located in UNESCO headquarters and receives some funding and other support from the agency. The Convention and the Committee, however, are independent of UNESCO. (The director of the World Heritage Centre reports to and is responsible to the director general of UNESCO.) The entire Committee, which takes action on all nominations as well as makes program policy decisions, meets only once a year. As the Mount Nimba case illustrates, development and enforcement of effective conservation plans may require a long-term perspective as well as technical knowledge. But many delegates who attend the Committee meetings are diplomats rather than substantive experts—with a short-term assignment.

Despite the structural issues confronting the Convention and the continuing problems surrounding Mount Nimba, halfway around the world from West Africa, Australia offers a different, more positive model of the World Heritage system: an example of how environmentalists used the international treaty to safeguard sites in their own country and to stimulate public debate and awareness of environmental issues.

"Australians have a history of fighting in public about these things," says Andrew Turner, then-assistant secretary of the Commonwealth's (federal government's) Nature Conservation Branch, over breakfast one morning before the Committee went into session.

When the government proposed a logging ban in the Wet Tropics of Queensland, a World Heritage site, he recalled, "You couldn't walk into a pub without someone picking a fight about it, with someone else or with you."

Australia's constitution gives land-management power to the states, not to the central government. "In the early 1980s," Turner recounted, "the Tasmanian Hydroelectric Commission wanted to build a dam that would have flooded the valley of the Gordon River, including a lot of aboriginal caves with evidence of early habitation." The proposed dam was in the Tasmanian Wilderness, a World Heritage area that now encompasses about 10 percent of the state.

The Australian High Court set an important precedent in the 1980s in two decisions when it cited the national government's commitment to an international treaty—the World Heritage Convention—as grounds for approving the Commonwealth government's power to impose the logging ban in Queensland and prohibiting the proposed dam project in Tasmania.

Unlike most countries, the Australian government publishes a regular monitoring report on all of its World Heritage sites, describing the nature of the property; current issues, such as proposed construction or tourism growth; management plans; and the number of people who visited the site.

Most observers and participants in the World Heritage process agree that an important key to its future effectiveness is increasing awareness of the concept and the reasons for protecting natural and cultural monuments.

The United States played a key role in creating the Convention and makes the largest contributions to the program budget. But it took the meeting of the Committee in Santa Fe, 20 years after the formation of the treaty, to spur the National Park Service to commit itself to providing information about World Heritage to the millions of people who visit our sites every year.

In contrast, Spain, which has 15 sites, ranging from the prehistoric caves of Altamira to a twentieth-century Barcelona house designed by architect Antonio Gaudí, publishes a glossy, illustrated pamphlet describing each site and the purpose of the World Heritage Convention.

It may or may not be coincidental that one of World Heritage's most passionate advocates is a Spaniard, Federico Mayor, who is UNESCO's director general. "Each citizen of the world should become a defender of our world heritage," he said. "I like to imagine that the World Heritage message is a message of solidarity, of sharing, but that must come from the world level to the national and municipal levels."

Mayor said he's encouraged by the publicity given to conservation of the environment by the Rio conference and the possibility of increasing funding through the new Global Environmental Facility starting in 1994.

His vision for a vigorous, effective World Heritage program a decade from now emphasizes education and public awareness: "In Paris, at UNESCO headquarters, we have a clearinghouse for information, with publications from all over." In addition to the Paris Centre, he hopes to see five or six regional centers and national nongovernmental organizations, which would actively promote an understanding of the Convention and suggest actions to help preserve World Heritage sites. "In children's textbooks, World Heritage would be a symbol of sharing and general awareness of what is precious in one's own and other cultures."

'Will our grandchildren be able to visit the Taj Mahal or the Galápagos Islands? The rock churches of Ethiopia or the lagoon of Venice?'

The person most on the spot now to shape the future of World Heritage is Centre director Bernd von Droste, who became director in May of 1992. Equipped with his meager budget and the energy that comes from knowing you're right, von Droste has begun to address issues of public awareness and funding by negotiating for a major television series on World Heritage and seeking private-sector funding.

Von Droste also has a sheaf of dreams for the future. Stressing that these are his personal ideas, not official UNESCO or Committee policies, he offered the following vision of an effective World Heritage program 20 years down the road:

• A World Heritage Fund of $2 billion or more, with new mechanisms to fund it, such as an energy tax.

• Formation of an academy of "the world's leading personalities—beyond any suspicion—to see that World Heri-

tage is defended on the highest levels."

• Communication networks that will spread the World Heritage message.

• Proper management of tourism at all sites so that they continue to be protected at the same time that they contribute to economic development.

Will our children or grandchildren be able to visit and appreciate the sublime architecture of the Taj Mahal? Will they see the blue-footed boobies of the Galápagos? The rock churches of Ethiopia? The lagoon of Venice or the monoliths of Stonehenge? Or will they only be able to read about them in books?

In an ideal world, where we all recognize and appreciate natural phenomena and the achievements of humankind, where resources abound and protection of the planet is a shared value, our progeny would visit, learn from, and enjoy all of these World Heritage sites—and more. In the real world, points out IUCN's Thorsell, "World Heritage is a small player, taking in a small portion of the world's protected areas and the world's problems." But, he emphasizes, it's worth doing. "One thing that this world needs is more bridges. World Heritage helps build bridges."

When My Grandmother is Your Database: Reactions to Repatriation

Nathalie F S Woodbury

Certainly nothing concerning the past is more present than the issue of repatriation. Establishing federal and state policies of skeletal and artifact return (see January, March, April 1991 *AN*s) was not the result of a swift Indian raid on American museums, but of a long, steady campaign in the '70s and '80s by concerned Native Americans using communication, consultation and the legal system at both state and national levels. Confrontation, a form of communication, has been present, as has resentment, on the part of both Indians and anthropologists—among the latter, especially the archeologists, who dig literally into the past to reconstruct it, and the biological anthropologists, who use skeletal material to study such areas as disease, diet and genetic relationships.

The reaction of a senior archeologist to restraints on dealing with Indian remains is printed below. This letter from *The Teocentli* (January 1991) represents an extreme view.

Sixty-five years ago, when I began my archaeological career, I never dreamed that I would live to see the death of archaeology in the Northern Hemisphere. Fortunately, during the 46 years of my activities, I spent much of my time in the field, excavating some 100 major prehistoric sites in the northeast, and putting together a veritable jigsaw puzzle of data into a comprehensive picture of aboriginal occupations.

No longer is it possible to carry on such researches. It seems that everywhere there is an Indian waiting to look over one's shoulder and demand a halt to the work and the confiscation of one's discoveries. A classic example is going on right now (December 1990) at Wenatchee, Washington, where perhaps the most striking Paleo-Indian find on record is being closed down, unfinished, by the Colville Indians, whose possible ancestral relationship to the site is nil.

With only oral traditions, the actual history of the Indians rests almost entirely on the work of archaeologists, physical anthropologists, and ethnohistorians, a fact apparently completely lost on most Indians. They would have us believe in a pan-Indian religion, philosophy, and set of traditions, largely at variance with the findings of science.

Just as the archeologist quoted above is not altogether accurate in his appraisal of the situation, so neither is Vine Deloria Jr, a Standing Rock Sioux who is a professor of political science at Arizona and holds a JD and a theology degree. Deloria wrote "A Simple Question of Humanity: The Moral Dimensions of the Reburial Issue" in the *Legal Review* of the Native American Rights Fund (Fall 1989). The article includes a section, "How valuable are Indian remains for science?" from which I quote:

When Indian tribes approach museums and other institutions to seek return of human remains, they are often told that it is necessary to keep the Indian human remains because of their great value to science. Allegedly profound and sophisticated experiments are being conducted with these remains which promise great things for all of humanity. But what are these profound studies? In spite of the repeated attempts by American Indians to get a bibliography of the studies being done by these so-called scientists, scholars have yet to produce any significant materials which would justify their claims. Scientific arguments should therefore not be given credence unless and until a clear and concise statement is made explaining the urgency and hysteria behind the scientific opposition to the reburial of Indian human remains. At the present time the arguments used by museum directors and scientists appear to be merely a crude appeal to the authority status of science and little else.

Assuming, for the moment, that American Indian human remains are critical to scientific knowledge, no explanation has been given regarding the peculiar characteristics which make Indian remains more valuable than the remains of other races. What could possibly be learned exclusively from Indian bones which could not also be learned from the bones of other races? The answers that Indians generally receive to this question are superficial and unsatisfactory. Diet? The annual reports of the Commissioner of Indian Affairs, particularly the reports of the Indian agents, can provide much more accurate information on the diets of these people in historical times. For periods of time earlier than modern recorded history, it is a matter of such tenuous speculation that scientific tests would not reveal much of anything. It is a fact, recorded in the agents' reports, that many Indians starved to death on the reservations when Congress failed to appropriate funds for rations which were due Indians. To conduct tests to see whether or not Indians starved is superfluous and would be comparable to testing the bones of holocaust victims to see if they had died of malnutrition.

Some representatives of science claim that the prevalence of disease can be recorded using human remains in specific tests. But most of the diseases afflicting Indians in historical times are well recorded in government reports; discovering diseases of earlier Indians would produce information only mildly interesting and, in any case, speculative in the extreme. It is also suggested that by testing bones and other materials it is possible to demonstrate that American Indians actually came from Asia. But why should this proposition need to be supported by tests? It is absolute doctrine for most scientists in spite of the massive evidence in the oral traditions of the tribes that they had their origin elsewhere. In any case, tests on human remains cannot tell which way the footprints were heading and it may well be that Asia was populated from the western hemisphere, but no present test could confirm or deny that proposition.

Let us suppose for the moment that a great deal of information about disease can be elicited from human remains. Why use Indians remains when there are so many other, easily identified remains that would yield an incredible body of important and vitally needed information? In the 19th century the southern coastal cities were periodically ravaged by epidemics of typhoid fever and cholera. What actually caused these epidemics? Did they strike only the slaves, the free whites, or the slave-owning families? We have records and graveyards available. We can run precise tests on the remains of people who died of these diseases and those who survived them. Why isn't the Smithsonian Institution digging up the family graveyards of the first families of Savannah, Charleston, and New Orleans, perhaps even Mobile, in an effort to obtain this data?

It is a known fact that human beings in America are growing in average size and stature of skeletal structure. Soldiers who served in the American Rev-

olution were a bit smaller than those who were engaged in military service in the Civil War. The First and Second World Wars also saw a rise in the average size of the men in the military. What caused this increase in size? Was it the benefits of democracy, since most of these wars were waged to establish and protect democracy? Was it the rations or the military training? Did the size and capability of the weapons influence the growth of body size? These questions are important because we intend to continue waging wars and we should be at work now doing everything we can to produce future armies that are bigger and better than what we have historically fielded in our wars.

Douglas Ubelaker, a biological anthropologist at the National Museum of Natural History, and Lauryn Guttenplan Grant, Office of General Counsel, Smithsonian, published "Human Skeletal Remains: Preservation or Reburial?" in the 1989 Yearbook of Physical Anthropology; the abstract, included below, summarizes the article's coverage. It provides a balance to Deloria's. Incidentally, the literature cited is a good start on "a bibliography of studies being done," which Deloria claims American Indians are unable to procure.

Recent years have witnessed a surge of scientific interest in the biocultural analysis of mortuary sites and human remains. Concurrently, members of the American Indian community and others have questioned the merit of scientific study and argued for reburial of Indian human remains and associated artifacts. Strong differences of opinion have led to varied responses among museums, professional organizations, federal and state organizations, and individuals. This article addresses the scientific, ethical, religious, political, and legal issues raised by this debate.

Although archeologists (and physical anthropologists) grumble about "loss of the database," recognition of "traditional interests in human remains among a diversity of interests" is included in the formal statement on reburial of the Society for American Archaeology (Bulletin 1986). The American Association of Physical Anthropologists passed a resolution on the reburial of skeletal remains at its 1982 annual meeting. Both organizations urged

case-by-case consideration. More recently the SAA has published in the April 1990 Bulletin "A Perspective on Reburial and Repatriation," by Keith Kintigh, chair of the SAA Task Force.

The Yearbook of Physical Anthropology article includes a state-by-state summary of reburial legislation (p 275) and also provides a short section on international repatriation developments. The past decade has brought increasing activity in Australia where "the [1984] Archaeological and Aboriginal Relics Preservation Act of the state of Victoria was amended to make it unlawful for any person to hold aboriginal remains without government consent"(p 279). In 1988 a London auction house-sale of a tattooed Maori head was halted by court action brought by the Maori Tribal Council. Ubelaker and Grant write, "An open question now is the fate of the remaining 150 Maori heads extant around the world, including 30 at the American Museum of Natural History in New York" (p 279).

Anthropology Today, the bimonthly publication of the royal Anthropological Institute, reports on repatriation of Australian Aborigine remains in the February 1991 issue; the claims, attitudes and arguments are familiar.

The move to repatriate Aboriginal relics from the UK is reviewed in the Financial Times (8/12/90). Since the 1820s museums have collected Aboriginal skeletons, and Tasmanian and Australian Aborigines have increasingly campaigned for the return of these. "The campaign for repatriation of human remains makes the issue of returning the Elgin Marbles look like a genteel sideshow." Why? Curators who return the Marbles will know these will not be destroyed when handed back, but when the human remains are handed over these will almost certainly be cremated or buried. Aboriginal activists claim that Britain's institutions hold about 2000 items "which must be returned if the spirits of their land are to cease crying for them." The debate is a difficult one for members of both sides. Great steps have recently been made in the methods of analysis of human remains, but Bob Weatherall, a barrister who is leading the campaign, points out that it should be decided by the Aboriginal community what is "significant research." It looks as if the Aboriginal community is winning. The Australian government has announced in October that it will be asking overseas institutions to hand back human remains, and in March Irish premier Charles Haughey intervened directly to force the Royal College of Surgeons in Dublin to give up the skull of "Shiney," to which the surgeons were bitterly opposed. In June the Pitt-Rivers Museum returned five skulls and a penis, and in October the Kelvin Grove Museum in Glasgow returned remains of three individuals. Items were returned also from Bradford University and Peterborough City Museum. The campaigners are lobbying the Royal College of Surgeons in London for the remains of 53 unnamed individuals, the National Museum of Scotland with 160 items, and collections in France and Germany. The main criterion by which the remains are returned is whether the person issuing the request can be shown to be related, but it is exactly these well-documented remains which are considered by scientists to have the "best" scientific value. Scientists are now able to identify sex, kinship, racial affinities and medical history of 5000-year-old bones, and are able to detect information about diet, health and maturation from the sectioning of teeth. Archaeologists such as Don Brothwell hope that Aborigines too, as American Indians have increasingly done, take responsibility as custodians of irreplaceable evidence of their past; *FT* comment to this is that "the idea of educating Aborigines to take a different view of their past can have the ring of intellectual colonialism."

Tales from a Peruvian Crypt

The looting of a prehistoric pyramid stimulates an operation in salvage archeology, with unexpected scientific dividends

Walter Alva and Christopher B. Donnan

Walter Alva, a native of Peru, has participated in numerous excavations on that country's north coast and is the director of the Museo Brüning at Lambayeque. Coauthor Christopher B. Donnan is a professor of anthropology and director of the Fowler Museum of Cultural History at the University of California, Los Angeles. They are the coauthors of Royal Tombs of Sipán *(Los Angeles: Fowler Museum of Cultural History, University of California, 1993).*

In the fertile river valleys that relieve Peru's arid coastal plain, mud-brick pyramids stand as the most visible evidence of the prehistoric Moche civilization, which flourished between the first and eighth centuries A.D. Rising out of agricultural fields in the Moche River valley, the massive Pyramid of the Sun was the largest structure ever built in South America. With a ramp that led up to small buildings on its flat summit, it stood about 135 feet high and sprawled over 12.5 acres at its base. It once contained more than 130 million sun-dried bricks. Some of it has eroded away naturally, while part was demolished in the seventeenth century by Spanish entrepreneurs in search of rich burials or other treasures.

About ninety-five miles north of the Pyramid of the Sun, in the Lambayeque River valley, the Moche ceme-

teries and three pyramids near the village of Sipán have long been the target of looters. Over the years they have dug many deep holes with picks and shovels in hopes of locating intact tombs containing ceramic vessels, shell and stone beads, and rarer ornaments of silver and gold. By November 1986, they had nearly exhausted the cemeteries, and one group of treasure seekers decided to focus on the smallest pyramid. Working at night to avoid police detection, they dug a series of holes, but found little of value. Then, on the night of February 16, 1987, at a depth of about twenty-three feet, they suddenly broke into one of the richest funerary chambers ever looted, the tomb of an ancient Moche ruler.

The looters removed several sacks of gold, silver, and gilded copper artifacts. They also took some ceramic vessels, but they broke and scattered many others in their haste. Almost immediately, the looters quarreled over the division of the spoils, and one of them tipped off the police. The authorities were able to seize some of the plundered artifacts, but only a pitiful amount was salvaged from the find. The rest disappeared into the hands of Peruvian collectors or was illegally exported for sale in Europe, Japan, and the United States.

Building on civilizations that preceded them in coastal Peru, the Moche developed their own elaborate society, based on the cultivation of such crops as corn and beans, the harvesting of fish and shellfish, and the exploitation

of other wild and domestic resources. They had a dense, socially stratified population, with large numbers of workers devoted to the construction and maintenance of irrigation canals, pyramids, palaces, and temples. Their lords apparently received food and commodities from their subjects and distributed them to lesser nobles and to the potters, weavers, metalworkers, and other artisans who created luxury objects for the elite. In sculptures, decorated ceramics, and murals, archeologists have glimpsed many complex scenes of Moche life, including hunting, combat, and ceremonial practices.

The luxury items from Sipán that were confiscated by the police, including hollow gold beads of various shapes and sizes, hinted at the magnificence of the plundered burial, which must have belonged to one of the Moche elite. More fortune-hunters descended on the site in search of overlooked valuables. They hacked at the tomb walls and sifted through the excavated dirt. By the time the police secured the area, little was left except a boot-shaped hole. Nevertheless, with armed guards stationed around the clock, we hastily organized an archeological survey to learn everything possible of scientific value (author Walter Alva directed the project; coauthor Christopher B. Donnan was one of the many participants.)

We began by making a contour map of the three pyramids and what remained of their ramps and adjacent plazas. The small pyramid, where the

From *Natural History*, May 1994, pp. 26-30, 33-34. Adapted from *Royal Tombs of Sipan* by Walter Alva and Christopher B. Donnan. Los Angeles: Fowler Museum of Cultural History, University of California, 1993.

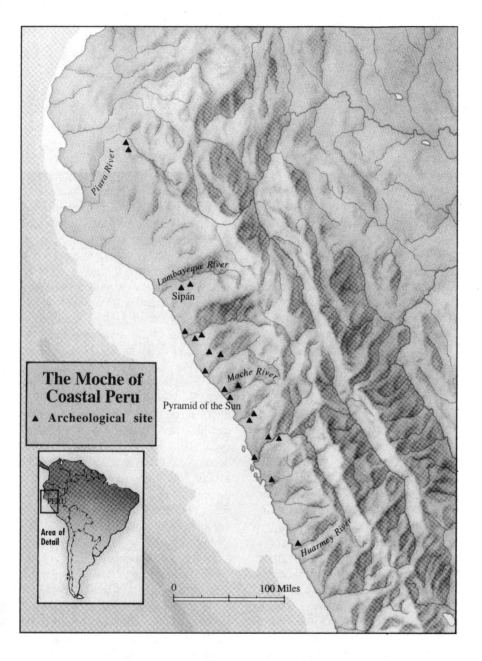

The Moche of Coastal Peru

▲ **Archeological site**

PERU

Area of Detail

0   100 Miles

Piura River

Lambayeque River

Sipán

Moche River

Pyramid of the Sun

Huarmey River

platform with a balustrade, surrounding an open-front building with one back wall and a peaked roof supported by posts. Seventeen double-faced human heads decorated the roof ridge, while depicted in relief on the wall was a supernatural creature, half feline and half reptile, copulating with a woman on a crescent moon.

Knowing that the pyramid would be further plundered once we left, we decided to open up a new section to methodical excavation, choosing a ten-by-ten meter (1,076-square-foot) area near the summit. Here we came upon a place where the mud brick had been carved out and refilled in ancient times. Digging down, we found eight decomposed wood beams, similar to those that had roofed the looted burial chamber. Buried beneath these, in the debris of what had been a small rectagular chamber, we found 1,137 ceramic bowls, jars, and bottles. They portrayed a variety of human figures: warriors holding war clubs and shields, nude prisoners with leashlike ropes around their necks, musicians with drums, and seated figures wearing beaded pectorals (biblike coverings). Some were arranged in symbolic tableaux, for example, musicians and prisoners ringing and facing noble personages.

As we removed the ceramics, we found several pieces of copper and, finally, a man's skeleton lying jackknifed on its back, with chin, knees, and arms pulled in toward the torso. Since the Moche customarily buried their dead in a fully extended position, we interpreted this individual to be a sacrificial victim, whose body had been shoved into the small chamber as part of the ritual offering.

Even as these offerings were being excavated, we discovered a second, larger rectangular area that appeared to have been carved into the pyramid and refilled. As we carefully excavated this, we found, about thirteen feet below the original surface of the pyramid, the skeleton of a man wrapped in a cotton shroud. He lay stretched out on his back and wore a gilded copper helmet. Over the right forearm, which rested on his chest, was a round copper shield. A little below we found the

tomb had been found, was riddled with looters' tunnels, but in some places, the piles of dirt they had excavated helped preserve the original contours. The tunnels also enabled us to examine the internal construction. The pyramid and the rest of the complex evidently had been built and rebuilt over a long period of time, undergoing many changes as the various parts were enlarged. The small pyramid seems to have gone through six phases, beginning in the first century A.D. and ending about 300.

Although the burial chamber had been gouged out of shape, we were able to determine that it had originally

been roofed with large wood beams, which had decomposed. To our great surprise, we were able to uncover some of the tomb's contents that had been missed by the original looters and the subsequent gleaners. Clearing along one side of the chamber, we found the remains of a large, gilded copper crown decorated with metal disks; four ceramic jars modeled in the shape of human figures; and a copper mask with inlaid turquoise eyes. In excavating these, we also discovered a heavy copper scepter forty inches long, pointed at one end and bearing a three-dimensional architectural model on the other. The model depicted a remains of seventeen parallel beams that, we dared hope, lay over a major, undisturbed burial chamber.

The discoveries that subsequently emerged surpassed our dreams. Buried in the chamber were the remains of a wood coffin that contained the richest grave offerings ever to be excavated scientifically in the Western Hemisphere. The body of a man between thirty-five and forty-five years of age had been laid to rest with a feathered headdress, banners of cloth with gilded copper decorations, beaded pectorals, nose ornaments and necklaces of gold and silver, ear ornaments of gold and turquoise, face coverings of gold, a gold backflap and a silver backflap that would have been hung from the belt, and countless other precious objects. In his right hand the deceased had held a gold and silver scepter topped with a large rattle, and in his left hand, a smaller scepter of cast silver. In relief on the rattle, which was shaped like an inverted pyramid, were scenes of an elaborately dressed warrior subjugating a vanquished opponent. The sculpted head of the smaller scepter echoed this theme.

Working six days a week, it took us four months to document and safely empty the delicate contents of the tomb. As our original budget became exhausted, we received some partial funding from a brewery and a truckload of noodles donated by a pasta manufacturer. At one point we were paying the fieldworkers with a combination of cash and noodles. We eventually secured new support from the Research Committee of the National Geographic Society and were able to proceed with further excavation.

All the while we had been working and moving equipment around the coffin burial, we had been walking only inches above hundreds of ceramic vessels, two sacrificed llamas, a dog, and the burials of two men, three women, and a child of nine or ten. Although we do not know this for sure, the men and the child might have been buried as sacrifices to accompany the principal figures. The remains of the females, however, were partly decomposed at the time they were placed in the tomb,

as evident from the way the bones were somewhat jumbled. They had probably died years earlier and their remains maintained elsewhere until this final interment.

As we excavated the tomb and cataloged its contents, we couldn't help wondering who was the important personage buried there. The key to the answer was a major photographic archive of Moche sculpture and drawings at the University of California at Los Angeles. As the tomb was being excavated, photographs of the objects were sent to UCLA for comparative study.

Many of the objects in the coffin suggested the man buried there was a warrior. The archive of Moche art contains hundreds of depictions from which we can reconstruct a sequence of Moche militarism and ceremonial activity. We can see processions of warriors carrying war clubs, spears, and spear throwers, perhaps on their way to battle. We can see warriors in combat, apparently away from settled areas. The essence of Moche combat appears to have been the expression of individual valor, in which warriors engaged in one-on-one combat, seeking to vanquish, rather than kill, an opponent. The victor is often shown hitting his opponent on the head or upper body with the war club, while the defeated individual is depicted bleeding from his nose or losing his headdress or other parts of his attire. Sometimes the victor grasps his adversary by the hair and removes his nose ornament or slaps his face.

As far as we can tell, the Moche warriors fought with one another, not against some foreign enemy. Once an opponent was defeated, he was stripped of some or all of his clothing and a rope was placed around his neck. The victor made a bundle of the prisoner's clothing and weapons and tied it to his own war club as a trophy. After a public parading of the spoils, the prisoners were arraigned before a high-status individual and finally brought back to the Moche settlements or ceremonial precincts. There the priests and their attendants sacrificed them, cutting their throats and drinking the

blood from tall goblets. The bodies were then dismembered and the heads, hands, and feet tied individually with ropes to create trophies.

Many representations of the sacrifice ceremony exist in Moche art. Although they vary, not always depicting all personages in the ceremony, apparently three principal priests and one priestess were involved, each associated with specific garments and ritual paraphernalia. The most important was the "warrior priest," generally depicted with a crescent-shaped nose ornament, large circular ear ornaments, a warrior backflap, a scepter, and a conical helmet with a crescent-shaped ornament at its peak. A comparison of these and other details with the contents of the tomb convinced us that the individual buried there was just such a warrior priest.

When the sacrifice ceremony was first identified in Moche art, in 1974, no one could be sure it was a real practice, as opposed to a mythical event. Now we had archeological evidence that this was an actual part of Moche life. Here was one of the individuals who presided over the sacrifices. Further, because the limited numbers of objects salvaged from the looted tomb were similar to some of those we had excavated, we could conclude that the looted tomb also must have belonged to a warrior priest.

As if this were not enough, during the excavation of the warrior priest's tomb, we located another suspected tomb elsewhere on the pyramid. We held off excavation until work on the earlier find was nearly complete. The knowledge we gained made it easier to anticipate the sequence of excavation. Again we found the residue of a plank coffin containing the rich burial of a man between thirty-five and forty-five years old. Among his grave goods was a spectacular headdress ornament of gilded copper, in the form of the head and body of an owl from which arched long banks with suspended bangles, representing the feathered wings. Nearby we found the remains of four other individuals: a male between fourteen and seventeen years of age, two females in their late teens or early twenties, and an eight- to ten-year-old child. Buried with the child were a dog and a snake.

The contents of this tomb were only a little less lavish than those of the warrior priest. They suggest that the principal individual was another of the priests depicted in the sacrifice ceremony—one we call the "bird priest." The major clue was the large owl headdress. He was also buried with a copper cup near his right hand, similar in proportion to the cups portrayed in pictures of the sacrifice ceremony.

Having identified these individuals as participants in the sacrifice ceremony, we began to wonder if such ceremonies took place in Sipán itself. The answer was soon revealed when, about eleven yards from the bird priest's tomb, we found several small rooms that contained hundreds of ceramic vessels, human and llama bones, and miniature ornaments and implements, mixed with ash and organic

residues. Among the human remains were hands and feet, quite possibly the trophies taken from dismembered sacrificial victims. Altogether these looked to be the residue of sacrifice ceremonies, which the Moche apparently carried out at Sipán, as no doubt they did at their other centers.

The looted tomb, the two excavated tombs, and the sacrificial offerings all seem to date to about A.D. 290. While excavating the offerings, we found a fourth, somewhat earlier tomb containing the remains of a man between forty-five and fifty-five years old, also richly endowed with grave goods, including a necklace of gold beads in the form of spiders on their webs, anthropomorphic figures of a crab and a feline, scepters, an octopus pectoral with gilded copper tentacles, and numerous other ornaments and objects. Nearby we found the body of a young, sixteen- to eighteen-year-old woman next to a sacrificed llama. This tomb

may also have belonged to a warrior priest, but not all the identifying elements are there. Possibly, this is simply because it dates to an earlier period than the depictions we have of the sacrifice ceremony, which are all from after A.D. 300.

Moche civilization collapsed suddenly, probably as a result of one or more of the natural cataclysms that periodically devastate coastal Peru—earthquake, flooding, or drought. The Moche had no writing system, so they left no records we can hope to decipher. They disappeared before Europeans reached the New World and could leave us eyewitness accounts. Yet with the scientific excavation of these royal tombs, we have gained an intimate portrait of some of their most powerful lords. Work at Sipán continues, now at a promising location near the tomb of the bird priest. As we dig more deeply, we look forward to our next encounter.

Indians, Archaeologists, and the Future

Vine Deloria, Jr.

Vine Deloria, Jr., Department of History, Center for Studies of Ethnicity and Race in America, Campus Box 234, University of Colorado, Denver, CO 80309-0234

The most recent encounter between American Indians and archaeologists, over the Native American Graves Protection and Repatriation Act (P.L. 101-601), has left hard feelings on both sides. From the Indian point of view, conflict will be inevitable so long as archaeologists maintain a stance that privileges their interests as scientists over all other human considerations. Nonetheless there are some areas where American Indians and archaeologists might develop cooperative ventures, for example, in the investigation of Precolumbian contact and diffusion, and in clarifying the status of sacred sites.

I realize that there is still considerable emotional baggage connected with the reburial issue that has been the most recent encounter between American Indians and archaeologists, and while I do not wish to reverse the progress made to date, I do feel a responsibility to represent some of the residual feelings that we see present in Indian minds across the country.

The Society for American Archaeology (SAA) did finally come to a compromise position that supported the Indian efforts to get the Native American Graves Protection and Repatriation Act (Public Law 101-601) passed, although not without some doing. Some representatives of the SAA feel that their final efforts of support should thereby mask what were some dreadfully arrogant attitudes earlier in the struggle. It may well be that we should simply move forward and make the best of the present situation, but we should also recognize that it will take more than a few representatives gathering together in civil conversations to erase the hard feelings on both sides of the issue.

Some of what I can gather as hard feelings from the Indian point of view stem back to the position that the scholarly community has enjoyed for the past century, i.e., that only scholars have the credentials to define and explain American Indians and that their word should be regarded as definitive and conclusive. Indians reject that attitude out of hand, and therefore when the reburial issue was first raised and we heard cries of "Science" and its sanctity given as the excuse for not considering the repatriation of Indian human remains and funerary objects, Indians naturally got their backs arched and resentments built quickly. We have been the objects of scientific investigations and publications for far too long, and it is our intent to become people once again, not specimens.

Science today has the edge in establishing itself as the primary source of truth because of the spectacular success of technology which, in the minds of the general public, is devised by people in white lab smocks busily providing us with more gadgets. Some scholars, particularly people in California, adopted the attitude that the Indian interest in human remains was purely political and had no emotional or religious substance while they, as scientists, were impartial and stood above the battle. Nothing could be further from the truth of course. Considering the vast financial and status rewards that the academic community bestows on its members, the chances are that scientists would lie, cheat, and steal in order to advance their personal careers. But the implication of crying out "Science" whenever reburial was mentioned was just the opposite—Indians were made to appear as if they were looting the scientific heritage instead of receiving back the remains of loved ones who had been illegally and

Reprinted with permission from the Society for American Archaeology from *American Antiquity*, Volume 57, Number 4, 1992, pp. 595-598. © 1992 by the Society for American Archaeology.

immorally taken from them a century or more ago.

Conflicts will always arise, and increasingly so, as long as a substantial number of people in the academic establishment insist that their careers and research come before all other human considerations. This conflict is probably inherent in the nature of the academic enterprise itself. We have a society so wealthy that we can pay people outrageous salaries to become experts on butterfly wings, verb tenses of obscure Indian languages, and custodians of fragments of old pottery abandoned by earlier people. But in the extreme example, only the National Socialist German Workers' party of the 1930s and 1940s in Germany insisted they had the absolute right to use and dispose of human beings and human remains without giving any other people a voice in the proceedings.

I wish some of you could hear the descriptions of the medicine men who conducted the reburial ceremonies for some of the tribes. In these ceremonies the spirits of the people whose remains were being returned appeared. They asked surprisingly practical questions for spirits. Some wanted to know if it was possible to get the indelible ink removed from their bones. Others said their remains had no feet or no head and they wondered at the kind of people who would remove these parts of the body and what they thought human life was. I don't much care whether any of you believe in spirits or a life hereafter. I think it is foolish to pretend on the basis of a wholly materialistic science (which can only measure quantities) that there is nothing spiritual and nonmaterial in our universe. It is this attitude, as much as anything, that distinguishes Indians from the rest of American society and most certainly from the scientific endeavor. Whether there is sufficient proof of the Indian beliefs and experiences or not, it is a hazardous thing to assume without good cause that the Indians are lying or simply superstitious. Indeed, large numbers of non-Indians are now embracing the Indian beliefs in increasing numbers, so in some sense materialists are on the losing side of this crest of the historical/emotional wave of sensitivities.

Archaeology has been a suspicious science for Indians from the very beginning. People who spend their lives writing tomes on the garbage of other people are not regarded as quite mentally sound in many Indian communities. And to define Indian civilizations by watching the change of pottery styles as archaeology once did is not exactly a process of compiling irrefutable knowledge; it is mere White man speculation and fiction and should be regarded as such. We all of us still carry the baggage of former days, and it should be a task in the days ahead for archaeologists who truly want cooperative ventures with American Indians to begin to communicate about some of the new techniques that are being used and the changes in dogmas and doctrines that are occurring as a result of the new instruments and processes available to you.

In this respect I wonder at the isolation of archaeologists today. I have in the neighborhood of 80 books dealing in one way or another with Precolumbian expeditions to the Western Hemisphere. These books range from utter nonsense to rather sophisticated and careful review of your own archaeological reports and the addition of new interpretations and efforts to interpret the anomalies that you seemed unable to understand at the time. I began to take this expanding body of literature seriously when I happened to mention Barry Fell's writing to people in the Smithsonian. Before I could even say whether I agreed with Fell or not, William Sturtevant and Ives Goddard got exceedingly heated and began to argue with me about Lybian verb tenses and some translation, or purported translation, of an inscription that Fell had made.

My rule of thumb is that the Smithsonian is the last bastion of nineteenth-century science, so if people there are against any new theory, the chances are they are dead wrong. Thus I have maintained a lively interest in the possibility of proving that some of the theories embraced by lay people regarding Precolumbian America will someday be demonstrated. I will willingly grant that we have nothing in the way of small artifacts at some of these sites and that seems puzzling if the other aspects of the site seem to hold. But the "official" explanation I have received about the stone chambers in New England and the ogam inscriptions which seem to abound in other places is simply ludicrous.

Without even examining some of these sites, scholars have told me that they are root cellars or simply marks made by colonists' plows or Indians sharpening their arrows. Now some of the locations where these alleged ogam inscriptions are found are on inaccessible cliffs, and I have great difficulty imagining colonists hitching up their teams and suspending their plows over some abyss in order to make these marks. Additionally, there seems to be an abundance of old coins found in various parts of the country but most noticeably in the eastern United States. If I were to accept the usual scholarly explanation I would come to believe that the ships that brought immigrants from Europe were stuffed with British, German, and French coin collectors who brought hoards of old coins to this continent and then casually scattered them all over Ohio as a joke. In fact so many of these sites have been declared to be hoaxes that American society seems to have been filled with practical jokers during most of the 300 years of European occupation. Looking at the presidential candidates every four years is almost irrefutable evidence for your present interpretation of the alleged Precolumbian sites but I am still uncomfortable with the idea that NO contacts were made between Europe and North America before Columbus.

As a side note to this problem, I have been told that there is great debate between diffusionists and others over the interpretation of some digs and that many people feel they cannot advocate Precolumbian contact for to do so would mean demeaning the Indians and suggesting that they could not have made discoveries on their own. Strangely this debate also rages in Indian circles, and a few of my best friends are adamant about maintaining the theory of isolation in order to enhance the achievements of our ancestors. Here I part company with other Indians and urge you to take a good look at all possible theories of Precolumbian contacts and even the transmission of every cultural trait that is found elsewhere. Samuel Eliot Morrison is now dead, and we need no longer cringe in fear that he will discredit us for believing that someone besides Columbus visited these shores.

Unpleasant though it may be to some Indians, we need to know the truth about North American prehistory, and indeed that of the Western Hemisphere. I personally feel that unless and until we are in some way connected with world history as early peoples, perhaps even as refugees from Old World turmoils and persecutions, we will never be accorded full humanity. We cannot be primitive peoples who were suddenly discovered half a millenium ago. The image and interpretation are all wrong, and we are regarded as freaks outside historical time. During the Wounded Knee trials I was forced to go along with Bering Strait advocates and argue that Indians had come across from Siberia, during one of those times that you people manipulate by increasing or decreasing the amount of water tied up in the glaciers, and bringing along a very sophisticated culture and a protoscientific technology.

Standing in the hall of the courtroom one day, a non-Indian approached me and said "I am very interested in this Bering Strait theory. It proves we are all natives." I said that being here perhaps 40,000 or even 100,000 years is a little more than having arrived in third-class steerage in 1920. I don't think he got the point since he was a Nebraska intellectual, and we all know that the "N" on Nebraska football helmets represents "Knowledge." But

the point I wish to make is that this migration from Siberia is regarded as doctrine, but basically it is a fictional doctrine that places American Indians outside the realm of planetary human experiences. So I hope you will stop being so staid and respectable and begin an era of courageous speculation and openness and try to give Precolumbian expeditions serious consideration.

Finally, in recent months I have been working hard with the coalition of American Indians seeking to get federal legislation clarifying the status of sacred sites, and naturally archaeology is involved or eventually will become involved in this problem. I must honestly report to you that many Indians are looking to your discipline for specific technical assistance in this struggle. One problem is the requirement of courts, at the present time, to insist that the location be a longstanding sacred site, and so it will make a big difference whether or not continuous or at least consistent use of the site is demonstrated by scholarly means as well as by traditional religious leaders. Some locations have very little evidence of use because they were considered of sufficient spiritual power that few individuals were allowed to go there. Consequently the locations show very little evidence of Indian use. It's not as if annual Methodist picnics and camp revivals were held at these locations.

You will be pleased to know that some very powerful Indian spiritual leaders have decided to find a reliable archaeologist or group of archaeologists who can help them completely cover and record what is present at some of these sacred sites. These people are very worried that if the site is declared sacred it will be invaded by hundreds of New Agers looking for a spiritual experience. So there is concern that plants, paths, shrines, rocks, and other aspects of the site be care-

fully and accurately recorded in case the place is desecrated by the curious in the years to come.

We can look forward, therefore, to creating a more constructive relationship between scholars and the people they study if we look at the present and future and make an effort to leave the past behind us. One difficulty in making this transition is that we already have a large body of data which represents the efforts of the previous century, and we are stuck with these writings and with the language they represent, which is often derogatory and demeaning to American Indians. Students continue to have access to these materials and consequently old attitudes and stereotypes are perpetuated even in spite of our best efforts. Archaeologists might well consider what the field of law has done in a comparable situation. In law we have what basically amounts to modernization of concepts through the device of scholars and practicing attorneys working to create "restatements" of the law.

One project that might be considered in the decades ahead would be a cooperative effort between archaeologists and interested Indians to rework and restate the findings of major importance in terms and language that eliminates cultural bias and attempts to give an accurate summary of what is known. That task seems formidable, but with some few exceptions is not only manageable but probably an effort that is easily funded. We may not be able to promote such a project on a national scale, but we can certainly consider the beneficial impact such a recasting would create with respect to specific tribes and scholars and perhaps come up with a solution or alternative way of establishing good relations for the future.

Damming the Past

*Are reservoirs destroying our archeological heritage? Scuba divers
give us an answer*

Daniel J. Lenihan

*Trained as both a diver and an arche-
ologist, Daniel J. Lenihan is chief of
the National Park Service's Submerged
Cultural Resources Unit. Recently his
team mapped and photographed various American, German, and Japanese
ships sunk in the 1946 atomic bomb
testing at Bikini Atoll.*

The movie light I hold in one hand
plays over a graffiti-covered wall in the
dark, concrete building. A scrawl in
balloon letters, "The Lord Cometh,"
reminds me of spray-can wisdom I
have seen on a hundred subway cars. I
float slowly through the flooded hall-
way, walking on the index and middle
finger of my free hand. Tiny clouds of
silt puff up as I leave my odd paw
prints. Another ghostly form, that of
my diving partner, rises effortlessly
toward the ceiling. He prepares to snap
a picture of the illuminated words.

The building was probably a foundry. The Lord may have been here, but
he's gone now. We linger for a second
photo, then we too move on. Gently,
silently but for the sound of our ex-
haled breaths splashing on the ceiling,
we glide through a series of doorways
devoid of doors and propel ourselves
through a glassless window. On emerging, we are in the light of day, subdued
by the twenty feet of water between us
and the air above.

What does it take to cover sixty
square miles of New Mexico desert
with water? Sometimes, an act of God,

but in this case it was the Bureau of
Reclamation. In 1911, Burec cameth
and made rise the waters of the Rio
Grande to create the Elephant Butte
Reservoir and Recreation Area. The
Southwest is full of these improve-
ments on nature. They harness indolent
rivers for electrical power, allow people to live in flood plains, and convert
desert scrub into profitable farmland.
Regaining the surface, I am reminded
that they also insure the popularity of
the outboard engine. Protective of the
student divers under my supervision, I
make obscene gestures at boaters who
come too close to our diver warning
flags.

I have visited many of these watery
worlds. From 1975 to 1980, I led a
National Park Service study of major
water-impoundment areas in the United
States, mainly in the arid Southwest.
Other researchers were charged with
assessing loss of habitat and scenic
values. My task was to determine if the
federal money allocated for salvaging
archeological sites was being pru-
dently spent.

The dozens of large reservoirs built
by the Army Corps of Engineers, Bureau of Reclamation, Tennessee Valley
Authority, and others throughout the
country impact river valleys, usually
the locus of past human activity. The
scope of this phenomenon is hard to
convey. The combined surface area of
just two of the artificial lakes on the
Colorado River, lakes Mead and Powell, for example, is more than 500
square miles, or about half the size of

Rhode Island. Sizable portions of these
two lakes are deep enough to cover the
Washington Monument. Beneath them
now lie some 2,000 known sites of the
Anasazi—the ancient ones—ranging
from the ruins of pueblos to scatterings
of stone tools. The sites identified in
surveys before the valleys were flooded
probably represent only a fraction of
those actually present. Apart from the
value archeologists attach to these remains, one can only imagine what living Indian peoples must feel when they
see their heritage, including sacred sites
and ancient landscapes, obliterated.

Even as the dams were being built,
the American preservation community
managed to impress upon Congress
that archeological remains are irreplaceable. This sometimes elusive point was
easiest to establish with politicians
from regions where the loss of impressive ruins would be noticed by their
constituents. One piece of legislation
in the early 1970s authorized the
spending of up to one percent of the
entire cost of a new reservoir on salvage archeology. Large-scale excavations of the most dramatic sites in the
deepest parts of the about-to-be lakes
seemed the remedy of choice.

The result, however, was warehouses
full of artifacts needing expensive cur-
ating, from sites dug for the wrong
reasons. A reaction to this process was
taking shape in the archeological profession about the time our study began,
culminating in the formation of the
American Society for Conservation
Archeology. These archeologists argued

for more focused use of available human and monetary resources—in essence, elegance of research design instead of energetic shoveling. Terms such as "partial-site excavation," "minimal impact archeology," and "problem-oriented research designs" started to replace "dig we must."

Were history and prehistory destroyed when covered by impounded river waters? Or were they preserved forever in an underwater data bank for future generations? Environmental impact statements authoritatively supported these two contradictory positions. With public funds going toward some very comprehensive and expensive archeological projects, federal reservoir managers wanted some definitive answers fast. The National Park Service was given the ball, and I, a diving instructor with a degree in anthropology, got to be quarterback. I moved to Santa Fe, where at the behest of Calvin R. Cummings, regional archeologist for the service's Southwest region, I assembled a team.

With more than a little dismay we realized that we had to define what was of archeological value before we could decide whether or not it was being destroyed. Is the stuff of archeology made up of only artifacts and bones and their relative locations? What about the texture and color of the soil they are found in—how does flooding affect such archeological clues? What of the soil chemistry, which helps to establish where humans performed different daily activities? What of the subtle properties of materials dated through arcane laboratory tricks? Heady fare for a handful of archeologists just out of graduate school, selected for the job largely because we could dive.

This foundry dive is a training exercise for a group of sport divers wishing to refine their underwater recording skills. As I struggle to remove my wet suit, however, I dredge up memories of reservoir dives past. My mind's eye takes me momentarily from the nearby shore of the placid Rio Grande to the mighty Colorado. It gives one pause to stand on the brink of Glen Canyon Dam and look down at the Colorado River on one side and Lake Powell on

the other. A raging river, a piece of raw wilderness, has been molded into a huge pond. At the bottom of the sixty-story concrete megalith, a reconstituted Colorado seems to shrug off the insult and strive to regain its personality. By the time it hits the Grand Canyon, it has become a serious river once more. Farther downstream it is dammed again to form Lake Mead, then Lake Mohave, and yet again to become Lake Havasu.

Hundreds of speedboats zooming in what seem to be long lanes of traffic give Lake Havasu the appearance of an aqueous turnpike. To cap the impression of some sort of surreal theme park, an entrepreneurial genius has placed the reconstituted London Bridge across a side channel of the impounded Colorado River. Moved stone by stone for the Thames, the bridge now stands as a monument to the general level of intelligence involved in our use of human energy and natural resources in the great American Southwest.

Below Lake Mead, released through the turbines of Hoover Dam, the Colorado rages through a narrow, steep canyon for several miles. For scuba divers, this is a challenging stretch. At Ringbolt Rapids the current drags divers down into a hole almost seventy feet deep before disgorging them back to the twenty-foot depth. Here, in the shallower reaches below the rapids, we tried to document the remains of an old river boat (such boats would winch themselves upriver using iron bolts set in the canyon walls). One of our group would try to take a photograph while holding on to the wreck with one hand, but if he relaxed his grip even slightly, the current would sweep him away, leaving behind only a swirl of sand and silt. And if he glanced back upstream, his mask would be ripped off. We eventually decided that a "preliminary evaluation" was sufficient, declared victory, and headed for more convenient sites to document.

The presence of historic shipwrecks in the desert is always cause for wonder. A few miles below Glen Canyon Dam, the *Charles H. Spencer* lies near Lee's Ferry, a popular point for rafters to begin their run through the

Grand Canyon. Near the ruins of the old mining camp, the craft lies in shallow water with most of its lower hull well preserved. At most water levels, the smooth, metal boiler is partly exposed, and Navajos fish from the perch it offers. Prefabricated in San Francisco, the *Spencer* was assembled at Lee's Ferry to carry coal to a gold mine. After the craft was launched more than a thousand miles from the ocean, its owners discovered it took more coal to fight the river than the vessel could carry as cargo. The craft was left to rot on the riverbank—a long-term proposition in this part of the world.

Newly impounded waters hold special surprises. I recall the hull of our small aluminum boat scraping over the tips of branches above Cochiti Dam, as Cochiti Lake filled just west of Santa Fe. These were the tops of ponderosa pines, their roots still embedded in the drowned soil sixty feet below us—New Mexico's high desert converted into an evergreen swamp. The Anasazi pueblos, which we had found on our foot survey through this valley years before, would know a strange requiem. While their descendants struggle to maintain an identity, selling their traditional wares on the plaza in Santa Fe, the Anasazi lie buried in earthen house floors, sleeping with the fishes.

Hiking along the ridgetops above Cochiti Dam, I have rested on smooth white logs hundreds of yards above the river. These convenient seats are driftwood, piled there when melts from heavy snowpacks in the Rockies raised the waters to levels unthinkable before impoundment.

During droughts in California's Folsom Reservoir, nature temporarily overrules the dam builders, as rivers fall to their original levels. Here, prehistoric house floors compacted from years of trampling resist the erosion of the receding waters better than the surroundings soils can. The curious result is that once-buried archeological treasures are left pedestaled above the adjacent terrain. Stumps of oak trees stand beside them on their tap roots. Raccoons, nature's opportunists, have done their own excavating in the hardened house floors, placing snail shells and potsherds in neat piles outside their burrows. One suspects they are less interested in scientific analysis than in extracting the mollusks that took up residence in the house floors during inundation, but their precise digging technique would put some archeologists to shame.

Underwater in Texas, I have flutter-kicked through old ranch houses, cut my way through barbed-wire fences, trailed old railroad tracks into the depths, and followed asphalt highways (still feeling some compulsion to keep to the right of the yellow line). In some places I have even seen old dams that have been covered by the waters backed up by new dams. These reinforced concrete monsters that gobble up river valleys devour their own with equal indifference.

Several tense, cold winter days spent searching for a drowned diver in the submerged powerhouse of a dam near the Mexican border will stay with me always. A hundred feet below the surface, my colleague Larry Murphy and I entered through glassless windows much more forbidding than the ones in the Elephant Butte foundry and felt our way cautiously through murky water. Our tanks scraped against hazardous wires and steel bars hanging from the ceiling. Blinded by disturbed sediment that even our powerful lights couldn't penetrate, we felt our way down a flight of stairs, ran our hands over commodes, and searched restroom stalls. With equal caution we made our way back out before our double tanks emptied of their precious air.

We found the young man's body a day later, wedged in a corner between a glass partition and the electrical switch cage. Larry and I felt especially compelled to remove a fellow diver from this alien environment. Muttering words of encouragement to the lifeless form, we maneuvered him through the many obstacles to the surface.

The official conclusions of our National Reservoir Inundation Study, while voluminous, can be boiled down to a few general observations. The most surprising is that one of the lowest impact zones is in the bottom of a lake, particularly if it has been flooded quickly. Most of what has archeological value is preserved intact, except for soil chemistry, which loses its analytical use after inundation. Access, of course, is compromised, but the findings are reassuring, at least if the goal is to bank sites for future research.

The places worst hit turn out to be the zones where the water level varies up and down, subjecting sites to alternate wet and dry cycles. Little of archeological value survives that sort of treatment. In addition, this is where park goers have their greatest impact. As reservoir levels fluctuate seasonally or over the years, campers follow the beach line, parking their RVs side by side. At Roosevelt Lake in Arizona, for example, stones that marked the ancient house outlines of Hohokam and later Salado peoples for hundreds of years are piled helter-skelter by unknowing tourists to form campfire pits. Even areas outside the maximum flood pool are highly affected, as sites formerly exposed only to occasional visits of Native Americans and backpackers become available to anyone with a bass boat and a sixpack.

Our inundation project also taught us something about American values. Underlying the whole program was the premise that reservoirs were going to be built, archeological sites or endangered snail-darters notwithstanding. Society had already made its fundamental choices; we were providing answers that would improve the efforts to mitigate the impact.

Many reservoirs are beautiful places, although those who love wild rivers may find that hard to swallow. Some people, like the late writer and "eco-warrior" Edward Abbey, have such an intense hatred for dams that they would take satisfaction in seeing them blown up. The heroes of Abbey's *Monkey Wrench Gang* attempt just that, to the vicarious delight of many readers. They could just as well take solace, however, in contemplating the fragility of human-made structures. The ghosts of drowned rivers stir restlessly beneath the placid waters of reservoirs. In the eye-blink of a few thousand years, they will sweep away the concrete and earthen plugs that hamper their quest for the sea.

As I cram the last of the dive gear into our van at Elephant Butte, one of our students approaches me to ask a parting question. She points across the lake at the white line that runs along the steep shoreline just above the present water level—the bathtub ring common to many water impoundments. "What is that anyway?" she wants to know. I tell her it's blue-green algae bonded with calcium carbonate, and if she'd like a closer look, she can glance down at her feet, because she is standing in it. Like many of the things that affect us most, it isn't noticeable until we're removed enough to gain perspective.

Archaeologists as People

Everyone knows that archaeological digs are filled with mystery and romance. What they do not know is that the mystery is usually determining how the pencils disappear from the digging kits at the rate of one per day. It is like the socks that go into washing machines as pairs and come out as singles. The greatest archaeological find someday may be that of the millions and millions of single socks and the civilization that they have founded. The solution to the mystery will probably have something to do with avoiding inbreeding.

As for the romance of archaeology, it occurs, but it rarely has anything to do with archaeological finds. It has everything to do with being away from home, away from loved ones and close friends, and being placed in tight quarters under strange and uncomfortable circumstances among a bunch of people from Wack-o-land overseen by sadistic digging masters from Bootcamp, Inc.

Life on a dig is like life among tribal peoples being played by people who have the wrong set of rules. The rules of civilized behavior do not apply when the singular modern possession of privacy is taken away. Communal living can be communal hell. Life becomes filled with bad food, sickness, sunburns, bug bites, nasty parasites, and bad vibes; hot water and indoor plumbing become artifacts of some past life.

Still, people adapt to it. Especially those in the habit of camping in swamps. Physical discomfort aside, there is a job to be done, and as long as the dig lasts, that job is imminent, pervasive, and all-consuming. The dig animates the soul like a perpetual adrenaline explosion driven by the fear of the possibility of leaving an artifact undiscovered.

Homesickness, culture shock, discomfort, and obsession pale beside the need to live as a social human being. So the dig becomes something like high school run on fast forward. Couples fall in and out of love with the same certainty that a 40-pound metate will fall when dropped into a pit. Some people are popular, some are not. Cliques form and reform in a world that has shrunk from thousands to 20 people. A world in which each and every social exchange, word, look, or touch is magnified far beyond its social weight in the now lost horizons of pre-dig life. Time stretches and snaps back into a nanospace, like Alice, of Alice in Wonderland, down the rabbit hole. The hour of humiliation when a student drops and breaks the most important pot in the collection lasts a hundred years. And that last day, when good-byes must be said to the greatest love of a lifetime, feelings dissolve faster than drinking a glass of homemade lemonade on a hot day. A whole lifetime is lived in an average six-week field session in which each week becomes a decade and social perceptions are wired up so high it is a wonder student digs do not end in a massive electrical storm.

On the student dig, even if ever so fleetingly, the heights and depths that life can offer will be experienced. No, this is not an exaggeration. Seriousness of outcome does not correlate with depth of feeling. If it did, nobody would ever make it past childhood. It is the closest thing to knowing the true expanse of human nature, short of going to war. Or until the next dig.

Yet, when it is over, the necessary *rite of passage* that all wanna-be archaeologists must go through is completed. The first dig. And even if it is the last dig, it will be an experience in social learning that will never be forgotten. It could also be that first little opening of Earth's crust with a Marshalltown that awakens a fierce and permanent curiosity about the great expanse of the human past.

This unit is presented in order to facilitate the ability to experience archaeology from the inside out through literature written by archaeologists and/or writers about archaeological experiences. The articles chosen range from straightforward autobiographical reporting to satirically presented truths about the experience of doing archaeology.

Literature is a rich and often ignored resource for the teaching of archaeology. Used carefully, it can put the sensory experience back into archaeology without sensationalism. Archaeology involves sensation; it is made of the gooey stuff that is being dug through, the touch of a hand on that million-year-old hand ax. The sound, for a moment, of the distant and rhythmic ringing of the flakes being chipped away from this ancient tool. The quick turn of the head to catch the sound again in the wind, but it is gone. The really lucky ones might know that one ecstatic moment of oneness with that ancient cultural being.

Looking Ahead: Challenge Questions

What was Mary Leakey's role in the discovery of "Zinjanthropus"? What was the importance of this discovery?

Under what circumstances did Donald Johanson discover "Lucy"? What was the significance of this discovery?

Why do you think modern people continue to be so fascinated with Neanderthals?

What are the possible relationships between modern humans and Neanderthals?

What relationship between these two forms of humans does Jean Auel present (see "The Clan of the Cave Bear")?

Why is Jean Auel's novel about humans and Neanderthals a commentary on racism?

The Beginning of a Partnership

Mary Leakey

It was Gertrude Caton-Thompson who introduced me to Louis. She was pleased with the drawings I had produced for her Fayoum book and was anxious to further my career in any way she could. I am not sure whether she knew that Louis was specifically looking for a draughtsman to produce illustrations for the popular book *Adam's Ancestors* that he had recently started writing, or whether she thought perhaps he could use my services in due course. In any case she thought it would be good for me to meet him and a few other leading figures of the archaeological world on the occasion when Louis was to give a lecture at the Royal Anthropological Institute in Bedford Square. Plenty of interesting people would be there, for Leakey had caused quite a stir with the expeditions he had already made to East Africa, and with his discoveries of early Palaeolithic material and even of remains of early Man himself. One of the most notable finds was the Kanam jaw, which had received wide publicity and about which there had been only very recently a special meeting of the Institute's human biology section in Cambridge. This lecture was to be about his work in Africa and would probably even mention that remote place Olduvai Gorge, which he had succeeded in reaching. So Gertrude invited me to the lecture as her guest and of course I gladly accepted. Further, being herself a leading member of the Institute by virtue of her own achievements, she arranged that we should both attend the dinner that followed the lecture, with the speaker as the chief guest, and she even arranged that I sat next to him.

It would have been appropriately romantic to think that I fell dramatically in love, there and then, at first sight; but it simply was not so. I liked Louis and talked a lot to him, and it did seem a little odd that he was directing so much of his conversation to me when there were more senior and important people there. But I thought little of it. He did indeed ask me to help him with the *Adam's Ancestors* drawings, and of course I delightedly agreed and we made some arrangement for me to collect the specimens, but again I cannot recall what it was. And that was really all there was to it at that stage.

In that can be seen my complete naïvety and preoccupation with prehistoric archaeology at the time; I was just 20 years old. My mother was certainly beginning to get restive about finding me someone suitable to marry. She had occasionally sent me to a dance, partnered by one or another young man who in her view fell into the 'suitable' class. I cannot recall the name of a single one, and I classified them all as spotty youths. I had nothing against men in general, and got on splendidly with people like Thurstan, but my mother's attempts to start me on boyfriends as such were if anything counter-productive. Louis was ten years older than I, fully mature and an established and experienced archaeologist. Moreover he had a taste for wild places, working in the field, and being alone among wild animals about which he knew a great deal: all things that appealed to me. Above all he seemed from the very start, like Gertrude herself, to treat me as an equal and a colleague to be consulted. How could I fail to like him? My naïvety concealed from me two things that were relevant, and which were known to many others. Firstly, Louis had throughout his life that powerful if indefinable quality of attractiveness to women that is perhaps ultimately a matter of chemistry. Secondly, he was certainly on the lookout at this moment for the solace of a new girlfriend in whom he could confide, because his marriage to his first wife, Frida, was proving to be from his point of view a complete failure, notwithstanding the birth of their daughter Priscilla in 1931, or their recent move to a larger house in Cambridge, or even the fact that Frida was in the earliest stages of expecting a second child. In fact I knew later that Louis had several girlfriends at about this time, though they all melted away over the next few months. My commitment to the *Adam's Ancestors* drawings would certainly have assured Louis that he could count on seeing me regularly for some while to come, if his first impressions were indeed as favourable as they seemed, but the drawings were a quite separate issue and he would undoubtedly have commissioned me to do them for him whatever he had thought of me. Soon afterwards I went with Miss Liddell to the Meon Hill excavation, with my innocence intact and also with some African hand axes to draw in my spare time in the evenings. They presented a pleasing challenge because they were made of volcanic rocks, not flint, and their different surface texture demanded quite a change of technique.

The Meon Hill dig was a summer one, and in Britain the end of the summer is a time when various annual meetings and conferences occur. One body that has a large gathering at this time is the British Association for the Advancement of Science. It selects some suitable centre, usually a city or town that has a university and a surrounding region of varied interest, and there a conference is held for a week or a fortnight with many sections, including geology and archaeology. There are excursions, scientific sessions and the usual social events: quite an occasion, and more so in the 1930s perhaps than now, rising costs having somewhat changed the nature of the event. In 1933 the British Association had its meeting at Leicester, and there Louis and I met again.

Because of my work on the drawings we had corresponded throughout the summer, but we had not actually met. Were his letters perhaps just a little more frequent than was strictly necessary? I always replied at once, and the correspondence was certainly friendly, with minor exchanges of news as well as details concerned with the drawings, but if it had a pleasant warmth it had nothing further. It was, in fact, quite independently that I decided to go to the meeting at Leicester. No doubt Louis had mentioned that he would be there, but I had no preconceived plans concerning him when I set out. Yet from the time we met up soon after our arrivals we became inseparable companions, and it was here that I first felt and instinctively recognized something that was new to me: the mental stimulus and physical thrill of having Louis with me. Yet no proprieties were breached. Louis lived in one set of conference accommodations and

I in another: to these we returned separately each evening, and our final farewell was entirely proper. But it was clearly understood between us that we would meet again, soon and frequently.

As summer drew on into autumn, Louis found more and more material for me to draw, some of which was to appear in later books, since *Adam's Ancestors* was nearly complete. The relevant material was at the British Museum in Bloomsbury, and there we used to go so that I could work on it, in a room that was also occupied by Sir Thomas Kendrick and Christopher Hawkes, both members of the Department of British and Mediaeval Antiquities ('British' having the archaic special meaning of 'belonging to the Ancient Britons'). There I worked, and Louis would look in from time to time so that inevitably the nature of our relationship became clear to the other two occupants of the room, both of whom were to become major names in British Archaeology. Christopher Hawkes chose to turn a blind eye, or at least not to interfere, but Tom Kendrick, who was the senior of the two, felt it incumbent upon himself to do something. He was clearly worried for me, assuming that I was simply dazzled by Louis and that I might well be hurt, which was kind of him. So one day he invited me to lunch as his guest at the old Holborn Restaurant, which has long since disappeared, and he set himself to open my eyes and warn me. The one sentence of his that sticks in my mind referred to Louis: 'Genius is akin to madness, Mary: you must be careful.' Those were his words, and there was much more along the same lines; but he might as well have saved his breath for all the notice I took.

Inevitably it was not long before my mother found out what was afoot, and naturally it shook her to the core and upset her beyond measure. It is one thing to hope that your daughter will attach herself by a bond of fondness to a suitable young man and end up married to a charming, distinguished and possibly wealthy husband, but quite another matter when she takes the whole thing into her own hands and forms an attachment to a married man

ten years older than herself. In fact the ten years difference would not have mattered in the least to my mother, since my father had been just that much older than her. But she simply could not stand Louis and mistrusted his stability, even when she had met him. That event was not long delayed, for during that autumn he began to come to Fulham Road to take me away for weekends. So my mother remained in a state of total dismay and set herself to change my mind, right up to the time Louis and I got married; and even after that she never really reconciled herself to the situation. My aunts too, so often my allies in the past, were quite against the whole thing from the moment they got to hear about it. My grandmother never heard the news at all. She was getting very old, and they rightly decided to keep it from her.

One of the visits that Louis and I made together during that autumn was to Cambridge, and he took me to meet his wife. That may sound like the most foolhardy undertaking, especially when I add that I was taken actually to stay at their house, The Close, at Girton just outside Cambridge. I stayed there for something like a week. Officially, I was going with Louis to see the remainder of his African collection, and to learn about certain aspects of palaeontology in connection with my assistance to him in preparing his various publications. What was more natural than that the young colleague, who could hardly afford hotel accommodation, should be invited to stay at the host's own home? In any case, Frida Leakey had become used to erratic behaviour by her husband, who was working extremely hard, as he always did, and kept unconventional hours. Louis was at this time a Research Fellow at St. John's College, and in that capacity had rooms there in New Court, just across the famous Bridge of Sighs. He would often work late and decide to sleep there instead of going home, and apart from that he made frequent trips to the Royal College of Surgeons in London, to work on material relevant to his studies of human evolution. This he had been accustomed to do for some while before he met me, and there, too, work and perhaps other attractions would sometimes detain him. I recall that during this week he quite suddenly disappeared for a couple of days. It seems to me that even then he and Frida were almost living separate lives. Yet I might have been any casual visitor in the home of an unremarkable Cambridge academic family. In the evenings Louis used to teach me string figures ('cat's-cradles'), which remained a hobby of his and later on to a lesser extent became one of mine: at one time I could do sixty or seventy different ones, mainly of African or Eskimo origin.

Thus would the scene at Girton have appeared to any onlooker. But when Louis and I were alone in his rooms in College we might have been two quite different people. Tension mounted until on a day when the atmosphere was almost electric he told me, quite suddenly, that he now knew the one thing he wanted was to end his marriage to Frida and marry me. I cannot remember exactly what I replied, if indeed I heard myself speak. Such a thing had simply not entered my head and I felt more a sense of shock than of exhilaration. Eventually I managed to gasp out something that I intended as acquiescence and he clearly understood it as such. After that for some moments neither of us was really in a position to speak at all.

With this understanding between us, the course of events became inevitable, though not particularly rapid as it turned out. Immediately, during the late autumn and the winter, we began to spend weekends together regularly, in spite of my mother's protestations. And from his point of view, if, in the 1930s, one had decided to get oneself divorced, adultery was the only practical means to achieve one's end.

There can be no doubt that Louis felt bad over the way he was treating Frida, and it would be quite wrong to suppose that he had no thought at all for her feelings. Things were complicated by the fact that she was expecting their second child. I think that even before the baby, his son Colin, was born on 13 December 1933, Louis had made the act of separation by moving completely from The Close to his rooms in College, and Frida perhaps knew that he had no intention of returning. But of me he still said nothing, and he waited until the new baby had settled in before he confessed the true situation. Frida was every bit as furious as any wife would be, and indeed she was fully entitled to be. She summoned us both to The Close and told us with admirable clarity exactly what she thought of each of us. I do not remember her words clearly enough to quote them, but the upshot was that Louis was a cad and a traitor to her and to his own children, while I was a worthless hussy, utterly lacking any moral sense, who had seduced him. She then walked out of the room. Louis and I heard her out—I was not, thank goodness, required to undergo the ordeal alone—but the only conclusion we ultimately drew was that she did not wish to see either of us again and that we could therefore proceed along our chosen path and take the consequences.

Frida's friends in Cambridge were soon informed. The whole story quickly became widely known there, and no one, without exception, had a good word to say for either of us. This was naturally a far more serious matter for Louis than for me, for I had little connection with the world of Cambridge. But there was one very saddening consequence for myself, which was that I lost the regard and friendship of Gertrude Caton-Thompson, and indeed I really only fully regained them towards the end of Louis's life and after his death. This was a heavy blow. Gertrude, who had a Fellowship at Newnham College and lived in Cambridge, knew Frida at least as well as she knew Louis, and Frida told her the story directly. Gertrude, for all that she was entirely blameless, was absolutely appalled at the terrible consequences of her act of kindness in introducing me to Louis, and she felt, understandably, that I had betrayed her. She now did her level best to get me to turn back, urging among other arguments the effect that it was all likely to have on Louis's parents out in Kenya. They were missionaries; Canon Harry Leakey and his wife Mary, the gentlest and finest of people, and in 1933 just retired from active service and about to come to England to visit Louis and his family. Yet even Gertrude's appeal to me fell on deaf ears. I had no intention of turning back for anyone, and nor had Louis.

I have never before told this whole story in such detail, and I hope and believe that my account is as accurate as I can make it. In its origins and also in its development, both up to this point and later, the whole affair was intimately mixed up with the progress of my incipient career as an archaeologist. Without the latter, none of it could or would have happened. I can now, not without relief, let the archaeology for a while become the dominant theme of the story. For 1934, after this somewhat torrid start, was to see a good deal of progress under that heading. For much of the time Louis was with me and he also gave me a good deal of useful advice and practical help. That, of course, was as between archaeologists. When his parents arrived in England later in the year, Louis had inevitably to tell them that he and Frida had separated; but somehow he managed to conceal my existence from them entirely. The news of the broken marriage was a heavy enough blow to them by itself.

My fieldwork in 1934 was at Hembury in the spring, at Swanscombe in midsummer and at Jaywick near Clacton in the early autumn, where I directed my own dig for the first time. Because the finds at Olduvai over the past 25 years have been so exciting, many people seem to think of me as entirely a Palaeolithic archaeologist. In fact I have worked on sites ranging in time from the Miocene fossil beds of West Kenya, something like 18 million years old, to those belonging to the African Iron Age of just a few centuries ago, and I have become deeply involved at one time or another with problems that interested me in virtually every period. It has always been the existence of a fascinating problem or an interesting body of material, regardless of age, that has provided my motivation—not dedication to any single period.

I was conscious that the 1934 season at Hembury was my last training excavation, for the work at Jaywick was already firmly planned, so I gathered all the experience I could. Thurstan was there again, being by now an undergraduate at Cambridge, and he knew Louis too; he recalls visiting him at St John's and Louis showing him something he had never seen before; hand axes of the same types as the flint ones in Britain and France, but made from African volcanic rocks. This greatly impressed Thurstan, whose own thoughts had already turned in the direction of Africa: Louis was able to open his eyes to the enormous possibilities that African archaeology held. Louis and I each separately confided in Thurstan, telling him what had happened to us and what our intentions were for the future. Notwithstanding his upbringing at the Devonshire vicarage, Thurstan says that he was far more intrigued than shocked, and this is worth mentioning because we were so used to universal condemnation as each new person came to hear the story. Louis would come down to Hembury and spirit me away for weekends. Dorothy Liddell liked him, and watched with approval and deep interest when on one visit he gave a demonstration of flint-knapping. Thurstan has a vivid memory of Louis standing on top of one of the Hembury ramparts, with a great block of flint at his feet. Knapping had early become a special skill of Louis's and throughout his life he loved to demonstrate it: he was an eagerly anticipated sideshow at many an international conference, and sometimes the demonstration included butchery of some animal with stone tools he had just made. Now that it was spring our weekends were no longer spent at pretty country pubs or little boarding houses, but camping with our own small tent, just big enough for two, here and there in the beautiful unspoilt places of southwest England. Louis did the cooking (another special enthusiasm and real skill of his) and we would walk to look at hill-forts, or find foxes or other animals to watch, which reminded me of the *causse* at Cabrerets. Could that really be only eight years ago?

In 1934 too, we both worked at Swanscombe. It was really Louis's dig in which I joined, not only to help him and be with him, but also to gain experience and information directly relevant to my own dig, which was soon to begin at Jaywick. The main work was done by undergraduates from Cambridge, chosen by Louis, and they camped at the site. Louis and I made frequent visits, together or independently, and many other people came to see the work, including some who were already, or soon afterwards became, well known in British Palaeolithic studies. One blazing hot day Tom Kendrick came down from the British Museum, with Christopher Hawkes and his wife Jacquetta. Another visitor was the amateur archaeologist A. T. Marston, who the following year found the first fragments of the famous Swanscombe hominid skull. The skull itself was found at Barnfield Pit, which we visited briefly in 1934, but our own work was at another gravel pit nearby. Louis was hoping to solve certain problems concerning the nature of the so-called 'Clactonian' industries of the British Lower Palaeolithic, but the operation was no more than a moderate success and Louis never got round to publishing the results as they were more or less superseded by those from my own dig at Jaywick.

I had become interested in the Clactonian myself through Louis, and it was in the cause of solving some of the same problems that my own project had been planned. Jaywick is adjacent to Clacton, in Essex, where Clactonian material had first been discovered. Because Clacton was a favourite English holiday resort, certain areas of land that could be expected to yield good archaeological and geological information were rapidly being built over, as estates of seaside bungalows and chalets spread, so the dig had an element of urgency about it.

The work at Jaywick was to be mine and Kenneth Oakley's, whom I had first met during my brief stay at Wheeler's dig at St. Albans. At this time he held a post in the Geological Survey, though he was afterwards to spend most of his working life at the British Museum of Natural History. At the time of which I am writing, one of his special projects concerned the Pleistocene geology of the Lower Thames Valley, and hence arose his particular interest in Clacton. Kenneth himself had little training in archaeological excavation while I had little specialist knowledge of Pleistocene geology, so our roles at Jaywick were complementary to one another.

During the reconnaissance stages, Kenneth and I went down a number of times to discuss the site over picnic lunches with S. Hazzledine Warren and his wife. Hazzledine Warren, usually called 'Hazzy' by his friends, was a charming man and a most gifted amateur archaeologist, well respected far beyond his home county of Essex. He had studied the Clacton site since as long ago as 1910 and had made most of the important finds himself. These picnics were delightful, but I still shudder at the memory of Mrs Warren's 'Camp' coffee. Most of Warren's best Clactonian sites lay on the foreshore and could only be examined at low tide, so no conventional form of archaeological excavation was possible. We, however, were to dig a little way inland, where we knew that an extension of the deposits lay. It was not a large operation, but it was a successful one. We had about four labourers, I think, and a few undergraduate assistants, of whom Thurstan gladly agreed to be one. My mother came down and kept house for me and some of the others in a seaside bungalow, and clearly enjoyed doing so, and the arrangement had the additional bonus that I need not be parted from my dogs. Louis came for weekends, and so did Kenneth Oakley.

As the dig progressed we found some good faunal remains. In particular, I remember the uncovering of the largest elephant tooth yet discovered in Britain; a fine and complete specimen. I had never before seen an elephant tooth, and although it was so obviously something very particular I was quite unable to identify it—rather a loss of face for the young Director! Fortunately Louis turned up while we were considering the problem and not only identified it but also helped us to lift it undamaged by encasing it in a plaster-of-Paris jacket.

The Clacton dig was a very happy occasion, and the technical report on it was published, in the *Proceedings of the Prehistoric Society* for 1937, jointly by Kenneth Oakley and myself. It was my first publication. Had I remained in England, I am sure we would have had other seasons there. The finds were good and we lived well in our simple way, thanks largely to my mother's cooking. I remember with particular pleasure a special kind of mushroom that grew in early autumn among the tufts of grass not far from the sea. We loved them, all except one member of the team—Kenneth Oakley, who sometimes could be extremely fussy. It seemed that this was not the kind of mushroom that grew where he lived, and nothing would make him try them. This was the only time I ever worked directly in the field with Kenneth, but I always kept in touch with him and visited him when in England during his later years. He made many outstanding contributions to archaeology and was one of those responsible for unmasking the Piltdown fraud.

With the end of the season at Jaywick came a turning point in both my life and career. Louis had succeeded in raising money for his next East African expedition, his fourth, and he was to leave by boat in October, taking with him three young assistants, Peter Kent (later Sir Peter Kent) as geologist, Sam White as surveyor and Peter Bell as ornithologist. One of the main reasons why Louis had received generous financial support for this trip was his previous spectacular success in discovering hominid fossils at Kanjera and Kanam in 1932. But certain doubts had since arisen over the age and status claimed by Louis for the famous Kanam mandible in particular, and among the other aims of the expedition, Louis was to conduct Professor Percy Boswell to the Kanjera and Kanam find-spots in January 1935 to check the relevant evidence. In fact it all turned out disastrously for Louis, who was shown in Boswell's subsequent report to have made unfortunate and unavoidable errors, through experience, during his 1932 fieldwork, although some of the errors of which he was accused were due to circumstances beyond his control.

So Louis left in October 1934, but before he did so we made an arrangement that I should join him in April 1935 in Tanzania. By then Louis would have finished the first part of the expedition, and would be ready to go again to Olduvai Gorge. On the basis of his previous visit, Olduvai clearly seemed to offer the greatest potential for exciting early Palaeolithic discoveries anywhere in East Africa, and therefore perhaps anywhere in the world. He wanted me with him, and from the descriptions he had given me I could hardly wait to see Olduvai. Meanwhile, I was not to be left kicking my heels for five or six months in the Fulham Road. My mother had not been won over by Louis, not even in the happy atmosphere of the Jaywick dig, and she still had aspirations of getting him out of my mind and indeed out of my life. It was therefore arranged that she and I should go in January for a visit to South Africa and Zimbabwe (then Southern Rhodesia), where we would see prehistoric sites and also some of the other tourist attractions. No doubt my mother hoped that with Louis out of sight and out of reach I would find other attractions and come to my senses, and that when April came she would bring me safely home with her. From my point of view it would be an easy enough journey in April from Zimbabwe to Tanzania, and much quicker than going from London. Louis gave us various introductions for use on our arrival in Cape Town, and I looked forward to the trip with excitement and a light heart. My mother ended our rental of the Fulham Road flat, and she and I moved with the dogs for a short stay in a flat in Hamilton House, near Hyde Park Corner, for the final period of preparation. January 1935 came at last, and while Louis was having a difficult time at Kanjera and Kanam, my mother and I, having left the two dogs in safe hands, joined a Union Castle liner at Tilbury and set out via St. Helena for Cape Town and, more importantly, for Africa.

Lucy

The Beginnings of Humankind

Don Johanson
and Maitland A. Edey

Prologue

In some older strata do the fossilized bones of an ape more anthropoid (manlike) or a man more pithecoid (apelike) than any yet known await the researches of some unborn paleontologist?

T.H. Huxley

On the morning of November 30, 1974, I woke, as I usually do on a field expedition, at daybreak. I was in Ethiopia, camped on the edge of a small muddy river, the Awash, at a place called Hadar, about a hundred miles northeast of Addis Ababa. I had been there for several weeks, acting as a coleader of a group of scientists looking for fossils.

For a few minutes I lay in my tent, looking up at the canvas above me, black at first but quickly turning to green as the sun shot straight up beyond the rim of hills off to the east. Close to the Equator the sun does that; there is no long dawn as there is at home in the United States. It was still relatively cool, not more than 80 degrees. The air had the unmistakable crystalline smell of early morning on the desert, faintly touched with the smoke of cooking fires. Some of the Afar tribesmen who worked for the expedition had brought their families with them, and there was a small compound of dome-shaped huts made of sticks and grass mats about two hundred yards from the main camp. The Afar women had been up before daylight, tending their camels and goats, talking quietly.

For most of the Americans in camp this was the best part of the day. The rocks and boulders that littered the landscape had bled away most of their heat during the night and no longer felt like stoves when you stood next to one of them. I stepped out of the tent and took a look at the sky. Another cloudless day; another flawless morning on the desert that would turn to a crisper later on. I washed my face and got a cup of coffee from the camp cook, Kabete. Mornings are not my favorite time. I am a slow starter and much prefer evenings and nights. At Hadar I feel best just as the sun is going down. I like to walk up one of the exposed ridges near the camp, feel the first stirrings of evening air and watch the hills turn purple. There I can sit alone for a while, think about the work of the day just ended, plan the next, and ponder the larger questions that have brought me to Ethiopia. Dry silent places are intensifiers of thought, and have been known to be since early Christian anchorites went out into the desert to face God and their own souls.

Tom Gray joined me for coffee. Tom was an American graduate student who had come out to Hadar to study the fossil animals and plants of the region, to reconstruct as accurately as possible the kinds and frequencies and relationships of what had lived there at various times in the remote past and what the climate had been like. My own target—the reason for our expedition—was hominid fossils: the bones of extinct human ancestors and their close relatives. I was interested in the evidence for human evolution. But to understand that, to interpret any hominid fossils we might find, we had to have the supporting work of other specialists like Tom.

"So, what's up for today?" I asked.

8. ARCHAEOLOGISTS AS PEOPLE

Tom said he was busy marking fossil sites on a map.

"When are you going to mark in Locality 162?"

"I'm not sure where 162 is," he said.

"Then I guess I'll have to show you." I wasn't eager to go out with Gray that morning. I had a tremendous amount of work to catch up on. We had had a number of visitors to the camp recently. Richard and Mary Leakey, two well-known experts on hominid fossils from Kenya, had left only the day before. During their stay I had not done any paperwork, any cataloguing. I had not written any letters or done detailed descriptions of any fossils. I *should* have stayed in camp that morning—but I didn't. I felt a strong subconscious urge to go with Tom, and I obeyed it. I wrote a note to myself in my daily diary: *Nov. 30, 1974. To Locality 162 with Gray in AM. Feel good.*

As a paleoanthropologist—one who studies the fossils of human ancestors—I am superstitious. Many of us are, because the work we do depends a great deal on luck. The fossils we study are extremely rare, and quite a few distinguished paleoanthropologists have gone a lifetime without finding a single one. I am one of the more fortunate. This was only my third year in the field at Hadar, and I had already found several. I know I am lucky, and I don't try to hide it. That is why I wrote "feel good" in my diary. When I got up that morning I felt it was one of those days when you should press your luck. One of those days when something terrific might happen.

Throughout most of that morning, nothing did. Gray and I got into one of the expedition's four Land-Rovers and slowly jounced our way to Locality 162. This was one of several hundred sites that were in the process of being plotted on a master map of the Hadar area, with detailed information about geology and fossils being entered on it as fast as it was obtained. Although the spot we were headed for was only about four miles from camp, it took us half an hour to get there because of the rough terrain. When we arrived it was already beginning to get hot.

At Hadar, which is a wasteland of bare rock, gravel and sand, the fossils that one finds are almost all exposed on the surface of the ground. Hadar is in the center of the Afar desert, an ancient lake bed now dry and filled with sediments that record the history of past geological events. You can trace volcanic-ash falls there, deposits of mud and silt washed down from distant mountains, episodes of volcanic dust, more mud, and so on. Those events reveal themselves like layers in a slice of cake in the gullies of new young rivers that recently have cut through the lake bed here and there. It seldom rains at Hadar, but when it does it comes in an overpowering gush—six months' worth overnight. The soil, which is bare of vegetation, cannot hold all that water. It roars down the gullies, cutting back their sides and bringing more fossils into view.

Gray and I parked the Land-Rover on the slope of one of those gullies. We were careful to face it in such a way that the canvas water bag that was hanging from the side mirror was in the shade. Gray plotted the locality on the map. Then we got out and began doing what most members of the expedition spent a great deal of their time doing: we began surveying, walking slowly about, looking for exposed fossils.

Some people are good at finding fossils. Others are hopelessly bad at it. It's a matter of practice, of training your eye to see what you need to see. I will never be as good as some of the Afar people. They spend all their time wandering around in the rocks and sand. They have to be sharp-eyed; their lives depend on it. Anything the least bit unusual they notice. One quick educated look at all those stones and pebbles, and they'll spot a couple of things a person not acquainted with the desert would miss.

Tom and I surveyed for a couple of hours. It was now close to noon, and the temperature was approaching 110. We hadn't found much: a few

teeth of the small extinct horse *Hipparion*; part of the skull of an extinct pig; some antelope molars; a bit on a monkey jaw. We had large collections of all these things already, but Tom insisted on taking these also as added pieces in the overall jigsaw puzzle of what went where.

"I've had it," said Tom. "When do we head back to camp?"

"Right now. But let's go back this way and survey the bottom of that little gully over there."

The gully in question was just over the crest of the rise where we had been working all morning. It had been thoroughly checked out at least twice before by other workers, who had found nothing interesting. Nevertheless, conscious of the "lucky" feeling that had been with me since I woke, I decided to make that small final detour. There was virtually no bone in the gully. But as we turned to leave, I noticed something lying on the ground partway up the slope.

"That's a bit of a hominid arm," I said.

"Can't be. It's too small. Has to be a monkey of some kind."

We knelt to examine it.

"Much too small," said Gray again.

I shook my head. "Hominid."

"What makes you so sure?" he said.

"That piece right next to your hand. That's hominid too."

"Jesus Christ," said Gray. He picked it up. It was the back of a small skull. A few feet away was part of a femur: a thighbone. "Jesus Christ," he said again. We stood up, and began to see other bits of bone on the slope: a couple of vertebrae, part of a pelvis—all of them hominid. An unbelievable, impermissible thought flickered through my mind. Suppose all these fitted together? Could they be parts of a single, extremely primitive skeleton? No such skeleton had ever been found—anywhere.

"Look at that," said Gray. "Ribs."

A single individual?

"I can't believe it," I said. "I just can't believe it."

"By God, you'd better believe it!" shouted Gray. "Here it is. Right here!" His voice went up into a howl. I joined him. In that 110-degree heat we began jumping up and down. With nobody to share our feelings, we hugged each other, sweaty and smelly, howling and hugging in the heat-shimmering gravel, the small brown remains of what now seemed almost certain to be parts of a single hominid skeleton lying all around us.

"We've got to stop jumping around," I finally said. "We may step on something. Also, we've got to make sure."

"Aren't you sure, for Christ's sake?"

"I mean, suppose we find two left legs. There may be several individuals here, all mixed up. Let's play it cool until we can come back and make absolutely sure that it all fits together."

We collected a couple of pieces of jaw, marked the spot exactly and got into the blistering Land-Rover for the run back to camp. On the way we picked up two expedition geologists who were loaded down with rock samples they had been gathering.

"Something big," Gray kept saying to them. "Something big. Something *big*."

"Cool it," I said.

But about a quarter of a mile from camp, Gray could not cool it. He pressed his thumb on the Land-Rover's horn, and the long blast brought a scurry of scientists who had been bathing in the river. "We've got it," he yelled. "Oh, Jesus, we've got it. We've got The Whole Thing!"

That afternoon everyone in camp was at the gully, sectioning off the site and preparing for a massive collecting job that ultimately took three weeks. When it was done, we had recovered several hundred pieces of bone (many of them fragments) representing about forty percent of the skeleton of a single individual. Tom's and my original hunch had been right. There was no bone duplication.

But a single individual of what? On preliminary examination it was very hard to say, for nothing quite like it had ever been discovered. The camp was rocking with excitement. That first night we never went to bed at all.

We talked and talked. We drank beer after beer. There was a tape recorder in the camp, and a tape of the Beatles song "Lucy in the Sky with Diamonds" went belting out into the night sky, and was played in full volume over and over again out of sheer exuberance. At some point during that unforgettable evening—I no longer remember exactly when—the new fossil picked up the name of Lucy, and has been so known ever since, although its proper name—its acquisition number in the Hadar collection—is AL 288-1.

"Lucy?"

That is the question I always get from somebody who sees the fossil for the first time. I have to explain: "Yes, she was a female. And that Beatles song. We were sky-high, you must remember, from finding her."

Then comes the question: "How did you know she was a female?"

"From her pelvis. We had one complete pelvic bone and her sacrum. Since the pelvic opening in hominids has to be proportionally larger in females than in males to allow for the birth of large-brained infants, you can tell a female."

And the next: "She was a hominid?"

Oh, yes. She walked erect. She walked as well as you do."

"Hominids all walked erect?"

"Yes."

"Just exactly what is a hominid?"

That usually ends the questions, because that one has no simple answer. Science has had to leave the definition rather flexible because we do not yet know exactly when hominids first appeared. However, it is safe to say that a hominid is an erect-walking primate. That is, it is either an extinct ancestor to man,* a collateral relative to man, or a true man. All human beings are hominids, but not all hominids are human beings.

We can picture human evolution as starting with a primitive ape-like type that gradually, over a long period of time, began to be less and less apelike and more manlike. There was no

*In this book the general term "man" is used to include both males and females of the genus *Homo*.

abrupt crossover from ape to human, but probably a rather fuzzy time of in-between types that would be difficult to classify either way. We have no fossils yet that tell us what went on during that in-between time. Therefore, the handiest way of separating the newer types from their ape ancestors is to lump together all those that stood up on their hind legs. That group of men and near-men is called hominids.

I am a hominid. I am a human being. I belong to the genius *Homo* and to the species *sapiens:* thinking man. Perhaps I should say wise or knowing man—a man who is smart enough to recognize that he is a man. There have been other species of *Homo* who were not so smart, ancestors now extinct. *Homo sapiens* began to emerge a hundred thousand—perhaps two or three hundred thousand—years ago, depending on how one regards Neanderthal Man. He was another *Homo.* Some think he was the same species as ourselves. Others think he was an ancestor. There are a few who consider him a kind of cousin. That matter is unsettled because many of the best Neanderthal fossils were collected in Europe before anybody knew how to excavate sites properly or get good dates. Consequently, we do not have exact ages for most of the Neanderthal fossils in collections.

I consider Neanderthal conspecific with *sapiens*, with myself. One hears talk about putting him in a business suit and turning him loose in the subway. It is true; one could do it and he would never be noticed. He was just a little heavier-boned than people today, more primitive in a few facial features. But he was a man. His brain was as big as a modern man's, but shaped in a slightly different way. Could he make change at the subway booth and recognize a token? He certainly could. He could do many things more complicated than that. He was doing them over much of Europe, Africa and Asia as long as sixty or a hundred thousand years ago.

Neanderthal Man had ancestors, human ones. Before him in time was a less advanced type: *Homo erectus.* Put him on the subway and people would probably take a suspicious look at him. Before *Homo erectus* was a really primitive type, *Homo habilis;* put him on the subway and people would probably move to the other end of the car. Before *Homo habilis* the human line may run out entirely. The next stop in the past, back of *Homo habilis,* might be something like Lucy.

All of the above are hominids. They are all erect walkers. Some were human, even though they were of exceedingly primitive types. Others were not human. Lucy was not. No matter what kind of clothes were put on Lucy, she would not look like a human being. She was too far back, out of the human range entirely. That is what happens going back along an evolutionary line. If one goes back far enough, one finds oneself dealing with a different kind of creature. On the hominid line the earliest ones are too primitive to be called humans. They must be given another name. Lucy is in that category.

For five years I kept Lucy in a safe in my office in the Cleveland Museum of Natural History. I had filled a wide shallow box with yellow foam padding, and had cut depressions in the foam so that each of her bones fitted into its own tailor-made nest. *Everybody* who came to the Museum—it seemed to me—wanted to see Lucy. What surprised people most was her small size.

Her head, on the evidence of the bits of her skull that had been recovered, was not much larger than a softball. Lucy herself stood only three and one-half feet tall, although she was fully grown. That could be deduced from her wisdom teeth, which were fully erupted and had been exposed to several years of wear. My best guess was that she was between twenty-five and thirty years old when she died. She had already begun to show the onset of arthritis or some other bone ailment, on the evidence of deformation of her vertebrae. If she had lived much longer, it probably would have begun to bother her.

Her surprisingly good condition— her completeness—came from the

fact that she had died quietly. There were no tooth marks on her bones. They had not been crunched and splintered, as they would have been if she had been killed by a lion or a saber-toothed cat. Her head had not been carried off in one direction and her legs in another, as hyenas might have done with her. She had simply settled down in one piece right where she was, in the sand of a long-vanished lake edge or stream—and died. Whether from illness or accidental drowning, it was impossible to say. The important thing was that she had not been found by a predator just after death and eaten. Her carcass had remained inviolate, slowly covered by sand or mud, buried deeper and deeper, the sand hardening into rock under the weight of subsequent depositions. She had lain silently in her adamantine grave for millennium after millennium until the rains at Hadar had brought her to light again.

That was where I was unbelievably lucky. If I had not followed a hunch that morning with Tom Gray, Lucy might never have been found. Why the other people who looked there did not see her, I do not know. Perhaps they were looking in another direction. Perhaps the light was different. Sometimes one person sees things that another misses, even though he may be looking directly at them. If I had not gone to Locality 162 that morning, nobody might have bothered to go back for a year, maybe five years. Hadar is a big place, and there is a tremendous amount to do. If I had waited another few years, the next rains might have washed many of her bones down the gully. They would have been lost, or at least badly scattered; it would not have been possible to establish that they belonged together. What was utterly fantastic was that she had come to the surface so recently, probably in the last year or two. Five years earlier, she still would have been buried. Five years later, she would have been gone. As it was, the front of her skull was already gone, washed away somewhere. We never did find it.

Consequently, the one thing we really cannot measure accurately is the size of her brain.

Lucy always managed to look interesting in her little yellow nest—but to a nonprofessional, not overly impressive. There were other bones all around her in the Cleveland Museum. She was dwarfed by them, by drawer after drawer of fossils, hundreds of them from Hadar alone. There were casts of hominid specimens from East Africa, from South Africa and Asia. There were antelope and pig skulls, extinct rodents, rabbits and monkeys, as well as apes. There were one of the largest collections of gorilla skulls in the world. In that stupefying array of bones, I kept being asked, What was so special about Lucy? Why had she, as another member of the expedition put it, "blown us out of our little anthropological minds for months"?

"Three things," I always answered. "First: what she is—or isn't. She is different from anything that has been discovered and named before. She doesn't fit anywhere. She is just a very old, very primitive, very small hominid. Somehow we are going to have to fit her in, find a name for her.

"Second," I would say, "is her completeness. Until Lucy was found, there just weren't any very old skeletons. The oldest was one of those Neanderthalers I spoke of a little while ago. It is about seventy-five thousand years old. Yes, there *are* older hominid fossils, but they are all fragments. Everything that has been reconstructed from them has had to be done by matching up those little pieces—a tooth here, a bit of jaw there, maybe a complete skull from somewhere else, plus a leg bone from some other place. The fitting together has been done by scientists who know those bones as well as I know my own hand. And yet, when you consider that such a reconstruction may consist of pieces from a couple of dozen individuals who may have lived hundreds of miles apart and may have been separated from each other by a hundred thousand years in time— well, when you look at the complete individual you've just put together you have to say to yourself, 'Just how real is he?' With Lucy you know. It's all there. You don't have to guess. You don't have to imagine an arm bone you haven't got. You *see* it. You see it for the first time from something older than a Neanderthaler."

"How much older?"

"That's point number three. The Neanderthaler is seventy-five thousand years old. Lucy is approximately 3.5 million years old. She is the oldest, most complete, best-preserved skeleton of any erect-walking human ancestor that has ever been found."

That is the significance of Lucy: her completeness and her great age. They make her unique in the history of hominid fossil collecting. She is easy to describe, and—as will be seen— she makes a number of anthropological problems easier to work out. But exactly what is she?

Unique Lucy may be, but she is incomprehensible outside the context of other fossils. She becomes meaningless unless she is fitted into a scheme of hominid evolution and scientific logic that has been laboriously pieced together over more than a century by hundreds of specialists from four continents. Their fossil finds, their insights—sometimes inspired, sometimes silly—their application of techniques from such faraway disciplines as botany, nuclear physics and microbiology have combined to produce an increasingly clear and rich picture of man's emergence from the apes—a story that is finally, in the ninth decade of this century, beginning to make some sense. That story could not even begin to be told, of course, until Charles Darwin suggested in 1857 that we *were* descended from apes and not divinely created in 4004 B.C., as the Church insisted. But not even Darwin could have suspected some of the odd turns the hominid story would take. Nor could he have guessed which apes we are descended from. Indeed, we are not entirely sure about that even today.

A Novel Notion of Neanderthal

"Human unity is no idle political slogan or tenet of mushy romanticism"

Stephen Jay Gould

Stephen Jay Gould teaches biology, geology, and the history of science at Harvard University.

I am not insensible to the great American myth of wide-open western spaces (nurtured, in my formative experience, primarily by the closed domains of Hollywood backlots used for sets of B movies). Still, as a New Yorker now resident in New England, I tend to side with Frost on the correlation between good fences and good neighbors. Nonetheless, I must admit that, once in a while, the folks next door can actually outdo a resident on his own turf. I prefer T. H. Huxley or Charles Lyell—strictly as literature—to many Victorian novelists. Conversely, I regard one important area of my own profession as better enlightened by novelists than by scientists.

Science is constrained by its canons of evidence. Pure speculation, however reined by plausibility or pregnant with insight, does not lie within the rules of our game. But novelists are free, like Milton's "L'Allegro," the embodiment of good cheer:

> Come, and trip it as ye go
> On the light fantastic toe;
> And, in thy right hand lead with thee
> The mountain nymph, sweet Liberty.

(I was as happy as the namesake of this poem when I first read these lines during a dull college course, for they resolved one of those little puzzles that weighs, however lightly, on the intellect. I had never understood how you could "trip the light fantastic on the sidewalks of New York" because, in my streetwise parochialism, I had always pictured a traffic beacon.)

Many crucial events in life's history have provided no direct data for their resolution. Yet the art of plausible reconstruction has value to science because we must have frameworks to discipline our thoughts. Writers of fiction can enlighten us in this treacherous domain. No event so poor in evidence has so strongly captured our imagination as the meeting of Neanderthal and Cro-Magnon people in Europe some 30,000 years ago. The people of Cro-Magnon carved intricate figures of horses and deer and painted their caves with an esthetic power never exceeded in the history of human art. Some Neanderthals buried their dead with ceremony and may have adorned their bodies with ocher, but they had no concept (so far as we can tell) of representational art. We feel that something fundamental about our origin, and our "essence," must lie hidden in the character of this contact between our ancestors and our closest collateral relatives. But we have no data at all beyond the temporal and geographic overlap. We do not know if they murdered each other or met with the equivalent of a Paleolithic handshake, ignored each other or interbred.

This combination of fascination and mystery has spawned a minor industry of novel writing—from William Golding (*The Inheritors*), who explored another aspect of human nature in *Lord of the Flies*, to more recent works of the Finnish paleontologist and novelist Bjorn Jurten (*Dance of the Tiger*) and the saga of Ayla as depicted by Jean Auel (*Clan of the Cave Bear* and sequels).

Let me cite just one example, at my own expense, of the novelist's power to enlighten. In the racist tradition, all too common and often unconscious, Cro-Magnons, as modern conquerors, are usually depicted as light-skinned, Neanderthals as dark. In *Meet Your Ancestors* (1945), for example, Roy Chapman Andrews wrote of the Cro-Magnon people:

They have been called the finest physical types the world has ever produced. Probably their skins were white. In fact, if you saw a Cro-Magnon man on Fifth Avenue dressed in sack suit and a Homburg you wouldn't give him a second glance [well, you probably would these days, for his outdated apparel]. Or perhaps you might, if you were a woman, for artists depict him as a debutante's "dream man."

I had unconsciously adopted this stereotype in my mental picture of these people, but Bjorn Kurten's reconstruction explicitly depicts Neanderthal as white, Cro-Magnon as dark. This conjecture surely makes more sense—for Neanderthals were cold-adapted people living near the ice sheet of glacial Europe, while Cro-Magnons may have had a more tropical origin. Since we possess no direct data, a scientific treatise would have no basis for discussing the skin colors of these people. But a novelist is free, and Kurten's well-informed conjecture taught me something about prejudice and the hold of tradition.

For all their breadth and variation, however, one unchallenged assumption pervades the Neanderthal novels. The modes and reasons differ, but Cro-Magnons are superior, and they quickly prevail in all accounts. This contact of ca. 30,000 years ago is portrayed as the "first meeting" of primitive and advanced—and the Neanderthals rapidly succumb. Neanderthals are dazzled by the technological superiority of Cro-Magnons. Golding's primitives are awe-struck by a Cro-Magnon boat with sails, because they have never thought beyond a floating log when they needed to cross a river. Kurten's watch dumbfoundedly as a Cro-Magnon artist carves the likeness of an animal in wood. The brains of Auel's Neanderthals are so stuffed with memory that they cannot initiate anything new. Of the Cro-Magnon heroine, Ayla, Auel writes, "In nature's way, her kind was destined to supplant the ancient, dying race."

This notion of *temporal succession*—superior supplanting primitive— is common to both major theories about the biological relationship of Cro-Magnon to Neanderthal. In one view, Neanderthals represent an ancestral stage in a progressive sequence of general advance toward modern humans. (The next step to Cro-Magnon then occurs outside Europe. Neanderthals become primitive survivors in a European backwater, and the emigrating Cro-Magnons wipe them out.) In the second view, Neanderthals are a side branch, not an ancestral stock. Yet their early division from an advancing central stock guarantees their backwardness and rapid defeat. Thus, even the novelists, with the maximal range of reasonable conjecture, have never challenged the cardinal premise of conventional wisdom—that modern people arrived in Eurasia far later than primitive Neanderthals, contacted them once, and quickly prevailed.

In this context, a report by H. Valladas and five colleagues generated astonishment in press accounts throughout the world ("Thermoluminescence Dating of Mousterian 'Proto-Cro-Magnon' Remains From Israel and the Origin of Modern Man," *Nature*, February 18, 1988, pp. 614–16). Neanderthals are a Eurasian group dating from about 125,000 to 150,000 years ago, for their first known occurrence, to about 30,000 years ago, for their supposedly singular replacement by modern Cro-Magnons. Anthropologists have puzzled for a long time over a few Eurasian sites that yield anatomically modern human remains but seem to be substantially older than the canonical 30,000-year date for contact and conquest. For example, the Qafzeh caves of Israel contain anatomically modern humans in association with species of rodents usually considered to have been victims of extinction during the early days of Neanderthal in Eurasia. Nonetheless, the presumption of nonoverlap between moderns and Neanderthals (until the crucial and momentary 30,000-year replacement) has been so strong that these sites have remained in limbo, usually rationalized in the literature as "probably" 40,000 years old or less.

Valladas and colleagues have confounded this tradition by reporting a date of 90,000 years for the anatomically modern humans of Qafzeh. You might cling to the old view by arguing that the Levant is not Europe and lies close to the favored African source for modern human origins. Perhaps the Levant was a long staging ground for a western European invasion 60,000 years later. But this resolution will not work, because Israel and the Near East also house abundant and well documented remains of classical Neanderthals clearly younger than the Qafzeh moderns. Thus, the geographic potential for contact between moderns and Neanderthals must have existed for nearly 60,000 years before the novelists' western European apocalypse. Yet moderns did not supplant Neanderthals.

I must admit that I am not fully confident about the 90,000-year date for Qafzeh because the technique of thermoluminescence dating (called TL in the trade), although applied in the most modern and meticulous way by Valladas and colleagues, includes some intrinsic, theoretical uncertainty. (Press accounts, in their lamentable tradition of reporting only claims, and omitting any critical discussion of procedure and methodology, have bypassed this issue entirely—and simply reported the 90,000-year date as though it possessed the factuality of a new fossil bone. I do so wish that this tradition could be broken. Science is a methodology for the testing of claims, not a list of oracular pronouncements about the nature of nature.)

As natural materials are exposed to ionizing radiation, both from the external environment and from the breakdown of isotopes in their own composition, they accumulate energy in the form of electrons trapped at defects in the crystal lattices of their constituent minerals. When the materials are heated, these electrons are driven off, often producing a visible "puff" of light, called thermoluminescence and first reported by Robert Boyle in October 1663 after he took a diamond to bed and warmed it against his naked body. (I shall refrain from the obvious vulgarities, but must report that Boyle considered his diamond as especially sensitive because he viewed his own constitution as "not of the hottest.") TL is not the ordinary red-hot glow of conventional heating, but a distinct emission of light at lower temperature caused by release of these trapped electrons. In any case, the intensity of the TL peak might measure the age of a sample since these electrons accumulate through time.

But how could we use TL to date ancient humans? Clays and flints record their own age, not the moment of human use. Unless, of course, human use has heated the materials and released their TL, thus setting the TL clock back to zero. The subsequent accumulation of new TL will then record the time since human heating. Unsurprisingly, this method was first developed for dating pottery, since clays are fired at temperatures sufficiently high to release TL and reset the clock to zero. The method has been quite successful, but its application is neither straightforward nor unambiguous. In particular, no lawlike, universal rate governs the accumulation of TL; one has to measure the local influx of ionizing radiation from surrounding materials. This requires a firm knowledge of the postburial history of an artifact. In practice, gauges are usually buried for a year at sites where artifacts were found. The excess of an artifact's TL over this yearly dose should, in principle, determine its age.

But Neanderthals and early moderns didn't make pottery. However, they did occasionally drop flint tools and flakes into their fires. Thus, the reported TL dates at Qafzeh and other early sites are based on burned flints—and I am not entirely confident that human campfires invariably burned long enough or hot enough to reset the TL clocks to zero. However, I think that Valladas and colleagues have presented the best possible case, given intrinsic uncertainties of the method. They dated twenty flints from Qafzeh, and all fell in the narrow range of 82,400 to 109,900 years. Moreover, the associated mammalian fauna of Qafzeh, as previously mentioned, has been hinting for years that these anatomically modern humans predated the later Neanderthals of the Levant. (See M. J. Aitken, *Thermoluminescence Dating,* Academic Press, 1985. I also thank Tim White of Berkeley and John Shea of Harvard for their generous help in discussion and supplying references for several topics discussed in the essay.)

For the past thirty years or so, the main excitement in studies of human evolution has centered on discoveries about our early history—from the dawn of the first known australopithecine more than 3 million years ago, to the later transition to our own genus *Homo,* to the evolution and spread of *Homo erectus* from Africa throughout the Old World. The fascination of the opposite end—the much more recent origin of our own species, *Homo sapiens*—has received relatively little attention because no real breakthroughs have been made. This situa-

tion has changed dramatically in the last few years because two independent sources of data seem to be converging upon a firm, exciting conclusion that has been intensely surprising (but shouldn't be) to most people—*Homo sapiens* is the product of a relatively recent, discrete event of branching speciation in Africa, not the result of a continuous process of worldwide advance. The redating of Qafzeh provides a confirming link in this story—hence its status as the central item in this essay.

Genetics and paleontology are the partners of this reinterpretation. (For a good review of this important subject, see C. B. Stringer and P. Andrews, "Genetic and Fossil Evidence for the Origin of Modern Humans," *Science,* March 11, 1988, pp. 1263–68.) As discussed in my essay of June 1987, the genealogical tree of modern humans, as reconstructed from the evolution of mitochondrial DNA, contains two major branches: one with only Africans; the other with additional Africans, plus everybody else. This topology implies an African source for the most recent common ancestor. (Although origin in the Levant with multiple migrations back to Africa is not excluded, no data support this more complex reconstruction.) If we are willing to accept a constant rate for the evolution of mitochondrial DNA (unproved, but supported by data now available from other groups), then all non-African racial diversity in *Homo sapiens* is only 90,000 to 180,000 years old, while the common ancestral stock of all modern humans probably lived no more than 250,000 years ago, and perhaps a good deal more recently.

Genetic data cannot tell us what these ancestral people looked like or date their origin with certainty. Perhaps this ca. 200,000-year-old common ancestor was a brutish, small-brained fellow—and the selective blessings of mentality then promoted the evolution of modern characters in both great branches of our family tree. Only the direct evidence of paleontology can resolve this issue.

Happily, fossil data are beginning to suggest an interesting conclusion. The

oldest-known anatomically modern humans are probably the South African remains from the Klasies River caves, dated at some 80,000 to 130,000 years old. The redate of Qafzeh indicates about the same age for anatomically modern humans in the Levant. We still do not know the form of the ca. 200,000-year-old common ancestor, but if Klasies and Qafzeh are essentially us, then at least we can say that half the history of our species involves little change of anatomy. Mired in my own biases of punctuated equilibrium, I rather suspect that the 200,000-year-old forebear won't look much different from us either.

Where does this reinterpretation leave Neanderthal, who looks quite a bit different from us—not the Alley Oop caveman primitive of legend, but different nonetheless. Neanderthals have been controversial ever since their first discovery in 1856. (They were found in a valley of the Düssel River named for the minor poet Neander. Valley, in German is *Tal* or, in an older spelling often used in the nineteenth century, *Thal,* hence chronic confusion over the variant spellings Neandertal and Neanderthal. In any case, the word was always pronounced "tal" whatever its spelling, and the common pronunciation with English "th" is just plain wrong—a good example of the common confusion between orthography and content.)

Some leading anthropologists have interpreted Neanderthal as a stage in a general trend to modern humans, hence as our direct ancestor. This view was defended by the Czech-born leader of American paleontology earlier in this century, Ales Hrdlička; also by Franz Weidenrich in the last generation and by C. Loring Brace in our own.

The extreme version of the alternative was presented by the great French anthropologist Marcellin Boule. In a series of detailed monographs on the well-preserved Neanderthal skeleton of La Chapelle-aux-Saints, Boule constructed the apish stereotype later assimilated by pop culture as the brutish, stoop-shouldered caveman—club in one hand, wife's hair in the other.

Boule's Neanderthal, presented to the world just before World War I, slouched because he couldn't straighten his knees, bent forward because his backbone formed a single curve, slung his heavy head forward, and walked on the outer edge of his foot because his semi-prehensile big toe stuck out to the side and couldn't be used for proper support.

Boule's account was surely wrong, unfortunately mired in his own racist desire to compare these primitives with some modern groups that he wished to disparage, and partly based (though not so much as legend proclaims) on the arthritis, not the original anatomy, of his specimen. But in retrospect, bolstered by the redate of Qafzeh, Boule was probably right in his central claim—that Neanderthal is a branch of the human bush completely separated from *Homo sapiens,* and not at all part of our ancestry; and also that Cro-Magnons must have evolved elsewhere and lived contemporaneously with Neanderthals, long before their contact in western Europe some 30,000 years ago. The redating of Qafzeh is a vindication of Boule's primary conclusion:

Now these Cro-Magnons, which seem to replace Neanderthals abruptly in our country, must have lived before then in another place, unless we are willing to propose a mutation so great and so abrupt as to be absurd [from *Les Hommes fossiles,* 1946 edition, p. 267].

Boule's Neanderthal was an apish primitive. Modern anatomical reconstructions reveal a stocky, heavy-set, cold-adapted skeleton with a brain as big as ours—a creature well designed for the climates of glacial Europe. But while Neanderthals have been promoted from primitive to merely different, they have not—and this is the crucial point—become more like us.

During the twenty years that I have studied this field, general consensus has ranked Neanderthal within our own species, as a cold-adapted European race, *Homo sapiens neanderthalensis.* But if the dating of Qafzeh holds, and if the general view that ties all modern humans to a recent African root continues to gain strength, then this consensus must give way. If Neanderthals and modern humans lived in the Levant—and maintained their integrity without interbreeding—for 60,000 years before the great replacement in western Europe, then the two are separate species by the primary criterion of reproductive isolation. We shall have to return to the older view of Neanderthal as a separate species, *H. neanderthalensis.*

A much deeper issue underlies this entire debate. We are astonished to learn that all modern humans are products of a recent branching event in a single place, probably Africa. We are surprised that Neanderthal may be a separate branch of the human bush, not a more primitive ancestor. We are used to conceptualizing evolution as a tale of transformation within a continuous lineage—think of the museum parade of horses, from eohippus (fox-terrier sized, of course!) to Seabiscuit, or the line of human ascent from *Australopithecus,* naked in the African bush, to John Q. Businesssuit. Mired in this prejudice, for example, the *Auckland Sun* (February 19, 1988) reported the Qafzeh redating with this lurid leading paragraph (well, they do walk upside down out there in New Zealand, so maybe we shouldn't be surprised): "Evolutionary theories were turned back to front this week when scientists claimed modern humans existed before Neanderthal Stone Age cavemen."

We shall be truly wiser when we understand that the Qafzeh redate did not turn evolutionary theory upside down. Rather, the separation and prolonged simultaneous existence of Neanderthals and moderns as distinct species fits beautifully with a proper understanding of evolution. The only casualty of Qafzeh is a cultural prejudice of gradual, continuous advance as the canonical style of evolutionary change.

Evolution, at geological scales, is fundamentally about bushes and branching. Modern *Homo sapiens* and the extinct Neanderthals are two distinct branches, two contemporaneous species for most of their existence, if the data and arguments of this essay hold up to future scrutiny. Evolutionary trends usually work this way. The transition from reptiles to mammals, for example, is not the slow movement of a large population in lock-step from cold to warm blood, and from jawbones to earbones. Trends arise within a forest of distinct branches. Most of these branches die; a few are successful and produce more branches like themselves to fuel the transition. Trends are propagated by the differential birth and death of distinct branches, not the wholesale, gradual transformation of a single great entity. Mammals arose because the most mammallike species within a particular group of reptiles tended to live longer or branch off more daughter species. The robust australopithecines died: *Homo habilis* lived. Neanderthals became extinct; *Homo sapiens* survived.

Scientists are subject to the same biases of thinking; the press and general public hold no monopoly upon bloody-mindedness. Professional understanding of human evolution has long been hampered by a preference for viewing trends as the gradual transformation of "whole things," rather than the differential success of some kinds of little branches versus others. Stringer and Andrews, in the article cited previously, distinguished two basic views of human evolution. The "multi-regional model" embodies the older view of trends as gradual transformation. It holds that *Homo sapiens* evolved over a large part of the Old World in a coordinated transition from African and Eurasian *Homo erectus.* Contact and gene flow was sufficient, according to this view, to forge *Homo erectus* from Nairobi to Beijing to Jakarta into a functioning whole, then gradually transformed by natural selection into modern humanity.

The second view, often called Noah's Ark among anthropologists, holds that most ancestral lines died, and that modern humans descend from a local group that eventually spread throughout the world. Everything discussed in this article—from the redating of Qafzeh to the status of Neanderthal to genetic and paleontological evidence for a common, temporally shallow root of all humanity in

Africa—stands as a ringing confirmation of this second theory.

Yet as I advocate this second view with such delight (for its fits well with my own preferences for punctuated equilibrium), I strongly reject its designation as Noah's Ark. I have no objection to flippancy or to biblical metaphor, but only to the inappropriate implications of this name. The Deluge was a disaster outside the ordinary course of nature. If all modern humans stem from the fortunate survivors of a debacle, then our evolution seems unusual among the trends of life's history. But nothing could be more ordinary than the derivation of a successful stock from a single event of branching. Evolution works this way nearly all the time.

Human unity is no idle political slogan or tenet of mushy romanticism (I speak of the biological meaning, not the ethical concept that science cannot touch). All modern humans form an entity united by physical bonds of descent from a recent African root; we are not merely the current state of a tendency, as the multi-regional model suggests. Our unities are genealogical; we are an object of history. This insight is evolution's finest contribution to our greatest quest—the injunction inscribed as one of two cardinal precepts upon the Delphic oracle (according to Plutarch), and later invoked by Linnaeus as the very definition of the name he gave us, *Homo sapiens*: Know thyself.

The Clan of the Cave Bear

Jean M. Auel

The child turned over and began to thrash.

"Mother," she moaned. Flailing her arms wildly, she called out again, louder, "Mother!"

Iza held her, murmuring a soft rumbling undertone. The warm closeness of the woman's body and her soothing sounds penetrated the girl's feverish brain and quieted her. She had slept fitfully through the night, awakening the woman often with her tossing and moaning and delirious mutterings. The sounds were strange, different from the words spoken by Clan people. They flowed easily, fluently, one sound blending into another. Iza could not begin to reproduce many of them; her ear was not even conditioned to hearing the finer variations. But that particular set of sounds was repeated so often, Iza guessed it was a name for someone close to the child, and when she saw that her presence comforted the girl, she sensed who the someone was.

She can't be very old, Iza thought, she didn't even know how to find food. I wonder how long she's been alone? What could have happened to her people? Could it have been the earthquake? Has she been wandering by herself that long? And how did she escape from a cave lion with only a few scratches? Iza had treated enough maulings to know the girl's wounds were inflicted by the huge cat. Powerful spirits must protect her, Iza decided.

It was still dark, though dawn was approaching, when the child's fever finally broke in a drenching sweat. Iza cuddled her close, adding her warmth and making sure she was well covered. The girl woke shortly afterward and wondered where she was, but it was too dark to see. She felt the reassurance of the woman's body next to her and closed her eyes again, drifting into a more restful sleep.

As the sky lightened, silhouetting the trees against its faint glow, Iza crept quietly out of the warm fur. She stoked the fire, added more wood, then went to the small creek to fill her bowl and peel bark off a willow tree. She paused for a moment, clutched her amulet, and thanked the spirits for willow. She always thanked the spirits for willow, for its ubiquitous presence as well as for its painkilling bark. She couldn't remember how many times she had peeled willow bark for a tea to relieve aches and pains. She knew of stronger painkillers, but they also dulled the senses. The analgesic properties of willow just dulled the pain and reduced fever.

A few other people were beginning to stir as Iza sat hunched over the fire adding small hot stones to the bowl of water and willow bark. When it was ready, she carried it back to the fur, carefully rested the bowl in a small depression scooped out of the ground, then slid in beside the child. Iza watched the sleeping girl, noting that her breathing was normal, intrigued by her unusual face. The sunburn had faded to tan except for a little peeling skin across the bridge of her small nose.

Iza had seen her kind once, but only from a distance. Women of the Clan always ran and hid from them. Unpleasant incidents had been told at Clan Gatherings of chance encounters between the Clan and the Others, and Clan people avoided them. Women, especially, were allowed little contact. But the experience of their clan had not been bad. Iza remembered talking with Creb about the man who had stumbled into their cave long before, nearly out of his head with pain, his arm badly broken.

He had learned a little of their language, but his ways were strange. He liked to talk to women as well as men and treated the medicine woman with great respect, almost reverence. It hadn't kept him from gaining the respect of the men. Iza wondered about the Others, lying awake watching the child as the sky grew lighter.

While Iza was looking at her, a shaft of sunlight fell on the child's face from the bright ball of flame just edging over the horizon. The girl's eyelids fluttered. She opened her eyes and looked into a pair of large brown eyes, deep set below heavy brow ridges in a face that protruded somewhat, like a muzzle.

The girl screamed and squeezed her eyes shut again. Iza drew the child close to her, feeling her scrawny body shaking with fear, and murmured soothing sounds. The sounds were somehow familiar to the child, but more familiar was the warm comforting body. Slowly, her shaking stilled. She opened her eyes a crack and looked at Iza again. This time she didn't scream. Then she opened her eyes wide and started at the frightening, totally unfamiliar face of the woman.

Iza stared too, in wonder. She had never seen eyes the color of the sky before. For a moment she wondered if the child was blind. Eyes of older Clan people sometimes grew a film over them, and as the film clouded the eyes to a lighter shade, sight grew dimmer. But the pupils of the child's eyes dilated normally and there could be no doubt she had seen Iza. That light blue-gray color must be normal for her, Iza thought.

The little girl lay perfectly still, afraid to move a muscle, her eyes wide open. When the child sat up with Iza's help, she winced in pain from the movement, and her memories came flooding back. She recalled the monstrous lion with a shudder, visualizing the sharp claw raking her leg. She remembered struggling to the stream, thirst overcoming her fear and the pain in her leg, but she remembered nothing before. Her mind had blocked out all memory of her ordeal wandering alone, hungry and afraid, the terrifying earthquake, and the loved ones she had lost.

Iza held the cup of liquid to the child's mouth. She was thirsty and took a drink, and made a face at the bitter taste. But when the woman put the cup back to her lips, she swallowed again, too frightened to resist. Iza nodded approval, then left to help the women prepare the morning meal. The little girl's eyes followed Iza, and she opened them wider when she saw for the first time a camp full of people who looked like the woman.

The smell of cooking food brought pangs of hunger, and when the woman returned with a small bowl of meaty broth thickened with grain into a gruel, the child gulped it down ravenously. The medicine woman didn't think she was ready for solid food yet. It didn't take much to fill her shrunken stomach, and Iza put the remainder in a water skin for the child to drink while they traveled. When the girl was through, Iza laid her down and removed the poultice. The wounds were draining and the swelling was down.

"Good," Iza said aloud.

The child jumped at the harsh guttural sound of the word, the first she had heard the woman speak. It didn't sound like a word at all, more like a growl or grunt of some animal to the girl's untutored ears. But Iza's actions were not animal-like, they were very human, very humane. The medicine

woman had another mashed root ready and while she was applying the new dressing, a misshapen, lopsided man hobbled toward them.

He was the most fearsomely repulsive man the girl had ever seen. One side of his face was scarred and a flap of skin covered the place where one of his eyes should have been. But all of these people were so alien and ugly to her, his forbidding disfiguration was only a matter of degree. She didn't know who they were or how she happened to be among them, but she knew the woman was taking care of her. She had been given food, the dressing cooled and soothed her leg, and most of all, from the depths of her unconscious mind, she felt a relief from the anxiety that had filled her with aching fear. Strange as these people were, with them she was, at least, no longer alone.

The crippled man eased himself down and observed the child. She returned his look with a frank curiosity that surprised him. The children of his clan were always a little afraid of him. They learned quickly that even their elders held him in awe, and his aloof manner didn't encourage familiarity. The gulf widened when mothers threatened to call Mog-ur if they misbehaved. By the time children were nearly adults, most of them, especially girls, really feared him. It wasn't until they gained the maturity of middle years that members of the clan came to temper their fear with respect. Creb's good right eye sparkled with interest at this strange child's fearless appraisal of him.

"The child is better, Iza," he indicated. His voice was lower pitched than the woman's, but the sounds he made were more like grunts than words to the girl. She didn't notice the accompanying hand signals. The language was totally alien to her; she only knew the man had communicated something to the woman.

"She is still weak from hunger," Iza said, "but the wound is better. The gashes were deep, but not enough to seriously damage her leg, and the infection is draining. She was clawed by a cave lion, Creb. Have you ever known a cave lion to stop with a few

scratches once it decided to attack? I'm surprised she's alive. She must have a strong spirit protecting her. But," Iza added, "what do I know of spirits?"

It was certainly not a woman's place, not even his sibling's, to tell Mog-ur about spirits. She made a deprecating gesture that also begged his forgiveness for her presumption. He didn't acknowledge her—she hadn't expected him to—but he looked at the child with greater interest as a result of her comment about a strong protecting spirit. He had been thinking much the same thing himself, and though he would never admit it, his sibling's opinion carried weight with him, and confirmed his own thoughts.

They broke camp quickly. Iza, loaded with her basket and bundles, reached down to hoist the girl up to her hip and fell in behind Brun and Grod. Riding on the woman's hip, the little girl looked around her with curiosity while they traveled, watching everything Iza and the other women did. She was particularly interested whenever they stopped to gather food. Iza often gave her a bite of a fresh bud or tender young shoot, and it brought a vague recollection of another woman who had done the same thing. But now, the girl paid closer attention to the plants and began to notice identifying characteristics. Her days of hunger aroused in the young child a keen desire to learn how to find food. She pointed to a plant and was pleased when the woman stopped and dug up its root. Iza was pleased, too. The child is quick, she thought. She couldn't have known it before or she would have eaten it.

They stopped for a rest near midday while Brun looked over a possible cave site, and after giving the youngster the last of the broth from the water skin, Iza handed her a strip of hard dry meat to chew. The cave was not adequate for their needs. Later in the afternoon, the girl's leg began to throb as the effects of the willow bark wore off. She squirmed restlessly, Iza patted her and shifted her weight to a more comfortable position. The girl gave herself over completely to the woman's care. With total trust and confidence, she wrapped skinny arms around Iza's neck and rested her head on the woman's broad shoulder. The medicine woman, childless for so long, felt a surge of inner warmth for the orphaned girl. She was still weak and tired, and lulled by the rhythmic motion as the woman walked, she fell asleep.

By the time evening approached, Iza was feeling the strain of the additional burden she carried and was grateful to let the child down when Burn called a halt for the day. The girl was feverish, her cheeks flushed and hot, her eyes glazed, and while the woman looked for wood, she also looked for plants to treat the child again. Iza didn't know what caused infection, but she did know how to treat it, and many other ailments as well.

Though healing was magic and couched in terms of spirits, it didn't make Iza's medicine less effective. The ancient Clan had always lived by hunting and gathering, and generations of using wild plantlife had, by experiment or accident, built up a store of information about it. Animals were skinned and butchered and their organs observed and compared. The women dissected while preparing dinner and applied the knowledge to themselves.

Her mother had shown Iza the various internal parts and explained their functions as part of her training, but it was only to remind her of something she already knew. Iza was born to a highly respected line of medicine women and, through a means more mysterious than training, knowledge of healing was passed on to a medicine woman's daughters. A fledgling medicine woman of an illustrious line had a higher rank than an experienced one of mediocre antecedents—with good reason.

Stored in her brain at birth was the knowledge acquired by her ancestors, the ancient line of medicine women of which Iza was a direct descendant. She could remember what they knew. It was not much different from recalling her own experience; and once stimu-

lated, the process was automatic. She knew her own memories primarily because she could also remember the circumstances associated with them— she never forgot anything—and she could only recall the knowledge in her memory bank, not how it was learned. And although Iza and her siblings had the same parents, neither Creb nor Brun had her medical knowledge.

Memories in Clan people were sex differentiated. Women had no more need of hunting lore than men had of more than rudimentary knowledge of plants. The difference in the brains of men and women was imposed by nature, and only cemented by culture. It was another of nature's attempts to limit the size of their brains in an effort to prolong the race. Any child with knowledge rightfully belonging to the opposite gender at birth lost it through lack of stimulation by the time adult status was reached.

But nature's attempt to save the race from extinction carried with it the elements to defeat its own purpose. Not only were both sexes essential for procreation, but for day to day living; one could not survive for long without the other. And they could not learn each other's skills, they hadn't the memories for it.

But the eyes and brain of people of the Clan had also endowed both genders with acute and perceptive vision, though it was used in different ways. The terrain had been changing gradually as they traveled, and, unconsciously, Iza recorded each detail of the landscape they passed through, noting especially the vegetation. She could discern minor variations in the shape of a leaf or the height of a stalk from a great distance, and though there were some plants, a few flowers, an occasional tree or shrub she had never seen before, they were not unfamiliar. From a recess deep in the back of her large brain she found a memory of them, a memory not her own. But even with that tremendous reservoir of information at her disposal, she had recently seen some vegetation that was completely unfamiliar, as unfamiliar as the countryside. She would have liked to examine it more closely. All women

were curious about unknown plantlife. Though it meant acquiring new knowledge, it was essential to immediate survival.

Part of every woman's heredity was the knowledge of how to test unfamiliar vegetation, and like the rest, Iza experimented on herself. Similarities to known plants placed new ones in relative categories, but she knew the dangers of assuming similar characteristics meant identical properties. The procedure for testing was simple. She took a small bite. If the taste was unpleasant, she spit it out immediately. If it was agreeable, she held the tiny portion in her mouth, carefully noting any tingling or burning sensations or any changes in taste. If there were none, she swallowed it and waited to see if she could detect any effects. The following day, she took a larger bite and went through the same procedure. If no ill effects were noticed after a third trial, the new food was considered edible, in small portions at first.

But Iza was often more interested when there were noticeable effects, for that indicated a possibility of a medicinal use. The other women brought anything unusual to her when they applied the same test for edibility or anything that had characteristics similar to plants known to be poisonous or toxic. Proceeding with caution, she experimented with these too, using her own methods. But such experimentation took time, and she stayed with plants she knew while they traveled.

Near this campsite, Iza found several tall, wandlike slim-stemmed hollyhocks with large bright flowers. The roots of the multicolored flowering plants could be made into a poultice similar to iris roots to promote healing and reduce swelling and inflammation. An infusion of the flowers would both numb the child's pain and make her sleepy. She collected them along with her wood.

After the evening meal, the little girl sat propped up against a large rock watching the activities of the people around her. Food and a fresh dressing had refreshed her and she jabbered at Iza, though she could tell the woman didn't understand her. Other clan members glanced disapprovingly in her direction, but the child was unaware of the meaning of the looks. Their underdeveloped vocal organs made precise articulation impossible for people of the Clan. The few sounds they used as emphasis had evolved from cries of warning or a need to gain attention, and the importance attached to verbalizations was a part of their traditions. Their primary means of communication—hand signals, gestures, positions; and an intuition born of intimate contact, established customs, and perceptive discernment of expressions and postures—were expressive, but limited. Specific objects seen by one were difficult to describe to others, and abstract concepts even more so. The child's volubility perplexed the clan and made them distrustful.

They treasured children, reared them with gentle fond affection and discipline which grew more stern as they grew older. Babies were pampered by women and men alike, young children rebuked most often by simply being ignored. When children became aware of the higher status of older children and adults, they emulated their elders and resisted pampering as fit only for babies. Youngsters learned early to behave within the strict confines of established custom, and one custom was that superfluous sounds were inappropriate. Because of her height, the girl seemed older than her years, and the clan considered her undisciplined, not well brought up.

Iza, who had been in much closer contact with her, guessed she was younger than she seemed. She was coming to a close approximation of the girl's true age and she responded to her helplessness more leniently. She sensed, too, from her mutterings while she was delirious, that her kind verbalized more fluently and more frequently. Iza was drawn to the child whose life depended on her and who had wrapped scrawny little arms around her neck in complete trust. There will be time, Iza thought, to teach her better manners. She was already beginning to think of the child as hers.

Creb wandered over while Iza was pouring boiling water over the flowers

of the hollyhocks, and sat down near the child. He was interested in the stranger, and since the preparations for the evening ceremony were not yet complete, he went to see how she was recovering. They stared at each other, the young girl and the crippled, scarred old man, studying each other with equal intensity. He had never been so close to one of her kind and had never seen a young one of the Others at all. She didn't even know of the existence of Clan people until she woke up to find herself among them, but more than their racial characteristics, she was curious about the puckered skin of his face. In her limited experience, she had never seen a face so horribly scarred. Impetuously, with the uninhibited reactions of a child, she reached out to touch his face, to see if the scar felt different.

Creb was taken aback as she lightly stroked his face. None of the children of the clan had ever reached out to him like that. No adults reached out to him either. They avoided contact with him, as though they might somehow catch his deformity by touching him. Only Iza, who nursed him through his sieges of arthritis which attacked with greater severity every winter, seemed to have no compunction about it. She was neither repulsed by his misshapen body and ugly scars nor in awe of his power and position. The little girl's gentle touch struck an inner chord in his lonely old heart. He wanted to communicate with her and thought for a moment about how to begin.

"Creb," he said, pointing to himself. Iza was watching quietly, waiting for the flowers to steep. She was glad Creb was taking an interest in the girl, and the use of his personal name was not lost on her.

"Creb," he repeated, tapping his chest.

The child cocked her head, trying to understand. There was something he wanted her to do. Creb said his name a third time. Suddenly she brightened, sat up straight, and smiled.

"Grub?" she responded, rolling the r to mimic his sound.

The old man nodded approval; her pronunciation was close. Then he

pointed at her. She frowned slightly, not quite sure what he wanted now. He tapped his chest, repeated his name, then tapped hers. Her wide smile of understanding looked like a grimace to him, and the polysyllabic word that rolled out of her mouth was not only unpronounceable, it was almost incomprehensible. He went through the same motions, leaning close to hear better. She said her name.

"Aay-rr," he hesitated, shook his head, tried again. "Aay-lla, Ay-la?" It was the best approximation he could make. There were not many in the clan who could have come as close. She beamed and nodded her head up and down vigorously. It was not exactly what she had said, but she accepted it, sensing even in her young mind that he could not say the word for her name any better.

"Ayla," Creb repeated, getting used to the sound.

"Creb?" the girl said, tugging at his arm to get his attention, then pointed at the woman.

"Iza," Creb said, "Iza."

"Eeez-sa," she repeated. She was delighted with the word game. "Iza, Iza," she reiterated, looking at the woman.

Iza nodded solemnly; name sounds were very important. She leaned forward and tapped the child's chest the way Creb had, wanting her to say her name-word again. The girl repeated her full name, but Iza just shook her head. She couldn't begin to make that combination of sounds that the girl made so easily. The child was dismayed, then glancing at Creb, said her name the way he had.

"Eye-ghha?" the woman tried. The girl shook her head and said it again. "Eye-ya?" Iza tried again.

"Aay, Aay, not Eye," Creb said. "Aaay-llla," he repeated very slowly so Iza could hear the unfamiliar combination of sounds.

"Aay-lla," the woman said carefully, struggling to make the word the way Creb had.

The girl smiled. It didn't matter that the name wasn't exactly right; Iza had tried so hard to say the name Creb had given her, she accepted it as her own.

She would be Ayla for them. Spontaneously, she reached out and hugged the woman.

Iza squeezed her gently, then pulled away. She would have to teach the child that displays of affection were unseemly in public, but she was pleased nonetheless.

Ayla was beside herself with joy. She had felt so lost, so isolated among these strange people. She had tried so hard to communicate with the woman who was caring for her, and she was so frustrated when all her attempts failed. It was only a beginning, but at least she had a name to call the woman and a name to be called. She turned back to the man who had initiated the communication. He didn't seem nearly so ugly to her anymore. Her joy bubbled over, she felt a warmth toward him, and as she had done many times to another man she remembered only vaguely, the little girl put her arms around the crippled man's neck, pulled his head down to her, and rested her cheek against his.

Her gesture of affection unsettled him. He resisted an urge to return the hug. It would be totally improper to be seen hugging this strange little creature outside the boundary of a family hearth. But he allowed her to press her smooth, firm little cheek to his bushy-bearded face a moment longer before he gently removed her arms from around his neck.

Creb picked up his staff and used it to pull himself up. As he limped away, he thought about the girl. I must teach her to speak, she should learn to communicate properly, he said to himself. After all, I can't entrust all her instruction to a woman. He knew, though, that he really wanted to spend more time with her. Without realizing it, he thought of her as a permanent part of the clan.

Brun had not considered the implications of allowing Iza to pick up a strange child along the way. It was not a failing of him as a leader, it was the failing of his race. He could not have anticipated finding a wounded child who was not Clan and he could not foresee the logical consequences of rescuing her. Her life had been saved; the only alternative to letting her stay

with them was to turn her out to wander alone again. She could not survive alone—that did not take foresight, it was fact. After saving her life, to expose her to death again he would have to oppose Iza, who, although she had no power personally, did have a formidable array of spirits on her side—and now Creb, the Mog-ur who had the ability to call upon any and all spirits. Spirits were a potent force to Brun, he had no desire to find himself at odds with them. To give him full credit, it was just that eventuality that bothered him about the girl. He hadn't been able to express it to himself, but the thought had been hovering. He didn't know it yet, but Brun's clan had increased to twenty-one.

When the medicine woman examined Ayla's leg the next morning, she could see the improvement. Under her expert care, the infection was nearly gone and the four parallel gashes were closed and healing, though she would always carry the scars. Iza decided a poultice was no longer needed, but she made a willow-bark tea for the child. When she moved her off the sleeping fur, Ayla tried to stand. Iza helped her and supported her while the girl gingerly tried to put her weight on the leg. It hurt, but after a few careful steps, it felt better.

Standing up at her full height, the girl was even taller than Iza thought. Her legs were long, spindly with knobby knees, and straight. Iza wonder if they were deformed. The legs of Clan people were bowed in an outward curvature, but, except for a limp, the child had no problem moving around. Straight legs must be normal for her too, Iza decided—like blue eyes.

The medicine woman wrapped the cloak around her and lifted the child to her hip as the clan got under way; her leg wasn't healed enough yet for her to walk any great distance. At intervals during the day's march, Iza let her down to walk for a while. The girl had been eating ravenously, making up for her long hunger, and Iza thought she could notice a weight gain already. She was glad to be relieved of the extra burden occasionally, especially since traveling was becoming more difficult.

The clan left the broad flat steppes behind and for the next few days traversed rolling hills that grew progressively steeper. They were in the foothills of the mountains whose glistening ice caps drew closer every day. The hills were thickly forested, not with the evergreens of boreal forest, but with the rich green leaves and thick gnarled trunks of broad-leafed deciduous trees. The temperature had warmed much faster than the season usually progressed, which puzzled Brun. The men had replaced their wraps with a shorter leather hide that left the torso bare. The women didn't change to their summer wear; it was easier to carry their loads with a full wrap that eased chafing.

The terrain lost all resemblance to the cold prairie that had surrounded their old cave. Iza found herself depending more and more on knowledge of memories more ancient than her own as the clan passed through shaded glens and over grassy knolls of a full temperate forest. The heavy brown barks of oak, beech, walnut, apple, and maple were intermixed with supple, straight, thin-barked willow, birch, hornbeam, aspen, and the high brush of alder and hazelnut. There was a tang to the air Iza couldn't readily identify that seemed to ride on the warm soft breeze from the south. Catkins still clung to fully leafed birches. Delicate petals of pink and white drifted down, blown blossoms of fruit and nut trees, giving early promise of autumn's bounty.

They struggled through brush and vines of the dense forest and climbed exposed faces. As they mounted rocky outcrops, the hillsides around them were resplendent with greens of every hue. The deep shades of pine reappeared as they climbed, along with silver fir. Higher up, blue spruce made an occasional appearance. The deeper colors of conifers intermingled with the rich primary greens of the broad-leafed trees and the limes and pale-white greens of the small-leafed varieties. Mosses and grass added their shades to the verdant mosaic of lush growth and small plants, from oxalis, the cloverlike wood sorrel, to tiny suc-

239

culents clinging to exposed rock faces. Wild flowers were scattered through the woods, white trilliums, yellow violets, rose pink hawthorn, while yellow jonquils and blue and yellow gentians dominated some of the higher meadows. In a few of the heavily shaded places, the last of the yellow and white and purple crocus, off to a later start, still bravely showed their heads.

The clan stopped for a rest after reaching the top of a steep incline. Below, the panorama of wooded hillsides ended abruptly at the steppes expanding to the horizon. From their vantage point, several herds could be seen in the distance grazing on the tall grass already fading to summer gold. Fast-moving hunters, traveling light and unencumbered by heavily burdened women, could pick and choose among the several varieties of game and reach the steppes easily in far less than half a morning. The sky to the east, over the broad prairie, was clear, but scudding up fast from the south, thunderheads were brewing. If they continued to develop, the high mountain range to the north would cause the clouds to dump their load of moisture on the clan.

Brun and the men were having a meeting just out of range of the women and children, but the worried scowls and hand gestures left no doubt about the reason for the discussion. They were trying to decide if they should turn back. The countryside was unfamiliar, but more important, they were moving too far away from the steppes. Though they had caught glimpses of many animals in the wooded foothills, it was nothing like the tremendous herds supported by the plentiful fodder of the grassy plains below. Animals were easier to hunt out in the open, easier to see without the cover of forest to hide them, cover that hid their four-legged hunters as well. Plains animals were more social, tended to form in herds, not as isolated individuals or small family groups like the forest prey.

Iza guessed they would probably turn back, making their struggle to climb the steep hills all in vain. The gathering clouds and threatening rain cast a dreary pall over the dispirited travelers. While they were waiting, Iza let Ayla down and eased off her heavy load. The child, enjoying the freedom of movement her healing leg allowed after being confined to the woman's hip, wandered off. Iza saw her as she moved out of sight beyond the nose of a jutting ridge just ahead. She didn't want the girl to stray too far. The meeting might end at any time, and Brun would not look with favor on the girl if she held up their departure. She went after her, and rounding the ridge, Iza saw the child, but what she saw beyond the girl made her heart race.

She hurried back, casting quick glances over her shoulder. She didn't dare interrupt Brun and the men, and waited impatiently for the meeting to break up. Brun saw her, and though he gave no indication of it, he knew something was bothering her. As soon as the men separated, Iza ran to Brun, sat down in front of him, and looked at the ground—the position which meant she wanted to talk to him. He could grant an audience or not; the choice was his. If he ignored her, she would not be allowed to tell him what was on her mind.

Brun wondered what she wanted. He had noticed the girl exploring ahead—there was little about his clan that escaped his attention—but he had had more pressing problems. It must be about that girl, he thought scowling, and was tempted to disregard Iza's petition. No matter what Mog-ur said, he didn't like the child traveling with them. Glancing up, Brun saw the magician watching him and tried to discern what the one-eyed man was thinking, but he could not read the impassive face.

The leader looked back at the woman sitting at his feet; her posture gave away her tense agitation. She is really disturbed, he thought. Brun was not an unfeeling man, and he held his sibling in high regard. Despite the problems she had had with her mate, she had always conducted herself well. She was an example to the other women and seldom bothered him with insignificant requests. perhaps he should let her speak; he did not have to act upon her request. He reached down and tapped her shoulder.

Iza's breath exploded at the touch; she hadn't realized she had been holding it. He would let her speak! He had taken so long to decide, she was sure he was going to ignore her. Iza stood up and, pointing in the direction of the ridge, she said one word, "Cave!"

Index

Credits/ Acknowledgments

Cover design by Charles Vitelli

1. About Archaeology

Facing overview—United Nations photo by John Isaac. 23—Courtesy of the Library of the University of Virginia. 24—Courtesy of Jeff Hantman. Map source: David Bushnell, "The Five Monacan Towns in Virginia, 1607," Smithsonian Miscellaneous Collections, Vol. 82, Number 12, 1930. A reprint of a section of the 1624 original. 30—Photo courtesy of the McNitt Collection/State Records Center and Archives, Santa Fe. 31–35—Photos by Terrence Moore.

2. Thinking Like an Archaeologist

Facing overview—Photo courtesy of George Keller. 51, 53, 54 (bottom), 56-57—Photos courtesy of Caroline Malone and Simon Stoddart. 52—Photo courtesy of the National Museum of Archaeology. 54-55—Illustration courtesy of Caroline Malone and Steven Ashley.

3. Problem-oriented Archaeology

Facing overview—Photo courtesy of the American Museum of Natural History. 71-73—Photos by Neal Brown. 91-94—Photos, map, and illustration by Cemal Pulak and Donald A. Frey.

4. Experimental Archaeology

Facing overview—Photo by M. R. Harrington courtesy of the Museum of the American Indian, Heye Foundation. 108-110—Photos by Michael Lorblanchet.

5. History and Ethnoarchaeology

Facing overview—Photo by the Colorado Tourism Board.

6. Paleoanthropology

Facing overview—Photo courtesy of the American Museum of Natural History. 163-164—Photos courtesy of Sophie A. de Beaune.

7. Archaeologists Today

Facing overview—United Nations photo by Rothstein. 209—Map by Joe LeMonnier.

8. Archaeologists As People

Facing overview—United Nations photo by S. Stokes.

ANNUAL EDITIONS ARTICLE REVIEW FORM

- NAME: _____ DATE: _____
- TITLE AND NUMBER OF ARTICLE: _____
- BRIEFLY STATE THE MAIN IDEA OF THIS ARTICLE: _____

_____

_____

_____

_____

- LIST THREE IMPORTANT FACTS THAT THE AUTHOR USES TO SUPPORT THE MAIN IDEA:

_____

_____

_____

_____

_____

- WHAT INFORMATION OR IDEAS DISCUSSED IN THIS ARTICLE ARE ALSO DISCUSSED IN YOUR
TEXTBOOK OR OTHER READING YOU HAVE DONE? LIST THE TEXTBOOK CHAPTERS AND PAGE
NUMBERS:

_____

_____

_____

_____

_____

_____

- LIST ANY EXAMPLES OF BIAS OR FAULTY REASONING THAT YOU FOUND IN THE ARTICLE:

_____

_____

_____

_____

- LIST ANY NEW TERMS/CONCEPTS THAT WERE DISCUSSED IN THE ARTICLE AND WRITE A
SHORT DEFINITION:

_____

_____

_____

_____

_____

ANNUAL EDITIONS: ARCHAEOLOGY 95/96
Article Rating Form

Here is an opportunity for you to have direct input into the next revision of this volume.
We would like you to rate each of the 42 articles listed below, using the following scale:

1. Excellent: should definitely be retained
2. Above average: should probably be retained
3. Below average: should probably be deleted
4. Poor: should definitely be deleted

Your ratings will play a vital part in the next revision. So please mail this prepaid form to
us just as soon as you complete it.
Thanks for your help!

We Want Your Advice

Annual Editions
revisions depend on
two major opinion
sources: one is our
Advisory Board, listed
in the front of this
volume, which works
with us in scanning
the thousands of
articles published in
the public press each
year; the other is
you—the person
actually using the
book. Please help us
and the users of the
next edition by
completing the prepaid
article rating form on
this page and
returning it to us.
Thank you.

Rating	Article	Rating	Article
	1. The Quest for the Past		21. The Past as Propaganda
	2. The Golden Marshalltown: A Parable for the Archeology of the 1980s		22. Murders from the Past
			23. Post-Mortem at the Little Bighorn
	3. The Enlightened Archaeologist		24. Bones and Bureaucrats: New York's Great Cemetery Imbroglio
	4. Indiana Joans		
	5. 'Reverse Archaeologists' Are Tracing the Footsteps of a Cowboy-Explorer		25. What Was the Acheulean Hand Ax?
			26. Infants, Cannibals, and the Pit of Bones
	6. Archaeology and Relief		27. Ice Age Lamps
	7. Epistemology: How You Know What You Know		28. Lithic Technology and the Hunter-Gatherer Sexual Division of Labor
	8. The Death Cults of Prehistoric Malta		29. The Dating Game
	9. The Mysterious Fall of the Nacirema		30. A Primitive Prescription for Equality
	10. Living Through the Donner Party		31. The Antiquities Market
	11. Coming to America		32. Project Sting
	12. Who Were the Israelites?		33. An Anthropological Culture Shift
	13. Ever Since Eve . . . Birth Control in the Ancient World		34. Saving Our World's Heritage
			35. When My Grandmother Is Your Database: Reactions to Repatriation
	14. The Mummies of Xinjiang		
	15. The Search for a Bronze Age Shipwreck		36. Tales from a Peruvian Crypt
	16. Yes, Wonderful Things		37. Indians, Archaeologists, and the Future
	17. Paleolithic Paint Job		38. Damming the Past
	18. Bushmen		39. The Beginning of a Partnership
	19. Ancient Indians Sought Shadows and Ice Caves		40. Lucy: The Beginnings of Humankind
			41. A Novel Notion of Neanderthal
	20. The Arrow of Disease		42. The Clan of the Cave Bear

(Continued on next page)

ABOUT YOU

Name_____ Date_____

Are you a teacher? ☐   Or student? ☐

Your School Name _____

Department _____

Address _____

City _____ State _____ Zip _____

School Telephone # _____

YOUR COMMENTS ARE IMPORTANT TO US!

Please fill in the following information:

For which course did you use this book? _____

Did you use a text with this Annual Edition?   ☐ yes   ☐ no

The title of the text? _____

What are your general reactions to the Annual Editions concept?

Have you read any particular articles recently that you think should be included in the next edition?

Are there any articles you feel should be replaced in the next edition? Why?

Are there other areas that you feel would utilize an Annual Edition?

May we contact you for editorial input?

May we quote you from above?